D0900069

A SURVEY OF ENGLISH LITERATURE

1780-1830

BY

OLIVER ELTON

D.LITT., LL.D., F.B.A.,
EMERITUS PROFESSOR IN THE UNIVERSITY OF LIVERPOOL

'I have endeavoured to feel what is good, and to give a reason for the faith that was in me, when necessary, and when in my power. —HAZLITT.

IN TWO VOLUMES

VOL. II

LONDON

EDWARD ARNOLD (PUBLISHERS) LTD.

Printed in Great Britain by
Lowe and Brydone (Printers) Limited, London, N.W.10

CONTENTS

CHAPTER XIV

SOUTHEY AND LANDOR

CHAPTER XV

WILLIAM WORDSWORTH

CHAPTER XVI

THE COLERIDGES

CHAPTER XVII

BYRON

CHAPTER XVIII

PERCY BYSSHE SHELLEY

CHAPTER XIX

LEIGH HUNT AND JOHN KEATS

CHAPTER XX

OTHER POETS

CHAPTER XXI

OTHER POETS (*concluded*) AND DRAMATISTS

CHAPTER XXII

THOMAS DE QUINCEY

CHAPTER XXIII

CHARLES AND MARY LAMB

CHAPTER XXIV

WILLIAM HAZLITT

CHAPTER XXV

HISTORIANS AND OTHER PROSE WRITERS

CONTENTS

CHAPTER XXVI

SOME INFLUENCES: CONCLUSION

CHAPTER XIV

SOUTHEY AND LANDOR

I. Robert Southey : career ; affinities with other poets. Eclogues, ballads, short pieces.

II. Southey : plan and ambition of his long poems : *Thalaba* and its metre ; *Curse of Kehama* ; *Madoc* ; *Roderick*.

III. Southey's prose : discussion of his style ; its 'achromatic' quality ; *The Doctor.* Rough classification of his works. Books of travel, essays, *Colloquies on Society.* Works on Spanish and Portuguese subjects ; *Peninsular War, History of Brazil.* Biographies : the *Nelson* and the *Wesley* ; *Life of Cowper.* Character of his conservatism ; position in letters.

IV. W. S. Landor : his 'solitariness' ; divisions of his career, 1795-1824, 1825-1846, 1847-1864.

V. Landor : *Poems* of 1795; *Gebir* and *Gebirus*; manner and source and excellences ; 'arrestedness' of imagery ; plastic effects. *Poems*, 1802.

VI. 'Dramatic scenes,' or plays : *Count Julian, Andrea of Hungary*, etc. ; *Siege of Ancona.*

VII. Short lyrics, epigrams, elegies ; poems to friends and to old age. Economy of passion ; classical manner, affinities with Jonson.

VIII. *The Hellenics* : usage of the term ; those translated from the Latin compared with the others ; analogies with sculpture. Increase of naturalness ; imaginative quality.

IX. *Imaginary Conversations* : variety, range, length, possible models. Grouping under six kinds :—(1) Heroic action and passion depicted ; conversations of Greeks and Romans, and modern subjects of like kind. (2) Brutal and ferocious scenes. (3) Idyllic, gracious, and playful scenes. (4) Humorous and ironic.

X. *Imaginary Conversations* :—non-artistic, or non-dramatic : (5) political and constitutional, or ethical, disquisitions in dialogue. (6) Conversations of ' literary men,' and criticisms.

XI. Longer prose works, or protracted 'imaginary conversations' : *Pericles and Aspasia, Pentameron, Citation, etc.,* of *W. Shakespeare.*

XII. Robert Eyres Landor : *Count Arezzi*, etc. ; prose romances.

I

IT is easy and too true to say that Robert Southey [1] (1774-1843) is a dead poet, a bookman, a journeyman in verse ; that he has no magic, that he betrays his procedure, and that he sinks under his learning and his ambition. Still the picture of high poetical effort in this age is incomplete without him.

He has some of the qualities and aims which, had he only been a better poet, would have made him more considerable. First and above all, he has in a high degree the instinct for emancipating and purging language. He is a purer writer than many greater ones. We can measure in his average performance the success of the revulsion against the false eighteenth-century styles—the cumbered artificial style in verse, the pompous periodic style in prose. Southey carries out this new ideal in his verse and his prose alike. Any one can see how in his verse he failed nevertheless, and how well in his best prose he succeeded. He had no conception of the difference of his achievement in the two kinds. He was as sure as Milton that he was a poet born to last. Even of his prose not much has lasted; but this is our loss; though it is partly his own fault, for he wrote too much.

Prose he produced all his life, but the best of it comes after 1810, when he settled down to quarterly reviewing and to professional bookwork. Most of his verse is earlier; his ballads, lays, domestic idylls, and sonnets are in some instances earlier than the *Lyrical Ballads*, and are part of the same campaign in the interest of simplicity; they aim at using, with due qualifications, the 'real language of men.' *Joan of Arc* and *Wat Tyler* (printed later by a pirate) are earlier still; they belong to the Republican period, when Southey was still at Balliol and was vowed to 'Pantisocracy,' and they may be neglected. The big quasi-epical enterprises begin in 1801 with *Thalaba the Destroyer*; then follow *Madoc* (1805), *The Curse of Kehama* (1810), and *Roderick, the Last of the Goths* (1814). These appeared alongside of Scott's lays, and represent, however ineffectually, the impatience of the romantic spirit to be off to new continents, to great remote legends, and to capture their grandeur. The *Tale of Paraguay*, also written in 1814, belongs, like *Roderick*, to Southey's studies of exotic history and legend. He wrote other verse after this, such as the unlucky *Vision of Judgement* (1820), accompanied by the attack on Byron which provoked Byron's great satire. But Southey became more and more immersed in prose, and found time, in the midst of a vast mass of journalism and bookseller's jobs, to prove himself a born biographer, and to perfect, as it has been well termed, a style of all work of most remarkable quality. His poetry may be noticed first.

A tiny link between noble plain stories like *Michael*, and Crabbe's or Cowper's work, narrative or reflective, of lower pitch and fainter flame, is found in Southey's four *English Eclogues,* written between 1797 and 1804. In one, *The Old Mansion-House,* the blank verse is so near the ' real language of men ' that it has no plea left for existing ; indeed, few of the *Lyrical Ballads* are more liable to this reproach.

> That 's all you 'll quarrel with ; walk in and taste
> His beer, old friend ! and see if your old Lady
> E'er broach'd a better cask.

This might have served a reviewer for a parody of certain passages in Wordsworth. In another idyll, *Hannah,* Wordsworth's grave transforming touch is only just missed ; the subject, the death of a deserted girl, is like a tale in *The Excursion. The Ruined Cottage* is like the homelier and more playful descriptions of *The Prelude,* with a not unpleasant stroke added of Cowper-like moralising :

> Look, its little hatch
> Fleeced with that gray and wintry moss ; the roof
> Part moulder'd in, the rest o'ergrown with weeds,
> House-leek, and long thin grass, and greener moss ;
> So Nature steals on all the works of man,
> Sure conqueror she, reclaiming to herself
> His perishable piles.

The Alderman's Funeral, a satire upon a stony-hearted rich local man who dies unregretted except on his tombstone, is just like Crabbe without Crabbe's couplets. Surely, but for those long tyrannous epics, which consumed his life in tasks that were beyond him, Southey might have done more in these low-lying forms of poetry, which have a faint scent of the autumnal earth.

The best of his ballads have the heat and fling of his youth in them ; they were written before he kept office hours perforce for the production of books. Many were made in 1797-8 ; one or two, conceived in the German style, date from 1796, not long after Scott's. Few are ' Lake ' poems ; they were made in Hereford, Bristol, and the west country. The only features common to Scott, Coleridge, and Southey are a dependence, more or less direct, upon the form and style of the English folk-ballad, and the use of the motive of terror, derived from the supernatural and inclining towards the grotesque ; ' a spring,' remarks Sir Walter, ' which is peculiarly apt to lose elasticity by being too much pressed upon.' The three poets, in spite of these affinities, cannot be said to have much influenced one another ; but the enterprise of balladry was now active on all hands ; and though by 1801 it was slackening,

at least in the popular estimation, all three are found con-
tributors, under the editorial crook of Lewis, to the *Tales of
Wonder* in that year ; the miscellany which, as Scott tells us,
fell somewhat flat upon the public. It remains, however,
as we have seen, the most distinctive book produced by the
school, if school it can be called, and the differences between
Southey and his companions can be fairly judged from it.

Southey did not make use of the Scots language, and his
fleeting inclination (seen in the early *Donica* and *Rudiger*,
1796) to the odd false manner encouraged by the German
literary ballad did not last so long as Scott's. This was one
of the blind alleys of Romance, but Southey turned his back
on it. Nor does he, on the other hand, like Scott, echo, piece
out, and directly imitate the vernacular British ballad ; not
even in *Lord William*, which is dire downright bogus literary
rhyming. Nor does he aim at the poetical effects, the profound art, and the sublimation of the familiar, which Coleridge
achieved ; he is, when writing at his best, much more frankly
popular. These traits are best seen in the descendants of the
two poets. Coleridge is the ancestor of *La Belle Dame sans
Merci* and *Ravelston* ; Southey, of Lockhart's *Spanish Ballads*
on the one hand and of the *Ingoldsby Legends* on the other.
One of his pieces, *Queen Orraca*, is from a Spanish chronicle ;
and its direct ringing verse, devoid of subtleties, but excellently
fitted for quick narrative, is one of the first examples of the
kind. But his real triumphs are in the comic or terrible
grotesque, supernaturally induced. Here nothing, unluckily,
is left unsaid, but then all is well said ; there is not much
more atmosphere or poetic suggestion than in the ditties of
Lewis, though there is far more style ; nor is the work itself,
like most of Lewis's, absurd. Here again Southey stands at
various distances from the popular ballad. *St. Michael's
Chair* is primitive comedy, and has a true local ring ; the
shrewish wife climbs to the chair, in order to have the whip-
hand, as the legend ran, of her spouse, but is thrown out by
the shaking of the bells and killed, much to his relief. *The
Well of St. Keyne*, universally known, is a masterpiece of the
same sort. *Jaspar* is an effective little popular tract in rhyme,
with a good deal of ballad-language. But *The Old Woman
of Berkeley*, which was first published in 1799 and afterwards
adorned the *Tales of Wonder*, is in rattling anapæsts, which
run down to something like doggerel ; and here we stand at the
source of the *Ingoldsby* manner. *God's Judgement on a Wicked
Bishop* and *The Inchcape Rock*, again, are in quite a different

strain from the late and beautiful *Brough Bells*, which is written (1828) with the true tradition of the ' Lake poets ' behind it :

> What feelings and what impulses
> Their cadence might convey
> To herdsman or to shepherd boy
> Whiling in indolent employ
> The solitary day.

While at Nether Stowey, Coleridge and Southey one morning, at breakfast, ' in dingdong chime of sing-song rhyme,' knocked together the first and raciest version (in fourteen stanzas) of the squib usually known as *The Devil's Walk*, but published in the *Morning Post* (1799) as *The Devil's Thoughts*.[1] The wild, happy-go-lucky, jolting rhymes, and the bluff efficient satire of the thing made it justly popular. It was often reprinted, and often attributed to Porson ; and in 1827, wishing to state the true authorship, Southey diluted it into fifty-seven stanzas, most of which are inferior. The theme of the Devil walking abroad to watch with glee the vices of society and the professions was an obvious one, once it had been hit upon ; and Shelley in his *Devil's Walk*, and Byron in his *Devil's Drive*, produced rather forced imitations, each in his own satirical rhetoric. But none of their phrases have become proverbial like the original lines on the Devil's breeches and ' the pride that apes humility.' It is in this kind of writing that Southey's talent worked itself free, and we wish he had done more of it.

II

Richard Lovell Edgeworth (whose domestic history might itself have furnished forth a humorous ballad) observed to Southey, upon reading some of his lighter pieces, ' Take my word for it, Sir, the bent of your genius is for comedy.' Certainly Southey had the art of telling a grim yarn in a light and gleeful spirit ; of a wicked bishop eaten by rats, or an old crone summoned straight off to hell out of her coffin while it is resting in a church ; children enjoy such things, and Southey enjoys them like a child. In none of his long portentous epics, unless it be in *The Curse of Kehama*, is there a relieving glimmer of this cheerful frame of mind. But he had not Scott's vein of shrewd self-criticism, which saves a man from going on with huge wrong-headed tasks ; and his attitude towards the public, which was loftier and more rigid than Scott's, and which would have been his salvation had he only been an artist, sustained him in his error. The public, indeed, fostered it for some time and bought his long poems, but he lived to see his fame decline.

Not only can we respect a man who played, with a tenacity so unfailing, for so high a stake ; but there was some colour for Southey's self-deception.

While a schoolboy at Westminster I had formed an intention of exhibiting the most remarkable forms of mythology which have at any time obtained among mankind, by making each the ground-work of a narrative poem.

A terrible venture, from which Goethe himself might have shrunk ! Southey had neither the art nor the catholic intellect demanded for his task ; and the results seem all the more wasteful because from time to time, as we read painfully on, we start up and exclaim to ourselves that here is a real man of letters, who has mistaken his subject. It is more to the purpose now to point to these rare moments of success than to join in damning Southey's epics. Indeed, it is hard to say what is wrong with them, except that the one thing needful is absent. They are not ill planned ; *The Curse of Kehama* is very well planned ; they are not in an impure style, there is none of Coleridge's besetting rhetoric, none of Scott's facile false diction ; the intention, the spirit, are high ; but we cannot get on with them. By the critics they could only be admired in an age when official criticism was still far in the wake of poetry. *Thalaba* (1801) had, as we know, a passing attraction for Shelley, who borrowed for his *Queen Mab* the irregular blank metres that Southey had himself borrowed from Sayers [1] of Norwich. But Shelley soon outgrew the taste, and reshaped parts of *Queen Mab* into decasyllabics. It is pro-bable that the original error lay in the metre itself, rather than in Southey's handling of it. He makes the best of a bad business. ' No two lines,' he boasts with some justice, ' are employed in sequence that can be read into one ' ; there are no pseudo-Alexandrines, and so forth. But these are mere virtues of abstention. One critic has compared the effect of the metre to that of ' bread without butter, white-bait without the accessories, matches without heads, and a piano with hammers but without wires.' To speak more dully, the ear is not satisfied by a recurrence of iambs, which are plentifully varied, no doubt, by trochaic and anapæstic inter-ludes, but soon recur interminably, and which are cut across at capricious intervals by a pause in the sense. There is not enough recurrence ; nothing at all recurs but the iambs themselves. There are neither rhymes, nor equi-syllabic lines, nor strophic form; only feet, feet, feet, broken irregularly. We cannot bear it long. There is not the underlying law which we feel in many of Blake's almost lawless measures (see Ch. v.); nor again have we sheer rhythmical prose, which Southey, hard as it is, might have managed well. Perhaps in the multitude of three-foot lines, which pull Pegasus, as it were, upon his haunches, and are a bad variation, when too often repeated, upon a prevailing base-line of five feet, may be found the most serious technical flaw. There is therefore a kind of frustrate beauty in *Thalaba*; nor is it always frustrate:

> Meanwhile with fuller reach and stronger swell
> Wave after wave advanced;
> Each following billow lifted the last foam
> That trembled on the sand with rainbow hues;
> The living flower that, rooted to the rock,
> Late from the thinner element
> Shrunk down within its purple stem to sleep,
> Now feels the water, and again
> Awakening, blossoms out
> All its green anther-necks.

This is not unlike Landor's epic verse in dignity of intention —in its classical intention, which is by no means disguised by the Oriental and fantastic matter; but the moulding, when all is said, is inferior, and Landor achieved what Southey only attempted. The passion, too, proper to an Eastern tale of vengeance and fatality is absent; we have only to turn back to *Vathek* to see the difference. Except in his prejudices, the respectable and orderly Southey had little passion, or else he smothered it under his industry.

In *The Curse of Kehama* he allows himself to rhyme, and the rhyme brings some of the missing spirit and passion back with it. But it is intermingled with blank lines confusingly, so that we never know whether to expect a rhyme or not, and the curse of shapelessness is therefore still present and mars a powerful instinct for rhythm. In the Curse itself (' I charm thy life '), and in other spots, such as ' Jaga-Naut ' (xiv.) and ' Padalon ' (xxiii.), Southey rises to a true enchantment, to a true style; there is magnificence and onset; but the final effect leaves us cold through the writer's want of sympathy. Charles Lamb, though he liked the descriptions, was ' not made happier by reading the poem,' and thought ' there was too much trick in it.' Thus he is reported by Crabb Robinson, and we may well agree. In truth, these exotic legends, drawn from the ends of the earth and from the stores of Southey's reading, are a sign of the time, and show the cosmopolitan poetic interest which is attested by Hugo, by Chateaubriand, and by Goethe himself ; but this interest sits ill on Southey, who had no real touch of Indian, or Arabian, or Mexican sentiment, but got his subjects up as if for an article, and doggedly wrote a theme upon each of them.

The religion of the Hindoos . . . of all false religions is the most monstrous in its fables, and the most fatal in its effects. . . . In *Thalaba* nothing but moral sublimity could compensate for the extravagance of the fictions, and . . . all the skill I might possess in the art of poetry was required to counterbalance the disadvantage of a mythology with which few readers were likely to be well acquainted, and which would appear monstrous if its deformities were not kept out of sight.

This is hardly the right spirit ; but we need not throw scornful pebbles at Southey's cairn, or dwell on the consequences ; on the cold Orientalism, the heartless dealings in marvel. In *Madoc*, and especially in *Roderick*, there are passages of real loftiness, and the subject of the latter, which also occupied Scott and Landor, is a great and truly epical one. Landor strove to make it dramatic, as will be seen presently. The landscapes in *Roderick*, as well as the gentler passages, have a marked Wordsworthian ring, but are no servile following. The impression, however, left by the work as a whole is pallid ; and it is plain once more that the ' three indispensable purities of poetry,' cited by Southey in a triad that he found or invented, namely, ' pure truth, pure language, and pure manners,' are, however ' indispensable,' not sufficient.

III

Southey's prose is much more voluminous, and much better, than his verse ; yet little of it has lived. It is better, because the negative excellences of his verse—such as the level, workmanlike diction, so lacking in salience—become positive virtues in his prose. Here his subject is given to him ; he seldom has to create one. And where there is greatness in the subject, as in the *Life of Wesley* or the *Life of Nelson* there is, then the style is a perfect medium. We look through it as through pure gently-flowing water ; it does not distract our attention from the subject, and this is Southey's merit. It is pure eighteenth-century English, ranking high in its own high order. But

whether that order be the highest or no, Southey's prose is
not supreme within it. His mind is receptive and impres-
sible rather than originative, and this deficiency is mirrored
in his language. Swift has all the classical virtues, lucidity,
measure, adaptiveness ; but he also moulds and colours his
subject. Southey does not ; he has little genius ; and his
achromatic prose, with all its effortless ease and rightness,
leaves us impatient and dissatisfied. He is like Browning's
Andrea del Sarto, ' the faultless painter,' lacking in ' the play,
the insight, and the stretch' that are Raphael's ; except that,
unlike Andrea del Sarto, Southey never seems aware of the
deficiency. Some will say that this is grudging praise, and
that we must not ask for ' better bread than is made of wheat ' ;
and certainly it is more needful now to vindicate Southey's
fame than to slight him. There is room for a pleasing and
varied anthology from his prose works. Many delightful
passages could thus be saved from the mass of lumber. The
Life of Nelson, at any rate, is secure ; it need not figure in
such a treasury. This process could be well applied, for
instance, to *The Doctor*, where the style is not achromatic,
but tinted, wilful, and humoristic, and which Southey wrote
to please himself and wrote from his heart. In *The Doctor*,
however, he becomes tedious ; a little of it goes a long way ;
and it is a book to be ' tasted,' not ' chewed and digested.'
Besides, much of it is imitative. Southey has taken on, by
second nature, a comic rich Rabelaisian manner, or a whimsical
excursive Sterne-like manner, and becomes the creature of his
chameleon reading. We hardly feel, as we do with his favourite
Burton, whose vast learning colours his very essence, that
he is original in spite of it. But most of Southey's books
fall into the former class, and are in his even, limpid style.[1]

Otherwise, they almost defy classification. Some of them,
such as *Omniana* (1812) and the *Commonplace Book*, are
immense collections of ' notes and queries,' such as three
ordinary scholars do not gather in a lifetime. They give a
vivid picture of Southey's mental furniture, and of the kind
of material, ever easily at command, that he was ready to
give out, woven and shot and broidered, in *The Doctor*. Others
are travel diaries, either plain and simple like the *Letters from
Spain and Portugal*, published in 1797, or satiric after a
familiar model, such as the *Letters from England by Don Manuel
Espriella* (1807), wherein, after the manner of Goldsmith and
Morier, a foreigner's surprised impressions of England are put
on record. Others are kindly, over-generous introductions of

lesser men of letters, like the memoir of Kirke White, or the *Lives of Uneducated Poets*. Many are *Quarterly* or other magazine articles reprinted, like the solid *Essays* (1832) of an anti-Whig or anti-Radical type; those against Catholic Emancipation are perhaps the most fervent, and the least enlightened. *Sir Thomas More, or Colloquies on the Progress and Prospects of Society* (1829), is a series of imaginary conversations between Southey and the ghost of More, who appears amidst the most beautiful scenes, and talks, and hears talk, on the gravest topics. The landscapes are exquisite : they are Southey's best title to be called a 'lake poet'; and the engraving of his library, with the Keswick spire in the distance, is well in keeping. We do not know whether to laugh or not when these two interlocutors meet by Walla Crag and shake their heads over the educational proposals of Mr. Robert Owen, the Socialist of Lanark. At any rate the scene is natural enough, except that Sir Thomas More is a wraith ; for such solitudes no doubt echoed to long anxious discussions between Southey and his friends. Macaulay's review does little justice to this piquant feature of the *Colloquies*, or to their frequent charm.

Southey's dealings with the history and literature of the Peninsular races must not pass unhonoured. He had, as he says, 'intellectually naturalised himself' in that field of study, to a degree not up to then rivalled by any Englishman. He found in it a new realm of poetry, folklore, romance, and grandiose heroism. He had travelled in Spain, and knew its scenery, though his descriptions lack the intimate sympathy of Beckford's. He wove into English prose *The Chronicle of the Cid* (1808), embodying also passages from the *Poema*, and translated *Amadis de Gaul*, as well as the Portuguese *Palmerin of England*. In his long *History of the Peninsular War* (1822-32) he suffered from the proximity of Napier, whose great work (1828-40) eclipsed him. Southey's powers and defects are here conspicuous enough. His accounts of the French Revolution and of Napoleon, his two bogeys, are wholly puerile, and his reports of the debates in the Commons are frankly *Quarterly* and partisan. He only writes well when his imagination is touched, and his accounts of some of the battles, and of scenes like the death of Sir John Moore, are in his best vein. Another work of great and conscientious labour is his *History of Brazil* (1810-19), a theme hardly touched before in any language. At the close he promises himself the meed of fame, in a strain of high assurance which is like that of some Renaissance poet ; but the book has not been reprinted. It reveals, however, some of his best and most genial qualities. His rigid and blind anti-Romanism softens when he comes to the work of the Jesuits in Paraguay ; and his pictures of savage life and custom are most vivid and particular. The book is written with unusual zest, and Southey gallantly announces his intention—never fulfilled—to follow it up with the history of Portugal and its literature. One little episode, published separately, *The Expedition of Orsua and the Crimes of Aguirre* (1821), is a deftly-coloured and dramatic piece of narrative. In all this kind of work, founded often on obscure and crabbed chronicles, Southey shows something of the old conception, such as was cherished by King Alfred, of the translator's function. He wishes to be a presenter, an educator. He treats his material with an eye to the average reader, smoothing out the rough places and proportioning as he sees fit. He is, in this way, a really great populariser.

The *Life of Nelson* (1813), designed as a manual 'for the young sailor, which he may carry about with him,' and therefore studiously simple in language, was written before the materials for a true biography were sifted or available, and founded on authorities which are now pronounced most unsafe. It has to be checked from point to point by the conclusions of scholars like Hannay, Mahan, and Laughton. Southey shows his usual incapacity for appreciating Napoleon and the French, and he was not conversant with the science of naval warfare. Yet he achieved a classic memoir, which is not merely a romance. He has an intuition of Nelson's genius and greatness as a man, he writes with a noble measure and reserve, and the skill of his narrative, interweaving as it does history and biography without confusion, and unfolding the character of his hero from point to point through his actions, is memorable enough.

The *Life of Wesley and the Rise and Progress of Methodism* (1820), which is also a life of Whitfield and of many lesser lights, is not a work of art like the *Nelson*, but is a more durable piece of historical scholarship, and calls out many of Southey's rarer gifts. It is written, to begin with, from without ; that is, from the standpoint of his strict Anglicanism, here noticeably liberalised, and also in the spirit of a calm detachment which is wholly inaccessible to, and condemnatory of, the more passionate and violent forms of enthusiasm. It is not to be thought that a biographer, who described Wesley as having invented, in the ' outward signs ' of conversion, ' a new disease,' should give satisfaction to the Methodists themselves. But the analysis of Wesley's creed, given often through his own words, in the twentieth chapter, is masterly and even sympathetic ; the recognition of his quickening power and influence on conduct, and of the sources of comfort that he opened, is duly generous ; and the miniature biographies that are interspersed, of the first followers and the field-preachers, are planned with the utmost skill. Southey works from the printed sources with much diligence, suffers Wesley to speak for himself, and if necessary to condemn himself, and leaves a most luminous impression of his work and genius.

Of his other memoirs little need be said ; of the *Lives of the Admirals*, or of the briefer ones of Cromwell and Bunyan. The *Cromwell* is bigoted and unintelligent ; the *Bunyan* hardly worthy of the theme, though not disfigured in the same way. Southey was more at home with Cowper, his *Life* of whom is full of charm and kindness, though somewhat rambling ; and the thirteenth chapter, on the state of English letters about the year 1780, is most significant of the state of critical perspective in 1834.

If most of Southey's prose has fallen out of sight, the reason is less to be found in its mass and its air of taskwork than in a certain intellectual stiffness and sterility of view. His conservatism is unbending ; yet this is no bar to permanence, for the same might be said of Wordsworth, of Coleridge, and of Scott. But Southey's conservatism has not the geniality, the romantic chivalrousness, of Scott's ; nor has it the august stamp of fervid meditation which at times distinguishes Wordsworth's. Nor is it, like Coleridge's, rooted in a philosophic play of thought, which is alive to the last whatever we may think of the conclusions ; it is fixed and unreflective. In the same way Southey, though his enjoyment of books is deep, indeed is perhaps his master-passion, is not a critic of mark ; beside Coleridge he seems lifeless. In his endless quotations and accompanying expressions of relish we miss that reaction of thought upon the subject, that penetrative power as of radium-rays, which is felt in every page of the *Table Talk* or of *Anima Poetae*. For all this, Southey, if not in any strict sense a great writer, is often, nay, is instinctively, a sound and a good one, and is repeatedly a delightful one ; and he left the status of men of letters, and the tradition of their calling, higher than he found it. His correspondence, with its dignity, its naturalness, and its playful, affectionate touches of home, has all the virtues of his best writing, and reveals his friendships with Wordsworth, with Lamb, and with Landor.

IV

Walter Savage Landor[1] loved to see himself as a solitary figure, on the sky-line of the 'far eastern uplands,' where he 'walked meditating and remembering.' His famous impeccable phrases, 'I shall dine late, but the dining-room will be well lighted, and the guests few and select '—' I strove with none '—' I am alone, and will be alone, as long as I live, and after,' are not to be taken too solemnly. He was sociable and hospitable, and had hosts of friends, and the admiration of the best minds ; he adored children and dogs ; his tender chivalry towards women and his robust power of laughter among men did not desert him, and he lived to within ' two paces,' as he says, of ninety. He uttered the regrets of age with the freshness of youth. He passed most of his days in reading, writing, or talking. His life, in spite of all his quarrels, explosions, vexations, blindnesses, estrangements, and losses, cannot be called either tragical or lonely. The affectionate caricature of Charles Dickens, and the amused shrewdness that can be seen through the reverence and admiration of Robert Browning, serve to correct Landor's self-estimate. He was a splendid, insuperable old man, much loved, though much galled ; yet when he turned to his art, his troubles were ' but the fierce vexations of a dream ' ; and his art was such as to give him the utmost of pleasure that may consist with the torments of an artist.

In his art, certainly Landor does appear as somewhat of a solitary. It is hard to draw his lines of relationship with his contemporaries. He crosses, like a star from some other system, the more familiar orbits in which Scott and Wordsworth, Byron and Shelley, with their known attractions and repulsions, are seen moving. In his toughness, his sense of the heroic, and his jealousy for the rigour of the English language, he has affinities with Wordsworth ; but in his richer sense of beauty and Hellenism he is nearer to Keats ; and yet his presentation of beauty, and his treatment of the antique, are quite different from those of Keats. The same independence is seen in his public sympathies, and in the way he expresses them. He is with the poets and orators of freedom ; he is a child of the Revolution, inspired, he also, by the Greek and Roman ideals of republicanism. But, like Byron, he is also an aristocrat, though of a truer breed ; he ' hates the crowd,' and has a streak of Coriolanus, and also of the fastidious English gentleman, which is found colouring his admiration for Mazzini and Kosciusko. Here we pass into the region of his whims and prejudice, which have little to do with his genius ;. but he remains the poet of liberty and ' regeneration ' nevertheless. Landor's ' place,' therefore, in his age, as the phrase runs, is not easy to determine, for he refuses to be put in his place ; but we can at least ask what would be missed, if we could imagine his age without him.

His last publication, *Heroic Idylls*, appeared in 1863, sixty-eight years after his earliest (*Poems*, 1795) ; and *Gebir* (1798), his first real poem, was only three years later than these. He laboured for as long a span of time as Goethe, Hugo, Carlyle, or Hobbes. He outlived not only his own generation but the next ; he praised and survived Shelley, Keats, and Hood. His *Hellenics* first appeared in English in 1846, four years after Tennyson's *Ulysses* ; but we think of them as earlier, and in substance many of them are earlier, having been made in Latin long before. He owed little or nothing to any contemporary writer, and founded no school. It will be easier to see how, if at all, he touches his age after his curious, voluminous, un-equal, noble performance has been reviewed.

Landor's work falls, not very distinctly, into three periods, of which the dividing landmarks are the first series of *Imaginary Conversations* in 1824 and the *Hellenics* of 1846. The first twenty-six years he gave almost wholly to verse, of which not a little is in Latin. Amongst the volumes containing Latin are *Gebirus* (1803), issued five years after *Gebir*; *Simon-idea* (Latin and English, 1806) ; and two volumes, *Idyllia Heroica* (1815, amplified 1820), which contain the originals of many of the *Hellenics*. The English *Gebir* was succeeded by the *Poetry* of 1802, and the next volume of note was the tragedy of *Count Julian* (1812). Most of this earlier English poetry is in blank verse, exalted or tragical in tone, and ellipti-cal and rugged in utterance, but containing passages of a clear and vivid beauty. There is no steady conduct in the story, no even rightness in the style ; the qualities that we call classical only emerge here and there. The seeds of that kind of perfection which was afterwards to distinguish Landor's poetry at its best are to be found either in a few of his short English pieces, of the occasional, epigrammatic, or inscriptional order, or in the Latin works. There his genius is already beginning to be pure—his genius for uttering heroic emotion in the ancient way, and also for gentle, lovely, and idyllic portraiture.

He had already, by 1824, written prose, but chiefly in the shape of fugitive pamphlets or letters upon political affairs ;

and these give little prophecy of the *Imaginary Conversations*, except, indeed, of those duller ones that treat of similar topics. With the *Conversations* he was busied for the next five years almost unbrokenly ; and five volumes came out before 1830. These were followed by the three longer works, which are in essence protracted 'Conversations': *The Citation and Examination of William Shakespeare, etc.* (1834), *Pericles and Aspasia* (1836), and *The Pentameron* (1837); a triad rich in beauty, wisdom, and vivacity, and most original in plan, although in no case free from weary stretches. New short poems, and new sallies in political prose, had appeared meanwhile ; but the close of this second period is occupied with the three connected dramas, *Andrea of Hungary, Giovanna of Naples,* and *Fra Rupert*, which show the same species of power as *Count Julian,* now much clarified by time and practice. Landor seldom gave up for good any forms that he had attempted ; in his third and latest period there are examples, and sometimes the best examples, of them all.

In 1846, besides the collected edition of his *Works,* came out his first batch of *Hellenics,* augmented and modified both in the following year and again in 1859. His *Poemata et Inscriptiones* (1847) is the last volume that he published wholly in Latin. His English verses, *The Last Fruit off an Old Tree,* so misnamed, came in 1853, and his *Dry Sticks Fagoted* in 1858. He also poured forth dramatic scenes in verse, further *Imaginary Conversations,* including 'those of the Greeks and Romans,' on the whole the finest in workmanship of any ; and more prose scraps. In the year (1863) before his death the tireless old man issued *Heroic Idylls, with additional Poems.* Few English writers with any claim to greatness have been more voluminous. Hence Landor has never been completely edited, even by his faithful biographer Forster, who omits a few of his best things as well as not a little that can well be sacrificed.

V

Landor's *Poems* of 1795, and his *Moral Epistle,* an attack on Pitt, issued in the same year, are youthful exercises in the classical taste, and sixty years afterwards he relates his early likings : he was then

> Contented with the native lay
> Of Pope or Prior, Swift or Gay,
> Or Goldsmith, or that graver bard
> Who led me to the lone churchyard—

until, he adds, he was claimed by Spenser and Chaucer. These poets, indeed, ' affected him little enough as a writer,' almost as little as the ' Persian and Arabic ' bards from whom he pretended to have made his ' translations ' in 1800. Landor soon escaped from eighteenth-century classicism of this sort, and came towards the true antique ; liberated, as it would seem, by reading Pindar, who taught him to be ' compendious and exclusive,' and to be abstruse and elliptical and to hide his head in cloud ; and by reading Virgil, who taught him the heroic way of delineation ; and, above all, by reading Milton, to whom he was ever to offer a free man's allegiance, and whose blank verse shaped and ennobled but never overpowered his own. Parts of *Gebir* (1798) were written first in Latin,[1] and the whole was afterwards (1803) published in Latin as *Gebirus*. The lines upon the sea-shell, than which few of Landor's are more often repeated, were first conceived in Latin :

> Veteres reminiscitur aedes,
> Oceanusque suus quo murmure murmurat illa.

This became :

> It remembers its august abodes,
> And murmurs as the ocean murmurs there.

Such influences do not impair, but rather explain, the poetical independence of *Gebir*, a work as wonderful in its way, coming as it does in the age of Darwin and *The Anti-Jacobin*, as Blake's oracular books or the *Lyrical Ballads*. It does not mark a date like *The Ancient Mariner* or *Tintern Abbey*, for Landor founded no school or tradition : and none but he could carry forward, or purify, or perfect the manner that he invented. And it is a manner imperfect enough, with the imperfections and splendour of youthful strength and pride ; the language often half-hewn, rigid, hieratic, like some early monument in that ' land of Nile ' where the story is laid. The occasional drumming hardness of the decasyllables and the violent compression of the imagery are so unlike Virgil that comparison seems inept ; and yet many a passage leaves us regretting that Landor never translated into English blank metre the hunting-party in the Fourth Æneid, or the wrestling-match in the Fifth :

> Meantime, with pomp august and solemn, borne
> On four white camels tinkling plates of gold,
> Heralds before and Ethiop slaves behind,
> Each with the sign of office in his hand,
> Each on his brow the sacred stamp of years,
> The four ambassadors of peace proceed.

> Rich carpets bear they, corn and generous wine,
> The Syrian olive's cheerful gift they bear,
> With stubborn goats that eye the mountain-top
> Askance, and riot with reluctant horn,
> And steeds and stately camels in their train.

This is nearer than Dryden's *Virgil* to a Virgilian style, except that the pace is somewhat slower than Virgilian ; and we do not need the evidence of *Gebirus* to show that the author was steeped in Virgil. The story is formally laid out like that of an epic ; it is in seven books, and an idyllic underplot is woven into the main action, which itself is tragical in issue. We begin to ask whether the 'phantom epic,'[1] that haunted the poets of the English and French Renaissance—a dream that once came true when Milton dreamed it—was this, after all, to return into our literature ? We can hardly say so much. Landor, in his *Hellenics*, came to beat out a language and versification worthy of an epic ; but wisely, when he had done so, confined its use to episodes or short stories. And even this he attained slowly, for the mass of the *Hellenics* lies nearly half a century ahead of *Gebir*. Only two other poets were to show even the promise of such an epic style ; but *Hyperion* remains a fragment, and the *Idylls of the King* an allegory in episodes. Now and then *Hyperion* itself recalls *Gebir*,[2] perhaps because the younger poet had the elder in his mind. In Keats's lines on Thea such a debt has been traced :

> How beautiful, if Sorrow had not made
> Sorrow more beautiful than Beauty's self :
> There was a listening fear in her regard
> As if calamity had but begun . . .

The passage in *Gebir* forecasts Keats in other ways as well :

> There was brightening paleness in his face
> Such as Diana rising o'er the rocks
> Shower'd on the lonely Latmian ; on his brow
> Sorrow there was, yet nought was there austere.

These two poets may be said to have crossed on their journey : for Landor began with a stiff noble manner, which passed into something gentler and freer, while Keats began with a soft flowing manner, which passed into something potent and august.

The manner of *Gebir* is epical, but the theme is only strong enough for an Ovidian tale, so that the manner becomes too great for the theme. Landor found the sketch of the story in an appendix to Clara Reeve's *Progress of Romance*,[3] lent him by his friend Rose Aylmer. It is of Eastern origin, but the genteel Clara Reeve had not left much of the East in it. Her tale, says Landor, lacked simplicity and keeping ; *sed erat magnificum nescio quid sub crepusculo vetustatis*.[1] He altered freely what he found, and classicised it as much as he could ; adding, for example (not without aid from Dante), the incident of Gebir's visit to the underworld. The hero himself is a kind of gigantic shadow of Æneas ; he wins the unwilling love of Charoba, Princess of Egypt, and founds a city in her realms, which is destroyed by enchantments. His death is brought about by Dalica, Charoba's nurse, who gives him a poisoned shirt to wear upon his wedding morning. The hatred of Dalica is a weak occasion for so tragical a close ; it has nothing to do with Gebir's character, and is not rooted in the action. Landor had found a noble and picturesque but not a really heroic subject.

But the poem already shows that ruling passion for plastic beauty, and that distinctive way of shaping it into words, in which Landor stands alone amongst the poets of his time and country, and which meets us everywhere in his writing. The curious *arrestedness* of his pictures, if the phrase may be used, begins to appear. He has the air of representing not so much the imaginary object, as some marble or painted representation of it that he has first imagined. He chronicles the moment of checked motion that is proper to a solid group or to the figures on a vase. Keats might have taken examples for his great ode from Landor's verse or prose. Lessing, who had written his *Laocoon* thirty years before, would perhaps have said that the flow and continuity proper to poetry, as distinct from the other fine arts, are thereby impaired ; and certainly to read Landor is often like regarding a series of sculptural poses. But that this is lawful in poetry, is shown by the great and peculiar pleasure that it gives : as in the description of the nymph, who has outwrestled Gebir's brother, the shepherd Tamar, and carries off the prize :

> The sheep she carried easy as a cloak ;
> But, when I heard its bleating, as I did,
> And saw, she hastening on, its hinder feet
> Struggle, and from her snowy shoulder slip,
> One shoulder its poor efforts had unveil'd.
> Then all my passions mingling fell in tears.

And the image is equally distinct here :

> Haply and one among them with his spear
> Measures the lintel, if so great its highth
> As will receive him with his helm unlower'd.

This way of describing will meet us again in the *Imaginary Conversations*, and is essentially undramatic, or rather anti-dramatic, because it would be superfluous and irritating if the images thus told of were really to be seen upon a stage. It is all the fitter for the purpose in hand, which is to supply the lack of the bodily eyesight.

The hampered magnificence of *Gebir* is found again in the *Poetry* of 1802. The lengthy fragment entitled *The Phocœans*, which Landor never reprinted, has still more of the air of a constrained translation, and goes farther in the path of tangled obscurity. But *Chrysaor*, though liable to the same reproach, is the earliest of these Titan and rebel poems, founded on classical indications, which harmonised so well with the revolutionary temper, and in which Shelley and Keats were to triumph. In splendour of occasional phrase and in strength of rhythm it is a worthy prelude to their work : although, no doubt, the chisel is flung down too soon, and the effect is that of a giant face half-emerging from the rock, with the frown of the death-struggle already apparent, and with a voice issuing

> More dismal than the blasts of Phlegethon
> Below, that urge along ten thousand ghosts
> Wafted loud-wailing o'er the fiery tide.

The political peroration is ill in keeping, but *Regeneration*, a short piece in which the verse moves on a wing yet more elate and superb than in *Chrysaor*, marks plainly enough the new era in poetic sentiment. Collins, in his *Ode to Liberty*, sang of the land ' where holy Freedom died,' and attained at moments to a Greek beauty. But by 1802 the Revolution has come and gone, and Napoleon fills the scene ; and, almost in the same hour as Wordsworth, Landor reproaches his country for supineness in the struggle against despotism. Thus the passion for Greece and the passion for popular liberty are now one ; and despite some declamation, the hope of the Mediterranean peoples to regain a little of their ancient glory is hymned with an ardour as pure as Shelley's or Swinburne's, and with a lofty precision of language that is most unlike the familiar outpourings of Byron :

> We are what suns and winds and waters make us ;
> The mountains are our sponsors, and the hills
> Fashion and win their nursling with their smiles.
> But where the land is dim from tyranny,
> There tiny pleasures occupy the place
> Of glories and of duties ; as the feet
> Of fabled faeries when the sun goes down
> Trip o'er the grass where wrestlers strove by day.

Between Milton and Shelley, only two writers can be said
to have commanded the great *public* style in poetry. Burke,
like some of his fellow-orators, has it in prose, and Blake at
moments in his prophecies. But Wordsworth and Landor
have it to the full — Wordsworth, assuredly, much more
frequently and fully. But Landor has it here, ar in prose
he has it often, in the ' conversations ' of Penn and Peterborough, and of the two Ciceros, and elsewhere.

VI

The tragedy of *Count Julian* has a grandiose subject, and
also a tough and strong dramatic mainspring. Julian, a
Spanish patriot, is driven to attack his king, Roderigo, who has
outraged his daughter. This he can only do by striking also
at his country, and enlisting in alliance her Moorish enemies.
The Moors, on their side, distrust Julian and turn upon him.
This admirable theme is spoilt by Landor with ingenious
perversity. The action becomes too complex for the reader
to follow ; the cross-loves and internecine ambitions of the
Moors, and the position of Egilona, Roderigo's queen, in their
camp, are alike fatally obscure. Indeed the whole action of
the tale at any given crisis remains in a darkness which the
painfully compressed dialogue only helps to intensify. As a
whole, therefore, and despite the admiration of Southey and
the enthusiasm of some later critics, *Count Julian* is incurably
a failure ; it is wearisome, undramatic, wooden, and impossible. But a selection could easily be made of single scenes,
of lucid and inspired passages, and of exalted and priceless
similes, which would seem to brand such a verdict with im-
pertinence. *Count Julian* in this way recalls some of the high
Senecan tragedies of Daniel or Greville, and like them was
avowedly written only to be read. There are the same strain
and intricacy, the same frequent splendours and sudden
felicities, and the same promise, held to the lips and then
snatched away, of dramatic style and power. The great
speeches, such as Julian's upon the love of country (Act i. sc. 4),
have an epic rather than a dramatic ring ; and there is more
life and humanity in them than in all the *Alahams* and *Philo-
tases* of the old ' closet drama.' The brakes and thorns that
beset the approaches to this lofty play are so much more
apparent than the glades and fountains within it, that they
need no announcing. And the great style, though warped
and interrupted continually, is never far away ; and when it

comes, with its never slavish echoes of Marlowe or Milton, its relish for Eastern and romantic names, and its instinct for their rightful and stately use, the inalienable mark of Landor is perceived at once, like the cipher of some master-craftsman in steel or gold :

> 'Tis Abdalazis, son of Muza, prince
> Commanding Africa, from Abyla
> To where Tunisian pilots bend the eye
> O'er ruin'd temples in the glassy wave.
> Till quiet times and ancient laws return
> He comes to govern here.

The versification of Landor at this stage, and indeed always, is markedly regular. The endings overrun a little, and the single lines are usually intact, giving the effect of a sheaf of arrows of equal length. There is not yet, save in short passages, the more limpid flow and the more even sweetness and dignity of the *Hellenics* ; but at the worst we are far enough from the blank verse of Southey's *Madoc* or *Roderick*, so blameless in a neutral way, but so impossible to remember ; and at the best, we are led to think of the higher blank verse of Wordsworth ; Landor's has the same sort of chastity and beauty :

> Wide are the regions of our far-famed land :
> Thou shalt arrive at her remotest bounds,
> See her best people, choose some holiest house ;
> Whether where Castro from surrounding vines
> Hears the hoarse ocean roar among his caves,
> And, through the fissure in the green churchyard,
> The wind wail loud the calmest summer day ;
> Or where Santona leans against the hill,
> Hidden from sea and land by groves and bowers.

This is quoted not so much as something detachable for its own grace and music, but as rather an example of texture—a length from Landor's loom ; it is the kind of writing that will hold out well, despite a certain uniformity, as a vehicle for noble narrative or description. In the *Hellenics*, a quarter of a century later, this style or something like it has become habitual.

Landor's remaining plays, or 'dramatic scenes,' composed much later than *Count Julian*, are near akin to it, although they concede more to the weakness of mortal readers and are far more natural in language. The characters, if they do not grow or change during the action, at least reveal themselves under its stress. Nor does the poet now overlabour in revision work that is already pithy and pregnant to a fault. The most ambitious of these works, 'no better,' as he too modestly puts it, 'than imaginary conversations in metre,' are the three connected pieces, *Andrea of Hungary, Giovanna of Naples,* and *Fra Rupert*; of which the first two were very rapidly written in 1838, and the third in 1840, none of them being meant for the theatre. The high poetic drama that cannot be acted may be a doubtful and amphibious form at the best. It is meant to be read; but then the best plays to read are those which are also meant to be played, although, as with some of Shakespeare's, we may after all prefer reading to seeing them. It cannot be said that Landor writes even for his readers; he writes for himself, and perhaps for Forster and Southey and a few of the chosen; and there is no fear that too many will ever join that company, or share the rough and unmellowed but splendid fruit that he sets before them. But those who do so will wonder at the current disregard of many scenes, matching the most impassioned and salient of Landor's prose conversations, and written in verse that recalls the level gravity and sweetness of Massinger or of Beaumont at their best. While Byron's plays, mostly so dreary and broken-winded, are often reprinted, and known comparatively well, the explorers of this lofty trilogy have remained few enough. It is true that the poet's inborn weakness in conducting a dramatic action has not disappeared, and that there is enough confusion in the story to exasperate any patience that is short of Teutonic. But this obscurity leaves many a scene and situation untouched. The pictures of the light, frightened, flippant boy Andrea, Giovanna's consort, and of her kindly half-maternal pleasure in his lightness, and of his murder at their wedding-feast; of the fragile youths and maidens surrounding them, and also swept to death; of Boccaccio and Fiammetta, dallying by the way; and of Rienzi, who is tempted by policy, despite his wife's honourable reproaches, to countenance the monstrous charge that imputes Andrea's death to Andrea's bride; these passages, like the whole trilogy, are linked together by the dark and dominant figure of the monk Rupert, breeder of troubles and intriguer in the Hungarian cause. Rupert is Landor's version of the clerical villain, already so long vulgarised, as we have seen, in the contemporary novel and drama. But he goes back to the Elizabethans for his model, and not to the later, baser, and derivative sources. Rupert comes to his natural doom like some personage of Marlowe's or Middleton's, and in his weary, half-remorseful soliloquies there is undeniable force and splendour. The frequency of massy, exalted ethical

discourses in these plays reminds us rather of the poetic habit
of Chapman or of Jonson than of the more romantic among
our tragic dramatists ; but Landor's note in this kind of verse
is as personal and intransmissible as it is in his prose. Some
of the passages which were inserted after the first drafting
deserve Forster's praise of their ' extraordinary beauty ' :

> When sunshine glistens round,
> And friends as young as we are sit beside us,
> We smile at Death—one rather grim indeed
> And whimsical, but not disposed to hurt us—
> And give and take fresh courage. But, sweet sister,
> The days are many when he is unwelcome,
> And you will think so too another time.
> 'Tis chiefly in cold places, with old folks,
> His features seem prodigiously amiss.
> But Life looks always pleasant, sometimes more
> And sometimes less so, but looks always pleasant,
> And, when we cherish him, repays us well.

There is a similar strain in the scene where the wife of Rienzi
tries to shame him out of his projected infamy :

> If thou do this,
> Eternal is the stain upon thine hand ;
> Freedom through thee will be the proud man's scoff,
> The wise man's problem ; even the slave himself
> Will rather bear the scourge than trust the snare.
> Thou hast brought large materials, large and solid,
> To build thy glory on ; if equity
> Be not the base, lay not one stone above.

This was not, and is not, and will not be, popular writing.
It had not the flushed and irksome sentiment of the ' plays
on the passions' that were then the mode, and its very
faults, its condensation and restraint, were the opposite of
the faults that were then and are always popular. But
Landor, like Wordsworth, tries to work in granite ; and if
the material is often stubborn, and refuses to yield the curves
that lie hid in marble, and is loth to reflect the sun, it is monu-
mental notwithstanding. In these plays the spirit of pure
beauty, though by no means absent, is somewhat in abeyance.
It is not in drama, but in idyll, and epigram, and choric ode,
and prose dialogue, that Landor ceases to become an ' unsub-
duable old Roman,' and becomes a modern Italian or a Sicilian
Greek. But these rugged works, if we are to call them Roman,
are such in the sense that Jonson's or Chapman's tragedies
claim the title. The antique is there, but it has passed through
the Elizabethan mind ; and to many who open *Count Julian*
or *Fra Rupert* for the first time, there will come the same thrill,

the same sense of discovery, that greeted Lamb or Hazlitt when they revealed the less known of the elder dramatists.

Landor's scornful and voluntary roughness of handiwork is far less perceptible in the series of episodes called *The Siege of Ancona*, a one-act piece in which the action and style are as clear as they are heroic. It is perhaps the most faultless of his longer poems. ' No event,' he says, ' in the history of Italy, including the Roman, is at once so tragical and so glorious as the siege of Ancona ' in 1154. The city is beset by Germans and Venetians at once, and brought to the last pinch of famine. It is defended by the Consul, whose voice heartens the people and shames the cowardly Senate ; by an aged priest, Father John, who cuts the Venetian cables under water ; and by gallant women and youths ; and is at last relieved, just in time, by Marchesella and the Countess of Bertinoro. A high and regular beauty of execution distinguishes this play, rather than any separable patches of eloquence, nor can any passage be torn out for quotation from the scene in which the dying soldier brings the last cup of wine to the dying Lady Malaspina and her infant ; here Landor reaches the high-tide-mark of his pathetic power. The love-tale of Erminia, the Consul's daughter, and the young Stamura, is inwrought with the passages of ' grim-visaged war,' after Landor's favourite fashion and with more than his accustomed skill, and relieves the high spirit of patriot martyrdom that animates the work.

VII

Landor has left some hundreds of lyrics and brief occasional poems, many of them dating from his latter years, and forming together a sort of diary of his higher, gentler, or more playful moods, almost to the exclusion of those stormier ones which we know beset him in reality, but which he commonly preferred to forget rather than to versify. This trait is well described by Lord Houghton : [1]

Nowhere in the range of English literature is the glory and happiness of moderation of mind more nobly preached than in the writings of this most intemperate man ; nowhere is the sacredness of the placid life more hallowed and honoured than in the utterances of this tossed and troubled spirit.

In his lyric temper he is not a man of his time ; and is far indeed from Byron or Shelley, with their straining, their passionate confessions, and their desire to utter ' the pain of

finite hearts that yearn.' Instead, there is the record of
cheerful friendly hours and of chivalrous and controlled
affections, or else the harmonious sadness of retrospect.   Landor
was free from the ' malady of the century ' ; in fact, his tone
is of no century in particular ; some of his odes and lyrics
might be by Meleager.   Others, again, might be by Ben
Jonson, with whom his affinities, as has often been noticed,
are remarkable.   There is the same mixture of oaken independence and ruggedness with flowery grace and charm, and
even a similarity, perhaps not unconscious, of rhythm.   It
is impossible and impertinent to appraise Landor's short
poems in detail, and in his lines upon the critics he has warned
us against doing so :

> This takes me down his slate,
> Draws me a line and teaches me to write ;
> Another pats me kindly on the head,
> But finds one letter here and there too great,
> One passable, one pretty well, one quite.

Every man will make his own anthology amongst these verses ;
it is not likely to be a small one, and the art of the poetic
medallion has found few surer masters than Landor.

His love-poems range from a strain of lofty and steady,
rather than passionate, regard, to one of knightly gallantry
or compliment, mixed with a certain stately pleasantry that
is all his own.   Of women, Landor, Scott, Wordsworth, and
Shelley always write like gentlemen ; while Byron, Moore,
and Keats can never wholly be trusted to do so.   Such a
temper is not unfavourable to the nobler kinds of poetic form.
The sundry verses (many of them written from 1802 to 1806)
addressed to his oldest and longest-living friend, ' Ianthe,'
or Sophia Jane Swifte, afterwards Countess de Molandé, are
as pure in finish as in devotion, and are known to all.   They
tend to the briefer kind of Greek epigram, and of this kind
Landor is the greatest practitioner in English :

> Soon, O Ianthe ! life is o'er,
> And sooner beauty's heavenly smile :
> Grant only (and I ask no more)
> Let love remain that little while.

Rose Aylmer, which did not become perfect all at once, and
its second flowering *The Three Roses*, are above praise.   They
are epigrams in the high sense of the term ; that is, a complete and immortal utterance of a single passing thought, or
feeling which yet is the fruit of years : ' a moment's monument,' like the sonnet, but less complex than the sonnet,

and yet more intellectual in substance and pointed in form than ordinary lyric. Many of Landor's shorter pieces come under this description. They may be grouped roughly and not without cross-division into verses addressed to friends living or departed; verses in which the dominant note is that of musing old age; and incidental pieces, often written in sweet and fluent octosyllabics, upon matters of the moment—brief epistles or journal-entries which chance to fall into rhyme. There are also a few odes, such as those to Southey or to Ablett, of an ampler rhythm than the rest.

Landor's likeness to Jonson, and to those other stoical elders, Drayton and Chapman, who nurse themselves in a Roman pride, and 'hate the crowd,' and despise 'the dull ass's hoof,' comes out well in his little poems. It is a frame of mind learnt in part from Tacitus or Plutarch, and partly natural; and it may comport with prejudice and spleen, but never with envy. Smallness and oblique censoriousness, the vices of the writing man, are not found in such soldierly spirits; and Landor's just and cordial praises of Lamb and Wordsworth, of Browning and Dickens, like his generous and honest overpraise of Southey, recall Ben Jonson's openhandedness in speaking of Bacon or Shakespeare with those well-picked superlatives, which are often, after all, the truest criticism and honour most the giver. If we are to choose, the lines *To the Sister of Elia* may be thought to excel in the difficult quality of restrained sublimity, and to be the pattern of a memorial tablet inscribed to a great man; referring as they do only to the essence, and neglecting all things accidental. Of tributes to the living, the ode, or letter in verse, *To Joseph Ablett*, is the most Horatian, in the proper sense of the epithet; conciliating as it does the tone of personal talk with passages in a high and heroic mode, and being consummate in brilliancy and finish. It was much revised and amplified from the original draft,[1] which is given in Forster's *Life*; and whilst all the additions and burnishings are for the better, none of the removals are to be regretted, except the couplet on Coleridge, who died before the verses were first composed:

> Coleridge hath heard the call, and bathes in bliss
> Among the spirits that have power like his.

The poetry of old age,—the poetry, that is, which is written by the old about themselves, has Landor for its laureate. His power was enhanced and not dulled by the years; for they were themselves its inspiration. Some poets burn them-

selves out and die ; or are dumb if they survive ; or go on
writing, but the spirit is dead. Goethe, Hugo, and Tennyson
are amongst the exceptions, and Landor is with them. We
may fancy that Goethe would have delighted in Landor's
admirably pagan and perfect utterances on youth and death ;
for the natural process has never been so serenely faced by
poet as in the famous epigrams which were written by Landor
during the last twenty years of his life :—' The day returns,
my natal day '—' No, my own love of other years '—' To my
ninth decade I have totter'd on '—' Death stands above me,
whispering low.' One Latin quatrain[1] may be given to show
how naturally he wrote from his heart in either tongue :

> Una, Senecta, viximus multos dies,
> Una atque amice viximus :
> Quietiorem inveneris siquem locum,
> Id dic in aure, tunc abi.

One sometimes meets old persons who seem to have the same
secret, and Landor is their poet. This long and late survival
of his gift, while due in part to a potent vitality, also connects
itself with his special temper as an artist. It would be absurd
to speak of want, or even of economy, of passion, and of the
author of *Tiberius and Vipsania*, in the same breath; but
it was not in Landor to exhaust his heart, or to pierce that
of his hearers, by the intimate and personal outcry that meets
us in the romantic poets. There is a certain guarding of the
altar-flame, which keeps it unimpaired to the last ; and the
gales of Landor's anger and bitterness are spent upon levels
lying far below that still mountain shrine.

This impression is confirmed by the scores of verses of the
occasional kind, which he threw off as happily and incessantly
as Turner did his sketches. Gallant or playful, affectionate
and reminiscent, they keep alive the hours of happiness which
it is easy to forget. *Abertawy*, and the lines *To a Bride*, and
' My serious son,' and the *Apology for Gebir*, are but scattered
examples of his easy felicity in such chronicling ; and these pieces
form part, and perhaps the most consoling part, of Landor's
biography. The rapid and limpid variety of octosyllabic
couplet he often uses, and always with grace ; but he also
likes the old and impressive metre used by Jonson, with lines
of six and ten syllables alternately ; as in *The Genius of Greece* :

> Greece with calm eyes I see,
> Her pure white marbles have not blinded me,
> But breathe on me the love
> Of earthly things as bright as things above.

The regular heroic quatrain, in what may be termed its inscriptional form, he commanded always, and may be said to have made his own.

The humour of Landor is a pleasing mixture of the roguish and the stately. The latter epithet is indeed not always deserved, if, as appears likely, the blatant *Terry Hogan*[1] is to be imputed to him. He had an undeniable and vigorous vein of the Smollettesque in his composition. But in general his light verses are full of grace and dignity and most carefully cut, and their gallantry, as of a young-hearted patriarch writing to please a young girl or a child, is of the most chivalrous sort. The invitation to Tennyson, *The Gifts Returned*, and 'Yes, I write verses now and then,' are but examples. He is perhaps the most graceful payer of versified compliments in the language; the six lines *To E. Arundell* cannot be equalled in their kind :

> Nature ! thou mayst fume and fret,
> There 's but one white violet ;
> Scatter o'er the vernal ground
> Faint resemblances around,
> Nature ! I will tell thee yet,
> There 's but one white violet.

VIII

Landor, then, could write the short poem—nay, the shortest possible poem, of a few lines only—to perfection. To the long poem, or full-sized drama, he proved for various reasons unequal. The flower of his poetic art is certainly found in the best of those pieces of moderate length, inclining often to brevity, which he termed *Hellenics* ; a happy title, that appears to be of his own coinage. A ' Hellenic,' in Landor's usage, is a short story upon a mythic, heroic, or idyllic subject drawn from the Greek, and is commonly written in blank verse. Sometimes it is a dialogue only, without any narrative, in fact an ' imaginary conversation ' in metre ; such are *The Shades of Agamemnon and Iphigeneia* (distinct from the narrative *Iphigeneia and Agamemnon*), *The Death of Clytemnestra*, and *The Madness of Orestes* ; two of these have odes appended, and are so far outside his usual practice. It is never a dramatic monologue like Tennyson's *Ulysses* or Browning's *Artemis Prologuizes*, although one beautiful brief poem, *Artemidora*, consists of a single speech. The Hellenic, when written in Latin, Landor calls an *Idyllium*, or *Idyllium Heroicum*; it is in hexameters. A number of the English Hellenics—

not always the best or easiest, have Latin originals of this
kind. Such are *Coresus and Callirrhoë*, *Corythos*, and *The
Espousals of Polyxena*. Each of the Latin *Idyllia Heroica*
has an English counterpart. *Peleus and Thetis*, and *Achilles
and Helena*, may also be called translations, but they are
versified from Landor's English prose.

The *Hellenics* can be sufficiently enjoyed, though by no
means completely studied, in the collection of 1846, or better
still in the augmented one of 1847. But they occupied Landor,
in one way or another, during most of his life, their composition stretching out both backwards and forwards from those
central years. In English, the rugged *Chrysaor* of 1802,
named already, stands long alone ; but we begin to hear of
the Latin works in Landor's letters[1] as early as 1809, and
Sponsalia Polyxenæ he printed privately in 1817.

The three dialogues from the Agamemnon story might be
thought of as fragments translated from some lost old drama,
dug up in a papyrus. One of them is deliberately made, as
a Greek rival might have made it, to counteract the impression given by Sophocles of the character of Electra, whom
Landor, like some modern playwrights, makes furious and
vindictive. But most of the *Hellenics* follow the type, not of
the drama, but of the idyll, or of the short story in verse. The
Hero and Leander of the pseudo-Musæus is not unlike some
of them in point of scale and feeling ; with the difference,
certainly a deep one, that their grace is restrained, and their
beauty severe rather than luxuriant. They are not really
like anything ancient or modern except the rare imitations
of themselves. There is nothing Elizabethan about them,
nothing Ovidian or ' Italianate,' as there is about *Venus and
Adonis* or Drayton's *Endimion and Phœbe*. Their purity of
style forbids such a comparison ; and it is also a different
purity, less warm-blooded and frank than that of Marlowe's
own narrative, *Hero and Leander*; it is the purity of delicate and
' breathing marbles,' or else of heroic statuary. It is natural
and common to speak of Landor's style in terms drawn from
the plastic arts. The *Conversations* are a frieze of heroes and
poets in procession ; the epigrams and eulogies are medallions ;
the *Hellenics* are groups, not unlike some that are seen in the
' Street of Tombs,' or on the best vases. Two lovers, Enallos
and Cymodameia, are asleep ' upon an island tilled by peaceful
men ' ; Pan is seen embracing Pitys, ' and with sharp finger
parting her smooth hair ' ; Paris unawares in jealousy stabs
Corythos, his son by Œnone, in the presence of Helena ;

Rhaicos sits at draughts with his father, and brushes off the
bee sent to him by the faithful Hamadryad. The narrative
is a tissue joining together a series of such groups or poses.
This habit of Landor's imagination, already traced in a
rougher form in *Gebir*, has now found perfect expression. It
leads him to something like the 'distinct, sharp, and wiry
bounding line' commended by Blake. There is neither
twilight nor heat-haze, but tempered sunlight. There is
little motion, but what there is never becomes excited or
restless, even in moments of vehemence. The action is related
succinctly, and in little separate phases, with a pause between
each, and for each phase there is a picture. Thus Cymodameia
is cast overboard in a storm to satisfy the gods, and Enallos
follows her :

> They wrung her from his knee ; they hurl'd her down
> (Clinging in vain at the hard slippery pitch)
> Into the whitening wave. But her long hair
> Scarcely had risen up again, before
> Another plunge was heard, another form
> Clove the strait line of bubbling foam, direct
> As ringdove after ringdove. Groans from all
> Burst, for the roaring sea ingulpht them both.
> Onward the vessel flew ; the skies again
> Shone bright, and thunder roll'd along, not wroth,
> But gently murmuring to the white-wing'd sails.
> The shore was won ; the fields markt out ; and roofs
> Collected the dun wings that seek house-fare ;
> And presently the ruddy-bosom'd guest
> Of winter knew the doors : then infant cries
> Were heard within ; and lastly, tottering steps
> Patter'd along the image-station'd hall.

The beauty of this slow, vivid movement speaks for itself ;
and it is clear how far Landor's speech and versification has
unbent, not without an effort, from the rigidness of *Gebir* or
Count Julian. Often it is supple and even playful ; but one
other famous passage may be given to show how quick it is
to rise again into the statelier mood :

> Day after day the Hours beheld them blest,
> And season after season ; years had past,
> Blest were they still. He who asserts that Love
> Ever is sated of sweet things, the same
> Sweet things he fretted for in earlier days,
> Never, by Zeus ! loved he a Hamadryad.
>   The nights had now grown longer, and perhaps
> The Hamadryads find them lone and dull
> Among their woods ; one did, alas ! She called
> Her faithful bee ; 'twas when all bees should sleep,

And all did sleep but hers. She was sent forth
To bring that light which never wintry blast
Blows out, nor rain nor snow extinguishes,
The light that shines from loving eyes upon
Eyes that love back, till they can see no more.

Not all of the *Hellenics*, by any means, rise so high.   In many
there is heaviness, and a touch of the eighteenth-century
blank verse, not quite thawed out :

You will soon educe
Bolder assertion of important deeds
Who things terrestrial haughtily despise.

The poems translated from the Latin[1] incline much more to
this fault ; they are often literal and stark, but a beautiful
example of improvement by such translation is *Cupid and
Pan* ; and in one of the latest *Hellenics* of all, *Homer, Laertes,
Agatha*, published in 1863, the whole style has become more
natural and homefelt : this was never, apparently, in Latin :

I am content to stay in Ithaca,
Where the dogs know me, and the ferryman
Asks nothing from me, and the rills are full
After the rain, and flowers grow everywhere,
And bees grudge not their honey, and the grape
Grows everywhere, and figs, blue, yellow, green,
Without my climbing.

Landor's scholarship, and his acquaintance with the realities
of ancient life—its dress and ritual, its food and wine—give
him a favourite source of relief and decoration, that is used
as aptly in his poems as in the prose scenes of *Pericles and
Aspasia*. The austerity of *Thrasymedes and Eunoë*, and of
Catillus and Salia, is thus lightened, while in the lengthy
Corythos and its sequel *The Death of Paris and Œnone* (the
first translated from *Idyllia*), this happy ingredient is missed.
In such homely strokes Landor is always safe. At the
loftier extreme of language, he is only sparing in the kind of
imagination that carries us beyond the story itself into the
infinite, and that informs such a poem as Tennyson's *Love
and Duty* ; but he has it at least once, in *Catillus and Salia*,
in a passage which recalls Tennyson's

all the wheels of time
Spun round in station, for the end had come ;

and which may conceivably have been read by Tennyson.   It
is as high an instance as could be found of the ' pathetic

fallacy' rightly used :—nature is shown as in sympathy with
a condition of tense yet suspended feeling :

> Sharp was the splendour of the stars ; all heaven
> Seem'd moving as it never yet had mov'd.

It is the rarity of these touches that keeps Landor apart from
his contemporaries, and also from the greatest modern poets.

IX

The ' imaginary conversation,' in its freedom and its limita-
tions, is a form that was shaped by Landor in exact accordance with his genius as a writer of prose. It has only two
rules. First, there is no narrative, and as few stage directions
as possible ; and although the speakers sometimes tell each
other stories, the author does not interrupt them, except when
' Walter Landor ' comes forward himself as an interlocutor.
Secondly, the speakers must be real persons, living or dead.
That rule is at times broken, as it is in the conversation of *Peleus
and Thetis* ; and this, besides being a translation from Landor's
English verse, is transplanted into the heart of another conversation, where it takes the form of a dramatic piece recited.
Otherwise the *Imaginary Conversations* are as free as air.
Any one of the ' leading figures of time,' or any one else, may
appear, and may talk about anything. Hence the *Conversations* differ as much from one another as Cicero's Tusculan
disputations, a scene in Sophocles, a scene in Molière, or a
dialogue of Lucian. Some are quite short, and many are of
middle length, corresponding in scale to the *Hellenics*. Some
of the shortest are the most impassioned and dramatic ; the
bow is at full stretch, and the arrow is pulled home, and
even Ulysses cannot hold it long. Others are very lengthy ;
the conversations of *Southey and Landor*, or of *Penn and
Peterborough*, are little books in themselves. The *Pentameron* and the *Citation* are conversations much prolonged,
or rather aggregated, for the single dialogue is Landor's
unit ; and though he could string such units together, he did
not shape them into any larger dramatic whole. These conditions are modified only in *Pericles and Aspasia*, which may
be regarded as a dialogue in the form of letters. Clearly
these different kinds of colloquy must be judged by
varying canons, as they approach nearer to the idyll, the
tragic episode, or the disquisition. To distinguish them by
the rank or character of the speakers—statesmen, famous

women,[1] writers, and the like—is little help towards an artistic estimate.

The plan of the *Conversations* has been compared to that of Boethius, *De Consolatione Philosophiæ*. But the dialogues of the martyr with his majestic visitant are unlike anything that Landor wrote, and if he really has any model, it is Plato, against whom he harbours one of his perverse crazes, and whom he seems only to praise in order to give some colour of justice to his abuse. His opinions on[2] the *Republic* and *Banquet* are unworthy and pettifogging. This is ungrateful, for to Plato as an artist he is in debt ; he is, indeed, the only English writer, except Berkeley, who can be claimed as in any sense of Plato's tribe. He has learnt from him many strokes of the craft of dialogue—the cunning overture, the power of keeping characters distinct, and of interveining an abstract discussion with beautiful or lively human touches ; the use of allegory, or idyll, by way of interlude. For all this Landor must surely have studied the master to whom he is unfair. His tact in the choice of background—the gardens of Epicurus, the slopes of Florence, and the bathrooms of Lucullus, is certainly worthy of Plato. The likeness, of course, cannot be carried further, for, not to name the total difference of scope, the style of Plato has the freedom of life itself, but Landor's, even while expressing the most ardent or gracious feeling, remains a thing carven.

The eighteenth-century makers of dialogue cannot have counted for much to him. Berkeley and Hume discussed first principles, which he does not ; besides, their personages are imaginary, and shadows with Greek names. It is true that many of his conversations turn on political theory ; but Landor deals less in first principles than in 'middle axioms,' as Bacon calls them, or generalisations of a secondary kind, midway between the schools and the market-place. His discussions are always lofty, and his endless aphorisms strong and pithy, but they derive from a few simple tenets which he assumes and does not argue. He is a republican with an aristocratic temper ; anti-despotic, anti-clerical, and a mob-hater as well. His ethical reflections and axioms move on the same level ; they are less monotonous and more inspiring than his political ones. The conversations, indeed, which are devoted to argument or theory are among the longest, dullest, and most shapeless. He did not learn much from the dialogues of *Hylas and Philonous*, or those *Concerning Natural Religion*. The compositions of Lyttelton and Hurd can only have touched

him faintly, though superficially nearer in purpose. The range
and power, like the plan and execution, of the *Imaginary
Conversations*; the marshalling of warriors and poets, of
heroines and sages, in not less than one hundred and fifty
separate colloquies, and the new, incomparable harmonies
that are won for English prose; all entitle Landor to the
praise which many great, and some greater, writers have not
earned—that of inventing a new form of art, of which he remains the chief master. No catalogue of this huge gallery is
here possible, but the grouping on the walls can be observed,
and a few of the masterpieces. There are some half-dozen
rooms, each with a character of its own.

1. In its highest form, the imaginary conversation represents a short episode, in which heroic action rules with its
accompanying passion, usually involving, but not necessitat-
ing, pathos; and which can be thought of as the climax of
some lost tragedy or epic. There is here no irony or argumentation. Prose is the medium. There is nothing, either
in the stuff or the diction, unsuitable to highly-pitched and
fervent verse. Yet for Landor prose is here plainly the right
implement; he is freer, more powerful, more natural than he
is in verse. To see this, it is enough to compare *Peleus and
Thetis*, or *Achilles and Helena*, with the verse into which he
transplanted them. In scenes of this order the Roman dialogues are richer than the Greek. The motive of *Marcellus
and Hannibal* is that of a heroic ballad; the generous Hannibal, like the Percy 'leaning on his sword,' looks at the dying
Roman, and tells him that his son is safe. His exclamation
over his enemy, 'I would rejoice, and cannot,' is almost beyond
a ballad; it is Homeric. The whole dialogue falls into short
breathless sentences, such as befit the stricken field. *Metellus
and Marius* contains the elaborate and magnificent pictures
of the dying sentinel and of Numantia destroyed by fire, but
is more visibly studious in phraseology; it is a recital, not a
piece of drama like *Tiberius and Vipsania*. Here the husband,
whom Landor represents as chivalrous and devoted, swiftly
takes farewell of the wife whom Livia and Augustus have
forced him to put away and exchange for another. Nor does
the action stand still, for Vipsania contrives to forgive both
him and them; and there is the atmosphere of an interview
stolen under suspense and peril. This dialogue might be
classified amongst those 'conversations of famous women,'
which give the fullest scope to Landor's powers. His portraiture of feminine bravery and patience can hardly be

matched, it is not too much to say, between the end of the old drama and *The Ring and the Book*. The sifted purity of his prose idiom well suits the lips of women, and their talk runs more easily than that of his men ; it has less the air of being a distinguished translation from an ancient classic. And the men often talk with the women more naturally than they do with one another. It is not easy to put words into the mouth of Dante ; and Landor does so twice, without our feeling that Dante has demeaned himself ; but the honours rest with Beatrice in the first dialogue, and in the second with Gemma Donati, his wife, who has named her own child Beatrice. *Tasso and Cornelia*, and also *Tancredi and Constantia*, are worthy companions to these masterpieces ; the sharp pathos of the first, and the high knightliness of the second, are of a kind that soon becomes familiar to the student of Landor. One of the loveliest and least often cited is *Beniowski and Aphanasia*, a good example of his simple and lucid habit of language in presenting poignant matter. The young exile, who is in the official charge of Aphanasia's father, vainly dissuades her from sharing the perils of his escape :

Aphanasia.—The seas are very wide, they tell me, and covered with rocks of ice and mountains of snow for many versts, upon which there is not an aspen or birch or alder to catch at, if the wind should blow hard. There is no rye, nor berries, nor little birds tamed by the frost, nor beasts asleep ; and many days, and many long stormy nights must be endured upon the waves without food. Could you bear this quite alone ?
Beniowski.—Could *you* bear it, Aphanasia ?
Aphanasia.—Alone, I could not.
Beniowski.—Could you, with me ? Think again ; we both must suffer.
Aphanasia.—How can we, Maurice ? Shall we not die together ? Why do you clasp me so hard ?

2. There is one well-marked and racy variety of these high dramatic conversations, on a lower level than the greatest. Landor loves great bullying scenes, where the tyrant lets his loose-lipped invective fly against the soft endurance or proud defiance of the helpless. His own spleen and masculine temper gave him a store of savage language, which, on the lips of his Henry the Eighth or his Catherine of Russia, though never on his own, becomes ferociously brutal. The ferocity is sometimes overdone and tumbles over into the consciously ludicrous, as in the dialogue of *Peter the Great and Alexis*, where Peter, on hearing that his son has died broken-hearted at his taunts, calls for

brandy, bacon, sturgeon, krout, caviar, and 'some good strong cheese.' The cheese is perhaps excessive. Landor accepts the legend, since rejected, of the Empress Catherine's guilt as her husband's murderess ; and, in his fierce concrete way, shows her listening at the keyhole to the drip of her husband's blood as she talks with her lover in her chamber. The ruthless imagination of Webster or Middleton has not gone further in this kind of effect ; perhaps, luckily, not so far :

My ears are quicker than yours, and know these notes better. Let me come.—Hear nothing ! You did not wait long enough, nor with coolness and patience. There—there again ! The drops are now like lead : every half minute they penetrate the eider-down and the mattress.—How now ! which of these fools has brought his dog with him ? What tramping and lapping ! The creature will carry the marks all about the palace with his feet and muzzle.

This will hardly bear being read in the cool morning ; it turns to the grotesque, and is long drawn out ; but a great actress might make it terrible, and purge disgust into fear. No such doubts arise over Landor's pathos ; he has a sure command of all the tones of martyrdom, and the sweet opposing fortitude of his heroines has no touch of mawkishness or exaggeration. His good women are alive, not mere patterns ; their suffering is itself action, and their persistence of soul Shakespearean. Such is his Anne Boleyn, and such his Godiva, whose story had fascinated him when a boy at Rugby. The same qualities, in the case of his male characters who suffer for country or for conscience, become a duly haughty resistance, or stoical dignity, in the face of the oppressor. It is so with Henry of Melctal, whose eyes are put out because, contrary to an unjust sentence, he has set them upon his son ; and with Francesco Madiai, who will not buy the freedom of his wife by abjuring his heresy to the Archbishop of Paris. But this last Conversa-tion also introduces Landor's favourite vein of anti-clerical irony or declamation, with which he passes out of poetry into satire, and becomes a man of the eighteenth century. Before reaching this, another and a gentler kind of his imaginative prose should be considered, in which he succeeds almost in-fallibly, and something of which he has learned, as to its scenery and temper, from the Greek idyll, from the Latin elegy, from Boccaccio, and from his own life in Italy. Some of his actual sources, or rather the hints in which he drew, have been traced [1] ; they are various and abstruse, but they seldom furnish him with more than an outline, and this is true of the *Imaginary*

Conversations generally. He treats his originals quite freely, far more freely than Shakespeare treated Plutarch, so that they count for little in his artistic procedure.

3. The class of dialogues which may be best entitled idyllic are near akin to some of the *Hellenics* in their playful or serious grace, which is often conferred on them by the feminine or girlish figures that predominate. The colloquies of such creatures with philosophic but courteous and fresh old men are like a page out of Landor's own life. Epicurus, discoursing with his young friends, Leontion and Ternissa, in his garden, is indeed sufficiently unlike Landor, although one of his favourite sages ; but the talk that strays through such pleasant alleys of poetry, philosophy, and gallantry, rising often to the higher mood, is Landorian in essence. The two Conversations of *Æsop and Rhodopè* have more unity, and are distinguished by Rhodopè's story of her enslavement—one of Landor's best pieces of brief narrative—and by many passages of his loftiest lyrical prose ; beautiful, detachable things, but best seen in their setting. Of such is the often-quoted descant upon death ('Laodameia died ; Helen died . . .'), which revives, though with a different music, the deep and harmonious elegiac prose of the Jacobeans. Another sort of idyll is seen in *Odysseus, Tersitza, Acrive, and Trelawny*, which is founded on a fact : Odysseus, the Greek patriot, having really entrusted his daughter and mother to Trelawny for concealment in the cave of Parnassus, whose grim recesses are lighted, in the dialogue, by the flitting presence of the Greek child Tersitza, just as that of the coquette Delia cheers the grave intercourse of *Tibullus and Messala*. The episode, or *novella*, of Euthymedes and Thelymnia, recited by Polybius in his dialogue with Scipio, is another gay idyll ; and in the apologue of Critobulus, inserted in the conversation between the two Ciceros, there is a faun-like humour despite its serious intent. There is the same redolence of Latin life and culture, and a picture of refined ingenious luxury, in *Lucullus and Cæsar*. There would be no end to such instances ; but the representation of Montaigne, whose conversation is with Joseph Scaliger, may be named as also in the high Epicurean style, and, though but a sketch, may worthily be contrasted with a more finished and subtle one—Pater's, in his *Gaston de Latour*. Landor, however, is more rapid, and not less refreshing in his diaphanous workmanship than the later and subtler master.

Landor's humour, which has been underrated, can be bold and biting as well as kindly and gracious. He likes some one to attack—a king will do, but a priest or pope is better. When he preaches or rails against dignitaries, he is tiresome ; but not when he lets them expose themselves and save him comment ; and he shows no little self-restraint, and, as it were, a loving patience, in this process, never breaking out undramatically or wasting strokes. In *Alexander and the Priest of Hammon*, the priest discomfits the claim of the monarch to have been begotten by Jove in the guise of a serpent, by offering him the sacred reptile of the temple for a bride. Here the churchman has the irony on his side ; but in *Louis the Fourteenth and Père La Chaise* it is evenly divided. Had it lain with Molière to mock at kings, we can fancy him delighting in the prescription of a sackcloth no bigger than a plaster, and of a royal *maigre* :

Six dishes alone shall come upon the table ; and, although fasting does not extend to wines or liqueurs, I order that three kinds only of wine shall be presented, and three of liqueur.

Louis.—In the six dishes is soup included ?

La Chaise.—Soup is not served in a dish ; but I forbid more than three kinds of soup.

Louis.—Oysters of Cancale ?

La Chaise.—Those come in barrels ; take care they be not dished. Your Majesty must either eat them raw from the barrel, or dressed in scallop, or both ; but beware, I say again, of dishing this article, as your soul shall answer for it at the last day.

This is perhaps more in the vein of the elder Dumas ; but the conversation of *Bossuet and the Duchess de Fontanges* is in a finer and higher strain of comedy, unlike but worthy of Molière. The half-naïve little favourite, over whom the superb funereal periods of Bossuet pass like a frightening peal of thunder instantly forgotten, is perfectly drawn ; and the courtliness of the preacher, who will not let her stoop for his fallen ring, is admirably mimicked. *Eugenius IV. and Lippi* is a prose precursor of some of Browning's Renaissance portraits, and *The Bishop Orders his Tomb*, conversely, can well be imagined in Landor's prose ; luxury, hypocrisy, wantonness, good nature, and connoisseurship are curiously blended. The bitter comedy of courts reappears in *Elizabeth and the Duke of Anjou*, and that of clerical rapacity in *Lord Coleraine and The Reverend Mr. Bloombury*. The raffish companion, turned canting preacher, waits on the dying Lord Coleraine to recover a gambling debt, and suffers the kind of repulse that Landor loved to depict. In all such work his humour is of the learned, hard-hitting and robust order, not unlike Ben Jonson's ; and

it is always dramatic, and helps the action, when there is an
action, forward. It is never the humour of mere ' humours '
or oddities. It also has its convivial and Rabelaisian side,
rich and loud, which any reader of the *Citation and Examination*, or of the odd and rambling but opulent dialogue between
The Duke de Richelieu, Lady Glengrin, and Normanby, may
discover ; a work that is more a string of episodes and *novelle*
than properly a conversation.

X

5. Heroic or idyllic, sardonic or severe, all these classes of
dialogue have at least an artistic framework. There is usually
a situation, a story, a point, or a theme. But in many of the
Imaginary Conversations there is no such bond. They are
tracts or disquisitions, in colloquial form, on politics, or
affairs, or literary criticism, and the interest lies in the opinions
uttered, not in the characters. There is no reason why these
deliverances should not go on longer, or stop sooner, than they
do. Most readers would wish them shorter. Landor, it is
true, cannot be mean or common ; but he moves on a level,
high, somewhat monotonous and stony tableland of historical
or constitutional discussion, and his speakers are often mere
masks, while the voice is his own. Lofty passages, grave
and sound aphorisms, eloquent sallies are seldom far off, but
often the form of the imaginary conversation is a mere pretext.
Prince Leopold and the President du Paty is a solid and pertinent
lecture on policy and jurisprudence ; Washington and Franklin
canvass the American constitution ; Boulter and Savage the
miseries of Ireland ; Penn and Peterborough, at vast length,
the principles of society ; General Lacy and Cura Merino, the
government of Spain. Earnest and instructed as Landor is,
the life of these conversations lies in the interludes, stories,
and human digressions that relieve them. An astonishing
number of the ' leading figures of time ' come upon the
stage. Among French notabilities, for example, are found
Bonaparte, Louis Philippe, Thiers, Guizot, Béranger, Talley-
rand, and Corbière. But they are often talking phantoms ;
and it is much the same with Solon, Xenophon, ' Aristoteles,'
and Æschines. We do not see them, as we see Leontion
and Ternissa, or Queen Elizabeth, who appears thrice,
and each time in a different mood, and who does not talk
statecraft.

6. Among the best of the dialogues on affairs is that of

Machiavelli and Guicciardini; and the easy-ranging talk between La Fontaine and La Rochefoucauld, with his cynical ethics, is human enough. These belong to the 'conversations of literary men,' amongst which are found most of Landor's deliverances on books and writers. Here he recovers himself, and though captious, whimsical, and often blind, he is never wearisome, except when he is vainly haranguing the world upon the improvement of English spelling (as in *Archdeacon Hare and Walter Savage Landor*). As a critic he would be unsafe in his dislikes, if any man could be imagined as accepting them. He cannot be reconciled to Milton's 'rollcalls of proper names,'

> Lancelot, or Pelleas, or Pellenore.

He sees nothing good in Boileau ; nay, he holds that of Shakespeare's sonnets 'not a single one is very admirable,' and compares them to 'raspberry jam, without cream, without crust, without bread, to break its viscidity.' He also states that 'Wordsworth has not written three poems so excellent as *Thalaba, The Curse of Kehama,* and *Roderick.*' But these Boythornisms need not trouble us. Landor's formal examinations of Wordsworth in *Southey and Porson,* and of Milton in *Southey and Landor,* though full of such whims, are not therefore worthless ; they are pieces of sharp, minute, textual comment, often censorious, always courageous, and again and again pertinent. Subtle Landor is not, but delicate he often is, and perhaps his best judgments are those conveyed by poetic metaphor. His well-known image for the genius of Spenser may be quoted, and that not merely for its music ; any one who has passed a night in an arrased room in an old castle will feel its felicity :

> Spenser's is a spacious but somewhat low chamber, hung with rich tapestry, on which the figures are mostly disproportioned, but some of the faces are lively and beautiful ; the furniture is part creaking and worm-eaten, part fragrant with cedar and sandalwood and aromatic gums and balsams ; every table and mantelpiece and cabinet is covered with gorgeous vases, and birds, and dragons, and houses in the air.

In prose as in verse, Landor is apt and cordial in his praise of younger poets, especially of Keats and Shelley. His occasional sayings are excellent, and have the air of real talk ; as when he makes Alfieri say of Dante, 'There is something of the Englishman in his austerity and sternness,' and Horne Tooke speak of the 'sweet temperature of thought' in Addison.

His verdicts on the ancient, especially on the Latin poets, are long meditated, and those of a scholar. In *Pericles and Aspasia*, as in the *Hellenics*, the temper of Greek literature is rather re-created than analysed, and this is the best kind of criticism.

XI

Thus, in that curious protracted experiment of high comedy or historical fiction, *The Citation and Examination of William Shakespeare*, etc., Landor tries to make Shakespeare speak. To say he half-succeeds, and also that the result is tedious, is a not wholly absurd paradox. The youth who defends himself with such slippery wit and insidious eloquence before Sir Thomas Lucy is at any rate not unlike some personage in *Love's Labour's Lost* or its companion comedies. Landor does not always mimic an existing style so well, but something of the same skill is shown in the conversation of *Hooker and Bacon*. Here the freedom and flying allusiveness of the talk of Shakespeare's wits and sparks is, if not reproduced, at least suggested. The recital indeed, by the young deer-stealer, of a long Puritan sermon (which he has heard or fabricated) in order to appease Sir Thomas Lucy and infuriate his chaplain, is a bold venture, and not too well in keeping. Landor is at his best when he is frankly Landorian. In the tale of the unhappy drowned Oxford boy, ' Joannes Wellerby,' the cadence, the pathos, are his own; and the landscape has the clear beauty of Homer's garden of Calypso, rather than the dim dreamy air of Shakespeare's own Athens or Sicily :

About half a mile from St. John's College is the termination of a natural terrace, with the Cherwell close under it, in some places bright with yellow and red flowers glancing and glowing through the stream, and suddenly in others dark with the shadows of many different trees in broad, overbending thickets, and with rushes spear-high, and party-coloured flags. . . . The long meadowsweet and blooming burnet half-concealed from me him whom the earth was about to hide totally and for ever.

The *Citation* goes on too long, and is in the nature of a feat ; but it is one of the freest and raciest of Landor's books, and is charged with life and spirit.

Landor's longest and most formidable single work, *Pericles and Aspasia*, also offers matter for an ample, delightful anthology. The bare statement of its plan, highly original but almost hopeless of performance, may serve to show why thus much must be said, whilst little more can be said, in its honour. The aim is to portray the Golden Age of the ancient world, and to deliver Landor's long-harvested opinions and impressions of it, through a series of imaginary letters. Most of these are exchanged between Aspasia and her distant friend, another intellectual lady, Cleone. Her grace and gaiety, her humanity and high-bred taste, are most delicately disclosed ; she sprinkles her letters, like Cleone, with lightsome and varied lyrics ; her gossip, and the little love-stories that she tells of Grecian youths and maidens, are full of sweetness and humour. It is a pity that in her dissertations, which do not soon finish, she is somewhat of a bluestocking. Pericles himself is a posturer, and also talks too like Dr. Johnson ; and an imitation, even by Landor, of the public speeches composed by Thucydides is a hard morsel. The other correspondents include Alcibiades, who is flippant and affectionate, and Anaxagoras, who is dull. Amongst the matters discussed in the letters (chiefly by Aspasia) are the Homeric question, the politics of the Peloponnesian war, the drama, and the early history of Rome. It was Landor's stubborn British whim to make this famous lady a mouthpiece for his own theories. It is a relief when he (or she) leaves discoursing and gets back to humanity and poetry. There are many green oases, full of fresh springs and flowers, in *Pericles and Aspasia*. They are not found in the most ambitious scenes. Sophocles, Euripides, Aristophanes, Socrates, Herodotus, and Thucydides are all introduced, and speak, and go their ways—a dauntless essay on the part of the author, on which he could not adventure, it is needless to say, without dropping many an exalted maxim or shrewd comment on the way—but they speak overmuch like Walter Savage Landor on stilts. It is otherwise with the first thirty letters, brief and swift and animated, which tell of the acquaintance and love of Aspasia and Pericles. The banquet of the fat comedian Polus (No. 78) is a genuine piece of Falstaffian, or rather Jonsonian, humour ; the trial and acquittal of Aspasia (No. 162) has the uplifted quality of the best among the Roman Conversations ; and the last scenes of the Plague, and the deathbed of Pericles, are a worthy climax. Landor is but once tempted into the kind of satire called topical ; and the account (Nos. 54, 55) of the barbarous Thracians, who have ' so imperfect a sense of religion as to bury the dead in the temples of the gods,' and put up ' flat marbles fastened with iron cramps against the walls ' in their honour, ' of all forms and dimensions,' and ' inscribed in an obsolete language,' is a pretty piece of irony in the traditions of the Addisonian essay.

The five dialogues of the *Pentameron* are thickly starred with beautiful and playful passages, such as the idyll of Assunta and her admirer, and the humours of Fra Biagio ; above all, the visions of Petrarca and Boccaccio, and the prose dirge upon Acciaioli, bring out all the music of which Landor's English is capable ; and he is supreme in his own kind of harmony. But these things are detachable, and best when detached ; and the truth is that Petrarca and Boccaccio are prone to talk too much like eighteenth-century essayists of the ponderous tribe, and their disquisitions on universal monarchy and the vices of the French are unrefreshing. Their dissection of Dante's poem is captious, and their very praises of him—being chiefly of particular ' beauties '—dissatisfy. Moreover, they say of him what Landor thought, and not what either of them could have dreamed of thinking. But we forgive and overleap all this for the profuse variety of happy homely incident, intermingled with eloquence, which the *Pentameron* gives us. The dreams are nearer to the allegories in Plato than to Petrarca's own frigid *Triumphs*, which no doubt suggested them in the first instance. Their light, lovely, and precise imagery, and their clarity of feeling, contrast them with De Quincey's, which ever have a shifting *penumbra* and suggestion of the infinite ; and the differences between the ' classic ' and ' romantic,' both as to sentiment and form, could hardly be better pointed than by such a comparison :

Love pouted, and rumpled and bent down with his forefinger the stiff short feathers on his arrowhead ; but replied not. Although he frowned worse than ever, and at me, I dreaded him less and less, and scarcely looked toward him. The milder and calmer Genius, the third, in proportion as I took courage to contemplate him, regarded me with more and more complacency. He held neither flower nor arrow, as the others did ; but, throwing back the clusters of dark curls that overshadowed his countenance, he presented to me his hand, openly and benignly. I shrank on looking at him so near, and yet I sighed to love him.

This third Genius is Death ; the others are Sleep and Love. De Quincey's Three Ladies of Sorrow have no such visible gestures or features, which could be struck upon a coin ; they are cloudily and terribly symbolic, and the imagination vibrates deep and painfully in the effort to fix them before it, instead of being filled and contented at once.

XII

Landor enlarged the dominions of our prose, not so much by inventing the imaginary conversation, in which he has had no real follower and which suited and satisfied his own genius, as by attaining in prose the goal which some of his fellow-poets were attaining in verse. The term ' poetic prose ' suggests something hybrid or florid, or some kind of usurpation—justified, perhaps, by the event, but still of doubtful title—on the part of prose, of the functions of poetry. This is misleading, for there is no usurpation, but a simple reclamation. Take away metre, with all its own deep-reaching power, and its ennobling reaction upon language and idiom ; put in its place ' the other harmony, of prose,' whose effect and reaction, while different, are equally potent ; and it is then, and then only, clear of what prose is capable in its own right. It cannot do all that verse can do ; but it is also true that it can do things that are denied to verse ; no subject is out of its province, and in prose the imagination can work as freely, under the law of beauty, as in verse. It would not be wise to question the conclusion, drawn from universal consent, that verse is essential to the highest of all utterance ; but that needs no affirming, while the lawful rights and proved possibilities of prose always need reaffirming. This may now seem a truism, but in 1800 it was not such ; for, despite Berkeley and Burke, the imaginative use of prose had been disregarded, or implicitly denied, for more than a century and a half. Nay, in 1820, when Lamb and Hazlitt and De Quincey were just beginning to give their measure and Landor had not yet done so, it still needed reaffirming, not as an abstract truth, but by the thing being done. In 1830 no doubts could remain. The *Opium-Eater* and the *Imaginary Conversations*, and the *Essays of Elia* and Hazlitt's papers, had appeared.

The make of Landor's prose will be best understood (see Ch. XXII.) by comparison with that of another rigorous and studious workman in the art, De Quincey. Much of it, no doubt, being devoted to severe converse upon politics, ethics, or criticism, is of the weighty eighteenth-century stamp, and may even be called Johnsonian. But it is less mannered than *The Rambler*, and more like the *Lives of the Poets* or the talk of their author. *Penn and Peterborough*, or *Demosthenes and Eubulides*, abound in such writing. An imaginary conversation between Landor and Johnson has yet to be written ; but it is piquant to hear the following cadences on the lips of a republican :

I know not upon what principle the Chancellor Clarendon called Cromwell a bold, bad man, unless it were to persuade us that he had read a play of Shakespeare's; in which we find the same words, rather more happily applied. People are good and bad relatively and comparatively. Oliver would have been a sorry saint, and no very tractable disciple or apostle; nor do I imagine you would have admitted him without a scruple into the Society of Friends: but he was a good father, a good husband, a good soldier. . . .

Landor's regular level prose, of the essay type, is more old-fashioned than that of his friend Southey, which is much easier and equally transparent. Southey shares with Wordsworth the wish to rid the diction of verse of the false classical fashion that clung to it, and only succeeds less, because he was less of a poet. In prose his aim is similar, and here he succeeds wonderfully. But Landor, though he does not achieve this in his ordinary prose, achieves it and much more when his prose is impassioned, or decorative, or idyllic. It is there that he is seen to be a true founder, or redeemer, of the art. There he justifies for prose its claim to share with poetry the dual control over the same imaginative province. The mass of his good or great writing in that province is very considerable. Much of it is now common property, thanks to his best critic and anthologist. The conversation of Essex and Spenser, the dreams of Scipio and of Petrarca, need no introduction. Perhaps Landor rises highest in the expression of *desiderium*, in short passages of the same scale as a sonnet or a verse elegy of the middle length. Thus Tasso speaks of Leonora:

Never will I believe she has left me utterly. Oftentimes, and long before her departure, I fancied we were in heaven together. I fancied it in the fields, in the garden, in the palace, in the prison. I fancied it in the broad daylight, when my eyes were open, when blessed spirits drew around me that golden circle which one only of earth's inhabitants can enter. Oftentimes in my sleep, also, I fancied it; and sometimes in the intermediate state, in that serenity which breathes about the transported soul, enjoying its pure and perfect rest, a span below the feet of the Immortal.

This *vox angelica* is heard a hundred times in the *Imaginary Conversations*. The harmonies in *Peleus and Thetis*, in *Lady Lisle and Elizabeth Gaunt*, in *Æsop and Rhodopè*, are new and incomparable. In all there is the expression of noble and heroic suffering, with its natural but still idealised rhythms. The constructions are not so long or involved as to give the effect rather of mere eloquence than of real passion; and if the passion is restrained, it is only by its own dignity, and by Landor's inveterate love for distinctness ; and also, perhaps, by the reserve already noticed in connection with his verse.

His ruling instinct as a prose artist, whatever the subject or mood, is an extreme purity in the choice of words, and a corresponding precision and keeping in, the imagery. This aim he cherishes the more, we cannot doubt, for his familiarity with the best Latin writing. His more finished passages of the imaginative order leave on us the same sense of perfection as Cicero's *Somnium Scipionis*. But his study of Italian counts for something too : the familiar Italian he heard around him, as well as what he read in his favourite Boccaccio, who may be called his fellow-citizen of Florence, and whose voice, along with that of Petrarca, is heard in the *Pentameron*. It is on this note that we can best take leave of Landor, on his note of country peace and cheerfulness, unlike Blake's, unlike Goldsmith's, because it is heard sounding through a lighter and more radiant air :

And now the sound of village bells, in many hamlets and convents and churches out of sight, was indistinctly heard, and lost again ; and at last the five of Certaldo seemed to crow over the faintness of them all.

The freshness of the morning was enough of itself to excite the spirits of youth ; a portion of which never fails to descend on years that are far removed from it, if the mind has partaken in innocent mirth while it was its season and its duty to enjoy it. . . . As they approached the walls of the town, the whole country was pervaded by a stirring and diversified air of gladness. Laughter and songs and flutes and viols, inviting voices and complying responses, mingled with merry bells and with processional hymns, along the woodland paths and along the yellow meadows.

Southey remarked on the 'intellectual family likeness' between Walter Savage Landor and his younger brother, Robert Eyres Landor [1] (1781-1869). A likeness there is, but no question of imitation ; the work of Robert Landor is simply the less sunned and favoured fruit growing from the same noble stock, and ripening reluctantly, or never, in the shade of a country rectory. The author of *The Count Arezzi*, a rapidly moving and loftily romantic, however ill-shapen, play in verse (1824), and of *The Fawn of Sertorius* (1846), a gracious and delicately told prose legend, 'collected from *Plutarch's Lives*,' is all but forgotten. Yet rumour assigned the first of these works to Byron, and the second to Walter Landor, until the honest avowal of the authorship was paid by an oblivion as quick as it was undeserved. *Count Arezzi*, sharing as it does in the encumbered richness and lofty abrupt transitions of *Fra Rupert* or *Count Julian*, could never have been either playable or popular ; but the dignified beauty of the scenes between Arezzi's mother and her ward Cicilia should have sufficed to rescue the work, even without the curious and dolphin-dyed fantasies of the poetry assigned to the young Cimbelli, Arezzi's confidant. Of Robert Landor's three other plays, published in 1841, not one is lacking in poetical ore. *The Earl of Brecon* has least of it ; but the singular and pleasantly extravagant *Faith's Fraud* contains one of the passages of filial piety in which Robert Landor excelled ; the device of an interview between the outcast father and the daughter veiled as a nun and vowed to strict disguise reminding us of some strained and passionate scene of John Fletcher's. The verse tragi-comedy called *The Ferryman*, chaotic or ill-jointed as it may be, is remarkable for the vigour with which the tempest of wild weather, and of the Danube in roaring spate, is realised through the terror-struck and broken speech of the supposed spectators. The author is said to have burned most of the copies of these three dramas, and was only too successful in his impatience.

Robert, like Walter Landor, is more sincerely at his ease in prose ; and his prose, if lacking the rhythm and colour and splendour of the *Imaginary Conversations*, is of a noticeably stately and leisured stamp. *The Fawn of Sertorius* has a silvery charm. It is a historical romance, relating the journeys of the general with his supernatural companion, who warns him of dangers, guides him through forests, and dies in presage of his death. The element of historic narrative has weighted down this tale, just as that of satiric or philosophic essay has weighted *The Fountain of Arethusa* (1848) ; but the quaint and fantastic felicity of conception in the latter story might well have kept it fresh. Two explorers of the mines in the Peak of Derbyshire are swept down a cataract into an underworld paradise, full of strange flowers and fruits, and tenanted by a multitude of Greek and Roman ghosts, whose day has lasted a cycle of eighteen hundred years ; and dialogues follow between the narrator, Cicero, Aristotle, and Alexander. Like other wanderers to Utopia, the Englishman makes a poor affair of explaining the consonance of Christian morality with the practice of the Christian world. The law of this habitation of sexless spirits is well invented, and Buddhistic in complexion ; it is, so the traveller learns, the law of ' memory, ever occupied about the transactions of that life not yet ended by yourself, which can dismiss nothing from your knowledge and disguise nothing from your conscience '; so that the offences of this life remain in clear vision and exact proportion, eternally retributive. The Ciceronian English of Robert Landor is now buried almost as deep as his Roman phantoms, so that a quotation [1] need not be excused :

Here is no growth, no decay, no change. Even in intellect, there can never be any other increase than by the accumulation of knowledge and the proficiency of experience. We are wiser than we were, only because we have had more time to learn. The vessel remains the same though it is better filled. Time may ripen the crude austerity of its contents, but time has no power by which clay can be transmuted into copper, or copper into gold. When we awoke from our last sleep, it was with amazement at the dream of death just ended,—at our lightness, feebleness, nakedness,—at the place in which we were, and the regardless multitudes by whom we were surrounded,—at organs so active, yet apparently so inefficient, and members as impotent for the infliction of injury, as impassive to its endurance—but, above all, at memory ever occupied about things which had been, till then, negligently lost, or imperiously dismissed by us. The young, the old, the millions between both, resume that personal and distinctive presence in which they died—excepting its decrepitude, its imbecility, or its accidental distortion and curtailment. You will see here no marks of casualty and deformity. We are what nature first meant us to be till some misadventure interposed.

CHAPTER XV

WILLIAM WORDSWORTH

I

THE habit of literary confession has two large historic sources, religious and secular. It came into English letters, not so much from the classical writings of the old faith, like those

of St. Augustine, as through the Protestants, to whom every
little scene in the history of their souls wore a serious importance ; for their lives were enacted in the presence of a jealous
and surely a weary God. The records even of their greater
men, Baxter, Bunyan, and Cowper, are sorry, humiliating
reading ; but the genius of these works ensures their fascina-
tion. Milton, the mightiest of the Protestant writers, differs
from the rest in essence. He tells us of his high purposes, his
noble sadness, and his celestial comfortings, but nothing about
' experience ' ; hence his dignity and harmony of spirit when
he gives us his confidence. Bunyan tells his tale with the
vivid vehemence, the minute self-torture, and the want of
proportion, that are part of his Puritan legacy. Wordsworth
is a Puritan too, but of Milton's breed and not of Bunyan's.
Though he writes a long poem to expound his inner discord
and how it was resolved, his struggle is neither theological
nor in the ordinary sense moral. His lapses are mental, and
failures of faith ; in their worst moments he falls into an
aridity, or want of hopefulness, which is not his fault so much
as that of the world ; he loses his primal sensibility to what
man and nature can teach him. His Urania, Nature, revisits
him at the last and for good and all. This is, no doubt, unlike
Milton ; but Wordsworth's dejection approaches Milton's in
that its source is largely due to the clouding of his political
and national hopes, though he is unlike Milton because it at
last ceases to weigh fatally upon him. What Wordsworth
inherits from the mass of the Puritans is the instinct to impart
to other men the means of liberation, and to tell their tale
exhaustively. He has nothing, indeed, to confess ; but what
Coleridge well called his ' own august and most innocent life,'
with its one inward crisis, he felt it a duty to chronicle. It
lies before us like a view of noble mountain country, with its
heights and valleys, and its bare patches too, in clear definition. A wonderful expansion and transformation, this, of
those purely evangelical records, without which it could hardly
have existed.

Nor could it have existed without the more secular tradition of spiritual autobiography. In this field the revelation
of a new uncharted world, the self, had been most fully made,
in modern times, by Petrarch, and varied in a thousand ways
by the poets of the Renaissance from Michelangelo to Shakespeare. During the age of classicism, after the middle of the
seventeenth century, this interest in the intimate history of
the secular self had died down, though the records of the

mystics continue and multiply. But in the eighteenth century it emerged stronger than ever. Rousseau's *Confessions* were published 1782-90. Written to ensure that one man at least should have told the whole truth about himself, they left the self-consciousness of Western Europe, it is not too much to say, permanently altered. A great sounding-board was hung over the confessional ; a new literary form was invented, or the old one formidably enlarged. Real autobiography was now possible ; there was no reason why it should not take in the whole of male experience. Goethe, Chateaubriand, and Wordsworth all practise it in diverse ways, but their common aim is to re-live their inward life before the world, and, in retrospective expression, to give to that life, itself often broken and motley, the unity of a piece of art. The task was easier for Wordsworth, not that he had more art than the others, but that his tale was less disturbed and his life more single. He does not mainly write, like Rousseau, to expose himself ; nor, like Goethe, from an interest in his past as a pageant and from the intellectual need for self-expression ; nor, like Byron, in order to ease his mind a while and to be noticed. He writes for the good of the world, and he is sustained by the enormous importance of his chronicle to himself. He is justified ; he has written, in *The Prelude* and the pieces that cluster round it, poetry that disinfects life for us. And it is all true ; there is no unconscious moulding of the facts ; from that he was kept by his sense of his responsibility to himself. His whole past was thus a possession to him, and the unity of his soul and work comes out in ever clearer, more stately light as he proceeds. His life was a poem in truth, though sometimes it was a very dull poem. Much is uninspired, but there is ' nothing but well and fair.' His self-opinion and self-engross-ment, which have made him the easy prey of critics, were needful for facing the long years of neglect. This seems to be a quality necessary to many North-country natures in the struggle for survival ; but in his case it was the best possible armour. It is in utter contrast with the restless, self-vexing sensibility of Rousseau and the romantic poets. Thus two traditional currents meet in Wordsworth, one springing from the Protestants, from the mystics and Milton, and the other springing from the secular Rousseau. The first gave him his temper and method of confession, the second gave him his larger scope, and also, though he might not have owned it, some of his seminal ideas—the ' education of nature,' the return to the simple affections.

II

The better genius of Wordsworth [1] is to be found, and its expansion to be watched, in some six publications, the contents of which were mostly written between 1796 and 1808. Thus, out of about fifty-three years given to composition, ten were poetically fertile. No other poet who has written so well has left evidence so copious of having outlasted his powers. But the aftermath is not to be slighted, and we cannot wish, for the sake of his reputation, that Wordsworth had been silent after his fortieth year. He died in 1850, aged eighty.

The volumes of 1793, *Descriptive Sketches* and *An Evening Walk*, are not amongst these five. From that of 1798, *Lyrical Ballads with a few other Poems*, the second distinct renewal of our poetry is often dated, if we assign the first renewal to the years 1780-6. *Tintern Abbey* and *The Ancient Mariner* make good the claim ; but the original and permanent beauty of these pieces was not confessed by the reading public for some time. Few of the other lyrical ballads are yet in their most perfect form. But the contributions of Wordsworth are signal, not only for the new scene of life he disclosed, and the new manner of language which he critically defended, but for his invention and execution of fresh species of poetry, the ' lyrical ballad ' being one, and the meditation, like *Tintern Abbey*, another. In 1800 these poems were reprinted with changes, and a second volume added, containing more faultless examples of the narrative and reflective lyric. Less is written to theory. while the critical preface is much extended and reaches its final form in a reprint of two years later. But most of the remaining poetry of Wordsworth's prime was in a style which he took no pains, and had no need, to defend on principle.

The Prelude, begun before the end of the century, was ended in 1805, but not printed till 1850. On *The Excursion*, published in 1814, Wordsworth had also been at work during many years. It therefore partakes both of his full and his declining powers. *The Recluse* is of his best, but, as a whole, it long remained unknown, till 1888. The three works together form part of what he intended to be his most imposing monument, a long philosophical poem ' on Man, on Nature, and on human Life.' This also was a great and a fresh invention. Alone, and despite some dreary ingredients, it would have been a sufficient memorial for one man ; and yet it gives no inkling of his lyrical greatness.

Meantime, in 1807, a pair of volumes had appeared, which reveal another, and the last, development of his genius. There are some reiterations, as in *Alice Fell*, of his early, starker manner. His retrospective and tender poetry is there also, and better than before ; ' She was a phantom of delight,' and *Stepping Westward* and *The Solitary Reaper* fail in nothing. *The Affliction of Margaret* is not excelled in form or in sub-limity of spirit amongst ' lyrical ballads ' or pathetic mono-logues anywhere. But the poet is no longer busy only with private lives, or with himself. The meditative patriotism of *The Prelude* has now its lyric counterpart. The passion for England, too long silent in verse, now finds heroic utterance in the sonnets to liberty. The same spirit becomes universal in *The Happy Warrior* and the *Ode to Duty*. Here, and also in the ode, *Intimations of Immortality*, Wordsworth's high metaphysical verse reaches its crown as it passes from meditation into song. In these volumes he is less afraid to be splendid ; he is not curbed by doctrine ; he has read more in our major poets, and has found that he himself is of their company.

Of his other books, *The White Doe of Rylstone* (1815) is the last that contains nothing unpoetical. *Peter Bell* (1819) is an old work, belated. During the years 1819-22 there appeared *The Waggoner, The River Duddon, Memorials of a Tour on the Continent,* and *Ecclesiastical Sketches. Yarrow Revisited* came out in 1835. He issued many collected editions, successively larger ; the first in 1815, the last in 1849. Work of early date, such as *The Borderers,* was rescued and printed in the course of these editions ; but their chief interest lies in the repeated recensions and alterations [1] of Wordsworth's best writings.

His critical outlived his creative power, and he turned it with curious effect upon himself. It was long before he con-sented greatly to qualify the nudity of diction, which he had written some of his poems to commend and had defined in his prefaces less and less absolutely. But the classic criticisms of Coleridge in *Biographia Literaria* (1817) gave him some concern, and went home. Yet many years passed before he showed his will to act upon them ; and in doing so, since his sense of style had now ebbed, he often fell back, in revising, from the trivial into the conventional. Another nine years, and in 1836 Wordsworth rehandled his work with fresh rigour, but to little avail. Yet a poet is never too old for his power, or his tact, to revive ; and in the edition of 1845 some of the new changes are improvements, as can be seen in such instances as *Beggars* and the second of the poems to the *Celandine*. The approved text, on the other hand, of the *Ode to Duty* had been reached earlier, by steady emendation, and without any relapses. By this incessant industry, Wordsworth tried to make good his native uncertainty as an artist in language ; and he partly succeeded, through force of character, through his faith in his value to the world, and through a self-confidence of which no reckoning is possible.

His blind censors ought not to have found it so easy to exaggerate the decay of his inspiration. No doubt, after 1807, a certain prosaic blight, already threatening, spread over his poetry, and lasted ; this was due not to misguided theory, but to sheer lapse of poetic faculty and of self-criticising power. The work lacks magic, and even feature ; and it forms the greater part of his writings. It does not in any true sense exist, except that it is bound in the same covers as the rest. Still it is untrue, though it is sometimes said, that all Wordsworth's good verse was made in the decade between 1798 and 1808. He certainly did not, after that date, invent any new kinds ; all his best work is in the old kinds or in some simple variation of them ; and, above all, it is found in the sonnets. 'Surprised by joy' (about 1812) ; 'I thought of thee' (*River Duddon*, No. xxxiv., 1820 ?) ; *Mutability* (about 1821) ; 'Scorn not the Sonnet' (1827 ?) ; 'Most sweet it is' (1833) ; 'Why art thou silent ? ' (1832) ; these are all sonnets of the great stamp ; and many more, like that on *King's College Chapel*, or even that on *The Projected Railway* (1844), either approach them, or are on that steady level of power—a kind of *Vorgebirge*, or middle range, leading from the blank plain to the summits—up to which Wordsworth sometimes climbed even in old age. His genius also revived in elegy ; the sonnet on Scott's departure for Italy has the same kind of nobility and solemnity as the poems (1835) on Charles Lamb and James Hogg. And the forms and moods of the *Lyrical Ballads*, with their distinctive excellences, are not lost. The latest Yarrow poems were written in 1831, and 'This lawn, a carpet all alive,' two years earlier. To the last it is unsafe to neglect Wordsworth, for his power is apt to reappear. The lines on the mountain-daisy, with

> The beauty of its star-shaped shadow, thrown
> On the smooth surface of this naked stone,

were written when he was seventy-four.

III

The tributes of his sister, and *Brougham Castle*, and many other things, show that Wordsworth was not soft, though he wrote of kittens and the little celandine, and that he was not naturally peaceful. His mother found him a ‘ stiff, moody, and violent ’ child. Carlyle[1] judged the look of his face in old age to be ‘ not bland or benevolent,’ but rather ‘ close, impregnable, and hard ’ :

A deep, earnest man, who had thought silently and painfully about many things . . . essentially a cold, hard, silent, practical man, who if he had not fallen into poetry would have done effectual work of some sort in the world. . . . ‘ A man of a softer mood, more sympathetic ? ’ No, not at all, he was a man quite other than that ; a man of an immense head and great jaws like a crocodile’s, cast in a mould designed for prodigious work.

Of course Wordsworth was not cold, but he had a strong head and an iron programme, and he reined and bitted in his temper only too much, because he thought it his mission to be tranquil. He took public affairs, especially when they were grievous, with Miltonic intensity. In *The Recluse* he says that he is instructed by Nature to ‘ be mild and cleave to gentle things,’ and to do so without fear that his natural attributes,

The longing, the contempt, the undaunted quest,

will thereby be enfeebled ; they will only be transformed to finer uses. And this they really are. They come out unweakened in his heroic and political poetry, and they give the sternness and definiteness that informs all his best verse. They made him conceive his ideas rigidly and slowly ; he never let go. These qualities of character are closely connected with Wordsworth’s strong memory,[2] on which every scene and incident was etched as on a plate. The notes he dictated to Miss Fenwick when an old man prove how easily, and in general how surely, he consulted his memory about the occasion of every youthful poem. Such a faculty may be thought to have quickened his steady self-absorption, and it certainly qualified him to write *The Prelude* ; for it retained not only outward things, but vanishing shades and impalpable phases of his inner life, which to him, to the world, it was so indispensable to have on record.

There is no artist like memory, which Blake falsely opposed to the imagination. In a poet like Wordsworth they are nearly the same faculty. The imagination of such a poet is his memory acting truthfully, that is, throwing off the dross of unmeaning fact, controlling and using the power of forgetfulness properly, and shaping into beautiful form what it retains. In the freer kind of creation, which is dramatic or fantastic, the chemistry is more complete, and the result is not biographical evidence. In much of Byron's poetry reminiscence, delusion, and invention seem inextricably mingled. But Wordsworth employs his memory in a very different way for the service of his imagination. We know when he is inventing, and when he is chronicling, and also that his chronicle is faithful. His memory weeds itself, and only becomes indiscriminate or dull when his genius fails him. He puts down everything that illustrates ' the growth of a poet's mind.' Shelley, partly under Wordsworth's influence, often tries to do the like, and what he achieves in *Alastor* or *Prince Athanase* is more piercing than anything Wordsworth wrote about himself ; but the effort is scattered and broken, and much in his inner story is unexplained. Wordsworth related the history of his mind and ruling passion thrice, and his imagination is used to light up what actually happened and to give the full force of it. No other English poet has attempted any such thing on the same scale, and so triumphantly.

The first of these records is the briefest ; it is found in *Tintern Abbey* (1798) which gives, in a few lines, the history with the struggle left out. The second is *The Prelude*, written between 1799 and 1805, in fourteen books, and in a kind of epical form ; here the struggle, with its antecedents and consequents, is the theme. ' Sing, O Urania,' he seems to say, the victory of William Wordsworth over despondency. This was not published till 1850. The third record is in *The Excursion*, which came out in 1814 ; the experiences of the Wanderer and the Solitary give much of the same record, again with the painful part mitigated. Besides, there is the fragment called *The Recluse*, written in 1800, but not published till 1888 ; this is connected closely with *The Prelude*. Further there are many fragments, often in blank verse, of various date, which enhance the impression. All this writing, except *The Excursion*, is of Wordsworth's best period, when his poetic power was at its strongest ; and in *The Excursion*, though it is later, that power survives.

But the spiritual history told in all this belongs to the period when he had *not* found his style ; what it recites, he was unable to utter at the time. His first perfect work, written when he had shed his false though remarkable youthful manner, was in *Lyrical Ballads* (1797-8) ; and by that time the struggle was past, the crisis was behind him, and he was writing in the full tide of the power and happiness produced by his relief from it. While it was going on, he was only capable of *Descriptive Sketches* and *An Evening Walk* and *The Borderers*, which give no real picture of his mind. Not till he had acquired his true language could he set down—nay he could not truly even recollect, since no memory is complete till it has found words —the great occurrences of his spirit. Now, his whole past seemed to flash into clear light and harmonious form. From this point of view Wordsworth's wrestlings with the theory of poetic diction, his efforts to write purely, and his dismissal of the style of the last age, assume a fresh interest.

It follows that Wordsworth has two histories, in which the critical dates and stages are different, and which cannot without confusion be told in the same breath. We may either follow the 'growth of his mind,' or, in a different order of development, that of his poetic power. And we must do both to understand him. At any rate, in order to see where he stood when he wrote *Lyrical Ballads*, we must use what he tells us, in verse and prose, at various times of his life, about his long mental journey up to that time ; beginning with the *Ode on Intimations of Immortality* and his explanation of it. This tale, which it is so unjust to abridge, is also too long to tell ; any summary is sure to foreshorten and perhaps to falsify it.

Wordsworth is one of the poets, like Milton, Pope, and Shelley, who has made, recorded, and kept a definite vow : he says that he was not more than fourteen when he first became aware

of the infinite variety of natural appearances which had been unnoticed by the poets of any age or country, so far as I was acquainted with them ; and I made a resolution to supply, in some degree, the deficiency.[1]

Other poets had lain in the lap of nature now and then, but Wordsworth would espouse her. He did so ; he wrote the story of the courtship and nuptials at length. What if he sometimes portrays her as a kind of severe governess, and proses about her power to moralise the young ? Oftener she is young herself, incarnate in some joyful figure, a Highland girl or a Lucy, who is moulded by the rhythm of waves or the lines of the flowers, and is thus in some sort their explanation ; a creature bred anew ' in every age,' as Blake would have said, for the refreshment of humanity. The soul of natural things, as it becomes conscious in such persons, was incarnate in his sister. At other times nature is grave, sad, not young, or if young only the sadder for that, and seems inarticulate until she has flashed into feeling existence in some Ruth or Margaret or Leechgatherer, who cannot be thought of away from the landscape which is incomplete without their presence. At other times, when Wordsworth is most himself, he is alone with a Nature in which there is no other living thing; but then she herself is alive, and the poet is absorbed in her, under the sunrise or on·the shadowy fells, and is afterwards moved, in the rite of sacred reminiscence, to find words for his experience.

Part of the interest of *The Prelude* and accompanying poems lies in showing that these visitations did not come at random, as we are apt to read them, but in a traceable order and development. The passion that first discloses itself is not that of humanity. There is no precocity of suffering, or even of sympathy. There is a long, unreflective, childish phase, which begins early. When but ten years old, says Wordsworth,

> even then,
> I held unconscious intercourse with beauty
> Old as creation, drinking in a pure
> Organic pleasure from the silver wreaths
> Of curling mist.

He is full of blind joys and of alarms; the shades of vague nascent feeling, so overpowering in its pressure, have never been so powerfully described. 'That dreamlike vividness and splendour which invest objects of sight in childhood,' and the dizzy feeling of their unreality, are set forth in the great Ode. He remembers 'not what he felt, but how he felt'; and traces all the vital moments and delicate degrees of his expansion. At sixteen he is submerged, like a Hindoo, in the feeling of impersonal existence, or Being—not yet thought of as Mind. Then his spirit ceases to be merely passive, but seems itself to contribute to nature, to be her tyrant; she is rather part of him, than he of her; the consciousness of self and the intuition of nature become indistinguishable. Next Wordsworth takes his fellow-men into the circle of his feeling, and is aware of a new 'human-heartedness' in his love of nature. Men now fall into their place in nature, being, in happy instances at any rate, formed and ennobled by contact with her. In all this Wordsworth inverted the usual course of growth; for most men begin with the primary affections, and the love of nature is an afterthought if it comes at all, which with most people it never does. But even after this stage Wordsworth often speaks as if he were not only alone with the universe but alone in it. This is the impression left by two of the loftiest passages of *The Prelude* ; once, when, in a college vacation, he comes out from a gay festivity into the night, and a vow from unknown sources, undefined but irresistible, descends upon him, and he knows that he will be ' a dedicated spirit ' ; and once in the verses on the Simplon Pass, which he crossed in the summer of 1790. Rain and wind, snow and vapour, all the works of the Lord, are then

> like workings of one mind, the features
> Of the same face, blossoms upon one tree,
> Characters of the great Apocalypse,
> The types and symbols of Eternity,
> Of first, and last, and midst, and without end.

This is the feeling that is otherwise expressed in the more than Virgilian Pantheism of *Tintern Abbey*. Virgil, whilst he celebrates the universal mind, does not describe any mystical experience of its reality. Goethe, the child of Spinoza, has a vaster share than Wordsworth of the plastic, multifarious, and generative spirit which he finds in the world. Bruno has a more headlong rapture, nay a kind of sensuous apprehension of the divine principle. But Wordsworth is the *vates sacer* of Pantheism. His firm rather than broad or flexible intellect glows like a white-hot star when he is inspired to revive in memory its central, eucharistic experience ; and the great metaphysical style, which he recovered for English poetry, is at his command for the expression of it.

These are the summits ; but meantime the road runs along a low rolling table-land, by the edges of the lakes, or descends into the pleasant if uninspiring Cambridge flats. The external narrative of the poet's life as a boy is well sustained, and interesting for its own sake, and even vivacious. But a new region is in sight. So far, up to his twentieth year, there has been no misadventure to the traveller, who has suffered only the happy pain of exertion well rewarded. But in one of the very sources of his joy lies the disappointment that is in store. Through his shaken faith in France Wordsworth was to become a voice, like Burke his master, of the conservative revulsion. He went through a stage of hope and enthusiasm first ; and this, along with the causes of its decline, and the further process of consolation for the disenchantment that followed, is the subject of *The Prelude*.

IV

Wordsworth was treated by poets of the next age like Byron and Shelley as a typical backslider [1] from the faith. But they could not know his real history, since *The Prelude* was not published. Also they had grown up when the first heat of the national reaction was over, and to them the Revolution was a piece of history. In fact, Wordsworth's political faith was more stubbornly founded than that of Coleridge, Southey, Dr. Moore, and others who were discouraged. He was shaken, but he held out longer. The shock when it came was all the greater. Even latterly, he retained more popular sentiment than many of his friends, and had, as he said, ' something of the Chartist ' about him. It may not follow that the medicine he found for his ' strong disease ' was a good one for any one but himself ; it has, indeed, only a psychological interest. Wordsworth did not win a new political faith when the old one had gone ; he in no small measure shirked the problem that had vexed him. He went to live with his friends and his sister in the country, and fell back on nature, and poetry, and the love of common humanity. This, no doubt, it was his mission to do, and the world is the gainer. But he never fortified himself by contemplating the permanent good that the Revolution and the Napoleonic rule had done, and in this respect he showed a less open and instructed mind than Mackintosh, his admirer, whose course of thought otherwise reminds us of his own.

The steps of Wordsworth's political hopes and dejection [2] have often been carefully traced. His heroic sonnets on public affairs, and his defence of the Revolution in 1793 in his *Letter to the Bishop of Llandaff*, must be read along with *The Prelude*. His tour in 1790 with his friend Robert Jones, amid the public rejoicings ; the visits that he paid a year later to Paris, where he saw the Legislative Assembly at-work, and to Blois and Orleans, where he met Michel Beaupuy ; his enthusiasm for the Gironde, which he would have joined but for shortness of funds ; his delight, after he had come home, at the news of the death of Robespierre ; these are the chief outward incidents of his period of ' hope and joy.' Wordsworth, the ' lost leader,' digested a good deal ; his faith, though it was horrified, survived the execution of the king, the September massacres, the Terror ; he thinking that beyond these things he still saw the light. It was a greater blow when the war began ; at moments he even wished for the defeat of British arms ;

he was divided between shame and patriotism when ' Britain put forth her freeborn strength in league.' But the invasion of Switzerland by France staggered him as a kind of fratricide ; and the rise of the Napoleonic power totally struck down his faith. Then indeed he was aware of ' a melancholy waste of hopes o'erthrown.' Byron and Shelley, amid all their democratic zeal, felt the greatness of the conqueror, but Wordsworth was too old and too far gone for that. On the other hand, he raised the noblest of his patriot strains, invoking the shade of Milton if so he might stir his country in her worst hours. But this was after his recovery from the dejection into which he had fallen.

Wordsworth's malady, in the years 1795-7, took a peculiar shape, which represents a relapse towards eighteenth-century logic and analysis. As poetry, his account of it is too bad to quote ; but it vividly reflects the state of an honest mind whose radicalism has fallen in ruins, and which yet cannot fall back at once upon unreasoned tradition. Wordsworth tells us how he turned social anatomist, and plunged into the primary disputes of ethical philosophy ; but the effort was sterile, for he found himself demanding ' formal proof ' for everything, and ' yielding up moral questions in despair.' This is only to say that he was not built for so critical a task. So he fell back on feeling, on the society and influence of Dorothy, and on nature, his first love. His final note is reassuring. Great poets, all poets, he himself, are the human voices and inter-preters of the soul of the world, of

> a mind
> That feeds upon infinity, that broods
> Over the dark abyss, intent to hear
> Its voices issuing forth to silent light
> In one continuous stream.

This power, exhibited in the workings of nature,

> is the express
> Resemblance of that glorious faculty
> That higher minds bear with them as their own.

The poet's theme and destiny are divine :

> Such minds are truly from the Deity,
> For they are Powers.

Here, then, Wordsworth joins himself to the long line of Platonists, like Sidney and Shelley, who ' defend ' poetry as the ' light, winged, and holy thing,' which Plato, in the *Ion*, had averred it to be.   Such a conclusion rounds off *The Prelude*, and brings Wordsworth to the end of his pilgrimage of the soul, which was also the beginning of his true career as a poet.

V

But meanwhile he had begun his craft.   The two volumes published in 1793, *An Evening Walk* and *Descriptive Sketches*, being at once a museum of all the errors which he was soon to put away, and full of a new energy struggling through that spurious style, are a link between two ages of poetry.   They represent an older fashion of verse than Cowper's *Yardley Oak*, and at the same time they show Wordsworth's power and determination to observe and his as yet unshaded sense of colour and music in nature.   Forced grammar, abstract personifications, poetic diction[1] of the deadly kind, ellipses, are there, and the couplets, with their sprinkled alexandrines, betray the influence of various models, of whom Goldsmith is the most genial.   Yet they are full of fresh and hard and tenacious vision, better guided by the sense of beauty than Crabbe's, but clogged by conventional expression.   *An Evening Walk* was finished three years sooner than *Descriptive Sketches*, which yet show no real advance in method.   The reader who begins with *Lyrical Ballads* can hardly believe that either of those works are by Wordsworth, for they are ' poetry without an atmosphere,' their very faults are not those of *Goody Blake*, there are no clear deep pools in them of fancy and brooding thought, and they bear no trace of the mysteries that were rehearsing in the author's soul at the time when they were written.   But they reveal the bright, quick, upper current of his experience.   So swiftly did Wordsworth's powers expand, that in the *Lines left upon a Seat in a Yew-Tree*, finished only two years afterwards (1795), he has already found out how to write ;   they are almost like a passage of *The Excursion*. *Guilt and Sorrow*, also composed early, chiefly exists in revised form, but enough remains of its original roughness and unshapely strength to show in what grim blind alleys the young poet had been casting about for a subject.   The story of the murderer who, after seeing and hearing many distressful events, is moved by his wife's dying blessing to give himself up to the gallows—a mean ending—is in the taste of Crabbe ; but the measure is the measure of Spenser, forecasting the not dissimilar tune of *Resolution and Independence*.   The bare style, quite different from that of *Descriptive Sketches*, seems to have been natural to Wordsworth before he found a theory to warrant it. In *The Borderers* (1795-6) the poet dabbles his brush in sufficiently acrid colours. In this drama there is a villain of the period, a reason-worshipping, unscrupulous infidel, Oswald, who dupes the young lover Marmaduke into thinking that his lady, Idonea, is to be sold into infamy by Herbert, her blind father ; it is, then, Marmaduke's duty to murder Herbert, but the act is averted. Such matter is grotesque, but the melodrama, though interrupted by philosophic stretches, is unwincing. In his later sad or tragical tales, Wordsworth's pathos is softened by the remote and ruminative tone that has gained upon him, and by the atmosphere of thought and beauty ; and a kind of afternoon light converts tragedy properly so called into a solemn tragic idyll.

VI

He was the greatest inventor, between Gray and Shelley, of poetical forms ; a service which his campaign for a simpler diction has too much obscured. Some famous practitioners have worked almost wholly in transmitted moulds ; thus Pope's forms are those of Dryden, or Rochester, or Boileau, which he uses with a new delicacy. Crabbe hit on the rhymed novel, but his verse and diction long remained of the regulation cut. Blake's only original species of verse, the ' prophetic book,' went bankrupt on his hands. Coleridge, after he had made his ballad and his lay, showed little invention in structure. But the short ' lyrical ballad,' the blank verse tale of middle length, the long psychological poem in epic guise, were discoveries, while to the ode and the sonnet Wordsworth, while taking over ancestral forms, gave a new life.

Whatever *The Thorn* and *Ruth* may be called, they are a new kind of poem. The old names do not fit them, neither does that of ' lyrical ballad,' though a few of them suggest the ballad measure and movement, and many of them have lyrical turns and flashes. When they have the passion proper to lyric, it is either dramatically conceived, as in *The Lament of a Forsaken Indian Woman* ; or it is the revived passion, kindling anew in retrospect, of the poet himself ; or it is passion diffused and repressed. They are mostly reflective narratives, of a great variety of forms, ranging up from the versified moral *Anecdote for Fathers* with the lesson appended, to the tragical tale, hung over with stormy light and telling itself without a comment. There had been nothing of the sort before ; the very faults

were new. The prosaic strokes, such as the 'weak ankles' of
Simon Lee, which produced a crackle of thorns in the reviews,
imply a different effect and purpose from the flatnesses of
Crabbe. They are not put in to ensure 'actuality of relation and poetry without an atmosphere'; they are put in,
wilfully, to see how far poetry can retain its atmosphere
whilst condescending in that particular manner. And though
Wordsworth retrenched some of them in later editions, some
remained; nor is it a paradox to say that his errors have
taught us almost as much as his successes; involving as
they did a descent below those lowest levels of poetry, with
which it is impossible to mix higher matter without a sense of
shock and discord, and which are thus more clearly demarcated
than before.

In most of these poems there is a more or less distinct intrusion and separate formulation of the moral idea, for the
sake of which each of them is written. But we must not say
that the more the idea intrudes, the worse the poem is; its
excellence does not depend upon that consideration. Nor
does it depend on the value of the idea regarded in itself. It
depends on the degree in which the idea is poetically conceived
and expressed. In *The Tables Turned* the idea, if treated as
implying a dogmatic conviction, is itself doubtful, resting as
it does upon a silly if passing mood of antipathy to science;
and moreover it is not poetically conceived or expressed, above
all in the stanza ending 'we murder to dissect.' In the lines
To My Sister, this taint is absent; the mood of happiness in
which they are written is not aggressive. In *Simon Lee*, though
the form is that of a story with a moral ('the gratitude of men
Hath oftener left me mourning'), the idea is profound and
sudden, and is imaginatively though overtly expressed. In
The Two April Mornings, and *The Fountain*, the idea suffuses
the whole expression; it is not disjoined, or inserted at the end;
a piece of human life is shown and speaks for itself. In *Ruth*,
also, theory makes itself heard; a theory about the good and
bad influences of quiet and tropical landscape respectively.
The vicious effects of living among the Red Indians are not
prosaically stated, but the view does not carry conviction.
On the other side, the operation of the 'rocks and pools'
upon the mind of the distracted Ruth is told with that union
of insight and poetic phrase which is Wordsworth's glory; for
he as well as Coleridge deserves Shelley's title of the 'subtle-
souled psychologist.' For Ruth those rocks and pools are the
'engines of her pain, the tools that shaped her sorrow,' but she

'never taxed them with the ill That they had done to her.'
This kind of analysis must be applied to each of the poems
in turn. There is no doubt that Wordsworth is greatest when
he lets himself go, forgets the educational value of mountains,
forgets his position as *spectator ab extra*, speaks dramatically,
and rises, with Blake and Coleridge, to pure lyrical passion and
mastery; when he becomes, in fact, a true romantic. 'Her
eyes are wild' and *The Forsaken Indian Woman* were written
in the society of Coleridge, whose richer sensibility may well
have acted like the sun in unloosing the philosophical mantle
of his friend, which no north-east wind from Edinburgh could
ever have penetrated:

> About that tight and deadly band
> I see thy little fingers prest.
> The breeze I see is in the tree,
> It comes to cool my babe and me.

And the Indian woman complains:

> Before I see another day,
> Oh let my body die away!
> In sleep I heard the northern gleams;
> The stars, they were among my dreams—

This confounding and interchange of the overwrought senses [1]
('the breeze I *see*,' 'I *heard* the Northern gleams') are brought
home by such figures of speech, which Coleridge called 'once
the offspring of passion, but now the adopted children of
power.' In these two short pieces there is no separation of
the thought from the story and the feeling, and there is a
rhythmical ebb and flow of the expression of pain, not a jading
and unrelieved iteration of it. In the longer tales also, of
slighter or less concentrated energy, such as *Michael* or *The
Brothers*, there is the same virtue. It is needless to refer to
the pieces, written after Wordsworth's artistic faculty had
begun to decline, where this saving power is lost.

There is a good deal of variety of pace in Wordsworth's
narratives, and the pace is set by the metre. *We are Seven*
and *Lucy Gray* go sedately but lightly, and the journey is
short; the blank verse of *Michael* lasts longer, moving forward
incessantly but with dignity, like the old shepherd climbing
to the cairn. In *Ruth*, a story interrupted by reflections, the
step is rapid in the narrative parts, but is arrested several
times, like that of a man who pauses in his walk to think
deeply. In the retrospective pieces like *Daffodils* or *To a
Highland Girl*, and in their companions like *Matthew* or *The*

Small Celandine, where the subject is a single impression, or the conversation of people strolling slowly, there is hardly any movement at all. A sort of balance has to be struck between the original objects of memory—the girl or the daffodils—and their present value to the philosophic mind ; and such a process is somewhat retarding. In this class, *The Solitary Reaper* is the greatest achievement, because in addition to the pictured figure that remains on the inward eye, and to the sense of this image being a possession to the soul for ever, there re-enters the note of piercing song, which in other such poems is weaker ; and it overpowers everything else with its for once direct and transcendent note :

> A voice so thrilling ne'er was heard
> In spring-time from the Cuckoo-bird,
> Breaking the silence of the seas
> Among the farthest Hebrides.

In the very worst of the *Lyrical Ballads,* and of Wordsworth's later pieces of the same stamp, there is usually some sort of poetry. But where they are bad, it is less because they are prosaic, than because the poetry itself strikes us as intrusive. The purpose in *Goody Blake,* and in most of *The Thorn* and *Simon Lee,* is to write a moving tale in a kind of chapbook style ; and Wordsworth could have attained this purpose well enough if he had not gone beyond it. The mistake was to put in the poetry at all. Most of *The Thorn* is out of keeping, as Coleridge observed, with the elderly seafaring man who is supposed to relate it. These works are therefore to be regarded, not so much as high verse with lapses into baldness, but rather as naïve yarns interrupted—nay, spoilt ! by unseasonable inspiration. The dreary jigging facetiousness which often gets into the double rhymes is a fault of a different class. And yet all these errors are the result of excess of doctrine and not of want of power.

The Idiot Boy, therefore, and *Peter Bell,* must be given over to the critical lions or jackals who may still care to spring upon them. But even here, and generally in Wordsworth's work, there are two qualities that remain unimpaired. He is a master of mental pathology, and he can tell a story. The thronging fears of the idiot boy's mother, and the obsession of Peter Bell, are as good in their lower, as 'Her eyes are wild' and *The Indian Woman* are in their incomparably loftier kind. This trait is a link with Coleridge ; but the difference is that Wordsworth watched such emotions, while Coleridge felt them. Again, even in the stories of debateable worth, there is seldom any failure in structure or proportioning. The clay may be poor clay, but it takes the shape. Surplus lumps are not stuck on in order to use up the material. Wordsworth is an economist in narrative, though in his reflective writing he can be at once heavy and wasteful. And the 'lyrical ballad' may be thought of as the original unit, or starting-point, of his poetic production in this field. For out of it, or by its side, he developed his story-telling gift in two distinct directions. One of these is represented by *Michael* and the episodes in *The Excursion*, the other by his lyric lays, where he comes into some sort of comparison with Scott; as in *The White Doe of Rylstone* and in *Brougham Castle*. In both directions he triumphs, and triumphs once more in a new kind of his own invention.

In the former variety the lyrical spirit has vanished. *The Brothers*, *Michael*, the tale of Margaret in *The Excursion*, are in blank verse. There is none of that safeguard against prolixity and weakness which the lyric form helps to ensure. The higher the tension, the swifter the pace; and the briefer the measure, the more surely the artist is driven to make haste and make an end. Yet, though this check has gone, Wordsworth's tales are not often, like so many of Crabbe's, long and tedious. Crabbe's matter-of-fact treatment was, indeed, a warning to his successor. Much that we relish keenly in Crabbe has, no doubt, departed in Wordsworth; the whole sardonic ingredient, the touch of warranted and experienced bitterness. But instead of this there is the idealising touch which it is Wordsworth's secret to blend with the calm veracity of his report. The sorrows of Michael and of the wanderer in *The Brothers* fall into their place in a large, tranquil, judiciously ordered scheme of things, and are to be read in the light of a hopefulness, which does not rest on such a simple piety as might console the sufferers themselves, but on a sense that such troubles are as recurrent as winter storms or floods :— 'and wherefore should we grieve'—since after all they are troubles nobly met ? This attitude may not console everybody, but there is no doubt of its value to Wordsworth's art. The philosophy that sees events and catastrophes so calmly, measuring all mischances by the firmness of spirit that is evoked to meet them, gives a kind of epic grandeur to these exalted homely idylls. Nor does the chorus intrude unduly. In his best pieces, Wordsworth is not like a lecturer who chequers a lovely tale with his own valuable remarks. His large comment comes in easily :

purple passages with depth (handwritten margin note)

> There is a comfort in the strength of love ;
> 'Twill make a thing endurable, which else
> Would overset the brain, or break the heart ;
> I have conversed with more than one who well
> Remember the old Man, and what he was
> Years after he had heard this heavy news.

That is from *Michael* ; in the story of Margaret there is more
garrulity, which does no good, and in *The Churchyard among
the Mountains* the tales are swamped by the commentary,
despite the beauty of both (*Excursion*, books i. and vii.).
But in the slight slow stream of narrative in *The Brothers*
there is no tedium, for the commentary is implicit and incorporate in the story ; and the ending leaves an exquisite sense
of *desiderium*, diffused rather than acute, when the stranger,
who has heard from the parish parson of his brother's life and
death, departs without revealing his identity. Here Wordsworth shows a Greek kind of tact in knowing what to say and
when to stop, just as he shows it in *Laodamia*, which is a poem
in an opposite style, a style of high but mannered dignity.
It is as slow-moving as any poem can well be and yet live ;
each of the stanzas is self-inclosed, like an inscription ; it is
written with Virgil in mind, and with Virgilian labour ; it
could hardly be longer without becoming heavy ; but, just
as in *Michael*, the sense of scale and length remains infallible.

VII

One other feature of these narratives must be attended to.
The whole presentation of evil and calamity is peculiar. It
has been written that 'Wordsworth's eyes avert their ken
From half of human fate.' Rather, he watches that half
through a glass as though from a kind of observatory. He
does not say, like Miss Austen, 'Let other pens write of guilt
and misery.' He is a man of very hard grain, and he does
write of them, and that with stubborn veracity. And for
some time he positively traffics in them, and fails to make them
more than half poetical ; as in *The Borderers*, and even in *The
Thorn*, which might well have been left for prose and told in
the way of Edgar Allan Poe. Then, in others of the *Lyrical
Ballads*, he exhibits pain and desperation rather than guilt,
and achieves piercing pathos rather than the tragical display
of character and motive. As time passes, the pathos is softened
by the more remote and ruminative tone that gains upon the
poet ; or else the tragic side of the matter is held at arm's

length, and any traits of baseness or degeneration are severely
or curtly dismissed. So it is in *Michael*, where the fate of
Luke, the boy who went wrong, is disposed of in a few lines:

> Meantime Luke began
> To slacken in his duty; and, at length,
> He in the dissolute city gave himself
> To evil courses; ignominy and shame
> Fell on him, so that he was driven at last
> To seek a hiding-place beyond the seas,

and beyond any concern of the poet's, who blots Luke out
of the *dossier* as a rigid headmaster might a profligate pupil.
The interest in *Michael* is fixed on the shepherd himself, whose
entire life, with its one sad discolouring incident, is shown
as in a late afternoon light. Wordsworth's account of his
stay in London, or of his journey through revolutionary Paris,
well shows this apartness of spirit, which yet is not a mere
shutting of the eyes. In *The Prelude* he blesses God that he
was first nourished on shapes of grace, delight, and worthi-
ness, and

> That men before my inexperienced eyes
> Did first present themselves thus purified,
> Removed, and to a distance that was fit.

Else, he adds in a line of profound insight,

> How could the innocent heart bear up and live!

A just doctrine, for the premature sight of real evil disables
the mind from a sound view of reality itself. But in Wordsworth the 'fit distance' was always observed. He held the
ill-doings of men at just such a 'distance,' and saw them in
large masses, and in rare and strong imaginative glimpses.
In the theatre, indeed, he was moved,

> yet the storm
> Passed not beyond the suburbs of the mind.

Once in London he heard a harlot curse, and mused painfully
on the divorce of humanity from itself that is disclosed by
such a scene. This is not like Blake's exclamation,

> The harlot's cry from street to street
> Shall weave old England's winding-sheet,

and stirs us much less. Yet Wordsworth does not merely
philosophise on misery: for in the same episode he says that
he probed it no further; for, as he nobly adds,

> The sorrow of the passion stopped me there.

In *The Recluse* he gives the key to his attitude :

> Such grateful haunts foregoing, if I oft
> Must turn elsewhere—to travel near the tribes
> And fellowships of men, and see ill sights
> Of madding passions mutually inflamed ;
> Must hear Humanity in fields and groves
> Pipe solitary anguish ; or must hang
> Brooding above the fierce confederate storm
> Of sorrow, barricadoed evermore
> Within the walls of cities ; may these sounds
> Have their authentic comment ; that even these
> Hearing, I be not downcast or forlorn.

He did well in abstaining to write the ' authentic comment,'
but his abstinence seems to define his place amongst the poets,
the readers of life, in view of the claims that have sometimes
been made for his pre-eminence. He does reach a lofty and
victorious state of mind, not without a certain struggle and
circuit. But the struggle is after all too simple, and the
circuit too narrow, for him to match a poet like Leopardi,
who has not indeed Wordsworth's happiness, but who goes
deeper, and whose artistry is surer. With the masters of
tragedy he does not come into comparison at all, either as a
sage or as a poet.

It is easy to connect this lofty temper with his hard-won
creed. The pantheist, to whom all things are portions of the
divine, has to include, whether by violence of reasoning or
by an act of faith, even that which to the eye is undivine or
evil. Wordsworth admits the presence of evil in the world,
but is unwilling to admit it as a *principle* in things. It is, he
says, only thus

> rashly named by men
> Who know not what they speak.

This, however, is mere dogma. It is tempting to refer such a
frame of mind to another distinctive feature of Wordsworth's
writing. He is the most reminiscent of all poets. Many of
the people in his stories are dead or old ; they are, or soon
will be, buried in peace, and also, but for the memorial the
poet gives them, in extreme oblivion. They are gone, they
are part of nature ; but then nature herself is alive ; she is
charged with mind, and also she is ever breeding new generations, themselves soon to pass likewise. The hand, therefore,
of the dead is kind and cool upon the memory, and a sort of
balsam. And there are established joys of the past, which
nothing now can prevent from having existed. Why, then,

not soften the troubles of the departed, and colour the tale
with some of the tranquillity they enjoy themselves, as they
sleep

> Beside the mountain chapel, undisturbed ?

In other cases the subject is an 'emotion recollected in tranquillity,' if it is not always a tranquil emotion. The tense is
often in the past ; as in the poems on Lucy and on Matthew,
in *Daffodils*, in *The Solitary Reaper*,—where, indeed, for
once, the full passion of the hour is magically revived ; and,
again, in much of the *Ode on Intimations of Immortality*, and
in many of the sonnets. *Westminster Bridge* is an exception,
and owes its force to its immediacy and present flame. Usually,
however, the edge is taken off the feeling, which, in recompense,
is shown to us clear and rounded in the magic glass of the past.
In *The Prelude* the tone is retrospective by the nature of the
case, and in *The Excursion* too, for most of the personages
have only the past to talk of. In *The Brothers* the whole life
of the countryside for a generation is beheld at once :

> A sharp May-storm
> Will come with loads of January snow,
> And in one night send twenty score of sheep
> To feed the ravens ; or a shepherd dies
> By some untoward death among the rocks ;
> The ice breaks up and sweeps away a bridge ;
> A wood is felled :—and then for our own homes !
> A child is born or christened, a field ploughed,
> A daughter sent to service, a web spun,
> The old house-clock is decked with a new face.

But even this process is selective. The bestial episodes of
country life, the pinhead smallness of its interests, are overlooked ; everything is of a melancholy, not unhappy grey.
It is easy to see how with such a way of looking back at life
a man may come at times to forget Caliban, and to think that
things upon the whole are pretty well.

VIII

What can be said of *The Prelude, The Excursion*, and *The
Recluse*, amounting together to over seventeen thousand lines,
but even so forming only part of a vast uncompleted design ?
The Prelude was to precede a long tripartite poem, entitled
The Recluse ; a name that is now given to the fragment that
was meant to form the first book of the First Part. The Second
Part, *The Excursion*, was finished ; the Third Part was only

planned, but most of its materials are wrought up in other pieces written later than *The Excursion.* The whole would have formed

a philosophical poem, containing views of Man, Nature, and Society, . . . having for its principal subject the sensations and opinions of a poet living in retirement.

Is the man who could intend to do this, and who actually did so much of it, an artist still ? Yes, he is, to our astonishment. With all its gaps and flaws and barren stretches, his *opus magnum,* consisting of these three long works and of the various splinters of blank verse that accompany them, is more of a work of art than *The Seasons,* or *The Revolt of Islam,* or *The Task,* or *Childe Harold.* This praise it earns on the strength of its style, of its intellectual unity, and of its spiritual energy, all reckoned together. It is true that there has been no perfect English poem of epic length since *Paradise Regained,* and that Wordsworth's cathedral, to which *The Prelude* is meant as an ' antechapel,' is not only unfinished, but amorphous. Even so, this poetic chronicle of his life considered in its reaction on his mind is one of the most impressive long works in the English verse of the last two centuries.

The Prelude is laid out not unlike an epic, with episodes and vicissitudes and a climax, in fourteen mortal books. It is skilfully ordered for its purpose, for it begins at the end ; the poet, at the age of twenty-nine, is now safe in haven, and relates his long past voyage of the soul and imagination. And he ends with the same passions and consolations which dawned upon his childhood, which have been deadened or clouded, but which have at last come back to him, ratified now by experience, for good and all. The poem thus goes a kind of circuit. The first eight books describe the unchecked progress and expansion of the writer's mind ; the fifth, upon ' Books,' is a review of his reading and admirations, and really falls among his critical utterances. The eighth, ' Love of Nature leading to Love of Man,' as long as a book of Lucretius, is wholly inward and psychological, and is the chief example of Wordsworth's power to keep up the interest in an entirely abstract story. It shows him at the height of his buoyant but untried faith. The tenth book shows his disenchantment ; it is a retrospect of his mental crisis, and occupies the same sort of place in the arrangement as the ninth book of *Paradise Lost.* The last two books, ' Imagination and Taste, how repaired and restored,' are *Paradise Regained*—the old paradise with a difference.

The Prelude, however, is not all analysis ; it contains plenty of description and incident ; the childish games, the pictures of Beaupuy and the royalist officers, and of the pageant of London, come just when relief is wanted. The ' antechapel ' is full not only of ' cells and sepulchral recesses,' but of paintings and mosaics, some of them sacred and severe, others joyous, while not a few are playful and even familiar in theme. Wordsworth has more humour, of a dignified stiff kind, but not unpleasing, than Milton. The charm of the poem is found in its soft interfusion of story, scenery, and high reflective matter. The last element no doubt preponderates, and is sometimes beaten out unendurably thin, and in some of the later books is lumpy with pedantry ; but the style recovers itself at the last, and on the whole is sustained with unexpected freshness. There is no more noble and lucid diary of a poet's soul. *The Prelude* is one of those books which banish all but the purged and stately emotions that they chronicle—emotions such as Wordsworth's Protesilaus felt among the shades, or as are divined on the faces of old statues. The verse, at its best, advances like a slow river in flood, which casts up a clear-tempered light from its moving levels. Wordsworth has made more of the long confessional poem than any one else. Without *The Prelude,* our language would lack its capital example of a new and impressive order of poetic architecture ;—developed, it is true, from the long solemn productions of the century before, the *Night Thoughts* and the others—but alive, whilst they are not.

The Excursion is a modification of a different type, the lawless and discursive type of *The Task* ; but both the philosophical and the narrative elements bulk much larger than in its models. Meditation, description, and self-disclosure are present, as in *The Prelude*, and some of the same mental history, as we saw, is repeated. The Wanderer suffers less than Wordsworth, the Solitary goes deeper into doubt and suffers more ; but both are nourished by the same scenes and principles as he himself, and both live more in the past than in the present. *The Excursion* is conducted both worse than *The Prelude* and better. There is much commonplace throwing up of the hands against Voltaire and the infidels ; there is more of the Wordsworth who was to harden into a far stonier conservatism than Scott's, and who lost, as Lord Morley has said, his interest in progress about the date of Waterloo. But there is also more of Wordsworth's gracious vein, which appears when he gets out of himself and takes a holiday from his theories and his mission ; when he tells stories of the countryside, when he is no longer hammering on ' the educational influence of natural objects,' but lets his mind run in those happy fields of antique or romantic beauty, from which he has too soon to drag himself back with a conscientious sigh. Such is the picture of the Minstrel :

> wandering on from hall to hall,
> Baronial court or royal ; cheered with gifts
> Munificent, and love, and ladies' praise ;
> Now meeting on the road an armed knight,
> Now resting with a pilgrim by the side
> Of a clear brook.

The young freshness of rediscovered romance is there ; and we remember that *The Excursion* was published in the same year as *Waverley*. Wordsworth foreruns Keats in his delighted and noble appreciation of old Greek religion ; of the faith in Apollo, and the Naiad, and the Oread, and the god Pan (book iv.). In these truancies lies the special beauty of *The Excursion*. The poet's delight in Latin fancy, in cool-sounding names like *Lucretilis* and *Clitumnus*, had already been seen in *The Prelude*. The country tales in the later poem, alluded to already, can quite well be detached from it ; indeed, it is essentially a poem for extracts. Its disorder and its often ruthless tedium deprive it of artistic greatness as a whole. But it is a work out of which perfect passages can be taken without injury ; and many of these enhance Wordsworth's honours in that difficult form, of which *Yardley Oak* is a classic example ; the brief meditation in blank verse. *Tintern Abbey* is the greatest of such things, the most artfully varied and fluid in its transitions, with the utmost clearness in its total effect. And we cannot, indeed, match it by isolating the finest parts of *The Excursion* ; but the accounts of Langdale Pikes and of the Chaldean shepherds watching by night are of the same kind, if not of the same rank, of inspiration.

The Recluse describes Grasmere and its birds and inhabitants, and the poet's own companions, and the state of mind of which he has already recited the ' prelude,' and the poetic purposes that he harbours, and the reasons for his choice of a topic. It is an artistic whole. It rises by due degrees from direct description to great metaphysical writing ; it begins in the quiet valley, and first climbs well above the flats, and soars, with quickened wing and without relapse, to the upper air. It adds to our knowledge of the poet's reasonings with his own soul. It contains, amongst other things, a purged and guarded statement of some of the ideas that he argues, with more exaggeration, in his prose. It explains in what way communion with nature reveals to him the subjects for his muse. Nature has dealt with him 'as with a turbulent stream,' but now, after a time, is leading him 'through quiet meadows.' His inborn daring is not to be enfeebled, but is to be diverted to lofty and peaceful uses. He is to sing :

> Of Truth, of Grandeur, Beauty, Love, and Hope,
> And melancholy Fear subdued by Faith ;
> Of blessed consolations in distress ;
> Of moral strength, and intellectual power,
> Of joy in widest commonalty spread.

Of these he will sing, instead of raising, as he had once intended, an heroic strain in honour of Liberty. But not for this will he be a tame singer. On the contrary, he will

> arouse the sensual from their sleep
> Of Death, and win the vacant and the vain
> To noble raptures ;

and he will do this in words which refuse falsely to idealise the scenes of common life, and 'which speak of nothing more than what we are.'

IX

Wordsworth's verse has not always the character of ' emotion recollected in tranquillity.' His distinctively heroic writing has the force of a passion which is recorded while it is still alive, and which yet has nothing hysterical about it—nothing of the taint that so often intrudes in the cases of Byron, of Shelley, and of Swinburne. Here again Wordsworth is a renovator. Since Milton and Dryden heroic poetry had faded down, to be revived in lyrical form by Burns and Campbell, and in both lyrical and narrative form by Scott. Several of the new influences that were working upon poetry at large contributed to this revival. First, there was that of the adventurous and romantic lay, made popular by Scott ; and to this Wordsworth gave his highly individual turn in *The White Doe of Rylstone* and in *Brougham Castle*, both of them written in 1807, two years after *The Lay of the Last Minstrel*. Secondly, there was the high classical spirit, renewed already in Landor ; this finds expression in *Laodamia* and in the colder *Dion*. Thirdly, there was the inspiration of the public crisis, which stirred him to the depths. The early sonnets, and *The Happy Warrior*, are among the results. Wordsworth began to write on such themes in 1802, in the sonnet ' I grieved for Buona-parte.' It was not so much gallant episodes, like the Battle of the Baltic, that moved him, as the fate of England and her great struggle for existence and honour. His genius for this kind of writing came to light later than his genius for ruminative or narrative verse, and also outlasted his general decline of power. Probably his heroic poetry will live as long as anything that he wrote. Besides its simplicity and its directness, it has the advantage of not being written or staked upon any particular theory about the language or subjects of poetry. The style of the sonnet to Milton or *To the Men of Kent* is nearer to the central and historic style of great verse than most of what Wordsworth wrote before 1800. At the same time the two kinds are often blended ; we do not feel as if they were the work of different men. The ' good Lord Clifford,' in the *Song at the Feast of Brougham Castle*, had been reared, in the fifteenth century, a sound Wordsworthian, being for ' the space of twenty-four years a shepherd in Yorkshire,' and taught by ' woods and rills.' But this epilogue of the poet's to the song of his minstrel does not improve it ; the shepherd's solemn pipe sounds meagre after the unwonted thrill and up-lifting, the incomparable clangour of the harp-strings. In the famed lines, ' Armour rusting in his halls,' Wordsworth rises to a spiritualised battle-ardour and an instinctive cunning of quickened and galloping cadence, which makes us sorry he did not oftener allow himself to be angry, but rhymed a thousand sermons instead, thinking that ' Nature ' had so bidden him. The same fire and onset, the same splendid romantic extrava-gance and colour, are perceptible even in those parts of the *Song* that relate the life of Clifford on the hills amidst the creatures that waited on him, and is a welcome release from the poet's stiller manner. But even this hardly prepares us for the final, lyric shout of war. Throughout, there is the same clear direct evolution of the story, and the same freedom from surplusage, as in *Lyrical Ballads*.

The same may be said of *The White Doe of Rylstone*, where there is good ballad fighting, and in which lines are inter-woven from the old poem, *The Rising in the North*, that Percy discovered. Wordsworth in his youth had wanted to go into battle among the Girondins, and there was somewhere a war-dance in his blood. There is no languor in the narrative, but, as he explains, the crises are spiritual rather than prac-tical. The reflective element does not form an interruption, but is rather a suffusion over the whole. There is a lovely

silvery light of fantasy about the figure of the doe, who is at
once a real personage and a symbol, ' raised,' as the poet told
Mr. Justice Coleridge, from its mere animal nature [1] into something mysterious and saintlike. We pass without shock
between what may be called the male and the feminine ingredients in the story. The writing is purer than Scott's ;
there is none of the made-up diction into which *Marmion*
tends to slide. In one way Wordsworth's heroic muse somewhat defeats his end, for the imagination lingers less over
the ' legitimate catastrophe,' which he tells us is the power
of the Lady Emily to

> finally secure
> O'er pain and grief a triumph pure

than over the fall of Francis as he clasps the banner of the
Nortons and defies the treacherous odds. But the last scenes
are in a vaporous, ethereal, holy strain unlike all else in Wordsworth. He is master there of an enchanted territory of which
we did not know before.

The Character of the Happy Warrior is an Elizabethan poem,
with echoes of Spenser's couplet, and of Daniel's sweet austerity.
Much of it is in that neutral style in which, as Coleridge pointed
out, both Daniel and Wordsworth often move ; the style
namely which, though common to good prose and to poetry
that is also good, is yet not written in that rarer, magical
diction only appropriate in metre. The character might have
been described, almost in the same words, in such prose as
that of *The Convention of Cintra*, without leaving the sense
that it was trying to do the work of verse. The result here is
a ' character ' rather than a picture ; the abstract traits of
a hero are accumulated, in rhymed sentences, rather than
harmonised ; and we remember them separately. It might
have been better for the poet to be silent, in his preface, concerning Nelson, whom he censures for his ' one great crime,'
while confessing that he had borrowed for the happy warrior
certain of his attributes. But these remarks Wordsworth
prefixed in his old age, when his mind had become rigid.

The *Ode to Duty* is one of those poems that must always win
a strong, an extorted admiration. Gray and Horace are its
models ; it has therefore great majesty of sound, and is designed
with much of the orderly and severe harmony that it celebrates. Wordsworth has forgotten his war against the
eighteenth-century diction, which here he uses with all its
apostrophes, periphrases, antitheses, and ceremonies ; but the

ending is that of a prosaic hymn.   Few lyrics contain so many
noble and proverbial sentences.   The thought, as old as
Stoicism, is yet that of his own day.   Duty is conceivèd as a
refuge from ' unchartered freedom ' and from ' chance desires,'
and as the principle which keeps man in unison with the
eternal, even with the physical, order of the world.   The
coincidence of this idea with the famous words of Kant, and
with the ethical inspiration of Fichte, is probably an accident.
But there is the same revulsion from the revolutionary spirit ;
a cold stern hand is laid upon the claims of passion and the
individual.   The other great idealist, Shelley, has no place
for the constraints of duty in his human paradise.   They are
needless in a society where love and fraternity are universal.
The collisions of human thought can hardly go further.

In the ode, *Intimations of Immortality from Recollections of
Early Childhood*, the author's gifts for lyrical and for metaphysical verse become perfect, and are for once united.   He
shows himself able to lift the burden of metrical freedom ;
using the historic species of the lawless rhymed ode, invented
by the Jacobeans, in whose conduct Coleridge is his only rival
of his own day.   The basis is the heroic line, which often serves
rather for impassioned thinking than for a true chant ; but
it is sprinkled with shorter and blither measures, varying from
eight syllables down to three, which are received by the ear
at first with joyful surprise and then with as joyful an expect-
ancy, but which do not drown the solemn fundamental march
of the composition.   These interludes task the poet, who
always sang with difficulty, nor is every one of them successful ;
the close of the third stanza and the opening of the fourth
have something of a false gallop, and even incorrect rhymes ;
jollity, holiday, sullen, culling.   But Shelley could not have
bettered, if he often equals, the *allegro* of ' The Rainbow
comes and goes,' with its sudden long-drawn fall into disenchantment.   And in the ninth verse, ' O joy ! that in our
embers,' there is an interweaving of solemn with gayer paces,
which shows Wordsworth's utmost reach in the expression
of contrasted emotions ; while even in the seventh, ' Behold
the Child,' which is purposely at a lower pitch and in a playful
strain, there is no fault if we consider its purpose.   And the
conduct of the whole, with its sober close as of a splendid
evening, gives at least as high a pleasure as the language.   It
is Wordsworth's single but supreme triumph in the highest
kind of lyrical architecture.

He has answered all rational attacks on the conception of

the poem. The combined radiance and unreality of outward objects, he had felt in his own childhood ; it is a portion of his experience. The doctrine of reminiscence, which some have objected to as groundless, he does not pretend to be true ; it is enough that the poet may write of it as though it were true. He took hold of it, he says,

as having sufficient foundation in humanity for authorising me to make for my purpose the best use I could as a poet.

We may doubt whether such ideas can bear to us, as they surely bore to Wordsworth, all the exaltation and fire that he put into them ; we may think that the address to the child, in the eighth verse, as a seer and philosopher, leaves nothing loftier in reserve to be said of Plato ; but we must admit that there is ' sufficient foundation in humanity ' for authorising such an expense of power, in a writer commonly so frugal of mere splendour.

X

It remains to consider his management of the sonnet. One day in 1801 he took fire on hearing his sister read the sonnets of Milton, and produced three of his own on the same afternoon. He made sonnets up to the last, and has left more than five hundred examples of the form. ' I grieved for Buonaparte ' is one of the first, and *To an Octogenarian* (1846) perhaps the latest. The first and greatest cluster was composed in 1802. It is chiefly on public affairs, and includes two poems of the first order and without flaw, *Milton* and *On the Extinction of the Venetian Republic* ; to which must be added *Westminster Bridge* and ' It is a beauteous Evening.' Four or five others are in a style less uplifted, but on a high studious level of thinking and accomplishment ; such are the first three of those written at Calais, and the pair which begin ' It is not to be thought of.' In some four others, imperfect and marred as wholes, there are passages in the greatest manner ; for instance in the sonnet to Toussaint L'Ouverture, and in that ' written in London, in September 1802.' The nine sonnets of 1803, the year of expected invasion, rise in no case to the highest pitch, but one, *To the Men of Kent*, is very spirited and distinct. The others fall into the more even, regular species, which we already divine that Wordsworth will use as his habitual medium for his reflections or ' effusions.' The group of 1806 is unpolitical and miscellaneous, but still has a certain unity of pensive and fanciful mood, which in one

instance, 'The world[1] is too much with us,' rises and bursts
into imaginative strength, like a sudden flame on a mountain-
top.   But in another of this set, namely, the first of the four
called *Personal Talk*, Wordsworth approaches Keats in temper,
matches his special beauty of phrase, gets away for once into
a dreamy irresponsible world, and shows a disinterested joy
in sensation :

> Better than such discourse doth silence long,
> Long, barren silence, square with my desire ;
> To sit without emotion, hope or aim,
> In the loved presence of my cottage-fire,
> And listen to the flapping of the flame,
> Or kettle whispering its faint undersong.

In 1809-10 comes another double series, made in honour of
liberty, and prompted by the struggles of the Tyrolese and
the Spaniards against Napoleon.   All these are noble in vigour
and pure in finish, if none is of a very high achievement, unless
it be the little-quoted *Feelings of a Noble Biscayan at one of those
Funerals*—the funerals where the dead infant was garlanded
on the bier to the sound of choral singing.   Two lines in this
poem might have been assigned, had they been found in an
old anonymous play, to the youthful Shakespeare :

> A garland fashioned of the pure white rose
> Becomes not one whose father is a slave.

In 1815-17, and again in 1820, come other groups, in which
the temper is not less high, but the skill and inspiration are
fading ; nor does the poet's continental tour re-quicken it.
After this begin the various premeditated series of sonnets,
where each number is based on a single scene or journey, of
which every incident is resolutely versified.   There are three
such series : the first, of thirty-three numbers, being that on the
River Duddon (1806-20).   It is full of tender and lovely things,
and shows a return to Wordsworth's early freshness of response
to landscape, and with it a certain recovery of his early style ;
but no single sonnet is of the rarest merit.   The second is
the much longer *Ecclesiastical Sketches*, of 132 numbers ;
and here the version from Bede (' Man's life is like a sparrow ')
and the first poem on *King's College Chapel* are on a wholly
different elevation of workmanship from nearly all the rest.
To these must be joined *Mutability* (' From high to low doth
dissolution climb '), a truly noble metaphysical piece on that
ancient Renaissance theme, the decay of outward form and
beauty ; a thought here applied to the corresponding decay

of the outward forms of Truth herself, and receiving once more the ' unimaginable touch ' that the writer seemed to have lost. But to the last we are never safe in dullness with Wordsworth ; there are descents upon him, and visitations, and unloosings of the tongue, when all seems hopeless. The last of these formal series, besides the pieces, mostly per- functory, written in the tours of 1823 and 1837, is the arid one, *Sonnets upon the Punishment of Death* (1839) ; but there are flashes even here.

The sonnet, with its freedom of choice in theme and emotion, united to its exacting discipline, and to its special need of a clear intellectual basis and articulation, was a predestined form for Wordsworth. The ruminative and the impassioned elements can figure in almost any variety of proportion. Many, in fact, of Wordsworth's sonnets are in the same temper as his other retrospective and commemorative verse. But he was drawn to this form by its capacities for prophetic, uplifted, and indignant utterance, where the emotion is present and not merely revived. For his inspiration he went back to Milton, and seldom farther back, though he was acquainted with the sonnets of Dante and Petrarch, and translated some from Michael Angelo. His letter to Dyce (1833) shows that he had pondered the varieties of sonnet-structure ; but of his five hundred and twenty-three examples only one is in Shakespeare's form. The rest are in the traditional Italian measures, or else in varieties of them invented by himself. In general, he feels free to extend the practice of Milton, which in one essential had departed from that of the Florentine masters. Milton, while keeping, in most cases, the orthodox rhyme-divi- sions, had often allowed the *volta*—the break in grammar and thought which forms the pivot of the poem—to fall beyond the close of the eighth line ; and Wordsworth suggests that

this is done not merely to gratify the ear by variety and freedom of sound, but also to aid in giving that pervading sense of intense unity in which the excellence of the Sonnet has always seemed to me to consist.

Accordingly, he often varies the position of the *volta*.[1] But in some of his noblest sonnets he keeps it strictly ; and indeed, if we apply to them the sort of formal dissection which Dante makes of his own poems in the *Convito*, we see what a perfect and harmonious balance of parts is constantly attained. One instance, where the subject is only a fleeting mood, must serve. The poet himself, in a letter to Lady Beaumont, has eloquently analysed this mood, and left nothing to add except on the mechanism (*abba abba cde cde*). The rhyme-arrangement here is one of the most familiar kinds.

> With Ships the sea was sprinkled far and nigh,
>   Like stars in heaven, and joyously it showed ;
>   Some lying fast at anchor in the road,
> Some veering up and down, one knew not why.

This first quatrain shows the happy crowd of ships, and also that the poet's fancy is ' veering up and down ' along with them :

> A goodly Vessel did I then espy
>   Come like a giant from a haven broad ;
>   And lustily along the bay she strode,
> Her tackling rich, and of apparel high.

The second quatrain thus introduces the ship, and the material for the poet's fancy is completed. ' She may,' wrote Wordsworth on this poem, ' be said to come on a mission of the poetic spirit.' The first tercet discloses what the fancy is, and how without reason he favours this ship above the rest ; the central thought of the poem being thus thrown forward to the eleventh line :

> This Ship was nought to me, nor I to her,
>   Yet I pursued her with a lover's look ;
>   This Ship to all the rest did I prefer :

' making her a sovereign or a regent, and thus giving body and life to all the rest.' But the fancy is not yet exhausted ; the poet asks concerning her voyage, and at last learns its direction ; the destination is left to the imagination. Quiet as the level of the whole sonnet is, the last line is the quietest of all, and this, too, is part of the sonnet-tradition :

> When will she turn, and whither ? She will brook
>   No tarrying ; where She comes the winds must stir :
> On went She, and due north her journey took.

Here the articulation is perfect ; each of the four elements is complete in syntax, metre, and meaning ; though the link is closer between the two tercets than between the two quatrains. The metrical analysts have shown that the *volta* is seldom obscured, though often somewhat displaced ; that in the octave, the favourite forms are the permitted ones, *abba abba* and *abab abab*, though in the later series the irregular form *abba acca*, and its variants, become very abundant ; that in the sestet the schemes, *cd cd cd*, *cde cde*, and *cde dce*, are well represented (these being the favourites of the great Italians), but that many other varieties occur as well, including some inartistic ones ; and, lastly, that Wordsworth's skill in breaking the individual lines is great and studious.   Often, in many of the greater achievements in this kind, the line is left unbroken, and is felt to be continuous and unitary.   But at need there is a rapid, almost choppy, certainly agitated motion, effected by shifting of pause : as here :

> England hath need of thee : | she is a fen
> Of stagnant waters : | altar, sword, and pen,
> Fireside, | —

or as in the poem to his dead daughter Catharine, where there is a wonderful correspondency of the rhythm with the for once half-unnerved mood, and where the normal partitions of the poem are shaken and shifted by the cross-currents of sharp disenchantment and self-vindication :

> Surprised by joy | —impatient as the Wind—
> I turned to share the transport | —Oh ! with whom
> But Thee, | deep buried in the silent tomb ;

Wordsworth thus reinstalled the Italian sonnet in our poetry after a long period of disuse, and founded its tradition amongst us more effectually than Milton himself had done.   For after Milton the rhetorical couplet came into power, and the sonnet was ignored ; but after Wordsworth came Keats and the Rossettis, who enlarged its borders by reapplying it to the expression of love.   It is in his avoidance of love as a theme that Wordsworth resembles Milton more than he does Petrarch or Dante.   The one example he has left of such a theme in sonnet-form, ' Why art thou silent ? ', was written, he says,

merely to prove to myself that I could, if I thought fit, write in a strain that Poets have been fond of.

XI

A full analysis of Wordsworth's versification [1] would be idle, for it would only pain us with evidence of his want of self-judgment.   It would be necessary to take heed of *Goody Blake* and of *The Armenian Lady's Love* :

> ' Grieved am I, submissive Christian !
>   To behold thy captive state ;
>   Women in your land may pity
>   (May they not ?) the unfortunate.'

> ' Yes, kind Lady ! otherwise man could not bear
> Life, which to every one that breathes is full of care.'

These things have been printed in Wordsworth's works for the sake of completeness, but to recount or deride them may be left to the shades of blue and buff reviewers ; for us they do not exist. Taking only his good work, it may be said that his metrical power and inventiveness are fitful, though at times very high ; and that, seeing that in his case all other qualities, nobility, subtlety, and power of diction (so far as this can be disjoined from rhythm) often remain when the music will only just pass muster, he is herein just the opposite of a poet like Spenser or Swinburne, in whom rhythm remains when everything else has departed. Wordsworth's masterly and sometimes splendid manipulation of the various ballad-like measures, of the irregular ode, of the stanzaic ode, and of the semi-falling measure of the *Extempore Effusion* (1835), is manifest. His blank verse it is easy to underestimate, so capricious is its power. We can see one reason of its failure, namely, that though he went back for his music to Milton, Milton's heroic line too often only reached him through the intervening, the deadening chorus, of Milton's imitators, as through a wall of felt. He easily drops into their rhythmical heaviness and dreariness, and he learned from them the bad habit of closing his period with the kind of wooden slam already noticed in Cowper ; as can be seen by watching the endings of the paragraphs through, let us say, the first four books of *The Prelude*. Very rare are final lines like

> We beat with thundering hoofs the level sand,

compared with lines like

> This labour will be welcome, honoured Friend !

or like

> In thankful blessedness, which yet survives.

But to say that he is unequal is to say that he often succeeds. In happy hour he can build up a sure, a concerted, and a varied music of his own :

> Near,
> The solid mountains shone, bright as the clouds,
> Grain-tinctured, drenched in empyrean light ;
> And in the meadows and the lower grounds
> Was all the sweetness of a common dawn—
> Dews, vapours, and the melody of birds,
> And labourers going forth to till the fields.

The liberties and modulations of Milton's line Wordsworth does not, indeed, appropriate ; it is the strength, or grace, of the *regular* decasyllabic that he secures. Sometimes it is of a famous pattern ; as in :

> No languor, no dejection, no dismay.

or in :

> Suffer my genial spirits to decay.

But more often he has made a pattern of his own. Sometimes it rises to a booming sound :

> Amid the heart of many thousand mists ;

or is like a long-drawn gust of air :

> Murmuring from Glaramara's inmost caves.

But he is somewhat afraid, except in the passages that are full of antique names and savours, of the purely sensuous pleasure of the heroic line, and is most successful when he is nobly abstract, or ideal in substance, or ruminative : of endless examples here is one, quoted already :

> How could the innocent heart bear up and live ?

XII

His poetic style, whether simple or sumptuous, abstract or full of images, luminous or lacklustre, is always *hard* of texture : harder than that of any one since Milton, and much harder than that of Milton's early poems. It has this quality even when Wordsworth is tender and pensive. Cowper and Coleridge handle words flexibly, with a sense of their fragility, afraid of their revenge if force is used upon them. Wordsworth's verbal material is like a store of seasoned, tough wood, sometimes plain, sometimes exotic, but taking, if need be, a high burnish, and not easy to bend or destroy ; it can be inlaid—to press the likeness a step further—with steel or gold. The result is sometimes plain and ugly, but not through weakness in the material. Yet, here again, we need not attend to the failures at all. This hardness and strength in Wordsworth's better writing, are they but the expression of his own nature, or are they an inheritance from Milton, or are they not also an inheritance from the despised eighteenth century itself, strange as it would have sounded to Wordsworth to hear of such a debt ? Purity and naturalness of diction are the achievement of the eighteenth century, and that not only in prose. Pope is a great sinner in his *Homer* ; but in his *Satires and Epistles* he wrought out a pure and natural diction, though

he applied it to subjects that are not monopolised by verse,
and that, but for his triumphant execution, might be thought
to fall below poetry ; to satire and epigram and the quintessence of free-flowing, spontaneous talk, where pedantry is
odious.   This secret was lost by Pope's followers, though it
was partially regained by Goldsmith and Crabbe.   He wrote
in this lowered, living, natural key about bores and fops and
himself and the mutton from Banstead Down ; Wordsworth
adapted it to the fates of the old shepherd and the huntsman,
and to describing the flowers of the forest and the sacred
things of memory.

Hardness and strength, purity and naturalness are the great
achievements of Wordsworth's diction, and are ever at his
command when his verse is good at all.   The last of these
qualities, naturalness, becomes transformed, when he is prac-
tising the intricate-sublime, into something that can only
be called rightness :

> Amid the groves, under the shadowy hills,
> The generations are prepared ;   the pangs,
> The internal pangs, are ready.

It would be a confusion to call this ' natural ' diction ;   it is
rather consummately right, in a large austere way.   But still
it is rooted in the plainer, natural kind of writing, which runs
up into it by fine degrees, so that it does not remain merely
isolated and precipitous.   Many passages show this continuity
between Wordsworth's more magnificent and his more speech-
resembling diction.   Sometimes a daringly wrought and figured
overture leads to a close of almost scriptural plainness :

> The horse is taught his manage, and no star
> Of wildest course but treads back his own steps ;
> For the spent hurricane the air provides
> As fierce a successor ;   the tide retreats
> But to return out of its hiding-place
> In the great deep ;   all things have second birth ;
> The earthquake is not satisfied at once ;
> And in this way I wrought upon myself,
> Until I seemed to hear a voice that cried,
> To the whole city, ' Sleep no more.'

But though this close is ' natural ' in the great style, what we
usually think of, on hearing such an epithet, is the regular,
level, subdued, diffused manner of narratives like *The Brothers*,
or of those chapters of *The Prelude* that speak of things seen,
or of the quieter *Lyrical Ballads*—the habitual voice of the
poet during ' the long, blue, solemn hours, serenely flowing.'

But within this range there are many different levels, and many elevations above that 'neutral zone,' where the vocabulary, the order and the syntax of the words are as close to prose as the presence of metre permits, while yet the work can truly be termed poetical. In this zone, as Coleridge points out, Wordsworth moves with delight and steady power ; he may be said to have reannexed it to our poetry. Below it, again, comes the point of danger, where either through meanness of topic or lapse of language the metre becomes superfluous. Beneath this he often sinks, and no more need be said about it. A good example of the low-pitched sort of writing, which still justifies the use of metre and remains beautiful, is from *The Brothers* :

> *Priest.* The little colour that he had was soon
> Stolen from his cheek ; he drooped, and pined, and pined—
>
> *Leonard.* But these are all the graves of full-grown men !
>
> *Priest.* Ay, Sir, that passed away : we took him to us ;
> He was the child of all the dale—he lived
> Three months with one, and six months with another,
> And wanted neither food, nor clothes, nor love :
> And many, many happy days were his.
> But, whether blithe or not, 'tis my belief
> His absent Brother still was at his heart.

This approaches danger ; a touch more, and it would have the air of prose into which some blank lines had slipped by inadvertence ; the diction would be right, the metre superfluous. But it is not superfluous ; the third line, for instance, is either prose or verse as we will ; but the surprise, the pang, the searching power, justify, if they do not enforce, the use of metre.

Some scorn has been spent upon another kind of prosaic line which is really well-warranted and pleasant enough, for it shows Wordsworth unbending, smiling, and gently parodying himself or the heroic manner.

> The Horse of knowledge, and the learned Pig

is of this kind, and so, too, is this, mocked at by critics :

> And at the *Hoop* alighted, famous Inn !

We must take many such passages as forecasting the playful parts of *The Princess*, and as no worse than they. Such, again, is the description of Wordsworth as a freshman :

> with hose of silk, and hair
> Powdered like rimy trees, when frost is keen.

The picture of the dame's school, and of the faces of the kings
and queens on the pack of cards, is of the same sort. The
last-named passage will bear comparison with the *Rape of the
Lock*, though there is no pretence at epigram. At the opposite
pole is the high speculative writing that fills so large a space
in all Wordsworth's work. This, it is true, was a current
eighteenth-century kind; it was the supposed and peculiar
boast of that century. It was the common coin of Young, and
Akenside, and Johnson, and Thomson. Here again Wordsworth's artistic energy had a purifying effect. Blake had
purified the poetry of ideas in his own way, but he crazed it
with symbolism, and he had no influence. Wordsworth,
along with Coleridge, or before him, recovered the art of shaping
abstract ideas, or abstractly stated emotions, into true con-
sistency with poetic law; and, after him, Shelley claims the
next honours for the achievement. Wordsworth found the
right way early; in *Tintern Abbey* he has found it beyond all
cavil. He also kept it, at intervals, to the end, as the sonnet
Mutability, already referred to, is enough to prove. He did
not argue the question, as he had to argue about his right to
use humble language in *Lyrical Ballads*; there was no need;
and he simply did the work. The critics of the *Edinburgh
Review*, of course, did not perceive what he had accomplished.
He was using, or building upon, a form of verse quite familiar
to them, and they did not see how differently he used it.

XIII

Thus it is well to have all Wordsworth's good poetry in mind
before approaching his famous declarations of principle[1] concerning the nature of poetic diction. These are found in successively expanded forms in his prefaces of 1798, 1800, and
1802. They were threshed at by the reviewers, and at last
dealt with by Coleridge in his *Biographia Literaria* in 1817—
perhaps the most determined effort in the language to fathom
a question that may be called the central one in the philosophy of literature. What is, or rather what is not, poetic
diction ? More exactly still, what are its lower limits, and what
is its relation, at or about those limits, to the ordinary diction
of prose ?

Working his way out of the more frigid and abstract
style of eighteenth-century verse—a style which at first had
spoilt his own—and having before him the simple life-like

described, escapes from his definition. What Coleridge never shows is this, that the bare vocabulary, on which Wordsworth bases his challenge, and which he describes as 'real language,' is overstepped in some of those *Lyrical Ballads* that are admittedly, intensely, and uniformly poetical ; such as *The Forsaken Indian Woman*, where such combinations as 'rustling conflict,' and such words as 'rue,' stand out as exceptions. There is much in the piece that no such woman could possibly say, at least in the same collocation of words ; just as she would not talk in verse ; but, with the exceptions noted, no one word in the poem is by itself beyond her resources. Wordsworth, however, never fully faced this ambiguity of the term 'language,' and his friend made the most of it ; luckily for us, since the exposition became in his hands not only a profound piece of poetic, but the most memorable estimate as yet written of Wordsworth's genius.

As for these trivial passages, which set the official reviewers howling in full pack, it is enough to say that they are incompatible with the author's own definition of real language ; since there the language is not 'purified,' or 'selected,' or that of persons 'in a state of vivid sensation.' It is not the too prosaic, but the too magnificent passages, that expose themselves to the penetrating ray of Coleridge's criticism ;—those, that is, which are too great in phrase or emotion for the occasion that prompts them, like the description of the child as a 'seer' in the great Ode, or even the conclusion of *Daffodils* ; as to which Coleridge remarks in effect, that the language should be attuned to some far higher and more far-reaching memory than even that exquisite one of a dancing field of flowers. But this fault proceeds from an excess, not a defect, of force, or rather from a temporary misapplication of force and a failure in the sense of proportion ; which we can connect, if we like, with Wordsworth's inordinate sense of the importance of everything, great or small, that had happened to himself : a sense which is woven up with his high grave assurance of his mission, but also with his want of humour, which is itself 'beyond all human estimate.'

Another result of the analysis in *Biographia Literaria* has been already indicated, in speaking of that middle or 'neutral' land of diction which is common to verse and prose ; in other words, to which the presence of metre makes the least assignable difference, whilst yet the result is indubitably poetic. This distinction is of great importance, since it rescues and defines for us a very large province of Wordsworth's writing, which is bounded on the upper limit by the more exalted and elaborate styles at his command, and on the lower by the perilously and needlessly prosaic, thrust in by his doctrine and not by his genius.

The conclusion then is, that Wordsworth, led by his dislike of 'glossy and unfeeling diction,' but still more by the wish to find a poetic medium for the life and speech of the simple, was led to proclaim that speech as the medium desired; that he guarded this chosen medium, not indeed from his own misapplications of it, but against the charge that it need be vulgar or trifling; that he also proved its nobility in practice; that he did not face the ambiguity of the term 'language,' or the full consequences exerted upon diction of the employment of metre; that he did not rule out other styles, either his own or those of other men, which are equally poetical, though he did not touch on their theoretic basis; and that in many of his actual triumphs, won in that sphere of diction which he does vindicate, he employs a stratum of words which in prose would not strike us as over-poetical.

XIV

Wordsworth's own prose is never too poetical, except in his youthful *Apology for the French Revolution* (1793). Even the pamphlet usually called *The Convention of Cintra*, with all its passion and intensity, is less strictly poetical in language than much of the political writing of Milton or Burke. Solidity, purity, excellence of texture, rather than splendour or decoration, are the marks of Wordsworth's prose, whether descriptive, argumentative, or critical. There is often also great loftiness, rising frequently to eloquence of the controlled and manly kind; a vehemence not rapid or wasteful, but steady and permeating; a manner, in fact, that accords with what we are told of his best conversation. This is well described by Sara Coleridge [1]:

There was much in him to know, and the lines of his character were deep and strong—the whole they formed, simple and impressive. His discourse, as compared with my father's, was as the Latin language to the Greek . . . it was intelligent, wise, and easily remembered.

This applies to Wordsworth's critical writings: to his prefaces to the *Lyrical Ballads*, his discussions on *Poetic Diction*, and *Of Poetry as Observation and Description*, and his notes, letters, and recorded talk ; the whole forming a considerable mass of literary comment. The *Essay on Epitaphs*, and the *Letter on the Kendal and Windermere Railway*, with its implied defence of the subjects of his own poetry, throw further light on Wordsworth's criticisms. Indeed, they can at no point be separated from the far more comprehensive, piercing, and enlightening work of Coleridge in the same field. It is often found that where the two men agree, as in their antipathy to the obsolescent style of classical verse, Wordsworth gives the conclusion with pith and vigour, while Coleridge throws a searchlight on the philosophic reasons for it. The same kind of relationship is found in their discussions on the nature of the Imagination, as distinguished from the Fancy ; a theme that is really central in their treatment of Poetic. Wordsworth is also, like his friend, rich in remark on particular writers, and all that he says about the masters who influenced himself, Chaucer, Spenser, Milton, is the frank criticism of a comrade and an equal.

Wordsworth's plainer verse can be seen to approximate to his more studied prose at many points. The interweaving of the two forms in the *Letter on the Kendal Railway*, and even in the *Guide to the Lakes*, brings out this likeness. The passages describing the weather and climate of the Lakes are like much in *The Prelude* ; and the emphatic ones in *The Convention of Cintra* are like some of the indignant sonnets. It would be ungracious to compare the duller stretches of his verse and of his prose. But that community of tone and diction between the two forms, to which he had pointed in the case of simple speakers, is seen to extend far in his own case.

XV

Wordsworth is one of our greater poets ; still, we need not feel that if we are to pick out faults in him, we ought, as Goethe said of Schlegel in referring to his treatment of Euripides, to do so only on our knees. For this is too much what Wordsworth would have liked us to do ; nay, he would not have endured us even so. But we must be careful of which faults we speak ; it is superfluous, at this time of day, to name those —such as his uncertainty as an artist—which occur to any man with the slightest poetic ear or sense of humour. These were always evident, and were threshed into chaff a hundred years ago. Nor must we attack him, either really or in seeming, when we are in fact only discounting the adoration of some of the Wordsworthians. Nor must we ask of him what he does not proffer, such as dramatic insight and expression. Nor, again, must we be misled by his saying that he is 'a teacher or nothing' into fallaciously taking him on his own ground, and making out that, in this or that, his teaching is flat or unsatisfactory. For this is not altogether to judge him as a poet. It is, however, fair and necessary to say that sometimes, when he is writing well, and is also making a poetic attack on our deepest feelings, he does not carry us away. He fails to do so, because he is not carried away himself. We do not get this sensation with Milton, lofty and proud as he is; there is the accent of strong and self-forgetful passion in Milton's personal preludes to various books of his epic, as well as perfecttion of speech. Wordsworth we must be content to praise, on another side, for the very quality owing to which he is denied the same power as Milton; that, namely, of high detachment and self-possession, which is never self-forgetfulness, and which makes him, as Coleridge said, *spectator ab extra*. The essential is that we should not honour him for the things that do not belong to him, for that way self-deception lies.

Good witnesses, for example, have spoken to his 'healing power.' John Stuart Mill, finding Benthamism and Byronism equally barren, wandered successfully to Wordsworth's poetry for relief. Sir Leslie Stephen, a man not easily carried away, says that he is the only poet who will bear reading in times of distress, because he

suggests the single thought which, so far at least as this world is concerned, can be called consolatory . . . the thought that even death may bind the survivors closer, and leave as a legacy enduring motives to noble action. . . . His favourite lesson is the possibility of turning grief and disappointment to account.

The poet thus cast his bread upon unknown waters; a believer himself, he seems especially to have appealed to those who were deprived of the comforts dependent on dogmatic belief. In this way he touches, unexpectedly, the nobler positivism of the mid-century, which was much engrossed with the ideals of ethical devotion and self-sacrifice, but which still felt the loss of the historic doctrines with which those ethics had been associated. Wordsworth's morality seems to be self-supporting, and not to be staked essentially—however it may have been to himself—on any particular tenets. He has, of course, his devoted public within the orthodox pale. But he has really, in his own despite, entered into the big, lay, central movement of our ethical thought, and his influence on poets and artists is only a part, or, at any rate, a sign, of this influence. We owe him, therefore, the honour of asking what he can still really do for us in the way of spiritual consolation, in view of the changes in the current of ideas since, let us say, the death of Mill in 1873.

Such a question belongs to the history of ideas and of religion rather than to that of letters. But it is just here that the two kinds of history coincide. For the best, the most cherished ideas of Wordsworth are actually found in his best poetry. This, we know, does not always happen. George Eliot's lines on the ' choir invisible,' which distil her inmost thinking and aspiration, are in form merely third-rate Wordsworth. The revised *Hyperion*, so imperfect in form, brings us near to the creed of Keats. But the immortal things in Wordsworth that come back to us always—' A slumber did my spirit seal '— and *Tintern Abbey*, and the farewell sonnet to the Duddon, with its ' unimaginable touch ' :

> We men, that in our morn of youth defied
> The elements, must vanish ; be it so !—

and the ninth stanza of the great Ode, and the benediction on Coleridge in *The Prelude*—these things are immortal, just because expression, thought, and feeling are all perfected together. In the highest that he has to say, Wordsworth's genius is working at its fullest. To ask, then, what he has to give us for consolation is not simply to treat a poet as a missionary.

On one side he is secure. Unlike the best verse of the eighteenth century, and of Coleridge, Byron, Shelley, and Keats, of most of the poets since their time, unless Browning be excepted, the poetry of Wordsworth is the poetry of happiness. It is not written in high spirits and gallant cheer, like Scott's ; nor with gaiety, like Shakespeare's poetical comedy ; but it is written in a spirit of happiness, pervaded, like his life, by ' the deep power of joy.' More than this, it describes, and talks, and preaches about the sources of its own happiness ; and yet, in spite of taking this risk, it remains poetry, it can still communicate the happiness of which it talks. These sources are always being lost by mankind, and always being rediscovered. They had been found, in some sense, by Rousseau, and have been found again, in another sense, by Tolstoy, who says :

One of the first conditions of happiness is that the link between man and nature shall not be severed; that is, that he shall be able to see the sky above him, that he shall be able to enjoy the sunshine, the pure air, the fields with their verdure, their multitudinous life.

But Wordsworth has a great advantage over these other proclaimers of the way to happiness, though their mental range may be wider than his, and their actual influence is incomparably greater, being indeed European. He associates his doctrine in this matter with none of the fantasy and paradox with which those others, Rousseau, or Ruskin, or Tolstoy, habitually insult our reason. On the contrary, he associates it in the most sane and natural way with real existence, and also with real persons; whose fates he takes as he finds them, and does not, like Tolstoy, doctor and predestine in order to suit a particular theory. He is more reasonable than all other preachers of the natural life.

We may, no doubt, ask how such happiness holds out against the shocks of experience. 'I will look unto the hills, from whence cometh my help.' But the hills do not help; they fail to do so just when they are wanted. On the contrary, sorrow destroys our pleasure in the hills. For many people Wordsworth's country scenes and personages are just about as consolatory as the same things painted on china. His high and solemn, but, after all, elderly and edgeless reminiscences of loss may do us good in the long run, but at the moment they may be an irritation. And for self-reproach, as we have said, he has no remedy at all in his wallet; he never had serious occasion for it. Wordsworth is the poet for very good people. But there are others, like Coleridge or Burns, who keep up no dignity, who are creatures of the naked sorrows and humiliations of Mother Earth, and who in recompense receive from her the words that sing home like arrows.

Wordsworth's lofty pantheism, too, is only for those who can believe in it. For others it is magnificent literature, and that may be enough; but if it is put forward also as religion, as something that admits of argument, the case is different. Some of the greatest minds, Spinoza, Goethe, have believed in something like it. But it is never enough that the greatest minds should have believed in a thing. To others the idea that Nature is really inspired, or animated with mind, must remain for ever a mere figment. Nature is, they may feel, quite unlike that. Either she is pure mirage, a flux of shows, created by the brain, or she is something hard, real, independent, lifeless,

and largely hostile.   This latter conception, moreover, is quite
congruous with poetry, as Lucretius has shown.

It would be unjust to so great a writer as Wordsworth, and
a mere wanton forfeiture of what he can offer us, to end in such
a strain.   His achievement is that he can remain an artist
whilst uttering a moral or a philosophical idea.   Often he
utters it in such a way that some one can always start up and
exclaim that it is unsound, or that, if true, it is of no use.   But
then Wordsworth does not always work in this mode ; he can
utter a poetic idea in a manner that admits of no refutation,
because it does not admit of argument.   He speaks, like Shakespeare, without any designs upon us, or even upon himself.
There is no question then

> Of blessed consolations in distress,

for the need of them does not arise.   Such a need itself is
trampled down or swept away, and the imagination moves in
a free world ; as in the end of the sonnet to Toussaint
L'Ouverture :

> thou hast great allies ;
> Thy friends are exultations, agonies,
> And love, and man's unconquerable mind ;

or in *The Affliction of Margaret* :

> Or hast been summoned to the deep,
> Thou, thou and all thy mates, to keep
> An incommunicable sleep ;

or in the lines on Hartley Coleridge :

> A gem that glitters while it lives,
> And no forewarning gives ;
> But, at the touch of wrong, without a strife
> Slips in a moment out of life.

Who could be ungrateful for this ?   We must not slip into
slighting Wordsworth because too much has been claimed for
him, or because he is praised for the wrong things.   We should
not, on any account, let slip a crumb of the daily bread of
poetry which he gives us so generously, or a drop of the festal
wine, which he gives, it is true, more rarely, on high days.

His influence on the English poets was immediate, and it
still continues.   It is very distinct from the pure tradition of
romantic lyric, which comes straight down from Chatterton
through Coleridge, Keats, the youthful Tennyson, and the
' Pre-Raphaelites,' though it is here and there found working
upon the same persons.   Nay, it is in some sort a complement

and counterpoise to that tradition ; the ethical gravity, the patriot heroism, of Wordsworth, as well as his concern with the spiritual side of common life, and, on the other hand, with exalted philosophic matter, contrast with the absorption in beauty for its own sake, the frequent indifference to public matters, the life lived in an enchanted self-created world, and the carelessness of metaphysics, which have distinguished many of the romantic poets.   Such a description of them is, of course, but a general one ; Keats and Rossetti are both often occupied with abstract but poetic thought, and Tennyson commands a metaphysical style of high distinction.   But to press these comparisons home might only increase the sense of difference from Wordsworth.   That difference, however, is plainest in the region of style and diction ; for much of Wordsworth, even when he lets himself go, is of a Roman or Miltonic austerity—he is ' classical ' in that sense ; and his ' gleams like the flashing of a shield,' his excursions into colour and pure enchantment, are, though not very rare, exceptional, while *The Ancient Mariner* and *Kubla Khan* are a fountain-head of romantic style.   In this way he founded, more than any single writer—for Landor, who in some qualities is nearest him, had little audience—a way of writing strong, pure, and usually plain, but strong and pure also when splendid, which, together with his characteristic ideas and interests, makes him, nay, must permanently leave him, a ' poets' poet ' as well as a poet for us all, and also, in his own field, one who has earned the right to be described in his own phrase as *the acknowledged voice of life*.

There is no recounting the writers whom he has affected. The influence of Wordsworth and his writings upon Coleridge alone is matter for a whole chapter.   The likenesses between *Intimations of Immortality* and *Dejection*, and between the *Lines to a Gentleman* and *The Prelude*, are apparent ; and it is the manner of Wordsworth that is the starting-point.   Coleridge's odes and his reflective blank verse would have been different but for Wordsworth, while *Love* and *Kubla Khan* and *Christabel* would have been the same without him.   The criticisms in *Biographia Literaria* show Coleridge's mind, as ever, rebounding and reacting upon the influence that had coloured it.   The tie was strengthened not only by the force of a broken friendship restored, but by the common share of the two friends in the political and intellectual reaction.

The writers of the rebellion were differently touched.   Byron came to treat Wordsworth as a hireling poet and a prince of dullness; but he also professed 'reverence' for him, and in *Childe Harold*, as will appear, was for a time deflected from his natural temper by Wordsworth's poetry—working, it is true, in part through the medium of Shelley; and Shelley himself, though the same note of derision is heard on his lips, is consciously Wordsworth's debtor. The poet of *Tintern Abbey* left his stamp upon *Alastor*; and Shelley's special kind of pantheism, though of divers origins, flows partly from the same source. The like may be said of Tennyson's 'Flower in the crannied wall.'

Tennyson was grateful to Wordsworth for the aid his poetry had given him, and honoured him in his own verse. The direct influence of the elder laureate is seen here and there in his work. *Dora* is very nearly an experiment in 'the real language of men,' purified as Wordsworth desired that it should be, and applied to a simple passage of contemporary life. High ethical verse, written in a plain manner and in blank metre, Tennyson sometimes attempts in the *Idylls*; such barer parts stand out markedly amidst all the decoration. The plainness of manner, however, is not wholly natural to Tennyson. In Matthew Arnold the filiation of style and spirit is more direct. The relieving power of Wordsworth he tests upon a melancholy that Wordsworth never dreamed of, a melancholy 'compounded of many simples' and fed by the sight of a different world. Nor is Matthew Arnold, while he remains a poet, ever cured of his malady, for the seeds of it lie too deep; it remains, but it finds an utterance which in form, and perhaps in imperfection of form, often recalls Wordsworth's own. Arnold makes a false and exaggerated estimate of Wordsworth's place amongst the poets of modern Europe, but it must be forgiven to him for the admirable things that he says by the way. Other disciples and debtors of Wordsworth abound in the last half of the nineteenth century. From Aubrey de Vere to Frederic Myers, and from Coventry Patmore to Mr. William Watson, many poets have drawn from the same springs; and the Anglican muse of Keble and Faber long haunted them.

CHAPTER XVI

THE COLERIDGES

I. S. T. Coleridge : phases of his career : (*a*) till 1797 ; experimental poetry, Unitarian tenets, and idealistic bent. (*b*) 1797-1802, period of poetic genius and production ; drift towards political conservatism ; visit to Germany. (*c*) 1803-17, confused and indistinct period, but beginning of literary lectures and criticism. *The Friend, Statesman's Manual*, etc., and *Biog. Literaria*. (*d*) 1817-34, partial recovery of poetic power ; *Lay Sermons*, etc. ; position as talker and intellectual rallying-point.

II. Vein of gentleness and simplicity ; the dream-faculty, and strain of melancholy ; the 'subtle-souled psychologist.'

III. Early verse. *Ancient Mariner, Christabel, Kubla Khan, Love, Dejection.*

IV. Later verse : *Garden of Boccaccio.* Dramas : *Osorio (Remorse)* ; *Zapolya* ; translation of *Wallenstein.* Poetic prose.

V. Coleridge's prose ; digressiveness ; incompleteness of his books. Psychological cast of his reflections. His criticism, its creative quality. *Biog. Lit.* ; the 'fancy and imagination.' Work upon Shakespeare ; lectures on literary history.

VI. General course of Coleridge's philosophical thought ; nature of his 'originality' ; doubts cast on it. His 'missionary prose' ; *Aids to Reflection*, and *Confessions of an Inquiring Spirit* ; moral psychology, and estimate of the Bible. Conception of the State and National Church, their *Constitution according to the Idea of each.*

VII. Hartley Coleridge : Sonnets, criticisms, prose. Sara Coleridge, her critical instinct ; *Phantasmion.* Charles Lloyd.

I

SAMUEL TAYLOR COLERIDGE[1] (1772-1834) touches almost every shore of thought ; for besides being a great poet, critic, and psychologist—and this, rather than Charles Lamb's phrase ' logician, metaphysician, bard,' expresses the order of his activities in their importance—he strove to revitalise the old order of ideas in philosophy, theology, and political theory ; becoming thus the most eloquent and suggestive voice in England of the conservative reaction, or attempted reconstruction. In each of these fields of thought he travelled through several phases ; and he was, as Ferrier says of Plato, ' large in design, and magnificent in surmises.' The history of his life is largely one of designs unfulfilled—mere broken arcs—and of surmises thrown out rather than worked out. His performance as a thinker lies in fragments, and his great influence is hard to define or evaluate. Hence Coleridge's career fails to arrange itself duly into the ' periods ' beloved by the expositor. We can distinguish broadly four acts in the history of his mind ; remembering that he was always a poet, always a critic, and always a philosopher, though his utterance in each character was less baffled at some times than at others.

The first stage, which is one of formation, lasts until his meeting with the Wordsworths in the west country in the summer of 1797. Before this his verse is experimental, though his talent flashes to light here and there. He published a youthful play, *The Fall of Robespierre*, and two volumes of *Poems* (1796 and 1797), to which Lamb and Charles Lloyd contributed. In politics he was radically inclined, though never after the first a real ' Jacobin ' ; opposed the war for a time, but lost his political faith and began his long course of revulsion against Liberalism. He became a kind of pantheist ; though preaching, as a Unitarian,[1] with the eloquence that awakened the pent soul of Hazlitt. Already Coleridge admires Boehme and Spinoza ; his bent for large, monistic systems, and for a spiritualistic reading of the world, can be seen ; but in fact he halts, not with much decision, in the half-way house of opinion represented by Hartley, after whom he named his son (1796) ; a temporary conciliation of materialism and determinism with a belief in disinterested action and with a good deal of orthodoxy.

The second period opens in the summer of 1797, and may be taken to end in 1802, with *Dejection, an Ode*. It covers the flowering-season of Coleridge's poetic genius. He now produces not only *The Ancient Mariner* and other pieces in the *Lyrical Ballads* of 1798, but *Christabel, Love, Kubla Khan*, and *Osorio* (afterwards recast and acted as *Remorse* in 1813) ; besides *The Three Graves* and many minor poems. *France, an Ode* (April 1798), and *Dejection* tell us most about his moods and sympathies during this period. The first is an indignant and lofty recantation of his belief in France, and from this time forth Coleridge becomes an ever fiercer critic of all things French, and swings back towards conservatism. As Napoleon rises, Coleridge parts company with the new Whiggery, and his affinities with Burke become clearer. His political articles in the *Morning Post* (early in 1800) showed him to be a journalist of high talent. But meanwhile he had received the chief philosophical impulse of his life during his visit to

Germany (1798-1800). He learned to read German, translated *Wallenstein*[1] nobly but in a libertine fashion (1800), and came home prepared for the study of Kant and Kant's successors. His great dream, the reconstruction of philosophy and theology (we can hardly say their reconciliation, for to Coleridge the two were always much the same thing) on an idealistic basis, became more distinct. He broke entirely with the old associational psychology, which dissects the phenomena of mind into a mechanical play of forces, and did not profit by James Mill's development of that psychology. He was to pass through strange waters, and his dream was unfulfilled.

For four years he was in the Lakes, with intervals of absence; and by 1802 his slavery to opium—taken, at the outset, as a relief from pain—and his estrangement from his wife, seem to have become confirmed. His stay in Malta and Italy (1804-6) was not visibly productive ; and this confused indistinct period lasts until his settlement at the Gillmans' house in Highgate in 1816. He produced the periodical called *The Friend*, published in its first form in 1809 ; and in 1808 gave the first of those series of public lectures, in which he showed himself one of the greatest of English critics. In 1816 came *The Statesman's Manual*, embodying his maturer political creed, and in 1817 *Biographia Literaria*, containing his famed chapters on Wordsworth ; this is the most permanent, profound, and distinct of his prose writings.

The last phase fills the remaining seventeen years. *Lay Sermons*, the revised *Friend* (1818), and *The Constitution of the Church and State*, were among his publications. Coleridge wrote much that only appeared posthumously : the *Confessions of an Inquiring Spirit*, which contains many of his seminal ideas on theology, the *Notes on English Divines*, the *Essays on his Own Times*, as well as many scattered criticisms, fall into this class. The width and far-reaching scope of his mental interests, whilst fatal to his hope of writing a considered masterpiece, were also the source of his unique and diversified influence. His great, renovated scheme of metaphysics, ethics, and æsthetics remained in splinters, which flew far and pierced deep ; and his disciples tried, with little success, to piece it out after he had gone. But meanwhile he talked endlessly, often intangibly and obscurely, but with a potency of suggestion hard to parallel, quickening the English mind at one of its critical periods as with a new, stimulant air, rather than by any definite communication of truth.

II

We must not think of Coleridge too much as a master-dreamer, fond of working in emblazonry and 'witch's oils,' and full of curious painful self-knowledge for which the words never fail him. He was naturally good and simple, expansive and humble, and lived in the daytime, and was happy with his children when he saw them. He could write verse in a thin, tender, old-fashioned water-colour kind of English, and his homefelt passages recall the best of his son Hartley's. He had not Wordsworth's armour of noble pride, or of self-confidence, and was not, like him, manly and self-contained. But Coleridge says truly of himself, 'My many weaknesses have been of some advantage to me.' When he gives way, it is without shame, and he has no dignity to silence his poetry :

> Such griefs with some men well agree,
> But wherefore, wherefore fall on me ?
> To be beloved is all I need,
> And when I love, I love indeed.

His strength is so near his weakness that often it does not hold out, and we are always afraid for him. His defects of bearing, even of breeding, tell chiefly at the cost of his prose, and are worst when he is joking or declaiming ; for he can steer too close to vulgarity and sanctimony, and is not naturally quite a gentleman, while Wordsworth, though often narrow, can never be vulgar. But Coleridge craves like a child for a listener and for happiness, and some of his best verse comes when both are granted to him. *The Nightingale*, written at Stowey, is inspired by innocent pleasure, and the tone is one of warm pensive contentment. Even in *The Ancient Mariner*, with its shooting lights and far-off scenery, this infantine touch is present, as in an old wives' tale. Coleridge is not trying to put us to school, or concerned with the prevention of cruelty to albatrosses, but is dreaming of a golden time before the Fall, when all the creatures were friends :

> He loved the bird that loved the man
> That shot him with his bow.

Coleridge never lost the style appropriate to this frame of mind, though he did lose, all too early, the enchanted diction of *Kubla Khan* and of *Christabel*. We hear the same accent in the lines written in 1790 upon his sister's impending death, as in those written in 1827 to Mary Pridham :

Dear tho' unseen ! tho' hard has been my lot
And rough my path thro' life, I murmur not—
Rather rejoice, Hope making a new start.

This simple, instinctive element enters freely enough into
his more subtle and adorned poetry, serving, as he wished, to
' interest the affections,' while the imagination is carried out
of familiar life into tropic seas and ' caverns measureless.'

In a letter of 1816[1] he dissects the nature of stage-illusion,
which approaches to that state of dream wherein we neither
believe nor disbelieve ; or rather, to that ' willing suspension
of disbelief ' which he elsewhere tells us ' constitutes poetic
faith,' and in which poetry like his own, at any rate, is to be
read. This dream-state Coleridge is able to induce in us
better than any writer of his own tribe, unless it be Edgar
Allan Poe, and he has also explained it better than other
philosophers. It was here that he found Romance ; and he
saw also that just as the facts of life and daylight demand the
artistry of reverie if they are to become truths inspired, so the
realities of dream demand selection, and logic, and the rule of
the waking brain, if they are to be more than tumbled and
disordinate images. Hence the rigorous laws of beauty and
structure that he tries to impose on his visions, his *calentures*,
especially in *The Ancient Mariner*. Hence, too, the wholeness
and greatness of that poem, which leaves our mind satisfied,
but still at work when it is ended ; while the fragments called
Christabel, though separately deeper in idea and more intricate
in music, are written under varying inspirations, and there is
no logic or unity, the story struggling on and perhaps being
from the first incapable of a finish. The poetic honour of
Coleridge in his best days is this perfect union of dreamwork
and brainwork. Those days lasted from about 1797 to 1801,
when he was still not altogether unhappy at home, and when
his sense of force in reserve was still unimpaired. Even his
bad dreams did not overpower him, and were little worse than
part of his imaginative capital. Happiness had served him
to write his one sustained, long poem. Unhappiness inspired
his deepest and soundest single passages, like that on broken
friendship in *Christabel*, or like the ode *Dejection*. Happiness
had given him his magic, his joy, his fresh intensity of colour
and cadence, and had braced him for a moment to plan, and
finish, and compose. Unhappiness, while it deprived him of
this power, revealed to him the pains of sleep, hitherto untold
of, and made him the great transmitter, before Shelley and
Keats, of that traditional eighteenth-century melancholy, to

which he gives a new and far deeper turn, just as he does to the poetic style that expresses it.

Goethe[1] tells us, as we saw (Ch. I.), how in his youth he was nourished on the strain of melancholy and complaint that runs through those eighteenth-century writers. It is a melancholy 'compounded of many simples.' In Gray it is the scholar's mood, not really sad, the mood of the Penseroso, not 'a creature of a fiery heart'; it is what we feel when looking at the softly limned tops of English elm-trees under the moonlight. Macpherson put, or found, in his 'Ossian' another melancholy, wilder and less homelike, and less defined in expression; and in spite of Wordsworth's condemnation Europe was not moved by Ossian for nothing. The hard healthy gloom of Crabbe is at the other extreme. But Coleridge's real ancestors are none of these. Strangely, he is nearer to two spirits who otherwise are far from him and from one another, Johnson and Cowper, in whom melancholy has the touch of religious malady and of a conscience that goes beyond reason. We hear its voice in Johnson's diaries, and in Cowper's letters, and in Coleridge's confessions and *The Pains of Sleep.* But a difference soon appears; for Coleridge has not only more of the spirit and body of poetry than the other two : and not only has he more reason to be sorry, for Johnson and Cowper never injured a soul; but his sensibility, originally happy and simple, yet darkened and subtilised by pain, is of another make, owing to the peculiar play upon it of his restless self-dissecting intellect; so that he turns his searchlight inwards upon new, unheard-of moods, and finds words for them, in which the expression clings to the substance like a kind of Nessus-shirt. For the word will out; Coleridge was the first *decadent* in later English literature ; it is one of his glories.

He came to know too well the blankness and misery that may supervene when dreams ebb and depart, and when the will, though now and again awake, is powerless either to dismiss them or to range them in obedience. And when the dream itself is bred of drugs or indolence, and the waking brings to his schoolman's conscience the memory of the lapse, he becomes the prey of a self-watching remorse, which in turn increases the palsy, whilst it quickens the torture, of the will ; but which also, happily for the world's curiosity, provokes a revulsion, and eases itself, for the time, in expression ; the fruits being not only the verses that show what Shelley calls the 'subtle-souled psychologist,' but many an outpouring in his letters, and also his insight into Claudius and all such 'limèd souls.' When the power of poetry leaves him, he can write the prose of abject self-portrayal, tinged always with the memory of a once unspoilt happiness and with the recollected power of his ' shaping spirit of imagination.' The extent of Coleridge's failure has been too much dwelt upon—the bankruptcy of the huge intellectual plans which he never seems to have lost the illusion that he could carry out. But, besides his fertilising play of thought upon a whole era, his dire personal experience helped to make him one of the great critics of modern times, even while it kept his criticism from being much more than shattered gems and their dust. Thriftless nature broke and wasted him as if with the intention that he should at least achieve the power of a precise expression for his pain. This psychological genius is the link between Coleridge's art and his thinking, and works most surely of all when his thinking is turned upon art itself, in the analysis of his intuitions of Shakespeare or Wordsworth. His instinct for truth is made effectual, and his words concrete, by his hold on beauty and his watchfulness of its effect on himself ; and his passion for beauty, through this co-equal and reacting instinct for truth methodised, ends in more than a string of scattered impressions ; for this instinct reaches into his poetry itself, and gives it definiteness, and also freedom from the vanishing subtleties that abound in Shelley. Coleridge, then, should first of all be judged as a poet.

III

The poems of 1796 and 1797 are tentative, but there are plain intimations of Coleridge's power. At moments he is no better than a ' Della Cruscan,' of the kind that Gifford trampled on. At other times, as in the *Monody on the Death of Chatterton*, he is full of eighteenth-century abstractions and stock sonorities, some of which remain even in the last edition (1829) of the *Monody*. Or this style is heightened into a real if charged magnificence, as in the sonnet to Burke :

> Thee stormy Pity, and the cherish'd lure
> Of Pomp, and proud precipitance of soul
> Wildered with meteor fires.

The soft and true feeling, the sense of home and English landscape, which Coleridge found in Bowles, also begin to appear, and sort well with his vein of goodness and simplicity. Such an influence is shown in the lines *To the River Otter*, or in these :

> How are ye gone, whom most my soul held dear !
> Scarce had I loved you ere I mourn'd you lost.

Already Coleridge is at home in both these ways of writing, and he uses them both for those bursts of despondent self-reproach, which are also natural to him, and which precede all use of opium. And here his language sometimes shows its mature stamp.

At twenty-two he forestalls the note of *Dejection* ; he has been gifted with a patriotic and tender soul, with ' energic reason ' and with a ' shaping mind ' :

> Sloth-jaundiced all ! and from my graspless hand
> Drop Friendship's precious pearls, like hour-glass sand.

And again :

> Was it right
> While my unnumbered brethren toiled and bled,
> That I should dream away the entrusted hours
> On rose-leaf beds, pampering the coward heart
> With feelings all too delicate for use ?

In the ambitious longer pieces of this period, *Religious Musings* and *The Destiny of Nations*, such flashes are rarer ; but in those of a more homelike tone, written after Coleridge's settlement at Stowey, such as the lines addressed to his brother George, simplicity is gaining ground, and the sudden efflorescence of *Lyrical Ballads* approaches. The distance travelled in a single year may be seen by comparing together the two poems to Charles Lamb, *To a Friend* and ' This Lime-tree Bower my prison ' (1797). The epithet, thrice iterated, of ' gentle-hearted,' justly provoked the recipient ; but every line is in the clean, pure, Wordsworthian diction, warmed and coloured by the tremulous happiness of the writer, as he drinks in the scents of the bean-field, ' silent with swimming sense,' and gazes ' till all doth seem Less gross than bodily.' This verse is reflective and self-descriptive ; what is yet lacking is the lyric sound, the narrative movement, the dream-pageantry, that came soon afterwards and came as it were in a moment. There is more than a hint of them in *Lewti, or the Circassian Love-Chaunt* (1794), the only poem Coleridge had yet written which is entirely in a beautiful and characteristic style. The cloud-vapour, ' thin and white and very high,' is a symbol of the poet's dream, and the rocking rhythm is its accompaniment. The colour and the sound are there ; the subject, the story, have still to be found.

France has a story ; it is not unlike Wordsworth's in *The Prelude*, when he tells of his disenchantment and disgust at the French invasion of Switzerland. But Coleridge's conclusion is loftier ; he asks the forgiveness of Freedom for having

identified her with France, and asserts her life to be unquench-
able, even if she must be driven for her resort to the elements
themselves :

> Thou speedest on thy subtle pinions,
> The guide of homeless winds, and playmate of the waves.

This is like Shelley ; but not all is so well said. A good deal
of *France* is oratory, of the gong-like eighteenth-century
kind, recalling the few resonant lines that give to Smollett
his fragile title amongst the poets. It is a reversion to
Coleridge's earlier style, though it is better in that style than
anything he had done. It is unlike his true, magical writing,
and almost as unlike that of *Dejection*.

It is easy to see the distance of *The Ancient Mariner*, not
only from the work of the Mallets and Mickles, but from the
rarest things in the popular supernatural ballad, like *The
Wife of Usher's Well*. It is a great, a concerted and complex
composition, playing at once on the simplest matters of the
heart and conscience, and on the strangest visions of the
senses, with the depth of colour and changing recurrent
rhythms that we know. Still its debt to the folk-ballad
remains. Coleridge knew his *Reliques*, and by instinct got
behind the false manner that Percy had not failed to encourage ;
cancelling, for instance, in the second edition of the *Mariner*
the cruder archaisms of the first. He learned from popular
verse not merely how to keep the story foremost, or to sprinkle
in stray beauties of diction, but also that habit of repeated
clause and echoed sound,[1] which in *Fair Annet*, or *Sweet William*,
even if only a harping upon a musical conventional run of
words, still makes half the charm. That habit he turned into
an art. Each of the seven sections of his ballad returns to
and enforces the theme,—the slaying of the Albatross, with
re-modulated phrases and long-drawn reiterated tunes, 'their
soft response renewing ' :—' The Albatross about my neck
was hung '—' He 'll shrieve my soul, he 'll wash away The
Albatross's blood '—' O shrieve me, shrieve me, holy man ! '
The offence, the penance, the expiation, the hope, the release,
and the fitful return, after all, of the evil dream, form an
intricate moral and rhythmical harmony. In the same way
the use of words—the suddenly redoubled rhyme, the resump-
tion of a word or sound only just forgotten, the initial and
medial alliterations—could we think these away, the poem
would lose its touch on the senses altogether. It is thus a
series of cunning sound-patterns, which recall and forecast

the emotional theme on which the rapidly, dreamily moving story hangs.

The Ancient Mariner more than fulfils the author's purpose of inducing a ' poetic faith ' in its reality, and of ' interesting the affections by the dramatic truth of such emotions, as would naturally accompany such situations, supposing them real.' This is partly achieved by the vividness with which such feelings interpret themselves, without effort, as to such a narrator they might well do, in sheer physical sensations —reported, however, through a poetic medium. The poor body and nerves, with their thirst, and drowsiness, and light-headed tension, and torment, and relief ; the sheer terror of the veins :

> Fear at my heart, as at a cup,
> My life-blood seemed to sip !—

the ' swound ' that fells the Mariner when the ship lets go ' like a pawing horse ' ; the English air upon his cheek ; the agony that ' burns ' him when he must tell his tale :— here, indeed, is at last the long-wished-for, the untrammelled renewal of the artistic senses, after a century of struggle against the indistinctive, the half-realised diction which had stifled them.

What Coleridge avoided so happily, in his supernaturalism and in his presentment of the terrifying and fantastic, may be seen partly by his corrections, in the second edition, of the merely gruesome features of the phantom ship, which only deaden the imagination ; and also by his fragment, begun about the same date as *The Ancient Mariner*, called *The Three Graves* ; where the theme of a wicked mother's curse, sinking into the minds of her innocent victims until they pine under it, is worked out with a kind of hectic strength. The style is there touched, one must say infected, by Wordsworth's balder one, and therefore sinks often below the necessity of metre, to rise now and then to a plain formidable directness :

> Be blithe as lambs in April are,
>   As flies when fruits are red ;
> But God forbid that thought of me
>   Should haunt your marriage-bed.

But the literalism of the piece, as well as the unshaded and insoluble horrors of the motive—a mother her daughter's rival and destroyer—show by contrast how Coleridge made of *The Ancient Mariner* not only a triumph of enchantment made real, or of dream-reality filled with enchantment, but something spiritually complete and satisfactory; an effect his own words might leave us underestimating, when he says that the ' moral sentiment ' intrudes on the reader too much ' as a principle or cause of action.' It ought, he says, to have had no more moral than the Arabian Nights' tale, in which the genie says that he *must* kill the merchant who was eating dates, ' *because* one of the date shells had, it seems, put out the eye of the genie's son.' This was in reply to Mrs. Barbauld, who had objected that the poem ' was improbable,' and had no ' moral.' [1]

On the face of it, and in regard to moral cause and effect, or the proportioning of the crime to the sequel, *The Ancient Mariner* is doubtless as irresponsible a tale as that of the genie. Yet its dream-world is truer to humanity, and therefore to the feelings of charity, pity, and remorse, than that ' lifelike ' Eastern one of bazaars and palaces, where nothing happens but at the instance of tyrannous will, or under the impulse of sheer surprising chance. An offence more real and less symbolic, say the murder of a human being—judge how that would have broken up, not only the dream-world—making us think of sacks and yard-arms,—but also the satisfying sense of justice—here, if anywhere, truly of the ' poetic ' sort ! It was Wordsworth who suggested the story, after reading Shelvocke's old *Voyages*, where the slaying of an albatross, and the ill-luck with which such an act is credited by navigators, are recorded : an act, therefore, which at once fastens on the fancy, and one whose supposed effects are quite well enough rooted in the folklore of the sea to beget a probable train of troubles. Such a ' yarn,' to which the deck-hands, even, might be thought to listen credulously, is the poet's crude material ; and in spinning it he marshals, he harps on, he plays with, universal and beautiful emotions of love and repentance, of pain and forgiveness ; coming back to them, as we said, through many a verbal echo. Viewed thus, the final ' moral,' ' He prayeth best who loveth best,' is seen, despite Coleridge's misgiving, not to be intrusive at all, but as a naïve expression and summary of the leading mood, or *Stimmung*, of the poem ; which throughout shows a kind of Brahminical love and respect for the ' happy living things ' that are not human, and an astonishing new sensibility to their motion and colouring ; not so new, however, but that here, fully uttered for the first time, though anticipated in Blake, is the *mystical* side of the extension of man's sympathy with the animals.

irresponsible life he had discovered in the *Decameron*. He
is here in the central line of the romantic poets ; the next to
follow was the author of *Isabella*. The heroic couplet in *The
Garden of Boccaccio*, so rapid, so lightly poised, steering so
perfectly between the extremes of the dissolute-meandering
and the snappish-rhetorical, is itself a recovery of one of the
old secrets of the romantic craft. The versification has some
of the brilliance that Keats came to learn from Dryden ; and
in the closing lines Coleridge is even seen casting back to the
happier variations of the classical rhetoric :

> Rich, ornate, populous, all treasures thine,
> The golden corn, the olive, and the vine.
> Fair cities, gallant mansions, castles old,
> And forests, where beside his leafy hold
> The sullen boar hath heard the distant horn,
> And whets his tusk against the gnarled thorn ;
> Palladian palace with its storied halls ;
> Fountains, where Love lies listening to their fa' s ;
> Gardens, where flings the bridge its airy span,
> And Nature makes her happy home with man.

This is worthy of *Lamia*, and has more nerve than much of
the verse of William Morris written in the same measure.

It is best here to name Coleridge's dramatic essays, divided
though they are in date. The play at first entitled *Osorio*
was begun before the *Lyrical Ballads*, and declined by Sheridan ;
but in 1813, at the instance of Byron, it was acted at Drury
Lane with success under the name of *Remorse* ; having been
meanwhile revised by Coleridge, who changed the names of
the persons, transposed some of the scenes, and re-wrote
and added many passages. It is poetry on a basis of melodrama, and the action is sufficiently absurd ; but of poetry
it is brimful, and also of an ambitious intricate psychology
that sorts oddly with the flushed feeling and the overwound
tension that prevail from first to last, as the mode then was
in 'plays of the passions.' Osorio is a fratricide in intention ;
but his brother is saved, and comes back in disguise, and his
vengeance consists in awakening some spark of remorse in
Osorio's stupefied soul. He succeeds, but Osorio atones with
his life, being slain in reprisals for another crime—a murder that
he has really committed. Some unessential passages in the
play were printed separately in *Lyrical Ballads* as *The Dungeon*
and *The Foster-Mother's Tale* ; but the true power of Coleridge
is better seen elsewhere, above all in Osorio's invocation,
during the ridiculous altar-scene (III. i.), of the air-haunting
spirits of the dead,—'ye numberless and rapid travellers.'

As a whole, this play is a wonderful excursion of Coleridge's creative powers from their usual path, and increases—if anything could do so—our sense of what he might have accomplished. The song in the same scene, 'Hear, sweet spirit!' like that of Glycine in *Zapolya*, just named, has all his golden music and all his aëry enchantments; and *Zapolya* itself was one of the first-fruits of his partially retrieved powers. It was published in 1817, never acted. The stage, indeed, could only have brought out the crude conduct and inexperienced melodrama of this generously and romantically conceived little tragi-comedy, which Coleridge presents merely as a 'Christmas Tale,' modelled, as to its idyllic circumstance and conclusion, on the tale of Florizel and Perdita. If the poetic richness of his earlier day is felt only in the two songs just mentioned, still his grasp of high and impetuous diction remains, or is renewed; and *Zapolya* remains his longest flight in verse after his partial self-recovery.

More of such examples could be quoted, where the gift of poetry is relumed; but one sign of the change that befell Coleridge, besides the general transfer of his interests from creation to speculation and criticism, is the transfer of the poetic spirit itself from the form of verse to that of prose; or, to speak more properly (since both media had always been, and remained, at his command), the concentration of that spirit within the field of prose. The description of the voice of Maria Eleonora Schöning, in *The Friend*, shows the same gifts as the passages on sound and music in *The Ancient Mariner* :

If you had listened to it in one of those brief sabbaths of the soul, when the activity and discursiveness of the thoughts are suspended, and the mind quietly eddies round, instead of flowing onward (as at late evening in the spring I have seen a bat wheel in silent circles round and round a fruit-tree in full blossom, in the midst of which, as within a close tent of the purest white, an unseen nightingale was piping its sweetest notes), in such a mood you might have half fancied, half felt, that her voice had a separate being of its own ; that it was a living something, the mode of existence of which was for the ear only ; so deep was her resignation, so entirely had it become the unconscious habit of her nature, and in all she did or said so perfectly were both her movements and her utterance without effort, and without the appearance of effort !

This style, over which images and emotions flow like reflections on a pure mirror, but in which reflective and discriminative subtlety is never absent; a style formed of ample, expansive,

complex, but not antithetically or artificially built clauses ; is
used by Coleridge from first to last, and is his natural utterance.
It is found in his letters from Germany (*Satyrane's Letters*)
written in 1798, but printed in *The Friend* ; in *Biographia
Literaria*, as, for instance, in the comparison of the genius of
Wordsworth to *Magnolia grandiflora* ; in *Anima Poetae* and
Table Talk, the garlands of notes and memoranda saved for
us by family piety.   It was indeed the way in which he spoke ;
and the tones of his easier conversation and of his equally
spontaneous preaching are readily distinguishable, not always
to the advantage of the latter, in his written words.   Lamb
' had never heard him do anything else ' but preach; and the
well-known account by Hazlitt of his first impression of the
sermon, when the voice

> Rose like a steam of rich distilled perfumes

is confirmed by all the reports of his exalted monologue.
Illustration is hardly needful, it can be found anywhere ; but
a passage characteristic in temper and movement may be
taken from the political prose.   The idea is that so often
expounded by Burke,—the slow, august, and painful growth
of a national existence ; but it is here set forth with a freer,
more luxurious oratory, belonging rather to the pulpit than
to the platform :

> But whence did this happy organisation first come ?   Was it a
> tree transplanted from Paradise, with all its branches in full fruitage ?
> Or was it sowed in sunshine ?   Was it in vernal breezes and in gentle
> rains that it fixed its roots, and grew, and strengthened ?   Let
> history answer these questions.   With blood was it planted—it
> was rocked in tempests—the goat, the ass, and the stag gnawed it
> —the wild boar has whetted his tusks upon its bark.   The deep
> scars are still extant on its trunk, and the path of the lightning
> may be traced among its higher branches.   And even after its full
> growth, in the season of its strength, ' when its height reached to
> the heaven, and the sight thereof to all the earth,' the whirlwind
> has more than once forced its stately top to touch the ground ;
> it has been bent like a bow, and sprung back like a staff.

There is no doubt danger in this way of thinking in images ;
it can become a terrible tradition : and in Ruskin the danger
is sometimes ruinous ; and the passage has less intellectual
quality than is usual with Coleridge.   The mere manner of
it descends, plainly enough, from the great pre-Augustan
prose-writers, on whom Coleridge's sense of construction and
rhythm was nourished ; from Jeremy Taylor, in especial,

who often embarks, though with less of Hebrew parallelism, on just such prolonged and musical similes, perhaps as a substitute for reasoning. Coleridge was deeply read in these divines, in Barrow and his favourite Leighton as well as in Taylor, as his published *Notes* upon them show. We are reminded, too, of Sara Coleridge's words, quoted already, that Wordsworth's talk was to her father's as the ' Latin language compared to the Greek.' Coleridge's style and mind, at their best, have really in them something of the Greek ; the flowing, impregnating, Platonic quality, following precisely in words the windings of very refined matter. There is a body of logic and exact thinking—often, even of prosaic sense— full of distinctions unthought-of before but self-evident when uttered ; and there is also the same kind of *aura* round, or emanation from within, the words (usually wanting in writers of mere acumen and scientific habit), which bestows on Coleridge's best criticism the same kind of power as on his poetry, and seems to make it the only possible expression of the truth which it communicates. This, no doubt, is true not of the great bulk of his prose, but only of the ' balmy, sunny islets of the blest and the intelligible,' which Carlyle remarked upon. There is little evidence, indeed, that Carlyle could much avail himself of that blest sunshine.

V

Coleridge (with one exception to be named presently) hardly wrote anything in prose that can be called a book, though we can carve one out of the midst of *Biographia Literaria*. His *Friend, Aids to Reflection*, and the like, are mostly aggregations of formless discourses, circling in each case round certain leading ideas, but scattering off into meteor-fragments. We are seldom sure that his lectures on Shakespeare and the poets are saved for us in his actual words, as they are mostly preserved by dutiful reporters. But they were evidently discursive in essence. Even a stronger will than Coleridge's would have had much to contend with, in the task of shaping the rich material given to him by his far-ranging, accumulative, and illustrative intellect, which continually throws off new ideas, like the ' vortex-rings ' of smoke, that propagate yet others by a strange process, till they are lost in vanishing film just as the beauty and structure of the pattern is eluding our sense. This digressive spinning of thought out of thought

is most marked when Coleridge is moving amongst theological
or metaphysical ideas ; whilst when he is actually describing
mental processes, however evanescent, his hold of lucidity
and of language is much greater. This is because he is on the
ground of observation, and is watching Hamlet or himself, and is
nearer to his work as a poet or artist. In prose, he can hardly
utter a feeling without noticing its birth ; a procedure that
in his case is not the bare desiccating analysis, which destroys
the feeling itself in the act of reflection ; but the words are
charged with the feeling they describe, which Coleridge holds
in the mind as a man holds a flower or a butterfly, intact,
enjoying as well as noting it. No one has ever possessed this
double machinery in such perfection as he : it is the source
of his greatness as a literary critic both of form and matter ;
for he can re-word the artistic process of creation, both in
himself and others,—the very process which the creator himself
is commonly the last to apprehend distinctly. The faculty,
no doubt, could be a curse to the possessor when his material
was his own will and conscience in a state of degeneration ;
but even so it was preserved.

It is easy to show from absurd examples how inveterate
was this habit of mind. Coleridge is describing his love for
Mary Evans, in a letter to herself :

At first I voluntarily invited the recollection of these [your]
qualities into my mind. I made them the perpetual object of my
reveries, yet I entertained no one sentiment beyond that of the
immediate pleasure annexed to the thinking of you. At length it
became a habit . . . my associations were irrevocably formed, and
your image was blended with every idea.

What a lover ! And this was said in youth, the season of
pedantry, when Coleridge was still a Hartleian in theory ; but
Blake, his contemporary, gives the comment :

> He who bends to himself a joy
> Doth the winged life destroy :
> But he who kisses the joy as it flies
> Lives in Eternity's sunrise.

Later, the same process is applied to the unlucky Mrs. Coleridge,
in a letter to Southey :

For Mrs. Coleridge's mind has very little that is *bad* in it ; it is
an innocent mind ; but it is light and *unimpressible,* warm in anger,
cold in sympathy, and in all disputes *uniformly projects itself forth*
to recriminate, instead of turning itself inward with a silent self-
questioning.

What a husband ! We are ready to call him a Mr. Pecksniff
of genius. One thing that disappears under such a micro-
scope is the sense of humour. The jokes which Lamb made
or saw, his friend could explain admirably on first principles :
as when he says that an Irish ' bull ' gives ' the sensation
without the sense of a connection.' But Coleridge's own jests,
always prompted by self-observation, are toilsome enough, as
may be seen from the three sonnets parodying himself, which
he printed over the signature of ' Nehemiah Higginbottom,'
in order to gibbet his juvenile faults of doleful 'egotism,' the
use of ' low, creeping language and thoughts, under the pretence of simplicity,' and ' the indiscriminate use of elaborate
and swelling language and imagery.' These things are easily
said ; yet watch him at work upon any of the poets, applying
the same kind of calculus. He is here a great revealer ; for
here he ' kisses the joy as it flies ' ; the creative power, no
longer granted to him in act, is yet present in memory, and he
knows the process of its birth into utterance ; and he relates
it, not from without, by contemplating the result, but by
thinking himself back into the moment of conception : his
sensibility to form keeping pace with his perception of meaning.
Few critics are equally alive to both these things.

Much of Coleridge's theorising in *Biographia Literaria* is
taken up with his distinction between the Fancy and the
Imagination, which he developed on the same lines as Wordsworth, but more deeply ; striving to ground it philosophically
on the one side, and on the other to apply it as a touchstone
for the difference between the false, or at least the lower, mani-
festations of poetic faculty, and the higher, or truer ones. The
distinction, on his own showing, seems to be really one—though
a definite and fatal one—of degree ; but it serves as a link
between Coleridge's psychology (which is otherwise unsyste-
matic) and his criticism ; and in the course of drawing it he is
taken back to an analysis of the Associational philosophy at
large, through which he had worked his way, and is tempted
to shadow forth a more valid theory, as he judges, of his own,
together with its metaphysical basis. His view of the nature
of imagination grew and changed, and its origins in German
philosophers, or coincidences with their thought, have been
carefully traced.[1] It became to him, in this form, and in
contrast with the ruder exposition he supersedes, the most
living type and proof of the conquest over the ' mechanical '
reading of life and mind by the ' dynamic ' or spiritually
progressive one ; and this theory in his hands, is at least a

triumphant proof that there need be no break in the long chain between the abstract truths of æsthetics, and the judgment or intuitive enjoyment, yielding its own reasons, of a great passage in Shakespeare or the *Book of Job* ; a refutation, by the way, of the merely subjective notion of poetry, which reduces criticisms to arbitrary, or at least unarguable, likes and dislikes. The outline of a reasoned theory may be found, along with many illuminative sayings, in the fragmentary papers *On the Principles of Genial Criticism*, *An Essay on Taste*, *An Essay on Beauty*, and *On Poesy or Art*. The last of these flashes a more than passing light on almost every issue of æsthetic discussion—the nature of artistic pleasure, the demarcations between the various arts, and the Kantian conception, which Coleridge took with a gloss of his own, of Beauty as the source of ' disinterested,' or undesiring, pleasure. By these papers, and by innumerable glancing and scattered rays of insight in his books and talk, Coleridge, without ever bringing his speculations to a definite head, or into a series of propositions, opened a new era in our philosophy of criticism.

In his valuation of particular schools, writers, books, poems, passages, and images, he is, in spite of some caprice and much divagation, equally great. Or perhaps greater still ; for, after all, this gift matters more to art than even the best theories ; which, taken alone and without the perception of the facts of art, may be sterile enough ; while that perception, however intuitive and unreasoned, can do nobly and well without any theories at all, as we see in the case of Charles Lamb ; being a thing given to such a man in immediate and inborn vision, and ' felt along the blood.' In this kind of perceptiveness, Coleridge, though much wider than Lamb in his survey, is less sure, and his style in conveying it is more unequal, since he is sometimes led away by theory, and much oftener falls into his irritating moonshiny rhetoric, or talks like a somnambulist. But on the whole, there is no greater English critic, and there are few greater in the modern world ; and his historical importance and service in this way, high as they are, are swallowed up in the positive, the present, the enduring value of what he tells us. His criticism, in fact, ranks with the best of his poetry, and remains the most solid achievement of his prose.

An effort to value Coleridge's valuations, besides its presumption, would mean following in his steps over the whole sacred ground of Shakespeare, Wordsworth, and sundry large fields of literature, and also commenting on a thousand scattered remarks, dropped in conversation or in his endless digressions. In his accounts of Hamlet, or of his own image in Hamlet, and of Shakespeare's plays and characters generally, he always tries to probe to the essence of the idea, without losing his enjoyment of the workmanship. His training under Boyer at Christ's Hospital had taught him that poetry has its own 'logic,' which is 'more subtle, more complex, and dependent on more fugitive causes' than that of science itself; and this idea he applies to Shakespeare, arguing that his 'judgment is commensurate with his genius,' and that his plays have a self-evolved inner law of their own, and are by no means, as the 'classical' critics in their helpless admiration had declared them, some wild disorderly product of tropical 'nature,' to be contrasted with the symmetries of 'art.' Others before him, even Pope and Johnson, had said that Shakespeare was not to be bound or judged by rules; this was 'like trying a man by the laws of one country, who acted under those of another.' But Coleridge was the first, at least among Shakespeare's countrymen, to show that a great work of art not only creates but reveals its own law, and is rational in the highest sense, a piece of ordered brainwork and not of blind inspiration. He was unjust to the eighteenth-century critics, who had, at any rate, cleared the way for him, and he fell at times into a German kind of idolatry of Shakespeare, being ready to prove upon first principles that all his works were perfect and could not have been different. His views, too, of the Shakespeare canon, and of the probable order of the plays, are pre-scientific; but these subjects were not his task. His comments are always of price, and cannot be counted; as we read through the notes in the huge modern 'variorum' editions, they stand out from that dun chaos in letters of light. The remarks on Romeo's love for Rosaline, on the 'intellectual feminineness' of Richard the Second, on the 'mock fortitude of a mind deluded by ambition' in Macbeth, and on the comic matter in *Love's Labours Lost*, are but cupfuls caught from the endlessly-veering shower and fertilising spray of Coleridge's mind. It is in this state that most of his critical observations remain; but once or twice, by his own act, or through the preservation of notes by others, they have been gathered into order.

One of these pieces of salvage is the *Biographia Literaria*, with its treatment (already noticed) of Wordsworth's theory of diction, and its description, never yet improved upon, of Wordsworth's genius. Another is found in the series of lectures given in 1818.[1] These are in part historical, ranging over many of the great humourists, novelists, and poets, from Dante to Milton, from Rabelais to Defoe and Fielding. The paper on prose and on its successive forms and schools in England remains one of the best examples of Coleridge's enfolding and penetrating vision ; a faculty shown continually, although in the shape, as old stage directions run, of ' music dispersedly.' Whim, prejudice, intrusive didactics, verbiage like a bright mist, are seldom long absent. But in the power to quicken and liberate the artistic perceptions, and to find words, not so much for what we had felt but were unable to express, as for that which, to our shame, we ought to have seen, but did not, Coleridge is without a rival, and almost without a companion.

VI

In the course of his sympathies and convictions, he is profoundly representative, and for that reason one of the moulders, of national thought during his own lifetime. To Mill,[1] writing in 1840, he seemed to be the voice of the whole, far-reaching revulsion, which carried away Mill himself, against the characteristic English schools. The revolutionary doctrine, in ' first philosophy,' theology, ethics, and politics, had been grafted in England upon the stock of insular materialism, scepticism, and rationalism. A hundred curious and freaked varieties resulted ; but the general type and growth of the plant was clear. Coleridge wished to root it out ; he went behind all the presuppositions of the school. It was crude in its metaphysics ; and in his desultory but effectual way he revived or imported metaphysics, not treating them as a mere historian, or resting in them for their own sake, but seeing them in their outcome and bearing upon the rest of philosophy, especially on divinity and ethics. He turned his back on the old psychology of association. He tried to unite metaphysics once more with positive theology ; and this became in his hands *a priori* and scholastic theology over again, at the opposite pole to Paley's, which might be described as theology judged by results. While giving in his adhesion to Christian orthodoxy, Coleridge wrought out, after much mental wandering, a creed of his own. He passed away from his Unitarian belief, and forged, out of Plato and Schelling, a doctrine swaying now towards Pantheism, now towards a peculiar Trinitarian view of his own—unofficial enough, and founded in part on Fichtean metaphysic. In his Christian ethics he returns often to the tones of the evangelical revival, and in this sense we can fairly say that he 'never did anything else' but 'preach.' He certainly falls, with unpleasant ·facility, into something like the twang of the conventicle, even when talking to himself ; but this is an excrescence ; and at bottom, perhaps, he feels the need for a type of doctrine which is grounded upon, and developed to console and strengthen, his sense of personal weakness.   His utterances about mysticism [1] vary ; it would be quite an error to class him amongst the regular *illuminati* who appeal to some unique revelation of the divine being, or momentary identification with it, in the hour of ecstasy.   From this the strain of hard sense, so often outcropping in Coleridge, revolted ; yet his language is often coloured theosophically, and stands at the opposite extreme of human speech to that of Bentham, his only English rival in point of contemporary influence.

Coleridge's originality as a thinker has been much questioned, and the doubt is increased by his powers of self-delusion and forgetfulness, which have the effects, though not resting on the motive, of dishonesty.   His 'plagiarisms,' from Schelling above all, but also from other recent German writers on philosophy, do not prevent the resulting amalgam from being his own, especially when it is tinted by his eloquence ; but they are enough to discount his services as a contributor to general thought.   In the case of August von Schlegel,[2] to whose lectures on the drama, given at Vienna in 1808, Coleridge vehemently denied his debt, the charge is made out ; for after he had read those lectures in 1812 he often translated from them almost verbally, and made no acknowledgments.   But he deepened and ennobled what he took, adding poetry and psychology of his own ; and the very parallels often show his own supremacy as a critic, the blunter thinking and set elo- quence of the German writer becoming subtilised and only serving as a point of departure.   The treatment of the nurse in *Romeo and Juliet*, and of the whole play, is an example.

Much of Coleridge's distinguishing eloquence and many of his seminal ideas can be found, in all their disorder, in the strange publication called *The Friend*,[3] issued in 1809-10, and recast in 1818.   As a book it is impossible, and as a periodical it was still more so ; words would be wasted on its shapeless- ness and its profusion of digressive rigmarole.   It consists of three series of essays, of which the aim is to lay down the true and explode the false bases of moral science, political theory, and international law.   There is thus a trunk with many branches ; but it is much hidden under the parasitic plants

that grow too luxuriously into or out of it. Some of Coleridge's keenest dialectic is thus surrounded. The objections
to the social contract as conceived by Hobbes, and to Paley's
valuation of morality by its consequences, are brilliantly
enforced. The inevitable ' distinction between the reason
and the understanding ' is fully formulated, and *The Friend*
throughout shows the decisive influence of Kant. Amongst
the essays are dispersed ' landing-places,' or lighter articles,
into which Coleridge puts anything he may have in his wallet ;
one of them is the long story, imaginative but over-sentimental,
of Eleonora Maria Schöning, and another is a chronicle of
Coleridge's friend, Sir Alexander Ball, the governor of Malta.
In these interludes, and in the essays themselves, there are
many oases of ' the blest and the intelligible,' worthy of the
author of *The Ancient Mariner.* The description of the hues
of the ice on the Lake of Ratzeburg (written during Coleridge's
best years) is wonderful in rhythm ; while those of the prose
style of Mrs. Quickly, and of Luther's state of mind in the
presence of the Devil, are triumphs of analysis. It is hard to
think of *The Friend* save as matter for an anthology. But
nothing gives a better notion of the famous monologues, or
of the patience that Coleridge exacts and rewards. His genius
is ever waiting round the corner ; it is almost impossible to
hear him through, and never safe to leave him unheard.

His views on current politics [1] are full of interest, but cannot
be detailed here. He wrote copiously on the Revolution and
its issues, on Napoleon, on Pitt and Fox, on Ireland and on
Reform. He broke with his early revolutionary creed, and
became a somewhat blind ' Anti-Gallican and Anti-Jacobin.'
He had deplored the first war, and wrote strenuously in favour
of the Peace of Amiens ; and steered a course of his own,
going further than the Whig opposition, avoiding stagnant
Toryism, and drifting more and more away from Radical
sympathies. His articles in the *Morning Post*, especially his
formidable ' Character ' of Pitt, published in that paper on
March 19, 1800, show great skill in the loftier order of journalism,
and a good judge of the craft has lamented the loss in Coleridge of a great leader-writer.[2] He might have harnessed
himself to the press, and was offered high wages, but chose
his life of fatal freedom. These articles in the *Post*, for which
Coleridge had had some training in his essays (1795) in *The
Watchman*, he wrote, it must be recalled, while at the height
of his powers. Those contributed much later to the *Morning
Courier* show his genius more fitfully, but are noteworthy in

the development of his opinions. By 1811 he became much
more fiercely anti-Napoleonic, but also a more tolerant judge
of Jacobinism, by then an extinguished force. The best of
his political writings are still more than readable ; they are
lucid, rapid, edged, perfectly fitted to the average educated
reader, and yet informed with large ideas. The influence of
Burke is always apparent, though Coleridge's judgment
revolted against the whirling words and frenzy of the *Regi-
cide Peace* and its companion tirades. Indeed, his early
review of the *Letter to a Noble Lord* ranged him for the hour
among Burke's sharper critics. But as a philosophic conservative he is, with Wordsworth, Burke's true successor.
Each in his way is a mystic, and grounds the claim of historic
institutions and beliefs on something hardly expressible, on
moral emotions and imaginative awe and the needs of human
kind. But Coleridge seeks to supply that metaphysical basis
for religion, politics, and ethics which Burke distrusted ; and
this is to be set against his weaker appetite for the concrete
facts of history.

What may be called the missionary prose of Coleridge is
also well seen in his *Aids to Reflection*, which aims at sketching,
for the plain, convinced, and cultivated rather than scholarly
Christian, a rational groundwork for his faith, in its connections with pure philosophy on the one shore, and on the other
with the truth given by spiritual experience ; the bridge being
laid, as we should expect, across the depths of moral psychology,
in which Coleridge is so painfully at home. The Kantian
distinction between the ' reason ' and the ' understanding,'
he interprets as severing the faculty that gives us the higher
truths immediately, from that which works in a lower and more
limited way, in the empirical field and through logical cate-
gories. The destructive analysis of the last century was the
mere work of the 'understanding.' It had pretended to explain
away everything; but the really unexplained residue, the content
of the deeper, moral, religious, and political consciousness, only
lay open to the eye of 'reason.' On the ethical side, there arises
the other distinction between mere prudential morality—which
Paley and his school applied to both worlds—and a secular code
of the higher sort ; and a further one, again, between this and
the religious sanctity, which is intimately and transcendentally
rooted in the heart. Such differences fall into their place in
Coleridge's intricate theology, which is by no means orthodox
in form, but keeps him a member of the Christian community.
His own memories of his failures and consolations are eloquently

uttered in *Aids to Reflection*, and also in the *Confessions of an Inquiring Spirit*; and his scheme of belief, while justified to him by his 'reason,' is clearly and almost confessedly commended to him by his heart,—itself in his eyes a true organ of revelation. He swings clean away from the utilitarian divines; the joys of well-doing and the pains of sin are not to be computed by their effects on the sum of individual happiness, on earth or in hell; and he adopts something like Kant's conception of the good, or pure, will, as the basis of right conduct. Likewise the ordinary 'evidences' *a posteriori*, and the objections to them, recede in importance. Coleridge might now be termed a kind of 'pragmatist,' justifying Christianity by its meetness, as shown by centuries of experience, for the inward needs of mankind.

In his view of the Bible he anticipates a later position. He may be said to have striven to purge evangelical theology of its literalism and extravagance, whilst holding to its essence. He repudiates literal inspiration and text-worship; he shuns the more isolated and ignorant claims of 'enthusiasm,' and the quicksands of vulgar mysticism; clinging, all the same, to the intimate, personal side of Protestantism, and 'finding' more in the Bible that 'speaks' to him than in any other book or literature. He is as far from the level, reasonable Tillotson as from the visionary Fox; and reverts by choice to the more spiritual, scholarly divines of the seventeenth century. Above all, the lofty patristic eloquence of Archbishop Leighton attracts him, and the 'aphorisms' of that great preacher, who is a somewhat solitary voice in the age of the Restoration, he blends, not incongruously, with his own. In these passages of the *Confessions* we come near to the kind of English upon which Coleridge's, in his devout and meditative moods, is moulded; though he does not always preserve the measure, the clearness, or the refinement of his model. His conception of the national church is moulded on the historic one derived from these Anglican divines, on whom his volume of *Notes* is instructive. The precise form that Coleridge gave to these ideas, and their later influence, is to be traced by the historians of English theology; but it is clear how he touches, and even rises above, the various schools, 'high,' 'broad,' or 'low,' which came soon after his day into a kind of triangular antagonism.

One shapely and orderly work in prose must be credited to Coleridge. The tractate *On the Constitution of Church and State* is the most lucid and able product of his reasoned con-

servatism. It is a most skilful attempt to rest Church and
State, in their British guise, on a high philosophic basis, by
defining and connecting the essential 'Idea of each.' The
process of justifying the existing fact by an appeal to eternal
reason is familiar enough, but Hooker himself did not employ
it more ably. Coleridge's analysis of the State, in its narrower
sense, into the classes of the landowning nobility who furnish
forth the Lords, and the mercantile, labouring, and professional ones, who constitute the Commons; with the sovereign
as head, or rather as the 'beam of the balance'; and his
recital (with suggestions of moderate reform) of the duties
and privileges of each class;—this account leads at once to
his vindication of the clergy, or what he calls the 'clerisy,'
as a kind of co-equal fourth estate, of which the king is also
head. This Church, together with the secular groups described,
forms the State in its larger and comprehensive meaning.
For his 'idea,' or ideal, Coleridge in effect goes back to the
Middle Ages. The 'clerisy' have not merely to do with theology
(the crown, indeed, of the sciences) and with worship; men's
brains, as well as men's souls, are their affair, and almost
their monopoly; they are the clerks, the learned class, the
preservers of the treasures of the past, the bringers of light,
the providers (and controllers) of education. They are to
sustain

the true historical feeling, the immortal life of the nation, generation linked to generation by faith, freedom, heraldry, and ancestral
fame.

His diatribe against the age is like one of Ruskin's or of Carlyle's;
it is an age of mechanical improvement, of uppish empirical
science, of talent without genius, of 'understanding' without
'reason,' of social misery and vice unfathomed and uncured,
and of 'the Ouran Outang theology' instead of the first ten
chapters of Genesis. All this chaos is due to the absence of a
'dynamic' and spiritual conception of the State and the
Church in their vital relationship. Nothing can be remoter
from the dominant thoughts of to-day, or more eloquently
said.

In Coleridge, then, better than in Wordsworth or Shelley,
is seen how the new current of Continental thought reaches
our shores, how our poetry and prose are affected by it, and
what is meant by such a phrase as the 'Romantic philosophy.'[1]
There is no such philosophy; there is a philosophical tendency;
and this signifies a convergent impulse of creative art and of

speculation, each acting on and colouring the other.   The *unexplained* in human life ; in the desires of the intellect, and in ' the thoughts of the heart ' ; in the mystery of the moral will, and in the forces that shape traditional creeds and polities —things that are not invented but grow ; this is the novel sphere both of art and philosophy.   Each works in its own way, one representing in plastic form, and the other attempting a methodical synthesis ; but they both explore.   The whole world of the senses, both in its moral and æsthetic aspect, is seen, as well as the world of ideas, in a new import.   In the process, old schools are thrown over ; both the philosophy whose last word is mechanical analysis, and the poetry that is abstract in tissue and logical in movement, distrusts the seen world, and is cold to the principle of beauty.   Such changes go on for a while independently and fitfully, in all ages ; but after a time minds arise which feel them both, and attempt to interpret their connection.   Such a mind was Coleridge's, perhaps equally, and beyond doubt signally gifted for either side of his task.   To its immensity his broken achievement was partly due.

VII

In Coleridge, not least when he suffers, there is something of the child ; and this element, together with the poetic voice he gave to it, descended to his son, Hartley Coleridge[1] (1796-1849) ; as well as the tremulous fineness, though not the intellectual grip and energy, of his critical sensibility.   But in his verse, and also in his delicate and perceiving love for the poets, Hartley is no mere filial echo ; his writing has a shading of its own, like that of some flower that fears the daylight. His childish dreams and utterances prophesied genius, but in Wordsworth's famous lines, written when Hartley was six years old, he is truly portrayed as an alien in the world and living there on a fragile tenure.   His academic career bid fair, but was broken by intemperance, and something broke in Hartley himself ; yet his misfortunes, which tint his poetry, after all left, or made, him a poet, and it is not clear that without them he would have done more, or so much.   His harmless, elfish, vagrant life and gentle premature old age have left a delicate tradition in Wordsworth's countryside. He published some of his best verse in 1833.   It is hard to reckon with, partly because his voice, like Cordelia's, is low, and we have to listen for its undertones with purged hearing ;

and partly because he thought, perhaps, too little of himself always to endeavour after due poetic finish. His longest pieces are *Leonard and Susan*, a tragical 'English idyll' somewhat overwrought in feeling, but a link between the older generation and Tennyson's experiments ; and the fragment *Prometheus*, which shows, though fitfully, an unexpected kind of power. But most of his poems are short ;—little lyrics, of which *The Old Man's Wish* and the better-known 'She is not fair to outward view' are the best ; or personal and pathetic, like the beautiful lines in blank verse *To my Unknown Sister-in-Law*. Some of the *Sketches of English Poets* in heroic rhyme, such as those on Spenser, Drayton, and Dryden, rank with his finest criticisms. But the true bequest of Hartley Coleridge is found in his sonnets, and surely he is the best practitioner in this kind between Wordsworth and the Rossettis.

He often combines the Italian structure of the octave in closed rhyme (*abba abba*) with the final couplet ; a scheme which is supposed only by pedants to be inadmissible. He is by no means always careful to place the turn, or break, in the sense at the beginning of the sestet, which is a more disturbing heresy ; and the loftiest of his sonnets in feeling are not always the best composed. This is the case with the poem *To Shakespeare*, and with another noble one, 'In the great city we are met again.' But room may be found for one that is technically symmetrical (granting three rhymes in the octave), and in emotion most characteristic :

> Hast thou not seen an aged rifted tower,
>   Meet habitation for the Ghost of Time,
>   Where fearful ravage makes decay sublime,
> And destitution wears the face of power ?
>
> Yet is the fabric deck'd with many a flower
>   Of fragrance wild, and many-dappled hue,
>   Gold-streak'd with iron-brown and nodding blue,
> Making each ruinous chink a fairy bower.
>
> E'en such a thing methinks I fain would be,
>   Should Heaven appoint me to a lengthen'd age ;
> So old in look, that Young and Old may see
>   The record of my closing pilgrimage :
> Yet, to the last, a rugged wrinkled thing
> To which young sweetness may delight to cling !

Here, as in other places, the models of Shakespeare and Wordsworth count for something to Hartley Coleridge ; but he is most himself, and most faultless in form, when he is nearest to the earth and the simple affections, from the fulness of which his own lot cuts him off ; and when his spirit wanders like an air among the leaves and the lakeside rushes. We should choose the following for a brief anthology : the land-scapes in *Night, September,* and *November* (' The mellow year is hasting to its close ') ; ' Let me not deem that I was made in vain,' with its subtle and proud humility of tone ; the spirited and tender poem, *To a Lofty Beauty, from her poor Kinsman* ; that *To Louise Claude,* the homage of age to youth ; and the magnificent *Multum Dilexit,* worthy of Christina Rossetti.

Criticism, in both its elements of sharp sensibility and search-ing judgment, is in the veins of Hartley and Sara Coleridge ; and of the two, the learned sister is more decisive and dog-matic than her brother, and she has hardly the same flexible, open spirit. Hartley's gift of literary comment, though spilt and scattered, and never fully trained or concentrated, is most authentic, and all his prose is too much forgotten. In the *Biographia Borealis, or Lives of Northern Worthies,* who include such diverse figures as Ascham, Bentley, Mason, and William Roscoe, the biographical matter is now somewhat antiquated ; but the criticism is often startlingly fresh and fine, and worthy of the great company which Hartley had kept. The pages on the satires of Andrew Marvell, and above all those on the comedies of Congreve, do not deserve thus to have been buried alive. Hartley Coleridge is less oppressed than his father, or than his sister, by philosophy and reading, and is nearer to Lamb or Hazlitt in his direct plain utterance of what he feels. His style is purer and more dignified than Leigh Hunt's.

In his introduction to his edition of Massinger and Ford, his most sustained piece of commentary, there is the same quality ; and in his paper on Hamlet, and indeed in all he says upon Shakespeare, it is never far off. As a pure essayist he has the discursive ease and unobtrusive nicety, amidst a good deal of whim and surplusage. The best writing of Sara Cole-ridge is found in her letters, though in the little fairy tale, *Phantasmion* (1837), there is a rich and fanciful inventive-ness, and a feeling for colour unreal and magical, that beseems the daughter of Coleridge. Her opinions of books are frank and always well argued ; and her plain speaking about the diction and sentiment of *Laodamia,* her analysis of Shylock, and her notes on Cowper's *Homer,* on *In Memoriam,* and on *Vanity Fair,* are all worthy of resurrection.

The least remembered of the ' Lake poets,' Charles Lloyd [1] (1775-1839), may here be named. He lives rather in the letters of Lamb and Coleridge and in the reminiscences of De Quincey than by his own work; yet his almost frustrate literary gift is curious and distinctive enough. Lloyd begins as a sonneteer in the company of his two friends; the strain of juvenile melancholy, of fine-spun sentiment, and of an introspection that may easily defeat itself for want of material, is common to all three. Lamb and Coleridge escaped from this 'obscure wood' and found their genius; Lloyd never quite escaped, or expressed himself. His bent for analysis and psychology, recorded by several observers, seems to have been at its best in talk. 'He was,' says De Quincey, 'somewhat too *Rousseauish*'; and he is found, in 1795, exercised by the same kind of difficulties as Wordsworth in his early Godwinian stage. 'Oswald,' the hero of one of his poems, seems to be Lloyd himself; and the theme is

to trace the possible effects of the principal abuses of the social system on a Youth more accustomed to feel than to reason; who is doomed, when his sentiments had been raised to a high-toned enthusiasm, by contemplating the wildest features of nature through the magnifying medium of sensibility, to view not only the effects of the selfish principle in others, but to feel himself its unfortunate victim.

It would be hard to pack more of the floating doctrines and catchwords of that decade into a single sentence. Lloyd's *Desultory Thoughts in London* (1821), his best piece, written in a not very successful form of the *Don Juan* octave measure, contains some touching stanzas to Coleridge, with whom he had been at first intimate, then estranged, and lastly half-reconciled; and its topics are odd and thistly enough: 'Reflections on Unfortunate Females'—'The Philosophy of Penance'—'The Millennium.' More promising is 'The Folly of making Works of Imagination subservient to speculative Theory'; and Lloyd shows no little address in the conduct of these abstract matters. The 'Stanzas' ('let the reader,' he adds, 'determine their title') in his *Nugae Canorae* (1819) show the same kind of power, and vividly describe his solitude and dreariness. Lloyd continued to make sonnets, and *Nugae Canorae* contains many of the type he terms 'metaphysical,' sombrely and sincerely written, but lamed by some inborn and fatal failure in form. His novel, *Edmund Oliver*, is rubbish, and only of interest for its allusions, unpermitted and duly resented, to Coleridge's military escapade. Lloyd also translated Alfieri's tragedies.

CHAPTER XVII

BYRON

I. Byron's reputation, how far well founded. His personality in his works.
Literary phases: (a) lyric and youthful satire; (b) Childe Harold, cantos i.
and ii., and rhymed stories; (c) Childe Harold, cantos iii. and iv., poems on
Italy, and plays; (d) Don Juan, Vision of Judgment, etc. Songs and lyrics:
want of ear; reasoning on emotion. Hours of Idleness, Hebrew Melodies.
Early satires: English Bards and Scotch Reviewers; other invectives.

II. Childe Harold, i. and ii.; Byron's 'doppelgänger'; character of the
'Childe'; revisions of text; versification. Tales in verse: The Giaour,
Bride of Abydos, Corsair, etc. Siege of Corinth, Parisina, Prisoner of Chillon.
Rapidity of movement; metres; affinities with other romantic poets.

III. Childe Harold, iii. and iv.; changed spirit; confessions, history, and
descriptions interwoven. Cantos iii. and iv., how different. Points of contact with Wordsworth and with Shelley.

IV. Italy: self-revelation of Byron in The Dream, Darkness, etc. Byron's
private history; its bearing on his literary genius and mode of expression.
Are his utterances dramatic? Various views.

V. Plays: speculative verse; Byron's scepticism, its character: Manfred,
Cain, Heaven and Earth. Historical tragedies: Marino Faliero, etc. The
Deformed Transformed.

VI. The Italian medley-poem transplanted. Frere's Whistlecraft. Translation of Pulci. Beppo. The ottava rima and the wits; William Stewart Rose.
Don Juan: its ingredients; cynicism, scepticism, sense of beauty, insolence,
descriptive satire. Revanche on English society. Ending.

VII. Don Juan: Byron's mobility and self-consciousness reflected in his
management of the verse. The Vision of Judgment. The Island; sources.

VIII. Course of Byron's fame; his permanent qualities. His influence.

I

BYRON,[1] with his works, was the prey and wonder of all men
for a long generation, and his glory was only less than Goethe's.
He had a wider influence at the time than Goethe; he coloured
most of the literatures of the West, and his name grew abroad
while it faded in England. Can he have deceived Europe, or
at best can he simply have found it a voice for its passing needs
and emotions—for its melancholy, its 'Titanism,' and its self-
scrutiny? Was his influence of the same order as that of
'Ossian'—as transient, if on a greater scale? Is Byron still
wanted, and does he move us, and what has he left us that is

wearing well ? No Fathers or Councils have settled this
question ; there is no canonical view. On one side, there is
the liberal-cosmopolitan answer of a critic like Georg Brandes,
who makes Byron the centre of his canvas when delineating
the ' master-tendencies ' of the romantic period. The history
of letters, from Lisbon to St. Petersburg, during the first
quarter of the nineteenth century, can be cited in defence
of this estimate ; and Byron's mighty influence is beyond
question, it is a fact of history. It does not follow, all the
same, that his work endures, or that we can now read him for
his own sake. Can we ? Often the words Byron and art
seem to be incompatible ; he has been assailed and judged,
at home, by his peers, the poets themselves. His taint of
rhetoric, his commonness of diction, his want of ear, have been
censured repeatedly, and are undeniable. Where, then, does
he stand ?

The answer can at last only be a personal one ; but two
considerations may be named before surveying Byron's work.
One is, that we know a great deal about him ; and we cannot
judge of what he wrote as if it were nameless—as if it had been
dug up from the lava of a buried city. We cannot, if we would,
apply to him the strict and pure gospel of Execution. The
world—nay, the critic—will never do this, because Byron is
too interesting. We watch for him on every page, and when
we have found him, he remains greater than his work, which is
so perfect a mirror of his imperfections, of his elusive nature,
that we still gaze upon it. We read his writings with more
of human anxiety and sympathy than we do much that
possesses more infallible form, and is of a steadier sort of
greatness. But, in the second place, let us make no needless
concessions, even on the count of form. It is certain, surely,
that much of his performance will regain credit and honour.
It shows, if not a steady growth, still a true advance, a gradual
shedding of false experiment, a growing realisation of beauty,
a visible increase of veracity, and, in the long run, victory.
From the first he expressed himself faithfully in prose ; and,
before long, perfectly. In verse he started with a style that
was flawed and dubious ; often splendid, but very distant from
that of his prose, and by no means that of ' the real Byron.'
He followed out this style to the utmost, he made the best of
it ; and in doing this he travelled away from it. At length
he attained a poetic style that nearly approaches to his prose
style. Byron's artistic history lies in that sentence. But to
say this is not to give up his title as a poet. On the contrary,

his prose itself is worthy of a poet ; and further, when he uses
it for verse he adds the glory of poetry to his material. The
changes in his handiwork can be watched from this point
of view. The more we look at it, the more clearly, as time
passes, the features of Byron emerge ; and his voice, so
human under all its affectations, becomes more and more alive
to us.

This development of Byron's genius is not unbroken, it
suffers relapses and arrests. He was wont to try many things
at once, and to do one well and another badly, at the same
time. But for convenience four phases can be distinguished.
The first (1807-12) is that of poetical adolescence, and covers
his first experiments in lyric and in satire—two forms which
he is to practise to the last. *Hours of Idleness* (1807), along
with other miscellaneous work, and *English Bards and Scotch
Reviewers* (1809), the first book that indicates his power, are
the chief results. In the second phase (1812-16) he produces
the first two cantos of *Childe Harold* (1812), the diary of his
grand tour and its observations and emotions ; and then, on
the wave of success, pours out the series of rhymed lays, in the
following order :—*The Giaour* (1813), *The Bride of Abydos*
(1813), *The Corsair* and *Lara* (1814), *The Siege of Corinth* and
Parisina (1816). Then came his domestic catastrophe and
permanent ' self-exile ' from Britain, after which the stages
are less clearly marked. The first-fruits were the third canto
of *Childe Harold* (1816) and the fourth (1818) ; and by the side
of these come *The Lament of Tasso* and other poems of a serious
cast on Italian subjects. The lighter style opens in *Beppo*
(1818) ; in that year *Don Juan* was begun, and appeared at
intervals until 1824. But meanwhile Byron wrote two more
tales in verse, of finer workmanship than their predecessors ;
these are *The Prisoner of Chillon* (1816) and *Mazeppa* (1819) ;
The Island (1823), his last long poem, being a belated example
of the same kind. He also commenced dramatist ; and his
plays fall into two groups, *Manfred* (1817) and *Cain* (1821),
with *Heaven and Earth*, being in the true line of his genius,
while his historical and other dramas, *Mariño Faliero* and the
rest, are with a few exceptions a dull diversion from it. *The
Vision of Judgment* (1823), his greatest satire, is an accompaniment to *Don Juan*. Here Byron expresses himself entirely
without hindrance ; in all his other verse something essential
to him, his humour, his realism, his medley of qualities, is left
out. But at last his sardonic and critical spirit, the spirit of
his prose, finds its true medium, and his sense of beauty, which

increases to the last, is interwoven if not wholly harmonised with it. The medium in question, as will appear, he found in an Italian model. It was Italy that gave Byron not only his full personal and mental freedom, but artistic freedom as well.

It is best to speak of all his songs and lyrics together. They are not a large proportion of his writing; and many of them, such as the choruses in *Heaven and Earth*, might have been composed for pure love of discord. Often we are tempted to adapt Pope's line on Defoe, 'Earless, on high, stands unabashed' —Byron. If we let ourselves dwell on his failures, we might think that he is only a singer by chance, just as Shelley is a singer in essence. But his lyrical energy is great, if his lyrical execution is most fallible. He can control his energy so little, that it defeats itself. But it is there; it floods up in his tales, it bursts through his satire, it has the disquiet of a thwarted thing, and often it triumphs after all. At first it promises poorly. *Hours of Idleness* is little enough in itself; the whole book is not worth Gray's four lines of Latin, *O lacrymarum fons*, which Byron more than once shows his taste by quoting. But some of it shows how fast he is rooted in the eighteenth century—there are echoes of Gray, echoes of Ossian, and heroics after Pope—and how, all the same, a new flower is piercing through that exhausted soil. There is the first faint pencilling of the 'Byronic hero,' with his voice and gesture :

> I seek to shun, not hate mankind,
> My breast requires the sullen glen
> Whose gloom may suit a darken'd mind, etc.

And there is the beginning (as in the lines 'Why should my anxious breast repine') of the argumentative, expository lyric, which Byron was to make his own.

For even here he is a debtor of the age of rhymed reasoning and analysis. In his lyrics there is no brooding vision or evanescent imagery, but a kind of passionate thinking. The best of them, such as the verses addressed *To Thyrza*, could bear the apposition of a prose argument, like those which Dante made for the sonnets of the *Vita Nuova*; a process impossible with the songs of Shelley or of Beddoes, which leave no such precipitate, but vanish under our hand into wisps of cloud-wreath and rainbow; for such is their virtue, and their very being. This character attaches to nearly all Byron wrote in lyric form. It is found in 'When we two parted,'

written in 1808, and also in the farewell lines from Missolonghi,
' 'Tis time this heart should be unmoved.' This steady
ascendency of the brain over its own fever makes, after all,
for a clear perfection of form, or at least for a bare and moving
exactness of poetic language :

> The better days of life were ours :
>   The worst can but be mine ;
> The sun that cheers, the storm that lowers,
>   Shall never more be thine.
> The silence of that dreamless sleep
> I envy now too much to weep ;
>   Nor need I to repine
> That all those charms have pass'd away
> I might have watch'd through long decay.

The versification, too, often comes right, less through artistic
study than because experience has burnt itself clear and the
tune has been born without effort. Swinburne, who is Byron's
severest critic in this particular, never made anything more
cunning in cadence or composition than the ending of ' When
we two parted,' or the *Stanzas for Music* (' There be none
of Beauty's daughters '). It matters less that Byron can be
outrageous, that he can write

> Obscures his glory ;
> Despot no more, he
> Such territory
>   Quits with disdain ;

—when he can also write

> These lips are mute, these eyes are dry ;
>   But in my breast, and in my brain
> Awake the pangs that pass not by,
>   The thought that ne'er shall sleep again.
> My soul nor deigns nor dares complain,
>   Though grief and passion there rebel;
> I only know we loved in vain—
>   I only feel—farewell ! farewell !

Of a more popular and palpable order of merit, but still of
true quality, come the best of the *Hebrew Melodies* (1815).
Some of them, like *Jephthah's Daughter* and *Sennacherib*, are
heroic lyrics, and show the same kind of power as the rhymed
stories of the same period ; they seem like rapid, telling
improvisations. Like *The Isles of Greece*, they have a Latin
metallic ring which the lovers of high poetry must not be too
proud to love also. The song of the soldiers in *The Deformed
Transformed* is homely, strong, and rocky, and anticipates
the war lyrics of Browning. Soldiers do not rhyme with

finicking care, and 'vanguard' and 'Spaniard' go well enough
together on the march :

> The black bands came over
> The Alps and their snow ;
> With Bourbon, the rover,
> They pass'd the broad Po. . . .

It is hard to separate this style from that of *Mazeppa* and
the other long lyrical ballads, which must be thought of as
chanted or recited beside the camp-fire rather than sung.

Hours of Idleness was scarified with heavy archness in the
Edinburgh Review ; not unfairly, though the intention was
cruel. But *English Bards and Scotch Reviewers* was the reply.
The bards had done Byron no harm, but they suffered along
with the reviewers. This series of caricatures of most of the
literary personages, great or small, of the time, is written with
much gusto, and with a blindness not less remarkable. Byron
was never a critic, he had only likes and dislikes. But he was
capable of amending some of his more foolish dislikes, and also
of relapsing into them. He took back, for a time, his abuse
of Wordsworth (who had, indeed, detected some merit in the
Hours of Idleness) ; of Coleridge, whom he soon was to befriend
and afterwards to consider ungrateful ; of Jeffrey, with whom
he was to exchange eulogies, and who handsomely qualified
his own ill auguries ; of Scott, who generously perceived the
presence of ' noble merit ' in *English Bards* ; and, of course,
of Moore. Byron afterwards said, ' I am haunted by the ghosts
of my wholesale assertions,' and called the work a ' miserable
record of misplaced anger and indiscriminate acrimony.' But
he did not retract his praises of Rogers, who was to ' restore
Apollo ' ; or of Gifford, who is ' greater far ' than Burns ; or
of Wright's *Horae Ionicae* ; or of *The Aboriginal Britons*, a
poem by a Rev. Dr. Richards. He is, however, warranted
in his scorn of Darwin and Hayley ; and his well-known
tribute to Crabbe (' Nature's sternest painter, yet the best ') is
on the right side.

In this youthful work Byron is a young tiger-cub lashing
out with sharp and clumsy claws. He is trying to be like
Gifford, who had rabidly demolished small writers in the
Baviad, and like Gifford's master Pope, who had done the like
in the *Dunciad*. It was wise of Byron to copy the *Dunciad*
and not the *Homer*. But the Pope of the *Satires and Epistles*
was beyond his range ; and he does not really rival even the
Dunciad. He has not Pope's finish, or his malign instinct for
the real or colourable weakness of an enemy. He does ape

Pope's ineffable attitude as the champion of letters and virtue against dullness and imposture. But from *English Bards* we chiefly learn the names of many ephemeral writers of the year 1809. The faces of their betters are also to be seen, but as through a distorting and discoloured pane. In the poetry of hatred Byron still overreached himself. The bitter *Sketch*, which describes a real person ; *The Curse of Minerva,* in which the conveyance of the Elgin Marbles is reprobated ; the *Hints from Horace,* a dull adaptation of the *Ars Poetica,* and rated by the author above *Childe Harold* ; and *The Age of Bronze* (1823), a sally against the Holy Alliance, and a noticeable record of Byron's political antipathies ;—all these works may be described as the last flare-up of the old classical tirade. Not one of them is good. But meantime, as *The Vision of Judgment* (1823) is enough to show, Byron had changed his metre, deserting his heavy and maladroit heroic couplets for the nimble and motley octave rhyme, and had accomplished a new birth of satire. As usual, he often went on pounding away in the wrong style long after he had discovered the right one. But it is now necessary to go back to the verse of his second literary stage—that is, to the earliest that can be read with any satisfaction.

II

The first two cantos of *Childe Harold* (1812) are the rhymed diary of two years' travel ; most of the episodes being set down as they happened and stitched together afterwards. The same story is again told, without the rhetoric or the poetry, in Byron's footnotes and his correspondence. There he records the surface humours of the pilgrimage, and the light amours of the world-weary pilgrim ; as well as many hard facts of history and topography, which are more solidly set forth in his companion Hobhouse's *Journey through Albania, etc.* Byron was at first modest about his verses, but was persuaded to publish them by another friend, Dallas. They were therefore hardly written for the world ; so that if Byron poses in these cantos, he poses before his mirror in solitude. Here, at any rate, is an early sketch, at once blunt and uncertain, of that strange *doppelgänger,* who figures in so many of his writings down to *Manfred,* and whose features melt and waver but at last fix into some distinctness; whose literary origins[1] range from the old dramatists to Mme. de Staël and Mrs. Radcliffe ; who is sometimes as near to Byron, and as like him, as his shadow thrown upon the wall, and sometimes a huge disnatured image of him, like the same shadow thrown upon the mist ; but who, in either case, is the sole character that Byron ever fully conceived and realised until he thought of Don Juan.   There are reasons for crediting Byron with more sincerity and veracity in his self-portraiture than has always been conceded ; but, at this date, he denies formally that he is himself Childe Harold.   Harold is, in truth, at once less and more than Byron.   Less, for he is not the Byron of the letters, the satirist, the buck, the ex-dandy, the friend of Angelo and John Jackson ; and more, because he is in part a personage in the ' satanic ' tradition, of Vathek or Schedoni ancestry, harried by the memory of sorrows and follies, if not of crimes, and it comforts Byron to think himself such a personage.   At first the poet and the pilgrim are formally distinguished by the pronouns ' I ' and ' he ' ; but as the poem goes on the two figures approximate, so that the world and the reviewers were not patient to watch for the real divergence of language between the two.   But this is well seen in the descriptions of Ali Pacha,[1] the ' Mahometan Buonaparte.'

Here is what Byron observes :

His Highness is sixty years old, very fat, and not tall, but with a fine face, light blue eyes, and a white beard ; his manner is very kind, and at the same time he possesses that dignity which I find universal among the Turks.   He has the appearance of anything but his real character, for he is a remorseless tyrant, guilty of the most horrible cruelties. . . . He said he was certain I was a man of birth, because I had small ears, curling hair, and little white hands. . . . He told me to consider him as a father whilst I was in Turkey, and said he looked on me as his son.   Indeed, he treated me like a child, sending me almonds and sugared sherbet, fruit and sweetmeats, twenty times a day.

This is what Harold sees :

> In marble-paved pavilion, where a spring
> Of living water from the centre rose,
> Whose bubbling did a genial freshness fling,
> And soft voluptuous couches breathed repose,
> ALI reclined, a man of war and woes ;
> Yet in his lineaments ye cannot trace,
> While Gentleness her milder radiance throws
> Along that aged venerable face,
> The deeds that lurk beneath, and stain him with disgrace.

Here the prose is far better than the verse, and most unlike it ; it has the lightness, the naturalness, which only got into Byron's verse later, or which, when it did get in, he unluckily expunged. On the other side, it is rare that his prose echoes the high-pitched tone of his verse; but we find such an echo in the entry about the wounded eagle which Byron found by the Gulf of Lepanto :

It was only wounded, and I tried to save it—the eye was so bright. But it pined, and died in a few days ; and I never did since, and never will, attempt the death of another bird.

This has the true sound of romance, simply as it is said. It would be hard to imagine it written a century earlier.

Harold is pulled between his love for solitude and his love for the motley world, and so far he is Byron. But in the world he is lonely, and in solitude he is so much more lonely that he runs for relief to the pageant of history, whose wrecks are scattered over the lands that he visits. Herein, too, he is Byron, and also in his love for countries with a great remote past. He cares more for Greece than he does for the Peninsula, with its battlefields where the blood is scarcely dry, or for Albania, or even for Italy. Greece, where he is to die, is the home of his mind already. He cares somewhat for her myth and poetry, more for her scenery, and most of all for her lost freedom ; not like Shelley, transcendentally or with more than mortal passion, but with a living spirit aflame, ready to taunt the degenerate Hellenes, the 'hereditary bondsmen,' into activity. This was in 1809 ; in 1824 Byron might have done better ; he might have led them ; but he was cut off.

In these first two cantos he dashed off a number of alterations. Some of the flippant things which he was unluckily persuaded to omit, such as the lines on the warriors of Cintra or on 'digging Gell,' the antiquary, distinctly forecast the style of *Don Juan*. In its original shape the poem was more of a medley, and therefore a truer picture of Byron's nature. The lines upon the British Sabbath (i. lxix-lxx), which to Moore's horror were retained, have this touch of light-heartedness. The portrait of the Childe himself contains others, and it is a relief from his 'strange pangs' and 'disappointed passion' to find him an inmate of the Castle of Indolence :

> Ah me ! in sooth he was a shameless wight,
> Sore given to revel and ungodly glee ;
> Few earthly things found favour in his sight
> Save concubines and carnal companie,
> And flaunting wassailers of high and low degree.

This usage of Spenser's stanza for jest and derision is confessedly learned from James Thomson and Beattie. The measure soon ceases to be Spenser's except in its mere anatomy of rhyme-arrangement. The cunning alexandrines of *The Faerie Queene*, with their intricate alliteration, are not often heard :

> Nor from his lips did come
> One word of wail, while others sate and wept,
> And to the reckless gales unmanly moaning kept.

In general a new and original tune is heard, and Byron's oratorical style emerges. The archaisms diminish, the openings of the lines are apt to be repeated, like the phrases of a debater. When Byron spoke in the Lords, Curran told him that he should have taken to parliamentary eloquence, and we can well believe it. His bent is seen in his adaptation of the Spenserian verse. He ceases to aspire to its undulating and interwoven music. He likes to break up the stanza into separate ringing lines, and to end it with a crash. The onset is like a row of even, charging lances. He has as yet no inkling of his own later versification, where the pace and mood alter with every sentence, and which is broken and supple. The metrical climaxes of the stanza, at the fifth and eighth lines, he manages quite otherwise than Spenser. This technique, if somewhat rigid and obvious, is most favourably seen in the more uplifted and fervent passages, one of which may be quoted to show it :

> When riseth Lacedaemon's hardihood,
> When Thebes Epaminondas rears again,
> When Athens' children are with hearts endued,
> When Grecian mothers shall give birth to men,
> Then mayst thou be restored ; but not till then.
> A thousand years scarce serve to form a state ;
> An hour may lay it in the dust ; but when
> Can man its scattered splendour renovate,
> Recall its virtues back, and vanquish Time and Fate ?

This may be called oratory in verse, rather than poetry ; but then it is transporting oratory, because it is sincere, and more-over it is true ; and poetry and oratory touch, whenever they rise high enough. With the choruses of *Hellas*, it is true, we are in another world of language.

Between the second and third cantos of *Childe Harold*, while Byron was at the height of his vogue, like a ship cresting the waves,—a period closed by the wreck of his short married life, his departure from England, and the birth-hour of his deeper soul and genius,—came the series of his rhymed romances, usurping on the fame and borrowing from the verse-craft of Scott, but transferring the scene from Britain to the East and South, and the interest from action to passion. The appetite of the contemporary public for these stories, and the hot haste of their production, are well known. In three years there were fourteen editions of *The Giaour* (1813), ill-joined as it is and obscure in conduct. *The Bride of Abydos* was written in a week. Ten thousand copies of *The Corsair* (1814), another poem almost improvised, were sold on publication, and six thousand of *Lara* in the same year. *The Siege of Corinth* and *Parisina*, which show a distinct progress in skill and certitude of style, came out in 1816, just before Byron's domestic catastrophe.

These tales in verse, containing as they do little that is perfect, and leaving little durable impression on the mind, except a general one of disquiet and power and splendid turbulence, like that of a charging horseman ; for behind all that dust and murky discharge there is a young warrior armed : these poems, which embody Byron's memories of his grand tour and his reading, rather than the life which he was living when he wrote them, or the scenes of which he hoarded up unconsciously for the last cantos of *Don Juan*—were read by all the world ; and it can still be noticed that Byron's lot amongst our poets has been to include in his public many persons who care little for other poetry than his, or even, as some may add, for poetry at all. Such admirers are more alive to power than to art, and love to watch for the man behind the book ; they look rather for the utterance of passionate sensation, interveined with adventure and colour, than for the dramatic, or even the psychological, portrayal of passion. And what they wanted, Byron now gave to them, in these headlong extempore pieces, where we can still feel, hardly abated by time, the swift pulsation of the blood ; in contrast to the stillborn deadness of the deliberate, exotic narratives, epical in their ambition, which were begotten by Moore and Southey. The East had long been known in the prose of the historians and travellers and romancers, to all of whom Byron was in debt. But he too had travelled, and prided himself on the rightness of his costume and trappings, and on the probability or historical reality of the events, which he relates with such energy, but which in most instances move us feebly. In any case, he created for the tale in rhyme a new variety in which he has not been excelled or matched. Since his day this kind of poetry has not been acceptable without the exquisite uniform finish which Keats and Tennyson and Morris have given to it, and which Byron invariably lacks. He is

often hasty, patchy, common ; but no verse narrative of his
time has the same pace and energy and flame, the same Mazeppa
quality by which horse and rider seem as one. In Scott the
flame is fainter, if the pace is there ; though there is more
open air and more of simple humanity in Scott's lays. Crabbe
and Wordsworth in their stories display other virtues ; they
pay the price of their patience and reflectiveness. *The Prisoner
of Chillon* and *Mazeppa*, though later, may be considered with
the six earlier tales already named.

Byron was craftsman enough to feel the vital importance of
his choice of metre, but when he chooses it wrong he cannot
leave it off ; he goes on stubbornly with heroics or with blank
verse, so that self-criticism comes too late if it comes at all.
With him, even more than with most poets, ' metre,' in Coleridge's phrase, ' paves the way to other distinctions,' and
carries a whole atmosphere and cast of diction along with it.
Byron's general poetic power varies in close accord, rising or
fading or holding its level, with his felicity of cadence or rightness of prosodic touch.

The Giaour and *The Bride of Abydos* are in the simplest of
Scott's measures, the octosyllable in simple or alternate rhyme,
which Byron uses with less than Scott's relish for pure plain
sound, but with a kind of fiery facility of his own. Unluckily,
he has also far too much of Scott's conventional phraseology,
which is itself descended from the pseudo-noble, roundabout
style of eighteenth-century verse, though it is now applied to
the scenes of Eastern adventure. Plain words like *face,
clothes, blood, horse,* are discouraged :

> His swarthy *visage* spake distress,
> But this might be from weariness ;
> His *garb* with *sanguine spots* was dyed,
> But these might be from his *courser's* side.

Nor does Byron spare to multiply his personifications, *Grief,
Passion, Woman, Misery,* or his beloved detestable italics, with
their false emphasis that covers the want of art. Indeed,
emphasis is the palpable fault of all these stories : and yet
how genuine must be the power that we feel in spite of it !
The Giaour was written as it remained, in fragments, and was
spun out by successive insertions and accretion ; ' this snake
of a poem,' Byron calls it, ' which has been lengthening its
rattles every month.' He printed it with misgiving, and judged
it more truly than his first readers. But some of its pages
keep their glory and freshness. ' He who hath bent him o'er

the dead ' has been blamed for its grammar, but its ' trailing anacoluthon ' is not the least of its beauties ; for wild regret does not always remember the beginning of a sentence, and Byron's unusually studious polishing of the lines may show that if he sinned he sinned on purpose.

The Bride, such as it is, is my first entire composition of any length (except the Satire, and be damned to it), for *The Giaour* is but a string of passages, and *Childe Harold* [in 1813] is, and I rather think always will be, unconcluded.

The Bride of Abydos is a more satisfactory story than *The Giaour,* with no lack of romantic beauty in its theme and execution. It is not invented or taken from a book, but founded on ' observations ' of Byron's own. Selim, the cousin of Zuleika, whom she supposes to be her brother, loves her contrary to the will of her father the Pacha, and both lovers perish. Byron at first had meant Selim to be Zuleika's brother indeed, and to face the consequences ; but with some regret and sense of weakness he shrank from thus following his ' observations,' whatever they may have been, and also the precedents of Ford and Alfieri :

On second thoughts, I thought myself *two centuries* at least too late for the subject ; which, although admitting of very powerful feeling and description, yet is not adapted for this age, at least this country. . . . I have therefore altered it as you perceive, and in so doing have weakened the whole.

Byron thus shunned the artistic perplexity, and the demand for exceptional sureness and purity of treatment, which the abnormal subject exacts from a poet—one wrong word may mar all—and which he successfully faced afterwards in *Parisina.* But he also shirked the problem caused by the change of theme, and his tragic idyll remains incomplete. For though Selim knows the truth of his relationship to Zuleika all the while, Zuleika, up to the moment of the disclosure, still thinks herself to be his sister. The wrench of feeling caused in her mind by the tidings that she is not, would have given no pause to Fletcher or to Massinger, who ride so jauntily over these questions of piety. Byron gives Zuleika no time to be thus troubled, for the Pacha appears on the scene the next moment. Yet this is but a mean evasion. The result is undramatic, though a nicer psychologist than Byron might have failed in the task ; and instead of drama there is a slurred pathos and a passionate rush of words. *The Bride of Abydos* is better told, however, than *The Giaour,* and more various in

rhythm, lapsing into heroic couplets, and being prefaced with
an unskilful, much-quoted imitation of Goethe's ' Kennst du
das Land ? '

In the preface to *The Corsair*, it is observed that

Scott alone, of the present generation, has completely triumphed
over the fatal facility of the octosyllabic verse ; and this is not the
least victory of his fertile and mighty genius.

But Scott's victory, as we have said, was not at all a complete
one ; and Byron had managed the measure in his own way
quite as luckily as Scott ; with more momentum and colour,
if without the same emphatic ring upon the rhymes. It was
not for his good that he now went back, in *The Corsair* and
Lara, to heroic couplets. They are narrative and not satirical
heroics. The voice is that of Crabbe, not of Pope ; and moreover it is the voice of Crabbe moralising, rather than of
Crabbe observing. Such a tune assorts oddly with the Byronic
mood, and with the grandiose figure of Conrad-Lara, ' link'd
with one virtue and a thousand crimes.' The habitual movement of the verse is heard in such a passage as this :

> There is a war, a chaos of the mind,
> When all its elements convulsed, combined
> Lie dark and jarring with perturbed force,
> And gnashing with impenitent Remorse ;

and it is bad enough, but it is Byron's own. But it often
changes to another movement, which is pure Crabbe :

> Then rose his band from duty—not from sleep—
> Equipped for deeds alike on land or deep ;
> While lean'd their leader o'er the fretting flood,
> And calmly talk'd—and yet he talk'd of blood !

Or to this, which is worse still :

> One thought alone he could not—dared not—meet—
> ' Oh, how these tidings will Medora greet ? '

But in *The Corsair* there is the glory of motion, and the flush
of battle, voyaging, and rapine ; it does not seem long for
all its eighteen hundred lines. Its ten thousand readers were
not wholly dupes, though they were not critics ; and the knowledge that the poet was living there in London, in the midst
of the legends that swarmed about him, was itself part of the
poetry.

The long story of *Lara* is nothing ; we care less for Byron's
stories, as stories, than for Scott's ; and he might have said,

like Maturin, 'emotions are my events.' In one passage
(i. 312-360) he inserts a full-length portrait of Lara, who is
probably the Conrad of *The Corsair* in a second incarnation.
These forty lines break the regular movement of the lay ;
they are a ' character ' of the old classical, eighteenth-century
sort, standing out amidst a turbid flood of passion and incident. They may be taken to represent the Byronic ' hero '
in his penultimate form : that is, before his ' positively last
appearance ' in *Manfred*. Byron's journals of the year 1814
give a clue to the notion he had formed of himself at this time :

> The more I see of men, the less I like them. If I could but say
> so of women too, all would be well. Why can't I ? I am now six-
> and-twenty ; my passions have had enough to cool them ; my
> affections more than enough to wither them ;—and yet—and yet—
> always *yet* and *but*—' Excellent well, you are a fishmonger—get thee
> to a nunnery.'

We can well see how this figure is elaborated in Lara ; the
versified ' character ' represents not so much the man that Byron
thought he was, as the man that he feared and dreamed
he might become ; magnified, of course, and draped with
rhetorical frippery :

> His early dreams of good outstripp'd the truth,
> And troubled manhood follow'd baffled youth ;
> With thought of years in phantom chase misspent,
> And wasted powers for better purpose lent ;
> And fiery passions that had pour'd their wrath
> In hurried desolation o'er his path,
> And left the better feelings all at strife
> In wild reflection o'er his stormy life ;
> But haughty still, and loth himself to blame,
> He call'd on Nature's self to share the shame,
> And charged all faults upon the fleshly form
> She gave to clog the soul, and feast the worm :
> Till he at last confounded good and ill,
> And half mistook for fate the acts of will.

Whether the picture be accurate or no, it is sincere ; and it
is only because Byron's critics were Englishmen or Scotsmen
that they could ever have doubted that. The foreign reader,
the reader of Chateaubriand, was not sceptical or surprised at
such a candour in self-analysis. And it is accurate after all ;
it really expresses the temper of Byron at the time he wrote ;
his scorn, his early compunction, his loneliness, and especially
his fatalism, always real if also a little stagey, which was
remarked upon by Lady Byron and was imputed by her, not

unplausibly, to a streak of early Calvinistic training. It is as
sincere as Dryden's self-reproaches in *The Hind and Panther*,
and is also in the same tradition of style. The final couplet
of the passage quoted might have come from one of Dryden's
rhymed plays. At other points *Lara* is a weariness, with its
forced misanthropy and Udolpho trappings :

> The waving banner, and the clapping door ;
> The rustling tapestry, and the echoing floor ;
> The long dim shadows of surrounding trees ;
> The flapping bat, the night-song of the breeze.

The thud of these lines is Crabbe's once more, but had Crabbe
written them it would have been in sarcasm. Possibly Miss
Austen read them as well as Mrs. Radcliffe ; *Northanger
Abbey* appeared four years later than *The Corsair*.

In *The Siege of Corinth*,[1] which is full of excellent fighting,
routing, and forlorn defending, Byron was on the firmer
foundation of history and local legend : a solid masonry for
which he was always the better, since it took him away from
his real or imagined self, and brought out those welcome hard
elements in his composition, of which the true destiny lay in
action. Alp, the renegade, a shadowy invented personage of
the old stamp, stands to the story somewhat as the title-
figure of *Marmion* does to Scott's poem ; he is equally pervasive, absurd, and distracting ; and the comparison suggests
one more debt of Byron to Scott, whose weakness it was to
fabricate, though on duller lines, and without anything in his
own nature to build upon, these lowering heroes, whom he,
in his turn, took from the fiction current in his youth. The
form of *The Siege of Corinth* is instructive. In going back
to the octosyllabic rhyme, Byron embroiders upon it the variations which Scott [2] had practised after hearing *Christabel* recited.
Byron assures us that he had neither heard that poem at the
time, nor read it in manuscript, and he is moved to give us
this assurance by noticing the coincidence of his lines on the
night-wind (*Siege*, 520-2) with a famous passage in Coleridge's
poem. He is therefore not guilty of having blunted or blurred
the tune of Coleridge with the original in his ears ; on the
contrary, he used and strengthened the inferior modulations
of Scott upon the same tune. This fact does not make Byron's
lines any better, but it removes our prejudice against conced-
ing their native power. In spite of the occasional clumsy
creak of his anapæstics and dactylics, they are not easy to
forget ; and the passage of which his idol, the egregious Gifford,

disapproved, is a splendid triumph of 'representative metre' in its coarser form. There is a touch of Ingoldsby jingle about it, and also of boyish delight in purely gruesome matter:

> And he saw the lean dogs beneath the wall
> Hold o'er the dead their carnival,
> Growling and gorging o'er carcass and limb, . . .

This kind of realism was to be carried further and more cynically practised in *Don Juan*.

In *Parisina* Byron faces a story of love within the forbidden degrees, that of stepson and stepmother; and there were reviewers of the day who could not pardon the choice of theme. The true defence is not that the culprits are put to death by the vindictive and self-publishing justice of the injured husband; but that Byron has shown a kind of dramatic sense, which for him is uncommon, in the whole treatment. The weight is laid neither on the crime nor the offence, but on the pleading eloquence of the young bastard Hugo, the chief sinner. Azo, Hugo's father, had first grievously wronged Hugo's mother, and then had stolen from him Parisina, his destined wife. Thus the fault of Hugo becomes intelligible without being excused, and the tale is lifted from the region of mere transgression and pathetic calamity into that of drama; it resembles, indeed, the last act of an unwritten play. Death is the solution that satisfies the tragic sense; and the shadow of death, apparent from the first, gives an almost scornful purity to the handling. The style is very plain and swift, and it is also metrically simple save in the more scenic passages like that which relates the execution of the lovers. There, the movement of *Christabel* is again heard, and is again in place.

Echoes of the style of *Lyrical Ballads* were noticed at the time in *Parisina* and *The Prisoner of Chillon*; and there seem really to be affinities, which are due to more than chance, with that heightened and impassioned diction, so bare and yet so magically shot, in his use of which Wordsworth occasionally draws near to Coleridge, and which is heard in such poems as *The Lament of a Forsaken Indian Woman*. For Byron being thus in debt the evidence is purely internal. In any case, he has moved forward from his own earlier style, and from a partial dependence on that of Scott, to one that fairly recalls 'the real language of men in a state of vivid sensation'; this 'real language' being, as Coleridge showed in his criticism of Wordsworth, inevitably exalted out of the region of possible uttered speech into that of speech idealised; the agent, or occasioning impulse, being the presence of metre. In *Parisina* we come on passages such as this, where the awkward constructions do not efface the resemblance with Coleridge :

> She feared—she felt that something ill
> Lay on her soul, so deep and chill;
> That there was sin and shame she knew;
> That some one was to die—but who ?
> She had forgotten ;—did she breathe ?
> Could this be still the earth beneath,
> The sky above, and men around ;
> Or were they fiends who now so frowned
> On one, before whose eyes each eye
> Till then had smiled in sympathy ?

And also in *The Prisoner of Chillon* :

> A light broke in upon my brain,—
> It was the carol of a bird ;
> It ceased, and then it came again,
> The sweetest song ear ever heard,
> And mine was thankful till my eyes
> Ran over with the glad surprise,
> And they that moment could not see
> I was the mate of misery.

Byron's powers of pathetic or heroic narrative, moreover, seem to have blossomed and grown, as he rid himself of his incubus, the Byronic hero : who, henceforth, is relegated to *Manfred*, and does not cast his shadow upon the rhymed tales. For *The Prisoner of Chillon* there was a historical suggestion in the imprisonment of Bonnivard ; but the experiences and emotions of the prisoner are invented. *The Prisoner of Chillon* is less a tale than an imaginary reminiscence in monologue, all high temper and lofty tenderness. The scheme of *Mazeppa* (1818, written in the year when *Don Juan* was begun) is similar ; and the piece marks the passage from Byron's earlier to his maturer narrative style. In *Mazeppa* there are embers of the lowering and revengeful hero ; but there are flickers also of the jauntiness of *Beppo*. It is the poem of a soldier ; no sedentary bard could have imagined it. Coleridge knew the pains of sleep, no man better ; but only Byron and Shakespeare, and perhaps Scott, could have described the blackness that comes and goes over the senses of the bound victim as he rides before the wolf-pack, the ' uncouth noises ' that fill his ears before his brain is ' rebaptised ' by the icy plunge in the river, and the ' sickness curdling o'er his heart ' in his final swoon. The tale is supposed to be

told by the old warrior to Charles the Twelfth, as they bivouac
in the flight after Pultowa. Byron takes the outline from
Voltaire. Four years earlier he would not have suffered
himself to be playful, nor would a story of *The Corsair* kind
have closed with the line ' The king had been an hour asleep.'

<h2 style="text-align:center">III</h2>

Before printing these two stories, and after he had left
England for ever, Byron wrote and published the rest of
Childe Harold, the third canto appearing in 1816 and the fourth
in 1818. He had this further trait of the orator, that only
to a huge audience, to the public, could he say all that was
in him ; to his friends and in his journal he is less articulate.
And he now had much more to say. Conrad and Lara, and
the earlier Harold had, after all, nothing particular to say ;
they were sick or remorseful for reasons that remained a
riddle ; their self-accusations were not proved. But in 1816
his public disaster, in which he did not feel he was at fault,
had been punished by English society, as Macaulay well
says, in one of its periodical fits of morality ; the yelp of
the world was after him, and he was credited with many
infamies. Thus the world put itself in the wrong in his eyes.
Humanly enough, he snatched at the chance of a counter-
charge to balance his self-reproach. He appealed to Europe,
which ' counted every moan,' and he became, after Goethe,
and outside politics, the personality best known in Europe.
' Self-exiled Harold wanders forth again,' and the old mask,
thinner and more transparent now, and also older and more
seared, is re-assumed. Confession and travel are again interwoven, and the poetic energy is increased tenfold, winged now
with contempt and anger, and also with a nobler insight and
ambition. It is not that of a modest, quiet nature allowing
its agony to be just overheard, or of a stoic who only breaks
his silence once and then irresistibly. There is endless clamour,
and emphasis, and repetition. Of saying a thing once for all
in its right and final form, and then holding his peace, Byron
has from first to last no idea whatever except in satire ; and
the same thing is true of Carlyle. This, rather than his broken
metre or blemished diction, is Byron's greatest failing as an
artist. His force of honest and imperious feeling far exceeds
his power over words ; and it soon becomes plain that the kind
of harmony, which he had already achieved between his style
and his materials, especially in parts of his romances, and

in his better lyrics, is disturbed (as often happens, and as is exemplified on a greater scale by the passage from Shakespeare's histories to his tragedies) by a new inrush of passion and experience, with which his language cannot cope ; so that the opening of the third canto of *Childe Harold* is noticeably harsh, and even obscure, and often positively ill-written. This fault is above all evident where Byron speaks of himself, while in the descriptive or memorial passages, which are of the kind already familiar to his hand, only that they are loftier in pitch than before, and more fervent in their power, the style is truer and more correct. How much surer, at this date, Byron's language is in observation and portrayal than in reflection or analysis, may be seen by comparing his lines on the character of Napoleon with those famous ones on the Duchess of Richmond's ball, ' There was a sound of revelry by night ' : on which the popular taste has rightly fixed, so perfectly is the balance held in them between the visible scene and the obvious yet transcendent emotions pervading it ; although the last touches of transfusing imagination of which the subject is capable might only have found words if it had fallen to De Quincey. Byron's intuition of the character of Napoleon, or of the Napoleon whom the poets saw, is, indeed, penetrating, and that by virtue of Napoleon's kinship — certainly not wholly imaginary — with himself, of their common loneliness and sombreness. But the execution is inadequate, partly because Byron will not yet allow himself the relief of irony or mockery ; although there is already plenty of it in his nature, and in his prose ; and the omnipresence of those chequering elements in Mr. Hardy's panoramic tragedy, *The Dynasts*, makes the picture a hundred times as real as Byron's. Likewise, Byron's presentment of himself, and of his vain search at the breast of nature for rest and for forgetfulness of his ' wretched identity,' whilst accurately truthful, suffers as to expression, not only from his innate carelessness of finish, or impotence to ensure it, but from the perturbing weight of his disquiet, of which he is not for a moment the master. Nor does he give himself the relief of that jesting and deliberate motley bathos, which in *Juan* is his easy resource : so that his mind remains, after all and despite his sincerity, half-expressed. But through all this imperfect or fitfully sustained handiwork there pierce the real greatness and misery, which may be called Promethean, at least in respect of their incessancy and power, although they are unconsoled by the memories of Prometheus. When all

superficial posturing is allowed for, there remains a vast and
warranted egoism, manlier far than Rousseau's, and, if less
august, nearer to us all than Wordsworth's, by virtue of the
suffering involved in it : and this egoism, luckily careless of
offending, gave a noticeable and still unexhausted impulse
to the enlargement of the European spirit. This it did, not
by making current any new and fertile thought, but by the
spectacle of a large nature, at issue with itself, and losing
itself, at least for passing solace, both in the pageant of the
past, and in a vision so splendid of the banded peoples
of the world, as should even now steel us against all the
allurements of Reaction, that sterile temptress. Carlyle's
counsel, ' Close thy Byron, open thy Goethe,' implies a
false contrast. For to open Goethe[1] is to read the song of
Euphorion, and the praise of Cain ; and thus we are led
to see Byron's emancipating power better, and to open him
again after all.

The third and fourth cantos differ in spirit : they are not
one poem, or even a poem and its sequel ; they are two
poems written in the same metre, and with certain points in
common. In the third canto the poet is alone with nature ;
and nature makes him think of Rousseau, over whose country
he has travelled, in Shelley's company and with the *Nouvelle
Héloïse* in his hand. The idealised sketch of Rousseau is the
heart of this canto ; for the sequel, describing Gibbon and
Voltaire, is but versified epigram. In Rousseau Byron saw
something of his own likeness, and that is why he is hard upon
him. Certainly *Childe Harold*, like so many other books,
could not have been written but for the *Confessions*, and would
have been more faithfully written had it been more like the
Confessions. But there is a strain in Byron's nature-worship
which comes from another source. The religion of the hills,
set forth in the thirteenth and following stanzas (' Where rose
the mountains, these to him were friends '), had been sown
in his mind when a boy, as he watched the Highland ranges
or the Malverns. He had also by now read and admired
Wordsworth. The result is Byron's noble excursion into
metaphysical poetry. It is only an excursion, though he
repeats it partially in *Manfred* and in *Cain*. He was to go
back from it to the real world which was his sphere. But
whilst making it, he attains an unwonted purity of form and
loftiness of meditation. Through communion with the hills
and the sky he escapes for a time from the chains of the body.
He is, it is true, ' a link reluctant in a fleshly chain.' But

this is snapped when the mind is set free by death, and then
he will be at home in nature :

> When Elements to Elements conform,
> And dust is as it should be, shall I not
> Feel all I see less dazzling but more warm ?
> The bodiless thought ?   The Spirit of each spot ?
> Of which, even now, I share at times the immortal lot ?

This is not the idea of *Tintern Abbey*, where the poet, in the
hour of trance, has an immediate vision of the one Being, or
immanent spirit, that animates both man and nature.   Byron
thinks rather of the naked soul revisiting the scenes in which it
had been an impassioned sharer before it became discorporate.
His lines have a touch of the rarefied flame that quickens the
poetic reasonings of Shelley, his fellow-traveller.   But his
conception is different from that in Shelley's essay *On a Future
State*, perhaps written about this time, in which any kind of
posthumous consciousness is denied.   In *Adonais*, six years
later, Shelley's Pantheism was to include, at least as an image,
the notion of a semi-personal disembodied spirit.

IV

To tell at length how Italy perfected the genius, amused the
senses and wits, and for a time consoled the heart of Byron
would be to tear whole pages out of his biography.   In the
fourth canto of *Childe Harold*, the alternate rhythm of personal
and historic passion still continues : but the proportions are
altered, for the poem is less a ' pageant of his bleeding heart '
than of Italian history and poetry.   Byron invokes the memories
of Venice, of Ferrara, of Arquà, of Rome, and of Florence.
Tasso and Ariosto, and the three great Florentines, and Rienzi,
and the Apollo in the Vatican, and the Niobe, and the death
of Venetian freedom, are shown in a series of descants and
descriptions ;   and   the   clamorous flood   of the   narrative
sweeps us over all the snags and shallows of the style, with
its frequent false splendour.   The oratory of the third canto
has become louder, hardly finer ; it has the emphasis of a man
who is resolved to forget himself : the workmanship will often
not bear looking into at all ; but then it is all meant to be
heard rather than read.   Byron's favoured scheme, by this
time, is to begin and end a stanza with a loud, memorable line,
antithetic or climacteric, and often alliterative, and to keep
the intervening lines at only a shallow depression of pitch ;

the whole verse commonly containing a single thought or
feeling, but often running over, even grammatically, into the
next for its completion. The poet whom Byron most recalls,
in his regular manner, is Dryden : in both, even when they
speak most intimately, there is the same ring, bronze and not
silver-sounding. An average stanza will show this likeness :

> The field of Freedom—Faction—Fame—and Blood :
> Here a proud people's passions were exhaled,
> From the first hour of Empire in the bud
> To that when further worlds to conquer failed :
> But long before had Freedom's face been veiled,
> And Anarchy assumed her attributes ;
> Till every lawless soldier who assailed
> Trod on the trembling Senate's slavish mutes,
> Or raised the venal voice of baser prostitutes.

There is the same carelessness, the same amplitude, though
the range of ideas is different. Dryden commanded something
like this kind of *political* diction in his verse ; but his application of it to personal portraiture and satire is beyond
Byron, who only found his power in that kind of work when
he got to the octave rhyme and the vagrant or picaresque
poem. The fourth canto, taken as a whole, is a panoramic,
slowly-passing show without any progression but that of
travel, or any unity but that of tone ; but it ends with the
lines to the ocean, where the performance does not equal
the wrath and splendour of the inspiration. The lines translated, or rather diluted, from Filicaia ('Italia, O Italia')
are one more proof of the hold Italian verse was gaining
upon Byron.

Several themes of the third and fourth cantos are taken up
at more length and leisure in separate poems of this period
(1816-1818). Some, like *The Dream*, and *Darkness*, and the
lines to Mrs. Leigh, count amongst Byron's memoirs in verse.
Others, like *Manfred*, while they grow out of and are rooted
in such personal confessions, tend to be metaphysical poetry :
Cain and *Heaven and Earth* approach this class. A third set,
such as *The Lament of Tasso*, the *Ode on Venice*, and *The
Prophecy of Dante*, are like larger and more imposing monuments set amongst the commemorative tablets and inscriptions of the fourth canto. Add to all these the letters and
journals written by Byron during the same years, with his
accounts of his loves and amusements, of Marianna Segati
and Margarita Cogni, and of his studies in the Armenian
monastery ; and we have a completer picture of his life and

spirit ; and we also see how, when once he had sounded and
shaken off his graver moods, he was ready by revulsion, and
equipped with material, for the last and greatest phase of his
production, the satiric and observant. The three types of
poem mentioned above as accessory to *Childe Harold* may be
taken in turn.

To be hated, or even to be loved, by Byron meant, as he
knew, a world-wide publicity. He had some of these vices
which, according to the code of his own class, are the worst.
Delicacy, privacy, forgiveness, he could not understand where
his foes were concerned, and he had some excuse considering
his experience ; but he should not have attacked women. He
could only work off a poisonous memory by putting it into a
poem, which he was ready to publish, or not careful to suppress. Such is the peril of crossing the path of such a man.
He assailed his wife, and her household companion ; he
gravely embarrassed his half-sister, Mrs. Leigh, by printing her
praises ; he gave to the world in *The Dream* his love for Mary
Chaworth, and related her marriage, and her insanity ; and it
is possible that he refers to her, and to injuries he had done
her, in other places. His loose tongue is his worst fault, though
he spares himself as little as others. His ruling passion was
not solitude, or travel, or misanthropy, or women, but self-
expression ; to that, like Rousseau, Byron would sacrifice
anybody and anything. It is a distinctive vice of the literary
class, with whom Byron did not like to be confounded. Poetry
is often the gainer ; and shall we strike the balance in such a
reckoning, or say that we would wish enduring verse not to
have existed, in order to save the feelings of transitory persons ?
But we may at least say that only an enduring quality in the
poem can turn the balance. *The Dream* has that quality. It
is a series, not of dreams at all, but of memories in the mask
of dreams, each of them flashing over the screen, in exquisite
outline and colour, for a moment. They are memories idealised, not distorted. For our sorrows have this universal
quality, to which our joys more seldom attain, that if they
remain quick and keen, or may stick all the deeper when
their present edge becomes blunted, yet memory, the supreme
artist, may recompose them in larger masses and nobler outline, to be a possession for ourselves if we cannot utter them,
and for the world also if we can. The coincidence of style
between the plainer and stronger parts of this poem and
similar passages of Wordsworth may easily be overlooked,
because the memories that Wordsworth hoarded were happier

and calmer; but the chosen simplicity of the rhythm and
language are like Wordsworth at his best:

> The Maid was on the eve of Womanhood;
> The Boy had fewer summers, but his heart
> Had far outgrown his years, and to his eye
> There was but one beloved face on earth,
> And that was shining on him: he had looked
> Upon it till it could not pass away;
> He had no breath, no being, but in hers;
> She was his voice; he did not speak to her,
> But trembled on her words; she was his sight,
> For his eye followed hers, and saw with hers,
> Which coloured all his objects:—he had ceased
> To live within himself; she was his life,
> The ocean to the river of his thoughts,
> Which terminated all.

Byron's blank verse has been underrated, though no doubt
it is the measure which at times he not only marred but mauled
most seriously, and which he was prone to associate with a
specially dreary kind of rhetoric. In *Darkness* (1816) there is
a miscarriage of power, but not a little force and nobility also,
which find their way into the cadence. Amongst the other
personal verses which accompany the similar passages in
Childe Harold, the *Lines on Hearing that Lady Byron was Ill*
are as meanly composed as the *Epistle to Augusta* is grave and
beautiful in finish. This *Epistle* must be separated from the
Stanzas to Augusta, with their mournful, rather juvenile,
Moore-like jingle. It is written in a slower form of the octave,
which was afterwards to be Byron's chosen instrument, and
which as yet has none of its glancing and chameleon effects of
Don Juan.

It is well to ask here whether our reading of Byron's genius
is affected by our judgment on those matters in his private[1]
life that are still under debate (1912). Do these concern the
critic as well as the biographer? In one sense they do not,
for the execution, the verse and the words, are unaltered—
they are neither better nor worse however Byron may have
lived. But to say this is not enough. For one thing, to judge
what he wrote, and even how he wrote, we must know what
was in his mind when he wrote, and this only his biography
can tell us. For another, Byron presents himself as a different
kind of artist, according as we read his poems about himself
and the feelings he imputes to his tragic heroes as a confession,
or as a dramatic invention, or as a self-deception, or as an
inscrutable compound of the three. To urge this is not to be

Byron's moral censor; the business of criticism is not to
judge the man through his works, but to understand the works,
through knowledge of the man; a clue that in Shakespeare's
case is almost denied to us. It makes a difference whether the
lyrics spoken in the first person are mainly dramatic, like
Browning's, and whether Manfred is as much a being outside
Byron as Sardanapalus. It matters whether we are to suppose
a unity of remorseful memory running through his productions,
or whether he simply takes a trait or emotion of his own, works
on it, shapes it into something that has no counterpart in fact,
and yet allows himself to be taxed with it, not caring what
men may suppose. That was the way of some of the Elizabethan sonneteers. The latter view has the merit of recognising the existence of the imagination, and of shunning the risks
of those who rake amongst false creations of the ' heat-oppressed
brain ' for evidence to lay before a jury. In the case of almost
any other writer, it would seem rational to conclude that
where the material veracity of a poem is not proved either by
documents outside itself, or by internal proof beyond all cavil,
it should be taken simply as a fabric, and be judged purely by
its performance, without that judgment being coloured by any
pretence to mark the exact line where chronicle shades off
into fantasy. This is our state of mind in presence, for example,
of Tennyson's *Love and Duty*.

Byron, however, stands apart. Macaulay and the old
reviewers saw coarsely and said bluntly that he could only
represent himself. They meant this for blame, but it is the
point of interest in Byron. The more we read him, the more
we are forced to think that he wrote sincerely when he wrote
of himself; that he was accurately true to his mood of the
moment; that he did not write dramatic lyrics; that when
he said his peace was poisoned by memories, he meant it, and
that when he said he had done amiss he meant it; that the
passions of his tragic heroes, as distinct from the occurrences
in which he fancifully set them, reflect his own—magnified,
no doubt, and melodramatised; that he really had some reason
for remorse as well as for anger; and that his way of working
off the poison was not to turn to religion, or philosophy, or
action, but to make the world his confessor.

The evidence for this interpretation is found in his letters
and journals, as well as in his poems, and in facts independently
established or inferred. Criticism is bound here to notice two
alternative theories. According to the first, the offence of
Manfred's love for Astarte is that they are brother and sister,

and Manfred is said herein to represent Byron. It is noted that *Parisina* and the first scheme of *The Bride of Abydos* show him preoccupied with themes of this order, and it is alleged that the outcries and self-reproaches of Conrad and other such personages are in truth those of Byron himself ; reflecting the torture of his mind, on which he ' lies in restless ecstasy,' sorry for the crime of Manfred. The *Epistle* and the *Stanzas* already named are, on this view, distorted from their natural and fraternal meaning. This spectral old scandal, supposed to have been laid long ago, has been again revived, and again controverted ; it is enough to say that there is no conclusive evidence that it is anything but a misconstruction. It may therefore be with satisfaction dismissed to the limbo of things unproven.

On the second view, for which the circumstantial evidence is powerful, and in some measure fresh, the clue to that profound disturbance of soul, which Byron both utters himself and imputes to his characters, is found in his feeling for the lady celebrated in *The Dream*. It is argued at length that she was the one woman whom he can properly be said to have loved, out of the many of whom he was the lover ; that their acquaintance was renewed before his marriage and after hers, and then broken off again ; further, that this breach, and her passing mental illness, and his own conduct, caused his mind the wound which wrings from him the cries of his heart ; and that his offences, whatever they were, are thus kept within the bounds of the normal. There is thus, on any theory, a core of veracity in the Byronic hero ; he does not 'take up wickedness as a subject.'[1]

The poems on Dante and Tasso may be read as interludes to the last canto of *Childe Harold*, and as fruits of the same pilgrimage. Tasso, in the high-pitched *Lament*, is made to talk like Byron and not like himself ; but his 'sacred argument,' as well as the ' bright dream ' of Ariosto, is celebrated in *The Prophecy of Dante*. Byron did not understand the graver art of Italy so well as its lighter and more motley poetry ; but the patriot soul of Italy he did understand, and in the *Prophecy* he gives expression to it. This work was written to please the Countess Guiccioli, who was shocked by the beginning of *Don Juan* and wished to turn Byron (from the true line of his genius) to higher things. We may thank her for this diversion ; it did not last long, and meanwhile it disclosed a new and lofty strain of musing in Byron. In the *Prophecy*, indeed, he unwisely attempts to copy Dante's *terza rima*. No one who

felt the secret of that measure could thus have mishandled it,
or have ignored the pause at the end of the tercet, where the
last and third wave is flung upon the shore like thunder, leaving
a silence before strength is re-gathered for the new onset.   We
feel that Byron is for ever trying to fit the movement and
copious phraseology of *Childe Harold* upon a metrical frame
that is much too strict for it, as here :

> And you, ye Men ! Romans, who dare not die,
>   Sons of the conquerors who overthrew
> Those who o'erthrew proud Xerxes, where yet lie
>   The dead whose tomb Oblivion never knew,
> Are the Alps weaker than Thermopylae ?

Yet there is greatness in the plan of the *Prophecy*, and sometimes in the execution also.   Here and there the spareness
and equilibrium of Dante's language are really suggested, as
well as the height of his temper :

> But the sun, though not overcast, must set,
> And the night cometh ; I am old in days,
> And deeds, and contemplation, and have met
> Destruction face to face in all his ways.
> The World hath left me, what it found me, pure,
> And if I have not gathered yet its praise,
> I sought it not by any baser lure ;
> Man wrongs, and Time avenges, and my name
> May form a monument not all obscure.

These lines Tennyson might have envied for their heroic
height and their purity of form ; if all had been like them,
Byron might truly have called the *Prophecy* ' the best thing
I ever wrote,' though not, perhaps, the thing that he had
written best.   He never wrote anything higher, or fuller of
historical imagination.   Few Englishmen have put themselves
in the place of Dante considered as a patriot and prophet.
The union of a free Italy, with one polity reigning and one
ennobled speech in use from Venice to Calabria, was Dante's
dream, and Byron has it also ; so that he takes, it may be
fairly said, a certain place amongst the poets of Dante's country.
His personal labours in the cause of national emancipation
were embroiled and fruitless.   But his mind had already
begun to pass on to another phase of the Italian spirit, so gay
and yet sombre, so positive and cynical and yet so fully charged
with poetry all the while : and here he was to write his best
and to do his utmost.

V

Before reaching the mighty medley of *Don Juan*, Byron's other essays in that high speculative verse, which in *Childe Harold* was a kind of parenthesis, fall to be considered. These are found in three of his dramatic pieces—dramas he carefully shuns calling them—*Manfred*, *Cain*, and *Heaven and Earth*. All of them moved Goethe's admiration and interest, which contrast with the distant and forgotten uproar of the British reviews. But are not the poems forgotten too? Certainly they contain elements of decay. The scenic-supernatural requires a great artist for its management, like the author of the *Book of Job* or of *Faust*. The sceptical audacities of *Cain* are now beatings at an open door. It might seem as if only style and craftsmanship could save such poems; and there, as we know, Byron is not to be trusted. His blank verse is capable of falling to the level of his lyrical choruses, than some of which nothing can be worse. What then remains, and was Goethe wrong in his enthusiasm? No, he was not wrong, though the lapse of time may permit us to say that he was generous. But each of these three pieces must be judged apart, for they differ in aim and in quality.

In *Manfred* the features of Byron's strange companion, half-fire and half-shadow, his ' hero ' who is so like himself, have become more gigantic, and startling, and distinct. It has been argued above that the poem may embody real memories, and the dead Astarte represent the idealised figure of an actual woman. The punishment of Manfred, who has wronged and lost Astarte, is purely mental. His death and doom appear to come, not as a last penance, but as a release from penance, and in the wake of his tameless resistance to the spirits he has conjured up. This invocation of the elemental powers, and finally·of Ahrimanes, the presiding spirit of evil, is doubtless in part suggested by memories of Goethe's *Faust*, fragments of which Lewis had translated to Byron at Coligny in 1816. But Byron disclaims any further debt, and Goethe justly praised *Manfred* for the original turn given to his own conception. For Manfred seeks in magic the secret of oblivion, but cannot learn whether it exists beyond the grave ; he too, like Faust, has been the round of human experience, and is dissatisfied ; but his experience has been that of action and emotion, not of the brain ; he has not studied, any more than Byron himself had studied ; but like Byron he has lived and thought, and has rediscovered the old enigmas, and—

whether like Byron or not, we may never accurately know—
he has known remorse for a grievous offence. Faust commits
his offence, with which his final release and salvation are
mysteriously woven up, in the course of his quest for new
experience, and it is part of the drama ; but Manfred has
sinned before the drama opens. At the crucial point Byron's
meaning is indistinct. It is not clear what is the doom or
temptation which Manfred resists when he stands up against
the demons. It is not hellfire ; and it seems to be simply the
abandonment of his will. He remains indomitable, and finds
it is ' not so difficult to die,' a phrase which, Byron protests,
contains ' the whole effect and moral of the poem.' In parts
of the work there is a fresh and wonderful beauty, to which
none of the usual criticisms of Byron's verse and language
apply ; the overture, the appeal to Astarte, the last defiance,
and even some of the lyrics claim this praise to the full. The
immortal form of Marlowe's poem, which Byron had not read,
he does not reach ; but it is only by such a comparison that
his best passages could be dulled.

  Cain, like *Heaven and Earth*, is called a ' Mystery ' ; but it
is no more a Mystery than *Paradise Lost* ; nay, not so much
of one. Like Milton's epic, it is a mixture of cosmic pageantry,
argumentation, and idyll. But, leaving aside the differences
of power and structure, it is a poem that depends much more
for its value than *Paradise Lost* does upon the argumentation,
or rather upon the poetical treatment of argument. Abstract
ideas, especially if they are controversial, can only become
poetical in one of two ways. They may form the essence or
ruling passion of characters like Marlowe's heroes or Milton's
devils ; or else they may be poetically moulded, as they are
by Lucretius, through a consummate power of style. The
two methods coincide in the speeches of Hamlet or of Satan.
Byron cannot be called a master of either. His Cain too often
resembles an eighteenth-century heretic who rediscovers some
elementary objections to the cruder forms of orthodoxy, and
states them in the most dissonant blank verse. The metrical
deafness of Byron in this play has been repeatedly censured,
and examples of it need not be given. He is uneven enough ;
but he sometimes rises to the height of the subject, and that
not only when he catches for a moment the Miltonic ring :

> *We* must bear,
> And some of his resist—and both in vain,
> His Seraphs say ; but it is worth the trial,
> Since better may not be without :—

but also when his verse is musical and his own, and when he attains the naked strength and pure pathos that are so often blurred and overlaid in his writing :

> Then what have I further to do with life,
> Since I have taken life from my own flesh ?
> But he cannot be dead !—Is silence death ?
> No ; he will wake ; then let me watch by him.
> Life cannot be so slight, as to be quenched
> Thus quickly !—He hath spoken to me since—
> What shall I say to him ?—' My brother ! ' No :
> He will not answer to that name ; for brethren
> Smite not each other. Yet—yet—speak to me.
> Oh ! for a word more of that gentle voice,
> That I may bear to hear my own again !

Cain himself, in such passages, is a living man, not merely a self-described personage. He is not merely a doubter who has read the articles in Bayle's *Dictionary* upon Abel and the Paulicians, and who is inclined to criticise the curious bargain that has been struck between the good and the evil principles of the world ; he becomes august and tragic. Byron's Byronism and Titanism almost disappear for a time. The character of Cain comes out point by point and changes ; it is not fixed in advance. And the action is kept moving by the device of quick and instantaneous retorts, which ricochet in the dialogues with Lucifer and with Abel :

Cain. Why should I speak ?
Abel.   To pray.
Cain.   Have ye not prayed ?
Adam. We have, most fervently.
Cain.   And loudly ; I
        Have heard you.
Adam.   So will God, I trust.
Abel.   Amen !
Adam. But thou, my eldest-born ? Art silent still ?
Cain. 'Tis better I should be so.
Adam.   Wherefore so ?
Cain. I have nought to ask.
Adam.   Nor aught to thank for ?
Cain.   No.
Adam. Dost thou not live ?
Cain.   Must I not die ?

This *staccato* sort of conversation shows no failure in dignity, and it is more satisfactory than the grandiose visions of the pre-Adamite inhabitants of Earth. Better written throughout, *Cain* might have been one of the great super-terrestrial dramas in the language ; indeed, with all its faults, such it is. *Heaven and Earth,* a kind of uncompleted sequel to *Cain,* has a stately subject, the mating of the sons of God with the daughters of men, and it has some of the same exaltation of tone. But it is marred by its notorious lyrics, already deplored. Byron did not go on with the biblical drama, and it may have been as well. He came back to this world, and to the bazaars, and the harems, and to the isles of Greece, and there he found his true and final habitation. But with his usual perversity, while in the act of writing *Don Juan,* he had another series of artistic escapades, of which it is well to notice the redeeming features.

Despite their narcotic dullness, Byron's historical tragedies contain some pages of clangorous rhetoric, a little poetry, and no lack of his manly spirit. The heroes are not all made in his image—which may account for the dullness—and the work served to take him out of himself. It was not only when he read Armenian in the Mekhitarist Convent that his ' mind wanted something craggy to break upon '; he flung himself on the available authorities and documents, and like Ben Jonson piqued himself on accuracy. He had also the same heed for symmetry of construction, and proved himself once more a child of classicism in his craze for the ' unities.' He is like Jonson in little else, unless it be in a fondness for huge monologues ; for the speeches of Marino Faliero are nearly as long as those of the earlier dramatist's Catiline. There is no Roman rigour, however, in Byron's style, but a diffuse monotony broken by a few passages highly wrought. *Marino Faliero,* in spite of the author's excuses, suffers from insufficient motive, for the insult offered to the Doge is altogether too petty to account for his treason ; and Byron's lively page of examples in his Preface, where he proves that small occasions, like ' the basin of water spilt on Mrs. Masham's gown,' may alter great events, only shows that such themes are real, but by no means that they are dramatic. They are, in fact, only justifiable in a novel, or at best in a comedy. There is some pathos in *The Two Foscari,* but it is frittered away; and the verse, not unlike that of Massinger, moves along a low, level, tiresome tableland. But Massinger's theatrical sense is absent. Indeed, Byron resented these dramas being acted, and wrote them only to be read. *Sardanapalus* is much fuller of poetry and pageantry. It may be noted with how little relish Byron describes mere luxury. The poet of *Don Juan* was too fierce and virile to be a true voluptuary : there is more of that character in Coleridge, or even in Moore. The

orgies of Sardanapalus therefore leave little impression, and he
only ceases to be a puppet when he begins to play the hero.

Byron's two remaining dramas are founded on forgotten
novels of the hour. In the endless and lugubrious desert of
Werner there are some springs of fresh water; but much of it
is merely the prose of Harriet Lee's *Kruitzner* strung into slow
iambics. There is little in the piece except an idea which
might have been made dramatic. A father commits a theft,
and his son, without his knowledge and in order to screen him,
commits a murder and then fathers it on an innocent man.
The son further falls in love with the daughter of the victim;
this is Byron's precious addition to his original. He crowds
the full revelation of the plot into the very last page. The
story had fascinated him while a boy, and he chose this merciless fashion of discharging it from his mind. *The Deformed
Transformed*, on the contrary, is full of poetry, and also of a
dæmonic energy which is explained by the subject. Arnold,
the deformed hunchback, sells his soul to the powers of evil
in exchange for the gift of beauty, and assumes the shape of
the young Achilles. The tempter is a coarse version of Goethe's.
The scene between the hunchback and his cruel mother has all
the virulence of Byron's boyish memories, which are incomparably well imagined in Disraeli's *Venetia*. They were
deepened by his incessant reflection on his lameness, which all
observers have agreed was a lifelong poison to his happiness;
a poison which, after all, is not so strange as might be thought,
if we remember his passion for the perfection of physical
beauty. Seen in this light, Byron's self-consciousness becomes
less purely morbid. His hunchback, thus transformed, comes,
incongruously enough, to share in the Sack of Rome. The
poem remains a fragment; for how could it have ended save
in Marlowe's fashion, and who could rival Marlowe? But
meantime Byron had hit upon the only form that left him quite
free to do what he was born to do.

VI

This task was to transplant the Italian medley-poem, with
its vehicle the *ottava rima*, into English, and therewith to enlarge
its scope indefinitely. In a Scottish dress, the measure had
been used for *Anster Fair* by Tennant. But Byron found his
immediate pattern in the witty and curious sally of John
Hookham Frere,[1] Canning's accomplice in *The Anti-Jacobin*,
and afterwards to be famed as the most vivid and congenial

translator of Aristophanes. In 1816 Frere had retired from
diplomacy, after twice acting as plenipotentiary in Spain and
facing much criticism during and after the campaign of Sir
John Moore. He settled down at home, and in 1817 produced his *Prospectus and Specimen of an intended National
Work, by William and Robert Whistlecraft, of Stowmarket in
Suffolk, Harness and Collar Makers. Intended to comprise
the most Interesting Particulars relating to King Arthur and his
Round Table.* Of this ' national work,' whose title recalls the
pleasantries of *The Anti-Jacobin,* two cantos were first published, and two more followed in 1818. Frere's fancy had been
fired by reading some extracts from Pulci in Ginguené's
Histoire littéraire de l'Italie; and

it appeared that his ingenious and humorous assumption of the
vulgar character and vernacular phrase and rude popular attempts
at poetry among his countrymen were capable of being transferred,
mutatis mutandis, to the English nation and the present time.

In this spirit Frere, after translating scraps of Pulci, produced
Whistlecraft; but the poet is always overpowering the burlesquer,
and the spirit of grace and beauty invades his fantastic legend.
The giants who dwelt near Carlisle, and the ladies whom they
stole, and the knights who rescued the ladies, and the friars who
finally repulsed the giants, are an excellent cast of mock-romantic
dramatis personœ. The conduct and spirit of the story, which
is no story at all, often remind us of Peacock, and so does the
scholarly finish of the wit and versification. The fishing
Brother John, and the quarrel over the intrusive abbey bells,
are in somewhat the strain of *Maid Marian.* There is the
same love of streams and mountains, and the same uncertainty whether the next sentence will be serious or playful.
Frere, however, has a larger poetic sweep than Peacock, and
his management of the octave is effortless and full of variety.

The steps of Byron's initiation into this style are told by
himself. He had read Merivale's[1] scraps from Pulci, published
in 1806-7, and his *Orlando in Roncesvalles,* and some of Casti
and Forteguerri ; but he was first inspired to write by Frere
rather than by Frere's Italian creditors :

Mr. Whistlecraft has no greater admirer than myself. I have
written a story in eighty-nine stanzas in imitation of him, called
Beppo (the short name for Giuseppe, that is, the *Joe* of the Italian
Joseph), which I shall throw you into the balance of the fourth canto
to help you round to your money ; but you had perhaps better
publish it anonymously (To Murray, Oct. 1817).

The light, good-humoured, and gently malicious *Beppo* came
out in 1818 : it is dashed, harmlessly enough, with Byron's
ready vulgarity. *Beppo*, unlike *Don Juan* and *The Vision of
Judgment*, is without a sting. The long-lost husband, bronzed
like a Turk, returns to find his wife and her lover : accommoda-
tions follow, and there is no tragedy. It is like some anecdote
in Byron's letters, and the more his verse resembles his letters
the more it expresses him. This is not to say that in his letters
he is not a poet ; but he is a poet whose eyes glance with the
mischief of the satirist, a poet who is not at the moment sick
with his own disenchantment, but who is, rather, sick of it ;
and this is the mood of *Beppo* itself. The ground-tone is
observation and free, cheery irony ; high poetry is in the
background, or it breaks out from the irony rather than
reproves it. In *Childe Harold* the irony, when it came (as
in the omitted passages), had disconcerted and defeated the
poetry. This gradual inversion and approximation of the
two elements in Byron is, as we have implied, the great event
in his history as a poet. It is a change that did not come all
at once ; and it was much interrupted ; for *Cain* and the
heavy dramas were written in the same years as *Don Juan*.
But it worked steadily all the time and became at last complete.

Here, though it was written after the beginnings of *Don
Juan* and did not appear till 1822 (in *The Liberal*), may be
noticed the translation of the first canto of Pulci's *Morgante
Maggiore*. The literal, somewhat wooden performance is far
inferior to its precursor *Beppo* in gaiety, in lightness, and in
the reckless clink of apparently improvised rhymes. Nor is
it equal to Merivale's earlier rendering from Pulci, which is
dexterous enough and also fairly close. If Byron had read
Merivale, he forgot or did not profit by him. The verse is
not so lively as the notes ; there is nothing so good in it as
Byron's reference to his translation of 'un gran punzone in
su la testa ' as ' such a punch upon the head':

It is strange that Pulci should have literally anticipated the
technical terms of my old friend and master, Jackson. . . . [It]
is the exact and frequent phrase of our best pugilists, who little
dream that they are talking the purest Tuscan.

Beppo was published in February 1818, and *Don Juan* was
begun in the autumn. Meanwhile Byron was encouraged in
the vein by another English practitioner, William Stewart
Rose,[1] whose translation, or rather adaptation, of Casti's
Animali Parlanti did not come out under his name till 1819,

but who had made the style his own, The rhyming letters
of Rose to Byron and to Walter Scott in the octave are in the
manner of Frere, with a jigging boldness of their own added.
In May Byron received the lines describing the boredom of
Venice :

> And yet we dine at half past one or two ;
>   Not that we 've either heart, or hope to eat,
> But that we do not know what else to do ;
>   For when at that long-wish'd-for hour we meet,
> We gaze despondingly on roast and stew,
>   Exchange sad looks and curse the carrion-meat,
> The stall which fed it, and the grass which fill'd it,
> The slave who cook'd it, and the knave who kill'd it.

This epistolary talk of a wild companion, whose notions run
quickly into rhyme, and catch the ennui of the moment, or
its undignified hunger, or its fleeting improper quip, or its
petulance, is the very basis of *Don Juan* itself ; it is the note
to which that poem returns, after whatever bursts of poetry,
passion, or serious satire. No wonder Byron wrote of these
verses :

> They are good and true—and Rose is a fine fellow—and one of the
> few English who understand Italy—without which *Italian* is nothing.

We understand *Don Juan* better when we think of its style
as a kind of dialect of these Italianised wits, and the proper
instinctive medium for the humours, shrugs, spurts of temper,
and tales of the country. Whilst writing it, Byron seems to
have read deeper in Berni and Ariosto, though his debt to
them must not be overrated. He talks about them rather
than uses them. Ariosto he praises nobly in *The Prophecy of
Dante*, and he leans upon the precedent of *Orlando Furioso*
when he is driven to the wall to defend his inclusion of venture-
some and ribald matter. In truth his aim, like his ground-
tone, is quite different. Ariosto's purpose in his medley is to
create a thing of beauty touched with lightness and humour ;
and his supple and profound plastic instinct rests upon the
love of beauty. Byron wishes, in the main, to jest and pierce
and scarify ; his interludes of beauty and tenderness are many,
and some of them long, but they are still interludes. His
plastic power is not less than Ariosto's, but it is otherwise
directed. His trick of self-interruption by means of abrupt
bathos is unlike the delicate drops and easily moulded transitions of the *Orlando Furioso*. It is this difference that makes
Don Juan, with its appanage *The Vision of Judgment*, the
clearest mirror of Byron himself.

For if *Don Juan* is not the loftiest in spirit, it is the greatest, because the freest and the richest, of Byron's writings ; the most enduring, and the most perfectly done, and the longest ; shoreless in its talent, and the fullest and final expression of the man.   That it should have been written at the same time as his dramas, points to a curious dualism in the poet who could thus work off, in a fashion often prolix and ponderous enough, his more factitious and rhetorical vein, whilst, as though at another table in the same room, he was coining his real mind into the verse that will for ever form his greatest glory.   He does not seem to have known the difference between the two species, at one of which he plodded away, making plays which are not meant to be played and often can scarcely be read, while the other is the vehicle for all his passion, irony, and knowledge of the world.   Here, once more, he is at the mercy of the form that he happens to be using.   In *Don Juan* he found a form that excluded nothing which he had to say, whereas the tale, the pilgrimage, the vision, and the drama, had each of them excluded one thing or another that it was in him to say.   The planless, limitless poem, with its motley scene, was the only kind whose moods could and must change as fast as Byron's own.   It fed and satisfied his passion for the unrestrained and the universal, while it demanded, in particulars, the utmost vivacity of tone and rightness of finish.   It gave him also something which even his prose could not give him ; for he might now, on occasion, rise as high as he would, without feeling that he was going beyond the powers of his medium ; in his prose he feels this risk, and rarely rises ; or when he does, he can become turgid.   His range of tone in *Don Juan* is thus even wider than Ariosto's. He is only called upon to do each thing well as it comes, and not to flag ; and to this call he is equal.

Don Juan begins with the high-spirited, cynical comedy of Donna Julia, continues with the ruthless Defoe-like realism of the shipwreck, and rises next into the noble and ardent beauty, touched with defiance and pleasantry, of the idyll of Haidée.   Each of these episodes is on a different level of art, and answers to a different kind of literature.   The first canto is matter for a play somewhat of the type of Machiavelli's *Mandragola*, except that it is bitterly gay instead of being, like the Italian's, at bottom cold.   The long tirade, uttered by Donna Julia whilst her husband is searching everywhere for Juan except where he ought, is of a comic boldness which no English audience since Congreve's would have endured ;

but it is, in its essence, of the theatre. The flashes of poetry, like the description of Julia as she sinks back after her speech, strike us as incongruous, or as wrung from the poet in spite of his mood. The shipwreck and cannibal interludes that follow are of another make, being pieced from various voyages recording real incidents ; and Byron sometimes versifies, with the bare change into rhyme, long stretches from his documents, in the perverse manner he had adopted in *Werner*. Defoe would not have ramped and gibed over the man-eating episode, but would have trusted to bare recital. We need not have weak nerves to find something less than human in Byron's jokes, which fall so jauntily on the rhyme :

> And such things as the entrails and the brains
>   Regaled two sharks, who followed o'er the billow—
>   The sailors ate the rest of poor Pedrillo.

There is something of the cub in glee of this kind. But when he is telling the story of Haidée, Byron only drops in a discord when he remembers that he has sworn to do so. He is describing one of the few things that he still spares ; and his spirit here is that of Gautier's saying : ' Il n'y a rien de plus sacré que les caresses de deux êtres qui sont tous deux jeunes et tous deux beaux.'

Too seldom does he thus yield himself to the charm of pure beauty, too seldom does he care to bring us under it ; his plastic power is marred by his passion of anger ; his hand shakes ; he does not see steadily ; and he talks away, splendidly it may be, but without any clear message to the poetic senses. Or he deals in large, garish eastern scene-painting, doubtless accurate, but easily-fading. Or he sets in the middle of his stage persons who are not simple or real, or at least are not detached from himself. Not so here ; Juan and Haidée are themselves, and yet for once they are neither creatures of satire, nor yet are they the men and women of Byron's lays, who are made indistinct by a kind of fiery mist ; they sit clear and distinct in the evening light. The touches of pleasantry are, for Byron, gentle ; he is paternal, and, though not for long, he is solemn ; and the style is perfect, beautiful, and natural for a longer time than it remains anywhere else in his writings. The negative, defiant strain is excluded by the conditions in which he has placed his lovers ; on that coast there are no laws to break, except those of Lambro the buccaneer, who is to take his own kind of vengeance ; but for the moment all such omens are forgotten. Discord soon re-enters, and Byron drops to one of his cheap and candid descants against marriage. Yet in a moment, in course of the fourth canto, he reveals a new power, and invents for us a new pleasure. The home-coming of Lambro, and the description of the festivities he finds awaiting him, of the dancing and the feasting and the dresses, in its happy and lively truth, crossed with ill auguries and with bloodshed threatening at the season of prayer, is one of Byron's greater achievements ; and Lambro, if he has touches of the Corsair, is a being full of human rage and sorrow. The fate and death of Haidée are terrible but probable, as the novels of Hope and Morier are enough to show.

This was an idyll with a tragical close ; in the scenes with Gulbeyaz and the ladies of the seraglio, which form the next great episode, the proportions of the beautiful and the comic are quite different. Beauty is present, but intermittently : and there is abundance of comedy, broad, rich, not ill-tempered, and of course voluptuous. 'I can't help that,' wrote Byron ; ' Ariosto is worse.' He could only have helped it by leaving out the story ; if he was to tell the story, he could not have told it better. For in making his Eastern women creatures of one emotion at a time, Byron knew of what he was speaking ; and they are here individualised as far as may consist with the truth. Writing for men and travellers, and not for any kind of *théâtre blanc,* he would not leave the Oriental senses undescribed : but he never glances at their perverser side, and the unnatural has no place in the pages of *Don Juan.*

Byron's long and lively account of the Siege of Ismail is only here and there depressed by his use of his documents, or recalls in its literalism his treatment of the shipwreck. His declamations against war are commonplace, and do not accord with his extreme relish in portraying it. There is plenty of sarcasm on ' those butchers in large business, your mercenary soldiers '; but the story might have been told, as far as its spirit goes, by one of themselves—by a hard fighter not insensible to the heroism of the Turkish scorn of death or to the pathetic tale of the child who is just rescued from the Cossacks. The sheer fun of killing and pillaging is not forgotten either ; and the bewildered confused perception of the fight by those who are engaged in it recalls the description of Waterloo by Byron's acquaintance, Beyle, in *La Chartreuse de Parme.*

The *Keckheit,* or nimble impudence, which the venerable Goethe applauded in *Don Juan,* vowing that it excelled Ariosto's own, comes to its height in the picture of Catherine of Russia. Byron moves with wonderful freedom and lightness in this veneered barbaric world, of which he only knew through books published in his lifetime, or perhaps from the recollections of acquaintance. It is, no doubt, a 'nefarious empirical world,' like that which the laudable Eckermann found in *Beppo*; but the sense of its vanishing sparkle and transiency is never suffered to flag. And Juan, though he does not resist what no youth could have resisted, is made to keep a kind of soul of his own; he has enough of his servitude, of his 'duty'; for

> perhaps, in spite of duty,
> In Royalty's vast arms he sighed for beauty;

and, to escape too long a humiliation, he is made to fall sick and is hurried off to England. Byron had left his country for more than six years; he now started to pay the last instalment of his dues to her memory.

He had worked off much of his mere fume and blind self-defeating wrath before he thus sat down to join the novelists. His latter cantos are a half-way house between the stout, male fiction of the eighteenth century and the satiric social writing of the nineteenth. The scene on Shooter's Hill where Juan pistols the highwayman is like a page of Smollett, and must have been relished by Scott. But the pell-mell picture of town society and the marriage market, of 'Norman' (which is Newstead) Abbey, with its party of noble persons and eccentrics, touches Peacock on one side and Disraeli on the other, though Byron's aim was different from theirs. He had a resurgence of his younger, pre-diluvian memories, which had been working clear underground whilst the Cains and Manfreds were taking shape, and which his immersion in Italian life must have sharpened by contrast. His earlier diaries are full of the sort of material on which he now drew. In one (18th Dec. 1813) he describes the patrician ladies whom he saw in the boxes at Covent Garden, some of them divorced, and others 'divorceable.' It is just like a page of *Don Juan*. He now meant to turn the tables on the world that had cast him out, and to give his poem some show of serious reason for existing. It was not all self-deception when he said that his task was to expose hypocrisy, to show London its own face in a glass, and to prove that the English are 'not a moral nation.' Who were they, that they should throw stones at Byron? So he takes the old Regency life, with its dashing, brutal surface, more or less ceremoniously whitewashed, and its dandyism, and its arbitrary code, and its greed for enjoyment, and he does his best to represent it. Yet across this purpose cuts still another strain of reflection. In those six years of exile things at home had altered, had passed away, with amazing speed, and Byron is the chronicler who saves them from being forgotten :

> Where is Napoleon the Grand ? God knows !
>   Where little Castlereagh ? The devil can tell !
> Where Grattan, Curran, Sheridan—all those
>   Who bound the Bar or Senate in their spell ?
> Where is the unhappy Queen, with all her woes ?
>   And where the Daughter, whom the Isles loved well ?
> Where are those martyred saints the Five per Cents ?
> And where—oh, where the devil are the Rents ?
> Where 's Brummell ? Dished. Where 's Long Pole Wellesley ? Diddled.
>   Where 's Whitbread ? Romilly ? Where 's George the Third ?
> Where is his will ? That 's not so soon unriddled . . .

But the Babel still goes on, and is fuller of cant than ever, and Byron is the man to give it a parting kick. The last cantos (xi.-xvii.) are thus in effect a new poem ; a sequel to the first ten, but penned in another spirit and with another, a more concentrated purpose.

At first Byron is tired and slow in getting to his new task. The style flags, the rhymes, especially in the critical fifth and sixth lines of the stave, are oftener forced, and once he writes a whole canto, the thirteenth, which is pure disquisition without incident. London cramps him more than Asia or St. Petersburg ; he has to move chafing amidst stiffer social forms. But Lord Henry and Lady Adeline, the cold, admirably bred English public man and his spouse, are portraits worthy of the author of *Coningsby*. The set picture of the Abbey and of the shadowy humourists there assembled is ordinary work ; but all is retrieved when the Duchess of Fitz-Fulke comes on the scene. Until the other day *Don Juan* ended with a true surprise of comedy or farce, the appearance of her ' frolic Grace ' in Juan's quarters in the disguise of the local ghost or Black Friar ; and the two closing lines are the most audaciously bad in the whole poem. A broken sequel, however, is now unearthed, and forms a seventeenth canto. The by-play of the Lady Adeline, and the portrait of Aurora Raby, who plays no part in the tale, refresh the interest meanwhile (cantos xiv.-xvi.), and the end of *Don Juan* is as lively, after all, as the beginning. In Aurora Raby Byron makes the amends to his countrywomen which he owed. To the last, he is ever ready to return upon his own cynicism, and then to return to it, with that shuttle-like swiftness of revulsion which lies at the midst of his nature and is a clue to his poetic method.

VII

Behind this whole body of writing lie Byron's two central traits, his mobility and his self-consciousness. Every observer, from Trelawny to Lady Blessington, from Medwin to Shelley, and from Lady Byron to Mrs. Leigh, bears witness to one or other of these traits, or to both. Often he seems to have no self to come back to, unless it be some diseased core of sensibility, intensified by his lameness, his exile, his wrongs, his losses, and his regrets. But then this impression is not final, and is even false. Stand at a little distance, and the larger traits of Byron's nature come out clearer. Its two great facets, each with endless *reflets* of its own, are soon to be distinguished :—passion and satire, the ' romanesque ' and the positive, dream and description, engrossment with his own heart and watchfulness of the world. Each of these is ever ready to flash out ; so that Byron's mind is like a double-coloured light, revolving now slowly, now so quick that both lights are blended into a composite third, but never long at rest. Only in *Don Juan*, and perhaps in *The Vision of Judgment*, do we see the whole Byron ; and yet not even here the whole ; for already his passionate self-consciousness has taken a different hue, its red spark is altered, and Byron has worked off most of his ' Byronism ' and left it behind him. To the last the style and metre remain the precise expression of his new consciousness and of his everlasting mobility. The anticlimax, the cynical parenthesis in the midst of sentiment, the mischievous clang of the rhymes, single, double, triple, and even quadruple, are the technical expression of his soul. He never long forgets himself either in romance or in realism, though the realism is in the ascendant. Juan is sea-sick, in the midst of remembering Donna Julia, and the verse lurches with the ship. He is restive and dreams of beauty and youth even in the arms of an empress. If he submits to Catherine, he refuses Gulbeyaz : 'the prison'd eagle will not pair' : but the scene in the seraglio follows at once ; a piece of pure beauty and roguery, stained with the vulgarity which in Byron is never far off and into which he falls so deep. This inherent changefulness of *Don Juan*, it is no paradox to say, gives the poem its unity.

For Byron's medium to reflect him so perfectly, he has to manage it to perfection, and this he does. The full and splendid sail of the rhythm, its varied and harmonious dip and rise, its union of faultless single stanzas into a continuous and unflagging though ever-broken movement, have been praised by the masters, who are also the judges, of versification. The rhyming measures of *Childe Harold* lacked ease and naturalness ; those of the narrative lays were too facile and lacked salience. Wit, humour, and irony were almost absent in both. But now, dancing in the free, loose chain of the octave, Byron whirls and flings it into infinitely altering and glittering curves, which yet preserve the common law determined by the framework of the rhymes. Starting from the refined and dexterous craft of Frere and Rose, and beckoned forward by the larger freedom of Ariosto and the Italians, he enlarges for English the liberties of the measure, and crashes wickedly into depths of metrical bathos, or rises nobly to a summit of metrical rightness and beauty, in such a fashion as to have warned off all effectual rivals. *Don Juan*, therefore, is one of the larger achievements of poetry in Byron's time, and is to this hour as fresh as the more delicate or the loftier things of Wordsworth or of Keats.

The Vision of Judgment (1822), despite its likeness of form and temper, is more than a mere splinter of *Don Juan*. There is the same swift alternation or confusion of moods, and they are echoed by the versecraft in the same way, but there are new ingredients added. The poem is not merely a parody, point by point, of Southey's tribute to George III., but a gay burlesque of Milton's celestial scenery and persons. Yet neither is it this entirely ; for it becomes at moments a serious and passionate echo of Milton, whose strain Byron for the moment assimilates ; though at the next moment, ashamed of being in earnest, he claws and profanes Milton in revenge for the power that Milton exerts upon him. This does not matter to Milton, nor does it much hurt Byron. At any rate, with the interview of Satan and Michael the strength of the poem begins. After the blunt farcical opening, and the political oratory aimed at King George (which reminds us oddly of Macaulay's against Charles the First), there enters ' a Spirit of a different aspect.' The influence of the epical figure of Satan upon romantic verse and fiction, and upon Byron's preconception of himself, has often enough been noticed already. Here, he is just beginning to return upon it, to take it humorously ; and yet some of the old spell is still upon him. The heroic style is heard in the encounter between the two potentates :

> There was a high, immortal, proud regret
> In either's eye.

That is sincere, but it is the old Byron ; and here is the new
one :

> Yet still between his Darkness and his Brightness
> There passed a mutual glance of great politeness.

The pageant of the ' cloud of witnesses,' and the conjura-
tion of Wilkes and Junius and Southey, is a wonderful performance in the savage-grotesque, and perhaps it was this
part that Goethe, when Crabb Robinson read him the poem,
' enjoyed like a child,' exclaiming *Toll ! Ganz grob ! Himm-
lisch ! Unübertrefflich !* Stanza 24, the picture of Satan, he
declared ' sublime.' In his treatment of Southey Byron, like
Dryden in similar cases, keeps his temper well in hand, and
wins by his artistic control of his hatred : it is otherwise in
his prose preface, where he merely declaims. There is a true
Aristophanic glee and buoyancy in the ending, when the
Laureate's production of his MS. sends the whole assembly
shrilling away into the inane, and King George slips quietly
into heaven : a consummation that is meant as a display of
not ill-humoured tolerance for King George, and not as a
criticism upon heaven. Charles Lamb must have had such
passages in mind when he 'said that Byron had written only one
good-natured thing, and that was *The Vision of Judgment.*'
The element of travesty becomes drowned in comedy, as the
dance of the rolling and clashing stanzas quickens to a riot
of laughter.

The poetry and prose, it may be added, of Byron's nature
are intertwisted in the octave stanza, whose make and tradition predestined him for its consummate use. Its great secret
is the anticlimax, which slips in everywhere ; sometimes in
the middle of the stanza, oftener at the end, falling on the
chime of the couplet ; now and then it is deferred for two
stanzas or more. It is always surprising, though always
expected, and is the rhetorical counterpart of Byron's ingrained
habit of watching and returning on himself. It is sometimes
painful ; it can be, with some inveteracy, vulgar ; but it is
all the more Byron for that, and it is an honest trope in his
hands. There is nothing gradual about his anticlimax, no
delicate transition, but a downward jerk from the beautiful
to the harshly humorous—to what the Germans call *das Derbe*.
Now and then, as we have seen, the process is reversed ; Byron
escapes from satire into a harmonious world of imagination.
But usually he prefers to complete his fall, and to start again
on a new flight which is broken by a new fall. This habit
would be tiresome but for its sincerity and lively wit. Byron

has more vivacity than most of our narrative poets between Chaucer and Browning ; he is one of the few masters of sarcasm and jesting delineation who have used English verse in a large way ; and he will be read for this achievement when the names of most of his censors are forgotten even by the learned.

Whilst finishing *Don Juan* he wrote his last story, *The Island* (1823), which contains some of the same ingredients —a mutiny at sea, a fight, an idyll, and exotic scenery ; and there is the same mixture of romance and pleasantry. The language is sometimes artificial, and the couplets often old-fashioned in strain. The first part of the tale is taken from Lieutenant William Bligh's sober *Narrative of the Mutiny on Board the Bounty* (1790), and Byron's feverish manner is in quaint contrast with the original. Bligh observes, of one critical occasion : ' The guard around me had their pieces cocked, but on my daring the ungrateful wretches to fire, they uncocked them ' ; and this becomes in the poem :

> The levelled muskets circle round thy breast
> In hands as steel'd to do the deadly rest.
> Thou dar'st them to their worst, exclaiming ' Fire ! '
> But they who pitied not could yet admire, etc.

This is bad in its own kind ; and not much better told is the incident of the sailor who held a shaddock to the thirsty lips of his captain while in durance. It might seem as if the lesson of *Lyrical Ballads* had been preached in vain, when we watch this degenerate reversion to an else obsolete poetic diction :

> But, soon observed, this guardian was withdrawn,
> Nor further Mercy clouds Rebellion's dawn.

Byron does not go on to paraphrase Lieutenant Bligh's story of his voyage of four thousand miles in an open boat. He turns for his sequel to another authority, the *Account of the Tonga Islands* (1817), by William Mariner, one of the most absorbing and best-told records of travel in the language. Mariner was marooned on the islands, stayed four years, learnt and remembered the language, the customs, and the politics of the natives, and on his return to London, using the competent and friendly pen of Dr. Martin, set down his experiences. His book is of scientific value, and the instinct of Mariner and his colleague for the points of human and picturesque interest is never at fault. From it Byron took his picture of the isle of Toobonai, which is not full of witchery or ' noises ' like Prospero's, but of breadfruit and feasting, of life and

colour, of love and bravery, of white sailors and dark women.
The idyll of Neuha and Torquil, faithfully repeated by Mariner,
glows like a jewel in the poem, and Byron's romantic workmanship is here at its very best. This belated story in verse
shows that he was not exhausted, and that new springs of
poetry, a new sense of beauty, were quickening in him when
he died.

VIII

At home Byron's glory has declined, and the reasons are
intricate. Perhaps there are few to whom, as to the present
writer, he remains an inspiration and a living force. The
taste of the delicate, under the sway of Wordsworth, Tennyson, and their successors, has been led to demand from poetry
a conscious nobility of thought, or a consummate finish, which
Byron does not give. (The frank, mocking representation of
society on a large scale has been taken from poetry and given
over to the novel. But the novel, in the hands of Dickens
and Thackeray and their contemporaries, was timid beside *Don
Juan*—as timid in comment as in topic.)Nor does the novel
in any case admit of the soar and glow, the personal outbreak
and confession and fleer, and the rush of language, that belong
to poetry, any more than it admits of the glory of metre. But
the truth is that no English writer of either verse or prose
since Byron has had at once the courage, the zest, and the
aptitude for the same task. Poetry may have become franker
in the record of casuistical passions and intimate lusts ; but
it has never again broadened to the business of depicting
battles and seraglios and the high comedy of intrigue, and of
enveloping these things in a buoyant and bitter commentary.
This decline of energy, combined with the change of taste, has
hurt Byron's fame. The flashy side of his romances and their
personages has been all too painfully seen, and despised, and
indeed exaggerated. The futile, delighted horror with which
his first outpourings were received was bound to provoke
revolt and excessive censure ; such a critical reaction was
needful ; but there has never been a sufficient reaction against
the false censure of Byron. His satires, too, were at first read
with a silly kind of reprobation, or with a callow kind of
wonder, but not with the alert and mischievous sympathy,
crossed with protest, which they demand. His frequent and
portentous blemishes of form were also sure to be found out,
and in their turn over-blamed.

To these drawbacks the foreign readers of Byron are

naturally not a little blind. All the same, the foreign estimate of his greatness is truer and sounder than the English estimate. It would take a syndicate of scholars to describe his influence.[1] He has affected the spirit of poetry more than any modern man except Shakespeare and Goethe, and on the whole he has deserved to do so. His service was not of the same character as Scott's. He did not create a new literary form capable of infinite life and development. His pilgrimage-poems, his romantic narrative-poems, his medley-poems, were copied often enough; they have proved ephemeral kinds. But three traits in Byron contributed to the impression that he made upon Europe. There is, first of all, his 'Titanism,' his rebellious, impassioned self-description and self-assertion. To this instinct, coming straight down from Rousseau and *Werther*, he gave more potent expression than all other poets put together. This is the lyrical, introspective Byron, who makes the world his confessional. In Lamartine and Heine, in Espronceda and Leopardi, in Scandinavia and in the Slav countries, his voice is echoed. Secondly, there is Byron the satirist and observer, the Byron of *Don Juan*, in whom the passionate and lyrical element is blended with something hard and outspoken and courageous—blended, that is, with the revulsion from itself. This is the real, the great, the ultimate Byron, and yet has affected literature less than the other, because to write a *Don Juan* it was necessary to be Byron, and not enough to be Alfred de Musset. But, thirdly, there is Byron the liberator, the poet of the 'Isles of Greece,' the hero of Missolonghi, the prophet who cried that 'blood will be shed like water and tears like mist, but the peoples will conquer in the end'; the voice of the uprising against the Holy Alliance and the advocate of insurgent nationalities. This Byron did not write so much, or so good, poetry as the other two; but it was he that struck the imagination and kindled the soul of patriot poets everywhere; and it is he who has earned a permanent place in the modern history of the struggle for liberty.

If we come ‘back to literature, and to Byron's permanent place in it, the song of Euphorion is still his epitaph :

> Scharfer Blick die Welt zu schauen,
> Mitsinn jedem Herzensdrang,
> Liebesgluth der besten Frauen
> Und ein eigenster Gesang.

—‘A song of his very own’;—Goethe's words are true, and yet the greatness of Byron as a writer is not mainly a greatness

in song. Nor is his poetic greatness, again, achieved in the
highest fields of all. He only does his best, he only fully
utters himself, in a mixed and discordant sort of poetry, which
he writes better than any one else. Hence his feeling for
beauty and his power to clothe it in form are broken, are
interrupted, and we do not know if they would ever have
been otherwise. The paradox is that when his feeling for
beauty is in the ascendant, he fails to master his form, or does
not master it for long ; he never, indeed, masters it completely
for more than a few pages. He is only perfect when this feeling
is not paramount but is jarred and crossed with something
antipathetic to it. He is most faultless in his letters and
familiar prose, and in the verse which corresponds to them.
To read his prose brings us nearest, perhaps, to the fountains
of his power, which are not exhausted. Yet Time, the trier
of poets, has, even so, left much of Byron intact. The discrimin-
ations here essayed are only the impressions of a single critic ;
and it will be long before Byron's account is balanced ; for
there is always the sense of his personal power to be reckoned
with.

CHAPTER XVIII

PERCY BYSSHE SHELLEY

I

PERCY BYSSHE SHELLEY[1] (1792-1822) has his place, apart and secure, amongst the English prophets, in the great line from Alfred to Carlyle. He is blind to much in the history of human effort and in the conditions of human life; but he has a clear and sublime vision of the hopes of humankind. He wishes to see the world released from all the enslavements of the brain, and from the sloth that besets the heart and imagination. He dreams of an age of mental light, with the law of love and beauty for its principle. To this vision of a regenerate earth he comes by many paths. The revolutionary doctrine of his day counts for much; but his study of Plato leads him

in the same direction ; and his reading of the character of
Christ, apparent in *Prometheus Unbound*, is also a powerful
influence. He ignores many things close at hand, but no
man sees the stars clearer, and he is the most religious of men.
Yet, were this all, he might not concern the history of letters.

He is an artist as well as a prophet. He does not, like so
many others, keep his second-best form for his highest ideas,
and his most perfect form for his second-best ideas. He is
more constantly a poet than any Englishman of the idealising
type, except possibly Spenser ; and his teaching is rarer and
more inspiring than Spenser's, while his style is not less instinctively right and lovely. He is much more constantly a
poet than Wordsworth ; this is not to say that he is a greater
one. But he leaves the impression, more than any other
writer between Blake and Swinburne, that he could not help
being a poet. Even Keats does not suggest this so strongly,
although his ultimate achievement is as great as Shelley's ;
for in Keats it is long before we lose the feeling of effort and
experiment. Shelley, too, has his phase of experimentalising,
but once it is over he is hardly ever unpoetical.

But he is not an artist only when he is a prophet. Much
of his best verse seems to be, and is, quite foreign to his creed.
It is not ' prophetic ' at all—if the term be used to imply, not
that ' didactic ' writing which he tells us is his ' abhorrence,'
but the interposing and transfiguring power of the imagination
upon religious and moral ideas. He is not only the poet of
ideal love, of freedom triumphant, and of the reign of justice
upon earth. Pieces like *Mutability* and the *Stanzas Written in
Dejection* reveal a primitive melancholy and elemental remoteness which are perhaps deeper in him than all his aspirations
and philanthropies. Or we can call this, if we please, the
other Shelley ; and imagine in him the kind of dualism which
is present in us all, though we cannot put it into song. Both
sides of it can be traced, in more or less separate development.
The apostolic vision has its own history, from *Alastor* to
Prometheus Unbound and *Hellas*. The ' other ' Shelley can
be traced also, from the date (1814) of his first really piercing
and individual lyric ('Away, the moor is dark beneath the
moon ') to the poems of 1822, such as ' When the lamp is
shattered ' and the *Magnetic Lady to her Patient*. These
opposing moods, or themes, appear in turn, kaleidoscopically,
in the lyrics ; they clash and fall into confusion, in *Laon and
Cythna* ; and once at least, in the *Lines Written among the
Euganean Hills*, they coalesce in a wonderful harmony, which

too soon is lost again. The course of Shelley's genius may be regarded as an effort to attain this coalescence, and to find a form that should express at once all he dreamed of for humanity, and all he knew about himself. Cut off at twenty-nine, he hardly did this; but a sort of rhythm[1] can be traced in his poetic progress, or a race between these competing impulses.

Such a statement must be well guarded, for Shelley's mind is not to be packed into a formula. First of all, his mood of dejection and solitariness is often simply one of revulsion; an ebb of his high tide of hope, that leaves the foreshore for a time blank and the rocks gaunt and bare. It has this character, no doubt, in *Alastor*, where it is the inevitable counterpart of a young faith in its hour of disappointment. But this is not always, or generally, its character; and the poems where Shelley wails like a disembodied spirit, or pines to be one with the west wind or to perish away like odours or music, express, not a revulsion from anything, but rather something innate and temperamental; the voice, as it were, of those very winds and odours themselves, could we fancy them to have consciousness. Nor, secondly, is this trait in Shelley less fundamental, because it does not happen to be the earliest to find words. He was an apostle long before he was a sad solitary, and indeed before he was, to any purpose, a poet at all. His faith was formed before he could write in the least well. While at Eton he had made his vow[2] to be 'just and free and mild,' and to serve his fellow-men; and he was also early sworn to the service of intellectual, or ideal, beauty. And his first noticeable verse, from the date of *Queen Mab* onwards, is mainly devoted to these aspirations. But they are not for that more profound than his other and contrasting impulses, which are most naturally breathed out in his lyrics. In the third place, these two master-feelings must not for a moment be taken to exhaust, between them, the nature of Shelley. Often he is neither a visionary and idealist, nor yet an elemental, sorrowing spirit. Many of his poems can only be connected remotely with either frame of mind. In *The Witch of Atlas*, as intimate a poem in its way as he ever wrote, he moves in a world of almost wholly free fantasy and ethereal sportiveness. In *The Cenci* and *Charles the First* there is an unexpected power of dramatic self-suppression. Everything shows that we have to do with a genius that had not yet come to the full and whose future direction cannot be guessed. To the last Shelley was always beginning afresh.

He was a precocious scribbler[3] both of prose and verse, but not, like Pope or Chatterton, a poet very early. Few will turn to anything that he wrote before *Queen Mab* (1813), except to see what food his mind had already rejected. The lines called *Cwm Elan*[1] honestly echo the spirit of Wordsworth and the ring of Scott. But *Ruth* and *Michael* were no pattern for Shelley, who was never deceived, or attracted, by Wordsworth's theory of diction ; his own simplicity of style, which he lays aside at will, was of a different order. Nor did he as yet, or for a long while, care to portray any one but himself, or a bodiless double of himself. ' As to real flesh and blood,' he said at a later date, ' you know I do not deal in those articles ' ; and the confession, until he created Beatrice Cenci, was not too modest. Shelley afterwards treated Wordsworth as a political apostate, who was punished by his own dullness. But he always honoured the writer of *Tintern Abbey*, as it became him to do. He is not merely in debt to the philosophy of that poem. *Tintern Abbey*, in style, is the ennobled descendant of the abstract, declamatory verse of the eighteenth century, to which the heroic blank line had been appropriated ; and it is out of that verse, thus ennobled, that the verse of Shelley, on its intellectual side, arises. But Shelley, while a devotee of nature and Plato, has also a new thing to say, though it is long before he can say it well. The positive and negative dogmas, expounded in the discoloured prose of Godwin,[2] are proclaimed in *Queen Mab* in a rude shape with which Shelley soon became impatient, but which only slightly caricatures much of his lifelong creed. The history, the condition, and the hopes of the human race, and the obstacles to those hopes, are beheld with much the same eyes in *Prometheus Unbound* as in *Queen Mab*. No English poet, except Blake, of whom Shelley seems to have been ignorant, had as yet been inspired by these conceptions and aspirations, which were to have a long life in our literature. The notes to *Queen Mab*, wholly unoriginal as they are, are of more interest, in this aspect, than the text, and are written in prose which comes of a good stock. They repeat much of the argument of *The Necessity of Atheism* (1811), which cost Oxford his presence. The opinions of Godwin on war, property, and marriage, of Hume on miracles, of Condorcet on the perfectibility of man, and of Holbach on the crimes of Providence, are faithfully copied down. His materialism, indeed, Shelley soon gave up, but his attachment to theoretical fatalism[3] not so soon. Metaphysical idealism was more native to him, but he managed still to pin on to it the ethical and social views of Godwin, which thus survived their

original scaffolding. He was afterwards to strike living water
from these seemingly arid rocks ; but everything in *Queen
Mab* shows that his faith had grown quicker than his genius.

'The rhythm of *Queen Mab*,' says Mary Shelley, ' was founded
on that of *Thalaba*,' and the blank uneven iambic lines, in
which most of the poem is written, have a kind of frustrate
music. But, like those of Sayers and Southey, they cry out
in vain either for regularity of length, or for rhyme, or for the
absence of metre. They fall into exalted, over-metrical prose :

Upon the couch the body lay wrapt in the depth of slumber. Its
features were fixed and meaningless, yet animal life was there, and
every organ yet performed its natural functions. 'Twas a sight of
wonder to behold the body and soul. The self-same lineaments,
the same marks of identity were there, yet oh ! how different !

That no one who might be told that this is verse could say
where the lines conclude, is fatal to its claim to be printed as
metre. The passages of true verse, which announce the undoubted style of Shelley, therefore strike the ear as deviations.
Most of them occur in the setting, which describes the sleeping
Ianthe and the magic car, and which has a pale moony beauty
of its own. But the Fairy Mab, with her Shakespearean title
and fragile texture, is a strange guide over battlefields and a
quaint declaimer against commerce. Shelley, perhaps feeling
this incongruity, suppressed her in a later recension which he
made of portions of the poem (the first two sections, and the
eighth and ninth), and put in her place the 'Dæmon of the
World ' ; a dreary personage enough, and one fitter for the
declamation in hand. There is now a larger allowance of true
blank verse. Some of it is fresh and fine, but most of it is
still in bondage. The style of Shelley disengages itself from that
of his models, of Thomson or Wordsworth, like a child who
passes through a fleeting likeness to some ancestor before coming
to his proper voice and features. This process can be seen in
The Dæmon of the World. In a few lines we see the mixture
of *The Seasons*, of *Tintern Abbey*, and of Shelley himself :

> Yet, human Spirit, bravely hold thy course.
> Let virtue teach thee firmly to pursue
> The gradual paths of an aspiring change :
> For birth and life and death, and that strange state
> Before the naked powers that through the world
> Wander like winds have found a human home,
> All tend to perfect happiness, and urge
> The restless wheels of being on their way,
> Whose flashing spokes, instinct with infinite life,
> Bicker and burn to gain their destined goal—

—there it is at last! After the abstract jogging old diction, with its tedious final stop—*the gradual paths of an aspiring change*—and its prose book-phrase, *tend to perfect happiness*; and after the Wordsworthian lift into upper air, by *the naked powers that through the world wander like winds*; after this, suddenly comes Shelley's own, inalienable speech, when the words themselves *bicker and burn to gain their destined goal*; as they were to do thenceforth, and as they begin to do in *Alastor*,[1] *or the Spirit of Solitude* (1816), Shelley's next long, and his first great poem; a poem of the ebb, expressive of disenchantment and not of hope.

II

The model is here still the exalted, ruminative verse[2] of Wordsworth; and that of Landor's *Gebir* is perhaps audible too; but the lucid and pure flame proper to Shelley is everywhere underneath. His heroic verse, too, is seen taking shape, and he has a noticeable new liking, perhaps derived from Milton, for slow spondaic cadences. There are many lines like

> The lone couch of his everlasting sleep

Or

> And wasted for fond love of his wild eyes

Or

> Hang their mute thoughts on the mute walls around.

There is a new poise, a new resonance, almost an emphasis, which in Shelley's later work is softened. *Alastor*, though digressive, is not shapeless: indeed is better moulded than many of Shelley's maturer pieces.

And there are more rapid, dramatic lines, which indicate a different model altogether, like

> The eloquent blood told an ineffable tale;

Or

> With fierce gusts and precipitating force.

And in general there is a poise, a leisureliness of rhythm, indeed a prevalent hammer-like emphasis, to which Shelley does not again return. The deft employment of ringing Eastern names, *Oxus, Aornos, Chorasmian*, was nobly remembered by the poet of *Sohrab and Rustum*, whose ungrateful and incapable judgment upon Shelley, if it must be mentioned at all, shall not be controverted here. The obscurities of

Alastor are chiefly due to the intermittence of the allegory, which at times, and especially in the incidents of the Poet's voyage, vanishes without warning, in a way to which the reader of Spenser is accustomed. But the larger drift is plain. Shelley's hopes for the human race at large are here almost silent. The Poet is one of his many projections of himself— one of the first of the *radiated* Shelleys, half dream and half substance, who keep appearing till the last. He is at first contented with the solitary enjoyment of nature, and of thought, and of dead history. But the dream of perfect love and beauty intrudes and craves for real embodiment. Other men and women, with their simple human love, are dissatisfying shadows and fall short of the ideal. The poet is pursued by Alastor, the avenging spirit of solitude. ' He seeks in vain for a prototype of his conception. Blasted by his disappointment, he descends to an untimely grave.' Thus *Alastor* is a cry of revolt against the terms of our human life. It utters the passion, at once hopeless, imperative, and fatal, which lures us on to seek in mankind what nature cannot give and yet forces us to ask. This feeling may be transcendentally stated in the poem ; but so far being inhuman or remote, it is the ordinary burden of thinking men. That Shelley, in his preface, sees the deadly result of such a ' self-centred seclusion,' if carried to its utmost, does not remove the burden. The style of *Alastor* is nobly responsive to the expression of these subtleties, and for the first time Shelley floats, unhindered by his reading, in the dazzling and changing world of his own imagery.

The *Dedication* of *The Revolt of Islam* shows that in the story of *Alastor* Shelley had stopped short of the critical event in his own life, his meeting with Mary Godwin, whose love seemed to him, at least for the time, to offer what the Poet in *Alastor* had missed. The shorter pieces of 1814 and 1815 show this new influence, and the lines *To Mary Wollstonecraft Godwin* breathe of repose. But *Mutability* is again in the spirit of *Alastor* ; a spirit coloured, says Mrs. Shelley, ' by the recent anticipation of death ' ; and this dalliance with the thought, rather than the desire, of death became recurrent in Shelley. The verses written at Lechlade are full of it ; they are a gentler and softer salutation of the same idea :

> Thus solemnized and softened, death is mild
> And terrorless as this serenest night :
> Here could I hope, like some enquiring child
> Sporting on graves, that death did hide from human sight
> Sweet secrets, or beside its breathless sleep
> That loveliest dreams perpetual watch did keep.

But the wilder, the inveterate Shelley, ever breaking away from his own consolations, is also heard ; and the lines ' The cold earth slept below,' prove how far the spirit of Romance, by this time, has travelled, and what, in the kingdom of lyric, it has made of itself :

> The moon [1] made thy lips pale, beloved—
> The wind made thy bosom chill—
> The night did shed on thy dear head
> Its frozen dew, and thou didst lie
> Where the bitter breath of the naked sky
> Might visit thee at will.

Of the other poems written in 1816, the *Hymn to Intellectual Beauty* is the most imposing. The record of Shelley's pledge to be the servant of Beauty is worthy of him, and there is no need to answer his question, ' Have I not kept my vow ? ' But the form is hardly adequate, and he does not manage the irregular, apostrophic, metaphysical ode so well as Words-worth or Coleridge. Parts of the poem read too like a magnificent exercise. In *Mont Blanc*, a fiery and soaring piece in the manner of *Alastor*, the wanderer's spirit is ' driven like a homeless cloud from steep to steep.' The music throughout is great and exalted ; but the capricious spacing of the rhymes, unlike the same device as used in *Lycidas*, vexes the ear. Shelley's longer poems are best studied along with the showers of lyrical star-dust that attended their launch into space. Many songs of the year 1817, when *Laon and Cythna* was written at Marlow, are often unfinished ; ' many a stray idea and transitory emotion,' says Mrs. Shelley, ' found imperfect and abrupt expression, and then again lost themselves in silence,' and they are often melancholy : *Death* and *Unsatisfied Desire* are among the titles given by the editors, and are express-ive. But in one, which is happily complete, *To Constantia, singing*, the lyric genius of Shelley rises splendid and buoyant from the waves. It not only describes but communicates the rapture awakened by a golden voice ; and the rhythm of every stanza, rising in triumph, and slowly, lingeringly, but inevitably falling, conveys that sense of disembodiment for which few other poets have found language.

III

Laon and Cythna, which Shelley unwillingly altered, was published in 1818 in its new form as *The Revolt of Islam*. In the revised version the lovers are no longer brother and sister, and the changes involved are all for the better. 'Incest,' says Shelley elsewhere, in a comment on Calderón, 'is, like many other incorrect things, a very poetical circumstance.'[1] That depends on the treatment; in *Laon and Cythna* it is a circumstance of no poetical interest. The real subject is the liberation of mankind from bondage by the power of thought, love, and beauty; and this event is symbolised by Laon and Cythna's 'liberation of the Golden City.' But Shelley's purpose in his first draft, ' to startle the reader from the trance of ordinary life,' is only fulfilled in either version by lulling him into another trance, in which things happen with less than the logic of dreams. *The Revolt of Islam* does indeed relate, like *Alastor*, the mental travels of the poet, as well as the holy war to which he is dedicated. Othman is a type of the oppressors of the earth, and his outrage upon Cythna, the embodied principle of love and devotion, explains itself. The final sacrifice of the lovers, and their translation to the ' Temple of the Mind ' and the ' Senate of the Dead,' signify the martyrdom of the freethinker, whose one reward is in the tardy memory of men. But what is meant by the child of Cythna ? Why are the incarnations of free thought assailed by that strange regiment of founders, ' Joshua and Mahomet, Moses and Buddh ' ? The incoherence at times recalls Blake's miscreate epics ; and there is much in *The Revolt of Islam* to disgust the artistic reason. But if we let the reason sleep and are content to watch a succession of dissolving views, the poem is seen at once to overflow with beauty, from the faultless dedication to the last voyage of the reunited spirits whose bodies have perished on the pyre. The measure is Spenser's,[2] but Shelley has made it anew. The Elizabethan cadence he seldom reproduces ; and there are some traces of the clanging oratory of *Childe Harold* ; but the stream of the narrative, equable yet varied, lovely but not languid, with its reflections of starry imagery and rainbow colour, is utterly unlike Byron's boisterous torrent.

At this stage of his art Shelley can well be charged, like Byron, with representing only one character, himself. In *Prince Athanase* the Shelleyan hero, as he may be called, reappears with a difference. Athanase has been brought up, in painful remoteness from his fellows, upon Greek philosophy and poetry, and is for long disappointed both of earthly love and of its ideal counterpart. We learn from Mrs. Shelley's note that the fourth portion of this fragmentary work was to have ended with a consoling visit paid to Athanase, just before his death, by the spirit of intellectual love. This, then, is a variation of the theme of *Alastor* and *The Revolt of Islam*, where there are similar 'impersonations of the beautiful and the just.' One trait in all these figures must be mentioned. They suffer pain, solitude, and disappointment, but never self-reproach. Byron is always called an egoist, and so he is ; but he seems to have been sorry for something. Shelley is often called a saint, and he had, or came to have, some of the qualities of the saint. But he also shows an astonishing kind of egoism, like that of a child, who only knows that it is hurt, and cannot see when it has hurt its playmate. The evidence has never clearly shown in what measure Shelley's action can be called responsible for the fate of his first wife ; but nothing points to any trace of the self-blame, which might arise from the knowledge of having been a link, even an irresponsible link, in that fatal chain of occurrences. The point is only named here at all in its bearing on Shelley's art, and not from any wish either to excuse or condemn him as a man. Perhaps he had no occasion to be able to imagine a will or conscience at odds with itself ; it is certain that he cannot do so. His dramas give little opening for such a portrayal. It is, however, an artistic disability.

Not to overstrain this point, it may be added that Shelley's heroes, like Byron's, only express one half of himself. The letters and the poem *To Maria Gisborne* complete the picture in the happiest way, and correct our sense of the strain and fever in which he might seem to have lived. The life at Rydal is hardly simpler, or more natural, or even blither, than much of the life at Pisa. Shelley's frank friendliness and comrade-ship ; his clear-witted tact and good feeling in his intercourse with persons as difficult as Claire, Byron, Godwin, and Leigh Hunt ; his odd and fitful but genuine gaiety ; his eager simplicity and naturalness :—we must get all this into our minds if we are to see him aright. He had a *prose* existence, of which his letters are the most alluring record. He was not always in pain, or in some lonely paradise of dreams, or militant. The evidence of Trelawny confirms this impression, and remains the most faithful and distinct record of Shelley, alike on his angelic and his human side. It should be said that his correspondence becomes much more attractive, and wins the natural sweet ease for which it is famous, as well as being far saner and more measured, after the year 1817. Before then it is often tiresome and turgid, and its faults have been imputed wrongly to the adult Shelley.

IV

Rosalind and Helen[1] was also begun at Marlow, but finished at Lucca, after Shelley had left England for good. It is meant for an idyll of real life ; but he laid no stress on it, and the texture is no better than that of a weak romantic novel. It is the expression of Shelley's Godwinian revolt against loveless marriage custom. The ' incurable want of subject ' is not to be denied. The two women exchange their piteous stories, Rosalind telling of a tyrannical husband, the other, Helen, of an unwedded union with a lover, Lionel, who is dead. Rosalind's child is taken from her by wicked men, but at last mysteriously restored, and she lives in peace with it and her friend Helen ; in a melancholy peace, with a sort of hope. Given the story, Shelley shows an almost dramatic sense of feminine diction and feeling ; and the character and death of Lionel are drawn with idealising affection. He is a creature of the Laon or Athanase type, described this time from the point of view of his beloved. That is, he is a kind of trans-figured Shelley ; what Shelley would fain have made himself, or seemed to himself to be. The measure is that of Byron's or Scott's lays, the freer octosyllabic, with longer or shorter lines interspersed, and is rapidly written, as if extempore, with occasional strokes of phrase that go home. The lines

> Alas, we know not what we do
> When we speak words

might have come in some pathetic scene of Dekker or Heywood ; and the rites paid to the faithful dog, in the Temple of Fidelity, by the lady whom he had saved, close with a Coleridgian touch of romance :

> And the lady's harp would kindle there
> The melody of an old air,
> Softer than sleep ; the villagers
> Mixt their religion up with hers,
> And as they listened round, shed tears.

In *Julian and Maddalo*, written in 1818, there is the accent of Shelley's real and remembered talk with Byron,[2] or Count Maddalo, at Venice. The overture and close, and the picture of Allegra, are of this kind, and for the first time Shelley uses his supple and beautiful adaptation of the heroic couplet for the mingling of things serious and familiar. But these keen actual memories melt into excited fantasy and rhetoric when the two friends visit and overhear the mysterious ' maniac ' ;

a being who seems to be the wreck of a man distraught by domestic misery and the evils of society as it now is. Shelley's weakest style of high-pitched wailing and railing has only too much opportunity here, and his own calamities and aspirations are shadowed forth in riddles that disturb our sympathy ; for the story has neither the weight of truth nor the charm of free imagination working upon truth.

But in the lyric lay or monologue, composed in the same year, the *Lines Written among the Euganean Hills*, there are both these things ; there is ' truth in beauty dyed.' Nothing Shelley wrote in verse or prose, long or short, discloses him so fully as this descant of less than four hundred lines. Not only has each of his habitual moods—that of hope for man and joy in beauty, and that of solitary shivering and sorrow—the fullest play, but they are for once harmonised, and harmonised not by logic, but in a real and rememberable experience. It is a mystical revelation made articulate : and though it passes —for everything passes—and though its elements disintegrate into discord, and assert themselves again separately in other poems (such as the *Stanzas Written in Dejection* of the same date, and *To Misery*), still, there it was, and the words remain. Nowhere else is Shelley so nearly what he is always striving to be—one with the thing he contemplates. He is on one of the rare ' flowering islands ' that ' lie in the waters of wide Agony.' But he is not wholly alone amidst the beauty of the hills. He is also outside himself and his own lot, looking on Venice and Padua, and thinking on Byron and Petrarch and the fate of Italy. Thus fortified, he comes back to the glory of midday that bathes him ; and Shelley, and the sky, and the sun, ' interpenetrated lie ' with the living principle of the world :

> Be it love, light, harmony,
> Odour, or the soul of all
> Which from heaven like déw doth fall,
> Or the mind which feeds this verse
> Peopling the lone universe.

This poem is perfectly put together, and it is an intellectual pleasure to see its firm development, even apart from the rapid, impassioned, shimmering brilliancy of the imagery, which resolves itself into the emotions of the poet. In form the piece is like a prolonged simile which becomes a metaphor, or a metaphor which becomes a reality. But the things seen are not the reality, they are the metaphor : the reality is Shelley's own soul, with its deadly ebb of dejection, and its strong resurgence of a hope which at first can scarcely believe in itself. The natural scene and its beauty do not so much suggest certain feelings as give them colour, vesture, and extension. This distinction gives a clue to Shelley's way of regarding nature in his lyric verse, for instance in his *Ode to the West Wind.*

In *Prometheus Unbound*[1] (1820, written 1818-19) nature is thought of in a larger way, as filled with joy and gaiety at the freeing of mankind. The whole life of the earth is unbound with the unbinding of Prometheus. Nature, figured as Asia, the long-severed bride of Prometheus, is reunited with man in their common freedom ; and Shelley has no greater poetic invention than that of the second act, when in dreams and flushings of the blood the earth and nature presage the general liberation ; afterwards to join, throughout the fourth act, in a *Benedicite* over the event.

Prometheus Unbound is the greatest of our esoteric dramas. A play it is not, for none of Shelley's creatures, unless it be Prometheus himself, can ever reach the general mind, nor could they be staged except for the curious. Æschylus told a tale as familiar to Greeks as the Hebrew tales are to us, and equally august ; while Shelley, so far as he did not adapt Æschylus, had to create his own associations. But more happens in his play than in *Prometheus Vinctus*. The Greek sufferer merely defies, listens, and is stricken down, the true action being kept for the sequel which is lost to us. But Shelley's Titan unseats Jupiter ; by a machinery, it is true, of which the noble style cannot hide the grotesque poverty and weakness. Demogorgon, who is somehow the son of Jupiter, and is yet also the eternal principle of things, spurns him into the void. The whole connection of Prometheus and Jupiter before the play begins is obscure ; it is not simply that represented by Æschylus, for Prometheus is at once the installer of Jupiter and his victim. This is very well in the interpretation, which is that man has invented the gods of false theology, who become his tyrants ; but in the myth it is confusing. The meaning of the drama is thus much clearer than its mythical story : the contrary effect is produced by the *Faerie Queene*. It is this meaning that ranges Shelley, once more, amongst the great spirits of England ; and it shines in clear outline through the inadequate symbolism.

There seem to be two types of those spiritual minds that arise from time to time to prove that in man, who can form the conception of eternal goodness, there is some portion of it still resident. One type is steeped in the knowledge of life and of man as he is, by watching the world, and by the experience of that inner discord from which man seeks emancipation. A reforming sinner and saint, like Augustine ; a religious statesman, like Alfred ; a practical mystic, like St. Teresa : the varieties are endless, but they are all, in the high sense of the term, *realists*, with their roots laid in experience of the urgent needs of men. Of the other type is Plato, who watches life with profound intelligence, but only detachedly, and who rejects it. Such minds quarrel with reality because it is there and in the way ; they mould their hopes on the negation of it ; they foreshorten, therefore, the distance of their ideal ; they fling themselves on that ideal, and try to give it transcendental and universal form. They preach absolute love, unlimited sacrifice, the impossible because it is impossible ; and hence their power. We call such minds idealistic, and amongst English writers it is natural to think of Shelley and of Ruskin. The total absence of men and women in Shelley's picture of a redeemed mankind is characteristic. Ione, and Panthea, and Asia, and the Earth, and the Spirit of the Earth, and voices of the air innumerable, are his personages. Only the figures borrowed from the Greek, Prometheus and Mercury, have outline and are themselves ; but they again are barely persons. Yet it is hard to say in *Prometheus Unbound*, broken-backed as the story is, whether the meaning or expression is the more sublime. Those who cannot away with Shelley's disbeliefs must yet acknowledge the positive side of his ideal. The release of Prometheus is the dethronement of Christianity, but its dethronement by the spirit of Christ [1] ; and Jupiter himself is the whole body of insolent, traditional belief and institution which seeks covert under the falsely-claimed authority of the founder. On this destructive side Shelley's creed, an inheritance from the sceptics of the preceding century, is noticeably like that of Tolstoy. But his picture of the perfect man and the new earth is far more generous and sound than Tolstoy's, being, in fact, free from the element of insanity :

> To suffer woes which Hope thinks infinite ;
> To forgive wrongs darker than death or night ;
> To defy Power, which seems omnipotent ;
> To love and bear ; to hope till Hope creates
> From its own wreck the thing it contemplates ;
> Neither to change, to falter, nor repent ;
> This, like thy glory, Titan, is to be
> Good, great and joyous, beautiful and free :
> This is alone Life, Joy, Empire, and Victory.

Nothing less than the semi-divine figure of Prometheus, as adapted by Shelley, could embody these ideas. The reconciliation of Prometheus with Zeus, as effected by Æschylus, could only seem to him a ' feeble catastrophe.' The traditional service of Prometheus to mankind, as the giver of culture, he repeats, or rather re-creates, and adds to it the notion that is the mainspring of the drama. Prometheus is man considered as a loving and thinking being who aspires to liberate himself. It is his fate that he shall earn his release by suffering and defiance, and by forgiving, whilst he overthrows, his tyrant. The notion of Condorcet and the other *philosophes* is here in its quintessence, but it is transformed by the added presence of the Christian ideal which they discarded. Mrs. Shelley well explains the conception of her husband :

That man could be so perfectionised as to be able to expel evil from his own nature and from the greater part of the creation, was the cardinal point of his system.

So huge and typical a figure must needs lose in sharpness of outline something of what it gains in scope of meaning. He is less real than the hero of Æschylus, who is again less real than the hero of *Paradise Lost*, from whom Shelley borrows obvious traits. The other *dramatis personæ* are ' begotten upon the embrace of a cloud.' They are voices ; and yet they are voices carefully distinguished and concerted. Given the superterrestrial world chosen by the poet, the variety and distinctness of the scheme are most nobly sustained. With easy skill Shelley interweaves heroic monologue, lyrical recitative, and choric song. The story comes to an end with the third act ; but the fourth, though an afterthought, is not a superfluity. It is not only beautiful in itself, but completes the design, as a ' hymn of rejoicing in the fulfilment of the prophecies in regard to Prometheus.' The third act is in blank verse, and there is a limit to the rush and rapture which blank verse can express continuously. Shakespeare may have felt this when he made Romeo and Juliet fall into rhyme. Here a kind of ritual of song is needed to celebrate the emancipation of the world. The interfusion of descriptive blank verse in this fourth act prevents monotony, and the speech of the Earth, ' It interpenetrates my granite mass,' is Shelley's masterpiece in the difficult kind of poetry which is half-way between the pictorial and the lyrical.

Had we to choose between the varieties of perfect song in this drama, it might be felt that the passages which are most thoroughly stripped of doctrine, of definite ideas, and even of humanity, are the most perfect of all, and that Shelley is there most himself. With all the beauty of the more ode-like measures, their residuum of opinion or definable aspiration removes them by so much from the tone of song ; these ingredients being better fitted for recitative or for dramatic speech. Yet even here there are distinctions. The intrusion of social or anti-clerical reflections, in the chorus of the Furies in the first act, can doubtless be objected to ; but the same element in the address of Prometheus to the vision, or wraith, of Christ is supremely well managed. And the chorus of the sixfold band of spirits, the 'gentle guides and guardians' of mankind, with its measures gradually prolonged and solemnised, shows a command of lyrical orchestration that makes us think of the second part of *Faust*. Indeed, the transporting power of *Prometheus Unbound* as a whole is hard to parallel, and Shelley himself tells us how he came by it :

> The bright blue sky of Rome, and the effect of the vigorous awakening spring in that divinest climate, and the new life with which it drenches the spirits even to intoxication, were the inspiration of this drama.

V

In *The Cenci* (1819) he tries to portray absolute evil, as in *Prometheus* perfect goodness ; and our belief is repelled, not so much because the character of Count Cenci is out of humanity, as because it is undramatic. It is a compound of envy and revenge, with portentous unnatural cruelty thrown in :

> Add thereto a tiger's chaudron
> For the ingredients of our cauldron.

Still, Beatrice and not her father is the protagonist ; and in Beatrice Shelley drew at any rate what Shakespeare never tried to draw—a woman pure, tender, strong, and profoundly real, who is the chief actor and sufferer in a tragedy. He had a true story to work upon, or a story taken as true—'not to be mentioned in Italian society without awakening a deep and breathless interest,' as well as the portrait of Beatrice, which he so well describes in his preface ; and he explains his reading of her character :

> Beatrice Cenci appears to have been one of those rare persons in whom energy and gentleness dwell together without destroying

one another; her nature was simple and profound. The crimes and miseries in which she was an actor and a sufferer are as the mask and the mantle in which circumstances clothed her for her impersonation on the scene of the world.

Neither Webster nor Tourneur, whose school of poetry Shelley had clearly been studying, would have treated the outrage with the 'delicacy'[1] that he truly claims to have observed. But he has attained this delicacy (if that is the right word) not by shirking the fact, but by making us see it from the point of view of Beatrice herself, who holds it at arm's length, veils it in the mist of the horror that enwraps her, and yet does not let it for a moment weaken her purpose. Shelley also pleads that Beatrice is a truly dramatic character, because she *ought* not to have avenged herself—a point open to doubt; and also that she would have been 'wiser and better' had she not done so—only then she would have been undramatic; and that the drama consists in the

restless and anatomising casuistry, with which men seek the justification of Beatrice, yet feel that she has done what needs justification.

The interest, however, may not lie precisely or merely where Shelley suggests. His treatment requires a wider theory. Until the last act there is, properly speaking, little drama at all, though there are pity and terror, poetry and tension, in the highest degree. Except for the momentary thought of suicide, there is little division in the will of Beatrice:

> All must be suddenly resolved and done.

We have little hope or fear that she will not resolve and do. But the drama reaches its highest, not in the play of her scruples, but in the scene where she is at bay before her judges; when her patience and sorrow turn to warranted cunning and steely defiance; when she seizes every point in a losing game; and when, with apparent evasiveness but essential truth, she puts by the direct question:

> *Judge.* Art thou not guilty of thy father's death ?
> *Beatrice.* Or wilt thou rather tax high judging God
> That he permitted such an act as that
> Which I have suffered, and which he beheld;
> Made it unutterable, and took from it
> All refuge, all revenge, all consequence
> But that which thou hast called my father's death ?
> Which is or is not what men call a crime,

Which either I have done, or have not done ;
Say what ye will—I shall deny no more.
If ye desire it thus, thus let it be,
And so an end of all.   Now do your will.

This is drama ; and if Shelley learnt something from the
Jacobean master, inverting the arts of the splendid miscreant
Vittoria baffling justice, and applying them to the uses of
a noble heroine defying law—which oppresses her because
she has done the justice that the law would never have
awarded ; and if he has sharply united the dreadful and
heroic with traits of dissolving pathos, this is only to repeat
that he is the one co-equal master in Webster's kind since
Webster's day.   But he comes nearer to Shakespeare than
to Webster in the last impression that he leaves.   It is
not that of a lowering or stifling fatalism, according to which
' we are merely the stars' tennis-balls ' ; it is the sense that
the mind is above the fate which it courts and suffers, and
that Beatrice, when she is led off to die, has somehow an
advantage over death, revealing as she does new facets of
her radiance up to her last word,

My Lord,
We are quite ready.   Well, 'tis very well.

In this play Shelley has put aside the weaknesses which he
felt might have beset him.   All ' mere poetry,' he says, is
sternly kept out.   There is but one song, that of Beatrice,
' False friend, wilt thou smile or weep ? ' and it is in deep
accord with her and the situation.   There is not one lyrical
phrase in the whole work which is there for its own sake ;
and the diction is noticeably naked of imagery—much more
so than that of *Macbeth*.   The style and verse have a controlled force and a transparent purity which Shelley had not
yet secured, and which he did not, save in *Charles the First*,
again attempt.   The blank metre of *The Cenci*, while as clearly
affected in its general manner by the old drama as that in
Prometheus is by Milton, is original in stamp, or rather a new
variety of the great traditional species.   If it lacks the
bitterer felicities of Webster's, it is more flowing and lucid ;
and yet it is free from the dissolute overflow or loose liquidity
into which the versification of the silver age declined.   Neither
has it the free undulation and lapse, so miraculously like the
gusts of actual speech, yet never breaking from the fundamental scansion, which appear in Shakespeare's greater
tragedies ; resembling, instead, the verse in his best history
plays, where the separate harmony of the single lines is clearly
felt without any arrest of continuity.

> The deed is done,
> And what may follow now regards not me.
> I am as universal as the light;
> Free as the earth-surrounding air; as firm
> As the world's centre. Consequence, to me
> Is as the wind which strikes the solid rock
> But shakes it not.

VI

The Cenci swerves as little from its main action, and has as
little of what is called relief, as *Phèdre* or *Britannicus*; it is
in this sense, but in this only, a classical play. The writer of
such a tragedy needs relief as much as the reader; and Shelley
found it by turning to satire and parody. He lightened the
months after which he composed *The Cenci* by also making
Peter Bell the Third, in seven parts. He had his share of odd
gaiety and of the burlesquing instinct; he was not always too
exalted to be playful, or too sad to jeer. *Peter Bell the Third*
is aimed at Wordsworth, and is in a simple ballad-like measure.
Had it been in octaves, it would have come still nearer than
it does to the rhymed letters and sallies of Frere, Rose, and
Byron. In his demeanour towards Wordsworth and Coleridge, Shelley is on common ground for once with the author
of *Don Juan*; but he is a gentler and better critic, if his
satire is not so well kept up. He can be savage: Peter Bell's
timorous courtship of nature, and the 'double damnation'
of dullness which comes upon him through his service to the
Devil, are in the vein of the *Vision of Judgment*. As early as
1814, Shelley, in an austere sonnet, had deplored Wordsworth's
'desertion' of his service to 'truth and liberty,' and was ever
impatient with his theory of poetic diction. The wearisome-
ness of his later verse Shelley, not wholly in jest, treats as a
punishment for his lapse; and Peter Bell, the literal man, is
identified with his creator; yet not all ill-naturedly, or in
oblivion of Wordsworth's inspired years and of Shelley's own
debt to him:

> At night he oft would start and wake
>   Like a lover, and began
> In a wild measure songs to make
> On moor, and glen, and rocky lake,
>   And on the heart of man—
>
> And on the universal sky—
>   And the wide earth's bosom green,—
> And the sweet, strange mystery
> Of what beyond these things may lie,
>   And yet remain unseen. . . .

> He had also dim recollections
>   Of pedlars tramping on their rounds ;
> Milk-pans and pails ; and odd collections
> Of saws, and proverbs ; and reflections
>   Old parsons make in burying-grounds.

This is not ferocious ; it is a private coterie-poem to which
Shelley did not wish to put his name. His Aristophanic
attempt, *Œdipus Tyrannus, or Swellfoot the Tyrant* (1820), to
ridicule the king and the affair of Queen Caroline, is dismal
and unreadable ; the jokes do not show ability. His principal
other work of this sort is *The Mask of Anarchy*, ' written on
the occasion of the massacre at Manchester ' in 1819, which
reveals a gift, as unexpected as it was unpursued, for the sort
of satire which is both popular and high-poetical. There is
a likeness in it to Blake's which has often been noticed ; the
same kind of anvil-stroke, and the same use of an awkward
simplicity for the purposes of epigram :

> Next came Fraud, and he had on,
> Like Eldon, an ermined gown ;
> His big tears, for he wept well,
> Turned to millstones as they fell.

> And the little children, who
> Round his feet played to and fro,
> Thinking every tear a gem,
> Had their brains knocked out by them.

But this grim and gnomic style is for Shelley only a feat.
He breathes more freely when he is rid of it, and his appeal
to the English people to rise against the tyranny of the Government permits him to summon those elements which are never
sullen to his spell :

> Let the horsemen's scimitars
> Wheel and flash, like sphereless stars
> Thirsting to eclipse their burning
> In a sea of death and mourning.

The last years were the richest of Shelley's life, and mark
more than one fresh disclosure of his power. For his new
moods and thoughts, or the old ones changing and blending,
beget new poetic forms ; and thereby we know that an artist
is not marking time. This expansive power goes on at a
startling rate of progression till the end. *The Sensitive Plant*
(1820) is a reshaping, though not a reiteration, of familiar
images and musings, the poet figuring his own lonely spirit
this time as a mimosa in the heart of an earthly paradise,
and the ideal, satisfying loveliness, of the kind sought by

Alastor and Laon, as the Lady of the garden. She fades,
the garden is left bare, the plant withers, and so far the ending
is parallel to that of *Alastor* ; but by a sudden afterthought,
or *revirement*—marked by the slowing and smoothing down
of the quick trisyllabic ripple of the lines, which thus lose
their plaintive, nay slightly infantine and vexing sing-song—
the poet questions the reality, not this time of death, but of
life, in view of the eternity of beautiful things, of which he
thinks for the moment as self-subsistent apart from the enjoying mind. Shelley's wasteful expense of his powers in describing the horrible gives an immature effect to this otherwise
delicate poem.

The Witch of Atlas (written 1820) is, on the contrary, the
rarest of all his fantasies,—perhaps the most flawless of all
his writings of moderate scale. The Witch is a new creature
of his dream of beneficent loveliness ; a calm but kind, a
passionless but compassionate watcher of human fates ; a
gatherer of all the innocent and splendid things that visit
man in reality or day-dream, of all sweet odours and visions ;
and a president over the gaieties of fire and the sports of the
elements. The poem is complex in its inspiration. Shelley
starts from that playful, light, mischievous kind of Greek
humour, of which he shows so quick a sense in his versions of
the *Cyclops* and the *Hymn to Mercury*. The Witch's half-
solemn mythic parentage, part-solar and part-Atlantid,
serves for a mock-epical theme, which is wrought out with
the warm life and changefulness that belong to such fancies.
Beings of the antique brain, they shift under the hand of
each new poet who, like Shelley, can make good his right
to fashion them. Spenser's *Garden of Adonis* is well matched,
and perhaps remembered, in the recital of the Witch's possessions. Next follows a rainbow fabric of purely Shelleyan
vision, ending in the creation of the Hermaphrodite, a symbol
uniting the qualities of beauty that transcend sex. All this
is far removed from the most dexterous and glittering of
mosaic-work, like *The Rape of the Lock,* by its essential gentleness, and also by Shelley's freedom of movement in the world
of the pure elements. It is fantasy, not discernible from the
higher work of imagination except by its streak of ingenuity.
In the last section Shelley's native or habitual vision of a
restored world of love and kindness receives a new and lively
variation. The voyage of the Witch amidst the sleeping
human souls, whose 'naked beauty' is laid open to her ; her
Mab-like portioning out to them of elfish but medicinal visions ;

and her preservation of the chosen dead in a happy slumber, 'living in its dreams beyond the rage Of death or life'—all shows that Shelley, who had done his utmost in *Prometheus* for the majestic and imperial expression of his creed, was now free to play with it, and so to give it final warrant. The Italian octave in which the poem is written may perhaps be felt, towards the close, to run into a purely satiric vein ; but Shelley masters it in his own way, gives it new powers, and avoids letting it run riot in that traditional anti-climax which is Byron's favourite and disenchanting trick.

The *Letter to Maria Gisborne*, composed in the same summer mood (1820), also reveals Shelley at his ease, and, as we have said, serves, like his letters in prose, to give the lie to any misconceptions that may linger concerning his character. The ' shrill,' ' hysterical,' ' humourless ' personage, who is but ' the poet of clouds and sunsets,' is heard speaking, strangely enough, as humanly and familiarly as Charles Lamb :

' No humour ' :

> a china cup that was
> What it will never be again, I think,
> A thing from which sweet lips were wont to drink
> The liquor doctors rail at—and which I
> Will quaff in spite of them—and when we die
> We 'll toss up who died first of drinking tea,
> And cry out—heads or tails ?—where'er we be.

Shelley may now be shrill :

> Memory may clothe in wings my living name
> And feed it with the asphodels of fame,
> Which in those hearts that must remember me
> Grow, making love an immortality.

' Clouds and sunsets ' :

> Custards for supper, and an endless host
> Of syllabubs and jellies and mince-pies,
> And other such ladylike luxuries—
> Feasting on which we will philosophise !
> And we 'll have fires out of the Grand Duke's wood,
> To thaw the six weeks' winter in our blood.
> And then we 'll talk ; what shall we talk about ?

' Ineffectual angel ' :

> And here like some weird Archimage sit I,
> Plotting dark spells, and devilish enginery,
> The self-impelling steam-wheels of the mind
> Which pump up oaths from clergymen, and grind
> The gentle spirit of our meek reviews
> Into a powdery foam of salt abuse,
> Ruffling the ocean of their self-content—

—all this, interrupted by the gusts of Libeccio and the Contadino's song, makes a most harmonious medley ; and the lines slip from Shelley's pen without forethought for the rhyme, which infallibly comes.

In the unused scraps of *Epipsychidion*[1] there are traces enough of this conversational, even jesting speech, and allusions to the *Quarterly Review* ; but in the completed poem (1821) the lighter tone only survives faintly. The differences of cadence, poetic pitch, and emotional level are nevertheless well marked, and form a clue to the changing moods in which the work should be read. Those enforcing the doctrine that love need not be tied to one object at one time, and that we need not be faithful after the fading of love, which in its essence passes on from each embodiment of its own ideal to a fuller one—to a soul that complements[2] and fulfils the soul of the lover—are written mostly in the kind of luminous epigrammatic manner, quite serenely assertive, that Shelley may possibly have learnt from Marlowe's *Hero and Leander* :

> True love in this differs from gold and clay,
> That to divide is not to take away. . . .
> If you divide suffering and dross, you may
> Diminish till it is consumed away ;
> If you divide pleasure and love and thought,
> Each part exceeds the whole ; and we know not
> How much, while any yet remains unshared,
> Of pleasure may be gained, of sorrow spared.

There are even touches of almost playful artifice, perceptible when Shelley is haunted by rhythms of the despised school of Pope. Mary and Emilia, the Moon and the Sun, are in turn to share his devotion ; and who can read these lines in a ponderous and legal spirit ?—

> So, ye bright regents, with alternate sway
> Govern my sphere of being, night and day !
> Thou, not disdaining even a borrowed might ;
> Thou, not eclipsing a remoter light—

—the greater light, it would seem from the sequel, in defiance of scripture and physics, to be the rule not of the day but of the night. Shelley's remark, however, that ' the poem is not flesh and blood, for you know I do not deal in those articles,' must not be taken to mean that his doctrine of free love is not proclaimed in earnest ; it is so proclaimed, but in what kind of earnest may readily be mistaken. It is certain that one of the dry roots of this strange blossom of poetry is *Political Justice*, the book of Mary's father, where it is argued with solemn but sincere paradox that legal marriage is morally not binding when love has gone, and is indeed an evil in itself, like other institutions. This Shelley simply believed ; and the doctrine of free love is inwrought by him with the other doctrine, adapted from Platonism, of ideal or intellectual love, which had so often appeared in his verse already, and on which the best comment is his subtle and fragmentary essay *On Love.* His study of Dante's *Vita Nuova* and *Canzoniere,* with their history of a rarefied and spiritualised love, counted also for much. Apart from the designed but inartistic obscurity of some personal allusions, most of the darkness of *Epipsychidion* vanishes if we suppose that Shelley means in it neither more nor less than just what he says. It is a real if metaphysical expression of his absorbing though not lasting passion for Emilia Viviani ; of passion, nevertheless, never perhaps made actual by his practical will, or so meant to be, but fully realised —in imagination, and by that faculty carried to its extreme. In verse they are united. All the while, Shelley is in love not so much with two or more women as with Love, which they successively, and even at the same time, embody ; and for the moment the new woman embodies it more than his wife ; yet they are both beloved, and both are told that it is only reasonable that they should be. Shelley's aspiring and flaming fancy, moreover, passes to and fro, swift as a weaver's shuttle, between Emilia and that for which she stands, the discarnate ideal of love and beauty. He showers image after image upon her as the type of such beauty ; nor is his lavishness wasteful, for it is of the essence of the case that no image suffices ; and on these images he rises to those great heights of metaphysical impassioned speech, where ' cold performs the effect of fire.' At the end he comes back to Emilia, and imagines their life together, not now with any squandering of metaphors, but with a luminous and lovely distinctness of portraiture. Her features, and all human features, at last vanish in the consuming devotion of the poet to beauty for its own sake ; and this devotion is the living principle of his language.

The subtle and fervent writing which Shelley commanded in his psychological verse here reaches its highest power. The swiftly-soaring and never-flagging heroic rhyme is a thing of pure beauty, and will bear any criticism. The transitions to and from the more familiar style—the dips earthward and then upward—are not jarring or disconcerting, but part of the rhythm of the flight. Shelley's lyrical, like Shakespeare's dramatic language, often gives the peculiar effect of a train of fire, one metaphor kindling another as it goes ; this is not the case with Keats or in Wordsworth, who economise and give one impression. But Shelley, like Shakespeare, is also clear-cut when he chooses, as in the vision of himself and his beloved conversing ' under the roof of blue Ionian weather.' But the other, the accumulative manner, is more characteristic of *Epipsychidion*.

We must take what the gods give ; yet it is not the best fortune that the longer and greater English elegies should all have been framed with artifice, and written with a conscious elaborate splendour, as though uttered to a huge audience rather than to the poet himself. Sometimes a song of Webster or of Cowper hits harder than the threnodies of Milton, Shelley, and Tennyson. Each of these poets is not only sincere but highly impassioned ; yet it seems to be a law that we are moved so much the less sharply by any expression of loss, as it fails to keep to the object and eddies out into larger contemplations. Goethe's dirge on Byron, as Euphorion, is free from this drawback, though he did not know Byron in person, and does not affect the tone of bereavement ; for it keeps to the object. It has to be said that both Shelley and Tennyson are also masters of the brief lyric of personal sorrow, and have paid their dues that way. A prolonged elegy—unless, indeed, like *In Memoriam*, it consists of a series of separate poems sewn together—almost demands some sort of machinery. In *Lycidas* and *Adonais* there is the classical, traditional machinery with its formal structure. Invocation, sympathy of nature, procession of mourners, personal digression, lament, climax, change of mood, and final consolation :—each poet adapts the scheme to his own genius. And the likeness to the type is increased by the note of invective which dignifies *Lycidas* ; but it spoils *Adonais* ; for even had Keats been killed ' by an article,' which was not the case, what have Quarterly Reviewers to do with that which is written and conceived *sub specie æternitatis* ?

For thus *Adonais* [1] (1821) is really written and conceived ; that is its peculiar glory amongst English elegies. The framework, charged though it be with memories of Bion and Milton, is from the first etherealised, and at last is quite burnt away in superterrestrial fire. The style, at first marked by a certain note of oratory, which perhaps is affected by the blunt style of *Childe Harold*, becomes rarer and clearer ; the ' many-coloured glass ' gives way to the ' white radiance.' If not higher than *Epipsychidion*, this poem is more firmly based in thought and humanity. And certainly it is richer in substance ; for Shelley, save in the famed lines where he describes what he dreamed himself to be, and in the sudden prophetic close, escapes from himself ; and he speaks here not of love, but of glory and death and his fellow-poets and of the plastic spirit of the world. Some of these things he had not treated in verse before, and the manner in which they are now wrought into a symphony would ask for long analysis. The first thirty-eight verses, which form the lament, are in a different tone from the last seventeen, which form the consolation. They are in a style (except for the mistaken attack on the reviewer) of singular and individual magnificence. Shelley, with his unequalled refining and severing power, endows as with the life of faint separate souls the Dreams and Desires and Adorations of the dead poet, which hover round his bier ; they speak in sweet wailing voices like his own. The subsequent procession of the poets, however loftily managed, is purely an ideal one, for Byron was not intimate with Keats, and Leigh Hunt was not present at his death ; so we can but wish with Shelley that he had known in time of the devotion of Severn, and paid him honour in verse. We are not too indistinctly told in what sense Adonais ' wakes or sleeps with the enduring dead ' ; or rather, we can clearly see Shelley's fluctuation of thought on the matter. Adonais has won glory, and his spirit, through his poetry, works among men. He also is ' made one with Nature,' and lives because she is alive. He shares, in some sense, in the eternal labours of that Spirit which shapes all forms of beauty ; and he is absorbed in

> that sustaining Love
> Which, through the web of being blindly wove
> By man and beast and earth and air and sea,
> Burns bright or dim, as each are mirrors of
> The fire for which all thirst.

The poet has, at any rate, to work in figures that imply some kind of personal life, though it is not the kind we know. The last lines refer, not to the station of Keats among the poets, nor to his intensified individual existence after death, but to his pre-eminence among great souls—' the Eternal '—who, because they are eternal, share all the more fully in the universal and immanent principle of life. The form of *Adonais* is nobly adequate to these high themes.

Shelley, since *The Revolt of Islam,* has made a new thing of Spenser's stanza. He has made of it an heroic metre, applied to a metaphysical purpose, full of sound and weight, and impetuous as well. Concentration, rather than his frequent hurrying flow, marks the diction and the tune. He thought *Adonais* one of the best of his writings ; and it is one of the greatest, if some others are more suggestive of his natural voice.

VII

Hellas (1822), which he accurately calls a 'series of lyric pictures,' is not much like the *Persae*, 'the first model of my conception,' save in the circumstance that it celebrates the delivery of Greece. It was inspired by the news of the insurrection of 1821, and was perforce a prophetic rather than a justified thanksgiving. The ending, therefore, is not that of a drama ; and in the greatest of his impersonal lyrics, 'The world's great age begins anew,' Shelley sees an earnest of the hopes of mankind in the future destiny of Greece. The whole work is thus a visionary forecast. There is much soaring blank verse, but the special grace of the poem is in its clustered songs. The lyrics of *Prometheus Unbound* are more ethereal ; they suggest inexhaustible showers of light raining from some magic urn. But those of *Hellas* are more cordial and quickening to the soul, because their theme is more concrete. They are hymns of political faith and hope, 'songs before sunrise.' The faith may be vain and the hope deferred, but both are noticeably definite, and concern actual countries and historic struggles. There is accordingly more for the brain to take hold of than is usual in Shelley's songs. 'Worlds on worlds are rolling ever,' and 'Darkness has dawned in the East,' testify anew to Shelley's unspent stores of lyrical invention, and forbid us once more to fear that his powers were more than midway in their orbit when he sailed on the fatal day. The first of these pieces is from the hand that translated Goethe's *Prologue in Heaven*, and has the same kind of music.

The fragments of the abandoned drama on *Charles the First* (1822) can only increase our regret for the world's loss. It is indeed no more than the shattered limbs of a play ; but the new promise of sculpturing power and dramatic style is undeniable. The careful modelling of the court scenes upon Shakespeare's more stately and untroubled type of historical drama is proof enough that Shelley was feeling his way in an art that was still unfamiliar ; but the success in this effort, not only of stray lines but of whole passages and speeches, is of quite another order to that of Lamb or Beddoes when they 'catch the spirit' of Elizabethan verse.　The first long speech of the Queen in Scene 2, were it dug out of an anonymous sixteenth-century play, might well pass for the work of some young disciple of Shakespeare who had won his approbation.　Shelley has constrained himself to feel a true dramatic sympathy with Charles and Henrietta ; but his Puritans are commonplace, and his Hampden talks pure Shelley.　The piece was dropped, the poet's strongest bent being still for the disembodied and the processional, not for reality and drama ; and he turned to his other and final fragment, which as he left it is the hardest of his poems, *The Triumph of Life*,[1] written in 1822.

The 'triumph' is a pageant, in the Petrarchian sense of the term ; whether it is also a victory is uncertain, for Shelley does not try to answer his lifelong question,

> Then what is Life ? I cried.

For life, in the poem as it stands, is a mere rout, a scene of bewilderment, a blind dance towards a goal of darkness, leading from distracted youth to powerless age ; unredeemed by any Prometheus, though lightened by the presence of some rare spirits who ' could not tame Their spirits to the conquerors.' The 'conquerors' are the leaders of men, the royal 'anarchs,' such as Napoleon and the popes.　Such a view of history shows the weak digestion that was Shelley's chief intellectual disability.　But it was a condition of the advance of the human spirit, that for a time it should make short work of the past ; the contempt for the historical spirit had been a well-known symptom of the 'enlightenment'; and for a prophet like Shelley some such weakness was almost necessary, if his mind was to be light and free and to fix itself on the new heaven and new earth of which he dreamed.

In this unfinished poem there is no new earth in sight.　But the prelude suggests that, as in *The Euganean Hills*, some Paradiso might have succeeded that Inferno which our present life is represented as being.　And the words of salutation to Dante accord with this probability :

> Behold a wonder worthy of the rhyme
>
> Of him who from the lowest depths of hell,
> Through every paradise and through all glory,
> Love led serene, and who returned to tell
>
> The words of hate and awe ; the wondrous story
> How all things are transfigured except Love.

This and other passages make us say to ourselves that Shelley might have been an ideal translator of the *Paradiso*, supposing him to have mastered the *terza rima* as Dante understood it ; that is, as a chain of grammatically independent, or at least cleanly sundered tercets, with the single lines firmly marked and weighty, yet with a continuous interlinkage of sense as well as of rhymes. Shelley regards the pause at the end of the tercet, not as a rule that admits of relaxation, but as an obstacle to evade ; and this evasion is also seen in *Prince Athanase*, in the beautiful *Woodman and the Nightingale*, and in his translation of a passage in the *Purgatorio*. In all these cases the stanzas constantly run over. The habit has a beauty of its own, but does not make for restraint of style. Yet the strong hand of Dante is again and again perceptible, combating Shelley's natural expansiveness, and helping him, as Keats advised him, to ' curb his magnanimity, and be more of an artist.'

> And ere she ceased
>
> To move, as one between desire and shame
> Suspended, I said—If, as it doth seem,
> Thou comest from the realm without a name,
>
> Into this valley of perpetual dream,
> Show whence I came, and where I am, and why—
> Pass not away upon the passing stream.

Here the stanzas are not severed as Dante usually severs them ; but the poise and balance of the single lines, and their great dignity of sound, as well as their modulated pauses, counteract the overrunning and make the medium a perfect one of its kind. But Shelley's own rapider, laxer, lyric manner is always breaking through, and pervades most of the poem.

The vision itself has by no means the clear march or proportioning of its Italian models ; either of those cold *Trionfi* of Petrarch, or of Dante's pictures. It is not merely that it is unfinished, with rhymes sometimes unsupplied, personal riddles unexplained, and ' shapes ' and ' spirits ' uninterpreted. But the whole tale is put out of joint by the intrusion of Rousseau, who suddenly appears to explain the pageant, but only succeeds in relating, in like symbolic form, his own life's pilgrimage, which soon melts into Shelley's own. Greatness no one can fail to see in *The Triumph of Life* ; but that it could have been a good poem, unless it had been put back into the crucible, is difficult to suppose.

VIII

Shelley's supremacy amongst our lyrical poets hardly needs asserting, but its nature and title are less speedily defined. For one thing, the lyric impulse, like some nameless and subtle ray, penetrates, much more with him than with other writers, into alien kinds of verse—the pictorial, or the epical, or the analytic, or the dramatic ; as it also does with Swinburne, and as it does not do with Wordsworth, or Byron, or Keats. *The Witch of Atlas* and *Epipsychidion* are often only kept by the metre from being actual lyrics. This tendency is naturally felt least in regular drama ; as in *The Cenci*, where Shelley was on his guard against ' mere poetry.' But it is felt almost everywhere else, and is in general a quickening and propelling influence, though it also (as in *The Revolt of Islam*) makes for diffusion and weakness. But in *The Witch of Atlas* it is just what is wanted, for there it leads to a harmony and not to a confusion of styles.

In all kinds of true lyric, from the complex ode down to the smallest shining fragment of short-lined verse, Shelley is a master who owned few models. He did not, like Blake, apprentice himself to the Elizabethans. His boyish essays tell us little ; but, once he had begun to sing, it cannot be said that his sheer instinct for lyric language was greater at the end of his days than it is in the volume containing *Alastor*. He found more and more things to say in song, he invented more and more tunes. But his work of 1822 is not perceptibly more perfect than his work of 1815. He did not, like his own skylark, chant without labour. He rewrought and rejected incessantly, and left much unfinished. But his writing hides what it may have cost him ; it seems as effortless as breathing. The art of narrative or meditative verse we can to the last see him learning ; but his lyric art we seem to see him merely exercising.

If there be one exception to this mastery of Shelley's in the field of lyric, and one species less congenial than the rest, it is the elaborate and strophic ode ; and in the intricate but irregular form of ode he is still less at ease. The *Ode to Naples* is an example of the first kind, and the *Hymn to Intellectual Beauty* of the second. The strophic poem, with its corresponsive members and prolonged development, has been proclaimed by the heir to Shelley's singing robes as inherently the loftiest sort of lyric verse ; and Mr. Swinburne has gone far to make good this preference by his own achievement.

Shelley's own work of this sort is not his best. Noble, in his hands, it could not fail to be ; but it hardly shows his full spontaneity or ease of flight. He is more himself in stanza than in strophe. The greatest of his more highly organised stanzas is surely that of the *Ode to the West Wind*, which falls into four equal verses of chain-rhyme and a couplet, with an overture, a refrain, and a climax ; a scheme of his own making, which answers to the natural articulation of feeling and passion in the poem, and is carried through without break or blemish. Shelley thus seems to steer the element which he invokes, and with which his own soul sweeps along in wild but not lawless union. The first three verses follow the west wind on its course ; the fourth calls upon it to bear the poet away from ' the heavy weight of hours'; the last prays for absorption in the west wind (' be thou me, impetuous one '), so that he may rekindle his dead song and scatter it among the hearts of men. This is the greatest of all those lyrics of Shelley, which do not, in brief compass, convey a single and a simple emotion.

To a Skylark he does not call an ode, and it is rather one protracted jet of song, or, as Bagehot says, ' a clear ring of penetrating melody.' There is not the same body and cunning orchestration of sound as in the *Ode to the West Wind* ; the tone is sadder and more piercing. It is not, as absurd reciters make it, an expression of delight, but of a pain too keen for men's ordinary senses to apprehend. The contrast between the frustration of the poet and the triumphant happiness of the bird is never surmounted, and the conclusion is a cry for the impossible. The alexandrine at the end of each verse gives the fulness and weight which the breathless shorter lines leave us desiring and expecting ; but the charm of the piece lies in its crystalline diction, which is very full of grammatical inversions due to the claim of the soon-recurring rhymes. This diction is still of the kind *où la passion parle toute pure* ; of that most human passion, which would fain be rid of the burden of humanity. In his utterance of this desire Shelley comes home to all. He is not a remote or unreal writer, as he is sometimes made out to be ; but universal feelings come to him in rare and subtle forms. His pain, which in its essence is common to all men, is so sharp that the faith and solace which he finds in the future of mankind have to be strong indeed to ease it ; nothing less than such a faith will serve, and it does not always serve. In this poem, indeed, the faith is absent.

In *The Cloud* and *Arethusa*, both of them pure pictures,

or rather embodiments of elemental speed and movement,
in which the poet and his emotions do not appear at all, it
may be impious to see anything amiss ; but there is often
something singsong, even infantine, about Shelley's anapæstic
poems, which makes one think that they have gone on long
enough.   Their beauty, at any rate, is that of a playful and
incomparable feat ; the great executant turns virtuoso, rejoicing, without too much feeling, in his tyranny over his instrument.   It is a relief, at the same time, to see Shelley thus
at play and forgetting himself, and his technique is ever
consummate in each kind.   *The Cloud* is of the same structure
as the Old English or Latin ' Riddles,' in which the swan,
or the storm, or the Rood, speak of but forget to name themselves.   The essence of this kind of writing is an intense
identification with the subject : Henry Vaughan's *Tree* is
another instance ; but Shelley's way of brilliantly reiterating
and turning over his imagery is curiously like that of Anglo-
Saxon verse.   *Arethusa*, on the other hand, is a verbal and
rhythmical utterance of the joy of galloping waters.   Arethusa
and Alpheus, are they rivers or river-deities ?   We never ask ;
the two things are one ; and so Shelley recovers that primitive
confusion which begets a myth.   The musical tact with which
the lovely Greek names—*Dorian, Ortygian, Erymanthus*—are
spaced among the verses, is not less than that shown by Milton
in his *Nativity Ode*.   Shelley seldom keeps himself, or human
feeling, so triumphantly out of the life of these bright and soul-
less elements, which here seem to speak only for themselves.

But when he chose he could make quite another thing
of his four-foot anapæstic rhymes.   In the seldom-quoted
fragment, *A Vision of the Sea*, they labour, like Browning's,
in the expression of struggle and heaviness ; of the plunging
ocean, and the writhing serpent, and the toiling ship.   The
piece is a conscious exhibition of power, as *The Cloud* is of ease,
in language and versification.   And the power has a fierce
and concentrated quality which Shelley, in his lyric, hardly
ever displays, and which he in this instance attains partly
by the deliberate crash of consonants and a daring use of dis-
cords, and partly by arresting and overloading his trisyllabic
feet with fully-vowelled, or ' long ' syllables, in places where
light ones are expected :

> The foam | and the smoke | of the battle
> Stain the clear | air with sun | bows ; the jar, | and the rattle
> Of sol | id bones crushed | by the in | finite stress
> Of the snake's | adaman | tine volum | inousness.

Amid such images of violence and terror beauty resides, on a frail ark of safety. The picture of the mother and child floating upon the wreck reminds us of De Quincey's *Dream Fugue*, where the endangered figure of the young girl he had seen from the mail-coach visits him in all manner of ominous conjunctures ; and there, too, as in *A Vision of the Sea*,

> Death, Fear,
> Love, Beauty, are mixed in the atmosphere.

Shelley's briefer songs and lyrics will not bear separate description, or the touch of prose. No one can come nearer the limits of the unwordable ; the substance is of the frailest. In such a piece as ' Life of Life ! ' the screen of language is thin indeed ; the idea has no existence save in the words that are used. Yet he does not make words do the work of pure tune ; he always says something, and his brain keeps pace with the music. The lyric just named occurs in *Prometheus Unbound*, and gives the essence—almost volatilised—of the poem. Many of Shelley's songs, which are in all the anthologies, approach this character, and express, as hinted before, those fleeting but recurrent emotions which are his real self and are often far-withdrawn behind all his stock of beliefs, and friendships, and even loves. His love-lyrics, however, are often enough of this elusive kind, and are generally sad. ' Rarely, rarely comest thou,' and ' Swifter far than summer's flight,' and ' O World ! O Life ! O Time ! ' are perhaps the ultimate expression of his temper. The *Bridal Song* (' The golden gates of sleep unbar ') is midway, from this point of view, between Shelley's more private and personal and his more objective lyrics. In one sense it has a universal and eternal application ; yet we need only set it beside the old Elizabethan hymeneal odes to see how winnowed and rarefied its sentiment is. The poems in *Prometheus Unbound* and *Hellas*, that are so rich in apostolic hope and humanitarian fervour, have been mentioned already. They show no lapse, but a different and splendid order, of power. Amid their ringing call to arms and rounded melodies, they discover Shelley's peculiar fineness and aristocratical quality of mind. Commonness, of one sort or another, in execution if not in spirit, we could, if we stooped to take the trouble, easily pick out in Byron and Keats, in Coleridge or Wordsworth ; but in Shelley, except sometimes when he is satirising, never ; nor yet (with the same reserve) in Landor. And in his friendly, sportive, and colloquial lyrics or monologues, the same safety of note is evident. In these, too, he comes nearest to some of his contemporaries : to Wordsworth in *The Invitation*, and to Keats in the lines called *With a Guitar*. These pieces, along with the *Letter to Maria Gisborne*, bring us back to Shelley's daily life and talk, with its gentle play and soft sparkle.

He translated much, and for amusement, and rapidly ; but his handicraft does not desert him in such labours. More of a reader than most poets, he is not weighed down by study. He reads like a poet, preferring works of high imagination, or classic grace, or philosophic charm. Most of his versions are from the Greek. In prose, he did the *Banquet* of Plato, and parts of the *Republic* and *Ion*. Here, too, his high breeding in language served him well, and also his love of beauty and relish for subtle argument. The scholarship is by no means exact, but the translations read like originals, and it is obvious how such tasks and studies affected his original writing. Plato's view of love and beauty is always reappearing in Shelley, not as a fixed doctrine, but as a living and varying inspiration. In the same way *Adonais* is full of the tradition of Sicilian elegy, and the *Witch of Atlas* of the gaieties of old mythology. In verse, Shelley translated the *Cyclops* of Euripides,—the comic songs with particular success ; also the *Hymn to Mercury*, and some of Moschus, and several pieces from the Anthology. Of the ancient authors whom he did not translate, he was most influenced by Æschylus, as the *Prometheus* and *Hellas* show. Spanish and German were in his day still uncommon acquisitions amongst Englishmen. The scenes from Calderón's *Magico Prodigioso* and from the First Part of *Faust* are freely and dashingly rendered ; and the music of Shelley's famous lines from the *Prologue in Heaven* has the most glorious of his lyric qualities.

IX

Shelley's letters cover his whole life from 1810 onwards ; but most of his formal prose, except the *Defence of Poetry* and his fragmentary romance *The Coliseum*, seems to have been written before he finally left England in 1818. And apart from an occasional youthful ambitiousness, such as appears in the Preface to *Alastor*, his prose in general advances from a barer to a richer manner. Godwin at first affected his form as well as his ideas, though he always wrote more warmly and less sententiously than Godwin. The frog-like temperature of *The Enquirer* is not reproduced in Shelley. Still, in his notes to *Queen Mab* and in his Irish manifestos of 1812-13, he starts with an eighteenth-century manner, with a rather ample and flowing sentence, and with a good transparent sort of diction. But his prose at this date is not salient, and does not arrest the ear. Later—we cannot say when, for some of his best pieces such as *Love* are only to be dated by guesswork—he gathers colour and intensity, as the influence of Plato and other imaginative writers tells upon him ; such passages as the descant on love in *The Coliseum* have the *Symposium* behind them. The same richness, as well as a clear natural flow and ease, is found in his introductions to *Prometheus*, *The Cenci*, and *Hellas* ; these belong in fact to Shelley's critical writings, of which the *Defence of Poetry* is the chief.

His metaphysical, moral, social, and religious speculations[1] in prose remain mostly shards and splinters. Many of them do not so much show his genius as throw light on its development. Some are merely more or less eloquent decoctions, like *A Refutation of Deism*, which is in fact a plea for atheism. The *Essay on Christianity* is one of the most complete, and can be read as a kind of prose gloss on *Prometheus Unbound*. The *Speculations on Morals* come nearest to a formal and systematic statement. Shelley wrote little, in this polemical kind, with a perfectly free play of intelligence, except perhaps the piece *On the Devil and Devils*, which rings with his strange laughter. Often his ideas are borrowed, but receive new life and fire when his imagination works upon them ; and this is especially the case when he writes of love and beauty, or of the poetic imagination. But as his habit of mind, luckily, led him away from a methodical to an artistic treatment of such ideas, it is impossible to write a coherent history of his opinions. Yet their general course is clear enough, and they shaped his art and style too powerfully for them to be ignored.

He began with the tenets of Godwin and of Godwin's masters. These he found too stark and uninspiring, and he threw over their materialistic basis, and the doctrine of necessity. He became a philosophic idealist in the train of Plato and Berkeley. But he kept some of Godwin's cardinal doctrines all the same, and turned them into poetry. He continued to think that persecution was wrong because all error is involuntary, and all vice ignorance ; and that reasoning, or the mere letting in of light, would cure both vice and error. He continued to think that history revealed little but a blind effort on the part of mankind to ruin its own happiness by setting up creeds and governments ; that these must go ; that Reason, impelled by universal

Love, and emerging into forms of Beauty, was the Demogorgon who should dethrone Jupiter. But already it is clear how Shelley ennobled the creed of the 'enlightenment,' bringing into it an ideal strain from quite other sources. His creed, as it finally took shape, was largely independent of its original scaffolding. The communion of saints and sages in the kingdom of earth, ruled by the law of love, is his ultimate vision ; and the thistle of dogmatic rationalism has here blossomed indeed. The objections to Shelley's vision, which are founded upon the elements that he admittedly leaves out, all prove too much ; they can be urged against every mind of the eager, prophetic, idealising type that refuses to see obstacles. Shelley underestimated, of course, the power of the irrational in man, and all the stubborn inherited traits of the brute. He did not see that progress is likely to be as slow as ever, and did not allow for relapses or for the need of coercion. All this is too plain for words ; and yet he is among the prophets, because he saw the goal.

Shelley's actual theology varies in its colouring. His revolt from monotheism and historical Christianity led him often into a kind of pantheism which he expresses with great power and beauty, as in *Epipsychidion* and *Adonais*. His rapture of conviction reminds us of Bruno, but his flame has less of earthly fume and sputter in it than that of the Italian thinker. But Shelley is usually a dualist and not a pantheist, and much of his poetry depends upon his dualism. The world is a scene of strife between the evil principle, so long in possession, and certain faint but struggling forces for good. In *Alastor* evil is left rampant, in *Prometheus* good prevails. Shelley does not try to reconcile these contending creeds, the pantheistic and the Manichean, by logic. They are only to be reconciled by his faith and hope that Ahriman, the ill spirit, will one day be vanquished, and the dualism disappear. But this faith and hope, once more, are readily discouraged. And further, as we have said, Shelley often moves in a world of feeling in which the struggle in the world, or the struggle among his own opinions, does not appear at all.

X

His conception of art and poetry, and of their business, is not a simple or consistent one. His *Defence of Poetry* (written 1821) is a series of eloquent sentences and often deep intuitions, not a reasoned argument. He holds, with Plato in the *Ion*, that the poet has a share of divine inspiration which is above

reason ; and by a ' poet ' he means, like all the Platonist
critics, a creator of anything fair, or great, or virtuous, in words,
or tones, or marble, or deeds, or legislation.   He tolerates even
institutions, when they have been built by the Romans ; for then
they are full of ' poetry.'   But he soon drops this idea and
says that poetry, in the stricter sense, is an art working through
language.   The language need not be metrical, though metre
introduces a beauty of its own.   But *what*, then, does poetry
convey in language ?   What has it, what have Homer and
Milton, to say ?   He answers, that poetry proper puts into
beautiful verbal shape some aspect or other of that ideal,
which poetry, in its big, comprehensive sense, is an effort to
convey.   Man is its highest subject ;   and ideal man is its
supreme object of portraiture.   It is clear, in passing, that
such a theory makes little provision for much of the verse
that Shelley wrote himself, which is pure, subjective lyric, or
fantasy, or natural description.   But apart from this his
theory, when he comes to explain his notion of ideal man,
varies like his practice.

The word ' ideal ' is a familiar trap.   Sometimes it means
spiritually perfect, as Shelley's Prometheus is represented to
be.   Sometimes it means universally true, or representative,
or stripped of accident and passing circumstance, like Michael
Angelo's great figures, or the Greek gods in sculpture.   Or
it means something midway, as when we say that the character
of Cordelia, or of Antigone, has received ' ideal ' treatment
from the poet.   In such persons the noble element is markedly
preponderant, but it is not carried to the point of unreality.
These figures are human enough ; they do not intrude into the
world of tragedy like abstract patterns or types.   Shelley,
in his *Defence*, does not work out these differences, and makes
unawares some profit out of the resulting confusion.   But
in the most enduring and precious passage of his book he
rises above them, and states the eternal problem of art in
its bearing on conduct with signal insight.   Few artists or
moralists have so plainly stated the issue.   He repudiates
didactic poetry, or the desire to write verses ' for the direct
enforcement of reform.'   But he would hardly have understood the later notion that art and ethics move in different,
in remote, in never-intersecting planes : a notion, by the way,
that leaves *Prometheus Unbound* and the *Paradiso* no reason
for existing.   He frankly says that his purpose in *Prometheus*
is to ' present beautiful idealisms of moral excellence'; the
hero is to be

the type of the highest perfection of moral and intellectual nature, impelled by the purest and the truest motives to the best and noblest ends.

But, in the *Defence*, we see how this type is to be shapen :

The great instrument of moral good is the imagination : and poetry administers to the effect by acting on the cause.

And again, in the Preface to *The Cenci* :

Imagination is as the immortal God which should assume flesh for the redemption of mortal passion.

It does not matter, after this, that Shelley should commit himself to saying that Prometheus is a better hero than Milton's Satan, because Satan's ' envy, ambition, revenge,' and the like, ' interfere with the interest.' This is merely the voice of his as yet undeveloped dramatic sense, and *The Cenci* was to follow to belie it. The virtue of his view of the imagination is that it applies so well to much of the poetry he could *not* write ; to *Macbeth*, and *The House of Life*, and *Modern Love* ; in all of which imagination ' administers to the effect.' As to the further relationship of the beauty to which the imagination gives form, and the good of which it is the 'great instrument,' Shelley does not theorise. It would seem that mankind are divided into the few to whom the good seems a species, or an appanage, of the beautiful, and the many who will only accept the beautiful if it is apparently a species of the good. Shelley seems to identify the two things metaphysically, without giving priority to either ; and so belongs to a third class. But the first view, which makes the beautiful the larger term, seems to have the advantage of excluding none of the facts of ethics, while covering most of the facts of art.

XI

Where, then, is Shelley's own imagination found at work most intensely and efficiently ? His skill in poetic architecture is variable enough. In *The Revolt of Islam*, his longest work, it is slight or null. It is at its highest in *The Cenci*, amongst his more elaborate works ; but the first three acts are not so much drama as a kind of dramatic narrative. In *Prometheus Unbound* the action is unimpressive, but there is a perfect mastery and proportioning of the various forms, lyrical, descriptive, and the like, which make up the texture. Shelley's power of construction is often at its highest in his works of middle length, of between four hundred and a thousand lines. *The Witch of Atlas*, in its lawless law, is the most perfectly built of all these. *Adonais*, where the traditional framework of pastoral elegy is adapted, is also nobly arranged. *Epipsychidion*, with all its impetuous flow, has a clear argument, and the balance between metaphysical and concrete poetry is maintained with the surest instinct. This plastic power becomes more assured, as the scale of the work is narrowed. In the *Euganean Hills*, for instance, it is triumphant, and also in the *West Wind* and *Arethusa* ; and in the short lyrics Shelley's art of overture, development, and close, and his choice of metre in its correspondence with mood and emotion, becomes infallible.

On his own language he has a note of interest, though he does not often speak of the implements of his art, or muse upon the power of words in themselves. In the Preface to *Prometheus* he says that he may unwittingly have modified his diction, owing to his study of other poets ; there is ' a peculiar style of intense and comprehensive imagery which distinguishes the modern literature of England ' ; something in the air, which is shared by many writers, without any conscious mutual imitation. We now see, a century later, that this remark is true ; yet it is not so easy to define the likeness in question. There *is* an element common to the styles of Byron, Wordsworth, Shelley, and Landor,—to go no further ; something which is absent in Tennyson and Rossetti. But it is not merely ' intense and comprehensive imagery,' which is also found in these successors, if not in all poets. What, then, is it ? The old opposition between ' classical ' and ' romantic,' such as may be said to obtain between Landor and Coleridge, considered as poets, must be left behind and transcended if the quality we are seeking is to be grasped. This may be described as a certain directness, clarity, and strength, which give us a large, rapid impression. There is little desire, except in Keats and his companions, to dally with language, to pause and taste it, to hunt for felicities, to be strange and arresting and curious. When Wordsworth and Shelley revise their verse, it is in order to simplify it, and to keep the large rapid impression undisturbed. They refuse either to linger or to hurry ; they will not fret and torture language. Read *Lancelot and Elaine*, and *The Stream's Secret*, and the odes of Coventry Patmore ; then turn back to *Achilles and Helena*, and *Alastor*, and *Dejection*, and *Cain* ; and you will breathe more freely, you will feel the same sort of relief as in going back to a page of De Quincey or Hazlitt from a page of Walter Pater or Robert Louis Stevenson. This large rapid impression is one of the gifts of the romantic writers ; and it allies them with the antique. Shelley produces it in a supreme degree. In his best writing it is associated with the essential flame and purity of his language, just as in Wordsworth's best writing it is associated with his majesty of character and continuity of power.

The varieties of Shelley's poetic style are of course wide. In a poem like the *Hymn of Pan* or *The Question* it can be called romantic in the more special sense ; it is rich, and joyous, and full of colours and odours and liquid bird-notes, approaching in character the style of Keats :

> The wind in the reeds and the rushes,
>   The bees on the bells of thyme,
> The birds on the myrtle-bushes,
>   The cicale above in the lime,
> And the lizards below in the grass,
> Were as silent as ever old Tmolus was
>   Listening to my sweet pipings.

There is much of this in Shelley, and it is always delightful ; his favourite visions of a refuge, green and scented and solitary, from the bitterness of the world of men, are full of such imagery. But this is not his highest, or perhaps his most characteristic sort of language ; of which the marks are a great purity and magnificence, and sometimes a great austerity. The purity and magnificence, without the full measure of austerity, are felt in the famed stanza from *The Revolt of Islam* :

> What then was I ? She slumbered with the dead.
>   Glory and joy and peace had come and gone.
> Doth the cloud perish when the beams are fled
>   Which steeped its skirts in gold ? Or, dark and lone,
>   Doth it not through the paths of night, unknown,
> On outspread wings of its own wind upborne,
>   Pour rain upon the earth ? The stars are shown
> When the cold moon sharpens her silver horn
> Under the sea, and make the wide night not forlorn.

Not many styles, it may be felt, are greater than this one ; any poet in the world might be proud of it. Nor need we pit any other against it, least of all anything of Shelley's own. But in some of the speeches of his *Prometheus* there is superadded the austerity, which does not mean bareness, that Æschylus had taught him ; and here again he takes his place with the supreme poets :

> Peace is in the grave.
> The grave hides all things beautiful and good :
> I am a God and cannot find it there,
> Nor would I seek it ; for, though dread revenge,
> This is defeat, fierce king, not victory.
> The sights with which thou torturest gird my soul
> With new endurance, till the hour arrives
> When they shall be no types of things that are.
> *Panthea.* Alas, what sawest thou ?
> *Prometheus.*   There are two woes,
> To speak, and to behold ; thou, spare me one.

This, no doubt, is not Shelley's natural vein; he requires, to attain it, the coercion of a great subject and perhaps also of a great literary model; but he does attain it. Ordinarily his language has less condensation, less sculpturing; it is poured out, lavished, and has the qualities now of flickering fire and now of rushing water. But in actual vocabulary it is almost unsurpassably pure, and this it is by nature and not by taking of thought or study. A note on some of its constituents may close this chapter.

His diction in general may be called, like Wordsworth's, central or classical, and it is also his own. It seldom aims at strangeness, and shows none of that anxious tasting and adoption of Elizabethan forms, which Leigh Hunt taught to Keats. Traces of Shelley's reading of Shakespeare and Milton may easily be found, but they do not bulk large, and they tend to disappear. He does not distil the older poets after the manner of Tennyson, or care like Browning for free bold coinages. A word like ' hupaithric ' is rarely found in Shelley. Certain types of compound he may be said to adore, but he makes them in quite a regular way, and such inventions of Keats as 'proud-quivered' and 'branch-charmed' would have offended his instinct. He is rich in words compounded with ' sea-' and ' tempest-,' and especially with ' all-' (' all-miscreative '). He is sparing, unlike Rossetti, in the deliberate use of long single words, though he likes them when they give him some large elemental image, such as ' tempestuous ' or ' adamantine.' ' Eternity ' and ' Omnipotence ' come frequently, of course, in his anti-theological poems. Certain classes of abstract words abound, and the opinions and sensibilities of Shelley are very fully reflected in the concordance to his poems. It is natural that he should have such favourites as ' custom,' ' free,' ' slave,' ' hope,' ' just,' with their derivatives, in one class ; and in another, as ' agony,' ' pain,' ' torture,' and ' hate ' ; with their opposites

' joy,' ' delight,' ' gentleness,' ' mildness.' He is over-fond of words that, in their abuse or excessive use, may be called hectic, such as ' demon,' ' curse,' ' mad,' ' poison,' and ' blood.' This streak of the romantic novel of terror he never quite lost.

No poet is richer in terms descriptive of the elements and their attributes. Those which communicate the pleasure given by light are abundant ; if we look down a page of his poetry, it is likely enough to be studded with ' bright,' ' beam,' ' fire,' ' flame,' ' gleam,' ' radiance,' and the like ; and, to a less degree with ' gloom ' and ' darkness.' There are endless ' chasms,' ' caves,' ' gulphs,' and ' abysses.' But he is more at home than any one in the upper air ; expressions like ' airy,' ' atmosphere,' ' cloud,' ' wind,' ' blast,' and ' rain ' are for ever on his lips. Like Dante, he is much with the ' sun ' and the ' stars.' It may be noticed, however, that he is richer in epithets that convey sensations, than he is in those representing things. Shelley's birds and beasts would fill but a small cage. His singers are the earth, and spirits, and voices of phantasms, rather than the nightingale ; though, of course, he has his skylark. He often speaks of odours, and is profuse in adjectives like ' dim ' and ' faint ' and ' keen,' or substantives like ' trance ' and ' Elysium.' Yet there is a certain sharpness of pleasure, which easily becomes pain, in his very languors ; and he does not, like Keats, ' fade far away, and quite forget.' It would be easy to carry this sort of analysis further.

The power and charm of Shelley could only be rightly expressed in figured speech like his own ; and to describe a portion of his nature we have to fall back on the lines in *Adonais*, where he calls himself ' a dying lamp, a falling shower, a breaking billow.' But even this is only half a description ; it does not tell us that Shelley and his poetry are also like a beacon, or a fruitful rain, or a radiant sea. If we apply to himself what he says of the West Wind, we are nearer to the impression that he gives ; nor can we take better leave of him than in the words of the only lyric poet who can be thought to have earned, soon after his departure, a place in the same sphere of the lyrical heavens, Thomas Lovell Beddoes :

What would he not have done, if ten years more, that will be wasted upon the lives of unprofitable knaves and fools, had been given to him ? Was it that more of the beautiful and good, than Nature could spare to one, was incarnate in him, and that it was necessary to rescue it for distribution through the external and internal worlds ? How many springs will blossom with his thoughts —how many fair and glorious creations be born of his one extinction !

CHAPTER XIX

LEIGH HUNT AND JOHN KEATS

I. James Henry Leigh Hunt : Italian reading : *Story of Rimini* : its under-rated merit. Value of Leigh Hunt's influence on Keats. Other romantic poems : sonnets. Hunt as a critic ; *The Reflector, The Indicator,* etc. Later works : *A Jar of Honey : Autobiography.*

II. Keats : identification of himself with Nature ; nature and art. Enjoy-ing temper ; the religion of beauty, and of sorrow. Elizabethan sympathies. The volume of 1817 : *Calidore,* etc.

III. *Sleep and Poetry* ; versecraft ; early sonnets, and later ones.

IV. *Endymion* : the story ; odes inserted ; Keats's declaration for romance.

V. Longer Tales : *Isabella, Eve of St. Agnes, Eve of Saint Mark, Lamia.* Varieties and rapid development of poetic mastery. *La Belle Dame sans Merci.* Poems of Fancy.

VI. Later Odes : *To Autumn, On a Grecian Urn, To a Nightingale,* etc. *Hyperion* ; study of Milton ; management and balance of blank verse. The story, why unfinished ? The 'revised' *Hyperion* ; allegoric significance.

VII. The language and coinages of Keats ; relation to the whole of his writing. Gradual perfecting of the expression of poetic pleasure. Different modes of such expression. Treatment of ' ideas,'

I

LEIGH HUNT,[1] whilst in prison for describing the Regent, 'bought the *Parnaso Italiano,*' and read it ; those fifty-six pleasant, evilly-edited, fairly-printed volumes, ranging from Dante to Cacasenno, which have won so many friends for Italian letters. It was here, doubtless, that he read Redi's *Bacco in Toscana,* of which he long afterwards made an excellent and congenial version ; and here, too, he may have seen Dante's seventy lines on Paolo and Francesca. These he was moved to inflate into a long story, leisurely and complaisant, in the manner of Boccaccio, and written in something resembling the heroic verse of Chaucer. We must forget Dante, if we can, when we open *The Story of Rimini* (1816), and it is best to forget Chaucer also, if justice is to be done to Hunt. Hardly a page but is stained by vulgarity, or by something that no artist should print. The whooping backwoodsmen tomahawked these errors nearly a century ago, and repetition is needless.

Enough that Paolo knocks at the bower of Francesca, asking
' May I come in ? ' and the reply is ' O yes, certainly.'   And yet
this poem, preceding by a year the first volume of Keats, is
in the true line—when so many better poems are out of the
true line—of romantic inspiration : the line that comes down
from Chatterton and Coleridge to Keats and William Morris.
It is a tale in verse, and, with whatever stumbles and dis-
graces, as a tale it moves; it has the spirit of beauty,
intermittent but undeniable ; it is full of natural imagery,
luxuriously felt and rendered ; it has no purpose except the
story, and the imagery, and the expression of beauty ; and,
amidst the most desperate lapses, it has style.   All this may
be said of most of Hunt's poetry ; but one quotation may be
given from the derided *Story of Rimini* :

> The days were then at close of autumn—still,
> A little rainy, and, towards nightfall, chill ;
> But now there was a moaning air abroad ;
> And ever and anon, over the road,
> The last few leaves came fluttering from the trees,
> Whose trunks, wet, bare, and cold, seemed ill at ease.
> The people, who, from reverence, kept at home,
> Listen'd till afternoon to hear them come ;
> And hour on hour went by, and nought was heard
> But some chance horseman, or the wind that stirr'd,
> Till tow'rds the vesper hour ; and then, 'twas said,
> Some heard a voice, which seem'd as if it read ;
> And others said that they could hear a sound
> Of many horses trampling the moist ground.
> Still nothing came ;—till, on a sudden, just
> As the wind open'd in a rising gust,
> A voice of chaunting rose, and, as it spread,
> They plainly heard the anthem for the dead.
> It was the choristers, who went to meet
> The train, and now were entering the first street.
> Then turn'd aside that city, young and old,
> And in their lifted hands the gushing sorrow roll'd.

The last four words are a lapse ; but otherwise all is more than
right ; it is an admirable staple narrative style, better than
most of *Endymion,* and of its own kind the earliest example
in English.   The versification is not ' effeminate ' or ' Cockney '
at all, neither is it too slippery and Jacobean in its use of
the interlinked couplet.   The overlapping of line and distich,
which could have been learnt from many a page of the *Parnaso,* or from William Browne, is free but not too liberal.
The whole passage is more salient than much of the *Earthly
Paradise* ; it sticks better in the memory.   Leigh Hunt could
by no means keep up this manner, but he could often return

to it, and his revilers of his own day and afterwards were
perfectly deaf to it, beyond all skill of aurist.

How Leigh Hunt's writing affected Keats for ill has often
been told : the touches of commonness or sickliness, the rhyming down-at-heel (in which Keats at first much outdid his
master), the want of poetic sureness and concision.   But Keats
gained far more good from Hunt than harm.   For one thing,
he was introduced by him to the enchanted gardens of romantic
poetry.   He saw ' beautiful things made new ' ;   he had an
example of verse that with all its flaws revealed an imperturb-
able, free delight in pure beauty, in telling a story for its own
sake, and in imaginative richness ;   and this delight, though
it had its snares, and had to be braced and lifted by higher
inspirations, was   to Keats invaluable.   Later, indeed, he
turned on Hunt and repudiated his ungirt style and temper ;
' He makes beautiful things hateful,' said Keats vehemently ;
and this verdict, though hardly just, represents the better and
higher genius of Keats casting aside its early preconceptions.
We shall see, in the case of John Hamilton Reynolds, the fate
of a talent which did not get beyond the stage of Leigh Hunt's
early foibles ; nay, we see it in the case of Hunt himself.   For
it has to be said that the foibles clung to him, though they did
not sink him altogether, and that Hunt never for long—unless
it were once, in the *Legend of Florence*—reached and kept the
kind of style, of which those lines from *Rimini* are a happy
example.   His true power on literature, after the first, was
exerted by his prose, which has its flowery niche amongst that
of the critics.   But his poetry had a liberating as well as a
hampering influence.

In his other romantic anecdotes, such as *Hero and Leander*
(1819) and *The Palfrey* (1842), Leigh Hunt unluckily quits his
couplet and its dignified possibilities, and uses lilting measures
which give only too much opening for his worst vein, his vein
of playfulness, which is too much of the smirking order ;   and
this accords ill with romance and luxury : nor did the years
cure him of the malady.   But the *Legend of Florence* (1840),
a romantic, quasi-Elizabethan play, contains much, as he truly
says, ' of what I regard as most approaching to poetry.'   The
story, indeed, is but moderately persuasive.   There is a brutal
husband, a Griselda wife who is at last driven to defy him, and
who seems to be dead ;   yet she is revived, and, despite his
penitence, she refuses to go back to him ;   but on the last page
he commodiously provokes a bystander to run him through,
and the lady finds her true love awaiting her.   Despite all

this, there is poetry in the *Legend of Florence*, and the style
is generally pure—sound, easy, imitative Elizabethan that
seems to Hunt almost second nature. But he was not made
for long flights—has indeed more of the flying-fish than the
swallow about him. His best things are short ones, in which
he has not room to go wrong, and in which now and then he
attains to beauty, finish, and at moments even splendour.
Abou ben Adhem, so often cited, has for companions *The Panther*
and *The Glove and the Lions.* The sonnet *To the Grasshopper
and the Cricket* goes well with the companion piece of Keats,
'The poetry of earth is never dead '; and *The Nile,* with its
superb line on Cleopatra—

> The laughing queen that caught the world's great hands,

excels the rival poems by Keats and Shelley. But Hunt
seemed to be fated to leave nothing without some blemish.
Even in these two sonnets there are phrases, ' the feel of June,'
' nick the glad silent moments,' ' their eternal stands,' and ' for
sweet human sake,' which cause despair. *Captain Sword and
Captain Pen,* though sometimes admired, will hardly bear
looking into ; and *The Feast of the Poets,* an early piece, is a
more or less floundering exercise in the manner of Goldsmith's
Retaliation. But just when we despair indeed, Hunt saves
himself by a flash, by a phrase, like the astonishing close to
that quaint and strange sally of petulant fancy, *The Fish, the
Man, and the Spirit* :

> A cold, sweet, silver life, wrapped in round waves,
> Quicken'd with touches of transporting fear.

The poetic suggestions, physical and other, of the word ' transporting,' are worthy of Keats himself.

Hunt's prose begins as soon as his verse, with his articles
in *The Examiner,* some of which were reprinted along with
Hazlitt's in *The Round Table.* *The Indicator* (1819-21) is a
string of weekly essays, afterwards reprinted in a volume
which is still most pleasant and soothing to read. The famous
periodical, *The Liberal* (1822-3), published at Pisa, lived a year
under his conduct, and contained *The Vision of Judgment,*
Shelley's translations from *Faust,* and many other good things,
but involved Hunt in difficulties with Byron. He stayed till
1825 in Italy, deepening his native sympathy with the gayer
and more gracious sides of its life and poetry. Among the
fruits were his translation, admirably faithful in rush and
rhythm, of Redi's *Bacco in Toscana,* and, long afterwards, his

Jar of Honey from Mount Hybla (1848), full of happy memories
of Sicilian scenery, story, and poetry, with excursions on the
pastoral verse of several nations. Hunt lost repute by his
too candid and not very gentlemanly book, *Lord Byron and
some of his Contemporaries* (1828). His life afterwards is that
of a literary journalist, ever struggling against penury; and
of his many ventures, *The Tatler, Leigh Hunt's London Journal,
The Monthly Repository*, few were popular. After 1847 he was
put on the civil list, had time for more connected work, and
wrote in somewhat less haste, though the habit and effects of
improvisation clung to his writing to the end. *Imagination
and Fancy* and *Wit and Humour* are anthologies from the
poets, with comments and essays interspersed. *The Town* is
a miscellany of agreeable talks about London and its literary
and scenic associations. In 1850 he published his *Autobiography*, which is his best and most vivid book; indeed, almost
his only real *book*: it won the praise and even the respect
of his neighbour Carlyle.

Hunt, as an essayist, derives from *The Spectator*, and is in
form, or rather in want of finish, liker to Steele than to Addison.
He seems to wager with himself that he will write pleasantly
about anything, and his subject chooses him, rather than he it.
The Indicator has papers on angling, Lady Godiva, dolphins,
shaking hands, Pulci, 'my books,' and 'military insects.'
The result, it must be said, is an abundance of rigmarole, and
with Hunt it is hit or miss. He is not strong in self-criticism.
Hazlitt, who is at first sight equally miscellaneous, has several
definite styles and interests; he is fighting, or moralising, or
describing humours, or talking literature and art. He does
not abandon himself, and run on about the first thing that
meets his eye in the street. Hunt's somewhat loose style,
and a certain bent towards effusiveness and sprawliness, have
even unduly hurt his fame, and kept him from often reaching
perfection. But his merit and charm still assert themselves.
He has a surprising enjoyment of life, of little fugitive things,
of toys, and daily trifles, and of the whim of the moment.
There is nothing acrid or dour in his composition; his comments on Byron err, but in a different direction. His most
curious book, *The Religion of the Heart*, shows him at his best.
It is a pathetic and early example of an effort to make a creed
and canon—nay, even a ritual, out of the sayings of saints and
sages, as a substitute for the orthodox (and suspect) forms.
Socrates, and Jesus, and Emerson, and Dr. Combe are laid
under contribution, and a family worship is invented, consist-

ing of 'aspirations,' or semi-scriptural versicles for recital.
Hunt has not the style for such a task, but he gives us the
thoughts of his heart at a manifest expense of its best blood.
His gospel is cheerful and optimistic ; he vaguely believes in
a divine spirit, and in a transmigration of souls ; would give
all men a chance, and advises them to face death easily ; and,
above all, preaches the cult of beauty.

This, indeed, is Hunt's distinctive note, and it connects
him intimately with the romantic movement. Denied true
creative power, he falls back on the enjoyment of fair and
pleasant things—including the practice of charity and kindli-
ness. The pleasantest and fairest things in life are perhaps
books ; which are a kind of distilment of spring, and youth,
and old wine, and the grace of childhood. His criticism consists chiefly in beckoning to the reader to share his intense
relish for high or fine literature. His taste is perhaps the
most comprehensive and catholic of his time ; and though
he is not a revealer, or a great discriminator, or a philosopher,
he has a wonderful instinct for good things, and rarely praises
wrong. Dante and Moschus, Chaucer and Jonson, Butler
and Keats, Montaigne and Spinoza—none come amiss to him :
his essay on *My Books* gives us the most vivid sense of his
ardent and genial connoisseurship, as he sits surrounded with
his pleasures.

II

John Keats[1] (1795-1821) has at length been treated, de-
servedly, like an ancient classic. He has been well and fully
edited, and the books, marbles, and pictures that quickened
his art are not likely to be much better known than they are.
Greatly as we wish he had lived longer, he is by no means one
of the 'inheritors of unfulfilled renown.' His fellow-poets
have praised and judged him beyond appeal. He has been
so much studied that we are in danger of losing him in the
commentary. There seems little more to say, unless we can
write of him as he wrote of Chapman or of Milton. It is lost
labour to explain the nightingale, or to become a scholiast
of the autumnal 'stubble-plains with rosy hue.' We can but
learn to share in his peculiar mode of enjoying these things ; and
the best way to do so is to understand it from his own lips.

No poet buries his face so deep in the lap of his mother
earth, or gets down so suddenly to the Nature to which
man, not too soon, has to return. Keats at times wishes to
die into nature—to 'cease upon the midnight with no pain ';

but this is not his ordinary mood—it is rather characteristic of Shelley. He seeks, instead, to live in nature, and to be incorporate with one beautiful thing after another. He seems to be the spirit of them all, which has attained self-consciousness and expression. This Pan-like temper is plain from the first. He is the 'wailful choir' of the gnats, and the wraith of Lorenzo on whose dead feet 'a large flint-stone weighs,' and the 'chuckling linnet,' and the 'yellow-girted bees.' All true poets, no doubt, penetrate into nature in the same way; but this is just what Keats himself tells us that they do; and his power of doing it may fairly be distinguished, not only by its superior intensity, which gives him a difference in rank and species from even the most accomplished and faithful of describers, such as Thomson; but by its idiosyncrasy, of which he is himself well aware, and which he sets forth in his famous letter to his friend Wood-house. This is no mere fling of fancy, or figure of speech, but the expression of a primal instinct in Keats himself. He is describing the 'poetical character':

It is not itself—it has no self—it is everything and nothing—it has no character—it enjoys light and shade—it lives in gusto, be it foul or fair, high or low, rich or poor, mean or elevated—it has as much delight in conceiving an Iago as an Imogen. What shocks the virtuous philosopher delights the chameleon poet. It does no harm from its relish for the dark side of things, any more than from its taste for the bright side, because they both end in speculation. A poet is the most unpoetical of anything in existence, because he has no identity; for he is continually in and filling some other body. The sun, the moon, the sea, and men and women, who are creatures of impulse, are unpoetical, and have about them an unchangeable attribute; the poet has none, no identity—he is certainly the most unpoetical of God's creatures (27th Oct. 1818).

Elsewhere he says:

I scarcely remember counting upon any happiness. I look not for it if it be not in the present hour. The setting sun will always set me to rights, or if a sparrow come before my window, I take part in its existence, and pick about the gravel.

From this point of view the difference between nature and art becomes unreal, for both give the same sort of enjoyment. They are confounded, and the confusion is worth all the philosophical distinctions that can be made between them. Keats does not, like Chaucer and Wordsworth, tell us to throw away our book and go out into the sun or shade. Nature is herself a delicious poetry-book, and *A Midsummer Night's Dream* is an unexplored forest, and *The Flower and the Leaf* is ' like a little copse.' Writing from Carisbrooke, Keats quotes Spenser, and lives on stray lines from *The Tempest*, and also on ' several delightful wood-alleys, and copses and freshes,' which he has discovered, and which do him the same kind of good. This is the true way to live. The affinity between natural and artistic beauty he states, with more than a pleasant extravagance, in his youthful couplets :

> In the calm grandeur of a sober line,
> We see the waving of the mountain pine ;
> And when a tale is beautifully staid,
> We feel the safety of a hawthorn glade.

Beauty may have passed through other brains, and taken shape as art, before it reaches the poet ; but that makes no difference to him ; with all its varieties, it is one in essence, and he is one with it.

In all this we may feel there is something unqualified and unripe ; an element due to youth and the infection of Leigh Hunt, and to a passionate discipline, as yet imperfect, in the work of the great poets themselves. But there is nothing affected in it, though we can hardly believe that there is not, because our ears have been dinned with later theories about the ' cult ' of beauty. With all their greatness, their seriousness, their immense achievement, and their curious vein of fun, there *is* something affected about the ' Pre-Raphaelites '—about Rossetti and Swinburne, and even about Morris—when they start to talk about ' beauty '; and also about Pater and some of his critical successors. The popular instinct took hold of this failing, and the caricaturists joked about it bluntly ; but it is there, and at moments it is rather sickening. Keats works his way through all sorts of faults, but he does not pose ; the love of beauty is really and truly an original passion with him, and he says so. But the matter is not so simple as that.

Taken by itself, the temper he describes may be merely that of the enjoying connoisseur, who need not be a poet, and whose very enjoyments are limited by his evasion of suffering. By his power of suffering, and of creating too, Keats is more than the ' poet ' he describes. In this he resembles his friend Hazlitt, to whose talk he liked to listen, and whose favourite word *gusto* he uses. Hazlitt's pleasures in life and art were intensified by suffering, and also by his creative power—a term which is truly applicable to criticism like his, although in a lower degree. Most men are keenly aware of their joys and pains, but separately ; and are more dimly aware of their satieties. Keats came to feel that his joys were not at the full until they were sharpened into pains ; this is the burden of the *Ode to Melancholy*. He feels, too, that beauty, like Thea in *Hyperion*, is made ' more beautiful than beauty's self ' by sorrow ; so that the religion of beauty speedily becomes a religion of sorrow. It is vain to call him a Greek, for no Greek could see or say this as clearly as Keats does in the *Ode to a Nightingale*. He has no Christian sentiment ; but his naturalism is not, except at first, merely passive and sensational, like that of an instrument (if we could imagine such) that delights in the tunes played upon it. His letters, and the more exalted of his sonnets, and the revised version of *Hyperion*, show how far he got beyond that stage. He was not a poet who rested in sensations, but one whose sensations were so rich that he was awhile embarrassed in thinking and working upon them. This process of clearance and self-discovery is the clue to the history of Keats's spirit ; and the corresponding process, reflected in his expression, is the clue to the history of his art. His native stock of impressions and enjoyments was so great and so constantly renewed during his short life, that no overplus of thought and reflection ever left him stranded as an artist. He never became abstract, though he left some nobly intellectual verse ; that is, he remained a poet. He had much to endure ; and he did not shirk it, or seek for creeds to deaden it, but drew it closer to him, and sought to express it ; and the grandeur of his writing, as distinct from its charm, consists in this achievement, and comes out clearer as his works are reviewed in order. If we remember that he was to die at about the age when Wordsworth was finishing *The Borderers*, we shall wonder that he travelled so far.

Keats's want of conventional education and of interest in politics, affairs, and philosophic theory leaves him a poet of a different range to Shelley ; but he is a man of his time for all that. His art is fed and impelled by that of some of his contemporaries—of Hunt in one way, and Wordsworth in another. Thirty years earlier, or later, he would not have come in the first flush of the discovery of the old English poets—especially those of our Renaissance, to whose spirit and vocabulary he owed so much. He began, partly under Hunt's tutelage, by seeing natural and verbal beauty much after their manner, and expressing it in their language ; and he never lost this imprint, though it became overlaid by other influences.

He walked down a London lane (such lanes then existed) and thought of it in the language of Chapman or William Browne, just as Lamb thought of a deer-forest, in his *John Woodvil*, in the language of *As You Like It*. This is a note of the period, of which we find more examples ; and Keats's poetic diction will claim a separate word. He is also of the time in his growing unrest, and in his reaching out after the infinite, and in that mixture of pain with his enjoyment which we have noted, and in his needless noble touches of fear and scruple lest he should become inhumanly wrapped up in his art. He could hardly have lived at any other epoch and written as he did. At the same time Keats is certainly less a thing of the age's making than any other of its great poets—less than Wordsworth, or Byron, or Shelley. The genius of Landor (as distinct from his opinions) is almost as independent of surroundings ; but Landor's genius, as well as his opinions, was inspired by the Revolution, which only touched Keats remotely if at all. Thus the work of Keats, whilst in one sense the poorer, is in another the more enduring, as it is the less staked upon interests that are not universal or eternal.

Many of the pieces published in 1817 are experiments, or first sketches, in the manner of *Endymion*, with the same richness and confusion of imagery, and the same beautiful but rather nerveless versification, and also with the same authentic tokens of future power. They represent, however, a stage behind that of *Endymion* itself ; there is less thinking in them, and less achieved beauty. The influence of the Jacobean poets and Spenser is even more predominant. These writers came to Keats, not only as revelations of a lovely dream-world full of chivalrous shapes, and tapestried with scenes from enchanted forests, but also as the very trans-mitters and voices of the antique. From them (and not only from the dusty Lemprière,[1] as used to be supposed) he learnt tales like those of Endymion, and Glaucus, and Syrinx, and Pan, and Hyacinthus. In this mixed, surcharged form the antique came to him, with the profusion, the heady perfume, the formlessness of nature herself, as of a bean-field over which bees are murmuring. Some of the most heroic tales in the world, moreover, came to him through Chapman's *Homer*, with its style that is so manly and magnificent, but is also so easily false—false every five minutes ! The poets were to lead him out of this bewildering enchanted ground— *Paradise Lost*, and Shakespeare, and Dryden too ; but mean-time the poets had led him into it, and it is no wonder that his style faltered between beauty and inefficiency, and that his inefficient reviewers, who did not even know where he got his style, were blind to its beauty.

At this stage Spenser stands out above all the other creditors of Keats, as is evident from *Calidore*, and the *Imitation of Spenser*, and 'I stood tiptoe upon a little hill,' and *Sleep and Poetry*. Yet he never learnt the best that Spenser had to give—the secret of evenness and purity in style. He inhales Spenser's mood and temper; he enters his magic regions, as we see in the *Specimen of an Induction to a Poem*:

> Lo, I must tell a tale of chivalry;
> For large white plumes are dancing in mine eye;

and he lingers in his sleepy gardens, where, by the lapse of waters, men wait and drowse, and forget the holy quest. But he does not learn his sureness and rightness of expression. He learns, later, a sureness and rightness of his own; but this Keats has to reach by gradually economising his native wealth, and not, like Wordsworth, by enriching his native ruggedness. The contrast between these two poets is always meeting us. The earlier colouring of Keats is that of the south-English lowlands — flower-paven, bee-haunted, water-lit; Wordsworth's is that of the hillside, at first seeming cold and monotonous, but coming out, like Helvellyn under the sunshine, into an exquisite stain of blue-grey and modulated rust, 'proceeding from the iron that interveins the stone and impregnates the soil.' Keats, therefore, is not Spenser's pupil in style, except for some special turns and coinages. Chastity of form he has not yet found, in the volume of 1817; but sometimes we see it coming, as in the sonnet on Chapman's *Homer*. The study of such gradual changes is one of our chief delights in presence of a great poet, especially when he dies too young, or is too happy in his growth for the reverse change ever to force itself on our notice—the dying down or petrifaction of his form, under the stress of age or of the world or of the mere habit of writing.

III

Shelley well said of *Endymion* that it contained treasures of poetry, but that these were 'poured out in indistinct profusion.' This is still truer of Keats's first volume, and not least of its chief production, *Sleep and Poetry*, which is the first half-articulate voice of his aspiration as a craftsman. Here he prays that he may have ten years of life, ' that I may over-

whelm Myself in poesy,' and forecasts his task.   First he will
pass the 'realm of Flora and old Pan,' and write simply a
'lovely tale' ; then he will 'bid these joys farewell' :

> Yes, I must pass them for a nobler life
> Where I may find the agonies, the strife
> Of human hearts.

But meantime he is interrupted by a vision of an air-borne
charioteer in whose train are mysterious and lovely shapes ;
yet it all vanishes, and leaves him in doubt whether the
golden, the Elizabethan age of imagination can ever revive.
But *redeunt Saturnia regna*, the age is renewed ; after that long
silence of poetry, which is (1817) compared to 'might half-
slumbering on its own right arm.'   Keats himself, with all his
fears, banishes 'Déspondence' and will do his part, heartened
by the company of like-minded friends.   Sleep, invoked at
the outset, comes with her train of visions—fauns, satyrs,
and nymphs, with the 'cold and sacred busts' of the old poets
ranged about the poet's house, which is 'pleasure's temple.'
All this, told with an 'indistinct profusion' of images, but with
abundance of perfect lines and phrases, prepares us for *Endymion* and its scenery and governing mood : and there, though
still indistinctly, the poet's quest is to be further symbolised.

The verse-craft of this early volume, and of *Endymion*
itself, well answers to the mood of which it is the vehicle.
More than five thousand lines are written in the 'heroic'
couplet, which is here mostly as unheroic as it can be.   The
Epistles to Keats's brother George, and to his friends Felton
Mathew and Cowden Clarke, suit it ; but in the other pieces
its familiar faults can escape nobody, in spite of its grace and
sweetness.   The couplet is of the free-running, overflowing
sort, practised by Browne and Chamberlayne, and already
exaggerated by Leigh Hunt ; where the rhymes, however full-
sounding, tend to be in the nature of accidents.   They only
just arrest the ear, for they do not go along with the sense.
Their rhythm is not that of the feeling ; the rhyme-emphasis
is on the wrong words, as here :

> Is there so small a range
> In the present strength of manhood, that the *high*
> Imagination cannot freely fly
> As she was wont of old ? prepare her steeds,
> Paw up against the light, and do strange deeds
> Upon the clouds ?   Has she not shown us all ?
> From the clear space of ether, to the *small*
> Breath of new buds unfolding ?

High and *small*, being rhyme-words, wrest undue attention to themselves. Keats would never have written thus in *Lamia* ; but still there is a premonition of the perfect balance he was afterwards to discover :

> The patient weeds, that now unshent by foam
> Feel all about their undulating home.

The misuse of double rhymes has often been reproached, and in some of the early poems they are one-quarter of the whole ; and though they are not used at random, but studiously, to carry images of rich passive pleasure and floating contentment, they become a drawback, because these images themselves bulk too large and cloy us. Besides, the double ending is apt to go with an unlucky sort of facetiousness, or of sickliness, which certainly, as the reviewers were prompt to cry aloud, beset the ' cockney school.' There is no reason to linger on these or other touches of vulgarity in Keats, which were due to mere adolescence and cheap society ; we need only marvel how quickly they were burnt away in him. The double rhyme itself, we have seen, was simply a sign of revolt against the mechanical or metronomic decasyllables of the ' classical ' school ; but, in the result, it came to be associated with other palpable flaws, such as the misuse of the colloquial adverbs, *quite, very, so*, and of over-honeyed epithet. These things need only be named once in reference to Keats ; but one result, in his first volume, is that the best passages seldom hold out for more than a few lines ; and when they do they are usually found in the sonnets.

It seems that Keats was nineteen[1] when he wrote his one contribution to heroic lyric, *On first looking into Chapman's Homer*, so faultless in its structure and athletic diction, and spoken as it were in the energy of a single breath. Three of the other sixteen early sonnets are in a more native mood— that of high poetic luxury. Two of them begin with the same spondaic tune—' Keen, fitful gusts are whisp'ring here and there,' and ' Small, busy flames play through the fresh laid coals,' but both drop into a less consummate diction. They really fall among Keats's letters, and are an intimate picture of him as he was amidst his friends and books. ' Eloquent distress ' is the happiest description ever given of *Lycidas*, making neither too much of Milton's grief nor too little. *On the Grasshopper and Cricket* (' The poetry of earth is never dead ') is another sonnet of luxury. Two more—' How many bards gild the lapses of time,' and ' Nymph of the downward smile and sidelong glance,' have at least a noble overture ; and, taken all together, the whole seventeen show Keats's metrical confidence in the Italian form of sonnet—studied, no doubt, from Milton.

It is convenient to touch here on his other sonnets, all posthumously published, and more than thirty in number. Many belong to these early years, including *The Flower and the Leaf*, and ' After dark vapours have oppress'd our plains ' : the beauty and weakness of which are what we should expect. The sonnet *On Visiting the Tomb of Burns*, though terribly jagged and imperfect, is at least welcome for its opposite excess of painful and powerful feeling. These again are in the Italian measure ; and two others of irregular make, *To Sleep*, and ' If by dull rhymes our English must be chain'd,' are worthy of Keats. Others are in Shakespeare's rhyme-arrangement, and one, ' Time's sea hath been five years at its slow ebb,' is a fervid and triumphant mimicry of Shakespeare ; and in *The Human Seasons*, at the beginning and end, there is the same element, but the middle is in Keats's own fashion. Of the remainder, two are of the loftiest rank, namely: 'When I have fears,' and ' Bright Star ! ' the last of his poems, completed on his voyage, under the shadow of death and the memory of unfulfilled love. ' When I have fears,' composed two years before, is a forecast, made as if by second sight, of this tragic issue—the frustration by death of his happiness and of his task ; but the mind of Keats rises above the chances of mortality. Two more of the sonnets in this metrical mould must be chosen out, ' The day is gone,' and ' As Hermes once.' The latter is inspired by reading of Paolo and Francesca in Cary's *Dante* ; and the sestet has more in it of Dante's essence than all the poems and dramas in which the story has been fingered to death. It is founded on an actual dream of Keats,[1] which he describes in prose that matches the verse of the sonnet.

IV

In *Endymion* the story fills the larger part of the poem, and is ill enough told ; while the moon-allegory, peering in places out of the moonlit clouds, is soon obscured, and is never at any point quite lucid. The pains and pleasures that come to the poetic soul in its search for ideal beauty [2] are figured under Endymion's adventures ; and the Moon herself is the image of such beauty. The old myth, a favourite of the Elizabethans, was told by Drayton more as a tale than as a myth, with a profusion of arabesque, lovely or strange conceit,

and leisurely episode, but also with sudden sallies of a pure and
sweet perfection. The same may be said of Keats's poem ; but
then such passages are much more frequent in it, and the reach
and ambition of the work are also far greater than Drayton's.
Repeatedly, from the rich but pathless woodland of the narrative, there rise higher summits, at first thickly clustered.   In
the opening book there are the overture, the feast of Pan,
with the great ode in his honour ; and the speech of Peona
to Endymion. In the second, amid the rambling and yet breathless course of the story, there comes at last the lovely and
lofty comment upon the birth of the Moon legend (828-853)
—an offspring of lakeside and forest—and of its first capture
by the antique unknown poet. Endymion, meanwhile, is no
further with his quest, and story and interpretation alike are
checked in the ' deep water-world.' The third book contains
the long digression on Glaucus and Scylla, which seems to
be a parable of the mortal but ideal love which is only crowned
by fate after long and strange vexations. Much of this is
told in Keats's weakest and most spun-out manner, and despite
the beautiful picture of Glaucus and his pursuits we are glad
when it is over. In the last book the allegory is more insistent
and more devious, but it leads at last to the vision of Endymion
and Phœbe mated. The poet, or aspirant, has at last reached
his goal, after struggling long between the call of human
love, in the person of the ' Indian maiden,' and that of ideal
loveliness or perfection, typified by the Moon. These claims
are reconciled, for the maiden proves to be Phœbe in disguise ;
but the identity is not revealed before Endymion has passed
through many a phase of despondency and infertile flatness,
caused by his mistakes. At one time he has tried to solve
the riddle by repelling his human nature, and at another by
mistaking a life of immersion in lovely material things for the
true religion of beauty. At last he enlarges both the human
and the ideal love till they are the same, like equal circles
superposed. Keats does not say how this reconciliation is
contrived, but only that it happens. The lyrics and odes,
which hardly touch the allegory, are the finest parts of this
concluding book. The so-called ' roundelay ' to Sorrow, with
its clear prolonged chime, is one of the few songs, properly
so called, of any value that Keats wrote ; but in the great
descriptive and processional ode upon the Bacchanals, with the
clangour and passion of its interspersed short rhyming lines,
there is the very frenzy of the dark old religions in their hours
of dancing orgy—an astonishing emanation from Hampstead.

> I saw Osirian Egypt kneel adown
> Before the vine-wreath crown !
> I saw parch'd Abyssinia rouse and sing
> To the silver cymbals' ring !
> I saw the whelming vintage hotly pierce
> Old Tartary the fierce !   ʼ

The living motion and hot colouring of this are worth as much to us as the eternal, arrested, and pathetic beauty that Keats afterwards discovers on the sides of the Greek urn.

Keats has been censured for the lines at the beginning of the second book of *Endymion*, in which he says that he prefers romance to history, the tale of Troilus to that of the Trojan war, and the ' swoon of Imogen ' to the ' death-day of empires.' He puts the case in a young petulant way which delights us, and is merely true to youth, and romance, and his own genius as it was at the moment, and to the earlier temper of Chaucer himself in *Troilus*. He dismisses subjects that do not yet suit him. It is curious, however, that in this passage he writes best when describing the matter he repudiates, which is that of Chapman's *Homer* :

> The woes of Troy, towers smothering o'er their blaze,
> Stiff-holden shields, far-piercing spears, keen blades,
> Struggling, and blood, and shrieks.

But from these things he turns to speak of Adonis ; with a want of passion, it must be said, which the excess of amorous description makes painful, if with an abundance of ' strangeness in beauty.' But Keats himself, in his preface, has forestalled criticism. Even while sending out the poem, he felt he had done with it. In conception and accomplishment alike, ' this youngster,' as he calls it, is the fruit of a wonderful adolescence ; and he has ' some hope that while it is dwindling I may be plotting, and fitting myself for verses fit to live.' At the date of writing this (April 1818), he was engaged on *Isabella* ; within a year he had drafted *Hyperion*, and written some of his greater odes, and *The Eve of St. Agnes*, and *La Belle Dame sans Merci*. Before the end of 1819 he had done most of what he had to do ; the volume of 1820, and the sheaf of posthumous and fugitive pieces, complete his legacy.

V

Isabella, *The Eve of St. Agnes*, and *Lamia* were composed in succession, and *The Eve of Saint Mark* was begun along with *Lamia*. These tales show a progressive increase of narrative

craft and poetic maturity, which we can watch in the summer
months of 1818, like some swiftly-opening flower. In *Isabella,
or the Pot of Basil*, Keats asks pardon of Boccaccio, much as
Spenser does of Chaucer in his sequel to the *Squire's Tale* ; and
with equally good reason, for the story is not always well told.
The bare and economical, yet complex and beautiful prose of
the original fits the subject perfectly, and so does the sober
romantic irony. Boccaccio as a narrator gives a greater
intellectual pleasure than Keats, who declaims jarringly or
comically against the wicked commercial brethren ; and in
the love-making there are remnants of the boyish luscious
style he was abandoning. But the colour and magic of the
English poem—the passion which, as Lamb says of Webster's
dirge, is ' of the earth earthy,' and ' seems to resolve itself into
the element which it contemplates '—the tale of the discovery
of the murdered body, which Lamb himself praised so well—
all this, though not outside the mediæval imagination, has a
touch more rare than is granted even to Boccaccio. Once
the crime is committed, the story glides along fast, with nothing
demeaning or superfluous ; the ghastly and *macabre* element
never becomes repellent through a single lapse of imagination,
and is also relieved by the final strain of pathos, which leaves
all that misery now far remote and matter for a country folk-
song :

> And a sad ditty of this story born
>   From mouth to mouth through all the country pass'd ;
> Still is the burthen sung—' O cruelty,
> To steal my Basil-pot away from me ! '

So, in *The Eve of St. Agnes*, the whole is thrown back into the
far distance, for

> ages long ago
> These lovers fled away into the storm.

In this story the imagination is more evenly and constantly
at work than in *Isabella*, and though it never reaches the same
pitch of suspense as in the forest scene, the total effect is stronger.
Keats had at best an old rhyme to work upon, and no story to
tell ; but he ' loads every rift with ore,' and every verse with
felicities ; and the movement, the suspense, quicken line by
line ; and the terror behind, the fierceness that lies in wait
though asleep for the lovers through their colloquies, is kept
as clear before the mind as it is in *Romeo and Juliet*. By now
Keats's love-scenes have lost their sickliness, and a Spenserian
clearness and chivalry are maintained, together with a glow
of colour—' warm gules '—that is more than Spenserian. Also

Spenser's measure is used, or re-created ; and the alexandrines
are of noteworthy magnificence :

> ' She comes, she comes again, like ringdove fray'd and fled.'
> ' For o'er the southern moors I have a home for thee ! '

A few months, and Keats was at work upon a new style, more
ringing and rapid, and full of metallic notes and verbal fashions
that he had learnt from Dryden, so that he is the last great
poet, and a strange one, to be Dryden's scholar ; a style not
wholly unlike the best parts of *Theodore and Honoria*, and
marked by the same bold, not highly subtle, treatment of the
supernatural.   The tale of *Lamia* is garnished with a para-
bolical meaning, which does not seem to be in the poet's mind
from the first, but to arise from the scene in which ' the myrtle
sickened in a thousand wreaths,' and the ' philosopher '
Apollonius withers the lady at the banquet ; having, ' by some
probable conjecture, found her out to be a serpent, a lamia.'
The old witch-story, thus handed down by Burton in his
Anatomy of Melancholy, and thence cited by Keats, has, with
its sudden transformations and vanishings, a good deal of the
dream about it ; and as such, or as a winter's tale, it is best
remembered.   Well as it is told, it will not bear too close a
regard.   Lamia, who is thus detected to be a serpent, has
persuaded Hermes that her true form is that of a woman, and
he changes her from a woman-headed serpent into a woman ;
an episode invented by Keats and marred by the fireworks
of indistinct colour and giddy motion in his picture of the
transformation.   As if in whim, Lamia is made out to be a
symbol of the charm of poetry and romance, which vanishes
at the touch of ' cold philosophy '—a theme that must not
be pressed too hard.   The true contrast is that of the sinister
marvel itself with the real and crowded pleasant city of Corinth
in which it happens ; and the less unearthly scenes are the
best delineated, such as that of the city streets murmuring by
night :

> Men, women, rich and poor, in the cool hours,
> Shuffled their sandals o'er the pavement white,
> Companion'd or alone ; while many a light
> Flared, here and there, from wealthy festivals,
> And threw their moving shadows on the walls,
> Or found them cluster'd in the corniced shade
> Of some arch'd temple door, or dusky colonnade.

The movement of parts of *Jason* or *The Earthly Paradise* is
forecast here ; but with Keats we are in a real city, and not

in one of musical shadows. The handling of the couplets in
Lamia is perfect, and the actual echoes of Dryden's rhythm,
though unmistakable, are not so frequent as to disturb :

> while he, afraid
> Lest she should vanish ere his lip had paid
> Due adoration, thus began to adore ;
> Her soft look growing coy, she saw his chain so sure.

But the real lesson learnt from Dryden is that of co-ordinating
the measure with the sense, and bracing the formerly often
enervate rhymes, and resting strongly upon them ; while at
the same time the mere rhetoric of epigram and antithesis is
repressed.

But a finer poise of rhythm and a rarer touch on words are
found in *The Eve of Saint Mark*. Throughout this fragment there
is a purity of image that is never chill, a real and achieved
harmony between beauty and playfulness (the latter hitherto
too often a snare for Keats), and a perfect hold on the short
measure, which neither slides into over-fluency, nor is broken
into couplet-epigram. This skill, no doubt, is partly learnt
from Chaucer's use of the octosyllabic verse ; and the beauty
of Keats's impossible Middle English verses upon the nature
of dreams mocks at the pedant. Memories of Winchester
colour the poem, which, says Keats, ' is quite in the spirit of
town quietude. I think it will give you the sensation of walking about an old country town on a coolish evening.' Here
may best be seen the kind of spell Keats exercised on the
romancers of the next age. *The Eve of Saint Mark* is no col-
lateral or remote, but a direct and near ancestor of Tennyson's
St. Agnes' Eve and the drawings by Millais and his companions. The delicacy, the ease, the harmony are the same ;
and that somewhat studious accumulation of 'beauties,' which
is felt even in *The Eve of St. Agnes*, is lightened, and the style
is effortless as well as concentrated. Instead of simply moving
from one felicity to another, the mind takes in the whole
harmony of the picture. The actual subject is never reached.
The belief was that on that evening the phantoms of those
persons who are to sicken during the coming twelvemonth are
seen to pass in at the church door. Keats only gives us the
prologue—the Sabbath scene, and the girl reading the legend,
and her ' uneasy ' shadow on the walls :

> From plaited lawn-frill, fine and thin,
> She lifted up her soft warm chin,
> With aching neck and swimming eyes,
> And daz'd with saintly imageries.

Rossetti may well have learnt from this something of the slow beat and packed imagery, and also of the virginal atmosphere, of *Ave Mary* and his other verses in the same measure.

La Belle Dame sans Merci is another of the poems of Keats that found a great following ; but the experiments of Rossetti and his friends in the style of the 'literary ballad' sound forced and cramped after it.   It is in fact further from the folk-ballad than *The Ancient Mariner*—the conventions, the diction, the burden, are left far off, although the use of the echo, or refrain ('on the cold hill-side'), is essential to the effect. The ballad metre is there, with a difference that is everything— the last line of each verse being reduced to four from six syllables, with a spondaic, tolling close.   Keats weakened this great poem in some particulars when he printed it ; it should be read as he wrote it out in his 'journal-letter' to his brother George (1818). The art is felt in the economies and omissions, as in *The Wife of Usher's Well*, the most imaginative of our supernatural popular ballads.   The fairy has no motive except to add to her slaves ; the knight no reason for returning ; there is no leaden moral, and the lady is an elf, not a symbol.   The ancient subject of the mortal captured by such an elf, as Thomas the Rhymer was, must have been familiar to Keats ; and the well-known plight of the man who is restored desolate to our earth, so that he belongs neither to the inside nor the outside of the magic hill, is perhaps the starting-point for his imagination.   *La Belle Dame sans Merci* remains a touchstone for this kind of composition.

The four poems *Fancy*, 'Bards of Passion and of Mirth,' *Lines on the Mermaid Tavern*, and *Robin Hood*, printed in the volume of 1820, should be read in the letters in which they were first sent ;—they are less considered works of skill than impromptus, the poet taking up his silver pen in the midst of telling familiar news.   The trochaic couplets are swift and gay, and each rhyme seems to be flung down before its mate is thought of.   All four pieces celebrate older English verse and story ; and *Fancy*, in the earlier sense of playing with images, or ingeniously brooding on outward things till the pleasure of doing so brings the right words—fancy is the note of them all :

> Thou shalt see the field-mouse peep
> Meagre from its celled sleep ;
> And the snake all winter-thin
> Cast on sunny bank its skin.

This shows the same sort of vision as Marvell's verse upon 'the brooding throstle's shining eye,' or Breton's on the rabbit that washes its face with its fore-feet. In the other pieces the Elizabethan poets are saluted, and in *Robin Hood* the makers of the outlaw ballads. These verses were written several years before *Ivanhoe*, and some months before Peacock began his *Maid Marian*. The tragic piece, *Otho the Great*, and the fragmentary *King Stephen*, are further tributes to the old poets, but are imitative, and do not show Keats's power except in stray phrases, or suggest that he might have become a dramatist.

VI

The later Odes,[1] as small but complex works of art, challenge as close a scrutiny as if they were sonnets. They are a new and original variety of the genus Ode, with their intricate rhymed stanzas. The metre of one is never repeated in another, but in all except the *Ode to Psyche* and the fragment *To Maia* the stanza is regular. These stanzas, too, have the character of members of a sonnet-series ; they are poems linked together, but usually each is complete in itself. Generally, Keats tries to concentrate, as far as ever the law of beauty permits ; every line is like a bough that is weighed down with fruit to the breaking-point. This effort is best seen in the most impeccable of all, *To Autumn*. The scented landscape in the first stanza, and the symphony of natural sounds in the third, would have been enough for most poets ; but the effect would have been dispersed or confused without the slowly-moving or resting figures, in the central verse, of the winnower and gleaner ; these make the picture human and universal ; for the eternal labours of man, as he makes the most of nature, are kept before the eye by a profound instinct for plastic arrangement. The *Ode to Psyche* stands midway in style between *Endymion* and *Hyperion* ; for the lovers are painted in the earlier and less restrained fashion; but the statelier note is there too, and Milton would not have been ashamed or surprised to have written the opening :

> O latest born and loveliest vision far
> Of all Olympus' faded hierarchy !

Autumn is purely delineative, but in *Psyche* the poet appears himself as the builder of Psyche's 'rosy sanctuary' and as her priest ; thus he will find his refuge—from what, he does not here say ; but in the odes *On a Grecian Urn*[2] and *To a Nightingale* he reveals it, and most of all in the *Ode on Melancholy*. These three poems, together with one or two of the sonnets, and certain passages in his letters, tell us much of Keats himself, of his worship of beauty, and of the way in which he connects it with the sadness of experience. He has defined this creed more clearly than any Englishman, except Shakespeare in his sonnets. It is a good religion, though it has been vulgarised since. He 'speaks out loud and clear,' and it is at the foundation of his work, and there is no flaw in the masonry anywhere between base and pinnacle. Beauty, in his interpretation, has nothing in common with the Intellectual Beauty celebrated by Shelley, which is an ecstasy attained after an ascent of the giddy stairway which leads from sensuous experience to pure contemplation, and the clue to which is given by a transcendental refinement of Love. To Keats beauty is always concrete, though not always external; it lives in definite images, not necessarily of nature or the human form, but sometimes also of human beings acting or suffering—images of the soul at work. In this sense it is the same as Truth— 'truth in beauty dyed' is Shakespeare's phrase for their connection; and thus a larger than the apparent meaning is given to the doctrine uttered at the close of the *Grecian Urn*, that this is 'all ye need to know.' This conclusion, indeed, is too large for the main theme of the poem, which after all expresses a passing though recurrent thought : namely, of course, that the dead figures on the urn are more real, because more lasting in beauty, than the actual objects they represent ; and also happier, because their joy is ever still to come, while on earth joy passes. The 'unheard melodies,' the 'little town' which is not even on the urn at all, but is brought to mind, perhaps out of some Dürer picture, 'mountain-built,'—*these* are the eternal things. The beginning and the close may fall short of the stanzas that come between—but what would not fall short of them ? One thing perhaps equals them, namely, the ode to Maia, *Written on Mayday*, a simple and unalloyed wish, consummate in form, that the poet might join the old Sicilian or island company of bards.

If the beauty that is truth includes much of human trouble and action, and of the poet's own pain as well, a discord arises between the form, which gives delight, and the thing represented, which is tragic or causes despondency. What, then, can art and beauty do for the pains of life ? *To a Nightingale* gives an answer to this most practical question. Its tone is that of a high melancholy, which is inspired by the passing of youth and joy (as it is also in the lovely song 'In a drear-nighted December'), and which is only half-cheated out of itself by the bird's note ; the memory of which carries the dreamer away from the Hampstead garden and the English plum-tree under which he sits in the daytime to the perfumed midnight and the thicket overhung by the unseen moon. The divine defiance of logic in the seventh stanza, by which the individual nightingale is fancied as immortal, has arrested needlessly the enjoyment of some critics, whose patroness-bird is also from Attica. At the end the dream is out and the music fled ; but meanwhile sorrow has disappeared under the power of the very imagination that works upon it. This ode is the greatest, as a concerted composition, that Keats made, and is also the richest in variety of passionate expression.

Keats is not likely to have known much of any Eastern doctrine that consciousness is an evil, desire an illusion, and the beauties of sense a mirage ; nor might he have cared for it. But there is a touch of this feeling in the sonnet ' When I have fears,' and also in the *Ode on Melancholy*. There the pain of love triumphant is felt, and the transience of beauty ; for Melancholy also dwells with

> Joy, whose hand is ever at his lips
> Bidding adieu.

But the conclusion is not Eastern at all ; it is a sublime sort of Epicureanism ; for it is the enjoyer who knows Melancholy best :

> His soul shall taste the sadness of her might,
> And be among her cloudy trophies hung.

This ode is spoilt by the middle verse, with its comparative cheapness ; such a phrase as ' let her rave,' in its context, could only be redeemed by the high and faultless inspiration of the third verse just quoted. The vision of the three ' figures on a marble urn,' Love, Ambition, and Poesy, which opens the unequal *Ode on Indolence*, has no such deep import. They pass and vanish, after coming to life, back into ' masque-like figures on the dreamy urn ' ; better than them all is Indolence, a kind of trance without assignable record :

> Pain had no sting, and pleasure's wreath no flower ;
> O, why did ye not melt, and leave my sense
> Unhaunted quite of all but—nothingness ?

This is more like the youthful Keats ; but it is a mood that came back to him and remained characteristic, although he moved more habitually in the sharper and deeper experience of which the greater odes are the utterance.

Hyperion was written along with the tales and odes, and

though unfinished is greater than they. It is a length of
epic or mythic frieze, abandoned, re-wrought, and again
abandoned ; in either of its forms, perhaps, inherently incapable of being finished or even continued. It is the poem
that was to atone, and does atone, for the imperfections of
Endymion. It was to be great and heroic and pathetic, with
the heroism and pathos of defeated deities ; and like *Paradise
Lost*, where the fallen spirits regard themselves as godlike.
Milton here guards the way ; he saves Keats from treating
the tales of the Greek theogony in the style of Chapman and
the Jacobeans ; he lends a model for the verse and language,
and for the epical cast generally. This influence strikes deep,
far beyond the use of those ' inversions ' whose frequency,
according to Keats, induced him to drop the work ; and it has
been minutely traced[1] out by scholars. But in fact Keats
follows Milton too little rather than too much ; for after a
long and splendid triumph his style begins to waver, and in
spite of many glorious recoveries it does not keep up. The
spell of the Jacobeans reasserts itself ; the obsolete participial
epithets (' the rustled air,' the ridge ' stubborn'd with iron,'
and ' Enceladus tiger-passion'd ' are examples) thicken, and
the poet often falls into a bad rut of language—neither Miltonic
nor Jacobean, but something bad of his own. He does not
forge a diction that is fitted for the long wear and tear,
the time-and-wind-defying fabric, of an epic poem—even
such a short epic, on the scale of *Paradise Regained*, as *Hyperion*
would probably have been. This is only to say that Keats
was twenty-four and that he was trying to do what Milton
did when he was past fifty. Yet he has come nearer to Milton,
not only when he is following Milton, but when he is himself—
than any one else ;—nearer than Shelley or Landor. The opening three hundred lines of the First Book down to the speech
of Cœlus are in a great, original, and sustained style, full of
memories of Milton, but by no means too Miltonic. The
actual march is often more like Shakespeare's in his Histories,
the lines being separately spun rather than interlaced, but
not repelling one another or left in isolation ; they are accumulated, and the figure of enumeration is favoured by the poet :

> But it is so ; and I am smother'd up,
> And buried from all godlike exercise
> Of influence benign on planets pale,
> Of admonitions to the winds and seas,
> Of peaceful sway above man's harvesting,
> And all those acts which Deity supreme
> Doth ease its heart of love in.

What Keats has learnt, since he wrote *Endymion*, is to balance his decasyllabic line internally—one of the last secrets of the craft. In this passage the fifth line, ' Of peaceful sway,' is not perfectly balanced ; the first half weighs down the second, owing to the weak last foot. The beginning is very light in this one :

> As when, upon a trancèd summer night.

In Thomson's

> Come, gentle Spring ! ethereal mildness, come !

the balance is there, but it is mechanical. But it is perfect in Milton's line

> Hail, holy Light, offspring of Heaven first-born !

and in Keats's line

> Of influence benign on planets pale,

and in each line of the epic simile in the revised *Hyperion* :

> When in mid-day the sickening east wind
> Shifts sudden to the south, the small warm rain
> Melts out the frozen incense from all flowers,
> And fills the air with so much pleasant health
> That even the dying man forgets his shroud ;—
> Even so . . .

In this passage (and Keats wrote none nobler), there is also freedom, and not only balance ; the lines overrun, but not, as they once did, to the obscuration of the metre ; and the sweetness and gravity of the whole comparison—a brief poem in itself—are beyond praise. The dialogue of Titans in the Second Book of *Hyperion* culminates in the symbolic speech of Oceanus, which is another of Keats's triumphs, although it embarrasses the story ; and a certain flagging at the end of this book is redeemed in the Third, where the scene changes from gloom and discouragement to the summons of Apollo by Mnemosyne ; a contrast like that in the third book of *Paradise Lost.* But it breaks off [1] in the middle of a phrase. Why did not Keats go on ?

The question is more than curious, for it takes us into the heart of the poem, though the answer must be guesswork. The publisher stated that Keats was ' discouraged ' by the reception of *Endymion*; but this was contradicted by Keats himself. The excess of ' Miltonic inversions ' can hardly be the reason ; they are not so many, and could have been retrenched. When Keats took up the work again, it was not to continue but to re-mould it ; it was therefore not illness or conscious failure of power that told upon him. There was an obstacle in the subject, and, as a living poet[1] has observed, ' it is plain that the story was strangling itself.'

The subject, which is never reached, is the dethronement of Hyperion, last of the Titans, by the young Apollo, greater than he in might and melody. We are shown the decay of Saturn, the other fallen Titans, and the despondency of Hyperion, and the call to Apollo. So far the story ; but meantime it has become a symbol : Oceanus tells his fellow-sufferers that their fate accords with the eternal law by which every dynasty gives way to a better, fairer, and stronger one : ' so on our heels a fresh perfection treads.' This is the utterance of Keats's faith, or hope, that there is an eternal progress in the world. But Hyperion has to fade and disappear, under this very law. The poet was thus in a dilemma, into which he may have been led by Milton, in which Milton was himself partly entangled, but from which Keats had not Milton's ostensible way of escape. He may have preferred to stop rather than to plunge further.

We all know how Milton puts our sympathies on what is, officially, the wrong side. They are with Satan, not with God, and they are only in part transferred from Satan to Adam and Eve. We may say, as we please, either that God is too great to be realised in poetry, or that Milton's God is uninteresting ; the effect is the same. All through, Milton keeps falling back on theology, and on the importance to mankind of the event, in order to take the sting out of our interest in Satan. He manages to interest us in the event by humanising Adam and Eve, but this does not move us as the humanising of the fallen angels moves us. At the last he falls back on splendour and pageant, in the visions shown by Michael, in order to hide the decline of the interest. And he can always fall back on the belief of his readers in the story, when the poetic interest flags. The repetition of these points may be excused for their bearing on *Hyperion*.

Here, too, according to a story once believed, a race anciently established in heaven is cast out by one nobler. The Titans, of course, were not sullen servants like the angels, but were the *ancien régime* itself ; of a rougher, more sombre make than their dispossessors. Still, as in Milton, our sympathy is enlisted with the fallen, not with the victors. This interest, however, which in Milton's poem is both heroic and pathetic, in Keats's poem is much more pathetic than heroic, for the Titans can fight no longer. Hyperion himself is to fall, and might have fought, but there would have been difficulties in the foregone conclusion of a Homeric combat with Apollo. There is, in fact, no epic subject, such as Milton's story offered. There is therefore nothing in prospect which can increase our real interest in the Titans; nor is there any extrinsic interest, such as Milton possessed in his theology, to make this want good; nor can the interest be transferred to Apollo without Hyperion losing it. There remains only the symbolism; but this again is adverse to our caring much for Hyperion, who exists only to be outshone. Nor does the symbolism work out well, for no one believes that Zeus is really *better* than Saturn. Indeed Hyperion and Apollo, as Pope says of 'most women,' have 'no character at all,' but are god-like decorative figures. It is hard indeed to see how Keats could have gone on.

Yet his failure to go on hardly mars the success of what he did. From the first his achievement of epic majesty and style, and of a new heroic verse, were acknowledged; not only by Shelley, but by the sharp-eyed patronage of Jeffrey and the noisy spleen of Byron. *Hyperion* shows that Keats might have made a great epic poem, had he lived longer, and had he found a subject. He has the instinct for composition, the poetic oratory, the words, the music. Of no other English poet since Milton can this be so much as surmised.

When he took up the story again he did not go on with it, but prefaced it with a symbolic 'vision,' and started to alter the text of the story, presumably so as to accord better with the vision. In doing this he often spoilt the text so badly that the result was long supposed to be not a revision at all but an imperfect first draft. The evidence disproves this supposition;[1] and some few of the changes in the text of the story are, in fact, improvements; while the prefatory vision itself, written though it is most unequally, reveals new kinds of graver power and rarer workmanship, which it has been suggested are due in part to the inspiration of Dante. The general influence of the *Purgatory* (known to Keats in Cary's English) may fairly be conjectured. The poet is initiated by Moneta (the Mnemosyne of *Hyperion* glorified) into the secret of living. He feels keen bodily anguish, an emblem of mental suffering; mounts a stairway to be purified; hears wisdom from above; shows a high humility of acceptance; and speaks in close, significant imagery. All this is Dantesque, and perhaps Keats had put himself under the highest of all poetic disciplines.

The allegory marks the progress of the poet from his early contentment with the simple beauties or pleasures of the world, which are figured as summer fruits. He sleeps, and wakes in a vast natural sanctuary, which may signify nature seen with the spiritual eye. Far up is an altar, and a voice bids him mount thither, on pain of death, ere ' these gummed leaves be burnt '—a figure, possibly, for his own terribly brief span of life. (It was now or a little later (February 1820) that Keats recognised that he was suffering from arterial hæmorrhage.) With horrid pain he passes the test and learns the truth. Moneta tells him that

> none can usurp this height
> But those to whom the miseries of the world
> Are misery, and will not let them rest.

Others labour for mortal good ; but he, the dreamer, is apart, and ' venoms all his days,' and may only pass into safety after purgation. The rest is more enigmatical. He learns that the temple is the remnant of a great war in heaven, and Moneta ' sole goddess of this desolation.' She tells him that he shall behold the fallen Titans ; and the scenes of *Hyperion*, with alterations, begin, and the ' revision ' ends with the advance of Hyperion through his halls.

There is no saying how these scenes were to enforce the teaching that a poet must feel with the woes of mankind. The original parable, that the greater beauty succeeds the lesser, does not obviously fit into this teaching, and the Revision does not reach that point of the story. The Revision was begun and perhaps dropped before the volume of 1820 came out, so Keats may be taken as preferring his original version, or at least as preferring it to be known. We cannot see how either version would have ended. It may be added that Keats, in the Revision, is too hard on himself. He was not a dreamer ; he had long since left the stage of 1817 behind ; and though he had not, in a dramatic way, turned to portraying the human tragedy, he had taken the sense of it into his blood, as his odes and sonnets show ; and if this is to dream, he had done as much for mankind by his dreams as any man of action. He may, however, have felt that he was about to enter, with pain and stress, upon some other stage of his art ; and we can only be sure that from his art he would never have strayed.

VII

Keats steeped himself in nature, and treated the visions of the old English poets as part of nature, and for long hardly knew whether he looked at her through their eyes or his own.

It was natural that he should draw on their diction,[1] and he owes more to it than any contemporary—more than Shelley, or Byron, or Wordsworth, who after the first found their own language. The words—epithets, formations, compounds—that he learned from Chaucer, from Spenser, from Milton, from Chapman, and from William Browne, and also from, or through, Leigh Hunt, make an imposing list when put together, and have been studied with great fulness and precision. Many new coinages, often in harmony with the make of our language, but either archaic or invented by Keats himself, have been gathered and classified. He glides easily, but not always with poetic tact, from the natural to the more forced and daring forms. He has not only ' osier'd ' and ' honey'd ' but ' legion'd ' and ' tender-person'd ' ; not only ' bowery ' and ' spangly ' but ' surfy ' and ' liny.' That his inventions have not become established is not conclusive against them, but they have not ; he used them, though more sparely, to the last ; and when they come they often give a slight jar, as of something intrusive, to the style, though some are beautiful in themselves. But coldly to put them in a list may mislead us. They are, after all, only sprinkled in ; even in *Endymion* there are whole pages without them ; and the change of style and growth of power between that poem and *Hyperion* depends little on the fact that these locutions become more sparse. It depends on things less definable ; on the increase of purity and strength, of outline and clearness, in which the study of Milton and Dante and Dryden assisted the natural unfolding of Keats : an increase of astonishing speed, which will always leave the world wondering what might have followed later. Definite traces of other poets are seldom to be sought in his greatest passages. The fifteen lines of the *Ode to Maia*, the two sonnets ' When I have fears ' and ' Bright Star,' the description of Apollo in *Hyperion*, or that of the feast in *Lamia*, are in no imitated or imitable manner, and rest in their own perfection.

A poet's aim is to find words which will enable him to pass on to us, with the least of loss, the precise kind of pleasure —including, of course, painful pleasure—that he has received. Keats achieves this aim, not all at once. At first he tries to express all the modifications of warm, young, breathless, and passive happiness, and the sights, sounds, and remembered stories that enhance it. But though he finds many and lovely words for these things, they are often indistinct ones, and the effort defeats itself. Much of *Endymion*

is of this kind. The error is not in the feeling, but in the
medium :

> His every sense had grown
> Ethereal for pleasure ; 'bove his head
> Flew a delight half-graspable ; his tread
> Was Hesperean ; to his capable ears
> Silence was music from the holy spheres ;
> A dewy luxury was in his eyes . . .

Plainly the thing is not expressed ; the pleasure is not transmitted, only talked about ; and there are pages like this. But
at other times the message is unhindered :

> Sometimes
> A scent of violets and blossoming limes
> Loiter'd around us ; then of honey cells,
> Made delicate from all white-flower bells ;
> And once, above the edges of our nest,
> An arch face peep'd,—an Oread as I guess'd.

This kind of writing Keats perfected, as it became intensified
by passion and by the sense behind that such happiness is
rare and must be stolen or striven for. The close of the *Ode
to Psyche* shows the change, and that of the *Ode to Melancholy*
shows it still more. Here, and in the greater sonnets, the style
has not simply become impassioned and spiritualised ; it has
become so without any drifting into the abstract, or loss of
hold on poetic sensation ; no, there is an ever-keener edge on
poetic sensation, and the language rises to the double call :

> Now more than ever seems it *rich* to die.

Keats never lets go of these primal feelings, and attains a style
of the noblest sort for their expression when they are thus
lifted and transfigured—not deadened. This is one reason
why he comes home to us in a way that his great compeers do
not, and why ' he is with Shakespeare.'

No words but his own could express the profound satisfactori-
ness, the cordial and intimate effect, that Keats, owing to this
gift, in his best moments attains. He attains it best when
depicting things actually seen and felt, and less well when he
moves in a world that belongs more to Shelley, and is one of
superhuman fantasy. The picture of Hyperion's palace :

> his palace bright
> Bastion'd with pyramids of glowing gold,
> And touch'd with shade of bronzed obelisks,
> Glared a blood-red through all its thousand courts,
> Arches, and domes, and fiery galleries ;

—this is magnificent, but it is something excogitated ; the poet has not been there ; it is out of the line of his genius. The picture of the Bacchanals in *Endymion* is different ; he has seen something like it of Titian's, and that is enough to set him off :

> And, as I sat, over the light blue hills
> There came a noise of revellers : the rills
> Into the wide stream came of purple hue—
>   'Twas Bacchus and his crew !

Even this does not come home so close, or inspire so natural and homefelt a language, as the scene in *The Eve of St. Agnes* :

> The sculptured dead, on each side, seem to freeze
> Emprison'd in black, purgatorial rails :
> Knights, ladies, praying in dumb orat'ries,
> He passeth by ; and his weak spirit fails
> To think how they may ache in icy hoods and mails.

On Keats, with love in his heart, straying through some English abbey, Westminster or Tewkesbury, the chill of the dead sepulchral effigies has struck ; Blake's drawing of kings and queens thus at rest gives us the same impression. The ' dismal cirque of Druid stones ' near Keswick probably suggested the lines in the second book of *Hyperion* ; they come with startling freshness amidst the vague Titanic scenery, which we do not remember so easily. Students have delighted to track down such recollections, and there must be many more untraceable. Allowing for his transforming and creating power, Keats's mode of work sometimes reminds us of Tourgéniev's, who carefully hived his precise and actual memories for years, and had them at command. But Keats does not, like Wordsworth, make his verse a diary of his experience ; he does not brood on the past explicitly in the light of the value that it has retained for his soul—a method consistent with great poetic power, but one which involves a certain detachment. Keats is ever in the present ; every memory is charged for him with instant passion ; and it comes thus charged for us also. He tells a dream, and it is alive again :

> Pale were the lips I kiss'd, and fair the form
> I floated with, about that melancholy storm.

As to his treatment of ideas, strictly so termed, as distinct from memories and sensations, it is enough to say that it is always poetic, and often great. Metaphysical poetry, with its altitudes and dangers, he does not attempt ; that is, he does not speculate in imaginative form on the ultimate points of philosophy, or on subtle ones of psychology. There is nothing in his work like the latter part of *Adonais*, or Wordsworth's self-analysis in *The Prelude*. The ideas which he does handle are in a different region ; life and death, love and fame, beauty and sorrow are the chief of them. He does not argue about these, or expound them, but muses and shapes them, being concerned above all to remain an artist in doing so. Hence his profound rightness :

> O folly ! for to bear all naked truths,
> And to envisage circumstance, all calm,
> That is the top of sovereignty.

That is Shakespearean, in the sublime way ; it is the poetry of Stoicism. It is a direct moral utterance ; but Keats's way is usually not so direct. His more natural way is less direct ; and to ask then whether he is expressing a 'moral idea' is a verbal question ; if he is, so much the better for morality ; but he is certainly expressing a profound one in poetic form when he speaks of

> The moving waters at their priestlike task
> Of pure ablution round earth's human shores,

or cries :

> Ay, in the very temple of Delight
> Veil'd Melancholy has her sovran shrine.

These are his summits, and being summits are rare ; but they prove his claim to be numbered among the English poets who have given to permanent truths a form of supreme beauty ; and this, no doubt, is what Keats wished to do.

CHAPTER XX

OTHER POETS

I. Diffusion of poetry in this period; absence of definite schools. Cary's *Dante*: his use of Milton, and independence of style; his management of metre; his version of Pindar. Sir William Jones's Ode.

II. Sacred poets: Heber. James Montgomery's hymns, and his vein of talent. Keble, *The Christian Year*; his English character. Poetesses: Mrs. Hemans, Mrs. Southey. Wolfe's *Burial of Sir John Moore*. Blanco White, *On Night*.

III. Kirke White. Robert Bloomfield. John Clare: *Village Minstrel*, etc.; his true poetic touch, and rendering of simple natural things. Ebenezer Elliott, *Corn-Law Rhymes* and other pieces; declamation and poetry.

IV. The Irish Muse: John Banim, Callanan, Dermody. Thomas Moore: Moore's circle and its atmosphere; his satirical verse; *The Fudge Family* and *The Twopenny Postbag*, etc. Serious poems; *Lalla Rookh*. *The Epicurean* and other prose. *Irish Melodies*, and other songs. Their relation to the airs, and inequalities. The *Life of Byron*.

I

THE surprising diffusion, not only of the spirit and flame but of the spell and craft of poetry, throughout the first thirty years of the century, may be measured in its lesser, its remaining practitioners.[1] There is the same span of time between *The Shepherd's Calendar* and the appearance of Shakespeare's *Sonnets*. The ampler masterpieces of the English Renaissance are not rivalled during the romantic age; the gift of lyric was more pervasive in the day of Shakespeare than even in the day of Shelley; the proportion of true poetry in the whole mass of printed verse, which was then so much slighter than two hundred years afterwards, was doubtless larger; but it would still be hard to say that the seed was spread wider, or that the older flowering was more lovely or various. Certainly the future historian of the thirty years now ending (1912) will hazard no such comparison.

The greater poets of the time, though they have their true disciples as well as their parrot-followers, cannot be said to form schools, in the sense in which Pope or Tennyson have done so. Wordsworth's influence, in England, outlasted Byron's, and was better for our poetry, but it told most power-

fully later on. That of Shelley was also more restricted for the
moment. The attraction of Keats, strong as it was, especially
in his own circle, was much blended, during this period, with
the attraction of the old writers, Elizabethan or Italian, on
whom he drew, and it is not disengaged and seen in its purity
till afterwards, when it is working upon the youthful Tennyson
and then upon the 'pre-Raphaelites.' The minor writers, therefore, do not band themselves at all clearly under assignable
masters ; there is no Pleïade. The central strand, perhaps,
of the many-coloured cord is romance, in the historical sense
of the term ;—the revival of colour, of intimate passion, of
beauty for its own sake ; and of all this as beheld through the
old poets and their stories, now made new. Hood and Praed in
one way, Beddoes and Darley in another, show this complexion.
But there are other strands which cross and chequer the central
one. The romancers are also wits and parodists, the wits are
also singers. The writers of sacred or kindred verse form a
smaller section apart, the Irish lyrists another. But one surviving heir of the older Miltonic school must first receive a
tribute.

No more solid monument of English verse was built up
during the early years of the century than the translation of
the *Divine Comedy*, called *The Vision of Dante*,[1] by the Rev.
Henry Francis Cary (1772-1844). Already, in the *Gentleman's
Magazine*, Cary had shared with Bowles in the timid revival
of the sonnet-form ; and his versions of Italian sonnets and
lyrics, to be found in the notes of his greater work, are admirably turned and among the earliest of their kind. While a
Christ Church undergraduate, he had begun to study Dante
as well as Dante's authorities, contemporaries, and followers,
with a thoroughness that had then no parallel in England, or
perhaps elsewhere ; and in 1805-6 he published the *Inferno*
in blank verse along with the Italian text. Its excellence was
awhile unregarded, but in 1814 Cary, at his own cost, produced
his version (with commentary) of the whole *Comedy*. It now
caught the notice of the poets. Moore named it to Rogers, who,
as he informs us, told Wordsworth, who told Coleridge. An
article in the *Edinburgh Review* in 1818, by Ugo Foscolo[2] and
Mackintosh, and probably also a lecture by Coleridge, brought
the work into note, and its fame was soon assured. Editions
followed, and in 1844 Cary published his final revision. Dante
lore has swelled in the last seventy years ; but some of the
best modern scholars[3] have attested Cary's soundness of judgment and the wide sweep and pertinence of his erudition. Equal

honour must be paid to his work as a poem, despite the unending stream of verse translations that has flowed since his day.

Neither his diction nor his blank verse show any sign of the new age. He depends on the tradition of Milton. But he is not overpowered by Milton's greatness, and is often not infected by his stiffness, artifice, and other drawbacks ; and, what is still more to Cary's credit, he is also little led away by the vices of phrase and sound which encrust all Milton's eighteenth-century followers more or less. He uses his great model with a tact and discretion that is wonderful considering his date when he wrote, and that he himself had not exactly genius. Where he is conscious of the loan, he frankly states it in his footnote. At other times the echo, though no one passage may be copied, is so close as to need no avowal ; and if the metre was to be epical blank verse—and, after all, what other has ever been successful ?—Cary was wise in adopting its noblest known type, and in thus associating further two poets who, with all their difference, have the same incandescent passion and the same transcendent mastery of speech.

> He thus to me : ' This miserable fate
> Suffer the wretched souls of those, who lived
> Without or praise or blame, with that ill band
> Of angels mix'd, who nor rebellious proved,
> Nor yet were true to God, but for themselves
> Were only. From his bounds Heaven drove them forth,
> Not to impair his lustre ; nor the depth
> Of Hell receives them, lest the accursed tribe
> Should glory thence with exultation vain.'—(*Hell*, Canto iii.)

This is not to be bettered in its own way. But Cary's merit is to have forged a style which, whilst remaining even and serried throughout, adapts itself to Dante's varied purposes —description, simile, drama, invective, and abstract exposition. In the latter vein, above all, Cary frees himself more from Milton, and manages to keep, if not all the lofty and lucid march of his Italian original, which is impossible, at any rate the literal and faithful sense, and no little dignity besides :

> These tokens of pre-eminence in man
> Largely bestow'd, if any of them fail,
> He needs must forfeit his nobility,
> No longer stainless. Sin alone is that,
> Which doth disfranchise him, and make unlike
> To the chief good ; for that its light in him
> Is darken'd. And to dignity thus lost
> Is no return ; unless, where guilt makes void,
> He for ill pleasure pay with equal pain.—(*Paradise*, vii.)

This is surprisingly close ; the best literal prose is not much closer, and is prose after all. The verse is not imitative, nor yet is it strongly original, in cadence ; but it is writing of a most honourable stamp.

Cary's metrical problem was complex. Choosing blank verse, he had not only to write it well, but to leave such an impression of the original as consisted with his sacrifice of the *terza rima* with its interlapping waves of harmony. This he did, first of all, by making his version as *linear* as he could ; consistently, again, with keeping freedom of pause and movement. Sometimes, perhaps too often, he puts the tercet into three complete lines, coming to a dead stop at the end :

> ' My son ! observant thou my steps pursue.
> We must retreat to rereward ; for that way
> The champain to its low extreme declines.'
> The dawn had chased the matin hour of prime,
> Which fled before it, so that from afar
> I spied the trembling of the ocean stream.
> We traversed the deserted plain, as one
> Who, wander'd from his track, thinks every step
> Trodden in vain till he regain the path.—(*Purg.* i.)

This kind of fidelity is somewhat dear-bought, for it is unnatural to blank verse and it runs the risk of that jerk at the end of the paragraph, which we have seen to be one of the worst of the faults of the Miltonising poets. But as a rule Cary escapes this snare, and prefers to run the close of a tercet just over into a fourth line of blank verse, even at the cost of some expansion ; keeping, at the same time, a sufficient number of self-enclosed and impressive single lines, not more freely varied than Dante's own by the substitution of non-iambic feet, but seldom monotonous. Herein Cary is studiously restrained ; he either cannot or does not follow the bolder magic of Milton. The passage given above from the *Paradise* is a good illustration of his craftsmanship. A certain amount of creaking and constraint may doubtless be charged against him, but on the whole his performance wears the better the more it is scrutinised.

In his too little known translation of Pindar (1833) Cary was inspired by Gray, who had himself forged his noblest diction on Pindar's anvil. Thus, in Cary's hands, Pindar comes back to something of his own ; and though his rapidity and fire of onset are by no means reproduced,—partly because the flexible inversions of the Greek are too closely followed in the English and there retard the movement,—still his sound and majesty are often suggested, and the fulness of his vowelled language. Cary has the sympathy innate in a good translator, and succeeds best in the gnomic and reflective passages which are sown so thick in the Odes, and which celebrate the glory of venerated old age, or the power of the poet to immortalise his subject, or the certainty of the divine purposes. Perhaps this translation is the last good book of verse in the style which was not yet overlaid or supplanted by the fashions of Scott or Byron amongst the popular poets, or by the greater examples of Coleridge and Wordsworth. It is so rare a work that an extract is allowable :

> The simple paths of life be mine ;
> That when this being I resign
> I to my children may bequeath
> A name they shall not blush to hear.
> Others for gold the vow may breathe,
> Or lands that see no limit near ;
> But fain would I live out my days
> Belov'd by those with whom they 're past,
> In mine own city, till at last
> In earth my limbs are clad ;
> Still praising what is worthy praise,
> But scatt'ring censure on the bad.
> For virtue, by the wise and just
> Exalted, grows up as a tree,
> That springeth from the dust,
> And by the green dews fed
> Doth raise aloft her head,
> And in the blithe air waves her branches free.
>
> (*Nemean Odes*, viii.)

Ben Jonson would not have disdained this ; and many of the richer decorative passages are equally satisfactory.

Cary, it is plain, is of the lineage neither of Pope and Johnson, nor of Chatterton and the ballad-makers, nor yet of Thomson and Cowper. There is another pedigree, which almost dies out after *Lyrical Ballads*, though traces of it are found in the odes of their authors ; this comes down from Gray. It is inspired by Milton, and also by Pindar ; it is continued, ineffectively, in the pseudo-classical tragedies and odes of Mason, who lived till 1797. The diction is noble, if rather stiff ; it has, as Johnson said, ' a kind of cumbrous splendour that we wish away.' This diction Cary inherits and re-trieves. One link between Cary and these ancestors may be noted in the high-spirited *Ode in Imitation of Alcaeus*, written by Sir William Jones in 1781, and full of the best Old Whig oratory :

> Men who their duties know,
> But know their rights, and, knowing, dare maintain,
> Prevent the long-aimed blow,
> And crush the tyrant while they rend the chain :
> These constitute a state,
> And sovereign Law, that state's collected will,
> O'er thrones and globes elate
> Sits empress, crowning good, repressing ill.

There is more than a breath of this temper and style in Wordsworth ; but in Shelley's prophecies the temper becomes transcendent, and the style is raised on wings of fire.

The political and descriptive sonnets of Sir Aubrey de Vere [1] (1788-1846), mostly written before 1825, drew very high praise from Wordsworth. They are in his own following, well hewn, lofty in vein, severe in finish, and full of a conservatism recalling that of Burke. Such are those on Waterloo, and on the death of the Princess Charlotte, and on *The True Basis of Power*. In the sonnet *Rydal with Wordsworth* we seem to be present at the transfusion of spirit from the elder poet to the younger, as the two watch together

> Peaked mountains, shadowing vales of peacefulness ;
> Glens, echoing to the flashing waterfall . . .
> The moon between two mountain peaks embayed.

Sir Aubrey de Vere was also inspired by Petrarch and Chiabrera, and translated from them. As a sonneteer, accomplished as he is, he seldom crosses the line between sincere, fervent school-work and original poetry.

II

Reginald Heber [2] (1783-1826), bishop of Calcutta, is best known as a writer of hymns, many of which will last as long as the Anglican Church ; but they are in the eighteenth-century tradition, sonorous and finished rather than essentially poetic, somewhat obvious in their undoubted splendour, and vehicles, like the classical ode, of an emotion felt in unison rather than of the private feelings of the individual worshipper. 'From Greenland's icy mountains,' 'Holy, Holy, Holy,' and 'The Son of God goes forth to war,' are familiar examples. Heber's technique is careful, and his handling of full and open vowels and of ringing proper names is generous. His other poetry belongs for the most part to the transition, to the period of Campbell ; his college piece on *Palestine* (1803), and most of his other verses (*Europe*, 1809, and *The Passage of the Red Sea*), are in a light but conventional form of the

couplet ; and his translations from Pindar, less stiff but also
less strong than those of his contemporary Cary, are equally
in the following of Gray.

Many of the hymns, too, of James Montgomery [1] (1771-1854)
have rightly held their place in the popular collections, and
survived in the hard struggle for existence which besets this
kind of literature. 'Hail to the Lord's anointed,' and 'Go
to dark Gethsemane,' 'For ever with the Lord,' 'Prayer is
the soul's sincere desire,' 'Lift up your heads, ye gates,' and
many others, have remained in the standard hymnals, and
are good hymns and almost good poems. They are resonant,
not too subtle, deeply devout, and well suit the unison of
uplifted emotion proper to a throng of worshippers. Some of
them occur in the *Songs of Zion* (1822), a verse paraphrase
of the Psalter. There is no doubt that James Montgomery
(unlike his namesake Robert Montgomery, Macaulay's
victim) has his share of true poetical quality, though it is
diluted and too often lost. His long works, *The West Indies*,
The World before the Flood, *Greenland*, *The Pelican Island*
(the last of which shows some attention to the manner of
Shelley), are, indeed, little more than prize poems ; and his
essays in translating Dante are of no mark. But some of his
less aspiring verses upon children and dumb creatures are of
another kind. The lines *On Finding the Feathers of a Linnet*
(1796) precede Wordsworth's characteristic work of the same
sort ; and, as one critic has said, they are like Wordsworth
'without the unaccountable poetry' :

> Few were thy days, thy pleasures few,
>   Simple and unconfined ;
> On sunbeams every moment flew,
>   Nor left a care behind . . .
>
> Perhaps 'twas thy last evening song
>   That exquisitely stole
> In sweetest melody along
>   And harmonised my soul.

For its date, and even after Cowper had written, this is noticeable. The little series of epigrams, in the form of question
and answer, entitled *Birds*, have some of the cunning simplicity
of Christina Rossetti :

> Swallow, why homeward turned thy joyful wing ?
> —In a far land I heard the voice of spring ;
> I found myself that moment on the way ;
> My wings, my wings, they had not power to stay.

Montgomery, however, touches his highest note of imagination in some of the verses he wrote in defence of chimney-sweepers, and *The Dream* of one of the ' climbing boys ' has a few stanzas of signal intensity, not injured by the possible reminiscences of Coleridge or of *Sir Eustace Grey* :

> I trembled as I 've felt a bird
>   Tremble within my fist ;
> For none I saw and none I heard,
>   And all was lone and whist.
>
> The moonshine through the window show'd
>   Long stripes of light and gloom ;
> The carpet with all colours glow'd ;
>   Stone men stood round the room ;
>
> Fair pictures in their golden frames,
>   And looking-glasses bright,
> Fine things, I cannot tell their names,
>   Dazed and bewitch'd me quite.

Swamped as they are in the volumes of this forgotten and copious writer, such extracts justify themselves. Montgomery was by calling a provincial journalist, his headquarters being Sheffield ; he was a fervid reformer, and a humane and courageous advocate ; and he also had this intermittent streak of talent for verse.

John Keble, and also some of his poetry, belongs to the following age ; but *The Christian Year* came out in 1827, and has outlived, not wholly through its artistic merits, most of the verse described in this chapter. It is not (save for one or two famed and noble exceptions) a book of hymns. The familiar morning and evening hymns, as they are sung, are really hymns picked out of poems[1] by the rejection of unsuitable verses ; and show in a curious way how good poetry may be poor hymnody, being too solitary, or too literary and allusive, in tone. It does not face the peculiar requirements, lower in one way but harder in another, of hymnody ; it is mostly soliloquy, the communing of a pensive, eager, and pious spirit ; so that it asks to be judged as poetry. And as such it is not readily judged ; as a piece of art and style it is easily undervalued. There is plenty of thin, stopgap language ; the plan of making 'thoughts in verse for the Sundays and Holydays throughout the Year ' easily leads to writing per-force ; nor are the poetic observation and the devout comment always well soldered together. But Keble has not captured the world of religious readers, beyond as well as within his own communion, for nothing ; and he may be thought to have

done so, on poetical grounds, with a better right than George
Herbert. He has none of the chilling quaintness or tasteless
oddness that deforms the sweet fancies and swift exaltations
of his predecessor ; his faults, indeed, are in the direction of
flatness and faintness. But the grave and nice quality of
his language, his even but incessantly aspiring temper, and
the soft throb of diffused emotion in his rhythm, entitle Keble
to more than the rank among poets which his own humility
may have claimed. He is, above all, intensely English, the
flower of his caste. The English evening, the English tempered
sun, the blotted distance ; the near, surrounding greenness
and stillness of a thousand rectories ; they are all in his verse,
and we need not dwell in or near his world of belief to appreciate them. It is no use calling such a man ' Wordsworth
for women,' for he is not Wordsworth, and he is not particularly
for women.

Keble no doubt studies Wordsworth, and the ' religion of
nature ' is his also, perhaps derivatively. But he does just what
Wordsworth seldom did with success ; he turns the emotion
aroused by the contemplation of nature into the channel
of directly Christian and doctrinal sentiment, and he often
makes poetry of the result. Often too, and of course, he
leaves out the landscape, and utters the sentiment alone,
without much imagery ; but here, it may be, though Keble
is not the less a saint, he is something less of a poet. His
other literary models are not far to seek, Scott and Southey are
among them ; and he makes effective, though rather singular,
use of the rolling reiterated rhymes of the chivalrous lays for
his own purpose :

> Thou wilt be there, and not forsake,
>   To turn the bitter pool
> Into a bright and breezy lake
>   The throbbing brow to cool ;
> Till left awhile with Thee alone
> The wilful heart be fain to own
> That He, by whom our bright hours shone,
>   Our darkness best may rule.

Some other writers, once popular, attach themselves more
or less closely to the same schools. Robert Pollok's [1] *Course of
Time* (1827), a blank verse, and otherwise blank, history of the
world between the creation and the doomsday, is an impossible work. Mrs. Hemans [2] (1793-1835), born Felicia Dorothea
Browne, had an abundance of eager poetic emotion, a passion
for the obvious-romantic, an enthusiasm for foreign literature

and languages, and an endless flow of facile and not discreditable verse. Stories, lyrics, and plays (of which the chief is a too elegant tragedy, *The Vespers of Palermo*, produced by Charles Kemble) fill her six volumes. The best that can be said for Mrs. Hemans is that some of her subjects are good ; and that in a few of her briefer pieces, such as *England's Dead* and *The Graves of a Household*, her genuine exaltation of soul and temper, usually squandered and wasted, concentrates itself into fit and rememberable words. Less than this must be said of Letitia Landon (' L. E. L.') her contemporary, who wrote worse, in somewhat the same styles, and was still more read. But Mrs. Southey[1] (Caroline Bowles) is in a different class ; and her touch in poetry of the subdued, familiar kind, is genuine. *The Birthday* is a pleasant and playful piece of autobiography, a kind of feminine counterpart to the simple domestic parts of *The Prelude* ; but in its charm is more like Cowper. The *Legend of Santarem* is worthily told, which is much to say ; for it is the tale of the ' little Jesus ' who comes down from above the altar to share his meal with the children ; they go again with their old master, and are found kneeling dead before the image. *The Pauper's Funeral* is better known than *Ranger's Grave* (Mrs. Southey's elegy on her dog), or than *The Broken Bridge* ; but all are definitely poetry, if they are poetry in a whisper.

The Burial of Sir John Moore,[2] the one poem that is remembered, and is sure to be remembered, of Charles Wolfe, a young Irish clergyman, was written about 1814 and published anonymously. For a time it was claimed by pretenders ; and a French translation by Mahony was in sober jest passed off by that wit as the original. Wolfe deserved these tributes, and his fame ; and Campbell, whom he studied and admired, produced nothing more noble and finished in the same order. The power of the piece, it is easily seen, lies even less in the key of diction, which is plain, and yet chosen, and yet again not curious, than in the extraordinary aptness of the tune, which seems to spring out of the words themselves ; they are not first measured to fit it. The plummet-like fall of the heavy syllables of grief, as into an unknown depth, and the elastic rise, proper to the anapæstic measure, of the lighter ones, as though for heroic consolation, is worthy of the masters.

The poetic memory of Joseph Blanco White also rests upon a single piece, his sonnet[3] *On Night* (1829), which was enormously praised, and seemingly discovered, by Coleridge. It is indeed perfectly built (granting the final couplet to be admis-

sible in the Italian scheme of metre) and is of much beauty
and full of impetus, being spoken as it were in a breath.
Blanco White's prose is copious and not lively, though his
career and mental history are of interest. His progress from
the Roman to the Anglican, and from the Anglican to the
Unitarian fold; his letters, pamphlets, and articles on Spain,
which despite his Irish blood was in effect his mother-country;
and his later ties with the Tractarians, form a singular Odyssey.

III

Four writers may now be mentioned, who have little in
common except their struggle against poverty and want of
training. The memory of Henry Kirke White [1] (1785-1806)
might well have been allowed surely and gently to fade, and
has been poorly served by the mistaken praises of Southey and
Byron. They persisted in treating him as a minor Chatterton;
but White is not only not of the tribe of Chatterton; he
shows little sign of promising to be a poet at all. Southey's
limpid and kindly memoir, injudicious only in its estimate
of the boy's verses, created a kind of shadowy false reputation
for Kirke White. Against this later historians have revolted;
but their censures are almost as needless as Southey's funeral
laurels; for, in Kirke White's own words to the reviewer, ' Let
him remember he is holding the iron mace of criticism over the
flimsy superstructure of a youth of seventeen.' Kirke White
was precocious, and devout, and industrious, and struggled
against poverty and obscurity, and wrote a number of verses,
and overworked himself, and died very young. His *Clifton
Grove*, a 'local poem,' with echoes of Goldsmith and Crabbe,
appeared in 1803. He made sonnets and prose meditations, and
also some hymns after the manner of Cowper, which, though
not good poetry are quite good hymnody and have continued
in use. His schooling and forms are purely classical; he shows
no sign of the new poetical spirit except that he tries for a pure
and simple diction. Little more than this, if so much, can be
said of Robert Bloomfield, whose *Farmer's Boy* (1800) and
Rural Tales, Ballads, and Songs (1802) are in a conventional
enough manner. The public liked to find that this manner
could be united with a minute, direct, and rigidly accurate
notation of natural things, and for awhile did not feel the lack
of poetry. Bloomfield was a ' lady's shoemaker,' and his
English was polished for the press by his patron, Capel
Lofft. He follows Crabbe in *The Miller's Maid* and *John*

Gilpin in *The Fakenham Ghost,* not ill ; but his real style
is like this :

> The small dust-colour'd beetle climbs with pain
> O'er the smooth plantain-leaf, a spacious plain !
> Thence higher still, by countless steps convey'd,
> He gains the summit of a shiv'ring blade ;
> And flirts his filmy wings, and looks around,
> Exulting in his distance from the ground.

The false touch in the last line would have been impossible
to another ' peasant-poet,' who came twenty years after
Bloomfield, and whose vision of natural things was poetical,
not merely literal.

John Clare[1] (1793-1864), who was equally without advantages,
lived close to the ground—the flat soil of the Eastern counties
—with an eye for its less obtrusive flowers (pilewort, chickweed)
and an ear for the noises of its tinier creatures, and a sure hold
of the happy local words for the notation of such phenomena.
The ' drowking meadow-sweet,' the ' chumbling mouse,' the
' lumping flail,' the ' chelping gossip,' are epithets just as near
to the object as the Scots of Burns, and ' The yellow-hammer
flutters in short fears ' is an unimprovable description. But
the pulse of life in Clare, the ' Northamptonshire peasant,'
ran low and timid ; his life was crazily poised over the pit of
penury and madness ; his passing success was a cruelty, and he
was born in complete disharmony with his peasant life and
surroundings, except in so far as his genius lay in describing it.
His best verse has a faintness of tone—it is the only just audible
harmony of the underbrush, as we lean down and listen. A
gentle, playful pleasure in rustic gallantry and beauty—it
never rises higher than that in the way of joy ; and its sorrow
is the like thin note, too high for certain ears, of a wounded
small creature. Clare's moments of comfort are when he is
alone with the winds shut out, and dreams of the well-being
he has not ; in the *Address to Plenty*, he thinks luxuriously of
his usual self as a person outside the window :

> Needy Labour dithering stands,
> Beats and blows his numbing hands :
> And upon the crumping snows
> Stamps, in vain, to warm his toes.

It is then, too, that he dreams of poetry, and of what is in him :

> To think that I in humble dress
> Might have a right to happiness
> And sing as well as greater men :
> And then I strung the lyre again.

Clare began in 1820, with *Poems Descriptive of Rural Life and Scenery*. Many of these show his talent emerging painfully, as might be expected, from its dependence upon the preromantic models, Gray or Collins, and also upon Burns, whose favourite measure he practises imperfectly. But in *Noon* he expresses his real self, and lies on the 'spindles' of grass, 'fearless of the things that creep'; and in *Summer Images* he foregathers, like *L'Allegro*, with the rustics at nightfall : but Clare is one of themselves, and not a scholar-poet to whom they are but a masque or pageant. *The Village Minstrel* came out in 1821, and though just as good as the *Poems*, it did not do so well. *The Shepherd's Calendar* and *The Rural Muse* (1834) were little remarked. Clare left much in manuscript ; and the verses he made in his later days, from a lunatic asylum, appeared in 1873, nine years after his death. They have an elfish arresting sound, and are both in form and spirit the rarest of his writings. They are haunted by the figure of Mary Joyce, whom he had loved in childhood ; she appeared to his sick senses, and was more real to him than his wife Patty, with whom he had been happy so far as conditions permitted. *The Dying Child* is a 'song of innocence,' quite unlike Blake's, without any pictorial vision of the child itself, and with no sense of environing angels, but noting instead the 'whitenosed bee' that the child had captured :

> And then he shut his little eyes,
>   And flowers would notice not ;
> Birds' nests and eggs caused no surprise,
>   He now no blossoms got ;
> They met with plaintive sighs.

This awkwardness of speech, itself childlike, clings about all the best that Clare wrote, and goes to make its charm. His voice is low, but there is nothing else in English poetry that sings and murmurs from the same level.

Ebenezer Elliott [1] (1781-1849) is of the soil too ; his best work has the scent of it, of Yorkshire not of the Midlands. 'Art thou nigh, grey month of April ?' he cries ; it is a touch like Walt Whitman's. The 'flaskering duck,' the 'satin-thread flowers' of the bramble, the sloe-blossom; and again the heather, with the holidaying hands and their 'smoke-dried dog'; these he watches and likes ; and in several of his poems, such as *The Maltby Yew*, or *Wonders of the Lane*, the vision and relish of nature, in this unassuming fashion, are the main affair. Unluckily it is all much overlaid and spoilt. Elliott is not unlettered, but is only too much lettered, imitating Crabbe, or

Campbell, or Montgomery, as the case may be, with little discernment. Crabbe is his best teacher, and some of the things he does in Crabbe's kind are genuine, because he knows the humble life that he describes ; it is, indeed, his own life. *The Exile* has the familiar ring :

> Again he kiss'd me, and he turned to go ;
> But no—poor Emma would not have it so :
> He saw the boy on whom my sad eye fell,
> And kiss'd my little Alfred—then—farewell !
> I saw him not, but sobb'd, in sorrow blind,
> And heard his faint ' God bless thee ! ' in the wind.

There is the same approach to bathos, and it is redeemed in the same way. Usually Elliott tries this lowly style in lyric form, the form of the lyrical ballad, and he moves sometimes beneath, but often above, the danger-level. *The Death-Feast* is a good example :

> Some griefs the strongest soul might shake,
>   And I such griefs have had ;
> My brain is hot, but they mistake
>   Who deem that I am mad.
> My father died, my mother died,
>   Four orphans poor were we . . .

It hovers between poetry and the beggar-ditty. *The Death-Feast* is one of the *Corn-Law Rhymes*, for which Elliott is best known, though they contain many of his worse and only a few of his better things. He does not let the tale tell itself, but becomes passionate and declamatory, and his pure declamation is mostly bad. There are exceptions, such as the often-copied battle-song (' Day, like our souls, is fiercely dark '), of which the savage and splendid cadence is so far ahead of the clumsy angry diction. Elliott's way is often to set one of these rhymes to a familiar tune, of which he thus makes his advantage ; thus we have :

> Doctor said air was best,
>   Food we had none ;
> Father, with panting breast,
>   Groan'd to be gone,

to the melody of *Robin Adair* ; and his songs, partly through this device, struck home. In many of them the verse is a mere instrument, rudely strained, for communicating his indignation against the bread-tax and the landowner. There is no doubt as to the honesty or the humane rage of Elliott, and it was this that led Carlyle to admire some verses which are not poems, but in which he perceived the voice of a man.

Carlyle's essay upsets the balance a good deal in this respect; but it leaves no doubt that there is a seed of fire, as well as mere fume and dust-storm, in the *Corn-Law Rhymes*; and his words have the elegiac and heroic quality of his earlier writing:

A troublous element is his, a Life of painfulness and toil, insecurity, scarcity; yet he fronts it like a man; yields not to it, tames it into some subjection, some order; its wild fearful dinning and tumult, as of a devouring Chaos, becomes a sort of wild war-music for him; wherein too are passages of beauty, of melodious, melting softness, of lightness, and briskness, even of joy.

These qualities are scattered, somewhat unequally, over Elliott's volumes; the *Corn-Law Rhymes* appeared in 1828, *The Ranter* a year earlier, *The Village Patriarch* a year later, and his poems were finally collected in 1846.

IV

The Irish muse [1] during this age went often barefoot, though Thomas Moore was shod comfortably enough and not undeservedly. For the rest, the poets are often nameless, or struggle obscurely. They left much that is of pious and pathetic interest to their country, but little on the whole that remains in literature. They had to contend with distress and political distraction, and with their lack of schooling in the poetic use of English. The popular verse meantime written in the native tongue, and so well presented in ours by Dr. Douglas Hyde, was ample and beautiful. Several ballads that endure, like *The Wearin' of the Green* and *The Shan Van Vocht*, are assigned to the last years of the eighteenth century. John Banim's poem in praise of the ' priest dear,' *Soggarth Aroon*, is simple and fiery, and little the worse for its halting idiom. The first honours of translating Irish lyric into rapid English rhymes were earned, before Moore, by Jeremiah Joseph Callanan, who died in 1829. There is a lingering, Gaelic melancholy in the long lines of his *Gougaune Barra*; and his *Convict of Clonmel* and *Dirge of O'Sullivan Bear* have a most authentic ring, the one of pathos and the other of fierceness, though both betray the colouring of current English poetry. The unlucky, witty Thomas Dermody,[2] who died early in 1802 broken by drink, may well be called a lost singer, though his inspiration is by no means always Irish. A hedge-poet in temper and incurably vagrant, he was delightfully ungrateful to the persons of quality who gave him boots and banknotes, and he preferred to be free and not sober. He picked up tatters of the classics, and some of his hand-to-mouth ditties are in the classical manner, the best of them jaunty and reckless. His versification of the scuffle between Wolcot and Gifford in the bookshop is stingingly told and with much relish. There are many more names ; but until the writers of *The Nation* emerge in the 'forties, the stage is almost held by Moore, who in his inspiration is as much English as Irish.

The letters and journals of Thomas Moore [1] (1779-1852) give a disarming picture of himself, with his loyalty, tenderness, naïve pleasure in scampering from one celebrity to another, half-belief in his own greatness, and essential dapperness ; and a less engaging one of the society that cherished him and of the talk it liked ; in which, as ever in modish-intellectual English company, the perpetual jump is from mere anecdote, good or otherwise, to mere anecdote ; while the ingredients painfully peculiar to that day, the pun, the practical boorish jest, the rudeness carried off by audacity, and the insistence on grotesque points of honour—supported, in the last resort, by the challenge—figure quite sufficiently. It is a brilliant show nevertheless, of its kind, and has its *dramatis personæ*, mostly now forgotten save by students ; the accepted man of learning, Mackintosh, Macaulay's Whig precursor in omniscience ; Theodore Hook, the callous brutal joker ; Sydney Smith, who is more than the master of uproar and of the obvious ; Rogers, the institution, whose famed sarcasms now sound flat and hard enough ; the Whig noble patrons, including Lord Holland, the best and most generous of them, and others who cherish Moore, seldom too much for his liking ; the publisher, Murray, with the whole Byron circle and their questionings besetting him hard ; and many shadows more, to whom the breathless diarist gives a certain rather ghastly vivacity of outline ; leaving, after all and inadvertently, the impression of himself as not the least cheery and honest of that scarcely melodious society, with a true soul of music and song in him, and a heart untarnished under all his mobility.

The sparkle, the sputter, the disconcerting jump and vapour of Thomas Moore's squibs, which served for the entertainment and gratification of this lively crowd, are not yet wholly dead and damp to us as we read *The Twopenny Post-Bag* (1813), and *The Fudge Family in Paris* (1818), or those cantos from Horace, which are so 'freely adapted by George Regent.' *The Post-Bag* belongs to the history of the verse caricature, of which George Regent is the target ; and through Moore's pictures of his wig, his whiskers, his breakfast curaçoa, and his gallantries, the features of the 'First Gentleman' have become fixed in the memory of the nation, just as those of his father are fixed by Gillray and Wolcot. But a new refinement is attained; Moore shows a greater finish and dexterity in his insolence, and something less of essential vulgarity, than the lampooners of the last age; the satiric skill of Thackeray's verses and parodies is not yet there, but it is in sight. Moore, to vary the figure, has a gnat-like agility and pertinacity and blistering power, and a gnat-like music too; nay, *The Fudge Family*, with its mock letters from and to Castlereagh, and *The Twopenny Postbag*, with its epistle 'From G. R. to the E[arl] of Y[armouth],' sound like the chorus in Spenser's bog of Allan:

> Their murmuring small trompetts sounden wide,
> Whiles in the air their clustring army flies,
> That as a cloud doth seeme to dim the skies.

The Fudge Family is a deft and pleasing variety of the epistolary tale or sketch, used by Smollett in *Humphry Clinker*, and by Richardson before him, and by Mr. Henry James long afterwards in *The Point of View*. The father, Mr. Phil Fudge, the correspondent and creature of Castlereagh; the son and daughter; the young Irish patriot, the tutor, Phelim Connor, who half embodies and half burlesques Moore's liberal and shamrock sentiment, are all alive, and expose themselves naturally and without effort. Moore, in fact, is the best satirical improvisatore that we have, for ease, sharpness, and fertility combined. The little smirk and tumble of his verses, lyric or descriptive, is unfailingly carried through, and he is up again kissing his hand to the audience, and the pellets have flown into the eyes of his victims with so straight an aim that they too can hardly but applaud. Sometimes his lines rise beyond the scope of Whig personalities, and he rivals the nicety of Praed in his power of hitting off a social type, as in his *Fragment of a Character* on 'Factotum Ned,' who had a hand in everything:

> For though, by some unlucky miss,
>   He had not downright *seen* the King,
> He sent such hints through Viscount *This*,
>   And Marquis *That*, as clenched the thing. . . .
>
> *Childe Harold* in the proofs he read,
>   And here and there infus'd some soul in 't;
> Nay, Davy's lamp, till seen by Ned,
>   Had—odd enough—a dang'rous hole in 't.

But this strain is rarer, and Moore is best and most at home in his small conclusive rhymed sarcasms upon known persons of the opposite party. As to his liberal sentiment on broader matters, in which he is wholly generous, unoriginal, sincere, and rather commonplace, he is like some small swift silvery creature whisking dutifully alongside of the swordfish Byron; as in his *Fables for the Holy Alliance* (1823), a lively and well-turned set, seven in number, of which not the worst is the opening parable, *A Dream* of the symbolic ice-palace on the Neva. The fabric melts as the allied monarchs dance their turns, and they melt as well, and the river flows on 'happy as an enfranchised bird' without them. This kind of work came to Moore as naturally as breathing; and he left much of it, whence the life and coruscation has by no means departed —a life all surface and a coruscation full of sputter, it is true; but then these documents of the surface are as hard to write really well as odes or sonnets.

Moore won high estimation and profit from his *Lalla Rookh* (1817), a string of rhymed love-idylls, of which *The Veiled Prophet of Khorassan* and *Paradise and the Peri* were the most popular, and all of which are in a studious, book-learned Oriental setting, now unpersuasive enough. He had studied the Eastern poems of Southey and Byron; his ambition was to be at once erudite and 'glowing'; to be very amorous, and notwithstanding very pure. Unhappily this alliance can only be effected, not by the sentiment that he lavishes, but by the passion that he lacks, and the result is now tedious. There is more savour of the East in a page of Beckford's lesser tales or of *The Shaving of Shagpat* than in all *Lalla Rookh*, with *The Loves of the Angels* (1823) thrown into the balance. Moore succeeds better when he can infuse some raillery; and this he does in the prose interludes of *Lalla Rookh*, with their passages of love and conversation between the Princess Lalla herself, the musician and narrator Feramorz (a prince in disguise), and the chamberlain Fadladeen, who criticises the tales very much as they deserve but in the manner of a Scottish reviewer (see i. 392 *ante*). Moore's own Whiggery peers out oddly from under the stage turban, when he falls to praising liberty and denouncing tyrants in these exotic works.

In a strong and inborn feeling for music lies the source of whatever talent I may have shown for poetical composition, and it was the effort to translate into language the emotions and passions which music appeared to me to express that first led to my writing any poetry at all deserving the name.

Herein Moore differs from Burns, who, though he too started
with traditional melodies, had further the scraps and snatches
of old and wandering words to work upon, and who fitted the
one to the other with the freedom and skill of a poet. Moore
however had what Burns had not, the freedom and skill of
the musician ; he altered and recomposed many airs, to the
indignation of some who would fain have had him leave them
dead with their ' authentic dross ' about them. He also commanded a third art, that of the singer ; and his singing ' in
a style resembling recitative ' drew tears from himself and
others and pleased Coleridge, who praised such an union of
poetry and music—' the music, like the honeysuckle round
the stem, twining round the meaning, and at last overtopping
it.' This original dependence of Moore's own words upon
popular tunes led him to say that his verses ' are intended
rather to be sung than read,' but that

it is not through want of zeal or industry if I unfortunately disgrace
the sweet airs of my country by poetry altogether unworthy of their
taste, their energy, and their tenderness.

His interest in the tunes was not purely that of a musician ;
it was a wish to recover, so far as he knew it, the essence of
the Irish soul. He says that not many of them are very old,
and that most of them seem to date from the eighteenth
century, the period of Ireland's misery, and to be the voice,
most commonly, of her sadness rather than her gaiety. But
the words were unknown or unworthy, so that it fell to him
to create them. Later Irish scholars and poets have blamed
him for not having felt, what hardly any man of letters ever
felt till after Moore's time, the mysticism, the tremulous flame,
the spiritual and fairy touch which lie deep in the people
and which was already expressed, had he but known it, in
their tales and Gaelic verse. This he certainly does not feel ;
there is no trace of it in his composition. But the Irish people
has judged that Moore for all that has caught some of the
essence of their soul. *The Irish Peasant to his Mistress* would
go home to the heart of any dispossessed nation, and its deep
vibration is poetical and not rhetorical ; and, as to form, most
of it would satisfy an artist who cared for no country at all :

Through grief and through danger thy smile hath cheered my way,
Till hope ceased to bud from each thorn that round me lay ;
The darker our fortune, the brighter our pure love burned,
Till shame into glory, till fear into zeal was turned ;
Oh ! slave as I was, in thy arms my spirit felt free,
And bless'd even the sorrows that made me more dear to thee.

Moore in his modesty seems not to have been sure that his *Irish Melodies* would live simply as poetry ; he did not think of them, he could not think of them, apart from their music. But the best of them are not verses which are kept alive by their tunes ; and to judge of them as poems, they must be said and not sung, a test which they often triumphantly endure. They stand, certainly, at many different levels of poetic passion and workmanship. Some are perfect on a lower level, others imperfect on a higher level ; a few are perfect on a very high level. Many are merely deft exhibitions of ethical and sentimental routine, which are only saved by their accompaniments, and therefore are not saved for poetry at all.

What, then, as a lyric poet, can he still give us ? In judging of his power we must go beyond *Irish Melodies*. These pieces appeared in nine numbers or garlands, which cover a long space of years, ranging from 1808 to 1834. The success of the first numbers revealed the unguessed wealth of airs afloat in Ireland, and Moore's enterprise was prolonged by the abundance of the examples submitted to him for sifting ; so that in all he published 108 *Irish Melodies*. But in the intervals he also published *National Airs* (1818-27), drawn from many countries, and provided by him with words ; *Sacred Songs* (1816), of less interest, and many other lyrics, often not written for music at all.

In some few of these pieces—' Oft in the stilly night,' ' At the mid-hour of night,' *The Irish Peasant*—Moore rises throughout to a diction that is pure, noble, and piercing ; but this perfection is oftener won for only two or three stanzas at a time, and there is some intrusion of commoner and mechanical writing. *Echo*, and ' Poor wounded heart,' and ' Then fare thee well,' are favourable cases. But this class shades off into a much larger one, where Moore shows a rare technical facility in finding poetic phraseology for an obvious kind of sentiment, never ignoble and yet never transfigured. *The Minstrel Boy*, ' Go where glory waits thee,' ' 'Tis the last rose of summer,' ' The harp that once in Tara's halls,' and many more have struck home, and it is not every good poet who can draw even facile tears for more than a single generation. In many of these songs Moore recovers a stranger delicacy, a curious wail, by his metrical tact ; and, above all, by his use of long-drawn weighted syllables, or monosyllabic feet ; and these often redeem a commonplace style, as in such a verse as this :

The da'y | had sunk | in dim | sho'wers,
  But midnight now, with lustre meek,
Illu | mined a'll | the pale | flo'wers, etc.

Comparatively few of the *Melodies* are playful, but some of
the exceptions, like ' Lesbia hath a beaming eye,' are of proved
excellence, with an easy old conventional ' Irish wit and
tenderness.' We have to be thus miserly in speaking of Moore,
but it is the lapse of time that has worn down a vogue all but
universal in his day.

Moore was admired, as a lyric poet, by Shelley. When he
came into a Dublin theatre the house rose and shouted for him.
Elderly ladies, on a rough sea-passage, invaded his cabin for a
kiss. He was highly paid and pensioned and decorated, both
parties applauding. His bad work was saluted as eagerly as
his good. His verse was much translated, and his popularity
at home was next to that of Byron. Of his public there is a
remnant that sings his songs, or listens to them, rather than
reads them. But most of it is departed, and there is apathy
instead, or an inclination to treat Moore as an extinct standard
author ; and there is, as we have said, in his own land a certain
ingratitude, at least amongst the lettered. It would be an
error to set down his popularity to the bad taste of the multitude, which exists about equally in every age, though its objects
vary. But there was a certain critical bluntness amongst the
brilliant and lettered persons who surrounded him. The
Whig circle, the political wits, the cultured world, were in
general complacently set on a wrong track of poetical taste.
As ever, most of the work that endures was done by the solitary
artists, like Wordsworth and Shelley and Keats. It is always
so, save in the case where a true craftsman like Tennyson
chances, not always by his better work, to reach the public.
' There never was an artistic period ' ; Whistler's words are
true of the one we are studying.

The superiority of Moore's prose to his rhyme, for purposes
of story-telling, is again well seen from a comparison of the
unfinished poem *Alciphron* with the completed romance into
which he converted it. This is *The Epicurean* (1827), which
was translated into several languages, and illustrated by
Turner. Here the sham learning, censured by Peacock, is
lightly enough worn ; and the gardens of Epicurus, the sub-
terranean magic and mysteries of Egypt, and the martyrdom
of the Christian hermit and maiden, form a series of many-
coloured pageants. A thread is found in the love-adventures

of Alciphron himself, Epicurean and convert to the Gospel.
The book has the unreality of all Moore's tales, but it is sometimes saved by its rhythm, which is as a far echo of Landor's
or De Quincey's :

> Every plant and tree, that is consecrated to death, from the
> asphodel flower to the mystic plantain, lends its sweetness or shadow
> to this place of tombs ; and the only noise that disturbs its eternal
> calm is the low humming of the priests at prayer, when a new in-
> habitant is added to the silent city.

There is nothing of this strain in his other prose ; in his
curious naïve plea for his own faith, *Travels of an Irish Gentleman
in Search of a Religion*, which is full of his gentlemanly surface
reading, or in his patriotic *Memoirs of Captain Rock*.

His *Life of Byron* (1830) it is easy to underestimate.   It
does not come into comparison with the biographies by Boswell
or Lockhart, each of whom had a better comprehension of his
subject than Moore, while neither had the same enigmas to
face, or the same call upon his nerve.   But, up to the limits
of Moore's courage and capacity, and even beyond what we
might have expected of either, the *Life of Byron* is honest,
loyal, and accurate, if incomplete.   Moore no doubt wrote
on the wrong, the English principle : he shocks no more than
he must the conventions of that society which Byron had himself rejected.   They are Moore's own conventions, which also
had induced him to destroy, in his discretion, Byron's manuscript memoirs [1] ; and, as a faithful friend, he is always explaining and apologising for Byron, and making the best of him ;
so that though no one fact is falsified, the whole drawing is
feeble and wavering.   At the same time, Moore is far more
candid than most of our biographers : he notices, for instance,
that Byron's ' intellectual powers were increased ' by his
Venetian amusements.   And he has the great merit of letting
the story tell itself by letters, facts, and anecdotes, interposing
his own long commentaries from time to time.   A real life of
Byron has never been written ; it would require not only judgment, but a good deal of indiscretion, and something of the
spirit of *Don Juan* turned back upon its author.   Moore
remains Byron's best biographer : the rest have been pedantic
and academic, or vulgar and journalistic, or they have not
written on a large enough scale, or they have been biased by
political sympathy or antipathy.   His *Memoirs* of Sheridan are
incomplete and superseded.

CHAPTER XXI

OTHER POETS (*concluded*) AND DRAMATISTS

I. Wits, humourists, parodists: Henry Luttrell, *Advice to Julia*. James and Horace Smith, *Rejected Addresses*, and *Horace in London*. Praed: serious and romantic pieces; the humorous-grotesque; his social and satiric verse, and its tunes; political verses.

II. The romantic tradition: Mrs. Tighe; Thomas Hood. Hood, Keats and the Elizabethans: *The Two Swans, Plea of the Midsummer Fairies*, etc.; lyrics; poems of pathos and terror; pleasantries in verse and prose. John Hamilton Reynolds; *The Garden of Florence*; *The Fancy*. Wells, *Joseph and his Brethren*.

III. Other romantic poets, 1820-30; transitional period. Bryan Waller Procter ('Barry Cornwall'); dramatic sketches and songs. George Darley, *Sylvia, Nepenthe*, lyrics, and prose articles. Thomas Lovell Beddoes: the 'haunted ruin' of the drama; study of old dramatists; *The Bride's Tragedy, Torrismond*, etc.; *Death's Jest-Book*; no poetic wholes. His style in blank verse; its originality. Beddoes' songs; their varieties and unique quality; the *macabre*. Letters and criticisms.

IV. The drama; its weakness in this period. Dibdin's pieces and songs, and O'Keefe's. Comedies: Holcroft, Colman the younger, Morton. 'Serious' drama; Kotzebue and his influence; *The Stranger* and *Lovers' Vows*; attacks on Kotzebue. The literary drama; Elizabethan studio-work again; Joanna Baillie. Milman, *Fazio*. Sheridan Knowles, *Virginius, Hunchback*, etc.

I

WE now pass to the other wits and humourists who spoke in verse, and to the remaining romantic poets who wrote narratives, lyrics, and tragedies, concluding with a brief note on the comic drama and the relationship of the stage to literature.

Through the pages of Moore's *Journal* flits the figure of Henry Luttrell (?1765-1851), a fellow-satirist and an accepted wit, who outlived his generation, and also, somewhat undeservedly, his celebrity. The social verse of Luttrell is high-bred, light, and pointed, and is refreshing beside the blunter and louder jesting of Sydney Smith or of Hook. He lived, indeed, partly upon his puns, which were the toll taken of Laughter by Fashion in that day, and became as obsolete as the old-fashioned cravats of which Luttrell describes the momentous niceties. But his *Advice to Julia* (1820) is a link between the less ferocious sallies of *The Anti-Jacobin* and the verse of Praed. It merits revival, and is much better natured and better done than Horace Smith's *Horace in London*. It is in form a prolonged expansion of the ode *Delia, dic per omnes* ; but Delia becomes Julia, and Sybaris her husband Charles, a young, sporting, athletic buck who has been snared by Julia's eyes, and deserts Almack's and Rotten Row, and his Leicestershire hunting and his trips to Paris, and denies his old friends, and is the slave, as yet, of his young merciless mistress. Luttrell's picture of London, of his gay, summery, and dusty London, his cheerful and forgetful, his joyous and heartless London, which is now forsaken by his hero, is one of the best that remains to us from that day ; and amidst his light and pertinent effrontery he forgets neither its landscape nor its poverty, having indeed the essential kind-heartedness that goes well with dandyism. Even poverty, he adds, enjoys in town, and there only, the blessings of obscurity and of freedom from contempt. All this is told in Hudibras-measure, with an easy aptitude for difficult rhyming. Luttrell's is one of the last poems in this style, and the real scene is St. James's Street ; and he shows the Serpentine

> In winter when the slanting sun
> Just skirts th' horizon, and is gone ;
> When from his disk a shortlived glare
> Is wasted on the clear cold air,
> When the snow sparkles, on the sight
> Flashing intolerable white,
> And, swept by hurried feet, the ground
> Returns a crisp and crushing sound.

Luttrell also wrote *Crockford House* (1827), a mock-heroic description and a serious exposure of that famous gambling-shop, and *A Rhymer in Rome*, which appeared in the same volume. His pleasant lines on *Burnham Beeches* are in another vein, and familiar.

The mocking-bird performances of Canning and Frere in *The Anti-Jacobin* remained for more than ten years without a rival, but in 1812 the anonymously published *Rejected Addresses*,[1] *or the New Theatrum Poetarum*, took the town by storm, and renewed the craft of parody. With a difference : for one of the authors, Horatio or Horace Smith, explains in his preface to the eighteenth edition (1833) that

to avoid politics and personality, to imitate the turn of mind, as well as the phraseology of our originals, and, at all events, to raise a harmless laugh, were our main objects ; in the attainment of which united aims, we were sometimes hurried into extravagance, by attaching much more importance to the last than to the two first.

The Anti-Jacobins wished to do damage, Horace and James
Smith, his brother, to amuse ; and they managed to amuse,
amongst the authors they travestied, not only Scott and
Crabbe, but Byron. We have not the opinion of Wordsworth,
to whom Horace Smith in the same preface offers a kind of
apologetic tribute. But the famous verses on ' my brother
Jack,' if they are far nearer the mark than the imitations by
Hamilton Reynolds or by Shelley, must yield in felicity to the
profoundly mischievous and intimate reproduction by Catherine
Fanshawe,[1] in her lines ' There is a river clear and fair,' of Wordsworth's very tune and sentiment. Of the two brothers, James
appears to have had the nicer hand in parody, though Horace
was more of a man of letters by calling. Wordsworth, Cobbett,
Coleridge, Southey, and Crabbe are the prey of James ; whilst
in the heroic lay of Marmion-Higginbottom is found the chief
triumph of Horace. He also wrote most of *Cui Bono ?* a
poem which the author of *Childe Harold* might easily have
dreamt was his own, and which rivals the ditty assigned by
Peacock to his ' Mr. Cypress.' To the historian, the echoes of
forgotten poetasters like Fitzgerald, Dr. Busby, and ' Laura
Matilda ' (still, it seems, surviving in 1812) are hardly less
attractive. In the next year the brothers were encouraged by
their success to collect from the *Monthly Mirror* some imitations
under the title *Horace in London*. These are loose adaptations
of the first two books of the Odes. Without the finish of
Rejected Addresses, they are still a treasury of sprightly allusion
and mockery. Lewis, and Byron, and Johnson, and Busby,
and Cobbett figure once more as victims. The book is forgotten, and a few of the lines to Cobbett may be given :

> Hail, Botley Bifrons, sinuous eel !
> How shall the Muse your course reveal ?
>   In what Pindarics word it ?
> Round like a weathercock you flit,
> As interest veers, now puffing Pitt,
>   And now inflating Burdett.

Amongst others, Horne Tooke, and George Colman, and Lord
Elgin receive showers of rather stinging confetti, and lastly
' My Godwin ! ' ; and the fall of Godwin's fame is maliciously,
but all too truly, taken for granted. Horace Smith, who outlived his brother and died in 1849, wrote voluminously, pouring
out farces, novels, and more verses ; but nothing is remembered
except his resonant, not quite poetical *Address to a Mummy*,
his novel *Brambletye House*, and his genial reminiscent pages
on Shelley and Keats, on Hook and Matthews. Shelley's

praise of him in the *Letter to Maria Gisborne* is well known and well earned.

These masters of the lighter social verse had one disability which neither genius nor pains could make good. They were seldom, like Winthrop Mackworth Praed[1] (1802-39), born of the caste. Hood, like Dickens, is a gentleman in soul, but his humour runs easily into vociferation and caricature. Moore has the entry of the world he describes, and is not afraid of it, and chronicles its rumours deftly, but he does not truly belong to it, and is aware that he does not ; he is a kind of blue-bottle or ichneumon-fly humming about amongst the butter-flies. Praed is the embodiment of Eton and Cambridge and St. James's ; the very spirit of good English society without its insolence. He has the code, the wit, the manners, the way of taking itself for granted that belongs to the caste, but he is something more as well ; for in him the caste turns upon itself, and describes and mocks itself, though still it knows of no other self, and refuses to mock too hard. This mockery is conveyed in consummate verse, or rather, it might be said, in consummately good copies of verses ; for Praed, like Canning and Frere before him, is a schoolboy and undergraduate of genius, expert in Greek and Latin exercises, and even when grown up keeps something of the same tone and quality in his English. He is the pattern of clear-witted, fastidious youth holding up the mirror, untarnished, to the scene of life of which he is a part ;—but which he stands above precisely by this power of representing it. Except in his political verse, he is never ill-tempered. There is something of Addison in him, especially when he quits the town and depicts the country, with its life and leisured humourists—the squire, the vicar— who live away from the whirl, but are essentially part of the same British order of things as the men of the town. To them Praed is kinder than Jane Austen is to any man. He has no touch of the social passion of Hood, nor yet of his rhetoric, nor yet again of his gift of tears and occasional deep magic. He cannot sing like Moore, but his wit is better-conditioned, being rooted both in his breeding and his humour. This humour has several sides and modes, and through it, and hardly otherwise, he becomes aware, not immediately, of his true line in verse-craft.

Most of Praed's wholly serious and sentimental rhymes are those of a scholar trying to be a poet. They are in dead earnest, they never fail in finish ; but they do not go home, and we ask what is the matter with them. It is only when they are dashed

with irony that they acquire poetic virtue. Praed discovered
the need of this ingredient, and how to infuse it, somewhat
slowly. He began with romance, telling tales of Arthur and
Isumbras, and working in the style and measure of *Christabel*,
or of Scott's and Byron's imitations of *Christabel*. He goes
on quite single-mindedly awhile, and then suddenly remembers
and pulls himself back, flinging in, not too harmoniously, scraps
of modern satire. The unfinished *Troubadour* is full of pleasing chivalries and tuneful lay-making, charming enough in a
familiar vein ; but the lively picture of the alarmed scurrying
dwellers in the nunnery comes as a shock, though it already
shows Praed's curious skill in slinging into rhyme, quite naturally, fragments of shrill and confused feminine chatter. *Gog*,
another early piece, is wholly farcical, and *The Legend of the
Haunted Tree* is mostly serious. But the real bourne of such
experimental writing was the humorous-grotesque, and Praed
made himself a master of that species. *The Bridal of Belmont*,
and *The Legend of the Teufelhaus*, and above all *The Red Fisherman*, show this power in its fulness. The last of these poems
(originally named *The Devil's Decoy*) is more reserved, and less
boisterously rhymed, than the later and undeniable triumphs
of the *Ingoldsby Legends* ; but it is all the better for that. The
true *frisson* of comedy is attained in such passages as the final
doom pronounced by the devil-fisherman to the shaking abbot :

> O ho ! O ho !
> The cock doth crow ;
> It is time for the Father to rise and go.
> Fair luck to the Abbot, fair luck to the shrine !
> He hath gnawed in twain my choicest line ;
> Let him swim to the north, let him swim to the south,
> The Abbot will carry my hook in his mouth.

These romances were something of an excursion, and meantime Praed had been burnishing his other, his really more native
gift. We can watch his social poetry becoming, about the year
1826, ever more concentrated, freer from alien matter, more
classic—there is no other word—in its style, temper, and
proportioning. *The County Ball* is one of the best of the earlier
examples. Its theme is not the Rape of the Lock, but the
Dropping of the Comb ; and it is interspersed with those
character-portraits, in part no doubt of living friends and acquaintance, which Praed always much affected. We cannot
better ' catch the blossom of the flying terms ' than in the
sketches of Jacques the Cantab or Reuben Nott the blunderer ;
the latter reads like a bit of Regnard's comedies :—it is the

chaff of the best kind of young Englishman, endlessly familiar
yet free from false notes :

> He makes a College Fellow wild
> By asking for his wife and child ;
> Puts a haught blue in awful passion
> By disquisitions on the fashion ;
> Refers a knotty case in whist
> To Morley the philanthropist ;
> Quotes to a sportsman from St. Luke ;
> Bawls out plain ' Bobby ' to a Duke. . . .

The Bachelor : T. Quince, Esq., to the Rev. Matthew Pringle is
of the same quality. Praed seems to have written his best
between 1826 and 1832. He then settled down to his most
beloved and most effective metres, of which the chief is the
eight-line stanza with its characteristic double rhymes ;
perfects his device (since overtasked by other hands) of a
startling but not too violent anticlimax, often born of a pun,
and so attains in almost every verse the effect of a dance-
measure, with step and counter-step, which is at once gentle
and lively. One illustration may be allowed ; but almost
every page of the *Every-Day Characters*, *The Vicar*, or *Quince*,
or *My Partner*, would furnish another ; this is from *The Belle
of the Ballroom* :

> She talked,—of politics or prayers,
>   Of Southey's prose or Wordsworth's sonnets,—
> Of danglers,—or of dancing bears,—
>   Of battles,—or the last new bonnets.
> By candle-light, at twelve o'clock,
>   To me it mattered not a tittle ;
> If those bright lips had quoted Locke,
>   I might have thought they murmured Little.

Good-Night to the Season, and *Letters from Teignmouth*, are in a
different, a more lilting tune, that runs upon anapæsts, and
is equally apt—apter perhaps even than the other, for that
note of half-real sadness and solitariness that Praed interweaves with his satire. He has the feeling that these bright
things are transient, but he will not make too much of it. The
political squib *Utopia*, which is in a different rhyme again,
ends with a ring of real passion :

> O bitterness !—the morning broke
>   Alike for boor and bard ;
> And thou wert married when I woke,
>   And all the rest was marred :
> And toil and trouble, noise and steam,
>   Came back with the coming ray ;
> And, if I thought the dead could dream,
>   I 'd hang myself to-day !

The charm of Praed's best social poetry is that it is, or seems—
and in such a case ' being is seeming '—wholly unforced ; there
is, indeed, a kind of dew upon it, no hard sheen. It has the
freshness of a spirit that remains young, though it is undeceived.

Praed's political rhymes, which poured forth in a bright
stream from his college days until the end, have the same
qualities, slightly marred by a touch of fierceness which does
not always suit with his genius. Many of them, printed
anonymously in magazines and newspapers, are so allusive
as to be ephemeral. They have been carefully edited, but
light verse that requires a solid commentary is somewhat over-
weighted. They remain, however, to cheer not only the historian of parliamentary life and gossip, but the lover of gently
scarifying satire ; and they also reflect the change in Praed's
political sympathies. He began as a Liberal, or Radical, with
Whig leanings, in the camp of Austin and his set ; and the
sprightly lines to the Czar Alexander, to Lord Eldon, and the
official Tories, like the parody of the Duke of York's speech
against the Catholic Emancipation Bill, are of his best mintage.
Emancipation came, and Praed, who ' could never have supported a party opposed to ' it, was led by his growing distrust
of Reform to enlist under Peel. He sat in the Commons from
1830, with intervals, until his death, and was for a short time
Secretary of the Board of Control, founding though hardly
maturing a reputation in the House. He served his cause
very efficiently by his squibs on Lord Grey, and on the often-
rhymed ' Mr. Brougham [" Broom "] and Mr. Hume,' on Lord
Althorp and on John Cam Hobhouse. The best-tempered of
these pieces are usually the best. The *Nursery Song* (' Hume
has forgotten Waterloo '), *The Adieus of Westminster* (' When
first you came courting, John Cam, John Cam '), and the
Stanzas on seeing the Speaker Asleep, are in a mischievous,
dreamy, crooning strain that wins the ear. Of his more habitual
style and measure, with its sharp, blue-fizzing sparkle that
leaves a shock behind, there are many examples in his political
poetry. This manner is well applied to serious invective in
such work as the *Counsels of a Father to his Son*. The ' father,'
an official who had jobbed his son into a deanery, was also a
renegade from his early principles : and this Lord Plunket
suffered from the bludgeon of Cobbett as well as from the *épée*
of Praed :

> When I at last shall sleep in peace,
>   When life's consumption shall be o'er,
> When I shall fill that payless place
>   Where none shall plot or plunder more,

> Remember on what wings I soared
> To infamy's unfading crown,
> How I became a noble lord,
> And you became the Dean of Down.
>
> Professing disregard of self,
> I won the ermine of a Peer;
> Avowing carelessness of pelf,
> I earned some thousand pounds a year;
> I caught the favours of the Court,
> And seemed as honest as a clown;
> And though I fathered a ' Report,'
> I fathered, too, the Dean of Down.

There is more weight behind this than there is behind the
pasquinades of Thomas Moore, who uses the whiplash rather
than the steel. Praed, in his last years, perfected his art of
fence in three longer satires, of which *The Treasury Bench*,
addressed to Lord Palmerston, is the most biting.

II

In Praed the wit and ironist somewhat weighs down the
romancer, while in Hood the balance is in the other direction ;
and with him, and Reynolds and Darley, and the other Elizabethans striving to be reincarnate, we are back with the main
stream of poetry. There had been other such experiments
before, like those of Lamb or like that of Mrs. Henry Tighe,
whose Spenserian *Psyche* (1805) may be named here as an early
example. It is on the line between the older mode—Campbell's
mode—of appropriating Spenser's charm, and the newer, and it
shows the mixture of styles. Mrs. Tighe imposes on her Psyche,
instead of the familiar trials, duller ones of her own making, and
sends her wandering to the Coasts of Spleen and the Island
of Indifference, to be saved by a knight who proves to be
Cupid in disguise. There is not much romance in the work,
but Mrs. Tighe sometimes catches the ebb and resurgence of
Spenser's more equable verse with a pleasant ease.

Reading Thomas Hood's [1] (1799-1845) poems of pure imagination and summer fantasy, one might think at moments that his
master, Keats, had risen from the dead and was speaking once
more. *Hero and Leander*, with *The Two Swans*, doubtless owed
as much to Spenser and the young-eyed Elizabethans as to
their last and greatest disciple. In *The Two Swans* the stanza
and its whole tune and movement are Spenserian, while the
' gentle girl and boy,' and the ' serpent-sorrow ' that oppressed
them, and the release of these ' victims of old Enchantment's

love or hate,' are lovely after-coinages in Keats's own fashion ;
just as the verses on *Ruth* (' She stood breast high amid
the corn '), and the Ode, *Autumn* (' Where are the songs of
summer ? '), are modulations on some single phrase of Keats's
making.   But the rich heavy imagery of *The Two Swans*, and
the whole conduct of the tale—as of an oppressive dream at
last relieved—have a kind of romantic beauty for which Hood
is no man's debtor ;   and there is none of that bent towards
over-neat lyric epigram, or towards forced and overstrained
luridness, which elsewhere in his verse deters us.   A stanza
like the following shows the independence of his power—
unsure, alas, and interrupted, but beyond question :

> And forth into the light, small and remote,
> A creature, like the fair son of a king,
> Draws to the lattice in his jewell'd coat
> Against the silver moonlight glistening,
> And leans upon his white hand listening
> To that sweet music that with tenderer tone
> Salutes him ; wondering what kindly thing
> Is come to soothe him with so tuneful moan,
> Singing beneath the walls as if for him alone !

The later, longer, and better-sustained *Plea of the Midsummer Fairies* (1827) is so far less satisfying to the ear than
The Two Swans, in that the final alexandrine is shortened to a
line of ten ;   and this disappoints us a little in every verse.
Beautiful as this poem is in spirit and conception, and often in
single stanzas, it is a disappointment in other ways, falling
constantly behind in execution ;   and it must be said to live to
some extent on its fame.   The felicities, running into playfulness or deliberate quaintness, of Keats, are a dangerous
model for a poet given already to familiar rhyming.   But often
Hood keeps just the true pitch for the fantastic narrative style
that is midway between the gay and the melancholy, and we
can only regret that he never had time to perfect his power
over it, but had to jest for bread.   We would have given a
score of *Kilmanseggs* for a few more verses like this :

> Then Saturn, with a frown :—' Go forth, and fell
> Oak for your coffins, and thenceforth lay by
> Your axes for the rust, and bid farewell
> To all sweet birds, and the blue peeps of sky
> Through tangled branches, for ye shall not spy
> The next green generation of the tree ;
> But hence with the dead leaves, whene'er they fly,—
> Which in the bleak air I would rather see
> Than flights of the most tuneful birds that be.

The same kind of fancy, but less intense, is heard in *Hero and Leander* ; but *Lycus the Centaur*, the first of Hood's longer romantic pieces, seems to be influenced, as to its slow-galloping metre, by Shelley's *Vision of the Sea*, and perhaps also in its highly-charged attempt at dreadfulness. But the innocent poetry of the senses, of which it is also full, is still inspired by Keats. Indeed, this whole group of poems can only have fallen out of the general memory because it is crushed out, coming as it does in date between Keats himself, who begot it, and Tennyson, whose early writing of the same species eclipsed it.

That Hood turned away from this style before he had brought it to perfection is, no doubt, a sounder reason for its neglect. But it calls for some vindication, because the whole notion of Hood as primarily a dealer either in whims and points, or else in lyrical pathos and indignation, is a grotesque and obstinate one. It is true that he won his considerable share of fame, and his moderate share of bread, by *The Song of the Shirt* in one kind, and by *Sally Brown* and a myriad such things in another. But his romantic experiments are not mere uncompleted aberrations of his talent, for in them and not in the others is his real power to be seen. Much or most of the rest is in the nature of journalism, poetical or prosaic, high-minded or humorous.

But his serious short lyrics—a mere child's handful—show a rare and more personal gift even than the *Plea of the Midsummer Fairies*. It is true that they are apt to turn on some pun or play of words, but it is often in the large and untrivial Elizabethan fashion. It is thus with ' We watch'd her breathing through the night,' and in that last and noblest of Hood's songs, written under sentence of death, and entitled ' Farewell Life ! ' But this trick of language or pathetic antithesis is simply the natural or ingrained fashion of his thinking, and his emotion works irrepressibly towards it, from .some instinct of reserve, perhaps, or of courage ; and to die, or to speak of death, with this kind of jest on the lips, is by no means the worst way. In other pieces, again, there is no such inclination ; for twice at least, namely in the lines ' It was not in the winter ' and in those called *Autumn* (' The Autumn is old '), there is a pure rightness of form and a piercing music, a tone as of sorrow at once rooted and reflected in the beauty of the world without, which separates these pieces from the equally lovely, but after all more abstract lyrics of Thomas Moore.

In one well-marked class of Hood's pieces he seeks to bear hard upon the nerves, or, as the phrase ran forty years before during the vogue of Lewis and Mrs. Radcliffe, to 'touch the springs of terror.' This he does by a bold assault, and with effects of echoed phrase and threefold rhyme that remind us, afar off, of *The Ancient Mariner*, in *The Dream of Eugene Aram* ; a ballad that should be seen as Hood first printed it, with alarming cuts interspersed, and flanked by the actual reported speech of the learned Aram at his trial, in which he argued that the skeleton of his victim was the contents of an ancient prehistoric barrow. Hood, no doubt, invents the remorse, of which Aram was too cool a hand to entertain a spark ; but he makes an excellent scenic affair of it ; and more than that, makes it real and poetic : the echoes just mentioned play their part well in this stanza and elsewhere :

> My head was like an ardent coal,
>   My heart as solid ice ;
> My wretched, wretched soul, I knew,
>   Was at the Devil's price :
> A dozen times I groan'd ; the dead
>   Had never groan'd but twice !

It is not clear that just this effect has ever been so well attained again. In *The Elm-Tree* and *The Haunted House* the aim is less direct, and the poet operates by more allusion and by the unsaid. In the latter piece the refrain is not quite good enough to be a refrain, though it is a good verse ; and no doubt there is overmuch emphasis on the horrors :

> The Death Watch tick'd behind the pannel'd oak,
> Inexplicable tremors shook the arras,
> And echoes strange and mystical awoke,
> The fancy to embarrass.

This is too particular, and borders on the 'explicable,' but the tune and metre are masterly, and win their effect by iteration and by the clanging invariable double rhyme. *The Elm-Tree*, much less definite in its imagery, has a greater depth of fantasy, and though most unequal leaves a true sense of the inner pulsing life of the forest, at first magically disturbed and then restored.

Hood's social and indignant verses are less satisfactory and more popular. *The Song of the Shirt* and *The Bridge of Sighs*, and their inferior companions, *The Workhouse Clock* and *The Lay of the Labourer*, we approach with the same sort of respect and reserve as we do all other sincere and impassioned religious verse which is not well written. For religious, in the proper sense, they are; and well written, in any fastidious sense of the term, they assuredly are not. This has been no hindrance to their circulation. The tenet that the best art is the longest enjoyed is only true if we take very long views indeed; otherwise it is a superstition. This is evident from the fate of many hymns, and of many a page of Charles Dickens. But *The Bridge of Sighs* is a really bad treatment of a sacred subject, with its jarring tuneless dactyls, its *emphase*, and its grotesque phrase, ' Lave in it, drink of it,' which comes so near the climax. Or, if this view be thought profane, let us say that it is only saved, if it is saved, by its subject. Hood's quick, deep, and vehement humanity it would be impudent to question; but, as so often happens, it prevents him from doing his best. *The Song of the Shirt* is a far better piece, with a far better tune, and has a rhythm in it as of beating hands or stamping feet; its effects are obvious, like the theme—but then no one had thought of the obvious; it is, in truth, an act, a blow, a vindication, a piece of history, and has had its audience accordingly. So wide a fame is, indeed, no reason against a poem being excellent; but Hood is seldom quite certain of his words, and Kingsley's little poacher-piece, ' The merry brown hares came leaping,' shows a finer quality of the same sort of power.

Old fashions of dress may come in again, but old fashions of humour? It is fairest to say that the readers who can enjoy Hood's jokes have proved to be younger with each generation; and that he can hold even the young is no small accomplishment; while a few of his best rhymed punning yarns can still hold anybody who is not a pedant. *Faithless Sally Brown*, and *Faithless Nelly Gray*, and a few more, are the perfection of a kind that Hood invented; they are the survivors of a hundred, the rest more or less suffering shipwreck. No one else could do the thing well at all. The infallibly recurring pun and point, and the total want of apparent exertion, rank them high. They are the stray flower, we may say, of a long laborious life of pleasantry and quipping— industries that were at once Hood's livelihood and no doubt his distraction from ill health, pain, and worry. As we read his periodical and single-handed outpourings of the facetious sort, we may not often laugh—indeed we may despond; but respect remains,—respect, in particular, for the personal dignity that the humourist keeps through it all. His comic prose and his comic verse are both inexhaustible, and a weariness if we stay with them too long. The notes of English popular humour in the middle of the century,—the verbal somersault, the amusement felt over the acts of eating, drinking, bearing children, and dying, the delight in practical horseplay,—the whole repertory, in fact, of jests, that never lose their salt with an enormous majority of mankind—all are duly represented in Thomas Hood. Still there is a difference, for while Dickens, like John Leech and his precursors, is perused, Hood is not. His valiant breathless pages of high jinks and voluble light farce are seldom opened. The best prose pieces in *Hood's Own* are the *Literary Reminiscences* ; and the fourth of these papers admirably catches the spirit of the evening at Charles Lamb's which it describes—including the remark of the ' official gentleman ' who gave them his blessing—' Yes, yes, all very proper and praiseworthy—of course, you go there to *improve your minds.*' The portraits of Wordsworth, of Elia himself, of the poet Clare ' in his bright, grass-coloured coat, and yellow waistcoat,' of the ' Brobdignagdian ' (*sic*) Allan Cunningham, and of the ' mild and modest ' Cary, translator of Dante, and, not least, of Coleridge and his talk, are distinct and genial enough. The same kind of observing faculty, smothered overmuch under the pattering hail of jokes, is visible in *Up the Rhine*, a humorous letter-diary of travel. One species in *Hood's Own* that lifted its head after somewhat long oblivion is the ancient ' Character,' as of a ' Butler,' ' an Irishman,' and the like ; consisting of a string of detached sentences, each embodying a single trait and tumbling out destitute of order. As a whole, however, this body of work becomes melancholy reading.

Hood's most protracted adventure in funny verse is *Miss Kilmansegg and her Precious Leg,*—which, it is well known, was of solid gold, her carnal leg having been removed by an accident. It can still be read with astonishment and amusement, as a feat of reckless and successful impromptu rhyming, and as full of a certain savage-grotesque railing against the worship of gold and luxury. In satiric invective Hood went on too long, and was really too genial for the work ; but his *Ode to Rae Wilson, Esquire,*—a person who had, amazingly enough, rebuked the author for dangerous frivolity, contains some palpable hits. The typical preaching hypocrite, the first cousin in high life of Mr. Pecksniff, is raked with an honest broadside, and little is left of him. In all this preoccupation can be traced, what in Dickens takes a wider scope and emphasis, the note of the humanitarian fiction and verse of the mid-century,—the *return to the heart*, the vindication of the good feeling of the natural man, as against cold reason, frigid dogma, and modish hardness.

In John Hamilton Reynolds[1] (1796-1852), the poetic ally and intimate correspondent of Keats, and the satiric associate of Hood, we find, more than in its stronger members, the very complexion and accent of the circle. Very little of his work has been reprinted, and it is all immature ; he has in full measure all the weaknesses of his friends ; but he also has their impulse towards luxury and felicity of impression, and towards a somewhat far-sought and lingering beauty of phrase. He is a true poet, only half delivered from mannerism ; he is really in the central line of the tradition that runs down from the dreamier verses of Coleridge to the youthful verses of Tennyson. He feeds, no doubt, on the poetry of others as an insect on the leaves whose colouring matter passes into its wings. He began by imitating the Eastern tales of Byron (*Safie*, 1814) and Wordsworth (*The Eden of Imagination*, 1814) when little more than a boy, and afterwards related the growth of his own fancy in *The Romance of Youth*, his richest and most interesting work. The fairy-lore of Shakespeare sank into him early, and with it the spirit of romantic beauty ; despite mystical warnings, his young poet goes out into the world— Reynolds went, in fact, into a law-office—and on revisiting home he finds the fairies departed, and the glow of inspiration gone. In this picture, however, Reynolds was unjust to himself, for some of his daintiest things were produced after he had plunged into the dusty profession. It is the case, however, that he passed in the end from poetry to parody and satire, and that his true literary life ends about 1825.

It would be easy, in the spirit of now long mouldered reviewers, to show from the verses of Reynolds what was meant by the ' cockney school.' A line like

And he was very happy, as I guess ;

the gown which was ' simply button'd ' upon the ' easy shoulder ' of a lady, and her hand, ' so sonnet-sweet ' ; phrases like ' she did love him so,' and ' certes,' and coinages like ' buddingly ' and the ' gloss'd blackbird '—such things might be garnered, but they would give a false idea of Reynolds. He is, no doubt, not always ' manly,' and we fear he would have thanked God for it. But it would be hard to name any unregarded writer of that age in whom the poetic *will* is stronger and more genuine. The fairy verses in his volume, *The Naiad*, of 1816, are a worthy lyric overture to Hood's *Plea of the Midsummer Fairies* ; and the beginning of *The Naiad* gives a good idea of his manner :

> The golden sun went into the west,
> The soft airs sang him to his rest ;
> And yellow leaves all loose and dry
> Play'd on the branches listlessly ;
> The sky wax'd palely blue, and high
> A cloud seem'd touch'd upon the sky,
> A spot of cloud, blue, thin, and still ;
> And silence breath'd on vale and hill.

The Garden of Florence (1821) is one of the tales from Boccaccio (and *The Ladye of Provence*, in the same volume, is another) which Reynolds and Keats planned together, and is thus a companion to *Isabella*. But the theme will hardly bear the high romantic treatment that is essayed. It is that of the two lovers, who died, Pasquino first, and Simonida, who is falsely charged with his murder, afterwards, of eating the leaves of a sage-plant, under which a portentous and poisonous toad was resident. Not much could be made of this story ; but the heroic couplets of *The Garden of Florence*, grouped into irregular staves, and varied with alexandrines, are nearer to the firm, Dryden-like music of *Lamia* than to the weaker measure of *Endymion* ; and Reynolds was steeped both in Keats and in Keats's models. It would be harsh to say that the result is prize poetry, rather than poetry of a high order ; the note was rare in 1821, though soon afterwards many could strike it :

> O, lovers are long watchers of the night !
> Watchers of coiling darkness—of the light—
> Of the cold window-pane, whereon the moon
> Casteth her sallow smile in night's mid-noon —
> Of the unwearied stars that watch on high
> As though they were lone lovers in the sky.
> Passion lays desolate the fields of sleep,
> And wakes a thousand eyes to watch and weep.

Reynolds's most engaging volume is called *The Fancy* (1820), which is assigned by him to an imaginary person, 'the late Peter Corcoran.' It shows his vein of pleasantry ; *King Tims* is a kind of children's comic opera, and *Tothill Fields* confessedly a following of Frere's satiric octaves. Already he had produced *Peter Bell, a Lyrical Ballad* (1819), which was printed before Wordsworth's poem, and is a mosaic-parody, not without spite and spirit, of *Lyrical Ballads*. It has not the

spontaneity of the pegtop verses in *Rejected Addresses*, but is
pleasantly and vulgarly entertaining now and then :

> The flea doth skip o'er Betty Foy
>   Like a little living thing ;
> Though it hath not fin or wing
> Hath it not a moral joy ?

The same kind of light-hearted impudence is found in the
verses contributed by Reynolds to Hood's *Odes and Addresses*.
He also wrote sprightly prose articles—such as *The Royal Cockpit*
and *The Visit to Greenwich*—in the *London Magazine*, under
the name of Edward Herbert ; and, like Hazlitt, studied the
prize ring. Reynolds is so little read that room may be found
for his *Sonnet on the Nonpareil*, which might have been made
by Mr. Henley :

> With marble-colour'd shoulders,—and keen eyes,
>   Protected by a forehead broad and white,—
>   And hair cut close lest it impede the sight,
> And clench'd hands, firm, and of a punishing size,—
> Steadily held, or motion'd wary-wise,
>   To hit or stop,—and kerchief too drawn tight
>   O'er the unyielding loins, to keep from flight
> The inconstant wind, that all too often flies,—
> The Nonpareil stands.—Fame, whose bright eyes run o'er
>   With joy to see a Chicken of her own,
>   Dips her rich pen in *claret*, and writes down
> Under the letter R, first on the score,
>   ' Randall,—John,—Irish parents,—age not known,
> Good with both hands, and only ten stone four ! '

The prose counterpart of this may be found in Pierce Egan's
Boxiana (1818) ; and *Life in London* (1821), by the same lively
and agreeable rattle, contains Cruikshank's pictures of Jerry
Hawthorne and Corinthian Tom, and gives the gross material of
some of the humours noted by literary journalists and novelists.

One associate of Keats and Reynolds, moved by the same
poetic models and enthusiasms, has been a victim of poetic
fame in a singular way. This was Charles Jeremiah Wells,[1] who
died in 1879, aged about eighty, and in 1824 published the long
undramatic drama, *Joseph and his Brethren*. The diction and
blank verse of this lavish, impetuous, luscious poem often
recapture or mimic, in a startling way, that of Peele or even
of the youthful Shakespeare ; and the figure of Phraxanor, the
wife of Potiphar, is dressed out with great magnificence of
colouring. More it is hard to say fairly ; but the poem, long
forgotten, was detected and praised by Dante Rossetti, and
in 1875 was ardently proclaimed by Swinburne. The aged

author, despite his surprise, added further scenes. Most of
the work seems rather discoloured now, but the dye holds in
a few lines and passages.

III

It will be seen already that between the passing of Keats and
the coming of Tennyson not many fresh voices are heard in
our poetry. Those of the veterans, Landor, Coleridge, and
Wordsworth—the second romantic generation that had outlived the third—are still at times nobly audible. But the
others, apart from Hood and Beddoes and Praed, mostly
sound thin and batlike enough to our ears. Or rather there is
a something worse than silence ; for the air is full of imitative
tunes from the verse of the English Renaissance. Those old
writers inspired *The Cenci, Endymion,* and *The Plea of the
Midsummer Fairies.* But Wells, ' Barry Cornwall,' and even
Darley were too often to find in the Elizabethan drama and
lyric little but a refuge from their own deficiencies. They
now and then produced a startling and even beautiful piece of
mimicry ; and Beddoes did far more than this ; but, in general,
they are neither the old writers re-embodied nor yet themselves. It is hard to regenerate their fame, which was never
wide. This dubious time of suspense was to be ended by the
rich, true, and lovely singing of the youthful Tennyson, in his
volume of 1830, and above all in that of 1833.

The most popular new poet of this transitional decade
(1820-30) was also the most derivative. Bryan Waller Procter [1]
(1787-1874) wrote under the name of ' Barry Cornwall,' an
imperfect anagram of his own ; he lived long, and his writings
cover nearly half a century, but most of his verse appeared
between 1815 and 1830. He died full of honours, the survivor
of two or three of the elder generations, and the repositary of
many memories ; some of which are recorded, not over-saliently,
in the piece of autobiography published by Coventry Patmore
in 1877. His pleasing and affectionate *Memoir* of Lamb
has been absorbed in later biographies ; and he also wrote
the earliest sketch of the life of Edmund Kean, and some prose
tales and essays. The *Dramatic Scenes* (1819), which won the
friendly overpraise of Charles Lamb, draw upon Boccaccio
and the Elizabethans ; *Ludovico Sforza,* and *Love Cured by
Kindness* (the story of ' how Lisa loved the King '), are among
the best of them, together with *The Falcon*—the dish that was
served up to feast a lady by a proud and poor lover. It is
wonderful how close Procter's verse gets now and then to the

old poets, and how, nevertheless, it will not serve. A mother speaks of her child :

> He would have torn my pretty bird from me.
> I had but one—what could I do ? There was
> No other way—and this is blood for blood.

This is the very echo, but it is no more. The volume is best worth turning over in the edition, somewhat altered, of 1857, with the pictures by Tenniel, Birket Foster, Corbould, and others ; a friendly memorial to the old poet, rather than a sign of the vitality of his work. Of *Marcian Colonna* (1820) and *A Sicilian Story* (1821) and succeeding volumes, there is little else to say, except that these memories of the drama come more and more to be varied with memories of Procter's own contemporaries ; and no verdict more fatally final can be cited than Jeffrey's,[1] that 'the materials really harmonise very tolerably.' The *English Songs*, first produced in 1832, and afterwards with additions in 1851, show a different aspiration, and even at their best are divided from real poetry by some curious and frail but impassable barrier. They were deliberately written in order to make good that lack of genuine English songs (as distinct from Scottish ones, or ballads, or Irish melodies) which, according to Procter, then defaced our literature. It is clear that he is thinking of popular lyrics, and of such as can be set to music ; and he does not name Shelley. 'I recollect scarcely a single *English* song of high character, which has been ten years before the public.' His two hundred and three ditties are a modest effort to fill this gap, and were accepted at the time, but are mostly drawing-room stuff. They have their share of verbal melody, but are tantalisingly void of poetic style.

In the verse of George Darley[2] (1795-1846), with all his dependence on models—sometimes the fairy fantasias of Shakespeare (or rather of Fletcher), sometimes the soaring conceits of Jacobean lyric—there is an original, passionate energy of rhythm, very different from the facility of Procter or the art-school finish of Talfourd's *Ion*. Darley gives the impression—as well in his work as in his personal confidences—of a man ardently chasing an ideal of sound, missing it too often, but capturing it for many a precious minute ; never quite losing hope or inspiration, but on the whole discouraged by the blankness of the public and by a too finely tempered diffidence and pride. Darley's song does not seem, like that of Beddoes, the song of some naked and hovering sprite ; it is more human and fallible, but therefore nearer to us. His ideal of language is of something as rich and luxurious as it can be while still remaining pure. The purity is intermittent, the richness seldom fails.

His first work, *Errors of Ecstasie* (1822), has this quality, but is full of sediment still unsettled. He next made prose tales and articles for the *London Magazine*, and one of these tales, *Lillian of the Vale*, he developed into *Sylvia, or the May Queen* (1827), a bazaar-like mixture of many tasteless and more delightful things. He did not defend the grotesque parts or the prose Elizabethan fun, and they are tiresome now. The machinery of his fiends and fairies, who wage war over the happiness of the singing shadow, Sylvia, the heroine, is deftly enough contrived, and the blank verse is full of nimble and lovely short passages. Charles Lamb liked the scenical directions for being written in rhyme, and their octosyllabics have a pleasant sedateness and sweetness, free from the excitement into which Darley's language easily flusters itself, and which became the curse of Dobell, Alexander Smith, and other successors of this school. But the play is only a setting and occasion for the songs. Some of these we remember for their own sake, such as ' Wail ! wail ye o'er the dead,' ' Oh ! sweet to rove,' and 'Amid the valleys far away.' But oftener there remains but the inarticulate memory of a stream, which comes up again murmuring the same tune after a long passage underground. Darley's miscellaneous lyrics leave the same mixed impression. *Robin's Cross* and *The Maiden's Grave* have a ring of their own, incommunicable, not Elizabethan at all. The mock-antique, ' It is not beauty I demand,' which Palgrave once thought a true antique, is quite as good as if Palgrave had been in the right. The popular ' I 've been roaming ' has been almost needlessly popular. But in a score of others the true poetic essence, unlearnt, unborrowed, however clouded or diluted, is present—the essence that in Barry Cornwall's *English Songs* we as constantly miss. There is not much more to be said for Darley's later plays, *Thomas à Becket* and *Ethelstan*, than for Barry Cornwall's *Dramatic Scenes*, except that there are more brains in them ; the plots show no power, the painful effort is apparent.

Nepenthe, printed privately in 1835, but not published till 1897, is a failure of real nobility, clueless, and staggering under too great a pomp and ambition of language, but full of poetic instinct and splendid vibration, and bold even to rashness. There is that in it—a kind of drugged elation—which recalls *A Song to David* ; but instead of Smart's surging and falling stanza, it is in a regular roll of short-lined full rhymes. Darley's verse is now easy of access, but a few verses may be given to show his method. The first two lines are seventeenth-century, but the rest original :

> Thanks, Nepenthe fine, for this
> Living apotheosis !
> Hark ! above me I do hear
> Heavenly joy-bells ringing clear,
> And see their golden mouths, ding dong,
> Vibrate with a starry tongue.

> Welcome, welcome ! still they toll
> Syllabled sweetly in knell-knoll,
> While more deep, in undulous swell,
> Chimes unseen the burden-bell,
> Mellowing, in the mighty boom
> Of his huge sonorous womb,
> Their sweet clangour, like the din
> Of streams lost in a roaring lynn.

The tune, as ever with Darley, is safer than the words, which easily become amateurish. We feel that Poe would have hailed a kindred passion for cadence.

Darley's prose is not seen at its best where it is deliberately antique and motley. The poetry of the past is ever easier to re-create than its fun and quips. Darley had plenty of sprightliness of his own, as his tolerably fierce dramatic notices in the *London Magazine* are enough to show. He keeps his sharpest darts for the would-be Elizabethans, Procter and Talfourd. In his literary sympathies he was a true Elizabethan himself, and one of the latest to survive. His preface to Beaumont and Fletcher (1840) is, together with Hartley Coleridge's papers on *Hamlet*, the last sally of the critical genius of the older romantic generation. His mixture of enjoyment and strong-headed reserve is not unlike Hazlitt's, though Darley writes more loosely-girt and more whimsically than Hazlitt. He was also unlucky in his date ; Dyce's edition of Beaumont and Fletcher, with its close and judicious scholarship, came out a few years later ; and Darley is not in a position to distinguish duly between the handiwork of the two poets ; although, when all is said, much of the modern sifting is guesswork. Yet no one between Hazlitt and Mr. Swinburne wrote on these poets with such relish and sanity as Darley. Also, in earlier days, he produced some prose stories not without their charm. These were collected (still from the *London Magazine*) under the name of *The Labours of Idleness*, by ' Guy Penseval,' and the preface has a pathetic interest.   Here Darley seems to portray himself, with his outward angularity and diffidence, and his inward pride and sensitiveness.   He was the victim of an incurable stammer, and lived a pent life, although he was cheered by the friendship of Charles Lamb and Henry Cary.   To some of these judges, between 1820 and 1830, he seemed the most authentic and promising of the newer poets.   But Tennyson came.

He came, and few then attended to the Elizabethan revival, though it continued for some while.   But meantime an un-regarded poet was at work, in whom is visible the utmost that such a revival can achieve, and also perhaps how little is that utmost.   Thomas Lovell Beddoes [1] (1803-49) holds his patent far more on the strength of the songs and lyrics which he seems to have held in light esteem, than by the dramas at which he laboured so fiercely ; and yet, in these strained and congested tragedies, sometimes no better than the play within the play of *Hamlet*, he inherits lawfully from Webster and Tourneur, from the acrid but often magnificent Marston, and from the author of the *Second Maiden's Tragedy*.[2]   Like them, he builds on the motive of revenge ; and, while his philosophy is fatalistic or simply blank, he too nourishes his imagination on the idea of death, not less in its tender and pensive than in its more fantastic and pompous aspects.   Beddoes, in his piercing or terrific invocations, seems to raise the shades of these elders. But he is well on his guard, at least in theory, against mere midnight resurrection-work, and observes that 'these re-animations' (which in the years 1820-30 were rife) 'are vampire-cold.'

With the greatest reverence for all the antiquities of the drama, I still think that we had better beget than revive—attempt to give the literature of the day an idiosyncrasy and spirit of its own, and only raise a ghost to gaze on not to live with—just now the drama is a haunted ruin.[3]

This ruin Beddoes peopled with spectres singular enough ; but they are at least of his own conjuring, and he is a descendant not a slave of his Jacobean masters.   It is true that, like some of his dramatic ancestors, he stokes the furnace of his imagina-tion so fiercely as to hurt the eyes of the reader ; but the flame is there.

Beddoes read the old dramatists while a schoolboy at the Charterhouse ;   produced, while an Oxford undergraduate, two volumes called *The Improvisatore* (1821) and *The Bride's*

Tragedy (1822), and never published more. He worshipped
Shelley, and inspired the issue of his *Posthumous Poems* in 1824 ;
began soon after, but never finished, *The Second Brother* and
Torrismond ; and started work on *Death's Jestbook*, his chief
production, in 1825. He then went to Göttingen, Germanised
himself very completely, and studied medicine, his father's
calling, with much energy. He lived in Germany and Switzerland for some twenty years, wandering amongst the universities,
reading Goethe with mixed respect and disgust, developing
Radical opinions, working away at *Death's Jestbook*, penning
but never printing much other verse, writing letters home, and
becoming somewhat of a desperate eccentric and solitary. He
passed one more year in England, but returned in 1848 to
Germany. There he made more than one attempt at suicide,
and at last, deliberately and somewhat scenically, poisoned
himself with curare. His intimate friend and literary executor,
Kelsall, published most of his poetry in 1851.

Beddoes' miscellaneous work is of interest. He tried hard to
suppress all copies of *The Improvisatore*, which contains a Scott-
like minstrel, and is richly, gracefully, and harmlessly romantic.
Temporary traces of Leigh Hunt are easy to find in *Pygmalion*,
and of Shelley in *The Romance of the Lily*. But the debt of
Beddoes to Shelley can be overstated, though his admiration for
Shelley was profound. His motley rhymed epistles to friends,
and his quatorzains, show how natural his highly charged
manner had soon become, as well as the habit of verbal conceit
which he may have learned early from his favourite Cowley.

These plays and shreds of plays are all much alike, except
that *The Bride's Tragedy* does not prove that mastery of the
horrible and gleeful grotesque which is so prominent in *Death's
Jestbook*. Beddoes' letters show him incessantly mending and
patching this latter work, without ever making an end ; and
he left behind several differing drafts, but none that is ultimate.[1]
Nothing is more infantine than its composition—' its limbs,'
says the author, ' being as scattered and unconnected as those
of the old gentleman whom Medea minced and boiled young.'
A murderer-duke who turns into a more or less impenitent
pilgrim ; a murdered man who is summoned by the duke,
inadvertently, out of his coffin, and calmly walks among mortals,
of solid substance but able to vanish at will, and who at last
carries his slayer into the tomb ; a revenger disguised as a
court-fool, and chanting diabolical snatches of song—such are
some of the simples in the curious witch-broth that Beddoes
serves out to us. The poetry, therefore, is everything, for

there is nothing else left ; and, as with so many of the dramatists whom Lamb unearthed, when we turn from the anthology
to the text, we find, it is true, matter for another anthology,
but nothing else—no poetic whole at all. Beddoes commands
a variety of styles, which are portioned out amongst shadows
bearing sundry names ; and we are left with the sense of a power
that cannot be questioned but is working in the void.

Beddoes' blank verse has often a force and soaring splendour
that is not altered by our knowledge of its literary origins. We
may recognise the idiom of Tourneur, his peculiar use of
abstractions, in such lines as these :

> Though thou shouldst wed some hateful avarice,
> And I grow hoary with a daubed deceit,
> A smiling treachery in woman's form,
> Sad to the soul, heart-cankered and forlorn ;
> No matter, all no matter :

but though the gesture of an athlete can be copied, no man can
borrow his strength ; and here the strength is native and incon-
testable. So, too, the sweeter rhetoric and overflowing rhythms
of the silver age of our drama, before it had taken on too much
alloy, are easily heard in Beddoes' tenderer passages :

> I am a ghost. Tremble not ; fear not me.
> The dead are ever good and innocent,
> And love the living. They are cheerful creatures
> And quiet as the sunbeams, and most like,
> In grace and patient love and spotless beauty,
> The new-born of mankind. 'Tis better too
> To die, as thou art, young, in the first grace
> And full of beauty, and so be remembered
> As one chosen from the earth to be an angel ;
> Not left to droop, and wither, and be borne
> Down by the breath of time.

This is renovation rather than *pastiche*. Often little trace
of the poet's schooling remains ; he has fashioned a sure and
satisfactory style of his own. His mind circles, like that of so
many of his poetical creditors, round the thought of the grave ;
it is an abyss from which he can hardly keep aloof ; and, like
Shakespeare, or Donne, he presses the physiology and physics
of the day into the service of his fancy. But then the day
is a different one ; and some of what is most original in Beddoes'
poetical substance, and correspondingly so in his form, may
not unfairly be traced to this difference, as well as to his professional engrossment with scientific ideas.[1] He likes to trace
the progress of the mortal spirit, not only through the grave into

its disimprisoned state, but back into its pre-natal life, and
to and fro in its passage among the generations.   The following,
indeed, might have come from the hand of Donne :

> Adam, thy soul was happy that it wore
> The first, new, mortal members.   To have felt
> The joy of the first year, when the one spirit
> Kept house-warming within its fresh-built clay,
> I 'd be content to be as old a ghost.

But elsewhere the modern touch is felt :

> Or do you owe your life, not to this body,
> But to the sparks of spirit that fly off,
> Each instant disengaged and hurrying
> From little particles of flesh that die ?

One more passage may be given, from the close of *Torrismond*,
to show this persistent and daring rumination on the bodily
history of mankind :

> O father, father ! . . .
> Take of [1] my youth, unwrap me of my years,
> And hunt me up the dark and broken past
> Into my mother's womb: there unbeget me;
> For till I 'm in thy veins and unbegun,
> Or to the food returned, which made the blood
> That did make me, no possible lie can ever
> Unroot my feet of thee.

In spite of the intense realisation and clean consummate wording
of these conceptions, the twist in Beddoes is seen in his failure
to connect them credibly with any human personage or event.
They are isolated, they remain fixed ideas of his own, and they
have no dramatic force.   It is a pity that his blank verse is best
in fragments ; but the gods are jealous.

   The claims of Beddoes therefore do not, as is sometimes
thought, rest only, though they do rest indefeasibly, upon his
songs, which must by no means be regarded merely as a shower
of lyrical star-dust left in the shining wake of Shelley.   The
influence of Shelley, though perceptible, is in no way dominant.
Beddoes is as original a singer as Shelley himself.   His scope
and variety may be slighter, but his lyrics or lyrical scraps
number nearly seventy ;   and about half of them come in his
plays.   ' The swallow leaves her nest,' and ' If thou wilt ease
thine heart,' and ' Lady, was it fair of thee ? ' are found in
Death's Jestbook, relieving its grimness by their purity of
inspiration, like white birds flying and singing over a sepulchre.
The unmatched ' Far away,' and the classic *Dream-Pedlary*,
have no such dramatic or scenic setting.   These half-dozen are

quite of the first rate and flawless; they have the peculiar
purged and thrilling quality for which Beddoes is distinguished.
But near them might be named as many more, which have only
less of it, or which have it more in some verses than in others.
Such are 'Poor old pilgrim Misery,' 'Strew not earth with
empty stars,' 'As sudden thunder,' 'How many times do I
love thee, dear?' 'No tears, no sighings, no despair,' and
'A ghost that loved a lady fair'; such would be our anthology.
In many more the same touch is clearly present, and perhaps
in none is it absent altogether.

The experiments of Beddoes in lyric of the *macabre* kind are
made with the utmost relish, but they are apt to overreach
themselves and to tire and disgust the most willing imagination.
The well-known piece beginning 'Squats on a toadstool under
a tree' has been admired, but awakens only a reluctant harsh
sort of laughter. 'Old Adam, the carrion-crow, The old crow
of Cairo,' is, on the contrary, perfect in the keeping of its gallows-
music, like another lyric of which the burden is also 'The
ghosts' moonshine.' *Lord Alcohol* is the best piece of this
order, being a ghostly parody or echo of Beddoes' own habitual
and serious cadences:

> Love, quotha, Love? nay, nay!
> It is a spirit fine
> Of ale or ancient wine,
> Lord Alcohol, the drunken fay,
> Lord Alcohol alway!

In his lyric form, Beddoes has a preference for brief lines skilfully combined into intricate stanzas. He was too modest
when he said that he could not 'manage rhyme well or easily,'
or 'order complicated verse harmoniously'; for this is just
what he can do. His best songs are frail-seeming but unbreak-
able fabrics, like the fairy chain that was woven out of the
sound of cats' footsteps and the roots of the hills. They did not
come easily, but the result shows no effort; and not many
wise, not many learned amongst the English poets have risen
so lightly into so pure a lyric atmosphere as this specialist,
with his somewhat unblessed life and his death-engrossed
imagination.

The letters of Beddoes are precious, and are by no means
mad letters. This it is right to say; for the insane streak in
Beddoes is as questionable as it is in Hamlet; in his plays, we
may think, he 'put an antic disposition on,' although there was
that in him which made it easy to do so; and if it became
tyrannous over him, and the mask in the end grew to the face,

we need not wonder. In his letters, though they are wildly freakish in expression, he is not only full of clear-witted self-criticism, recognising his dramatic deficiencies as plainly as we do ; but he is a genuine judge of letters, not very wide in his sympathies, yet hardly deceivable by bad work. His eloquent Shakespeare-worship is that of his age, but his comments on dramaturgy rank with Lamb's ; and, like Lamb's, often evolve truth out of a paradox. An example is found in his notion that the actors' names should not appear on the playbills, in order that their identities should be sunk in those of the persons represented ; that it is a pity if a mask cannot be worn, in order to make Macbeth as ' absolutely distinct and independent an individual ' as Œdipus ; and that

Othello's colour is a sort of mask, and this is a reason perhaps why Shakespeare has given him so much less ideal language and more simple household truth than his other characters.[1]

His remark on the passage in Browning's *Strafford* (1837) in which 'two people describe Pym's appearance, action, etc.,' is of the same order. Beddoes calls this procedure artificial, noting how rarely it is used in Shakespeare, and also the reason for the exceptions ; for instance,

where the person whose actions are described must necessarily be laconic if not entirely speechless, and where the spectators in their doubt, fear and wonder, naturally communicate to each other their interpretation of the dumb show before them ; for instance, in Hamlet, where the ghost, unwilling *or unable perhaps* to speak to his son in the presence of Horatio and the watch, motions him to follow. *It is of some consequence to settle one's opinion on a question of this nature.*[2]

This is the true passion of the critic. The judgments of Beddoes on German writers are more capricious ; but he was early in the field, and his opinion is always independent, both of convention and of Carlyle.

IV

This is no history of the stage, or of the public appetite for plays, save in so far as literature may come into the question. The separation of the actable from the readable [3] drama during the period is only too complete. Indeed, hardly one play was produced during those fifty years which can now be both read and beheld without weariness. The exceptions, like *The*

Cenci, are but apparent; they are sometimes performed for
the few. We can read *Osorio*, and perhaps *Virginius*, and
while doing so can think of them as plays; and *The Deformed
Transformed*, and *Hellas*, without so thinking of them. But
where are Maturin's *Bertram*, and the tragedies of Sheil and
Milman, and of Barry Cornwall? Where, again, are the
comedies that so long held the town, and have sometimes
survived, veterans on sufferance, like *The Road to Ruin* and
The Heir at Law? Holcroft, the younger Colman, and
Morton as well, are in this limbo. Who, save some student,
flutters the closing volumes of Mrs. Inchbald's *British Theatre*,
or her *Collection of Farces*? It must be enough to mark one
or two of the points at which this mass of writing approxi-
mates to literature, or throws direct light upon it.

The songs of Charles Dibdin[1] (1745-1814) need, no doubt,
to be heard, and will hardly bear being read, but as songs the
best of them live all the same. He wrote many hundreds,
indeed more than a thousand, and inserted many of them
in his comic operas and nondescript boisterous entertain-
ments. The sea-songs, numbering close on a hundred, are
the best though by no means the only good ones. *Tom
Bowling* and *Poor Jack* and ' 'Twas in the good ship Rover '
are well enough known. Dibdin's skill and facility as a com-
poser told well upon his management of words and syllables,
and though he does not aim at or attain style he has an instinctive cunning in his treatment of burden, and quantity, and
pause. There is more poetry and as much gaiety in the
endless ditties of John O'Keefe (1747-1833), most of which
occur in the comedies and humorous operas that he improvised
without stint or care. It is melancholy to think that such
good spirits have become evaporated by time. O'Keefe has
abundance of rhythmical faculty of a simple, taking kind,
and is excellent at a tavern-catch, and in the tune of obvious
sentiment; his prose farce, *Wild Oats*, keeps a shadowy name
upon the stage; and wherever we open his plays we are likely
to find some headlong fun.

The genius of two great generations of actors, both tragic
and comic, could not of itself create an enduring drama,
though to such a drama, once in existence, it could have
responded. An equally great race of dramatic critics, including Lamb and Hazlitt, arose; but we find them usually judging
the actor and taking the play for granted. The sacred fire
of Mrs. Siddons and Kean, the dignified and potent playing
of John Kemble, and the creative humour of Elliston and

Munden, constitute a great tradition; but these artists either acted classic parts, which alone were worthy of their voices, and interpreted Shakespeare, Jonson, and Goldsmith, or else Sheridan, the only surviving dramatist of genius; or, again, they gave a hectic life to the passing plays of the hour,—to the bloodshot *Bertram,* and the adulterate imported wares of Kotzebue, or to topical and ephemeral jests. Good acting can make almost any bad thing go down, if only the badness be of the right sort. Hence, though the stage was never more popular or more brilliant, few of its glories abide, even on the stage, and in literature fewer still.

Sheridan's *Critic,* his last comedy, was produced in 1779, just before he entered parliament; he lived till 1816, ruled Drury Lane, brought out *Pizarro* (1799), and found, as a playwright, no true successor. The stage, indeed, teemed with comedies, but they tended to farce of a kind that is now melancholy, and they were often patched with fustian romance. Cheerful caterers of mirth abounded; besides O'Keefe, there were Holcroft, whose plays are livelier than his novels; George Colman the younger (1762-1836); Thomas Morton, and also Mrs. Inchbald. Their work, as a whole, is full of breathless action and bustle, and it would be pedantry to bear hard on writers who brought down so many hundred houses; but they belong to another history than that of letters. They rely much on the mechanical humours, or catchwords, to which artists as great as Jonson and Smollett have resorted when their genius was at a loss. Those who have seen a revival of Holcroft's *Road to Ruin* (1794), a melodrama of considerable skill and energy, and have pitied the actor who tried to carry off the parrot-saying ('That's your sort!') of Mr. Geoffry Wildgoose, will understand the impatience of one who has to read such works in cold blood. The brightest of these wits was Colman, whose Pangloss, in *The Heir at Law* (1808), has remained a type of the stage *savant,* and whose military apothecary, Ollapod, in *The Poor Gentleman,* is certainly a sprightly droll. In Colman's adaptation of *Caleb Williams,* called *The Iron Chest,* all the subtlety of the original is gone, and shoddy sentiment is substituted. The humours of his *John Bull* were relished by Scott as well as by many audiences. Besides endless comedies, operatic and other, Colman put forth a volume of rhymes, *Broad Grins,* which hardly explains his reputation as a witty companion, and whose title describes his general purpose. Another maker of tumbling, ridiculous comedies was Thomas Morton;

and one of them, *Speed the Plough,* is still referred to for a reason. The seeker for literary 'sources' will find in it the name of Mrs. Grundy, who is a character in the play only as Mrs. Harris is a character in *Martin Chuzzlewit,* and who is not specially a censor of improprieties. It is full of the high spirits and palpable hits of the time. John Tobin's pleasant piece, *The Honeymoon,* acted in 1805, is better than the average, with its comic steward and its rendering of the eternal shrew-taming story. It contains the tag 'The man that lays his hand upon a woman Save in the way of kindness, is a wretch,' etc.

In serious drama, or melodrama, two main influences became apparent towards the end of the century, and persisted more or less for a generation. One, the more salutary and lasting, was that of the Elizabethans; the earlier, for a while the stronger, and certainly the more curious, was that of Kotzebue,[1] who touches our literature at some points, although his true sphere is in the nether stage-world. August von Kotzebue was a playwright of alarming fertility, of much stagecraft, of some comic and satiric energy, and of no little impudence. He has a catchy eloquence, which being destitute of style does not lose in translation. He made farces, and also heroic tragedies; but his romantic prose melodramas are the vehicle of what stand to him for ideas. He affects Rousseau, nature, sentiment, and the religion of the heart; and all these things he edits for the gallery. His productions floated into England on the wave which brought not only the early translations from Schiller (*The Robbers, Kabale und Liebe*), from Goethe (*Götz*), and from Lessing (*Emilia Galotti*), but also the numerous tales of fairy, terror, and adventure. His vogue was greatest during the years 1780-1800. In March 1798 an adaptation of Kotzebue's *Menschenhass und Reue* was brought out by Sheridan, as *The Stranger,* with great success. At Covent Garden *Lovers' Vows* followed, constructed by Mrs. Inchbald, with prudent alterations, out of *Das Kind der Liebe. The Stranger* was acted nearly every year for half a century, and *Lovers' Vows* for about half as long. In 1799 Sheridan turned Kotzebue's highflown work, *Die Spanier in Peru,* into *Pizarro,* a patriotic opera, which was aimed against Napoleon and long outlived both Napoleon and Sheridan. The eloquence of Rolla, as played by Kemble, was greeted with approval by George the Third and by William Pitt; who, however, said that he had already heard it in the House of Commons. Many other works of Kotzebue were welcomed only less ardently by the British public, both in London and the provinces. Indeed, he exercised more influence on our drama, for the time, than any one except Shakespeare ; and for reasons that are now plain. Kotzebue, in the first place, was a facile and cunning master of effect, and, in the cheaper sense, of construction. Further, he arrived during the lean years of native talent. Thirdly, he managed to pass current some of the ideas and sentiments that had already found a narrower audience in the novel of doctrine and in the revolutionary pamphlets. His high tide was in 1799, when it is said that seventy editions or versions of his works were published in this country. Then the number fell ; but the chorus of jeers and denunciations continued, not soon to die down.

In *The Rovers* (1798), Canning and his friends tried to kill by derision the German imported play ; but *The Robbers* as well as Kotzebue gave them their materials, and they by no means gained their object. Their objections are not merely those of the humourist ; they regard their models as not only absurd but impious, and as examples of the ' new morality,' trifling with marriage and the sanctity of law. This ethical indignation appears in the oddest quarters. Byron, in *English Bards* (1809), calls upon Sheridan to

> Abjure the mummery of the German schools ;
> Leave new Pizarros to translating fools ;

and two years later, in a work called *The Quadrupeds of Quedlingburgh,*[1] *or the Rovers of Weimar*, the charges are put into shape. It is the task we learn, of Kotzebue and his fellows,

> To lull the soul by spurious strokes of art,
> To warp the genius, and mislead the heart ;
> To make mankind revere wives gone astray,—
> Love pious sons who rob on the highway ;
> For this the foreign Muses trod our stage.

Fanny Price, when *Lovers' Vows* was being rehearsed at Mansfield Park,

ran through it with an eagerness that was only suspended by intervals of astonishment. . . Agatha and Amelia appeared to her in their different ways so totally improper for home representation —the situation of one and the language of the other, so unfit to be expressed by any woman of modesty, that she could hardly suppose her cousins could be aware of what they were engaging in.

As is known, the performance did not occur, and Sir Thomas Bertram burnt all the copies he could find. Why all this alarm ?

Kotzebue is cheap rather than wicked ; he has a kind of slop morality, which might be worse, but which is of no dramatic value. If we turn over *Das Kind der Liebe*, we come on a bad baron who has misled a chambermaid (Agatha). She is driven forth to beg. Their son, Fritz, grows up, and suffers the disabilities of his birth ; meets, at last, his unknown father, and tries to rob him in order to find bread for his mother ; is arrested, but discovers and reveals his parentage ; forces his father (aided by the counsels of a virtuous minister) to marry the beggar-mother. The baron's wife has died meanwhile, leaving a daughter (Amelia), who marries, and in the original courts, the pastor. All this may have been too strong for Mansfield Park ; and, according to the censors of the time, it constituted an encouragement to ' rob on the highway,' and also tended to hold out false hopes to erring chambermaids. It is rather the pervading note of flushed rhetorical sentiment that offends us now. In *The Stranger*, a wife, duped by a villain, has left her husband. He, the husband, turns Timon —here is the ' misanthropy ' ; she changes her name, and lives a life of good works ; there is the ' repentance.' An ingenious train of occurrences brings them together ; the wife is forgiven and taken back, the husband believes again in mankind ; and why not ? It is the coarse and facile treatment, the mixture of tears and diatribes, the continual use of the wrong pedal, and the absence of real drama, that strikes the reader to-day. But these things were supposed to put a positive premium on infidelity ; and the inquiring can read, in Mrs. Inchbald's preface, the shifts to which she puts herself to defend its moral, and her surprising exploration of the delicacies of the case. Indeed, as we study *Die Edle Lüge*, or *Die Indianer in England* (which introduces ' Sir John Smith, a gouty man, once a rich merchant,' and ' Mistriss Smith, his wife, a German maiden by birth '), we smile at the craze for Kotzebue, and at the wrath he excited.

The Elizabethan influence struck deeper, though it is often found crossing and mingling with that of the Germans and doctrinaires. In Wordsworth's *Borderers* (written about 1795), the ideas are coloured by Godwin, but the verse imitates that of the best dramatic age ; as it is, for example, in that lofty and well-known speech, ' Action is transitory ' (act ii.), which Wordsworth afterwards prefixed to *The White Doe*. In Maturin's *Bertram*, a lurid, high-strained, ranting, popular, sometimes eloquent, and on the whole worthless composition, of which Coleridge hardly speaks too strongly, the old tragedy of blood and the modern romance of horror are brayed up as in a mortar. The precise ingredients vary, and also their proportion, in different writers ; but in most of the dramas of the time, from the ' plays of the passions ' up to the work of Beddoes, some such mixture can be traced. It is not an auspicious one ; it does not serve in place of original power, and does not work for the eliciting of such power ; and it might be expected to make for the sterility, which we have in fact to deplore.

Darley and the other dramatic poets who hardly wrote for the theatre have been reviewed. Of the rest the chief are Joanna Baillie [1] (1762-1851), Henry Hart Milman (1791-1868), and James Sheridan Knowles (1784-1862). There are others, among them Richard Lalor Sheil, the Irish orator, whose *Evadne*, produced in 1819, has, despite its absurd ingenious plot, a breath of romantic ardour ; and Miss Mitford, whose *Foscari* (1826) and *Rienzi* (1828) are by no means without true and touching poetry, which makes us forget their elementary machinery. Miss Mitford's tact keeps her alike from the tumidity of contemporary tragedy and from its ambitious blankness.

Miss Baillie was both early and late in the field ; the first series of her *Plays on the Passions* appeared in 1798, her last batch of dramas in 1836. She won huge esteem as a poet and dramatist ; her *De Monfort* and *The Family Legend* succeeded on the boards. Scott admired and praised her too fervently ; her accomplishments, high-mindedness, and personal charm are unquestioned ; and now no man reads her unless he must. Miss Baillie's plan, in her *Plays on the Passions*, was to start with one of the ' passions,' such as hate or fear, considered in itself, and to build round it a character who is landed by the said passion either in tragic disaster or in comic per-plexity : a procedure that is not unlike that of the comedy of humours run to seed. The aim, ruinous to drama, is to study the ' passions ' and deduce their social consequences. Miss Baillie further desires to be, unlike the playwrights then in fashion, simple and direct in language. This is an intention less fatal than the other ; but she has not the style to make it good. At the best she produces a surprising resemblance to a poem or a play ; and, as has been often noticed, she had a keen sense of stage mechanism and requirements. Her comedies are in prose, and though not without liveliness have not held their ground. Of the tragedies *Basil*, *The Family Legend*, and *De Monfort* were the most famous at the time. The plainer

Elizabethan manner is ever before Miss Baillie's eyes, and she merits respect for her aspirations. That she had some singing instinct, is seen especially in her Scottish lyrics, and in some small playful pieces she wrote in English.

Milman's [1] work as a historian belongs to the next age ; and of his five plays only his first, *Fazio* (1815), is worth looking at. The others, three of which are on biblical subjects (*Belshazzar* and the like), the fifth being *Anne Boleyn* (1826), are dreary and academic. *Fazio*, the work of a fervid young student, rather than a true descendant, of Fletcher and Shakespeare, also shows traces of *Faust*. There is a distinct coloured extravagance and rush about the writing, which Milman afterwards tamed down only too much ; there is some style, but it works in the void, without any hold upon character or situation. Sheridan Knowles [2] is a dramatist of far superior address ; he has both the sense of theatrical effect, and that *simulacrum*, as Carlyle would have called it, of a high tragic style, which a good actor can make his own and impose upon an audience. Knowles studied Massinger and profited, though he never learned either his skill, or the grave satisfying style—which moves on a kind of tableland—of *The Roman Actor* and *The Bondman*. He began with Roman subjects, and tried for a severe and unfanciful language, but only attained a tantalising kind of obvious oratory. His *Caius Gracchus* (1815) and *Virginius* (1820) made his name, and the latter work has preserved it in histories. *William Tell* (1825) was a triumph for the author and Macready. Knowles's comedies have remained longer on the stage, especially *The Hunchback* (1832), which is fuller of kindly sentiment than of fun ; while *The Love Chase* (1837) is a more cheerful and lively piece in the traditional style, a good deal tamed down. Knowles lived on into another age, and continued to write copiously, but it is hard to find poetry in him. There is more, perhaps, in the *Ion* (1835) of Lamb's friend and biographer, Sir Thomas Noon Talfourd. This has an excellent Greek subject, involving large conceptions of duty, fate, and sacrifice ; but despite the high spirit of the author it is almost frozen in the handling, like Matthew Arnold's *Merope*.

CHAPTER XXII

THOMAS DE QUINCEY

I. Affinities with the various 'Lake Poets.' Inequality of his writing; De Quincey, a *polyhistor*, dependent on the press.

II. Four phases of his work: (*a*) 1821-27: triple activity, in imaginative and reminiscent prose, in abstract reasoning, and in translation. (*b*) 1827-42: the *polyhistor* predominant: erudite articles; autobiographies expanded and continued. (*c*) 1843-50: culmination of powers; prose fantasies. (*d*) 1850-59: selections; works edited.

III. De Quincey's learning; transiency of his contribution to the 'literature of knowledge.' Dealings with German fiction and philosophy. Political and economic papers.

IV. The 'schoolman's intellect,' its effect on style; amplification and digression. Imaginative elaboration: *Revolt of the Tartars, Spanish Military Nun*: two drafts of *Confessions of an Opium-Eater*.

V. Reminiscent writing: memories of childhood; recollections of friends; Charles Lamb.

VI. The dream-territory; prose fantasies; *Suspiria*; *Daughter of Lebanon*; *English Mail-coach*. Character of De Quincey's visions.

VII. Diction, and 'mode of impassioned prose'; accumulation and antithesis within the grammatical period. 'Rhythmus' and vision co-operating; contrast with architecture of Landor's prose.

I

The Lakes hardly count in the scenery of Thomas de Quincey's[1] visions, and his medium is prose; but even so, he may be called one of the greater Lake poets,[2] and the last. His ties with the group whose neighbour he remained so long are more than personal. Southey, indeed, he only resembles in his conservatism, and in his versatile industry, reading, and production. But, like Wordsworth, he transfigures in the act of artistic creation the remembered events and faces of common life, which have lain long in his mind. Unlike him, De Quincey lets them undergo the 'chemistry of dreams,' so that they come out altered by fantasy, and with a glory upon them that is not of the daylight; he does not take them as they are, and let their poetry free itself as he muses upon them, so that the real earth we know is still there but is better understood. Like Coleridge, he watched the workings of his own mind, and the phases of its fever, and found, or made, colour and music for its visions ; and, like him, knew the struggle with opium and the ' pains of sleep.' De Quincey owned a profound debt to both writers, above all to Wordsworth, of whom he was one of the first proclaimers, and whom, as a man, he describes with vivid, amusing, and punctilious candour. But he was a vagrant, and he knew, better than Wordsworth, what it was to be sick and penitent, and to fall twice and again ; and in this he is nearer to Coleridge ; from whom, as a critic, he learned much and took his point of departure, and whom he resembles in criticising everything from the inner point of view of the artist. He is also a true humourist of the elfish and paradoxical sort, like his friend Charles Lamb, though he is not so sure of touch and is capable of being dismally jaunty and lamentably vulgar. De Quincey is nothing akin to Hazlitt, or to Shelley and Keats ; he outlived them all and understood none of them. He is equally remote from his coevals and fellow-masters of prose, Landor and Carlyle, though all three were for thirty years writing incessantly and concurrently. He is more of an artist than Carlyle, with more sense of cadence and structure and composition, although the disturbance that he caused in the waters of English thought is nothing in comparison. His phrase cannot be more beautiful, and in the proper sense classical, than Landor's, but his rhythm has a quicker and more intimate life. He survived till 1849, into the age of Newman and Ruskin, which did not exist for him at all.

De Quincey is also like Wordsworth in that he left behind him a mass of indistinct and transient writing, out of which a smaller but still ample body of perfect writing has to be sifted. But the two workmen are unequal for different reasons. Wordsworth, with his modest competence and his Roman way of living, was free to give his days and night to his art, and did so ; while his ' daemon, the spirit that kept him,' visited him, as we know, more and more rarely as time passed. De Quincey was the servant of journalism, as well as helpless in affairs ; he was forced to write endless magazine articles, which were too good for their hour but are impermanent nevertheless. He is the Renaissance type of *polyhistor*, or man of universal information, driven to become a modern pressman for bread ; the best-equipped, perhaps, of all the Englishmen then living who fell to such an industry. This necessity determined the form and scale of nearly all his works ; they are rarely books ; they are either of the length of articles, or are compounded of instalments originally planned to be of such a length. All

this meant waste ; and yet his genius, so far from declining
like Wordsworth's, stood the trial. It was renewed late in
his life, and had an autumn summer more splendid than its
June. We find the same thing in Landor and Tennyson ;
whilst the body and the brain hold together, 'the soul of sweet
delight can never be defiled.'

II

The bibliographers must enumerate De Quincey's hundred
and fifty articles and other compositions. Hard as it is to
trace any principle of development amongst them, some bearings must be taken by those who would steer through his
many volumes. His works are distributed over four phases,
which begin in 1821 and close with his life in 1859. Before
1821, when the *Confessions of an English Opium-Eater* came
out in the *London Magazine*, he had drafted [1] some notes to
Wordsworth's tract on the Convention of Cintra, and planned
a treatise, never to be written, *De Emendatione Humani
Intellectus*. As with Wordsworth, most of his vital experience
lay well behind him before he attained the art to write it down ;
the dreams, wanderings, and reminiscences, which are his
best material, came to him before his power of expression had
matured.

The first phase (1821-7) is marked by three distinct and
divergent interests, which answer to the three dominant
faculties in De Quincey's art and temper. First, there are
the *Confessions* in their original and briefer form ; these are the
earliest of his imaginative fantasias. Secondly, the *Dialogues
of Three Templars*, stimulated by the study of Ricardo, to
whom De Quincey had turned earlier as a distraction from
the pains of opium. These are the work of his finely-severing
and scholastic brain, and appeared in 1824 ; and twenty years
later he returned to the theme in his longer *Logic of Political
Economy*. Thirdly, he now began his translations, imitations,
and decoctions of German romance, which represent an
inferior play of his imagination, but exercised his craft (soon
to be consummate) of narrative. Now also begin his casual
but not infertile notices of Kant, till then in England little
known ; these constitute his furthest excursion in pure
philosophy.

The second phase lasts some fifteen years, from 1827 to
1842. On one side the *polyhistor* predominates ;—the disher-up
of curious, sometimes doubtful history and erudition for the
cultivated person who insists on having what is readable :

usually the public, as it proved, of *Blackwood's Magazine*. *Homer* and *Herodotus*, *The Essenes*, *The Traditions of the Rabbins*, the *Toilette of the Hebrew Lady*, are amongst the topics. The form is that of dissertation, lightened by anecdote and by De Quincey's humour, which too often betrayed him. *The Cæsars* is lofty in style, and *The Revolt of the Tartars* is worth all the rest as a composition. But within this period De Quincey turned to another and a far happier vein which he explored, with intervals, throughout the rest of his life. Working backwards from the record of the *Opium-Eater*, he began his reminiscences in the pages of *Tait's Magazine* for 1834. The *Autobiographic Sketches* relate his youth and childhood, lead us to the brink of his dreams, and reveal the moulding of the dreamer and his idiosyncrasies. The articles on his friends, Coleridge, Wordsworth, Lamb, Wilson, and others now also begin. They are not always to be trusted, but can never remain unread. To these he added papers in other journals, and (later in life) in Hogg's *Instructor* (1845). Equally noble fruits of the second period are the articles on *Style* (1840) and on *Rhetoric*, his most connected contributions to poetic, or the history and theory of criticism. *On the Knocking at the Gate in Macbeth* appeared in 1823. His tiresome novel, *Klosterheim*, which came out not as an article but a separate book, is dated 1832.

The years 1843-50 mark a third period, and the perfection of his powers. The old kinds are continued ;—the learned exposition, the reminiscences of friendship and childhood and youth, and the story ; in the last kind *The Spanish Military Nun* (at first called *The Nautico-Military Nun of Spain*) is the most noteworthy. Criticism also goes on ; the review of *Schlosser's Literary History of the Eighteenth Century* is one of his best articles of this order, and shows (1847) unflagging energy. But the highest work of his genius is found in his fantasies, of which *Suspiria de Profundis*, *Levana and Our Ladies of Sorrow*, and *Savannah-La-Mar* are the greatest (1845) ; together with the tripartite *English Mail-Coach* (1849), where nearly all De Quincey's gifts except the purely logical are seen combined and harmonised. Those gifts are the same as of old ; there is little change in essence, only an assured maturity of power ; these compositions are the work of one belated in his epoch because late in reaching his prime ; so that, though they fall beyond the limiting date of these volumes, they not only may but must be considered here, as the last great manifestation in prose of the earlier romantic spirit.

After 1850 till the last De Quincey busied himself with gathering and editing his writings, in the series of volumes called by him *Selections Grave and Gay* ; but death outraced his labours, and he left some of them incomplete. But not till he had nearly recast, with much cutting and expansion, his personal reminiscences, including the *Confessions* themselves, which came out in their new form (about thrice as lengthy as the first one) in 1856. Scores of his excursions and adventures in letters have been left unmentioned ; dictionary lives of Shakespeare and Milton and Bentley, discourses on duelling, war, Protestantism, oracles, astronomy, and many other matters. The habit of writing had laid hold on him, and he had to write in order to live. All this material, from first to last, has to be somewhat sternly sifted down, if we are to keep only what De Quincey contributed to the ' literature of power.'

III

Of most that he wrote to swell the ' literature of knowledge,' or in the cause of scholarship, the value is only transient and comparative. It is seldom hard to read, or lacking in spaciousness or charm of manner. It can be searched through, not in vain, for many gleams and sallies of his master-faculty,— namely, his union of logic, imagination, and narrative skill. The best of these papers, like *The Cæsars* and *The Revolt of the Tartars*, must be judged rather as works of art than of learning. De Quincey was up to a certain point notably well-equipped, moving easily not only in Greek and Latin but in German, a language which he saw becoming better known in England during his own lifetime. He helped to educate his day, and in range and oddness of information, as in power and grace of writing, his work much excels those tomes of heavier articles in the old magazines, which no man will ever again read or collect together. But he lived before the age of investigation, and had nothing in common with those of its pioneers, like Hallam or Finlay, who were his contemporaries. He left nothing for ' research ' to build upon. His aim was popular, and was capable of taking some dull or remote authority, saying nothing about it, and dressing it out, without scruple, for the readers of his journal. The result is usually antiquated, and is sometimes defaced by a certain wrong-headedness, which lay in wait for De Quincey like a mischievous sprite. The result can be judged from the paper on the Essenes,[1] in which, with some of the authorities open before him, he argues that they were no more and no less than a sect of Christians. But he is always curious, in either meaning of the term.

Before Carlyle, German romance [1] was freely commended to English readers by De Quincey's versions, imitations, and remarks. To name his worst deed and have done with it— he wrote of *Wilhelm Meister* in a spasm of domestic morality, reviewing the amours of the hero in the fatal strain of the comic man who has turned indignant. We have some respect for his master Wordsworth's remark that the incidents of the book 'wantonly outraged the sympathies of humanity'; but De Quincey's strictures are only vulgar. In this matter he compares ill, for critical digestion and for good sense, with Carlyle ; but then it sometimes so happens that the puritan has a better digestion than the fantast ; perhaps it is because he feels safer. Carlyle, however, is known to have been attracted to the study of Jean Paul Richter by De Quincey's praises. Tieck's tale, *The Love-Charm*, is also put into English, with a fervid eulogy of his talent (1825). Some other pieces ' from the German,' such as *The King of Hayti*, are of unknown source, and the source of such rubbish is not worth asking. From a then popular writer, Apel, comes *The Fatal Marksman*, whose hero is found again in Weber's opera, *Der Freischütz*. De Quincey must have been the last English satellite of this dreary school ; and in *The Avenger* and *The Household Wreck* there are signs of his power, and more than the spectre of his eloquence. But this kind of story, with its horrors, is apt at once to revolt the judgment and to leave the fancy tepid.

The same fault spoils the novel *Klosterheim, or The Masque*. The scenes of fighting and feasting, which are laid during the Thirty Years War, are not without their strongly coloured and swiftly moving pageantries ; and De Quincey can always give the impression of fatality and danger. But the plot is a mixture of convention and nightmare, and the evil trick of the old novel of sensation is revived, by which the object of terror is explained away into a thing of every day. A super-human appearance, which penetrates solid walls and enacts mysterious abductions, is found, in Jane Austen's phrase, to be nothing but 'a tall young man';—a noble young man, it is true, the rightful heir of the princedom, who dodges about the secret passages of a castle in a mask, with a band of fervent followers. The trace of the Waverley Novels is seen in the descriptions ; but we have only to think of the lifelike and motley picture of the same war which is to be read in

Simplicius Simplicissimus, that little prose epic of the seventeenth century, to find in De Quincey's experiment its dull
and painful foil. Another fantastic piece of fun, *The Somnambulist,*[1] from the German of Friedrich Laun, is also assigned
to him.

Outside the theory of art and style, De Quincey only paid
flying visits to pure philosophy. But with the works of Kant
he had a real if a somewhat vagrant conversance. He translated the essay *On the Idea of a Universal History*; his allusions to the *Critique of Pure Reason* are frequent, and in his
chapters on his Oxford days he relates his plunge into its
thickets. On its sceptical side, and especially by its doctrine
of the antinomies—cases ' in which two laws, equally binding
on the mind, are, or seem to be, in collision '—it impressed
and dejected him equally, leading him into a kind of blind
alley from which scarcely he found an intellectual exit.
The German idealism subsequent to Kant, which Coleridge
tried to import, did not touch De Quincey ; he found repose
for his affections in a kind of liberal Christianity. But his
essay on war, which he believes to be irremovable, shows something of the sternness of view which Kant may have taught
him. He perceives Kant's importance on the side of language.
Whilst humorously wrathful over his style, he sees the epoch-
making import of his fresh terminology, which re-stated the
whole problem of thought. This dialect, he says :

is not a re-baptism of ideas already existing in the universal consciousness ; it is in part an enlargement of the understanding by
new territory (of which I have spoken), and in part a better regulation
of its old territory. . . . In this way a terminology becomes, in a
manner, organic. . . . The new distinctions were so many intellectual problems to be mastered.

To consider De Quincey's papers of a theological or political
cast, which are also always singular, would only detain us from
the real play of his genius and mind. Those on the analysis of
modern party names, Whig and Tory, are less noteworthy than
the discursive essay, almost amounting to a small book, on
Dr. Samuel Parr, or Whiggism in its relations to Literature. This
is a most amusing, unfair study of a reputation that was already
extinct and only just remembered ; and it forms an epitaph in
English on Parr, much longer, more destructive, and more lasting,
than Parr's own Latin inscriptions on his friends ; to which,
be it said, De Quincey does handsome justice in passing. His
agile, rather undignified, and always unrespecting humour

finds in Dr. Parr a predestined victim. The papers on political economy are of more note, and have been praised by John Stuart Mill for their elucidation of Ricardo's theories. The subject belongs to science ; but both in the *Dialogues of Three Templars* and in the *Logic of Political Economy* De Quincey shows his power as a deductive reasoner in a form which if somewhat diffuse is bare, athletic, and elegant. At times he reminds us of Ferrier in his resolution to be clear, and in sharpness of style ; but the clearness is not what Nietzsche called the 'affronting lucidity' of John Stuart Mill, seemingly so composed and so remote ; it is the lucidity of the schoolman and disputant, who drives his point home in strict accordance with the rules. The work is fragmentary ; but the dialogue-form has hardly been used since the day of Hume, for pure dialectic, with greater finish. De Quincey hardly professes to be original ; he popularises Ricardo loyally, attacking Malthus, and adding a few distinctions ; and here also we have the impression of a high, razor-like, native faculty, which was just whetted and then allowed to rust. Economic theory has moved so far from Ricardo's abstract basis that the pages of his disciple have now chiefly value as an exercise.

IV

This finely-severing, deductive, schoolman's intellect is at bottom the same faculty as that which presides over some of De Quincey's narratives, in which every moment of the action and motive of the actors is anatomised, and where, in extreme instances like *Murder considered as one of the Fine Arts*, the events take longer to tell than to happen ;—with an increase, certainly, of the dramatic suspense, and no enfeebling of it. The outer expression of this habit of mind is the figure called by the books of rhetoric Amplification ; and of that figure, along with Burke, De Quincey is one of the great masters. Its abuses are easy to see, and indeed are gross. The chief blemish of all De Quincey's writings, which has discounted his fame by the mere tedium and irritation that it causes, is his proneness to word-spinning, digression, and dilution. He beats his story out so thin that he beats a hole in it, however precious the metal. This must be granted once and for all. Hence a frequent want of perspective, which spoils his naturally delicate sense of structure. But it is only the excess of a trait, which in its harmonious and temperate exhibition is his greatest excellence.

De Quincey's way of amplifying is different from Burke's. For Burke proceeds by turning an idea over and over, and by many-faceted allusion, so that the truth is at last presented solidly on all its sides and with all its qualifying terms. De Quincey proceeds by disquisition, and (so to say) by foliation. His main theme is like a trunk that throws off bough, and branch, and twig, down to the smallest shoot, without haste or pause. In *The Vision of Sudden Death* the theme is of the simplest : a heavy mail-coach, with the driver asleep, bearing down fatally in a narrow road upon two unconscious persons in a gig. This incident is told through many pages, though it is over in a minute. The disproportion is more than justified ; for we ' count time by heart-beats ' ; and into a few seconds are crowded those long vistas of ominous forecast and apprehension in the mind of the spectator which fly open at such a crisis. In this way the whole of the action is seen in its farthest issues, and these are registered on the brain so deep as to people the dreams of many a future midnight. De Quincey gives us the clue to this kind of second sight in himself :

> This accursed gift I have, as regards *thought*, that in the first step towards the possibility of a misfortune I see its total evolution ; in the radix of the series I see too certainly and too instantly its entire expansion ; in the first syllable of the dreadful sentence I read already the last.

So too, in the progress of Marr the murderer, his separate steps are counted, and there is a timing of each pulse of terror in the victim ; a recital that would have been perfect in its way but for that unlucky shrill joking with the King of Terrors, which is in De Quincey's worst fashion. In *The Revolt of the Tartars* the expansive and amplifying habit is managed with a splendid rightness and economy ; it is the best and swiftest of all De Quincey's narratives. It is mostly derived from a big and unfamiliar German work,[1] to which at the time he omits his acknowledgments. The tale is ordered, the intrigues laid bare, the proportions kept, the crises of the tragedy brought into relief, in a style worthy of the great historians. Immense numbers and distances, confused and gigantic sufferings, always appealed strongly to his fancy ; and here in a real, and recent, and tragical occurrence, enacted on a vast remote stage, he found his opportunity ;—in the record of the emigration of the Tartar hordes from the Volga to the Great Wall, of their decimation by the pursuing or environing armies, of the hopeless struggle of men, women and children, with cold and disease, and famine and the desert; of their final arrival under the wing of the Chinese emperor; and, after a last carnage, of their peaceful establishment in a promised land. In *The Spanish Military Nun*,[1] De Quincey once more goes playfully to work on his authorities, and like Defoe, delightedly confounds fact with fiction. This tale of Catalina, the roving, swashbuckling, escaped, disguised nun, with her duels and hardships, is based on fact, but takes its place amongst De Quincey's liveliest, not to say vulgarest, romances: the humour has a sort of ghastliness, and the author's shade continues to smile, with its queer *rictus*, at the scholars who have exposed his pretensions to be the critical editor of a ' genuine history.'

How the process of ramifying and expanding became almost a necessity of his intellect, appears on comparing the first form of the *Confessions* with the enlarged one of 1856. This is, as already said, thrice as long; and whilst the great poetic or tender passages remain, usually untouched, new ones are added of equal beauty. The actual story, at first as plain and simple as a page of Goldsmith, is now overlaid and carved, every foot of it, with fluent digressions and close traceries; and sometimes the result, in its own kind equally precious, might almost seem the handiwork of another man. De Quincey's conception of art has altered; he has forgotten the joys of thrift and symmetry; he thinks of his work not as a perfect whole, leading from austerity to splendour by right gradations, as the lines of a bare temple may point onward to some rich altarpiece, but as a complex irregular structure, decorated and recessed and many-celled, in which all manner of strange accretions and outworks are permissible. The manner, too, is more rhetorical, inversions are multiplied, and the voice is pitched higher throughout. Some early crudities are gone, but many of the new divagations and pleasantries are overfinely spun, and put off the suspense too long. The chief gain is that De Quincey tells us far more about his life and himself and others, time having removed the need of reserves and suppressions. His criticism on the earlier draft, that ' the main narrative should naturally have moved through a succession of secondary incidents,' explains his change of method. We can never be sorry for the recast; yet the earlier edition must remain the true starting-point for the reader. We must not, as is usually done, approach the later one first, and think of the earlier only as a maimed version or curious embryo.

V

Apart from those great compositions, of a kind that has no name, but approaches music nearer than any other art (ordinary ' poetic prose ' included) in its effects ; apart from his fantasias, as they may best be called, there is no doubt that De Quincey's genius shows best in narrative and reminiscence. The body of memoirs that surround the *Confessions*, leading up to them or away from them, and together giving an unrivalled, indeed the only picture of his early life, have the charm and arresting power of the best autobiography. They rank, it may be thought, even beside the personal and reminiscent sketches of his friend Elia ; for though Lamb works by condensation, by intensity, by sudden and piercing traits, and herein has no rival, De Quincey's stroke of wing is slower, longer, more sustained and leisurely, and if at times it is dilatory and feeble, he covers in the end a greater space of country. As he says in his affectionate essay on his friend, Lamb ' shrank from the continuous, the sustained, and the elaborate ' ; and it is De Quincey's honour that whether he failed or triumphed, the ' continuous, the sustained, and the elaborate ' were ever his artistic ambition. Between Gibbon and Ruskin no English writer, using the scale of the protracted article or essay, carried this ambition further than De Quincey ; and he always does best when he is telling of himself.

His imaginative life, as well as his studious temper of mind, was awakened far back in his childhood ; he was essentially precocious—not so much in expression as in reflection. Those who, without his, genius, have had the same fortune or misfortune, will recognise the painful sharpness of his memory. From the pictures of his home at Greenheys, of his sister's death and the daydream that came upon him as he saw her dead, of his games with his brother and their common war with the Manchester street lads, of his life and his masters and his discussions at the Manchester Grammar School, of his truant departure thence and wanderings—from all these things a singular charm disengages itself, as of some old-fashioned, rare, oddly-petalled herb or flower. De Quincey was thrust by circumstance now amongst persons of culture and caste, now amongst outlaws and equivocal traffickers, in both ways escaping from the rather prim-spirited middle-class comfort of his home. In the art of silvery, winding, eloquent, and considerate talk he had his own pre-eminence, differing therein from Coleridge with his monologues and Carlyle with his eruptions. His best articles upon himself and his friends have the character of such talk, with its eddies and excursions, and its backwaters sometimes too prolonged. Their noblest and also most disconcerting feature is a wide human fellow-feeling, before which class distinctions cease to count, combined with a pervading detachment and remoteness. Carlyle said, ' This child has been in hell ' ; but he was rather a kind of change-ling, one of the *good people*, who has married a human wife and conforms to the laws of our earth, but at certain recurring hours betrays his origin by some freakish trait or startling message from the world inside the hill.

In his recollections of his friends, published in some cases during their lifetime, he was often inaccurate, and cannot be denied to have shown some want of feeling. Only a changeling would have described Dorothy Wordsworth so precisely just as she had once been, when she was alive to read the description. He ought to have regretted doing so ; but can we regret that he did so ? We often find ourselves saying it is well that indis-cretions should come, but woe unto him by whom they come. In any case, De Quincey's are comparatively mild, and have been much exaggerated. We have a more convincing picture from his hand than from any mere worshipper of the Wordsworth household : and his account of the fashion in which an after-dinner sleep came upon Charles Lamb atones for much :

It descended upon him as softly as a shadow. In a gross person, laden with superfluous flesh, and sleeping heavily, this would have been disagreeable; but in Lamb, thin even to meagreness, spare and wiry as an Arab of the desert, or as Thomas Aquinas, wasted by scholastic vigils, the affection of sleep seemed rather a network of aerial gossamer than of earthly cobweb—more like a golden haze falling upon him gently from the heavens than a cloud exhaling upwards from the flesh. Motionless in his chair as a bust, breathing so gently as scarcely to seem certainly alive, he presented the image of repose midway between life and death, like the repose of sculpture ; and to one who knew his history, a repose affectingly contrasting with the calamities and internal storms of his life.

The passage, but for its rounder rhythm, might have come, in its tenderness and subtlety, from Lamb's own hand ; and the preceding estimate of his nature and literary idiosyncrasy is worthy of it. It is a pity that such things are not more numer-ous ; but De Quincey's habit of mind was too errant, and his judgment too open to the gusts of prejudice or caprice, to make him a trustworthy critic.

VI

The two shapes of the *Confessions* have already been noticed ; and they must be taken together with the fantasias written twenty years later than the earlier of the two drafts, namely with *Suspiria* and its companions ; and also with the denunciation of the Bishop of Beauvais in Joan of Arc, with the childish daydream in *Autobiographic Sketches*, and with *The Dream-Fugue* at the end of *The English Mail-Coach*. In all, it is not very much in mass ; but neither are *Urn-Burial* or *The Ancient Mariner*, or Bossuet's funeral sermons ; all of which works, it is not excessive to say, threw open a new kingdom of art, or crowned an old one that long had waited for its sovereign. By De Quincey the dream-territory of art is now increased or rediscovered ; in any case, it receives an unheard-of reality and definition. Many of the old literary visions, alleged to be beheld in sleep, are in fact the invention of wideawake satirists or moralists, like Jean de Meung or Addison. They forswear the laws of the daylight earth ; but not for that do they enter the borders of the night. Chaucer talks with quiet and learned irony about dreams, or uses them as poetic machinery. Once, in the *House of Fame*, he may be relating a real sleep, or building on the memory of one ; for he gives us the sharp sense of flying or soaring without surprise, and the zodiacal signs, equally without our surprise, are hung out in the sky in the form of actual beasts. Shakespeare, so often full of the sense that our life is only a vision, gives, in the dream of Clarence, the illusion of a real ominous nightmare, charged with the physical agony of helpless falling and drowning.

The romantic writers do not always invent their experiences of this order. Blake, as we have seen, invents only too little ; he records exactly what is given him in vision, and so often turns art into a kind of memory-work. *Kubla Khan*, however, is a true dream, where the words and images seem to have arisen in coalescence, and survived after waking ; and here the tune too must have been part of the revelation. De Quincey's imaginative prose does not seem to have been born thus easily in the bosom of sleep. With him the artistic process reshapes, cell by cell, the fabric of remembered images, in accord with the needs of a ' mode of impassioned prose ' that has its own literary associations and origins. At the same time, the artist traces for us the springs of the imagery to his previous waking life—to the drawings of Piranesi, or the face of the wanderer in Oxford Street, or the onset of the

mail-coach—so that the result implies a conscious reconstruction
at once of the dream and of its remembered causes. This
union of self-analysis, memory, studied rhythm, this history
of the progress of his soul through the strange regions it has
traversed, is found everywhere in De Quincey, and leaves him
a solitary amongst the visionaries of literature.

The wretched opium—save for the 'pleasures' and the
'pains' which are engendered, honestly and magnificently
enough, by the use of it—the opium and its symptoms, its
mastery of De Quincey and his struggle against it, not only
become, to say the truth, a pure weariness in themselves, but dis-
tracts us from the true genius of the writer, to which, after all,
the drug was but an accidental minister. To the victim himself, in the intervals of his repentance and self-excuse, and of
his anxious mean self-comparisons with Coleridge, the opium
becomes a portentous joke and an occasion for prolixities.
His dreams are greater than himself, and opium, no doubt,
it was that helped to unlock them, and also to make him less
worthy of them. De Quincey is a kind of 'psychic'—a channel
for these messages from the kingdom of the night. On the
other hand he is also the artist without whom they would have
remained mere nightmares ; and his art is greater than himself
and his character, just as it is with Whistler.

A few of De Quincey's fantasias, like *The Daughter of Lebanon*
and *Savannah-La-Mar*, are more strictly in the nature of
poems without metre, in that they stand alone, and begin
loudly ('God smote Savannah-La-Mar'), and never fall back
into ordinary prose at all. But these are not the best or most
impressive. Most of them arise naturally out of a level narrative which has prepared us for their reception. The 'pleasures'
and 'pains of opium' are explained by the long matter-of-fact
history that precedes. So *The Dream-Fugue* is the climax of
the three sections of *The English Mail-Coach*, of which the first,
The Glory of Motion, is humorous, external, and patriotic,
while the second, *The Vision of Sudden Death*, relates the actual
incident, with its swaying figures of the endangered youth and
lady, which forms the *motif* of the fugue. So *Levana and
Our Ladies of Sorrow* starts pedantically, with the etymology
of the words 'Levana' and 'education'; the last surely
a word that should paralyse any poet's vision in advance.
Then, by a forced transition indeed, we are led to the most
splendid and studious of all De Quincey's imaginations, in
which he triumphantly challenges his powers of imposing a
new climax upon one which already seemed insuperable. Our

Lady of Sighs, the embodiment of all human *desideria*, the goddess of the pariah, slave, and convict, has, after all, a yet more terrible sister, Our Lady of Darkness—the power, as we may think, that presides over *King Lear* ; and the true commentary on the following passage is that play itself, or Charles Lamb's criticism upon it.

She is the defier of God. She is also the mother of lunacies, and the suggestress of suicides. Deep lie the roots of her power ; but narrow is the nation that she rules. For she can approach only those in whom a profound nature has been upheaved by central convulsions ; in whom the heart trembles and the brain rocks under conspiracies of tempests from without and tempests from within.

There is a certain likeness amongst De Quincey's visions. Pomps he sees, and battalions, and multitudes of swaying faces ; and also foresees that they are advancing, waveringly but without remission, towards some dim tryst of disaster or betrayal. From their masses are detached, at rhythmic intervals, ' discs of light and interspaces of gloom,' and bursts of agitated colour, and also single groups or figures that shape themselves into passionate memories deriving from his time of youth ; and out of the murmur are distinguished, ever and again, sounding words which serve as a rallying-point to the ear :—*Consul Romanus*, or *Waterloo*, or *everlasting farewells*. This definite recurrent appeal, plastic or musical, amidst the general confused magnificence and clamour, is a feature of De Quincey's art ; nor is it solely a device of art. Just such concrete fragments of form or colour or sound are the waking salvage of real dreams, whose huge indistinct background is lost to memory with the coming of the morning ; and that morning wakes upon angry senses, and waits for the quiet progress of the day towards humanity. And in his picture, as in Coleridge's, of the ' pains of sleep,' diseased or artificially stimulated, there is a similar cast of imagery. The same armies and processions are there ; but through some physical cause, understood only as an incubus or oppression, they are now arrayed against the dreamer himself ; they are the enemy ; and in human or bestial or nameless forms they chase their victim down to hell, or up into space along ever-propagating spirals, or through unknown continents. Often the scenery is foreign or monstrous, Oriental or ' Nilotic,' and he is an alien from all homely safeguards, and a pariah amidst cruel Asiatic faces, and sundered from ' sweet far-off England.' The map of De Quincey's nightly wanderings reminds us, in its vastness

and strangeness, of the explorations made by Marlowe's Tam-
burlaine, or by Milton's tortured hero. To accompany him in
these journeys is like flying through a night lit by strange
auroras and meteors. We sometimes get a like impression
from the poets, especially from Shelley. With Milton we fly
by the map, taking our bearings amidst the evenly-whirling
spheres, and seeing hell and heaven at a measurable distance
in a certain direction. With Keats we fly like a bee, near the
ground, from one cup of honey to another, and with long
alightings. But with De Quincey we are in absolute space,
which has no bearings, or firm earth, or north and south ; and
yet it is peopled with human faces and memories and monuments—themes to fix and control the imagination, which else
would stray intolerably. The presence of these rallying-
points in a world otherwise without order, seems to define for
us the form of his visions or fantasias.

VII

The actual diction of these compositions is at all points
identical, or conterminous, with that of the highest poetry.
No word which Shakespeare or Milton would have admitted
is out of keeping with them. There is therefore an inverse
tendency to that which Wordsworth, in his earlier pieces,
attempted to encourage, when he drew the vocabulary of verse
nearer to that of spoken prose. And, apart from vocabulary,
the order of words as affected by inversion, apostrophe, com-
plication of dependent clause, and by all other modes of
heightening and channelling emotion, is as different from
ordinary prose even of high excellence, as is the order, similarly
conditioned, of high elaborate verse. So far, then, Coleridge's
rule that 'metre paves the way to other distinctions,' does not
apply, since those other distinctions are here equally present
without metre to stimulate them. But the rule, if we take a
step further, holds nevertheless. For, though both ' impassioned prose ' and impassioned verse vary from common prose
in these regards, the differences soon cease to be the *same*
differences. In prose the absence of metre sets the artist
free for a grammatical and rhetorical development foreign to
that which is followed by the poet. The chief distinction is
seen by reference to the historic law which lies at the root of
all our exalted and periodic prose, and which does not apply
to verse—rather, is inconsistent with it. Latin oratory, the
foundation of such prose, supplies the key. This is the law of

verbal balance, which takes the shape, not only of a simple antithesis of corresponding or contrasted clauses, but of a triple or fourfold accumulation of parallel members, and of a corresponsive series of echoes, or antiphonies. The guiding principle is seen at once by a study of the passage just quoted, or of this one :

I

a   b   c

The head, the diadem, the urn,

IIa

these all had sunk ;

IIb

at last over these also the cruel quicksand had closed ;

1.   and no memorial of the fair young girl had remained on earth,

IIIa   IIIb

except my own solitary tears,   and the funeral bells from the desert seas,

2.   that, rising again more softly, sang a requiem

IVa   IVb

over the grave of the buried child, and over her blighted dawn.

This is rooted in our English Ciceronian tradition of balanced clauses, which descends from Bolingbroke to Gibbon, and from Sir Thomas Browne to Samuel Johnson ; but the structure is different in both these branches of the tradition. It resembles more that of Jeremy Taylor, and no doubt owes something to his example ; yet, again, it is the demonstration of a new art—a new ' mode of impassioned prose,' as De Quincey himself claimed. The instance given is but one out of endless varieties. The triply-divided movement marked I is followed by a pair of clauses, parallel and in equipoise but of unequal length, IIa and IIb. Likewise IIIa and IIIb balance each other, more evenly ; and so do IVa and IVb, which run together also in actual rhythm. Single unbalanced sentences separate II from III and III from IV ; they serve as a kind of stem for the successive bifurcating sprays. A different web of single, double, and triple clauses is woven in the following sentence :

Ia

1.   The sea appeared paved with innumerable faces, upturned to the heavens ;

Ib

a   β   γ

faces imploring, wrathful, despairing ;

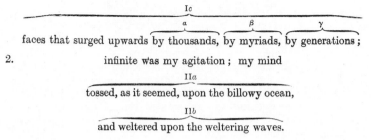

2.

               infinite was my agitation ; my mind

This kind of movement is only one, and perhaps the most definable, of those that recur in De Quincey's more exalted or 'impassioned' prose. In the staple of his writing, on whatever theme, the rhetorical elements are naturally less marked ; but his preference is always for more ample and sweeping—never trailing—constructions ; and of these his mastery is without effort and full of variety. The cadence is always heard, but it is never too emphatic for the subject ; and the chief secret of his art is the management of apt and expressive rhythm. 'Mysterious,' he says, 'is the life that connects all modes of passion with rhythmus'; and no one, not even Coleridge, had seen or said this so clearly, or had acted on it in the conduct of prose with so full a consciousness. 'Rhythmus' and vision in co-operation—therein is the essence of all his loftier work. The union of the two most potent among the artistic senses is the deepest thing in De Quincey's composition ; and though this fact is obscured by the frequent ascendency, already noticed, of the logical intellect, continually sundering and arranging, still he is at bottom an artist more than a reasoner. And in him rhythm is an even deeper thing than vision. In Landor rhythm is often perfect, though of less spacious and prolonged a kind ; but it often seems, with all its beauty, to be something studied and superadded, rather than to be incorporate with the feeling and to grow out of it. In De Quincey, as he intended, the art of rhythm approaches nearer to that of music ; it is more various, and even indeterminate ; it is closer to the infinite of pure feeling. The same difference of quality is found in the vision of the two writers. And in this difference, embracing at once imagery, cadence, and length of grammatical clause, are involved some of the stricter distinctions between the 'classical' and the 'romantic' treatment, as a pair of examples may show.

Epicurus (as Peleus). The wish of a divinity is powerfuller than the elements, and swifter than the light. Hence thou (what to me is impossible) mayest see the sweet Achilles, every day, every hour.

Ternissa (as Thetis). How few! alas how few! I see him in the dust, in agony, in death : I see his blood on the flints, his yellow hair flapping in its current, his hand unable to remove it from his eyes. I hear his voice ; and it calls not upon me! Mothers are soon forgotten! It is weakness to love the weak! I could not save him! He would have left the caverns of Ocean, and the groves and meadows of Elysium, though resounding with the songs of love and heroism, for a field of battle.

This passage from Landor is modelled, not on any one ancient author, but still on the antique. It has the firm, determinate outline that Blake loved ; and the emotion as well as the picture is defined exactly, with little of *penumbra* or unwordable suggestion. The units of phrase, while sometimes stretching out into pairs of melodious clauses, run to brevity. The moral tone, the feeling, or in other words the humanity, is heroic :—*mothers are soon forgotten—he would have left the caverns of Ocean for the field of battle* ; and this tone assuredly gives Landor a superiority over De Quincey, if we judge by the passage next to be cited, which is touched with commonplace pessimism. But it is chosen for his architecture and tune ; for its outlook into the twilight of fear and sorrow, and for its dying echo of confused and melancholy voices. It is a long musical movement, to be taken at a single breath, without exhaustion or hurry. It is in build an accumulation of clauses, separately not lengthy, but in most cases expanding and wavering on balanced wings rather than hanging, after Landor's or Johnson's fashion, in evenly-weighted scales ; the whole remaining at a true poetic pitch, whilst escaping metrical form:

What is life ? Darkness and formless vacancy for a beginning, or something beyond all beginning ; then next a dim lotos of human consciousness, finding itself afloat upon the bosom of waters without a shore ; then a few sunny smiles and many tears ; a little love and infinite strife ; whisperings from paradise and fierce mockeries from the anarchy of chaos ; dust and ashes, and once more darkness circling round, as if from the beginning, and in this way rounding or making an island of our fantastic existence,—*that* is human life, *that* the inevitable amount of man's laughter and his tears—of what he suffers and what he does—of his motions this way and that way, to the right or to the left, backwards or forwards—of all his seeming realities and all his absolute negations,—his shadowy pomps and his pompous shadows—of whatsoever he thinks, finds, makes or mars, creates or animates, loves, hates, or in dread hope anticipates. So it is, so it has been, so it will be for ever and ever.

De Quincey is less dignified than Landor, but is more tender, humble, and appealing, with his boundless sympathy with the outcast, the victim, the child, and the solitary. These tremulous and prolonged phrases, partly modelled on those of the pensive old seventeenth-century moralists (such as the unknown author of the essay on death,[1] once assigned to Bacon), are the true medium for such a sentiment. But in this whole business of the elaborate orchestration of prose De Quincey and Landor, with all their differences, stand apart and together. The exquisite fabrication of sentences and of pages on the ampler scale distinguishes them from their companions Lamb and Hazlitt, whose flights are briefer. De Quincey and Landor, along with Ruskin, also stand above all their successors in this craft. Their sweep and pace and compass, and their grave easy progress, separate them from masters of the inlaying and enamelling art like Pater or the lesser artist Stevenson, who overcrowd and clog their style. Prose in our day has inclined to this latter extreme ; and there seems little hope for it, unless it can recover some of its earlier greatness. It is capable of subtlety and beauty :

> but O how frail
> To that large utterance of the early gods !

VIII

STYLE has an *absolute* value, like the product of any other exquisite art, quite distinct from the value of the subject about which it is employed, and irrelatively to the subject. . . . It is a product of art, the rarest, subtlest, and most intellectual ; and, like other products of the fine arts, it is then finest when it is most eminently disinterested, that is, most conspicuously detached from gross palpable uses. Yet, in very many cases, it really *has* the obvious uses of that gross palpable order. . . . In these cases, meantime, the style is contemplated as a thing separable from the thoughts ; in fact, as the *dress* of the thoughts, a robe that may be laid aside at pleasure. But there arises a case entirely different, where style cannot be regarded as a *dress* or alien covering, but where style becomes the *incarnation* of the thoughts.

This passage, which occurs in the article on *Language,* is a good example of De Quincey's critical style, and throws light on his habit as a workman. In general he is associated, perhaps affiliated, with Coleridge, and also with Wordsworth, from whom the last sentence is taken. He realises the essential union of style and subject ; and also, what Coleridge and

Wordsworth never saw or said so plainly, the ' absolute value
of style.' He is not a greater artist than they are, but he is
a more conscious one. He handles words, at his best, like
' Scopas the Greek, or Cellini the Florentine,' and his temper
is more that of a critic of painting or sculpture than is the
temper of either of his friends. And when he says, ' mysterious
is the life that connects all forms of passion with rhythmus,'
here again, though not at variance with them, he goes beyond
them ; while in other respects, as in his treatment of Pope,
of the work of the discursive understanding in poetry, and of
eighteenth-century literature, he is, for good or ill, by their
side. His famed paper, *On the Knocking at the Gate in Macbeth*,
is much in the spirit of Coleridge ; but he has the double
advantage of here being in full possession of his peculiar
eloquence, and also of entering, by his more intimate bent
and sympathy, into the sensations of terror and suspense
involved. De Quincey's criticism, however, suffers almost
always from his darling sins of caprice and divagation, and,
as it has well been called, of rigmarole ; and, except for the
paper on Macbeth, has not left one critical composition that
is quite satisfactory. He is never quite sterile ; he always
drops some phrase or word that illuminates ; but he can
seldom keep to the point or finish in time.

The long articles on *Rhetoric* and *Style* exhibit all his critical
virtues and backslidings : let us dwell rather on the virtues.
In the first, he may seem needlessly to degrade the term
Rhetoric, treating it as a lower but still lawful species of writing,
different from chaos and want of art on the one side, and from
true eloquence on the other ; but it is hard to see what other
name he could find for what he describes. The historical
sweep, the survey of English ' rhetoric ' from Donne to Burke
(although it swamps his original distinction of this art from
eloquence), the praise of Taylor and the censure of Junius,
all rank this finely-conceived paper by the side of Coleridge's
chapter on the history of English prose ; [1] and even, by virtue
of De Quincey's greater leisure and clearer method, above it.
Again, the often-quoted distinction, to be found in the review
of Pope, between the literature of knowledge and that of
power, resembles that drawn by Coleridge between the aims
of poetry and of science, the first existing for the communication of knowledge, the second for the communication of
pleasure. But De Quincey gives the thought a new turn ;
he speaks not of poetry but of literature ; and in fact no one,
or no Englishman, had ever yet defined the ' literature of

power,' or made it so distinct a category.   When we read it, we forget his pitiable treatment of Goethe or of Shelley.   No one is so tricksy a guide, or sometimes so repellent ; but in his happy hours De Quincey is an artist who speaks not only of his own art, but through that art, and the effect is incomparable.

CHAPTER XXIII

CHARLES AND MARY LAMB

I. Point of likeness between Lamb and Keats. Lamb much investigated. Stages of his literary life (a) 1795-c. 1806: early tales and poems, and mimicries; (b) 1807-11: work with Mary Lamb; disclosure of power in prose; tales from Shakespeare and Homer; *Dramatic Poets*; (c) 1812-19: comparative quiescence; (d) from 1820: *Elia*, etc.; Lamb an essayist.

II. Connections with older generation; Godwin, Holcroft. James White's *Letters of Falstaff*. Sonnets, and other verse.

III. Reminiscent character of Lamb's best writing. *Rosamund Gray*. Books for children by Charles, or Mary Lamb, or both: treatment of *Tales from Shakespear*; reversal of Shakespeare's procedure. Poetic justice. Principles of diction. Method of tessellation: example. *Adventures of Ulysses.*

IV. *Poetry for Children.* Mary Lamb's handiwork. *Mrs. Leicester's School.* Lamb's dramatic pieces: *John Woodvil, The Wife's Trial*, etc.

V. Essays: early experiments. The *Essays of Elia* autobiographical, and essentially poems. Lamb a rescuer of persons and things forgotten. Character-portraits; method of the old humourists.

VI. Lamb's debt to eighteenth-century prose; the plain manner and the high-poetical: examples. Lamb's criticism: his preferences, and liking for situation. Comparison with Hazlitt. True attitude to Lamb's ' paradoxes.'

I

UNLIKE at first sight, Charles Lamb [1] (1775-1834) and Keats touch at more points than one; above all in being artists, who are resolute to do only what they were born to do and what no one else can do, and to let the rest pass. They are not, like Coleridge, De Quincey, or Landor, unfaithful to their stars through compulsion or perversity; they leave fewer masses of waste matter with their signatures; they do not spend upon enforcing the mere tenets that they share with a thousand others, or upon hack industry followed against the grain, the time that they might have given to their genius. We have not to reckon with anything like Shelley's minor pamphlets, or Hazlitt's political railings, or Browning's poetry that is not poetry. Lamb and Keats do not insist on playing the citizen, or the disputant, or the reasoner, when it is not predestined that they should. They mind their own business. When they go wrong, it is

within their own sphere, so that though much that they
have left is not good, it is never alien to them or inex-
pressive.   They do not seem to be under any real temptation
to swerve.

Lamb has been so well loved that the world (as may be
right) will not let him alone, and cannot have too much
of him.   His lightest things, tossed off in whim, or liquor,
or in familiar coterie-letters, have been unearthed and cased
and labelled in daylight print, and we are set down to ' appreciate' them in all soberness.   He tells us to 'give them fair
construction, as in an after-dinner conversation.'   We have
pages of his puns, like a glass case full of pinned-out ephemerids.
We can bear them, for we know enough of his way of life to
rebuild in fancy the kind of scenes in which they were brought
forth.   He had no Boswell ; but Hazlitt, and Talfourd, and
Le Grice, and many more, and above all Lamb himself, have
left their record, so that we can make up a picture.   It is wonderful how little, as a man, he suffers from this pious exposure,
and from the care of the editors who have burrowed into his
life and served his glory.

Lamb began to write about 1795, in the lifetime of Burke
and Cowper, and practised for ten years in verse, in fiction, in
drama, and in essay-making.   A few sonnets, a few lyrics, the
play *John Woodvil* (1802), and some stray papers, are the best
of these early fruits.   His youthful *Tale of Rosamund Gray*
(1798), his paid jokes for newspapers, and his farce that failed,
show some of his mind and gifts, which are still undeveloped.
Perhaps his mimicries of Burton, and of Shakespeare's prose
and verse, are the most original products of this period.   Then,
from 1807 to 1811, whilst he is working in frequent partnership
with his sister Mary, there is a sudden disclosure of power ;
a new master appears, a new prose, a new critic.   The *Tales
from Shakespear* (1807) they wrote together.   *The Adventures
of Ulysses* (1808) are by Lamb alone ; and these prose transcripts of poetry show the same richness, the same natural
insight and zest, the same affinity in mind and style with an
older day, as the notes to the *Specimens of English Dramatic
Poets who lived about the time of Shakspeare* (1808).   The same
sureness of power in reserve, and also a new vein of subtle
and tender reminiscence, are found in the works written by
the brother and sister for young people, in the prose of *Mrs.
Leicester's School* (1809), and in the verse of *Poetry for Children*
(1808) ; these and other works being printed for the ' juvenile
library ' of Mrs. Godwin, who was second wife of the philosopher,

and whom Lamb disliked not merely for her green spectacles. Lamb's distinctive humour is not yet fully apparent, except in his letters; but the faithful skill in pathetic or whimsical retrospect, which is a main source of his humour, is there already and cannot be mistaken. He published in 1818 such of his *Works* as he cared to save. For seven years (1812-19) he wrote little, but his power was ripening. The *Essays of Elia* began in 1820 in the *London Magazine*, and after its extinction in 1825 continued in other journals. The first series of twenty-eight was collected in 1823; the *Last Essays of Elia*, twenty-four in number, ten years later, and a volume of *Album Verses* in 1830. The fame of 'Elia' was assured in Lamb's lifetime, and has suffered little change.

II

Lamb thus belongs to the third generation of the romantic writers, and his prime, which begins with *Elia* in 1820, coincides with that of Keats, Shelley, and De Quincey; he reaches it later than his friends and coevals, Coleridge and Wordsworth. But in various odd ways he is connected with the older generation, the last writers of the eighteenth century. He came in by chance for a wild lash from the Anti-Jacobins, and figured in Gillray's caricature as a toad or frog. He was, in these early days, already an amused friend of old Godwin, 'the Professor,' sat through the performance of *Antonio*, and stuck to its author when he had become a kind of ghostly reputation, and raised money for him. Holcroft was also of the circle; but these personages were survivors, and had little to do with Lamb's tastes or opinions; they were 'characters' whom he liked, and humourists in the old meaning of the word. Lamb also strikes back to the age of *pastiche*. In 1777 had appeared Maurice Morgann's *Character of Sir John Falstaff*, a true and genial precursor of romantic criticism. In 1796 Lamb's-crony James White, the Jem White of *The Praise of Chimney-Sweepers*, published his *Original Letters of Sir John Falstaff*,[1] a now almost forgotten but sprightly mimicry of Shakespeare's comic prose, in which Mrs. Quickly, Pistol, Fluellen, and the whole company are boldly made to speak at length. Lamb greatly relished this work, and he also loudly praised it. The direct evidence of Southey confirms the suspicion that the roaring pleasantry of White is at times interrupted by a finer hand. Divesting the following passage of black-letter, we may conjecture its author:

Bote by the pryce sette upon your labours by the wyttes of the age, it sholde seeme lamentable matter of facte, how moche poesy, and the pryme phansies and conceipts of connynge menne are fallen into contempte in these the worldis last dayes. Natheless, Master Irelaunde, letten us not be fruitelesslye caste downe—The tyme dothe faste approche, nay even now is close at honde, when the overcharged cloudes of scepticysme muste incontinentlye vanish before convictione's serener Welkin, and Edmonde shall in vayne resume his laboures.

This spelling and idiom might pass muster at the time for Elizabethan ; and we may remember that despite the labours of Edmond Malone, Chatterton had not yet been dealt with fully by the stern philologist. So, too, in the Preface, we learn that that ' elderly maiden sister ' of Mrs. Quickly, to whom the Falstaff letters had devolved, was ' fond of roast pig ' :

A curse on her Epicurean guts, that could not be contented with plain mutton, like the rest of her Ancestors !

We see, at any rate, how early—he was but just of age—Lamb was dyed—at least superficially—in the diction of the old writers, which was afterwards to pass into his very blood, and to be re-created on his lips. His imitations of the style of Burton's *Anatomy* show a yet greater mastery. If he did not share in White's little book, he knew it, as well as its models, intimately ; yet meanwhile he was penning not prose but verse ; and his verse has the thin faint sweetness, at times youthfully sentimental, which was derided by the cheaper critics, but which contains many a foretaste of his later mind.

Lamb's sonnets, as we have seen (vol. i. p. 76), along with those of Lloyd and Coleridge, follow close on those of Bowles, Bampfylde, and their somewhat pallid company ; but even in his early experiments there is a new note of style and humanity ; there is less of mere gentle water-colour than in the work of his companions :

> For now to my, raised mind
> On wings of winds comes wild-eyed Phantasy,
> And her *rude visions give severe delight.*
> O winged bark ! how swift along the night
> Pass'd thy proud keel ! nor shall I let go by
> Lightly of that drear hour the memory,
> When wet and chilly on thy deck I stood,
> Unbonnetted, and gaz'd upon the flood,
> Even till it seemed a pleasant thing to die,—
> *To be resolv'd into th' elemental wave,*
> *Or take my portion with the winds that rave.* (1794.)

The lines italicised are from the revision of 1818 ; they are
curiously like Keats, and are worthy of him. But even in
its juvenile shape this poem (' O, I could laugh to hear the midnight wind ') is noteworthy. The blank verse of *The Gran-
dame* (who was Lamb's own grandmother), dated 1796, is in
the manner of Cowper : but there is a difference, which can
hardly be due to the influence of Wordsworth, and which gives
its flavour to the pretty and pious little memorial. The sonnet
to Mary Lamb, ' If from my lips some angry accents fell '
(1795), written in the Hoxton asylum, is of the sanest temper
and the purest simplicity of diction—a virtue not in that
decade too common ; and another of the same year, ' The
Lord of Life shakes off his drowsihed,' which, except for the
first line, is throughout plain and pathetic in manner, is one
more proof that Lamb's inward sad gravity, disguised under
a thousand quips, had settled on him almost in his boyhood.
Many of the pieces written after his domestic calamity (1796)
bear a tragic impress ; and they also disclose Lamb's essential
piety—as yet inevitably too high-wrought—which afterwards
disjoined itself more and more from all set forms and seems to
have settled into a sheer, strong-witted, secular goodness of
nature ; a change traceable also in his letters and conversation.
The form in two of these compositions is notable : in *The Old
Familiar Faces* (1798), which should be read in the original
shape, with its full note of tragic woe, and in *Hester* (1803),
a lyrical ballad equal to any of Wordsworth's (which is much
to say), and to the full as natural and homefelt in its language.
These are two out of Lamb's three most perfect—nay, of his
only perfect poems, the third by common consent being
the wonderful and much later metaphysical elegy on Thomas
Hood's dead baby, *On an Infant Dying as soon as Born* (1827),
which was assuredly ' written for antiquity,' and greeted by
the shades of Marvell and Vaughan, proudly, as a forgotten
thing of their own ; its sudden and remote but spontaneous
imagery, its octosyllabics with their alternate ripple and
arrest, being theirs by right. But when he wrote this, Lamb
had already shown himself a great prose fantast in the best
meaning of the word, and prose had become his medium ; so
that there is nothing else equal to this poem, or like it, except
the more whimsical and elaborate *Angel Help* and *The Christen-
ing*.

The rest of Lamb's verses, apart from those made for the
young, may well be here noted. While showing abundantly
the fineness of his temper and humour, they are scarcely those

of a poet born. He does not often move easily save in the lighter kinds, or when imitating the antique. His ballad, ' In a costly palace,' and *The Gipsy's Malison*, are powerful, but there is the fever in them of a man who is forcing himself out of his natural temper. The *Farewell to Tobacco* is an improvisation, also overdone and uncomfortable. Of his *Album Verses*, issued in 1830, the gravest, with its painful searchings of heart, is that written *In my Own Album*—surely the most groundless sally of momentary self-reproach ever chronicled by any heroic and self-sacrificing spirit—a clinging rag of the detestable poisoned robes of morbid introspection. These casual touches are the only serious effect upon Lamb's writings of his personal weaknesses—such as his inclination to liquor ; a habit unlucky enough, but hardly excessive as judged by the ignorant code of his day, and in its degree and effects wholly different from the disease that broke down Coleridge. Another ill effect, no doubt, must be found in the frequently thin and wearisome quality of his joking, which does not always represent his sober self, or his real and profound humour. A good deal of his funning, from first to last, is most comfortless to peruse, being a reaction from the strain and trouble of his life. It is of the lips only, maybe a gallant facing out of inward depression, or a revulsion from it for relief.

III

Apart from his criticisms and letters, the best of Lamb's prose and verse is reminiscent—the clear ethereal essence of memories that had lain by nearly a quarter of a century, from his childhood and youth, and had left no sediment. Viewed thus backwards, his life, passed among his beloved streets and ' old humourists, that had been long in their graves,' and also too soon in the company of dreadful shadows, shaped itself, his noble brain and nature emerging and conquering, into something like a piece of art which he found rather than made ; for we feel as if he came upon the *Essays of Elia* rather than sat down to make them up, the whole past of his early affections and laughters lying before him in a droll and tender light and with the right words ready. But while this process is beginning underground, he is seen printing much that only fitfully gives any intimation of it ; while, on the other hand, his correspondence, from its first records (beginning in 1796) to the last, gives Lamb as he really was, and is in no way studied or composed. Latterly, when his manner had become second

nature and reached perfection, Lamb's letters and his printed
work cannot thus be distinguished. His correspondence with
Coleridge after his personal tragedy at once shows his metal
as a writer, though he is there considering anything rather
than style ; and for many years his finest prose is that which
he pours out in this way without thinking.

The little story of *Rosamund Gray*, written when Lamb was
twenty-three, makes us feel upon how young a spirit the blows
of fate had already descended, and does not tempt criticism.
It is but one more of his links with a generation soon to become
dim ; that of Mrs. Opie, with her prim and tender moral tales,
written with an eye upon the young, and of the literature of
sensibility, which Lamb and his friends were already skirting
too closely in their verses. Something of this juvenile con-
strainedly simple style there is in *Rosamund Gray*, and also
something of incoherence and worse, that reminds us of the
malady which a year or two before had visited the writer.
But there is a curious pathos and true simplicity in the opening
pages, and in the idyll that follows, spoilt as it is by conventional
tragedy.

In the books written by the Lambs for young readers we see,
perhaps, the truest expression of their common mind ; a
perfume as of an old garden rises up from those pages, which
at first sight are merely a reduction of great literature to a
pleasant simplified prose—tragedy and epic made easy. In
Lamb himself, at any rate, the task is prompted by a certain
impatience, or even indignation, as he looks at the food offered
by the professional purveyors for children, and remembers how
one child, in his own experience, had thriven under more generous allowance, like Crabbe's young Peter in *The Happy Day* :

Mrs. Barbauld's stuff [1] has banished all the old classics of the
nursery ; and the shopman at Newberry's hardly deigned to reach
them off an old exploded corner of a shelf, when Mary asked for them.
Mrs. B.'s and Mrs. Trimmer's nonsense lay in piles about. Knowledge insignificant and vapid as Mrs. Barbauld's books convey, it
seems, must come to a child in the *shape of knowledge*, and his
empty noddle must be turned with conceit of his own powers when
he has learnt that a horse is an animal, and Billy is better than a
horse, and such like ; instead of that beautiful interest in wild tales,
which made the child a man, while all the time he suspected himself
to be no bigger than a child. . . . Think what you would have been
now, if, instead of being fed with tales and old wives' fables in
childhood, you had been crammed with geography and natural
history !

This was written to the poet of *The Ancient Mariner* in 1802 ; five years later appeared *Tales from Shakespear*, and then *The Adventures of Ulysses*. Lamb's mind during these years was full of some of the strongest literature in the world ; he was editing his *Specimens* of the dramatists. He understood the grave matters that in the *Tales* he left out, and gives the impression of a great force working delicately. *Mrs. Leicester's School, Poetry for Children*, and *Prince Dorus* at once show that where the Lambs are superior, not only to the Trimmers and Sherwoods,[1] but to the Opies and Edgeworths, is in their morality. Those ladies, some of whom possessed observant wit, had made 'moral tales ' ; they had trafficked without remorse in poetic or rather prosaic justice, rewarding the good children with cakes and gratified vanity and schoolroom approval, and with the satisfaction of seeing their bad brothers punished. Such, it was inferred, was the order of the world ; but this was really all a pack of lies, and not even what those ladies were fond of calling white lies ; but a house of painted cards, blown down by the first puff of reality, and leaving an honest child without any real code at all. But Lamb too is a moralist ; and whatever may be true for adults, no sane man will argue that children do not want, or gain by, his lessons :

What these Tales have been to you in childhood, that and much more it is my wish that the true Plays of Shakespear may prove to you in older years—enrichers of the fancy, strengtheners of virtue, a withdrawing from all selfish and mercenary thoughts, a lesson of all sweet and honourable thoughts and actions, to teach you courtesy, benignity, generosity, humanity ; for of examples, teaching these virtues, his pages are full.

This is not the kind of preaching out of which the bottom will be knocked by the hearer at the age of seventeen. Nor is it insipid just because it does not raise problems. A few years, and the youthful reader will open Lamb's notes on Webster or Middleton or *Macbeth* without any sense of having been cheated earlier by the *Tales from Shakespear* into a mere edited version. Life must be edited for the young ; and the test of the editing is whether they will afterwards look back with resentment, or with gratitude, on the version of life that was offered them. Lamb stands this test, and the Mrs. Barbaulds do not. He was an artist ; he had a peculiarly delicate and accurate gift of retrospect, and he therefore commanded—though he would have flouted the term—a sounder psychology. It has often been wondered how he could present *Othello* without shirking the story, and yet without introducing any element that would perplex the child's impression of ' the pity of it.'   Lamb seems to achieve this by figuring the adult passion, which to the child is hidden, purely as a kind of intensified affection—which in part it really is ; and this the child can follow, because it can imagine its own affections on a larger scale, though it cannot imagine anything beyond them.   Such a procedure shows faith in the child ; but to shift about, and sheer nervously off the question, is to show unfaith in the child ; while to blurt out the whole original, in parboiled prose, is to shock the child with an unmeaning horror, and to take his mind, after all, off the essence of the story.   It will be seen that by now we are talking, and indeed have been from the first, about fine art as well as about education.   In this kind of work the two things are one.

For one thing the Lambs do is to reverse Shakespeare's own way of working ; they turn a play back into an old story, such as he might have himself used to work upon, and such as seems an ' unhappy ' but yet a ' far-off thing ' to the child ;—as real as life, or more real, but still somehow pleasanter.   And to get this effect the language must be clarified, yet without being made foolishly simple ; else it at once attracts notice, as language, and is derided.   The Lambs always get the right sort of transparency, and have too much good sense and humour to tarry sentimentally :

And this innocent wife, as she lay at his mercy, begged for compassion, and to know her fault, and then he named Cassio, and the handkerchief which (he said) she had given him ; and as the guiltless lady was proceeding to clear herself, he suddenly would hear no more, but covering her up in the bedclothes, stifled her till she died.

Cinthio does not tell this catastrophe so well, since he had not Shakespeare behind him ; but it is just in the manner of some of those sound old French or Italian novelists—whom Lamb did *not* know.   The whole treatment of *Measure for Measure* shows the same kind of power ; it is meant for a somewhat older young person, and can only help to sweep his mind clean against the visits of experience.   And what of ' poetic justice,' which the child, we are told, surely demands ?   Well, there are two kinds of nonsense that can be talked about poetic justice.   There is the way of the Barbaulds, which falsifies tragedy.   But there is also the way of the cynic, the accuser of the world, a way which falsifies comedy and that part of life which justifies comedy. There, and also in tragi-comedy, poetic justice is the law; then let us have it, even to superfluity, whenever we can get it.

It only remains to be told, that Dionysia, the wicked wife of Cleon, met with an end proportionable to her deserts; the inhabitants of Tharsus, when her cruel attempt upon Marina was known, rising in a body to revenge the daughter of their benefactor, and setting fire to the palace of Cleon, burnt both him and her, and their whole household: the gods seeming well pleased, that so foul a murder, though but intentional, and never carried into act, should be punished in a way befitting its enormity.

Thus are enlarged and bettered the words of the venerable Gower:

> The gods for murder seemed so content
> To punish them; although not done, but meant.

And at the end of *Cymbeline* another turn is given to the 'moral': the punishment and death of the wicked queen

are events too tragical to interrupt this happy conclusion by more than merely touching upon. It is sufficient that all were made happy, who were deserving, and even the treacherous Iachimo, in consideration of his villainy having missed its final aim, was dismissed without punishment.

Here, as ever, the exact emphasis of the original is followed; an even harder matter than the creation of an adequate language, which shall face on one side towards Shakespeare and on the other towards the childish brain. The success of the Lambs in this latter effort is one of the best-known of literary miracles, and is worth considering.

Lamb explains the principles of his diction in the Preface:

Diligent care has been taken to select such words as might least interrupt the effect of the beautiful English tongue in which he wrote; therefore words introduced into our language since his time have been as far as possible avoided.

He adds that he has been able to borrow the poet's own words more freely in the tragedies than in the comedies, where it was scarcely ever possible 'to turn his words into the narrative form,' although he has here made free use of the dialogue; and that in some few places 'his blank verse is given unaltered, as hoping from its simple plainness to cheat the young readers into the belief that they are reading prose.' This business of tessellation is, of course, wonderfully carried through, the general principle being, as already hinted, to hold to the simpler parts of Shakespeare's speech—those innumerable simple things which, as he well knew, would go home to the whole audience, young and old—and to join them, as far as might be, with threads that might have come from the same spindle — with words, as we said, that would be appropriate to an old tale or to one of the poet's 'sources.' Much too is done by firmly omitting matter that would have tempted an adapter of blunter feeling. Thus, in Mary Lamb's version of *As You Like It*, there is no Jaques, and the wit of Rosalind becomes a kind of pleasant archness only ; and when she gives Orlando the chain, with a single word (' I am out of suits with fortune,' etc.), the following speech (' you have overcome more than your enemies ') is dropped wholly. All these contractions are right for the purpose in hand ; the obsolete Elizabethan quips and jests disappear ; no word is attempted that is for a minute out of keeping with the conditions of the task, which resembles the finest needlework.

Charles Lamb, who took in hand the tragedies, and helped out his sister in *All's Well*, is naturally more daring ; and his handling of *Timon of Athens* is not the least magnificent of his writings.. The prose is full of spacious periods and rushing rhythms, some of which are Lamb's own, and are credited to the supposed teller of the story ; who, by virtue of his indignant sympathy with Timon, can borrow as his own many of the words given by Shakespeare to Timon himself ; so that the whole is truly a compounding of the genius of Lamb and of Shakespeare.

For *the swallow follows not summer more willingly* than men of these dispositions follow the good fortunes of the great, *nor more willingly leaves winter* than these shrink from the first appearance of a reverse ; *such summer-birds are men.* But now with *music* and state the banquet of smoking dishes was served up ; and when the guests had a little done admiring whence the bankrupt Timon could find means to furnish so costly a *feast*, some doubting whether the scene which they saw were real, as scarce trusting their eyes ; at a signal given, *the dishes were uncovered*, and Timon's drift appeared ; instead of those varieties and far-fetched dainties which they expected, that Timon's epicurean table in past times had so liberally presented, now appeared under the covers of these dishes a preparation more suitable to Timon's poverty, nothing but a little *smoke and luke-warm water*, fit *feast* for this *knot of mouth-friends*, whose professions were indeed smoke, and their hearts lukewarm and slippery as the water, with which Timon welcomed his astonished guests, bidding them, ' *Uncover, dogs, and lap.*'

The words here in italics are in the original, the rest is Lamb's ; and few ignorant of the play could guess the seam between the two authors. The method is much the same in the other four tragedies selected—*Othello, Hamlet, Macbeth, Lear.* The histories, English and Roman, are all omitted, but of the comedies and tragi-comedies only *Love's Labour's Lost* and *The Merry Wives.*

In *The Adventures of Ulysses* the task was again to disentangle, and also to create, Elizabethan English ; for Lamb, he tells us, worked upon Chapman's *Odyssey*, not on Homer. There was little need here to pick his steps among grievous incidents ; he had only to condense and shape the tale into perspective, and, above all, to get behind the rich conceits of Chapman to the simplicity of Homer, whom he seems not to have used in Greek. But though he thus purges Chapman, he does not dismiss him wholly, but works upon him, and weaves in many a phrase and rhythm of that noble original ; feeling free also, since after all Chapman is *not* the original, to deepen the romantic element, and colour the fairy tale much as he will, so he preserves keeping in the English. And to do this, Lamb weaves in a turn here and there from Milton, from the Bible, and even from Fénelon, whose *Télémaque* he professes to be continuing. The result is something wonderfully shot and coloured, more inventive and original even than *Tales from Shakespear*, and yet leaving on us no feeling of forced archaism. The long-linked cadences of the prose, indeed, give a truer sense of the onset of Homer than Chapman's decasyllabic couplets :

Yet they singly bestirred themselves like men, and defended themselves against that great host, and through tables, shields, and all, right through the arrows of Ulysses clove, and the irresistible lances of Telemachus ; and many lay dead, and all had wounds, and Minerva in the likeness of a bird sate upon the beam which went across the hall, clapping her wings with a fearful noise, and sometimes the great bird would fly among them, cuffing at the swords and at the lances, and up and down the hall would go, beating her wings, and troubling everything, that it was frightful to behold, and it frayed the blood from the cheeks of those heaven-hated suitors.

This is Homer much foreshortened ; but a third delightful thing, neither Homer himself nor Homer seen through the eyes of Chapman, is the result, for a new poet is at work on the old story—a romantic poet, whose instrument is prose. *The Adventures of Ulysses* is little enough known, considering its beauty and the gusto of the telling.

IV

The little volume of *Poetry for Children*, 'by the author of *Mrs. Leicester's School*' (1809), is essentially Mary Lamb's book, though a few contributions are certainly known, and some few more may be guessed from their 'stronger savour,' to be from the hand of Charles. *Chusing a Name* and *The Three Friends* are amongst those ascertained to be his; and Mr. Swinburne's assignment to him of *Love, Death and Reputation*, which is founded on a passage in Webster, may be accepted with some confidence. The first two, at any rate, would almost sign themselves by their octosyllabics, which are of the stamp that Lamb had learnt from Wither, and by their tender tone of rumination. But the note of Mary Lamb is harder to define ; it is almost too nice to catch, like that of some shy bird in the hedgerow ; but nothing of its kind can be truer, or more unlike that of common invented nursery poetry. Most of her verses are, rightly, upon the tiniest things—little fables, counsels, anecdotes—homespun but perfectly wrought, and full of great good sense without flatness. The emphasis of brief quotation is almost enough to hurt them. No creaking, stiff-jointed, grown-up condescension is there ; but their effortless perception of the infantine point of view is without any intolerable pretence that the writer is herself a child, or anything but a kind and sagacious maiden aunt, writing to please and to show the virtue of kindness. This piece of 'taskwork,' as the Lambs called it, was, like most of their works for the young, published by Mrs. Godwin, and was soon submerged, leaving hardly a trace until it was rediscovered in 1877. Its purpose excluded full use of the gift that Mary Lamb had already shown for serious verse. *The Dialogue between a Mother and a Child*,[1] her most perfect production, is written not for a child but for a mother. In sureness of feeling, balance of temper, absence of excess, Mary Lamb, despite her recurrent infirmity, may well seem the more unvarying of the two partners, and (to be frank) the saner ; for in all her writing there is no touch of the over-strain of humour or pathos, that occasionally alters, though it cannot dominate, the fundamentally healthy and natural spirit of her brother. The fourteen lines of this *Dialogue*, in which the child refuses to be comforted by a second father, are worth many pompous tragedies—*Bertrams* and *Fazios*.

Mrs. Leicester's School, or the History of Several Young Ladies, Related by Themselves, has the quality and air of the

Dialogue rather than that of *Poetry for Children*. The tale
of *Elinor Forester*, indeed, is on a similar subject, but has a
different issue; for the good stepmother wins the heart of the
orphan after all, when she has got the impatient misunder-
standing father out of the way. Another tale of childish
grief consoled is *Elizabeth Villiers*, in which the little girl learns
her letters by studying her mother's gravestone. *Ann Withers*
is more of the conventional mint; Ann is a changeling, and
has to lose her wealth and station, because by her act the true
daughter is discovered; and Ann has to get over the wicked
feelings which (not unnaturally) ensue. But all Mary Lamb's
tales are written, and written nobly, from the heart; accurately
too, yet with no touch of hardness; they are like the best
things in *David Copperfield*, without the fun. Charles Lamb
had his share in this volume, and his *Susan Yates*, relating
the sensations of a little girl when she first goes to church, has
the same kind of grace as the personal remembrances in *Elia*.
The history of *Arabella Hardy*, who is brought home alone
on a ship from Jamaica, and becomes the sailors' favourite,
and loses her good friend Mr. Atkinson on the voyage, has a
different sort of charm, and explores a vein of pathos that
might have seemed foreign to the author. The retrospective
method natural to both brother and sister is brilliantly shown
in Mary Lamb's *Margaret Green*, which tells of the bewilderment
and alarms of a child turned loose in a library and perusing a
work called *Mahometism Explained*, which she literally believes
—why not?—until Mahomet is explained away by the elders.

The greenwood 'tragical-comical-pastoral' play of Lamb's
youth, *John Woodvil* (originally called *Pride's Cure*), which
was studiously revised, for all that it reads like a single spurt
of swift and happy invention, has a mere show of a story, on
which we must not bear too hard. The sudden death by
heartbreak of the old parliamentarian outlaw Woodvil, on
the pure unproven supposition that his son John has betrayed
him—the betrayal being indeed a fact, but caused by culpable
drunken inadvertence and not by treachery—becomes startling
enough in so tough a veteran and Protestant. It leads however to the scene, by far the most moving in the play, of
grave but gradually more joyous dialogue, in which John
Woodvil is brought back to a saner remorse, and rewarded
with a hardly merited happiness, by the sweet pleadings of
Margaret. The time is that of the Restoration, but the diction
is that of Elizabethan high serious comedy and roystering
farce—a division to which Lamb's verse and prose severally

correspond. The verse, both in its more even and in its richer passages (such as the noble description by Simon Lovel of the forest life in Sherwood), for a moment makes us forget that it is an imitation, and almost deceives us as it deceived Godwin—a poor judge doubtless, who hunted in the old playwrights to find Simon Lovel's speech. Beside this easy and sustained piece of mimicry, the work of Darley, Procter, and most of their company sounds made up. Neither here nor in the prose scenes did Lamb follow any dramatist in particular, though the influence of Shakespeare's open-air comedies is apparent. And even of the prose he makes something not only pleasant but acceptable and credible, thus escaping the fatal and frigid effect that commonly attends the fabricating of Jacobean jokes, too often to modern ear only jokes perforce. The same sufficiency of diction is found in the sedater verse comedy called *The Wife's Trial* (1827), founded on Crabbe's tale, *The Confidant* (1812). Indeed, we can here measure the distance between the later writing of the old school—a mixture of homespun and rhetoric—and that of the younger romancer, newly inspired by things old. The contrast is felt in the apologue by means of which the now enlightened husband, in his wife's presence, rids himself and her of their blackmailing tormentor. This is Crabbe :

> Then came augmenting woes, and fancy strong
> Drew forms of suffering, a tormenting throng ;
> He felt degraded, and the struggling mind
> Dared not be free, and could not be resign'd ;
> And all his pains and fervent prayers obtain'd
> Was truce from insult, while the fears remain'd.

And this is Lamb :

> The Secret, like a night-hag, rid his sleeps,
> And took the youthful pleasures from his days,
> And chased the youthful smoothness from his brow,
> That from a rose-cheek'd boy he waned and waned
> To a pale skeleton of what he was ;
> And would have died, but for one lucky chance.

The extravaganza called *Mr. H——* needs no mention save as a pleasant example of Lamb's readiness to blow up a mere soap-bubble of a joke, and clap at its painted show, and when it is pricked to death, to clap still harder. Nothing in *Mr. H——* is equal to the scene of Lamb relishing its damnation by the audience in Drury Lane Theatre. *The Pawnbroker's Daughter*, a little 'curtain-raising' farce never acted, contains a butcher who sentimentalises over Joseph Ritson's *Argument against the Use of Animal Food,* and a gentleman who, having been hanged, cut down, and revived, is too sensitive to the ridicule of his condition.

V

Lamb came late to the essay, when he was thirty-five, and groped about awhile, indeed for the best part of a decade (1811-20), before he was at ease in his own manner ; his earlier pleasantries in this form, such as the paper *On the Inconveniences Resulting from being Hanged* (of which only the title, perhaps, is good), being in truth dismal things. If this had been all, there would have been some colour for Carlyle's phrase, recorded long afterwards, about Lamb's ' ghastly make-believe of humour ' ; a verdict which, when all is said, sometimes comes into our minds even to the last, when the habit of jesting becomes a sheer effort of bravery, in the ebb of inspiration, and is simply, as we have said, Lamb's method —not the worst—of putting a good face upon life. But in these pre-Elian days that genius was, in one field, revealed to the full. Lamb was a critic before he was an essayist, and he is a greater critic than essayist, though his criticism, it is true, penetrates and informs his essays as it does his letters. The *Specimens,* with their imperishable comments, appeared in 1808 ; the paper on *The Tragedies of Shakespeare,* and that *On the Genius and Character of Hogarth,* in 1811. To compare these with the articles *On the Melancholy of Tailors, Edax on Appetite* (the forerunner of the popular but wearisome *Roast Pig*), of the same year, is to breathe again.

Lamb did not weary his friends with his troubles and reminiscences ; but many of them he has confided to the world, and to the world only. Like the poets of the time, he is under the necessity of making such confidences. We know as much of him from his own lips as of Wordsworth and Byron from theirs. They must record their hidden histories at any cost, and in the impulse to do this, which came down from Rousseau, Lamb, who is so unlike Rousseau in all other ways, fully participates. We have seen that such a habit is one of the deeper as well as the more palpable marks of the new literature. Thus the *Essays of Elia,* like Lamb's poems, are largely pieces of autobiography, determined as to their scale and haphazard mode of issue by the conditions of periodical writing.

It is, I think, probably unique for a man who had all his life meant to be a writer not to find himself until he was forty-five, and then to do so with material fetched from his teens.

These words (of an editor [1] whose service to Lamb's name cannot become antiquated) hit the mark. For five-and-twenty years the stuff of *Mackery End,* and *The South-Sea House,* and *The Old Benchers of the Inner Temple,* and *Barbara S——,* had been stored in memory against the hour of use, and rediscovered as if by chance. They and their companions are, in essence, *poems*; in so far, that is, as they are not the work of the 'understanding,' that mere arguing and expounding faculty against which Coleridge planned so many treatises, nor yet a mere Defoe-like reporting of the actual, hard and gritty in its vividness; but proceed from the brooding fancy, which softens the lines of the past, and purges its dross, mysteriously, without blurring or falsification of the truth. We have remarked on a similar hoarding of experiences in the writer of the Waverley Novels. If time bring any wisdom to a man, it is chiefly through this rejecting, adjusting, proportioning process, which continues for years below the levels of deliberate reflection. Something, however, may be done to encourage its workings. Lamb had not stifled or adulterated his memories, but cherished them as in a casket, the mere unsealing of which spreads a sense around of lavender and preservative balsams. Like *David Copperfield,* the *Essays of Elia* are a good example of what is meant by purity in literature; in none of those vulgar senses of the phrase, made current by casuists or confessors, by pedagogues or philistines; but understood as a kind of virtue of the whole nature, made possible by a long and delicate life of the intellect, and flowering only in due season.

Such writers are also the true historians. Persons, places, customs, humours, atmospheres, which the official historian of manners rattles past unregardingly, they rescue from utter darkness. They idealise these things, so as to save their essential truth. It is the sense of humour that steers them safe among the shallows of mere self-pity and false pathos. This is a faculty near allied to taste; and the humour of Lamb, at any rate, consists in this operation of his nice taste upon his recollections; so that in these papers he is as much a critic, in the due sense of the word, as when he speaks of Hogarth or Shakespeare. Such an instinctive rightness of taste gives the charm of charity to his descriptions; for his humour is not, like Hazlitt's, edged with too fierce a sense of what the unconscious sitter for his portrait is *not*. Lamb does not *expose* Samuel Salt or Mrs. Battle, but sees something harmless and piquant in them of which neither they nor the bystanders were aware, and he beckons the reader to share in the pleasure of this incongruity.

Sometimes ' Elia ' approaches the common forms of the *Spectator* essay, as in *The Wedding* or in *Popular Fallacies* ; and at other times he frankly goes back to the old character portrait, or string of recounted qualities with a string of ' He's,' which is the style of the natural man breathlessly describing an acquaintance. The account of the ' late Elia ' is of this sort, and so is the paper called *The Convalescent*.

He changes *sides* oftener than a politician. Now he lies full-length, then half-length, obliquely, transversely, head and feet quite across the bed ; and none accuses him of tergiversation. Within the four curtains he is absolute. They are his Mare Clausum. How sickness enlarges the dimensions of a man's self to himself ! he is his own exclusive object. . . . He has nothing to think of but how to get well.

The enumeration, the amplification, the turning over and over of the idea, the Latin conceit—it all might come out of Earle or Butler. And it is not a manner put on ; it is the writer's own habit of thought, or has become second nature. He might be some old humorous physician, a friend of Sir Thomas Browne, watching the patient, and talking in *staccato*, sonorous epigram. Lamb's relish in placing long learned words at the right spot in the sentence is extraordinary. Usually, however, he does not so fully submit himself to literary models, but embroiders and modulates quite in his own way, and can be mistaken for no one else. The regular staple of his English is plain eighteenth century, with an antique turn or two thrown in ; otherwise his language is of no particular period. But his habit of thought, underneath this level style, is that of an earlier time : the habit of stopping himself, whenever a fancy occurs that will bear working out and pirouetting round, in order thus to prolong and taste it. The ' Superannuated Man ' speaks of his release from the office :

I was in the condition of a prisoner in the old Bastile, suddenly let loose after a forty years' confinement. I could scarce trust myself with myself. It was like passing out of Time into Eternity—for it is a sort of Eternity for a man to have his Time all to himself. It seemed to me that I had more time on my hands than I could ever manage. From a poor man, poor in Time, I was suddenly lifted up into a vast revenue; I could see no end of my possessions; I wanted some steward, or judicious bailiff, to manage my estates in Time for me.

And Lamb goes on for a page dallying with the image of Time, and at last drops into that kind of playful logic, or mathematics, of the fancy which he had learnt, perhaps, from the *Religio Medici* ; and his words have a faint flavour of such old-fashioned musings :

The remnant of my poor days, whether long or short, is at least multiplied for me threefold. My ten next years, if I stretch so far, will be as long as any preceding thirty. 'Tis a fair rule-of-three sum.

VI

Lamb is so often called one of the Elizabethans that we forget how much better his prose can be, how much more in compass and manageable, than most of theirs—speaking, that is, of the authors who at all correspond to him, and not of the Hookers and Bacons who fly at high speculative matters. In other words, he has made his profit by the ages that come between, and especially by Dryden and the colloquial easy writers following in his train. Few of Dryden's predecessors, except Shakespeare, could talk naturally or easily in prose. They are apt either to trip entangled in the purple train of their long sentences, or to deal in curt and teasing short phrases without bearable transitions. There is current on this matter a good deal of antiquarian idolatry, in which Lamb, no doubt, as one of the great rediscoverers, himself genially shared. But what he has gained from the long intervening discipline of prose, is best seen from the lightness and rightness of his more imaginative papers, which are ' prose poetry ' in the lawful sense of the term. For sheer purity of immortal plain English, without anything to chill or let down the spirits, it would be hard to find anything of the same length in Renaissance times like *Dream-Children*. It is in this sense, and this only, that we can talk of any art as ' progressing ' ;—that is, when some craftsman arises, once in centuries, who can thus discern, and blend in use, the powers and accomplishment of different ages past. General progress there is none, nor can be, for there is no entail of genius. This purity and plainness of diction, as in *The Child Angel*, can go well with much poetic splendour and exaltation :

And it could not taste of death, by reason of its adoption into immortal palaces ; but it was to know weakness, and reliance, and the shadow of human imbecility ; and it went with a lame gait ; but in its goings it exceeded all mortal children in grace and swiftness. Then pity first sprang up in angelic bosoms ; and yearnings (like the human) touched them at the sight of the immortal lame one.

Elsewhere in this essay Lamb falls back upon a more elaborate architecture for the sentence ; but the whole is a noble example of the English *poème*, a species of which De Quincey and Landor are the other great masters. The pathetic speech of those writers who have had and lost children of their own can be just as high-inspired as Lamb's, but is different ; Lamb speaks of children as if they were 'things 'too dear for his possessing,' and the unbodied wraiths of those that might have been his float before him irremediably. The bare imagination of them, long-cherished, is to be counted amongst the personal memories, which formed, as we have seen, so precious a part of his artistic material.

At other times, when Lamb is not plain at all, but poetic in the great sumptuous style—and that without being in the least ' Elizabethan '—he reminds us once more of Keats ; in his thirsty ardour of appreciation, and in his power of re-creating through his own art the thing that he loves. This is best seen when he is criticising painting or poetry. Some of the fine things we read in Keats's letters about Milton, ' devoting himself rather to the ardours than the pleasures of song, solacing himself at intervals with cups of old wine,' might have been written by Lamb ; or rather they may be taken as uttered by the common voice of the age of Hazlitt and De Quincey— the age that ' solaced ' itself in such ways after the long fast, or *Ramadan*, of the ' age of prose.' Indeed, the onset of the new poetic spirit may itself well be figured in one of those images in which Lamb, drawing inspiration from the same picture as Keats himself, the *Bacchus and Ariadne* of Titian, finds words and rhythms as rich in their way as any in the great chorus of *Endymion* :

Precipitous, with his reeling Satyr rout about him, re-peopling and re-illuming suddenly the waste places, drunk with a new fury beyond the grape, Bacchus, born in fire, fire-like flings himself at the Cretan.

This affinity of the two artists need not be exaggerated ; but they seem to meet at one or two such fiery points, although Lamb's gift for analysis (born of his intuitions, ever faithful to them, and never going off either into bare abstraction or into Coleridgian first principles) takes him into a different field from that of the poet. Thus, whether he is talking of life or of art, his prose becomes the instrument of an emotion that never outstrips the accompanying brainwork. With Hazlitt, for all his cordial and passionate relish, the intellectual element is paramount, going wrong, when it does go wrong, through some shortcoming in sheer feeling.

With all his profound, instinctive sense for high or rare diction, and his power of appropriating it, so that it becomes part of his natural speech, and is most fully at his command in criticism, when he is speaking of Shakespeare or Webster in a tongue learnt from themselves ; Lamb is still not one of those critics who approach a work of art primarily through its style, and make their appraisal accordingly, disjoining, by an act of abstraction, the body from the soul, as some lovers use to do ; nor does he say much about beauty, and rhythm, and expression in themselves, but leaves that sphere to Coleridge. These things, rather, lead him through his hardly fallible taste up to what he admires ; but, when he has reached it, he is most concerned with its appeal to life and humanity, and to the ' moral sense ' ; interpreting that phrase, as he does in his Notes to his *Specimens*, to cover the whole imagined world— our own world, as the angels and Intelligences see it—of tragic stress or comic imbroglio, of conflicting passions, and of affections at full stretch. Lamb's love for the drama, or for fiction of the manlier type, means that he cared above all for *situation*, for scenes of a noble tension, represented in that imagined world ; just as, on another side of his brain, he cared for *wit*, in the old sense of the term, or the sudden verbal revelation, whether truly creative or merely fanciful, of curious remote lights upon human nature ; while he cared, perhaps, least of all for song like Shelley's, seemingly alien from the earth and its complexities. He loved literature and art that is ' immersed in matter,' and no one has spoken better of the beauties, as well as of the close-packed expressiveness, of Hogarth, who, indeed, was to him a maker of books more than of pictures : ' his prints we *read* ' ; so he says, in his essay on Hogarth's genius. No one, indeed, tasted fine fancies more than Lamb, and a phrase of Fuller or Wither would haunt him for days, and he would suck out and distil its essence into some phrase of his own bearing the same stamp. Hazlitt's zest and connoisseurship are equally keen, but he has something less than Lamb's re-creative power, and he identifies himself less with the thing he loves, though he loves it as much. He communicates his own enjoyment, and makes us a defiant present of it, as *his* ; but in Lamb the old poet speaks again, as though his spirit were but taking up a new instrument and breathing through it. We could not do without either of these minds. Lamb's temper is the same when he reviews *The Excursion* and *Lamia*, and in his essay on *Some Sonnets of Sir Philip Sydney*.

Luckily, Lamb did not mind if pedants read coldly what he said in the heat of his liking ; he wished to be listened to in the evening, and not in the judicial hours of the day. His saying on Ford is simply a thing thrown out in talk, by one of Ford's first discoverers. ' The first order of poets '! Hazlitt's judgment is here acute if harsh ; he sees the overstrain of the fantasy that defeats itself, in the scene of Calantha's dancing ; and he is harder on *'Tis Pity She 's a Whore*. Lamb's praise of this play is connected, certainly, not only with his love of sheer poetry, but with the strain in him that led to his defence of the Restoration drama. It is all an imagined world, a dance of creatures of the brain, whose wit, or whose wickedness, is only real in such a kingdom of the mind and has no relation to the solid world, the law-courts, and the peace of families. This is a mood, and a precious one ; and probably it is in this way that both the tragedy in question, and the school of comedy that Collier denounced, should be *played* ;—as something almost symbolic, a passionate dance-figure, or an arabesque of words and repartees. Once we step out of that region, the inhumanity of the thing becomes too apparent ; and an historian like Macaulay, with his blunt, vivid realisation of the facts, and his accompanying poverty in the faculty of fancy and make-believe, is within his rights in his protest : the mood is different.

Lamb's protest against acting Shakespeare is, on the other hand, well justified. That Shakespeare meant his plays to be acted, and acted in them himself, or that the acted drama is the greatest of the arts, is after all neither here nor there. There is an essence of the drama which is only tasted by silent reading, and is destroyed by even the greatest of actors. The actor tells us much we did not know, but he can never dream in our stead ; and the essence of Shakespeare's, or, we may add, Marlowe's poetry is to set up reverie unconnected with its actual subject. This power is only interrupted, not heightened, by presentation to the eye. To see and hear the play is a different pleasure,—perhaps a lesser one which inter-feres with the greater. Lamb's objection to the stage is not unlike Shakespeare's own sense of its inadequacy, expressed in the Chorus to *Henry the Fifth*. If we could imagine a similar apology prefaced to *King Lear* or *Othello*, it would seem natural enough, and it would not have been better said in verse than Lamb has said his apparent paradox in prose. Comedy, which Lamb feels to be a fabricated world, is not in the same position ; he hardly thinks of it apart from his affection for particular actors, for Munden or Elliston or Miss Kelly, who are the final cause of comedy. In his essay *On Stage Illusion*, this rightful and comparative unreality of the comic scene is brought home in another way, when he speaks of the kind of unconscious understanding, improper in tragedy, between the player and the audience, to whom he is ever speaking aside ; bearing on his points, and sharpening the sense of a common make-believe. In the letter of Coleridge [1] on the same subject, metaphysically treated, the difference and likeness of mind between the two friends are admirably seen. Together with Hazlitt, their fellow, they enlarged the whole horizon of English criticism.

CHAPTER XXIV

WILLIAM HAZLITT

I. Hazlitt's late discovery of his powers. Long prefatory stage (1805-15) of philosophical essays, political tracts, and journeyman-work. 1815-21 : the four series of literary lectures ; also *The Round Table, Table Talk, Letter to Gifford.* 1825-28 : *Liber Amoris, Characteristics,* papers on fine art, *Journey in France and Italy, Spirit of the Age, Plain Speaker.* 1828-30 : *Conversations of Northcote, Life of Napoleon.* Course of Hazlitt's political opinions.

II. His chosen form, the periodical essay, article, or review. Descent from the classical essayists. The maxim the integer of his style. Models : the Character-Writers ; the Johnsonian ' contrast ' ; examples. Habit of ' amplification.'

III. Love of quotations ; their felicity. Descriptive writing ; ruminative and fanciful essays ; appreciations of fine art and drama.

IV. Hazlitt and his troubles ; analogy with Rousseau. The habit of confession once more. *Liber Amoris.*

V. Literary criticism : width of scope. Hazlitt's principle as a critic. View of ' genius and taste.' Difference of his attitude from ' æsthetic ' enjoyment, as later understood. Indifference to ' scholarship.'

VI. Hazlitt on Shakespeare, on Elizabethan literature, on the poets and comic writers. Judgments on contemporaries : *Spirit of the Age.* Treatment of Burke, Coleridge, Bentham, etc. Skill in portraiture.

I

AN essayist and critic, like a novelist, we expect to be slow in the making. Life and manners cannot be taken in readily ; suffering must be not only undergone but understood before it is expressed ; books and art must speak to a mind prepared ; and a prose style should be seasoned like a violin. William Hazlitt [1] (1778-1830), like Bacon and Addison, is an example of this gradual growth ; up to the age of twenty-nine he wrote much, but seldom very well, busying himself with matters of the pure intellect which were a good enough discipline and stayed his hunger for utterance. The results are rather dull, and seldom declare his genius, though they illuminate the course of his opinions. In 1798 he was awakened by the voice of Coleridge discoursing. ' The light of his genius,' he says in *My First Acquaintance with Poets,* ' shone into my soul, like the sun's rays glittering in the puddles of the road.' Coleridge released his mind from the mechanical philosophy, but drew him for a time from his true path as a writer. One result of this influence was the closely argued, clayey treatise *On the Principles of Human Action*, not published till 1805. Hazlitt also, during this period of formation, cleverly decocted Tucker's lengthy *Light of Nature Pursued* ; began political pamphleteering with his *Free Thoughts on Public Affairs* (1806) ; tilted against Sterling ('Vetus') of the *Times* ; wrote a 'reply' to Malthus ; compiled *The Eloquence of the British Senate*, prefixing 'characters' of Walpole, Mansfield, and others, by no means formal, which give us a first relish of his quality ; made an English grammar ; finished Holcroft's *Memoirs* ; and began to notice plays and actors in the *Morning Chronicle* and the English novelists in the *Edinburgh Review*, coming thus ever nearer to his true bent. By 1815 he is visibly finding it, though little as yet shows his passionate idiosyncrasy of style. Long before, in 1802, he had begun copying pictures in the Louvre, and qualifying for an art critic. His uncongenial first marriage (1808) deepened his native streak of bitterness; but meanwhile he had found his friends. The Lambs saw him at Winterslow, by Salisbury Plain, the lonely workshop where many of his best essays were written.

During the next seven years (1815-22) Hazlitt entered into his kingdom. He perfected his two favourite and kindred forms of utterance, the essay and the lecture. Now came his four great series of discourses, *The Characters of Shakespeare's Plays* (printed in 1817), *The English Poets* (1818), *The English Comic Writers* (1819), and *The Dramatic Literature of the Age of Elizabeth* (1820). These have the vagrancy of the spoken word, but also its freshness ; and there had been no such body of catholic and vital comment upon English literature since the prefaces of Dryden. Hazlitt also produced his first two bundles of essays, *The Round Table* (1817) and *Table Talk* (1821-22) ; and between them came his *Letter to William Gifford*, an inky acrid retort of cuttlefish to cuttlefish, as well as the *View of the English Stage*, a collection of periodical articles. This is Hazlitt's golden hour. Swiftly, fiercely, delightedly, he overtakes the arrears of his growth as an artist ; becomes a critic of the greater order, and a master of the essay ; is no longer engrossed by hackwork, or by politics and ethics, which, however dear to him, recede to the outer parts or 'suburbs of his mind.' Such topics, no doubt, often distract him, and in spare moments he throws off many tracts and letters, which are gathered up in his *Political Essays* (1819). If Hazlitt is torn by his temper, by domestic jars, and by grievous public affairs, he has not much time to feel his unhappiness, and he has now the power to express it. Life excites him ; it is a play of which he is himself a part. It takes his breath away, like surf-bathing, but it takes him out of himself, so that he cannot say whether it gives more pain or pleasure. Such is the true temper of passionate youth. Afterwards he looks back on this time covetously, and lives much on his memories. ' Our existence,' he says, ' is a tissue of passion, and successive years only present us with fainter and fainter copies of the first proof-impressions.' Of those impressions, some of the sharpest are given by high literature, which is a kind of burning-glass for the more ardent rays of life ; and the pleasures of books, thus understood, last longer, and are more surely renewable, than most others. Thus Hazlitt's best later writing has the note of intense retrospection. And this temper reacts on his opinions. Such an intense, *rodent* mind as his was bound, upon looking into itself, to revolt against the cruder ' association-theory ' and its consequences. No such theory could account for the subtle shining filaments that bind youth to age, and restore it, when the glory seems to have departed, by a perfume, or a line of Milton, or the figures on a sundial. Of such associations Hazlitt is the prose poet. In the same way, his study of life and the drama makes havoc of the ugly egoistic ethics formulated by the school of Helvétius. In facing such questions he is not German or transcendental, nor again Gallic and doctrinal. He is here, as ever, English in mental texture, and his oft-repeated plea for the reality of ' disinterested action ' is moulded on his study of Butler's *Sermons* ; nor could the student of *King Lear* and of *The Old Law* have concluded otherwise.

The next five years (1823-28) began ill for Hazlitt. He chose, in *Liber Amoris* (1823), to publish the history of his thwarted and half-insane love-affair with Sarah Walker ; and during its progress he and his wife arranged their divorce. But his mind was thus freed ; the same year saw his composed and impersonal garland of maxims, called *Characteristics*. He remarried, and his *Notes of a Journey through France and Italy* (1826) were written during his brief companionship with the second Mrs. Hazlitt. They contain some of his best writing upon the fine arts ; and, together with Haydon, he contributed essays on painting to the *Encyclopædia Britannica*. He wrote *Sketches of the Principal Picture Galleries in England* (1824), and other such essays were published after his death. Like many, he found a new life in the study of pictures, could forget himself in their presence, and preferred their society to that of men. He also went on tirelessly with his essays: *The Plain Speaker* (1826) is the last collection printed in his lifetime, but some of the best were issued afterwards by his son under the titles of *Winterslow* and *Sketches and Essays*. *The Spirit of the Age* (1825) shows a recovery of all Hazlitt's wit, zest, pertinence, and lively prejudice. As in a 'steel glass,' if never without a twist, the features of twenty-five of his eminent contemporaries are there mirrored. His last two years were given over to compiling his long and unlucky *Life of Napoleon*; he also produced his *Conversations of James Northcote*, the painter. He died, like Shakespeare, at fifty-two. We need dare no other comparison; but Hazlitt also had lived much; his 'heart beat hard,' and his 'brain, high-blooded, ticked '—now a century since.

Hazlitt's political views and prejudices colour his writing angrily, and generously too. He ran an odd Ishmaelitish course. Brought up in the Unitarian and Radical camp, he was a precocious fighter. At thirteen he wrote to a newspaper to protest against the mob-violence done to Priestley, and was soon pondering an improved Benthamite plan of 'civil and criminal legislation.' Already his creed had taken its complexion. He was, perhaps, the last important Englishman of letters who 'started in life with the French Revolution,' [1] and never turned his back on it. Liberty, brotherhood, and natural rights are on his lips to the last. His shrewd rabid satires on rank and fashion, his hatred of almost all Tories, and of the Roman and the English churches, have the same origin. But Hazlitt in some ways, if a Jacobin, is an escaped Jacobin. He becomes shy of abstract programmes and doctrines, and of reformers who seem to wear blinkers. His witty though not unkindly treatment of Godwin and Owen [2] separates him from all their following. Bentham's tenets strike him as too grotesquely simple to apply to human nature, and he did not perceive Bentham's real influence. Often his ruling passion seems less a love of liberty than a hatred of all autocrats except Napoleon. He lives in a frenzy of reaction against the reaction. The Holy Alliance has blotted out the sun in heaven. The leading writers on the other side, from Burke to Southey, are as hateful as Pitt and his followers, or as the Duke of Wellington. Like Byron and Shelley, Hazlitt extended this feeling to the whole movement of reaction in Europe; but instead of hymns and satires, he wrote semi-insane prose tirades. On this creed he managed to engraft his worship of Napoleon, the crusher of the kings who crushed the peoples. Astonishing gusts of political fury sweep over his page amidst the most innocent literary criticism. Yet, on the whole, this violent interest in affairs gives a body to Hazlitt's thought, and an edge to his writing, that he could never have got from a diet of pure poetry and wit. The advantage is not all on the side of Lamb, so much his superior in harmony of soul, who ' damned the age ' and ' wrote for antiquity.'

II

Hazlitt lived by making articles, like De Quincey and Leigh Hunt and the young Carlyle. In the essay form, none of them wrote so much that wears so well. He is the essayist, as Shelley is the lyrist, *par excellence*. He has left more than a hundred compositions of this sort, and that apart from his lectures ; it is doubtful if Addison has left so many that can be read with pleasure as Hazlitt. No one approaches him in the kind of work that allies him with Fielding or Borrow, such as *The Fight* or *John Cavanagh the Fives-Player*. In the splendours and exaltations of elaborate prose, and in finesse of style, others of his tribe excel him ; but he bears them all down if range, and mass, and vitality are reckoned together. He was brought up on the eighteenth-century essay, of which the big quarterly review-notice is a scion. The essence of a paper by Steele or Goldsmith was to take a single text, or theme, of a sort neither too commonplace nor too remote, and work it out on a moderate scale. Hazlitt is much lengthier, but he often begins in the same way. His discourse buds out of an aphorism ; and he will face the hazard of a dull-sounding topic. He must have been the last good writer who sat down to pen a sheet on Envy, or Fame, or Depth and Superficiality. The tendency of such an essay is to fall into separate atoms of crystal. In his *Characteristics*, where he not immodestly challenges the ghost of La Rochefoucauld, he shows the integer of his style in all its bareness. The book is a series of detached maxims, numbered. Butler, Halifax, and Swift found this kind of thing hard enough to do well. Hazlitt comes not ill out of the trial ; but such imitations of proverbial or popular wisdom are risky. Truth, in English, seldom boils down to a dozen words. But out of Hazlitt's five hundred examples it is easy to pick some that betoken no common mind :

' We as often repent the good we have done as the ill.'—' It has been observed that the proudest people are not nice in love. In fact,

they think they raise the object of their choice above every one else.'
—' It is better to desire than to enjoy—to love than to be loved.'—
' To marry an actress for the admiration she excites on the stage,
is to imitate the man who bought Punch.'—' If the world is good for
nothing else, it is a fine subject for speculation.'

De Quincey reproaches Hazlitt for a certain choppiness in
his mode of composition—so different from his own complex
reticulation and embroidery of his themes. The curt, pellet-
like, uncompounded sentences grate on the ear of that master
of harmonies. It is true that Hazlitt thinks in such sentences.
But Bacon's method of hiving pros and cons in a notebook is
abhorrent to him. He gives, on the contrary, the effect of
living if abrupt speech. Each sentence smoulders like touch-
wood, and the next catches fire by attrition. A little wind of
passion comes, and the whole is ablaze. Such a habit of mind
and style, grafted on the approved manner of the *Tatler* or the
Bee, will explain some of the phenomena of Hazlitt's writing.

He does not think much of his own work, this late and bold
survivor of the classical age, with his new rebel temper burst-
ing through the ancient moulds. He is essentially modest
about his handicraft, though his modesty is dissembled by
pride and emphasis. He feels himself the inferior of the Indian
jugglers who can keep four brass balls in the air at once ; he
envies their professional skill :

What abortions are these Essays! What errors, what ill-pieced
transitions, what crooked reasons, what lame conclusions ! How
little is made out, and that little how ill ! Yet they are the best I
can do. I endeavour to recollect all I have ever observed or thought
upon a subject, and to express it as nearly as I can. Instead of
writing on four subjects at a time, it is as much as I can manage to
keep the thread of one discourse clear and unentangled.

Such self-distrust is often rewarded and refuted in the issue.
Hazlitt is in the ranks of the classic English writers whom he
knows so well. He has read Bacon, and Dryden, and Earle,
and Addison, and Swift, and has got something from most of
them ; for one thing, his manly strength and remarkably un-
defiled purity of diction; which cannot well be described, for it
is not strange or mannered, and for this reason defies parody.
It is good to go to school to him for vocabulary and idiom ; the
great distillers of language, the Elizabethans re-incarnate, like
Charles Lamb, may produce something more rare and wonderful,
but they are not such good models. Hazlitt simply uses right
English, and the only way to profit by him is to do the same.

Certain of his habits of speech, or rather of method, it is easy to notice. He has his favourite overture, which is of a traditional kind. Like Bacon, he is fond of starting with an epigram, of ringing down a solid gold coin upon the marble, to arrest or startle us ; and this he does because he knows it will make us go on :

'No young man believes he shall ever die.'—'Life is the art of being well deceived.'—'Food, warmth, sleep, and a book ; these are all I at present ask; the Ultima Thule of my wandering desires.' —'People have about as substantial an idea of Cobbett as they have of Cribb. His blows are as hard, and he himself is as impenetrable.' —'Footmen are no part of Christianity.'

Hazlitt sees to it that he does not lose the advantage which these openings afford. As he proceeds, his phrases sometimes fall, especially in his early essays, into the patterns set by the old Character-books, and practised by Butler and Steele and many others. Save in the best hands, this is the most monotonous and nauseating form in the world. It is a catalogue of traits and tricks ; the mere raw material for the dramatist or analyst. The order of the sentences is accidental or indifferent, and their syntax of the baldest. When the Character is taken up by a master like Clarendon, it acquires shading, and variety, and life ; but then it loses, while so justifying, its existence. This is said without disesteem to the witty authors of *Microcosmographie*, or of *A Duke of Bucks*, or to Hazlitt himself ; but he broke away from the habit, though pleasant traces of it can be found in abundance in his *Spirit of the Age*. The more formal species, well managed, can be seen in the essay *On the Clerical Character* : [1]

The Priest is not a negative character ; he is something positive and disagreeable. . . . He thinks more of external appearances than of his internal convictions. He is tied down to the prejudices and opinions of the world in every way. The motives of the heart are clogged and censured at the outset, by the fear of idle censure ; his understanding is the slave of established creeds and formulas of faith, etc.

This, however, is but the lusty shout of a Jacobin. But we have also the character of *A Jacobin, A Reformer, A Government-Man*, and the like. Hazlitt does better when he comes to real persons like Fox or Godwin ; and here he often deals in that excellent if old-fashioned form, descended from antiquity, and practised by Johnson, of the Contrast. Feature is paired off against feature, and if the effect is too like that of a row of handcuffs interlinked, it is definite enough. His comparison of Burke and Chatham shows what can be done with this figure, which has gone out of vogue, perhaps because no one can use it so well. Johnson's comparison of Dryden and Pope is in the same fashion, but its antitheses are much more mechanical; Hazlitt's, though formal, sound more like real speech :

> Chatham's eloquence [1] was popular ; his wisdom was altogether plain and practical. Burke's eloquence was that of the poet ; of the man of high and unbounded fancy ; his wisdom was profound and contemplative. Chatham's eloquence was calculated to make men *act* ; Burke's was calculated to make them *think*. Chatham could have roused the fury of a multitude, and wielded their physical energy as he pleased ; Burke's eloquence carried conviction into the mind of the retired and lonely student, opened the recesses of the human heart, and lighted up the face of nature around him. . . . The power which governed Burke's mind was his Imagination ; that which gave its impetus to Chatham's was Will (1807).

Such a style leads at once to the habit, as native to Hazlitt as to Burke himself, though he practises it differently—the habit of dilating. Burke, as we have said before, uses this figure of speech to enrich, and complete, and consolidate an idea ; to forestall objections to it, and give it in the round ; rather than simply to vivify it and drive it home. His best paragraphs are like fair wrought iron ; he turns his thought over on the anvil and hammers it into consummate modelling. Hazlitt's sentences, when he is reasoning, or assaulting, or moralising, fly rather like splinters from the axe ; the blows are clean enough, but they are all much alike. Hear him *On the Pleasure of Hating*,[2] where he takes a neglected half-truth—he has a passion for the racy and unnoticed sides of familiar truth—and persuades himself more and more of it as he kindles, and never has enough of it :

> Pure good soon grows insipid, wants variety and spirit. Pain is a bitter-sweet, which never surfeits. Love turns, with a little indulgence, to indifference or disgust ; hatred alone is immortal. Do we not see this principle at work everywhere ? Animals torment and worry one another without mercy ; children kill flies for sport ; every one reads the accidents and offences in a newspaper, as the cream of the sport ; a whole town runs to be present at a fire, and the spectator by no means exults to see it extinguished. It is better to have it so, but it diminishes the interest ; and our feelings take part with our passions rather than with our understandings.

This is in the good Montaignesque tradition of watching humanity in undress and telling the facts. Hazlitt has not

Montaigne's flexibility, or his wise readiness to return upon
and contradict himself; there is something of a *parti pris*
about it all. Still we feel that he is speaking faithfully as an
onlooker, a connoisseur in spectacles and sensations, and that
he enjoys the burning town like a play. The effect is higher
when he expands upon memories, and sorrows, and his imagination is freely at work. 'It is *we*,' he says somewhere, 'who
are Hamlet'; and a passage in his noble piece *On the Feeling
of Immortality in Youth* bears out the saying. This is an
unequalled utterance of the heartache which stamps Hazlitt
as a tragic and not merely a poetic soul. The same amplifying,
dilating method is here applied to matter which will bear it
well:

As we grow old,[1] our sense of the value of time becomes vivid.
Nothing else, indeed, seems of any consequence. We can never
cease wondering that that which has ever been has ceased to be.
We find many things remain the same: why, then, should there be a
change in us? This adds a convulsive grasp of whatever is, a sense
of a fallacious hollowness in all we see. Instead of the full, pulpy
feeling of youth tasting existence and every object in it, all is flat
and vapid—a whited sepulchre, fair without, but full of ravening
and all uncleanness within. The world is a witch that puts us off
with false shows and appearances. The simplicity of youth, the
confiding expectation, the boundless raptures, are gone; we only
think of getting out of it as well as we can, and without any great
mischance or annoyance.

In all this there is no monotony, but neither is there much
progression. At the end of the essay he is much where he
started; he has been his journey, in a circle, and said all there
is to say. As to the thought, we can but protest that such a
man can never be old. If the memory of youthful zest is so
sharp, however qualified with sour, then youth itself is not
gone. This, at least, is not the state lamented by the poet:

> When we are frozen up within, and quite
> The phantom of ourselves.

The same mode of descant is found in the best of Hazlitt's
meditative papers, like those *On the Fear of Death* and *On Going
a Journey*, though the shade of feeling is different.

III

One feature of Hazlitt's writing, namely his use of quotations,[2]
which are often given at length, and still oftener glimmer like
burnished threads in the texture of his prose, might have been

dangerous but for its naturalness and spontaneity. The passages are frequently familiar, and yet verbally incorrect ; they are given from memory. Yet they do not sound dragged-in or hackneyed, but rather, in Dante's words, *venusti et sapidi*, gracious and racy, because they are as much a part of the writer's mental furniture as his own diction. Quotation forms no small part, we may say, of Hazlitt's relish in life ; literature gives him perhaps the least alloyed element of his happiness, and good words are like a glass of wine to him. This we feel when he describes Coleridge reading ' with a sonorous and musical voice the ballad of *Betty Foy*,' and other things, in the year 1798 :

In the *Thorn*, the *Mad Mother*, and the *Complaint of a Poor* [*sic*] *Indian Woman*, I felt that deeper power and pathos which have been since acknowledged,

> In spite of pride, in erring reason's spite,

as the characteristics of this author ; and the sense of a new style and a new spirit in poetry came over me. It had to me something of the effect that arises from the turning up of the fresh soil, or of the first welcome breath of Spring,

> While yet the trembling year is unconfirmed.

Coleridge and myself walked back to Stowey that evening, and his voice sounded high

> Of Providence, foreknowledge, will, and fate,
> Fix'd fate, free-will, foreknowledge absolute,

as we passed through echoing grove, by fairy stream or waterfall, gleaming in the summer moonlight !

This is what is meant by a new birth, a new date, in literature ; and it was almost worth while having been through the dry years and long dearth of poetry, that such sensations might be possible. The passages cited come into the middle of the sentences, and are not intrusive ; they chequer the prose like Bible phrases well woven into some lofty thanksgiving. Hazlitt draws impartially on all sorts of authors ; Dryden and Pope and the prose comic dramatists provide him with what he wants, as well as the inspired poets.

He goes to work differently when he has something to describe. He revolves less than in his passages of *morale observatrice* or reflection. The incidents carry him on, and he keeps pace with things seen and heard. He steps lightly and athletically, and does not stop and tease language, like the precious writers ; indeed he likes just the scenes that they avoid as carefully as a

cat avoids dashing into fresh water. *The Fight* (between Bill
Neate and ' the Gasman ') will occur to every reader. Byron
and Meredith would have rejoiced to report such a heroic
event ; but Hazlitt's simplicity and keeping, and the perfection of his literary-colloquial English, they might not have
attained. The magazine articles of John Hamilton Reynolds
are nearest in spirit to his. We only wish that Hazlitt had
written oftener on such occurrences, which show us mankind
stripped and in a state of brisk competition. He reflects
rather too inveterately, and runs off into too many ' middle
axioms,' as Bacon called them, on life and conduct. But his
descriptions of pictures, or of play-acting, or of landscape,
or of ' still life ' are equally full of vitality. The *Notes of a
Journey through France and Italy* [1] are motley, pleasant reading ; happily innocent, as he says, ' of history or antiquities
or statistic.' He seems more at home in the Louvre or the
Pitti than even on the road ; or in describing, with a British
bias that he comically disclaims and reveals at every change
of horses, the weaknesses of the French national character.
His praises of our neighbours have the value of reluctance,
and his remarks, in contradiction to the vulgar view, on the
gravity, solidity, and taciturnity of that race are true and
happy. He often shows a bad, John-Bull-on-his-travels disposition, that reminds us of Smollett's :

> The women in Italy (so far as I have seen hitherto) are detestably
> ugly. They are not even dark and swarthy, but a mixture of brown
> and red, coarse, marked with the small-pox, with pug-features,
> awkward, ill-made, fierce, dirty, lazy, neither attempting nor hoping
> to please.

But when he is alone with art or scenery he recovers his
temper. He is not exactly a mystic in the presence of nature,
but he has been touched by the spirit of Wordsworth. Like
Gray and Matthew Arnold, he feels the peace of the Grande
Chartreuse ; it is in contrast with the fierce vexation of his
own fate. ' Life must there seem a noiseless dream ; Death
a near translation to the skies ! ' It is a ' country full of
wild grandeurs and shadowy fears.' The Apennines, and
Parma, and Siena, and Perugia tempt him out of himself,
and some of their beauty gets into his rhythm. This was in
1824-5 ; the voice of Ruskin was to be heard in the following
decades, and has inevitably drowned that of earlier travellers.
But Hazlitt has still the virgin brain, the freshness of sensation that meets us in the diaries of Gray and Beckford,—the

note of the man who is the first to see, or to mark, wonderful
things. These emotions had not yet become obligatory, like
going to church ; and the feeling for natural beauty was still
forcing its way under difficulties into the educated mind.
But Hazlitt is more at home in England, and apprehends many
of her beauties and humours just as well as Cobbett. His
papers on *The Letter-Bell* or on *Merry England* are pieces of
pure enjoyment and rumination, and his genius is at work
untroubled by bad dreams or didactics. In these essays, as
in poetry, there is no argument, and there is nothing concluded,
or which can be contested.

His appreciations of art [1] are not obsolete ; he is one of the
first English critics who reviews actual pictures and statues
and gives his impressions, instead of theorising on the picturesque or on the abstract nature of beauty. His training,
however, as a painter does not seem to help him much ; he
writes more, as the French say, *en amateur*, like a lover—
with the same rich and courageous superlatives of like or
dislike that he applies to books or persons. He revels in Claude
and ' romantic ' painting, and comes back again and again to
Titian ; hates the French mechanical school, but also kicks at
Michael Angelo ! In art he seeks at once for a reading of life,
and to escape from himself ; and to sit in a good gallery is for
him what Jeremy Taylor calls 'a little antepast of heaven ':

Here is the mind's true home. The contemplation of truth and
beauty is the proper object for which we were created, which calls
forth the most intense desires of the mind, and of which it never
tires. . . . There are only three pleasures in life, pure and lasting,
and all derived from inanimate things—books, pictures, and the face
of nature.

Hazlitt does not go to the Dulwich Collection, or to ' Mr. Anger-
stein's,' simply to form a professional judgment. He sees
the treasures of Hampton Court, or Blenheim, or Oxford,
and these places themselves get into the background of the
pictures he describes. Sometimes, as in his articles in the
Britannica, he is more formal, and canvasses the nature of
the ideal in art, or the true value of Raphael or Sir Joshua.
His curious streaks and fulgurations of prejudice throw into
relief rather than impair the essential catholicity of his taste,
and remove the kind of reproach that attaches to the priggish
official critic. His account of Hogarth's *Marriage à la Mode,*
which may be compared with Lamb's essay, is as good in one
vein as his appreciation of Poussin is in another. Sometimes

he talks more about his own sensations than about the picture, but this in Hazlitt we can bear :

At the sight of the first [Poussin], which I distinctly recollect (a fine green landscape with stately ruins), the tears came into my eyes, and I passed an hour or two in that state of luxurious enjoyment, which is the highest privilege of the mind of man, and which perhaps makes him amends for many sorrows.

IV

And these sorrows, which figure so much in Hazlitt's pages ? He often cries out like a man wearing the thumbscrew. He does not, like Lamb, take them heroically ; the pain, the wrath, are always ready to beset him. But he is not the less human for that, even though his woes are largely wilful ; and his unchangeable temper of revolt is not to his dishonour. It makes him, along with Byron, a romantic in the deeper sense of the term. What he writes of Rousseau [1] is true of himself ; he has

an acute and even morbid feeling of all that related to his own impressions, to the objects and events of his life. He had the most intense consciousness of his own existence. No object that had once made an impression on him was ever effaced. Every feeling in his mind became a passion.

This kind of temper, it is to be feared, encourages the vices of the writing man ; it does not make for dignified reserve or for chivalry. It fosters a ruling passion,—not ambition, or avarice, or any of the seven canonical sins, but simply the need of self-expression. To that everything must give way. To write, to publish,—that is the only vent, or purgation, of the feelings that really gives satisfaction. The cost to self or others is not counted. The world shakes its head, and truly says that a perfect gentleman would have restrained himself, and eagerly reads the book. This it has always done, and will always do, in the case of Rousseau. Perhaps Hazlitt consciously followed Rousseau ; at any rate, it was the age of confessions. 'Du moins je suis autre,' at least I am not like other people—that is the note in Cowper, and De Quincey, and in Hazlitt too. Hence the issue of *Liber Amoris*,[2] *or the New Pygmalion*, a work so often deplored as the worst sign of his incontinent temper and want of breeding ; or, more charitably, as a record of his temporary insanity. That Hazlitt should have printed and sold, instead of burning, this book, incurring the bray and blasphemy of his foes and embarrassing all friendly faces, is an act that leaves him an easy prey to his critics ; although, to be consistent, they should perhaps shut the page. That he should, short of publishing, have written the story down, may have been the best thing he could do, as a means of self-relief ; the thing that had 'overcome him like a summer cloud,' or caught him up as in a waterspout, passed away accordingly, leaving, so far as can be seen, his vision and his taste unaltered. That he should have got into the tangle he describes, must awaken our pity ; but in truth it might have happened to most men. He conceived a raging passion for the very common daughter of a lodging-house keeper ; she would neither take him (he meant marriage), nor hold him aloof, nor be true to him. She practised in the same way at the same time on another man. He comes to detect her cold angling, her sensual prudence, and her duplicity, but on the least sign of encouragement he lets his blood override his judgment once more, and false hope submerge the too obvious truth. Then he writes the whole thing down, in the form of more or less actual conversations with the woman, and of letters to his confidential friend. This, no doubt, is all too human. *Liber Amoris* shows, not indeed Hazlitt's higher or finer qualities, but his formidable power of satire and self-anatomy ; it is a piece of life ; the man really played the fool like that, and saw it, and suffered like that, and is able to report on his folly and suffering. A few men are too happy to speak, many are too unhappy, and most men cannot speak whether they are happy or not. Worst off, perhaps, are those who are unhappy, and think they can speak, and who speak incompetently ; Hazlitt, at the worst, is not of these. The affair passed ; he escaped from the squalid net ; and if we blame him for letting us hear the story, it must be remembered that we should not otherwise have understood him.

V

As a critic Hazlitt, like Lamb, stands above the rest in his sheer power of enjoyment. Here he refutes the proverb *vix sapere et amare* ; a sharp good sense accompanies his raptures, and is implied in his power of savouring the best things as they come. But he sits among them, from youth to age, re-reading with unabated 'gusto,' seldom altering his preferences, and keeping, what he is proud of, his freshness and 'continuity of impression.' It is like the joy of Adam in Paradise discovering and admiring the beauty of the animals.

This is why we do not mind his quoting and praising the best-known passages in *Othello* or *The Faerie Queene*. We remember that he really was a discoverer. Lamb's *Specimens* and the labours of editors had made the old dramatists much better known, and had created for them something like an audience. But Lamb's extracts and comments are precious fragments. The elder poets were much in the same case. The novelists had never been surveyed as a whole by any critic of genius, if we except the notices by Scott. Hazlitt thus had a noble field to cover in his lectures at the Surrey Institution, which he edited himself for publication, unlike Coleridge, whose addresses remain in reported scraps. The wit and glow, the insight and style of these discourses raise Hazlitt above the sphere of the expository lecturer, or of other educative persons, into a different heaven of literature altogether. He does not offer to be exhaustive ; he frankly talks, dwelling on what he likes or on what annoys him ; passing cavalierly over writers, and often good ones, for whom he does not care ; throwing over the whole baggage, which has since become so bulky, of 'scholarship' and 'sources' and dry exegesis ; giving only homœopathic doses of abstract theory ; and ever trying to revive in himself and his hearers the species of pleasure which the artists he reviews may have felt in the act of production. By the time he has done, he has managed to present a body of critical writing more than equal in mass to all that is saved from the pens of Lamb and Coleridge put together ; more panoramic in range, and more connected in view, and, at its best, as rare and revealing in its own fashion as theirs.

We may either say that Hazlitt has no principles as a critic, or else (and with equal satisfaction) that he has one, simple and comprehensive, which dispenses him from having any others :

I have undertaken [1] . . . merely to read over a set of authors with the audience, as I would do with a friend, to point out a favourite passage, to explain an objection ; or, if a remark or a theory occurs, to state it in illustration of the subject ; but neither to tire him nor puzzle myself with pedantic rules and pragmatical formulas of criticism that can do no good to anybody. I do not come to the task with a pair of compasses or a ruler in my pocket, to see whether a poem is round or square, or to measure its mechanical dimensions, like a meter and alnager of poetry. . . . In a word, *I have endeavoured to feel what is good and to 'give a reason for the faith that was in me,' when necessary, and when in my power.* This is what I have done and what I must continue to do.

And again :

I somehow felt it as a point of honour not to make my hearers
think less highly of some of these old writers than I myself did of
them. If I have praised an author, it was because I liked him ;
if I have quoted a passage, it was because it pleased me in the
reading ; if I have spoken contemptuously of any one, it has been
reluctantly.

This catholic enjoying spirit, in which Hazlitt resembles
Longinus, does not lead to anarchy in his judgments. That
he does not much philosophise, or like Coleridge refer his
pleasure to some æsthetic or psychological law, does not mean
that he records each hasty impression as it comes. It has
mellowed long in his mind. Moreover, he has been suckled
on argument and logic ; and he reasons a good deal about his
intuitions, though in artistic rather than in systematic form.
We may think his depreciation of Sidney and the *Arcadia*
perverse or indiscriminate ; but at least he refuses to treat
Sidney like Dr. Fell, and gives four pages which plead for the
faith, or unfaith, that is in him, and which boldly utter the
private qualms of many who have shrunk from saying aloud
that they are tired by that endless romance—which resembles
the animal a thousand miles long, that Aristotle says a play
ought not to resemble. Hazlitt, in his essay on *Taste*, puts
his creed in more connected form ; it is the orthodox one of
Dugald Stewart and 'common sense,' but with an added glow
that makes all the difference :

Genius is the power [1] of producing excellence ; taste is the power of
perceiving the excellence thus produced in its several sorts and
degrees, with all their force, refinement, distinctions, and connections. In other words, taste (as it relates to the productions of
art) is strictly the power of being properly affected by works of
genius. It is the proportioning admiration to power, pleasure to
beauty; it is entire sympathy with the finest impulses of imagination,
not antipathy, not indifference to them.

Thus he starts on the firm foundation laid down anew by Coleridge and Wordsworth (both men liable to be distracted, the
one by metaphysical, the other by strictly ethical considerations), that the aim of poetry is to produce pleasure. It is
implied that the aim of taste, or criticism, is to receive, define,
and re-impart the characteristic pleasure of each work of art.

To study Hazlitt should save us from more than one grave
misreading of this point of view. First of all, taste is not
merely a passive and receptive thing—the feminine of genius—

something which creative art simply impregnates. No, the critic reacts on the art he enjoys—reacts masculinely, ardently, even wilfully—if he is Hazlitt ; and so produces—if he be Hazlitt !—another work of art, of which the work he reviews is the subject-matter. He is inspired by it as one poet is inspired by another. This distinguishes him from the mere scholar and expositor, who does useful work of an inferior order ; and it disposes of the old sneer against the sterility of critics. But secondly, we must never confound this mode of critical enjoyment with that one of a later day, which has come to be called, in a sectarian sense, ' æsthetic,' and which was formulated in English (much more absolutely than he practised it) by Walter Pater, and also, with more paradox, by Wilde. These critics, who are named here, the one with all honour and the other with respect, have given a turn to the doctrine of artistic pleasure which is alien to Hazlitt and his age. They have (partly after French exemplars) extended the range of feeling from which that pleasure can be drawn, not without a preference, in one of these cases, for strange corners of experience ; whereas Hazlitt, the most unpuritanical of men, has a saving manly sense and a dislike of ' unfair subjects.' But much more than this ; they have managed to associate the idea of artistic pleasure, with that of its solitary (or coterie) enjoyment, and also with a studious, somewhat fingering calculation of it, which take us miles away from Hazlitt. *He* spoke to audiences, in order that they might share his feelings ; and he was most at home in the drama, which implies, more than any other form of literary art, and in at least the same measure as music or painting, a public—a communicated, a universal appeal, in which the consciousness of sympathetic emotion is half the pleasure. One man in the theatre (Hazlitt) may really fathom and appreciate the play ; but it reaches everybody more or less. This truth is not allowed for in the extreme form of æsthetic criticism ; but Hazlitt knows it very well.

We do not look to him for scholarship in the later sense of the term. It was the .age of Malone and Dyce, but he simply took their results and texts and did not trespass on their field. The age of more or less dogmatic criticism had gone before him : that of editors and antiquaries still survived ; that of concerted research, of monographs, classification of sources, investigation of the order of plays—the age of Skeat, Furnivall, and the societies—was to come. Hazlitt was innocent of all this activity, and as little troubled by it as

Lamb and Coleridge. It is surprising to see into how few errors of fact he fell. He is far more wary than Coleridge in his admissions of 'doubtful plays' to the Shakespearean canon. 'Sources' did not matter to him; he was intent on the play itself. The most serious drawback is his incompleteness. He omits, though he may have known, many a playwright and poet on whom we should wish to have heard him. Often they were unedited or inaccessible. We only get a rough conspectus—true and just as far as it goes—of the course of literature.

VI

But to dwell on this is to lose time and to miss what Hazlitt can give. His *Characters of Shakespeare's Plays* are the best-known rather than the most original of his discourses. They contain wonderful sallies, and he always rises to his topic. The analyses of Hamlet, of Othello, of Lear, and of the situation and dramatic sympathies in *The Merchant of Venice* and in *Much Ado*, are characteristic instances of his power. His defence of Helena in *All's Well*, and his incisive verdict on *Measure for Measure*, show as well as anything the inveterate freedom of his mind. But for his favourite work of pointing out and bringing home unfamiliar beauties he had more scope in his *Literature of the Age of Elizabeth*. We have indeed had Swinburne since; and in Hazlitt's swift dashing sketches a hundred things are left out, which the greater leisure and impassioned insight of the poet have recorded in his lyric prose. But with Hazlitt, as with Lamb, we have the sense that Dekker, and Jonson, and Heywood are his living friends, his companions at Winterslow, whose talk has given him golden hours, and that their very defects are set down with the clear vision of a comrade. There is abundance of sharp sense and of a feeling for ranks and gradations of excellence in all he says, if also plenty of whim and antipathy. His analysis of the weaknesses of Beaumont and Fletcher, whose splendours and successes no man can relish more, is the best account we have of a literary decadence. His condemnation of Massinger's 'hardness and repulsiveness of manner' is just enough in itself; but then he ignores nearly all his excellences—his dignity, constructive power, and theatrical instinct. In his friendly but seemingly insuperable difference with Lamb as to the merits of Ford, Hazlitt's dislike of the abnormal and extravagant carries him rather far, especially in his treatment of Calantha's 'uncalled-for exhibition of stoicism' in *The*

Broken Heart. Ford's world (despite the sobriety of his style and versification) must be treated as somewhat fantastic and preter-human ; he does not deal in ' probability and decorum ' ; he succeeds in transferring the pity and terror, proper to human tragedy, to beings who are not truly of human texture, by a kind of illusion to which Charles Lamb seems (consciously perhaps) to yield himself ; so that his praises, and Hazlitt's strictures, are alike sound, granting the difference of preconception (see p. 355 *ante*).

With all his love of pure poetry, and his eloquence in commending it, Hazlitt was bound by strong cords to the real world of men, and is perhaps most at home in the literature that describes it. ' I would have the reader understand,' he says over-modestly, ' I am deficient in the faculty of imagination ' ; and again :

In points where poetic diction [1] and conception are concerned, I may be at a loss, and liable to be imposed upon ; but in forming an estimate relating to common life and manners, I cannot think I am a plagiarist from any man.

We need not make too much of this diffidence ; but it is true that he is not greatly concerned, as the authors of *Lyrical Ballads* were concerned, with *words*—with the varieties, and the different admissible levels, of poetic diction, and with its subtle connections with ' the real language of men.' He takes his enjoyment in full draughts, and does not pause on matters of technique, which must needs absorb the poetic artist. He thinks more about ' life and manners,' and characters, and veracity of impression, and, as he puts it, ' the very web and texture of society as it really exists, and as we meet with it when we come into the world.' Hence he is the best critic we have of the essayists, of the novelists, of the observers, and of the poets like Dryden and Pope who most nearly resemble them. There are, indeed, always more good judges of poetry than there are of prose. For this reason his *Lectures on the English Comic Writers*—which include studies of Montaigne and Cervantes, of *Gil Blas* and of Hogarth—may be thought his most precious contribution to criticism. His account of Congreve (' there is a peculiar flavour in the very words, which is to be found in hardly any other writer ') ; of *Don Quixote*, with its ' indistinct keeping and involuntary unity of purpose ' ; of Richardson, who ' had the strongest matter-of-fact imagination that ever existed ' ; and of the superiority, as it seems to him, of the *Tatler* over the *Spectator*,—all these things, and many more like them, signalise Hazlitt, as the Notes in the *Specimens* of 1808 signalise Charles Lamb. Sometimes, when Hazlitt is writing on the poets, the gushing and dazzling flow of his enthusiasm drowns the thought ; but in speaking of *Crusoe* or the *Coverley* papers his discrimination is clearer, whilst his ' gusto ' is not less.

As Hazlitt approaches his contemporaries, on whom he has written profusely, and many of whom were his friends or adversaries, his opinions acquire a different interest. They are woven up with the history of his own development, and with his political passions and personal relationships, which are seen deflecting or emphasising his artistic judgments at a hundred points. He has scores of scattered references to Godwin, to the ' Lake poets,' and to Scott and Byron. His final views are shown in the twenty-five character-portraits published in 1825 as *The Spirit of the Age*. They are nearly all descriptive of persons then still living ; and it is well for Hazlitt's name that he did not include his discreditable attack on Burke (1817), whom he treats as one who has renounced his convictions for popularity's sake, and in whom he will allow nothing good but his style—of which, it is true, he has left the best descriptions in existence. Ten years before, in *The Eloquence of the British Senate*, he had written more nobly and reasonably ; but time deepened the ruts of Hazlitt's passionate prejudice. He is biased by it often enough in *The Spirit of the Age* ; and his account of Mackintosh, which has the false air of equity and allowance, and also the masterly sharpness, of a picture in *Absalom and Achitophel*, is one of the proofs. His virulent assault on Southey [1]—only the last of a long series—is in the same way printed with the pretence of being one of ' his sincerest and heartiest well-wishers ' ; but he has an eulogy, no doubt an honest one, of Southey's prose. Politics taint even his honourable mention of Scott,[2] which is otherwise acute and just enough ; but are happily absent from his pages on Wordsworth. To Coleridge,[3] his first inspirer, the attitude of Hazlitt is peculiar. He cannot leave him alone ; reviews him, portrays him, alludes to him, at different dates, with a constant ebb and flow between waxing impatience and dwindling gratitude ; and at last takes leave of him, in *The Spirit of the Age*, in a shower of fireworks, with a kind of disrespectful affection after all. Of Byron [4] and of *Don Juan* Hazlitt would never see the greatness ; he is as morbid about Byron's rank as Byron himself. ' He has intensity of power, but wants distinctive character,' is his odd summing-up.

We cannot, however, go through all the articles in this book ; as Charles Lamb said, ' the new ones are capitally done ' ; and these include Bentham and Godwin, Irving and Horne Tooke, Jeffrey and Cobbett, as well as Campbell, and Crabbe, Leigh Hunt, and Elia himself. Hazlitt's wit and humour are at their ripest and best in some of these portraits ; that of Bentham is a masterpiece, as vivid as one of Carlyle's, and much better-natured. The humours of Godwin and his fallen fame are perfectly indicated ; and the figure of Horne Tooke, with whom Hazlitt was of course in political sympathy, stands out as by an old master. Gifford he had already mauled in his *Letter* ; but the flaying in *The Spirit of the Age* is more effective, had it been necessary. The paper on Lamb is a fine example of a eulogy upon a living friend, and dignified and full of candour, and takes the metallic taste out of our mouth, which portions of the book must leave, and which never attends the words of Hazlitt on the old writers.

Hazlitt's [1] excellence in all this kind of work is twofold. When not goaded by temper or hatred, he is a true draughtsman of the intellectual character, as well as of the quaint or picturesque outer traits, of a man. But he is surer as a critic of form and language, not so much on their technical or scholastic side, but as an expression of mind. What can better his account of ' the great secret of his [Scott's] writing—a perfect indifference to self ' ? Or his coupling of Scott with Cervantes ; he says they both ' have raised the idea of human nature . . . by bringing out what there is really fine in it under a cloud of disadvantages ' ? Or his phrase on Coleridge, that ' his genius has angel's wings, but neither hands nor feet ' ? Or that on Cobbett's changes of view : ' He is not wedded to his notions, not he. There is not one Mrs. Cobbett among all his opinions ' ? Who would not think better of himself, if he had said such things as these ? Indeed, the very best of Hazlitt, whether he is witty or exalted, passionate or fanciful, arouses some of the feeling that he himself utters after finishing some vivid Elizabethan play :

It is something worth living for to write, or even to read, such poetry as this is, or to know that it has been written, or that there have been subjects on which to write it.

This is the spirit of Hazlitt in his happy hour ; and yet there is something more impressive in his sterner utterance, when he is self-withdrawn, and in the mood that may be detected in the sombre and splendid lines of his death-mask.[2]

CHAPTER XXV

HISTORIANS AND OTHER PROSE WRITERS

I. Mass of material. Various scholars and disputants. Dr. Samuel Parr: his Latin writings, and shadowy reputation. Horne Tooke: *The Diversions of Purley.* Richard Porson: *Letters to Travis,* etc.; lack of a biographer. Gilbert Wakefield. Quantity of translations from the classics; Frere's *Aristophanes.*

II. Historians: position of Gibbon in the march of ideas; his immediate successors. William Mitford's *History of Greece*; Sharon Turner's *History of the Anglo-Saxons*; Lingard's *History of England.*

III. Henry Hallam: temper and political complexion. Scope as a historian. His *Middle Ages, Constitutional History of England,* and *Literature of Europe.* His style, and restrained enthusiasm. James Mill, *History of British India.* Some other historians: William Roscoe, *Life of Lorenzo de' Medici* and *Life of Leo the Tenth.*

IV. Some divines and preachers. William Wilberforce's *Practical View.* Robert Hall, Edward Irving, and Thomas Chalmers; eloquence, not literature. Richard Whately, *Historic Doubts, Logic, Rhetoric,* etc.

V. Some travellers: copiousness of travel literature. Basil Hall, James Bruce, Mungo Park, Peter Dillon, Charles Waterton, Alexander Wilson; Sir Humphry Davy's *Salmonia.*

VI. Biography and memoirs. Lack of masterpieces between Boswell's and Lockhart's; stray examples of material; Wraxall, etc. Henry Crabb Robinson's *Diary.* Range of his chronicle, independence of his judgment; his importance as a student and importer of German thought and literature.

I

THERE are many more prose writers—pamphleteers, historians, travellers, men of science, biographers, and nondescripts—who have not yet been grouped or noticed, who often fall into the doubtful region between literature and scholarship, or science, or journalism, and from whom some rigid selection must here be made. No one critic, no three critics, could hope to overtake the mass of printed material; the controversial and periodical writing, the records of touring and exploration, the mass of memoirs, each calls for its own band of investigators. The authors now to be mentioned are sorted out by kinds rather than by dates.

The elaborate elfish jig danced by De Quincey on the tombstone of Dr. Samuel Parr [1] (1747-1825) has been alluded to before; but another word must be spared for this celebrity. Parr's methods as a schoolmaster were not wholly pedantic; it is said that the first Greek dramas acted in the original tongue in England were the *Œdipus Tyrannus* and the *Trachiniae*, presented at Stanmore (without the choruses) by his boys. As a professional talker of the blustering, quoting, dogmatic, sometimes jovial kind, he was famous in his day. Parr thought, spoke, and wrote in what De Quincey terms 'solemn antilibrations of cadence,' and was one of the last of the old Latinising sentence-mongers. His scanty English works, such as his 'characters' of Fox and his Spital and Assize sermons, exhibit this habit of speech. His classical learning is described as huge and sound but somewhat sterile of results. His Latin compositions—chiefly inscriptions, dedications, and the like— show his happier side. Among their themes are Johnson and Gibbon and Dr. Burney, Fox and Burke and North; but one of the best is upon a dog which saved its master from drowning. Parr's Whig principles come out in his Latin preface to his edition of the *De Statu* of Bellenden, the learned servant of James I. Together with his scholarship, they earned him a surprising share of recognition, and the list of his correspondents, famous, titled, and obscure, fills many pages. With all his brag and temper and mannerism Parr leaves a not ungenial impression.

A still earlier figure, that of John Horne (1736-1812), who assumed after 1782 the name of Horne Tooke, carries us back to the Wilkes and Junius quarrels, and to the treason trial of 1794, in which Tooke figured beside Holcroft and Thelwall. A Whig who developed into an impenitent Radical, a fighter of quick wit and genuine courage, Tooke was long known and dreaded as a speaker, agitator, and pamphleteer. His power of tongue, as well as his scholarship, now long since antiquated but singular in its day, can be seen in his Ἔπεα πτερόεντα, *or the Diversions of Purley* (1786, concluded in 1805). One feature in these philological dialogues, namely their 'nominalism,' or instinct for exposing fallacies of thinking through the definition and etymology of words, Tooke shares with his brother-Radicals. His etymologies are mostly pre-scientific; but he was early in the field with his knowledge of older English and other Germanic tongues. He was also the putative father of many epigrams and retorts, but it has often been lamented that he found no Boswell to record and sift them.

This lack is yet more sharply felt in the case of Richard Porson [1] (1759-1808). There should have been a table companion, to whom he could talk both in Greek and English, and who would have sat him out at nights ; not a half-seeing, gossiping, untrustworthy Beloe, nor yet a Boswell, but a humourist, a scholar, and in wit and pride and veracity an equal. Such a man could have been Porson's biographer. As it is, we have to decline upon anecdote that is half-legend and upon his scanty but precious English writings. The chief of these are the *Letters to Archdeacon Travis, in Answer to his Defence of the Spurious Verse* 1 *John* v. 7 (1788-89), and the reviews and skits on Hawkins's *Life of Johnson*, contributed to the *Gentleman's Magazine* in 1787. In both works can be admired Porson's classical economy of stroke, the value of every sentence to the attack, and the mock gravity of the compliments and apparent admissions ;—all executed in the best manner of Swift, and as careless in outward seeming as the *Modest Proposal* or the papers on Partridge the almanac-maker. Porson, though full of glee and mischief, is free from the saturnine humour of his master. That his literary judgment was of the keenest eighteenth-century kind, may be judged from his characterisation, in the *Letters to Travis*, of the style of Gibbon ; and, in the vein of parody, his imaginary conversation between Sir John Hawkins and Johnson's negro is of startling excellence. Modern scholars are agreed upon the nature of Porson's vast services to classical learning. His edition of Æschylus (1795) appeared anonymously, but the authorship was soon recognised. That of the *Hecuba* (1797) was followed by others of the *Orestes, Phoenissae*, and *Medea*, the last of which appeared with his name. These editions, as well as Porson's corrections and notes on Athenaeus and other late writers, and the flood of light that he cast on Greek idiom, grammar, and metric, have assured his reputation as one of the greatest of textual emenders and of modern Hellenists.

Gilbert Wakefield [1] (1756-1801), despite his rashness in crossing swords with Porson over Euripides and in his dealings with ancient texts, has also left a name of some mark in the progress of scholarship. His *Silva Critica* (1789-95), an effort to illustrate the Bible from Greek and Latin literature, and his editions of Lucretius and other writers, are still mentioned by the historians. Wakefield touches our chronicle on several sides, though he left no enduring work. He became a Unitarian, fervidly greeted the Revolution, assailed the war, Pitt, and the bishops, as well as Thomas Paine, and found himself in prison for ' sedition.' No one preached humane opinions with greater acrimony. His memoirs are dull and ostentatious, but his correspondence, largely upon classical topics, with Charles James Fox is much more engaging. Not many other scholars of this period fall to be named here ; Twining, the translator of the *Poetics*, a man of exceptional taste, has been referred to (Ch. I.). But one phenomenon, in which the romantic resembles the Renaissance age, told upon poetry and letters generally. A surprising number of translations [1] in verse and prose were made from the Greek and Latin classics. Few of these have lasted on their merits, and they do not seem greatly to have inspired the poets. But one at least must be named, Hookham Frere's versions,[2] privately printed in 1839, of Aristophanes' *Frogs*, *Acharnians*, *Knights*, and *Birds*. The partner in the *Anti-Jacobin* and the inventor of *Whistlecraft* was well equipped, with scholarship as well as with satiric and poetic energy, for such a task. The iambics of the originals are put into blank verse, and the choruses into rapid rhymed measures ; and Frere, though working freely and sometimes loosely on his originals, transfuses their life and riot with effortless fidelity.

II

For thirty years after the conclusion (1788) of *The Decline and Fall*, history flourished even less in England than pure philosophy, and remained an insignificant branch of science and letters. But in 1817-19 appeared Hallam's *Middle Ages*, Mill's *British India*, and the first volume of Lingard's *History of England*. Even then there is little to compare with the noble expansion of such studies in the country of Niebuhr and Savigny. One cause of this weakness was the apathy of our universities, which gave little teaching or stimulus to historical research. Another may have been the scorn of the sceptical doctrinaires, as well as of the Benthamite reformers, for the fabric of the past, which they only consented to study for its errors. The heightened national feeling inspired by the Napoleonic wars did not, as in Germany, lead to a methodical and zealous inquiry into the national records, but vented itself in poetry, fiction, and eloquence. One of the strongest impulses to historical studies in Britain came, in fact, from the historical novel, which focussed so many elements of the romantic revival. Scott's stories and their following affected historians in various ways. They moved Macaulay to make his chronicle as interesting as a novel ; while Ranke was led, by noticing the differences between *Quentin Durward* and

Comines, to formulate his canon of describing things as they really occurred. But this was long afterwards ; and there is little to say of the barren years between Gibbon and Hallam.

The Decline and Fall, though five of its six volumes were published after 1780, is a monument of the preceding age. How it nevertheless prepares us for the romantic temper, has been hinted in the first chapter (*ante,* i. 3-5). Bayle had placed learning at the service of destructive criticism ; Gibbon places criticism at the service of learning, in the interest of a great reconstruction of the past. The imagination is seen at work in a large and patient way. Gibbon's power of marshalling and ordering, his panoramic skill, and his studied variety of scene and topic, are admittedly unexcelled. His view of human life and destiny brings him to the verge of the new era, despite his cool temper and much-resented ' want of spirituality.' He often rises above the standpoint of prose and reason. He shares in the larger melancholy, and forgets the cautious curiosity, that mark the time. He writes like a poet of the Renaissance on the ruins of Rome, when he tells of the fire and flood, the invasions and feuds, the waste and luxury, that brought low the secular city. He is now known to have underrated the importance of Byzantine history ; but he becomes a poet when he exclaims that ' our immortal reason survives and disdains the sixty phantoms of kings, who have passed before our eyes and faintly dwell on our remembrance.' If Gibbon lingers more on the outward and processional than on the inward and vital part of history, at least he sees it in an epic vision, which is heightened by his power of assembling great masses of detail in due subordination.

His notion of history and of the light that it casts upon man's reasonable hopes is a product of the age of unfaith and 'enlightenment' ; but it is also his own. Religion he sees as a huge excrescence, producing casual charities and benefits, but on the whole a bar to civilisation and progress. And what, then, is progress ? Gibbon has no sense of evolution, and the conceptions of writers like Herder do not seem to touch him. But he believes in government, in education, and also (despite his tepid political views) in some measure of civic freedom. He can speak of ' Europe as one great republic.' He has a limited but real faith in the advance of the world. Often, he says, ' ages of laborious ascent have been followed by a moment of rapid downfall ' ; yet man can never again be a barbarian ; the rudiments ' of law and policy, of trades and manufactures, of arts and sciences ' must always survive, and we may therefore acquiesce in the pleasing conclusion that every age of the world has increased, and is still increasing, the real wealth, the happiness, the knowledge, and perhaps the virtue of the human race.

In Burke and Coleridge, a more poetic and transcendental view of history than this is seen unfolding itself ; but Gibbon's occasional influence on the romantic writers is to be remembered. Not only De Quincey, but the authors of *Childe Harold*, of *Hellas*, and of *Imaginary Conversations* are his debtors in one way or another. His style, in spite of the just criticisms of Porson, left a permanent mark on our elaborate prose. The long, slow-stepping, senatorial sentence, which came to him through Bolingbroke from the seventeenth-century masters, and to these from Rome, may lack the highest of all harmonies, and be open to the charge of a monotonous undulation ; but it is hardly equalled for its union of even perfection and recurrent splendour.

The historians who followed Gibbon could not, even when they tried to do so, 'wear the purple.' It is a sudden descent to his friend William Mitford (1744-1827), to whom Gibbon suggested the task of his *History of Greece* ; but Mitford claims respect as a true pioneer of Greek studies. His work, of which the first instalment came out in 1784, was not to be finished till 1810 ; it is carried from the origins to the death of Alexander the Great ; and it held the field until the admirable work of Thirlwall, which began to appear in 1835. Before then Mitford's only rival was John Gillies, whose *History of Ancient Greece* (1786) had censured the democracy of Athens from the standpoint of a Whig. Mitford, a Tory of the hot Anti-Jacobin type, drew an equally hostile moral from other premisses ; while Grote was afterwards provoked by the vogue and the bias of Mitford to the composition of his own great *History of Greece*. Mitford writes in a colourless, clear way, and keeps mostly to bare narrative. He is trite enough when he strays into philosophic commentary or into the portrayal of scenes and persons. Though he laboured minutely, he is not careful to give chapter and verse, and his work was obsolete within half a century of its appearance. His freakish spellings provoked the gibes of Byron, and his slips in chronology the corrections of Henry Fynes Clinton, whose *Fasti Hellenici* (1824-51) became an indispensable quarry for scholars.

The long and honourable labours of Sharon Turner (1768-1847) gave an epoch-marking impulse to the study of Old English and Old Germanic letters. The Norse poetry[1] had

already been touched by Mason and others in the wake of
Gray. In 1797 Amos Cottle produced a version of most of
the ' poetic Edda.' Turner, in his *History of the Anglo-Saxons*
(1799-1805), gave a learned and orderly description of the
institutions, customs, and life of the English, and a detailed
account, together with a number of texts and translations, of
their literature. *Beowulf* was published in Denmark after he
had finished ; but Turner's work long held the field, and it
was some little time before his labours were built upon in
England. He has been justly charged with trying and failing to
write like Gibbon ; but this reproach applies much less to the
valuable book just named than to his continuation, a *History
of England* reaching to Tudor times, which is of much less
importance.

Hume had written (1753-61) the first history of England that
is also a work of art. With all his Tory bias (deepened in successive editions), his apathy to spiritual forces, and his lack of
access to the authorities, his work is that of a powerful political
thinker. He puts the whole story in some, though often in a
false, perspective ; and for half a century he held the stage.
But beside Hallam he is pre-scientific. A genuine advance
was made by Dr. John Lingard,[1] a Roman Catholic priest and
professor, whose *History of England*, ranging from the origins
to the Revolution, began to come out in 1819 and was finished
in 1830. Lingard revised his work in three successive editions,
and in 1827, in reply to Protestant assailants, issued a *Vindication* of his treatment of the evidence. The abuse of some
ultramontane critics was to his honour ; but the strictures of
Hallam, to which Lingard rejoined, are more to be regarded.
Lingard's work on the earlier periods has long been obsolete,
and his chapters on the Stuarts and the Commonwealth embody a commonplace view of Cromwell and Puritanism. The
freshest and most useful part of his book deals with the English
Reformation and the Tudor Settlement. He had access to
manuscripts at Rome ; he worked honestly from his sources,
giving chapter and verse ; his tone in dispute is temperate,
and his sarcasm, except when he is attacked, is subdued ;
and he addressed himself to reasonable Protestants, who
were willing to consider the view of a reasonable Catholic,
when they had heard him speak roundly of the ' infamy ' of
the Marian persecutions and of the weaknesses of the popes.
Lingard is of course not detached ; he is loyal to his uniform ;
and his first concern is to secure that the historic case for his
own church shall be fairly presented. He keeps close to the

political record ; he has no philosophy, no rhetoric, and little colour. But his English is limpid and pleasant to read, with occasional traces of the antithetic manner of Gibbon. He is somewhat hidden by later historians, but his work is still spoken of honourably, and is not yet out of use.

III

The scholarly work of Lingard pretends to no philosophic scope ; and the reputation of Britain for historical studies is best upheld in this period by the three treatises of Henry Hallam (1777-1859). A trained lawyer, Hallam was most at home in constitutional questions ; but his vast and accurate reading, in which few were his peers except Mackintosh and Hamilton, carried him into almost every field of knowledge. He was more than erudite ; his judgment was ever abreast of his learning ; and his bent was to refer all historical phenomena to their place in the long process of human emancipation and culture. He was an opponent of slavery, and a convinced Whig of the solider and nobler type ; and his temper was aristocratic rather than radical, as is shown by his distrust of reform in 1832. Otherwise, he held many of the same tenets as Macaulay, while free from Macaulay's forensic bias and streak of materialism. He is also wholly without Macaulay's vivid feeling for the concrete, or his desire

> to call up our ancestors before us with all their peculiarities of language, manner, and garb, to show us over their houses, to seat us at their tables, to rummage their old-fashioned wardrobes, to explain the uses of their ponderous furniture.

To all such matter, and to battles, pageants, and great scenic occurrences, Hallam reveals a certain aversion. He cares for the growth of institutions and for the larger political issues. But he is also remote from the later schools that eschew moral comment and affect an impersonal treatment. History to Hallam is a great discipline for fortifying our faith in civilisation, in the slow but real advance of organised justice, and in the final achievement of an equilibrium, typified above all in the English adjustment of power as between King, Lords, and Commons. Individuals he judges by their service to these causes ; he awards praise and blame, freely but not lightly, after balancing the whole evidence with conspicuous skill and scruple. Rightly hailed on all sides as judicial in his temper, he is indeed dispassionate, but far from passionless ; for when he approaches any crisis in the history of liberty, a grave ardour[1] breaks through his somewhat frigid surface. His Aristides manner angered Tories like Southey, and did not give satisfaction to the Radicals of the day. There are not many glimpses of the man himself, and little but the externals of his life are known ; but his memoir[2] of his son Arthur, Tennyson's friend, reveals an intense and idealising affection.

The *View of the State of Europe during the Middle Ages* (1818) is not a continuous or even a connected history, but a series of nine surveys, in each instance self-contained. It aims at being ' a just outline rather than a miniature ' of the ' chief circumstances that can interest a philosophical inquirer during the period usually denominated the Middle Ages ' ; a span of some ten centuries, closing with the fifteenth, the first five of which, or the ' dark ages,' Hallam treats as on the whole a period of arrest or decline. From the tenth century onwards he traces a movement of advance, which soon quickens in the twelfth, and culminates perhaps in the fourteenth ; after which the mediæval polity and civilisation begin to dissolve into those of the modern world. Five of the chapters are narrative, comprising independent and perhaps too sharply isolated sketches of the history of France, Italy, Germany, Spain, and ' the Greek and Saracenic empires.' Here Hallam moves with a steady but not sluggish step, keeping close to purely political events, and never pausing to be picturesque. In his remaining chapters he has more scope for his gift of analysis and broad survey. They describe the feudal system, ' the progress of ecclesiastical power,' the English constitution, and lastly the ' state of society ' during the Middle Ages : a term covering the chronicle of letters and learning, of manners and superstitions, of education and commerce. The enlargement and subdivision of knowledge has made such large synoptic views less fashionable ; but Hallam's *Middle Ages* is still respected and used.

Two of these chapters were continued on an ampler scale by Hallam himself. His *Constitutional History of England* carries on the story from the accession of Henry VII. to the accession of George II. ; and there he stops, ' from unwillingness to excite the prejudices of modern politics.' It is just in the succeeding period that his equity and skill would have found happy scope. As it is, he fortunately strays beyond his title, and writes much more than a ' constitutional history ' ; finding that the study of law and government forces him not only to judge men and causes as well as measures, but also to trace the origin of the war-cries that had never died down. He does not shrink from the task ; and few books bring out more clearly the continuity, through all their transformations, of the great political divisions in our history. The analysis of the terms ' Whig ' and ' Tory ' in Hallam's sixteenth chapter is largely applicable to his own day ; and ' it will be obvious,' he says, ' that I have given to each of these political principles a moral character.' His own mental lineage is everywhere apparent ; but all parties admit that his temper qualifies him to act as a court of appeal. At the time he was attacked, and his stern sentence upon Laud was resented by those who forgot his frigid treatment of Cromwell, against which Macaulay protested. It may be urged that Hallam sometimes reproaches the men of the sixteenth or mid-seventeenth centuries with failing to serve political ideals which did not yet exist. The Whig settlement and its doctrines seem implicitly to govern his judgments of the Tudors and the Stewarts. But his task was to trace the establishment of these ideals and doctrines, the conquests of toleration, the growth of securities for civil freedom, and the settlement of the balance of power in the constitution ; and he had some right to measure persons and policies by their distance from this achievement. His want, however, of dramatic sympathy, as well as his special purpose, left ample room both for the pictorial, and also for what is called the ' objective ' method of relating history.

The width and sureness of Hallam's learning is nowhere more impressive than in the work which he calls an *Introduction to the Literature of Europe in the Fifteenth, Sixteenth, and Seventeenth Centuries* (1837-38), which in fact is an encyclopædic view of the knowledge, thought, art, and culture of the West, as recorded in print during those three centuries. Literature, in its distinctive sense as a fine art, forms only one section ; is subdivided into poetry, drama, and the like ; and is described as ' polite literature,' or the ' literature of taste ' ; and once, in a betraying phrase, as ' fine writing.' Hallam's competence in this field has sometimes been underrated, owing to his reserve of manner. But the admirer of Machiavelli's *Mandragola* and of Rabelais cannot be called illiberal ; and over writers of an ideal bent like Hooker, Spenser, and Milton, Hallam warms into chivalrous admiration and eloquence. His judgments are those of a catholic scholar rather than of an artist ; his temper is scientific and intellectual ; and though his cartography of what were then called ' belles lettres ' is of high value and often indispensable, it is not his most congenial work. He was more at ease in his survey of political speculation, theology, and classical scholarship, which he chronicles through the course of its revival and growth. These subjects fall into the neutral ground lying between pure letters and pure knowledge, and approach to one or other frontier according as they are excellent or otherwise in form. To the critic of letters in the narrower sense they accordingly give trouble. If he only includes good writing he mutilates the intellectual history. If he gives this history in full he must mention much that has no trace of art. Hallam's scheme, and a certain dullness in his sense of form, saved him from feeling this difficulty, and he passes from pastorals to mathematics with little sense of interruption. But the result is without a rival, in its own kind, for fulness, proportion, and lucidity.

His arrangement is peculiar, and he has to pay for its advantages. After a general survey reaching to 1400, he divides the period down to 1520 into sections of forty, sixty, and twenty years respectively, reviewing all that was written in Europe, of whatever kind, during each of those sections. Afterwards he proceeds by half-centuries, but cuts up each half-century into chapters, dealing with the history of ' ancient,' or of ' theological,' literature, or of ' mathematical and physical science.' The student of poetry or of law has only to desert Hallam's order and read in succession chapters that are distant in the book, in order to have a connected chronicle of the subject. Yet it is always a chronicle rather than a history. The grouping is clear, but there is little sense of growth, development, or even of change ; little notice of the vicissitudes of form and style ; and a decided obscuration of the decisive moments and epochs in the story. The same drawback is felt in his panorama of the history of thought. Here as elsewhere, though he is versed in philosophy and his standpoint is never petty, Hallam does not show himself exactly a philosophical historian. Save in constitutional matters, he does not seek for great generalisations or profound clues ; just as, on the other side, he rarely gives the living physiognomy either of men or books. But in his own realm, which lies midway, he shows a mastery that none of his countrymen has approached. And he had no real predecessors. Thomas Warton's valuable pioneering work—*The History of English Poetry* had been confined to one nation—stopped short in the reign of Elizabeth, and with all its fervour and value could not come into competition. Hallam in his preface enumerates the various writers or compilers, French and German, who had attempted parts of his task. But his scope was larger than that of the best scholars among them like Sismondi.

Hallam is a writer of mark ; his style wears well, and its placidity and coldness have been exaggerated. It is a good eighteenth-century style of the massive order, neither insidiously simple like Hume's, nor yet unduly Latinised and periodic, nor over-influenced by Gibbon. Its dignity is natural ; its conscious aims are plainness and succinctness ; and there is also a liking, after the facts have been solidly marshalled and the story told, for a restrained peroration, often in the form of a luminous retrospect. Hallam, with good right, indemnifies himself for his long row of qualifications and his nice dissection of the evidence by a summing-up with a ring of finality, like that of a Latin inscription. In his severe but not unjust (1808) review of Scott's *Dryden*,[1] he observes, in qualification of the praise usually given to Dryden's prose, that

change of measure may delight the fancy, but an equable sustained cadence will be found more effectual in keeping the attention steady through continued reasoning.

This well expresses Hallam's own practice ; his ' equable sustained cadence ' holds out through his many volumes, rising at intervals to a note of indignation or triumph, uttered as if by the voice of freedom or justice itself. It also attains a certain grace when he speaks of Ariosto or expounds, as Hurd and Scott did before him, and with evident affection, the code and spirit of mediæval chivalry ;[2] an unexpected point of contact between Hallam and romance.

The historical spirit seized, though in a strange and imperfect fashion, even upon the school of thinkers which had more or less formally broken with the past. James Mill, the chief missionary of Benthamism, spent ten years in amassing material for a record of the oldest of civilisations, and in 1817 produced his *History of British India*. His aim in the first instance was rather polemical than historical ; he wished to expose, by a faithful narrative, the misdoings of the Company and of the English governing class. Early in the course of his argument, it fell to him to give some account of the governed races ; and he defends in vain his personal ignorance of the East and of its languages. His scornful account, therefore, of Hindoo thought, religion, and character, written in the spirit of a literal and rigid rationalist, remains something of a curiosity, and his design to strip away the 'glamour of the East,' at the expense of enthusiastic scholars, remains abortive. But though Mill's authority as a historian is discounted in this and other ways, his industry and vigour and the worth of his labour as a pioneer are acknowledged. Here, as elsewhere, his manner of writing is almost wantonly dry and vigorous ; with all its force, it makes little concession to humanity.

There are many other historians in this period, whose labours belong more to erudition than to letters. Into this class, for example, fall William Coxe the traveller, a copious writer, whose memoirs of the Walpoles and *History of the House of Austria* (1807) are of solid value ; Dr. Thomas M'Crie, whose *Life of John Knox* (1811) shows great learning and much prejudice ; and Patrick Fraser Tytler, a far more judicial writer, whose *History of Scotland* (from Alexander III. to 1603) appeared in 1828. None of these are remarkable for form ; but mention has been deferred of one historian, who comes on the scene between Mitford and Lingard, and who stands apart as a finder of territory as yet hardly trodden. William Roscoe (1753-1831), the Liverpool banker, abolitionist, and philanthropist, a man of high personal credit, a devoted citizen, and in his way, though self-trained and not very critical, a genuine humanist, was one of the first writers in any country to attempt, on a big canvas, some picture of the Italian Renaissance. His *Life of Lorenzo de' Medici* (1795), beautifully printed in his own city, was within a few years put into German, French, and Italian, and won resounding applause. The stimulus to inquiry partly given by Roscoe himself did not serve his reputation well, and his book, like its successor *The Life and Pontificate of Leo the Tenth* (1805) has been largely superseded or absorbed. He did not visit Italy, though a certain number of original documents of value were copied for him by a friend. Much of his portrait of Lorenzo has been painted out by other investigators ; his mental habit, as an enlightened Nonconformist, did not qualify him perfectly to understand Italian statesmen and churchmen : and his language is rather stilted and deficient in grasp. Roscoe, however, did very good service by his sketches of poetry and letters, and if his translations from Lorenzo, Michelangelo, and others are free and over-elegant, the Italian texts which he printed in his histories were a revelation. His map of the literature is still worth consulting, although he does not think that Machiavelli was a great man. He published separately the text, with an English version, of Tansillo's *La Balia*, as *The Nurse* (1798)—a very early enterprise in this kind ; and wrote much verse of his own, of which the pleasing child's piece, *The Butterfly's Ball and the Grasshopper's Feast,* is remembered.

IV

The divines and theologians of the period achieve little that is lasting in the province of letters.   The great evangelical movement, both inside and without the Church, had reached and stirred the millions ; it had created and organised many communities, of which the Wesleyan was and remains the strongest ; it had manned the army of the abolitionists, and had given them conquering generals ; in Cowper and others it had inspired hymnody ; and it bred some notable preachers. But the Evangelicals seldom went far in learning or culture, they looked askance at philosophy, and they hardly, after Wesley, produced a writer.   The favourite manual of doctrine was Wilberforce's *Practical View* (1797), a lucid and well-spoken but somewhat narrow plea, of which the aim is to ' point out the scanty and erroneous system of the bulk of those who belong to the class of orthodox Christians,' and to drive home the spirit and articles of ' vital religion ' in reason-able accents.   Wilberforce is of the straiter and more indis-criminate sect ; he disapproves of the theatre as well as of the ' duello,' and proves the ' moral darkness ' of antiquity from a few lines of Cicero and Virgil.   He would fain dwell on the amenities and consolations of his creed, but manages to make it out a sombre affair.   His book well shows the kind of void, the distrust of reasoning on the one side, and of the imagination on the other, which the two other chief schools of theology, the Broad and the High, were to set themselves to fill.   The Tractarian revival, opening as it does with Keble, falls past our limits ; and before naming Whately, the chief early representative of the liberal bent within the Church, some note is due to the pulpit orators who were in more or less casual contact with literature.   Of these three are prominent, namely Robert Hall, Edward Irving, and Thomas Chalmers.

Robert Hall, the fighting Baptist, the friend of Mackintosh, and the reader of Plato, has been named in an earlier chapter for his vigorous and sometimes splendid *Apology for the Freedom of the Press.*   The amenities of divines reach their summit in the passage of the first version where Hall refers to Bishop Horsley as a capital example of the mystery of permitted evil. But his once famous sermons now hardly vindicate their reputation, though they are agreeably free from rhetoric and the baser kind of unction. Those *On Modern Infidelity* and *On War* (both 1802) are the best known, together with the elegy on the Princess Charlotte. Hall had in him a fiery and heroic element, which is betokened by his early ardour for the Revolution, and by his soldierly endurance of pain and illness ; and his *Terms of Communion* (1815) shows him to be catholic beyond the wont of his school.

The countenance of the meteoric Edward Irving is presented to us, with a kind of regretful and sarcastic head-shake, by both Hazlitt and Carlyle ; and he had a certain wasted greatness. His orations and sermons display, as Carlyle might have said, a surprising *simulacrum* of style and genius. It seems as though the ghost, but only the ghost, of Jeremy Taylor were addressing us ; there is the same gush of words, the same tender note of appeal ; there is the play of imagery, the rainbow in the fountain. Irving had schooled himself in Hooker and the old eloquent divines, and his acquaintance with Coleridge, which began in 1822, may well have encouraged this manner of speech, as it certainly drew his mind off into an atmosphere of fume and cloud. It is easy to see how he carried away his hearers and also himself. But his discoursing is all much alike, and as we go on it becomes fatally tiresome owing to the absence of intellectual stuff or basis ; and it is at last a desert of verbiage. Carlyle says that ' our great Babylon wore and wasted him, and it took her ten years.' But he was really worn out by the hopeless process of his own intellect, which sank more and more into an abyss of preternaturalism. What remains with us for consolation is the figure of Irving in his youth, the suitor of Jane Welsh, the encourager of Carlyle, rich in humanity, purpose, and promise, an apostle not yet tried. This was before 1822, when he departed to London, and his fame went up like a rocket from Hatton Garden. He had been brought up in the Scottish church and served under Chalmers, but broke away from these moorings or rather was cut adrift from them ; he gave the impulse to the ' Catholic Apostolic Church,' which was formally founded after his death.

The works of Dr. Thomas Chalmers (1780-1847) fill thirty volumes ; but he has even less to do with literature than Irving. He had a far tougher brain and was a far greater figure ; his work is part of the history of the Scottish church and nation. His power as an orator is attested by observers as different as Jeffrey and Lockhart, Cockburn and Dr. John Brown. As we open his *Sermons on Public Occasions*, or his elaborate rejoinders to Hume, we can rebuild in fancy some of the spell that he exerted. There is an imposing air of logic, a keen instinct for the stately enlargement and ramification of a theme, and a steady rising flood of passion and feeling, which bore his hearers away. But an orator must be great indeed who can prevail in spite of being an original thinker or a consummate artist in words. Bossuet had the style and yet prevailed; Burke had both the style and the ideas, and prevailed sometimes. Neither of these hindrances beset Dr. Chalmers. He did not contribute much to ideas, and he is difficult to read. His 'Bridgewater treatise' on 'the adaptation of external nature to the moral and intellectual constitution of man' is one of the most elaborate documents of the pre-scientific period. He drew up *Institutes of Theology*, Calvinistic in cast, and discoursed on Butler's *Analogy*. He wrote profusely and powerfully on questions of ecclesiastical organisation, and was a founder of the Free Church. All this is of historical mark. His vigour of soul and genuine largeness of temper are perhaps best seen in his *Astronomical Discourses*, where he descants on the smallness of man and the greatness of space and the ubiquity of God. It is as though a few sentences of Pascal were diluted into a volume.

With Richard Whately (1787-1863), who became Archbishop of Dublin in 1831, we are back again among the children of Reason :—not the revolutionaries, but the strong-headed, hard-hitting, unimaginative divines of the last century. The bankruptcy of this type has already been apparent in Paley ; but in Whately, a man of far wider mind and more liberal sympathies, it is regenerated. He can best be defined by his negations. He is anti-sacerdotal and anti-traditional on the one side ; and on the other, anti-mystical and in great measure anti-dogmatic. In his Bampton lectures *On the Use and Abuse of Party Spirit in Matters of Religion* (1822) there are passages that may be read either as cautiously agnostic or as a devout avoidance of inquiry into the mysteries of the faith. But he is also anti-sceptical, and his liveliest and shrewdest work, *Historic Doubts relative to Napoleon Bonaparte* (1819), is an attempt to push the argument against miracles, drawn from the weakness of human testimony, to an absurd conclusion. It may be regarded as a foretaste of the excellent chapter on Fallacies in his *Logic* (1826), a work which has not held its ground and does not count in literature, but which raised and impelled the study of logic in England more than any previous treatise. The *Rhetoric* (1828) is much more of a book ;

it is far more serried and acute than the most popular manual of the day, George Campbell's *Philosophy of Rhetoric* (1776), and is worthy of a student of Aristotle. The light is dry and the tone hard, but there are sallies of Whately's sharp bluff humour to enliven it. He follows his master in treating rhetoric as a craft whose aim is ' argumentative composition,' and as such morally neutral, being only concerned with persuasion irrespective of the end. In this way he rescues the term from its bad associations as the art of mere ornamentation, or of sophistry and emotional appeal. These devices, like Aristotle, he represents merely as tools of the trade ; while De Quincey, in his paper on *Rhetoric*, which is a nominal review of Whately, somewhat perversely drags the same associations in again. As would be expected, the art of working on the understanding is better set forth by Whately than that of capturing the feelings ; and his sections upon style and elocution, though they show his cool sense and rationality, are not such as an artist could have written. The chief work in pure theology that he published before 1830 is that *On Some of the Difficulties in the Writings of St. Paul* (1828), which once more shows his destructive bias. His life as a practical reformer and a founder and protagonist of the Broad Church belongs to the next period ; but Newman in his *Apologia* has borne witness to the power that Whately displayed in the early days at Oriel, of dusting and clearing, as with a besom well-wielded, the minds of younger men.

V

Among the professed men of letters a score of travellers have been named already, from John Moore and Beckford to Morier and Byron. But of those whose calling it was to travel and who have left their record no count or estimate is possible ; not even of those who wrote well, or better than well. During the half-century that is here reviewed, there is an immense increase of touring and exploration by sea and land. The result is a large library, but it is a library without a Hakluyt.[1] In every land then known, and in all waters, there are English observers and adventurers. Amateurs, watchers of the picturesque, missionaries, traders, exploiters, men of science, diplomatists, searchers for the missing, searchers for the pole and the north-west and the north-east passages, all play their parts. They are usually intent not on producing an effect by words, but on making their report ; which is, or is not, literature as the case may be, and irrespectively of its scientific or

anthropological value. Every shire and corner of the British
Isles has its note-takers ; Gilpin and Young, Pennant and Shaw,
are amongst them. The European tours are endless ; the
learned William Coxe, historian of the house of Austria, leaves
a ponderous valuable account of Switzerland, and another of
Poland and Russia ; and, at the other extreme, Mary Wollstonecraft sends *Letters from Scandinavia*. Eastern Europe,
the Levant, and Western Asia are portrayed from experience
by the novelists, Morier, Hope, Trelawny (see Ch. XII.) ;
Sir John Barrow, the encyclopædic, reaches and describes
China. The travels of Captain Basil Hall in Corea, Mexico,
and North America, published at various dates (1818-30), are
remarkably lively and arresting. Sir John Malcolm's works
on Persia are a good pendant to Morier's. Of those who go
furthest, it must serve to single out a few names from three
tracts that still tempted the imagination. These are the
Arctic regions, Africa, and Polynesia. The chronicles of
Franklin, at once veracious and graphic, are a classic, while
the faithful logs, geographically and otherwise precious, of
Parry and others accompany them well. The most noted
book of African travels in this age is that of James Bruce [1] of
Kinnaird, whose five volumes on his *Travels to Discover the
Source of the Nile* (1790), long questioned and flouted, after a
while took their place as an essentially true and classic chronicle.
Bruce was one of the great race of explorers, dauntless, adroit,
a trifle scenical, passionate and loud-spoken, watching and
describing everything without care for the proprieties, a master
in the portrayal of barbarian character, and also a precise
observer of fauna and flora. He wrote with apparent loose-
ness, and was assailable in the details of scholarship ; he
composed his work long after his return home, and evidently
idealised his memories of speeches and conversations ; but
later travellers have confirmed the truth and value of his
report. Bruce's successor, Mungo Park,[2] the friend of Scott,
who found and traced the Niger, and accomplished his desire
to ' die on the Niger ' if he could not ' discover its termination,' writes more lightly and simply than Bruce ; and his
Travels in the Interior of Africa (1799) have a natural ease of
style that ensures their permanence. The works in which he
enlisted a literary coadjutor are not so good in form ; but few
sentences in any story of travel move us more than those in
which Park himself relates how

I saw with infinite pleasure the great object of my mission; the
long-sought-for, majestic Niger, glittering in the morning sun, as

broad as the Thames at Westminster, and flowing steadily to the
eastward; and I hastened to the brink, and having drank of the
water, lifted up my fervent thanks in prayer to the great Ruler of
all things, for having thus crowned my endeavours with success.

The discoveries of Cook opened up Polynesia, and a multitude of navigators followed in his wake. The wanderings of
Bligh and Mariner, which were read and used by Byron, have
been referred to. These, again, are but survivors in literature
by natural selection ; their diaries were not written with the
expectation of earning the title of *books* ; and around them
are many other works—such as the weighty and useful *Tour
through Hawaii*, by the missionary William Ellis (1826), or the
bare *Voyage round the World* (1816) of Archibald Campbell,
or the earlier *Voyage to the Southern Pacific Ocean* in the *Duff*,
by Captain James Wilson (1799), a conscientious story ; but
few of these have much style or colour. Sometimes the
strength of the story serves well instead, as in Captain Peter
Dillon's *Discovery of the Fate of La Pérouse* (1829), a tale of
resolution and address sore tested by war, treachery, storm,
and sickness. La Pérouse had sailed with two ships out of
Botany Bay in 1788 and was no more heard of. In 1827
Dillon found remnants of those ships on the island of Mannicolo.
He had distrust and many obstacles to face, but he is seen
pushing on like fate, marshalling his proofs, and putting himself steadily in the right. The passages of his fray against
odds in Fiji (where he was nearly eaten), and of his unjust
trial in Van Diemen's Land, are told well and without emphasis ;
also his finding of the *fleur-de-lis* on the articles identified in
Mannicolo. The British captain's level way of telling his tale
is much the same in the sixteenth century and in the nineteenth, and is luckily not likely to alter. Of another type are
Charles Waterton's *Wanderings in South America, in the North-
West of North America, and in the Antilles, in the Years 1812,
1816, 1820, and 1824* (1825). Waterton is a naturalist and
a born observer, and also somewhat ambitious as a writer ;
there is not a little gloss upon his language ; and in describing,
for instance, the effects of the wourali poison he drops into
Latin quotation, and elsewhere into English verses of his own.
His beautiful quarto, with its frontispiece of the ' nondescript '
(a kind of Caliban), is in keeping with this quaint and
pleasant habit of narrative. His encounter with the over-
bearing customs officer at Liverpool is as well told as his
often-quoted ride upon the back of the cayman, or his description of the sloth hanging on the branches. There is a similar

elaboration, less humorous if more brilliant, in the writing of Alexander Wilson,[1] the Paisley poet and author of a classic work on *American Ornithology* (1808-14). Wilson, like Waterton, is happy when he can break into rhyme, his own or other men's; but the poetic eye and ear serve him best in his prose, when he has to tell of the song of the wood-thrush, or of the flight of starlings, or of the eagle feeding. These wandering naturalists, whose senses are all the keener because they carry their lives in their hands, partake, more or less unawares, in the artistic movement of the time; and herein also they are true successors of the peaceful Gilbert White, taking notes in his English village.

A different union of imagination and scientific power is found in the work of Sir Humphry Davy (1778-1829). His little dialogue *Salmonia, or Days of Fly-fishing, by an Angler* (1828) is in form, in simplicity, and in its mixture of free leisured talk and expert knowledge an avowed following of Izaak Walton. The speakers, a poet, a fisherman, a fowler, and a natural historian (' Physicus '), talk naturally, and do not betray the actual notes and conversations of which Davy, as we are told, here made use. His expository prose has the same qualities, and, like Faraday his younger contemporary, he was famous as a lecturer. He was the friend of Coleridge and other poets, and himself made verses; his piety was simple and of the old school; and his *Consolations in Travel* (1830) are the reflections of a clear and fervent spirit.

VI

Nearly half a century passed between the appearance of the greatest biography of the classical age, and the only great one of the period here surveyed. Boswell's *Life of Johnson* (1791) and Lockhart's *Life of Scott* (1838-39) have already been compared. The former is notable, if taken as a picture of the mind of the time, for the illusion that it creates by the very honesty and perfection of its workmanship. No one, after reading Boswell, would have an inkling of the forces whose operation our first chapter has attempted to describe. All is measured by Johnson and his ideas, and the occasional deferential demurrers of Boswell only enhance this impression. No one in the book has any notion of what literature was soon to be—of what it had begun to be—and the self-absorption and self-complacency of an age, a circle, a whole society have never been so fully mirrored. Boswell's *Johnson*, therefore, if read in this light, is the best possible preparation for the study of the romantic period, and thus to read it only heightens our opinion of its excellences.

The new age itself is remarkable for its profusion of memorial and biographical matter—far too large to be more than hinted at here—and still more so for its lack, until the appearance of Lockhart's work, of any masterpiece of biography. The poets and critics talk endlessly about themselves : Wordsworth, Coleridge, Lamb, Hazlitt, De Quincey, Byron do so. They also describe one another in a leisurely, refreshing, unmincing way that is only equalled in the time of Pope or of the de Goncourts. They do it in print, and in the lifetime of the persons of whom they speak. Still, there is no formal, complete, business-like biography or autobiography of any man of letters that can be called first-rate ; Moore's *Life of Byron* can hardly be so described. It may be doubted whether posterity has always supplied the lack. With all respect to the scholars and critics of a later day, where is the really great and ample Life of Byron, or of Landor, or of Hazlitt ? But we leave this dangerous ground.

Sometimes the men of letters did best with biographical subjects outside their own calling. The achievements of Southey and the pleasant sketches of Hartley Coleridge are cases in point. But most of this kind of work has remained a quarry for future labourers rather than in a chiselled state. Many diaries and records have been posthumously published, which throw much light on the personal side of political affairs. The papers of the Tory Croker are balanced and supplemented by those of Thomas Creevey, and those of Charles Greville are an indispensable document for the historian. The memoirs cannot be recounted, though some have been cited already. Those of the Miss Berrys, of Moore, of Rogers, of Lady Morgan, of Miss Burney—the last of these a work of art—and of Gibbon, are stray but representative instances. The *Historical Memoirs* (1815) and the *Posthumous Memoirs* (1836) of the traveller Nathaniel Wraxall are well known and valuable, and also agreeable. At the other social extreme there are odd and attractive chronicles ; Edward Topham's *Life of John Elwes*, the miser, and the story of George Barrington, the gentleman-pickpocket and literary convict, whose speech in court is inimitable, would have been admirable material for Charles Reade. But one work, indispensable to the student of letters, calls for further note.

This is the *Diary, Reminiscences, and Correspondence* of Henry

Crabb Robinson [1] (1777-1867), by profession at different times a barrister and *Times* correspondent, whose record of his numberless friends and their talk, and of the thought of the time, is of an extraordinary veracity, intimacy, and distinctness. Crabb Robinson is best known for his association with the group of Coleridge, Wordsworth and Lamb, and for his position as an interpreter of contemporary Germany to his own countrymen. His visits and talks with Goethe, Herder, and others, as well as with Madame de Staël, are unique. He has too often been regarded as a mere reporter, and too little as a mind. Receptive and reflective rather than originative, he nevertheless thought for himself and kept his head, and his criticisms are always strong-witted and pointed. His acquaintance with things German covered more than a whole generation. He knew William Taylor and his group ; he went twice to Germany, once in 1800, when he stayed several years, and again in 1829. To spread the knowledge of German thought and letters in England was the most distinct purpose of his life. He heard Schelling, and read Kant, and worked out a singular, half-sceptical creed of his own. His cast of thinking is more truly German than Carlyle's ; his comments have a ruminative, abstract, composed cast, which makes him an odd contrast to Lamb and Hazlitt. He held the ideal of self-culture, of *Bildung*, the great ideal of Goethe, steadily before him. At the same time he was a good man of business and very clear with himself and with others, and in this way noticeably English. His force of judgment, and not merely his curiosity and sympathy, can be watched in all he says of Blake or of Wordsworth. His acquaintances were everywhere ; Crabb Robinson had a gift for society and for attracting confidences, as other men have a gift for solitude. He came across Godwin and Holcroft, Tooke and Thelwall, and imbibed, discreetly but markedly, the radicalism of an earlier day. He also leaves his record of Sydney Smith and the Whigs ; and in his old age, at his famous breakfasts, he becomes himself a personage, like Rogers but far more significant, and the repositary of a thousand memories. The records left by De Morgan and Bagehot of his personality and conversation are as distinct as his own of Landor or Coleridge. His great bequest is his *Diary*, written steadily from 1811 onwards till his death. His *Reminiscences*, penned in his old age, are not less lively, but their value is of a different kind, owing to the selecting and softening processes of memory.

CHAPTER XXVI

SOME INFLUENCES: CONCLUSION

I. 'Anticipations' in Ch. I., how far borne out. Persistence of debt to the eighteenth-century style and temper; examples. Poetry and prose 'under the rule of the free imagination'; absence of poetic works on the larger scale. Poems of middle length, and lyrics. Comparison with the succeeding period (1830-1880).

II. The feeling for beauty, and the increase of human sympathy; coming change in poetry and fiction through association with a 'social purpose.' The movement of thought; the revolutionary and the 'reactionary' currents.

III. Note on the influence of Germany: its superficial effects on *belles lettres*. William Taylor of Norwich, his translations, articles, *Survey of German Poetry*. Carlyle, 1820-1832; his attitude to Schiller and Goethe, and his writings upon them. What Carlyle saw in Goethe. His articles on minor German writers. Beauty and power of his style during this period.

IV. Brief reference to the debts of English to other literatures. (1) Italian: study of Dante, and sway of Italy upon the poets. (2) Greek: the obligations of Shelley and Keats. (3) Older English writers; work of the scholars; Tyrwhitt, Thomas Warton. Exploration by the critics; the study of Spenser, Milton, and Shakespeare. Work of Malone and other scholars.

I

AFTER so long a journey, it may well be asked what has become, about the year 1830, of the 'anticipations' traced in the opening chapter. How has half a century of rich and brilliant production altered the mental and artistic forces that were beginning to stir in the time of Blake and Burke? How are the balance, and the connections, between prose and poetry affected? This theme would require another book; but we can briefly revert to some of the forces referred to and notice their transformation. In doing so, some of the influences that determine such changes will become more evident—the influence of new ideas, of other literatures, upon English men of letters. It will then be easier to judge the art of the 'romantic period' on its merits.

The debt of the nineteenth century to the eighteenth, in point of thought, form, and temper, may seem, in the latter days of Sir Walter Scott, to be somewhat covered up and obscured; but none the less it is there. Consider four of the books that came out in the years 1829-31, namely Mill's *Analysis of the Human Mind*, the last volume of Lingard's *History*, Cobbett's *Rural Rides*, and Miss Ferrier's *Destiny*. They have at first sight little enough in common ; but the style and habit of mind in each of them can be affiliated, in different ways, upon the age of criticism, observation, analysis, and hard sense. In the two last named there is an element that may be called romantic, but it is not of the essence ; and it would not have seemed strange, had all four been written forty years earlier.

The impulse of criticism, we have said, was followed by that of reconstruction ; and the great mark of our literature between 1780 and 1830 is (*ante*, i. 6) ' the reunion of poetry and prose under the rule of the free imagination.' On looking back, this view appears to be confirmed. There are, it is true, certain solid monuments of prose, built for use rather than for pleasure, in which the imagination, while still at work, is at work in the service of knowledge and ideas ; as in Hallam's histories, Southey's biographies, and the doctrinal works of Paley or of Paine. Some of these books are of tried excellence, but they do not bulk large in the whole mass of good writing, or even of good prose. They multiply visibly in the following age, which is that of Macaulay, Newman, and the younger Mill. One of the traits of that age is the prominence of historical, theological, or doctrinal works, which are very good literature, yet which are not primarily written for the pleasure of creating, and where the imagination is not the presiding power. But in the ' romantic period ' the leading trait is the predominance of poetry over prose, and of imaginative over other prose. Sometimes the imagination is at work in prose quite freely, and deals with life at first hand ; the result is fiction, fantasia, the imaginary conversation, or the essay. At other times it is at work upon existing products of its own, on poems, plays, tales, or pictures ; and then the result is criticism. But precious as these fruits are, the fruits of poetry itself, if not greater, are at least more numerous. And, as to the poetry, we have to ask how far the imagination has succeeded in producing perfect wholes, as distinct from simply exalting or enriching style. Here the answer is at hand. There are hardly any completed works in verse of the highest order and of considerable size : no *Paradise Lost*, no *Jerusalem Freed*, no *Othello*, no literature of the Periclean age. *Hyperion* promised to be something of this order, but it broke down. Perhaps *The Prelude* and *Don Juan*, in their almost absurdly different ways, are the nearest approach to such masterpieces. But *The Prelude* is a feat, though a mighty one—a psychological epic tracing ' the growth of a poet's soul,' and it sometimes drags. And *Don Juan*, after all, is perfect just through its persistent absence of plan ; it is a pattern of divagation—a wonderful quilt—a harmonious piece of anarchy. It is the poems of middle length, as observed before—it is *Peter Grimes, Michael, Adonais, Yardley Oak, The Ancient Mariner, Lamia, The Hamadryad,* that really do approach perfection. They answer in scale to the short prose story, and stories many of them are. Such a list, though it might be lengthened out, could soon be made. But of the lovely or admirable poems that are quite short the list could not so soon be made. Palgrave's, in the last book of his *Golden Treasury,* contains nothing that is not of the best ; but if the mesh were a little wider, and if playful or ironic verse were included, and also some things that were outside Palgrave's scheme—all the excellent short pieces, for example, of Landor and of Beddoes—then the true riches of the treasury would be seen. A reference to our account (Chs. xx.-xxi.) of the less conspicuous poets of the time would perhaps bear out this opinion. Much the same can be said of poetry in the age of Tennyson, Browning, and the mediævalists, except that the number of consummate long poems, though not large, has now increased ; this is seen to be true if we think of *Maud* and of the *Life and Death of Jason.* But there remains the old profusion of unimprovable short pieces, and there are many perfect idylls, elegies, and narratives of moderate span and harmonious in finish. Further, as just observed, in this later age the arrears of prose, especially of the prose that is not mainly the work of the imagination, are redressed. Thus the balance between the two kinds is better upheld ; and in spite of all the riches, the charm, the incomparable *newness* of the ' romantic ' writers, it might be pleaded that literature between 1830 and 1880 shows, at least in this direction, a real progress.

II

In 1830 there can be and need be no more talk about the ' convalescence of the feeling for beauty ' ; the feeling is everywhere ; and soon, after its temporary pallescence during the closing decade, it is to be found in fuller flush than ever. Tennyson and Browning are coming, and the great novelists, including Dickens, in whom the feeling is strong if it is not wholly pure. Literature can no longer be thought of without it, any more than painting. The old gropings after the ' picturesque ' are forgotten in the prose of Ruskin. And the same is true of those fresh, those enlarged or recovered sympathies with human hope and the human drama, which we have seen mirrored in art. They have been traced from name to name, they have taken twenty shapes, in Wordsworth, in Byron, and in fiction. They continue to grow. One transformation of these sympathies lies ahead. Art, whether in verse or in fiction or in prophetic and expository prose, becomes more nearly associated with the deep public questions, the problems of poverty and labour and war, that are moving the nation at large. Dickens and Kingsley, Carlyle and Ruskin, Morris and even Swinburne, exhibit this tendency powerfully. It is clear that the national life gained immensely by it, and it is not clear that art lost. In the romantic period there are omens of such a change, though they are not all on the surface, and art in general is devoid of a social purpose. The Irish novelists, and Shelley, and Bentham, foreshadow this engrossment in different ways.

The third of the forces that began to tell on art at the close of the eighteenth century was the movement of philosophic thought (*ante*, i. 23). In the course of the journey, this movement has been seen to be twofold ; and both of its currents, despite many confusing eddies, become at last still more clearly marked. The first of these may be called the revolutionary, and the second, without prejudice, the reactionary current. They may be treated to some extent separately.

By 1830 the revolutionary and Napoleonic eras have passed, and a generation is born to whom both are hearsay. The peace has come—peace abroad ; but at home there is a new war, generated by the pressure of the problems just adverted to—the conditions of labour, the demand for political privilege, and the gradual rise of the middle class ; all provoking a vehement discontent alike with the old order itself, and with the remedies prescribed by the Radicals and flouted by Carlyle. The old doctrinaires have passed too ; but they leave their offspring, who face such difficulties in a practical rather than an *a priori* spirit. These are the new Radicals, who close their ranks. The best of their writers, John Mill, is beginning to be heard. His early essays in the *Westminster Review* and the *Examiner* coincide with the spiritual crisis, in which he doubted whether mankind would be the better even if Bentham's heaven were seen upon earth. Before 1832 this crisis had gone by ; and Mill, heartened by Wordsworth's poetry, set himself to think out his reasoned groundwork for the science of human happiness. But the old, unadulterated radical spirit, needing no such consolation because touched by no qualms, went on by his side and goes on still, a direct inheritance at once from the older English philosophers, from the Revolution, and from Bentham.

Among the poets of the romantic age the revolutionary spirit persisted, with a difference. The gospel of universal love released from law, which Blake had proclaimed with Hebraic fervour, is preached by Shelley, with many modifications and in other tones. Shelley remained at this point of view, because he never shared in the full speculative movement of his time or came under the spell of German thought, but simply qualified his Godwinian creed by the study of Plato and high literature. Hazlitt, who thought that he remained faithful to the Revolution, but who also worshipped the great autocrat, and who coloured doctrine with the hues of passion and romance, was a survival and an Ishmaelite. This great race seems to have departed by 1830. But not so easily is such an ideal quenched. Within a quarter of a century, under the stimulus of new forces, it revives in a somewhat transcendental form, but still to be recognised, in the verse of Swinburne and the Utopias of Morris. *Songs before Sunrise* and *News from Nowhere* are a direct legacy from the Revolution ; they are romantic literature.

As for the ' reaction ' which has been watched in Wordsworth and so many more, it is in the nature of things far harder to seize or formulate. It is manifold, it is everywhere ; it is the manifestation of a mood which overtook not only England but Europe at large, and which left its large imprint on public as on intellectual history. In its bearing on ideas it has been well delineated by Georg Brandes,[1] who has surveyed both the revolution and the revulsion in the principal countries. The same story will have to be re-told some day in its more immediate bearing upon art, but this task is foreign to the plan or range of the present writer. In Britain, many ingredients of the reaction are well represented : the attempt to find a reasoned justification for the Church and the State as they are, and thus to put new life into them ; the return to metaphysics, founded on a deeper psychology and a wider observation of facts ; the return, concurrently, from the bare reason to the heart and emotions, at first for their own sake, but next as affording a surer revelation, and opening a window into the infinite ; and, lastly, the wish to fathom and vindicate

the workings of the imaginative power itself.   Many of these
impulses have been seen in Coleridge.   But neither Coleridge
nor any man left a perfect or well-shapen memorial, either in
prose or verse, of such aspirations; though *The Prelude*, once
more, is a kind of exception.   Instead, there is a great and
far-spread exaltation of thought and style, due to the currency
of philosophic ideas, and a true metaphysical poetry was
renewed (*ante*, i. 23) by Blake and his successors.

III

Remarkable coincidences[1] have been found, especially in
Wordsworth, with some of the leading conceptions of German
idealism.   It is hard to say how far, through Coleridge or
otherwise, such conceptions filtered through to him, and how
far they were independently evolved.   The musings, largely
common to the two friends, on the distinction between the
'fancy' and the 'imagination' (*ante*, ii. 122), supply one
point of contact with foreign thought.   The influence of
German[2] philosophy seems to have reached the other poets
in the most devious fashion, if at all.   But the whole mental
relationship between the two countries during this period still
awaits precise measurement.   Some of its more obvious
features may be collected from our studies of the 'Lake poets,'
of Scott and his earlier circle, of Byron, of De Quincey, of
Shelley, of Crabb Robinson, and of the translations from
Kotzebue.   In poetry and fiction the German influence,
though widely spread, was often superficial, transitory, or of
little service.   The effects of Scott's German ballad-monger-
ing on his poetic style, of Schiller's robber-hero on Maturin
and Mrs. Radcliffe, of minor fiction on De Quincey, and of
minor poetry on Coleridge are not altogether refreshing.   The
use that is made of Goethe's *Faust* in *Manfred* is more significant.   But throughout the dye is deeper in speculation
than in art.   This notice will be less imperfect, if two other
names are cited (though the difference between them is almost
grotesque), with whom the study of German writers in England
is identified.   These are William Taylor[3] of Norwich, and
Carlyle.

Taylor (1765-1836) was the most industrious and useful
middleman between the two countries—he can hardly be
called an interpreter—until Carlyle appeared.   Brought up on
the eager culture of Radical Norwich, he became an enthusiast for the Revolution, a passionate student of German

letters, and a not ungenial eccentric. His translation of
Lenore won an accidental importance ; and those of *Nathan
der Weise* and of *Iphigenie* were the first of a long series.
In the latter years of the century many works of Goethe,
Schiller, and Lessing were put into English by many hands ;
and Taylor, in the *Monthly* and the *Critical Review*, soon became
an acknowledged arbiter on all things German. His contributions were very numerous, and spread over many years.
All these versions and opinions, and much learning of a somewhat ill-digested and uncritical kind, Taylor at last gathered
up in his *Historic Survey of German Poetry* (1828-30). Such
a work, the first of its kind in the language, was of high value
for the time ; it was torn to pieces by Carlyle in the *Edinburgh Review* (1831), chiefly on account of its lack of insight
and its feebleness in proportion and perspective, and its reputation did not last very long.

Carlyle[1] had himself been already more than ten years at
work ; in 1819 he was already ' devouring Schiller and Goethe.'
Between his *Life of Schiller*, which appeared in book-form in
1825, and his elegy on Goethe (1832) his genius and style can
be traced unfolding to their first perfection. His creed and
characteristic ideas are also seen taking shape. Next to
life and experience, it was the German writers, whose work
he set himself to proclaim and penetrate, that had the greatest
share in the formation of Carlyle. Drawn in youth by Schiller,
with his more abstract, lyrical, and ideal bent, he soon passed
on to Goethe, and returned to him again and again, announcing him as the master of life and wisdom, the ' hero as poet,'
the richest and most harmonious of modern natures, crowned
with the power of song. No one would now go to Carlyle,
great portrayer as he is, for a distinct or convincing image,
a Rembrandt picture of his master. There was much in Goethe
—his science, his sheer curiosity—for which Carlyle cared
imperfectly. Still, as his defence of *Wilhelm Meister* shows,
it was by no means only the prophet and moralist and coun-
sellor that he admired. Carlyle himself was not only a prophet,
but equally, and in the high sense of the term, a realist ; one,
that is, who is never contented till he can see mankind as it
really is, in its rugged primitive foundations. Hence his
so-called ' worship of force,' and hence also his disconcerting
moods of tolerance. Goethe struck him as a seer of this order,
who was not to be blinded by ' formulae.' Across this dominant
influence, though somewhat later, struck that of Fichte and
the philosophic idealists. In the paper called *Characteristics*

their attraction is evident ; but it is only fully disclosed in *Sartor* (1837), which may be regarded as the last word and the bourne of Carlyle's early writing. Meantime he went on with his German evangel, spending on Richter, Tieck, Novalis, and lesser figures more pains and praise than they may now seem to merit, and, as Matthew Arnold noticed, disregarding Heine, a greater man than they ; expounding and introducing the *Nibelungenlied* to English readers ; and disposing by the way of poor old Taylor. All this hard labour of Carlyle's, whatever its shortcomings, did more than anything to establish communications between the English and the German mind. No one man has done so much in this direction since his day ; and to himself it had more than a purely moral or intellectual value. For he never writes better, or at least more beautifully, than in those earlier years. He is not yet, it is true, the greatest of describers, of engravers, and his full power as a humourist is to come. But in lyrical melody, in sheer plain purity of English, few things can stand beside his last words on Goethe ; and Carlyle is always great when speaking of death, a subject on which it is only too easy to be mannered. The growth of this gift of style is not hard to observe. The *Life of Schiller*, or much of it, might have been written by almost any competent and enthusiastic person of letters ; Carlyle afterwards called it ' insignificant,' and added that it ' pretends also to be very harmless ' ; but it is rather a thing of the ordinary mint of the day ; and yet he was already eight-and-twenty when he wrote it. The papers of a year or two later, on Goethe's *Helena*, and on the *State of German Literature*, are different ; and in those on Novalis and the *Nibelungenlied*, later still, the style has taken new colour, music, and personality, while it is hardly at all defaced by ' formulae ' (to which their great denouncer was soon himself to be prone). In these first years Carlyle is a craftsman in the ranks, and very high in the ranks, of the romantic critics and essayists.

IV

The debt of the English imagination to Italy is another field for the explorer, and has repeatedly been touched upon already. The achievement of Cary, preceded by the experiments of Mathias and the history of Roscoe, was but the noble firstfruits of a study which flourished more and more. The body of allusions to Dante [1] and his successors by poets, critics, and scholars, grows rapidly as the nineteenth century advances. This can be traced in the periodical writing ; and the activities of Ugo Foscolo,[1] himself a poet, give him a foremost place amongst the pioneers. It was on the third generation, that of Leigh Hunt, Byron, Keats, Shelley, and Hazlitt, that the spell of Italy wrought most fully. Some of the best they wrote was inspired by the land, or by its literature, or by both. Italy, as ever, was a school both of thought and of form ; supplying artistic moulds, uplifting poetic form and technique, and quickening the spirit by her memories, her struggles, her fine art, her scenery, and her poetry.

Only second in potency was the call of Greece, which in the mid-nineteenth century was to become stronger still. This again is slow but certain in its workings on the romantic writers. Cowper's *Homer*, and the allusions of Wordsworth to myth and fable, are by the way ; but the *Immortality Ode*, the greatest poem of its kind in English, rests in part on the antique. On the side of the arts, philosophy, and the drama, it is again Shelley and Keats who profit most profoundly by the Greek spirit ; Byron is chiefly stirred by the tradition of ancient glory and freedom. The work of Shelley, who was born to respond to the sublime, is inconceivable without Æschylus and Plato ; and the spirit of Keats overleaped the barriers of an unknown language. Landor, who was under no such disability, sat by the same fountains, and was inspired to create figures of heroic beauty or idyllic grace. Greece, too, inspired some of the critical searchings and revelations of Coleridge and De Quincey.

In this second English Renaissance, therefore, as in the first, there is not only a great and successful flowering of creative art ; but many of the seeds are brought from other lands, or else are handed down alive, after a long residence in darkness, from the ancient world. As before, the most precious of them come from Greece and Italy. Others are from the East, or from Spain, but these are fewer. And there are two new creditors : one is Germany, the other is the older English literature itself. This was now made more accessible by the labours of editors, historians, and antiquaries, who are seen working alongside of the inspired critics, and somewhat apart from them. The line of scholars comes down with little break through the eighteenth into the nineteenth century. Thomas Tyrwhitt's text of the *Canterbury Tales*, and his establishment, far completer than any hitherto, of the Chaucer canon (1775-78), laid a firm base for modern inquiries. Wordsworth's modernisations do not give the measure of his love for Chaucer, to whom

The Eve of Saint Mark is a less direct but a more real tribute. Warton's *History of English Poetry* (1774-81), which revealed the national treasures of romance more than any other book, bore many fruits. It mattered less that Warton was not always critical; the critics came afterwards, and he turned them into a wide pasture. They had to read and judge the mediæval and Renaissance poetry which he had discovered. It was owing to the efforts of Warton and others that the old writers were newly admired, honoured, and canvassed. It is hard to enumerate those who inspired the poets and appreciators ; among them are Drayton, Sidney, Chapman, Wither. Nor need we repeat what has been told of the quarryings of Hunt and Keats in Jacobean diction, and of Lamb among the playwrights, or of the debts of Coleridge and De Quincey to the masters of seventeenth-century prose. It would take a long chapter to describe the attention paid to Spenser, Milton, and Shakespeare by the scholars and writers of the time. The measure of *The Faerie Queene* proved its vitality by winning a new cadence from each of the greater poets who employed it. A whole anthology could be made of the praises of Milton, and he affected the romantic age more than any other poet. His style and verse, unlike Shakespeare's (though they are equally great and peculiar), have always had a mysterious power of self-transmission. They reappear transformed in the original work of other artists. In Blake, in Cowper, in Wordsworth, in Shelley, in Keats, and in Landor, this quality of Milton is apparent.

The deeper comprehension of Shakespeare[1] in his own country dates from Coleridge, Lamb, and their companions. At the same time, the honesty, diligence, and accuracy of Edmond Malone forestalled, and greatly furthered, the minute investigations of the later nineteenth century. His essay on the chronology of the plays (1790), and his critical edition (1790) of the text are scientific in method ; and the illustrations gathered by the younger Boswell into the ' variorum ' edition of 1821 are still a valuable mine. Malone's somewhat prosaic mind made him an excellent detective, and his criticisms of the ' Rowley poems ' of Chatterton, and also of William Henry Ireland's Shakespearean forgeries—including the practical joke, applauded, hooted, and confessed, of *Vortigern* (1796)— were undeniable. The tricksy operations of George Steevens, Malone's adversary, in the field of Elizabethan learning are of less credit, and have discounted his genuine acuteness and erudition. The diverse labours of Monck Mason the commentator and of the archæologists like Francis Douce and Nathan Drake did good service. It is not so easy to trace the influence of Shakespeare, at least for good, on the poets of the period, who seem to be either too strong or not strong enough to walk in his steps. It is on his inspired lovers, his apostles, his expounders, that some of his creative spirit descends, as if in the regal repayment of a debt.

NOTES

p. 1. **Southey.** The *Poems*, ed. by M. H. Fitzgerald (1909), contains all of importance or interest (though not the *Vision of Judgement* or a number of the lyrics, odes, etc.). The ed. of 1847, and the collected one of 1837-38 (10 vols.) can be consulted for the rest. The *Life and Correspondence*, ed. by Cuthbert Southey (1849-50), and the four vols. (1856), ed. by J. W. Warter, are the quarry for several selections, *e.g.* that of John Dennis (Boston, 1887). The prose works can never be collected ; the *Nelson* (ed. D. Hannay, 1896, and ed. H. B. Butler, 1911) and the *Wesley* have been oftenest reprinted. See E. Dowden's study ('Eng. Men of Letters,' 1880) and his small anthology ('Golden Treasury,' 1895) ; also Symons, *Romantic Movement*, pp. 148-60 (a destructive comment).

p. 5. **The Devil's Thoughts.** For the original version (*Morning Post*, Dec. 24, 1799) see Dykes Campbell's *Poetical Works of Coleridge* (1893), pp. 621-3 ; for the fuller one, *ib.*, p. 147 ; also Southey's *Poetical Works*, ed. Fitzgerald, pp. 420-5 and 757-8. Coleridge, whose memory was untrustworthy, says (*Poems*, ed. 1829) that stanzas 1, 2, 3, 15 were dictated by Southey (*i.e.* in the numbering of the enlarged poem). It is, anyhow, a joint-stock composition. For the ascription to Porson, see Dykes Campbell's note, and C. A. Ward, *N. and Q.*, 7th series, viii. 121. Several versions, more or less incorrect, were published in pamphlet as Porson's in 1830-31. I have seen one undated, 'edited by H. W. Montagu' (Marsh and Miller) : the editor quotes Beloe as his authority for the authorship, but I can find no mention of the subject in the first ed. of *The Sexagenarian* (1817). Cruikshank's pictures are of the blatant-grotesque order, like the poem itself.

p. 6. **Sayers.** See Preface to *Thalaba*, on Sayers's *Specimens of Northern Mythology* (1790) ; his unrhymed choric lines are stiff and dismal enough.

p. 9. **limpid style.** *The Story of the Three Bears* (*The Doctor*, ed. 1849, pp. 327-9) is a pattern of this, and an exception to the usual vein of *The Doctor*.

p. 13. **Landor.** Forster's *Life* (1869, 1879), and Sir Sidney Colvin's *Landor* in 'Eng. Men of Letters' (1881), are supplemented by Stephen Wheeler's two works, *Letters and other unpublished Writings of W. S. L.* (1897), and *Letters, Public and Private* (1899). There is no complete ed. of Landor's writings ; many are rare and hard of access. The ed. of 1846 in two vols. contains his own selection from the prose and verse he had written up to that time. Forster's in 8 vols. (1876, the first being the *Life*), and C. G. Crump's (1891-3), give between them almost all that is important. Mr. Crump gives only a selection from the verse, of which there is as yet no variorum edition (much needed owing to Landor's frequent revisions) ; he prints the 'longer prose works' entire and a number of the *Conversations*. These last were also separately published,

from Forster's ed., in 5 vols., in 1883 ; but a few are absent. Of selections, Sir
S. Colvin's ('Golden Treasury series,' first issued in 1882) gives the best
possible representation of Landor's prose and verse in a compact form, and the
introduction is of high value. The *Pentameron*, with some of the *Imag. Conv.*,
is conveniently reprinted in the 'Scott Library,' and more of the *Imag. Conv.*
in another vol. of the same series. See Sir L. Stephen's art. on W. S. L. in the
Dict. Nat. Biog., with its bibliography : a number of the scarcer works are in
the Forster collection at South Kensington. I have left several unmentioned or
undescribed in the text. For a good estimate of Landor see Lord Houghton's
Monographs (1873), pp. 63-150.

p. 16. **parts of Gebir first in Latin.** See *Ad Robertum Fratrem*, at the end
of *Poemata et Inscriptiones* : 'Sermone nostro incepi ; Latino deinde partes
aliquot tentavi.' Robert, he proceeds, on seeing a number of the verses in
Latin, persuaded him to finish it ; and Walter Landor, on the day after Buona-
parte was named 'Consul Perpetuo' (this was May 10, 1802) buried himself for
two months in the *Petit Trianon*, inhabiting Marie Antoinette's rooms, and
finished *Gebirus* pacing the gardens. The English *Gebir* was much cut down
in the second edition : Forster (1869), i. 102-4. It was finished first, as the
Latin reference above shows : see Lord Houghton, *Monographs*, p. 79, who
leaves the point open.

p. 17, note 1. '**phantom epic.**' For this phrase and its application to the
seventeenth century, see W. P. Ker, *Essays of Dryden* (1900), i. xv-xvii.

p. 17, note 2. **Hyperion recalls Gebir.** See W. T. Arnold, Keats's *Poet.
Works*, p. xxxiii.

p. 17, note 3. **Progress of Romance.** On Clara Reeve's book see *ante*, i.
244 ; and Colvin, *Selections from Landor*, pp. 362-4.

p. 18. **vetustatis.** See *Poemata et Inscriptiones*, as above (*Ad Robertum
Fratrem*).

p. 24. **Lord Houghton.** *Monographs*, p. 69.

p. 26. **original draft of** Ode to Joseph Ablett. See Forster, *Life* (1869), ii.
257-9.

p. 27. **Latin quatrain.** In *Dry Sticks* (1853), No. 330.

p. 28. **Terry Hogan.** This 'eclogue,' 'edited' by 'Phelim Octavius Quarle'
(1836) is assigned to Landor in the B. M. copy by an entry in the handwriting
of Prof. De Morgan.

p. 29. **Latin works named in Landor's letters.** See Forster, *Life* (1869), i.
252 foll.

p. 31. **poems translated from the Latin.** These, as finally collected in
Poemata et Inscriptiones (1847), are : *Cupido et Pan, Pudoris Ara, Sponsalia
Polyxenae, Dryope, Corythus, Pan et Pitys, Coresus et Callirhoë, Catillus et
Salia, Veneris Pueri, Ulysses in Argyripa*. But the English often betters the
Latin ; *e.g.* the lines quoted in text, ii. 32, 'Sharp was the splendour of the
stars,' etc., run :

> Splendor erat stellarum asper, totumque moveri
> Visum oculis alio quam quo solet ordine coelum.

p. 33, note 1. **statesmen, famous women,** etc. Forster's divisions (partly
Landor's own) are inconvenient and are not followed in the text. His 'miscellaneous' group (40 conversations) includes many that could go amongst his

other four—dialogues of 'Greeks and Romans,' of 'sovereigns and states-men,' of 'famous women,' and of 'literary men.' The famous women include some sovereigns, the Greeks and Romans include some writers. Certainly no classification can be exhaustive ; there is no pigeon-holing 'all the leading figures of Time,' as the Positivist Calendar shows. Sir Sidney Colvin's distinction between 'dramatic' and 'non-dramatic' conversations is the sound one, and is the basis of ours.

p. 33, note 2. **opinions on Plato.** See *Diogenes and Plato*, and *Aristoteles and Callisthenes*, also *Lucian and Timotheus*.

p. 36. **sources have been traced.** The notes to Colvin's *Selections* are a mine of this kind of investigation.

p. 46. **Robert Eyres Landor.** There seem to be no reprints, and since his own day few mentions, of this writer. His tragedies are not at all common ; I have been able to read them through the kindness of his grand-nephew, the Rev. R. E. H. Duke, of Maltby Rectory, Lincolnshire, who tells of the family tradition as to the burning of the plays. See art. in *Dict. Nat. Biog.*, and A. Symons, *Romantic Movement*, pp. 207-9 ; also the numerous mentions by Forster, *Life* (1869), especially ii. 363-9, where R. E. Landor's letters on his own plays are given, and the assignment of *Count Arezzi* to Byron is related.

p. 48. **quotation.** From *The Fountain of Arethusa* (1848), i. 152. R. E. Landor also wrote *The Impious Feast* (1820), a dignified but rather dull poem on Belshazzar in blank verse irregularly and unluckily sprinkled with rhymes ; a practice which he defends in the preface, wishing to show 'the possibility of extracting much which is desirable' from both measures.

p. 52. **Wordsworth.** The standard text of the *Poetical Works*, as revised by the author, appeared in 1849-50. Of modern editions may be named : that by William Knight (8 vols., 1882-86) with a *Life* (3 vols., 1889) ; one with introduction by Lord Morley (1888, etc.) ; the 'Aldine,' by E. Dowden (7 vols., 1892-3) ; the 'Oxford,' by T. Hutchinson (1904). For the text of quotations I have used the last of these, and also for indications of date. Knight's ed. and that of 1888 offer the poems in chronological order, which at some points is conjectural ; the 'Oxford' ed. is charier in assigning dates of composition, and follows Wordsworth's chosen arrangement and classification. Mr. Hutchinson has also published useful reprints, with notes, both of *Lyrical Ballads* (1798) and of the two vols. of the ed. of 1807. See too the reprint with notes by G. Sampson of the 1805 vols., *Lyrical Ballads, with Pastoral and other Poems*. Critical accounts are numerous : among them are conspicuous those of Matthew Arnold in the preface to his *Selections* ; of W. Pater in *Appreciations* ; of F. W. H. Myers, in 'Eng. Men of Letters' ; of Sir Walter Raleigh (1903) ; and of A. Symons in his *Romantic Movement in English Poetry*. One of the most illuminating is by E. Legouis, *La Jeunesse de W.* (Eng. tr., 1897). See also various essays by Sir L. Stephen, in *Hours in a Library* and elsewhere. *Prose Works*, ed. Grosart (3 vols., 1876). *Journal of Dorothy Wordsworth*, ed. J. Knight (2 vols., 1904).

p. 53. **recensions and alterations.** See the collations in footnotes of Knight's ed., and Dowden, 'On the Text of Wordsworth's Poems,' in *Transcripts and Studies* (1888). Wordsworth's recensions are an intricate matter, and the remarks in my text would need much expansion to do any justice to it. In the long run they are often for the better, but by no means always ; Prof. Dowden's instances go to show that his *additions* are seldom so questionable as his *changes* in existing matter.

p. 55, note 1. **Carlyle.** Sir C. G. Duffy, *Conversations with Carlyle* (1892), p. 55.

p. 55, note 2. **strong memory.** This often failed in reference to the dates, as distinct from the scenes and occasions, of the poems. The notes taken down by Miss Fenwick have to be corrected, where possible, from other sources. See Hutchinson, *Poems of* 1807, vol. i. pp. xxxiv-v, and 'Oxford' ed., p. ix, note.

p. 57. **the deficiency.** From the poet's note to *An Evening Walk*. In the sentences that follow in text, I had unpardonably forgotten Shelley's profanest reference in *Peter Bell the Third*, which yet may have given a suggestion.

p. 60, note 1. **backslider.** See Mrs. Shelley's note on *Peter Bell the Third* ; Byron, *Don Juan*, dedication, stanza vi. ; and, for Browning's not very satis-factory explaining away of the allusion in *A Lost Leader*, his letter (of 1875) quoted in Grosart, *Prose Works of W. W.*, vol. i. preface, p. xxxvii.

p. 60, note 2. **political hopes and dejection.** Best traced by Legouis, *op. cit.*, Eng. tr., pp. 190 foll. M. Legouis and M. G. Bussière have also written a monograph, which I have not seen, on Wordsworth's friend, *Le général Michel Beaupuy* (1891).

p. 62. **poetic diction of Descriptive Sketches** : *i.e.* of the first ed., which was afterwards greatly changed, and which is given (*e.g.*) in the 'Oxford' ed. See Legouis, *op. cit.*, for details.

p. 65. **interchange of the senses.** Of course this is in both cases eased and commended by the application ; the breeze *is* 'seen' ' in the tree,' and the gleams *are* 'heard,' at least by the inner ear, in their 'rustling conflict.'

p. 77. **raised from its animal nature.** See Grosart, *Prose Works of W.*, iii. 430 : 'He said he considered the *White Doe* as in conception the highest work he had ever produced.'

p. 80. **The world**, etc. Hutchinson ('Oxford' ed., p. 259) does not assign date ; I provisionally follow Knight here, and also in the case of *Personal Talk*.

p. 81. **the volta.** For full and excellent analysis of these sonnet-forms see Hutchinson's ed. of *Poems of 1807*, i. 208-26 ; I have drawn very freely on this. For the relevant letters and entries see Knight, *Life*, iii. 95, 231, 233, 258, etc.

p. 83. **versification.** See Saintsbury, *Hist. of Eng. Prosody*, iii. 71 foll., for a severer view.

p. 88. **declarations of principle.** Much has been written on this dispute, and Wordsworth's actual meaning is still contested. For a thoroughgoing state-ment of the adverse case see Saintsbury, *Prosody*, iii. 68-70 : ' When he obeyed his principles, he generally, though not always, wrote bad poetry, and when he wrote good poetry, he generally, though not always, betrayed his principles.' It depends on what the principles were, and on whether they are to be judged by his most extreme statement of them. See an exposition on the other side, with which I largely agree, in J. Shawcross's ed. of *Biographia Literaria* (1907), ii. 286-7 (notes by editor to Ch. xvii.).

p. 89. **one phase.** See C. H. Herford, in *Quart. Rev.*, Oct. 1910, on *Dante's Theory of Poetry*, p. 422 : 'and it was towards the spiritual freedom of a life at one with Nature that he looked when he [Wordsworth] prescribed for poetry a language purified to the utmost from the artifices introduced by man's meddling intellect and the glossy insincerities of urbane discourse.'

p. 92. **by Sara Coleridge**. See *Memoir and Letters of S. C.* (fourth ed., 1874), p. 391.

p. 100. **S. T. Coleridge**. See J. L. Haney, *Bibliography of S. T. C.* (Philadelphia, 1903, privately printed), which supersedes the older ones and forms a bedrock for the study of Coleridge ; the literature is very large and scattered. Of the *Poetical Works* the standard ed. is J. Dykes Campbell's, with memoir (1893) ; this memoir was afterwards expanded and separately published (1894). All Mr. Dykes Campbell's work is indispensable to the student ; see list in Haney, pp. 88-9, of his notes in *Athenaeum*. The prose works are most accessible (incomplete) in various vols. of Bohn's 'Standard Library' ; a fuller ed. is J. Shedd's (*Complete Works*, New York, 1853). The *Letters* have been edited by E. H. Coleridge, in a copious selection (2 vols., 1895), and in a supplementary one by A. Turnbull, *Coleridge's Biographia Epistolaris* (2 vols., 1911). A. Brandl's *S. T. Coleridge und die englische Romantik* (Eng. tr. 1887) is a valuable essay, but appeared before full biographical material was at hand. *Table Talk* (ed. H. N. Coleridge) is a common book, and *Anima Poetae* (ed. E. H. Coleridge, 1895) an equally precious one. J. Aynard's *La Vie d'un Poète* (1907) is a pertinent account of Coleridge.

p. 101. **pantheist . . . Unitarian**. See J. M. Robertson, *s.v.* 'S. T. Coleridge' in *Ency. Brit.* (eleventh ed., vi. 680), for a luminous sketch of these changes of view, and the same writer's *New Essays towards a Critical Method* (1897), pp. 130-90.

p. 102. **Wallenstein**. See complete *dossier* of the additions, omissions, blunders, and alterations by P. Machule, *Coleridge's Wallensteinübersetzung*, in *Eng. Studien* (1902), xxxi. 182-239 ; there is a full account of the MS. used by S. T. C., etc.

p. 104. **letter of 1816**. May 13, 1816 ; see *Letters* (ed. E. H. Coleridge), ii. 663.

p. 105. **Goethe**. See *ante*, i. 422-3 (note on i. 22).

p. 108. **habit . . . of echoed sound**. Exhaustively worked out in A. Eichler's ed. of *The Ancient Mariner* and *Christabel* (vol. xxvi. of *Wiener Beiträge zur engl. Philologie*, 1907), pp. 8-19.

p. 110. **'no moral.'** On all this see notes in *Poet. Works* (ed. Dykes Campbell), pp. 596-7.

p. 111. **Christabel**. For history, textual variations, and facsimile of MS., see the ed. of E. H. Coleridge (for Royal Society of Literature), 1907—a beautiful and complete production.

p. 112. **metre of Christabel**. For historical precedents and comment see Saintsbury, *Hist. of Eng. Prosody*, iii. 55-67 ; for a close analysis of the actual feet employed, H. D. Bateson, 'Rhythm of Christabel,' in *Manchester Quarterly* (1894). The criticism by R. Bridges, in *Milton's Prosody* (1901 ed.), App. F, pp. 73-5, on the 'conventional stresses' in this poem is ably met by T. S. Omond, *English Metrists* (1907), pp. 86-90. The sentence quoted in text, 'time can be felt,' etc., is Mr. Omond's, and I agree with his view that 'Coleridge's practice, if not his definition, restored *time* to its true pre-eminence ;' and may add my conviction that Mr. Omond's division of English verse into time-periods tending to be regular (without assigning impossible time-values to separate syllables) is far nearer the mark than either the bare accent-counting of one school of metrists, or the extravagant identification, by another school, of poetic with musical conditions.

p. 122. **carefully traced.** See *Biog. Literaria*, ed. J. Shawcross (2 vols., 1907)—a definitive edition. The connection of Coleridge's philosophy with his theory of art, and with the distinction between 'fancy and imagination,' is drawn out very fully. See too, for a selection, J. W. Mackail, *Coleridge's Literary Criticism* (1908), with introduction.

p. 124. **lectures of 1818.** In *Misc. Works* (4 vols., 1836-9), i. 216-40.

p. 125. **Mill.** In *Dissertations and Discussions* (4 vols., 1874), ii. 5-78 (art. on 'Coleridge,' orig. published 1840).

p. 126, note 1. **mysticism.** See *Aids to Reflection* (ed. H. N. Coleridge, 1848), i. 341-2, for the warning.

p. 126, note 2. **August von Schlegel.** See Miss Anna A. Helmholtz's thesis, *The Indebtedness of S. T. C. to August Wilhelm von Schlegel*, Wisconsin, 1907 (Bulletin No. 163 of the University of Wisconsin). The parallels cited at length show conclusively both the debt and the improvements of Coleridge. This is a thorough recital, and also a review of the previous (more or less incomplete) statements of the case. For a hostile account of the loans levied by Coleridge on Schelling, Maass, and others, see J. F. Ferrier in *Blackwood's Mag.* (March 1840), vol. xlvii.

p. 126, note 3. **The Friend.** The 1818 ed. is reprinted by Messrs. Bell, 1882. The numbers of 1809-10 were gathered up with a supplement in the 1812 ed., never reprinted, and not seen by me. The third ed. of 1837 contains some corrections : see Haney, *Bibliog.*, Nos. 12 and 13.

p. 127, note 1. **views on current politics.** Collected by Sara Coleridge in *Essays on his Own Times* (3 vols., 1850) ; these include most of Coleridge's political writings, though probably some articles in the *Morning Post* have escaped identification.

p. 127, note 2. **a great leader-writer.** See H. D. Traill, *Coleridge* ('Eng. Men of Letters,' 1884), pp. 84-7.

p. 130. **the 'Romantic Philosophy.'** See H. Höffding, *Hist. of Modern Philosophy* (Eng. tr. 1900, ii. 374-7) for this phrase, and for a judicial though severe estimate of Coleridge's intellectual importance ; the European point of view is urged, rather than the significance of Coleridge to English thought in its dead season.

p. 131. **Hartley Coleridge.** Derwent Coleridge in 1851 printed the *Poems* (2 vols.) and the *Essays and Marginalia* (2 vols.). *Complete Poems*, ed. Ramsay Colles ('Muses' Library,' n.d.), with introduction. *Memoir and Letters of Sara Coleridge*, edited by her daughter (1873 ; fourth ed. abridged, 1874).

p. 133. **Charles Lloyd.** None of his works seem to have been reprinted ; but there are extracts from *Desultory Thoughts* in Mr. E. V. Lucas's monograph, *Charles Lamb and the Lloyds* (1898), much of which is embodied in his *Life of Charles Lamb* (1905). The copy in the B. M. of *Nugae Canorae* has some depreciatory scrawlings by S. T. Coleridge.

p. 135. **Byron.** Hardly a bare indication of the literature can be given. The standard ed. of the *Poetical Works* is that by E. H. Coleridge (7 vols., 1898-1904), and uniform with this is the ed. of the *Letters and Journals*, by

R. E. Prothero (6 vols.) ; in both of these is a wealth of illustrative material,
and few English writers have been better served. See also *Poet. Works*, ed.
E. H. Coleridge (1 vol., 1905). Mr. Prothero prints more than twice as
many letters as Moore did in his ed. of the *Works, Letters*, etc. (17 vols.,
1832-3). But there is no good life and study of Byron on a large scale. Galt's
compilation (1846) succeeded Moore's well-known *Life*, etc. (1830) ; see *ante*,
ii. 278, on this ; Karl Elze's heavy and conscientious study (1872), J. C.
Jeaffreson's coarse and candid inquiry, *The Real Lord Byron* (2 vols., 1883),
and J. Nichol's brief brilliant sketch ('Eng. Men of Letters'), are in sundry
ways insufficient. There is a thick cloud of contemporary witnesses, not here
to be recounted ; Shelley, Trelawny (allowing for prejudice), and Lady
Blessington are among the most convincing. Of later judges, Georg Brandes
in his 'Naturalism in England' (in *Main Currents of Nineteenth Century Lit.*,
Eng. tr., 1905) is the most fervent, treating Byron as the centre and glory of
the liberal movement in letters. The well-known essays of Matthew Arnold
(*Poetry of Byron*, selected, 1902), and of Swinburne, have determined current
English opinion powerfully. Much of Macaulay's essay is external and
rhetorical.

p. 141. **literary origins** (of the Byronic hero). These become more evident
in the later personages like Conrad-Lara, than they are in *Childe Harold*. See,
in the *Literary Gazette* for Feb. and March 1821, Alaric Watts's article, which
detects suggestions from Massinger's *Unnatural Combat* ; for this reference
I am indebted to the late Prof. J. Churton Collins's article, *Quart. Rev.*, No.
cccciii (Ap. 1905). Collins also points out the borrowings in *Lara* from *The
Italian*, and the resemblances of Lord Nelvil in *Corinne*. The truth is that
Byron appropriated and heightened a type which was already afloat in the
consciousness of Europe, and Europe, gratefully, forgot all Byron's debts and
identified the type for good and all with Byron. See Kraeger's work, named
post, note on p. 419.

p. 142. **Ali Pacha.** Journal, in *Letters*, etc. (ed. Prothero), i. 282, and *Childe
Harold*, ii. 62.

p. 150, note 1. **Siege of Corinth.** See E. Kölbing's careful edition of this
poem (1893), and of *The Prisoner of Chillon*.

p. 150, note 2. **Scott . . . Christabel.** See *ante*, i. 448 (note to p. 313).

p. 155. **Goethe.** Goethe's reviews of *Cain, Manfred*, etc., and his Conversa-
tions with Eckermann, and the famed Song of Euphorion in the Second Part of
Faust, are classical ; the whole question is well surveyed by Alois Brandl in
Goethe-Jahrbuch, vol. xx. (1899), 'Goethe's Verhältniss zu Byron.'

p. 159. **Byron's private life.** For the older literature on this affair see Mrs.
Beecher Stowe in *Macmillan's Magazine*, 1869, and *Lady Byron Vindicated*
(1870). For the more recent controversy can be consulted : *Astarte* (1905), by
the late Lord Lovelace, Byron's grandson ; and rejoinder in *Lord Byron and
his Detractors* (1906, privately printed for Roxburghe Club), by John Murray,
with a chapter by R. E. Prothero, etc. ; Richard Edgcumbe, *Byron ; the Last
Phase* (1909). Also *Quart. Rev.* (Jan. 1910), 'Byron and Napoleon.' The matter
at issue is the charge of misconduct against Byron and his half-sister, Augusta,
Mrs. Leigh ; the original case on Byron's side is given, with contemporary documents, in the *Recollections of Lord Broughton* (John Cam Hobhouse) (1910),
vol. iii. Mrs. Stowe and Lord Lovelace are the accusers, the rest are for the

defence. After reading the literature I cannot see that the suggestion against Byron is made out. The alternative theory of Mr. Edgcumbe (partially adopted by the Quarterly Reviewer) is not authenticated save by circumstantial evidence, but has some real bearing on Byron's genius and poetry, and has the advantage of explaining a good many utterances in Byron's poems, letters, and journals. The essential point of this view that Byron's self-reproaches and standing remorse were caused by his tie with Mrs. Chaworth-Musters, formerly Mary Chaworth. The question has its literary importance, and is only touched on here for that reason. Mr. Murray kindly permits me to cite his work.

p. 161. '**wickedness.**' Moore's *Memoirs* (ed. Lord John Russell, 1853), iii. 235. An Italian lady said to Moore that Lord B. 'was much wronged by the world ; that he took up wickedness as a *subject*, just as Chateaubriand did religion, without either of them having much of the reality of either feeling in their hearts.'

But even here we are often baffled. Byron's character and demeanour as a man are hardly seizable, for the best and most intimate witnesses contradict one another. Contrast the often unsparing portraits of Trelawny in his *Recollections*, or of Lady Blessington, or of Galt, with the tribute written by Hobhouse, for his own private diary, just after Byron's death (Lord Broughton, *Recollections*, iii. 41). The strong-headed Hobhouse, accurate and not easy to impress, writes : 'His power of attaching those about him to his person was such as no one I ever knew possessed. No human being could approach him without being sensible of this magical influence. . . . There was a mildness and yet a decision in his mode of conversing, and even in his address, which are seldom united in the same person. . . . He was full of sensibility, but he did not suffer his feelings to betray him into absurdities.' The hero-worship of the Countess Guiccioli in her *Recollections* (1869) seems less extreme after such evidence ; but there is little distinctness in her picture. Shelley's, in *Julian and Maddalo*, and in his preface to that poem, may be compared.

p. 167. **John Hookham Frere** (1769-1846). His *Works*, ed. by W. E. and Sir Bartle Frere (2 vols., 1871 and 1874), contain an interesting memoir. The quotation concerning his reading of Pulci's poetry has been lately found in a letter of Frere to Ugo Foscolo, May 7, 1818, preserved in the Labronica Library at Pavia : given in F. Viglione, *Ugo Foscolo in Inghilterra* (Catania, 1910), pp. 171-2. The most elaborate recent study is by Albert Eichler, *J. H. Frere, sein Leben und seine Werke, und sein Einfluss auf Lord Byron* (Vienna, 1905) ; see pp. 129-49 for a truly exhaustive technical analysis of the metre of *Whistlecraft* ; a study valuable to the professional prosodist, even if it would have astonished the debonair author of the poem. For some personal details see Gabrielle Festing's work, named *ante*, i. 424.

p. 168. **Merivale.** His bits from Pulci are in *Monthly Mag.*, xxi. 204 foll. (1806), and are collected in his *Poems* (1844), vol. ii. ; he also translated Forteguerri's *Ricciardetto*.

p. 169. **Stewart Rose.** See these epistles in Byron's *Letters* (ed. Prothero), iv. 211 note, 212-4. He 'translated' Casti's *Gli Animali Parlanti* (1802) under the title of *The Court of Beasts* (first ed. anon., 1816), abridging freely and, after Pope's way, substituting English allusions from time to time. The seventh canto, for instance, contains a lively address to Scott, of which the first verse may suffice :

Dear Scott, I had a scheme to cross the Border,
And had, in fancy, swallowed many a mile,
But then some duct or gland got out of order,
And, in a thought, I was half swampt in bile :
From this account what you will understand is,
I had a sharp though short attack of jaundice.

The measure is the sextain here, but the run is the same as in the octave.
Rose also translated the *Orlando Innamorato* (1823), and the *Orl. Furioso*
(1823-31)—a step beyond the dead version of Hoole. All this Italian industry
should be studied along with the work of Ugo Foscolo (see Viglione, *op. cit.*).

p. 181. **Byron's influence.** I must content myself with some references to
the literature of this huge subject. *France* : E. Estève, *B. et le romantisme
français* (1907), a careful, elaborate monograph.—*Spain* : Philip H. Churchman, *The Beginnings of Byronism in Spain*, in *Revue hispanique*, tom. xxiii.
(1910), a patient examination of periodical and other literature, with a minute
bibliography of translations into Spanish and also of the journals consulted.—
Italy : G. Muoni, *La Fama del B. e il Byronismo in Italia* (Milan, 1903) (this
I have not seen, but it is severely described, and errors quoted, by Churchman,
op. cit., p. 4) ; G. Mazzoni, *Il Ottocento*, in *Storia letteraria d'Italia* (n.d.), pp.
710-2 ; and Max Simhart, *Lord B.'s Einfluss auf die ital. Literatur* (Naum-
burg a. S., 1908), for lists of translations, criticisms, etc.—*Germany* : bibliography of translations down to date in Cäsar Flaischlen, *Lord B. in Deutschland*
(Leipz., 1890), in *Centralblatt für Bibliothekswesen*, vii. 455-73 ; W. Ochsen-
bein, *Die Aufnahme Lord Byrons in Deutschland und sein Einfluss auf den
jungen Heine* (Bern, 1905), in O. F. Walzel's *Untersuchungen*,—a well-written
essay rich in materials ; R. Ackermann, *Lord B.* (Heidelberg, 1901), pp. 169-
82, for influence in Germany (the work is a compressed biography, and largely
descriptive, for the use especially of 'studious youth') ; H. Kraeger, *Der
Byronsche Heldentypus* (Munich, 1898, in F. Muncker's *Forschungen zur
neueren Literaturgeschichte*), dealing instructively with the influence of Schiller
and others on Byron ; H. von Treitschke, 'Lord B. und der Radicalismus,' in
Historische und politische Aufsätze (fifth ed., Leipz., 1886), i. 305-47 ; A.
Brandl, *Goethes Verhältniss zu B.*, in *Goethe-Jahrbuch* (1899), xx. 3-37. See
too *Byroniana und Anderes* (Erlangen, 1912), being articles by the English
Seminar in Erlangen, and including a note on the 'continuations' of *Don Juan*,
as well as a catalogue of the remarkably good Byron library in the University.
Prof. Robert Petsch has been good enough to put me on the track of most of
these German authorities.—*Russia* : A. N. Pypin and W. Spasowicz, *Gesch.
der slavonischen Literaturen*, tr. E. Pech (1880, etc.) ; references in K. Walis-
zewski, *Hist. of Russian Lit.* (Eng. tr., 1900) ; A. Veselyovsky, *Studies and
Characteristics*, pp. 517-64 ('On Byronism in Russia') ; W. Spasowicz, *Works*
(in Polish, St. Petersb., 1892), i. 311-21, 'On the Byronism of Mickiewicz,'
and v. 225-342, 'On the Byronism of Pushkin and Lermontov.'—*Poland* : Adam
Mickiewicz, *O poezyi romantycznej* ('On romantic poetry'), 1822-3 ; S. Krze-
minski, 'Byron,' in *Zarysy literackie* ('Literary Sketches,' Warsaw, 1895), i.
239-67 ; Ignacy Matuszewski, *Swoi i obcy* ('Polish and foreign Writers,'
Warsaw, 1898), 'Byron,' pp. 282-383 ; Maryen Zdziechowski, *Byron i jego wiek*
('B. and his Age,' Cracow, 1894) ; many translations of various works from
1820 onwards. For these references to works in Russian or Polish, languages

I cannot read, I have to thank my colleagues Mr. Hugh Stewart, M.A., and Mr. M. Trofimov, also my nephew Mr. A. Bruce Boswell. Mr. Stewart has furnished valuable detail which space compels me to omit. On the whole topic of Byron's influence there is a tentative dissertation by F. H. O. Weddigen, *Lord B.'s Einfluss auf die europ. Literaturen der Neuzeit* (Hanover, 1884), but it could only be duly handled by an able syndicate with an able editor.— *America*: W. E. Leonard, *Byron and Byronism in America* (Boston, 1905). I have not collected notices of Byron's influence in Scandinavia, which was very considerable, especially in Sweden.

p. 183. **Shelley.** Complete *Works*, 8 vols. (four verse and four prose), ed. H. Buxton Forman (1876-80); the verse also in 2 vols. (1882, etc.), same editor. Other edd. of *Poet. Works* by W. M. Rossetti (revised, 1878); by T. Hutchinson, with some fresh matter (1904); and by C. D. Locock (2 vols., 1911), with introduction by A. Clutton Brock. Mr. Buxton Forman's service to the text and bibliography (*e.g. The Shelley Library* (1886), in *Shelley Soc. Publications*), is invaluable. The many reprints, facsimiles, essays, etc., published by the Society are noteworthy; of these H. S. Salt's *A Shelley Primer* (1887) is one of the most useful. The standard *Life* is by E. Dowden (2 vols., 1886; 1 vol., abridged, 1896, etc.): the *Letters*, ed. R. Ingpen (2 vols., 1909), are indispensable. Among the most vivid of the older accounts are those of E. J. Trelawny, *Recollections of the Last Days of Shelley and Byron* (1858), re-issued as *Records of Shelley, Byron, and the Author* (2 vols., 1878; and 1906); by T. Jefferson Hogg, *Life of S.* (1858); and by T. L. Peacock, *Memoirs of S.* (ed. H. Brett-Smith, 1909). Amongst many critics can only be named A. C. Swinburne, 'On the Text of Shelley,' in *Essays and Studies* (1875); W. Bagehot, in *Literary Studies*; J. A. Symonds (1878); J. Todhunter (1880); Francis Thompson (1909); and A. Clutton Brock, *Shelley, The Man and the Poet* (1909), an able but somewhat rigid analysis of Shelley's character, and an often chary but on the whole fervent estimate of his genius. F. S. Ellis's *Lexical Concordance* (to the poems) should also be mentioned (1892).

p. 185, note 1. **a sort of rhythm.** This view, which finds in Shelley a kind of tidal ebb and flow between two radically different emotions, of solitary doubt and sick-heartedness on the one side, and on the other of faith and hope for human kind, differs somewhat from that of Prof. A. C. Bradley in his *Oxford Lectures on Poetry* (1909), p. 164: 'Clearly the lament which arises from loss of the ideal, and mourns the evanescence of its visitations or the desolation of its absence, is indirectly an expression *of* the ideal.' And cp. Clutton Brock, *Shelley*, p. 107: 'behind the despair of a great poet there is always an unconscious faith without which he could make no music.'

p. 185, note 2. **his vow.** Dedication of *Revolt of Islam*, iii.-v.; *Revolt*, ii. **xiv.-xv.**; *Hymn to Intellectual Beauty*, vi.

p. 185, note 3. **a precocious scribbler.** Shelley's youthful novels are named, i. 216 *ante*; and for *The Wandering Jew*, which has not yet found acceptance in the Shelley canon, and is in any case worthless, see reprint, *Shelley Soc. Publ.*, 1887, with preface by Bertram Dobell, who pleads for Shelley's authorship.

p. 186, note 1. **Cwm Elan.** The lines are also called *The Retrospect*; printed by Hutchinson, p. 970.

p. 186, note 2. **Godwin.** See Dowden, *Last Words on Shelley*, in *Transcripts and Studies* (1896). Prof. Dowden well shows that Shelley, in his forgiveness of Hogg, in his repudiation of the slanders of which he heard of in Italy, and in his relations with his first wife, was simply acting out Godwinian theory ; which, adds the same critic, attracted him by contrast with his own temperament. 'The fact that Shelley experienced all the troubles of an eager, never-satisfied heart, predisposed him to accept as a counterpoise to his own disturbing passions a philosophy so strict in its ideal of duty, so free from the riot of temperament and its consequent relapse into depression, as was the doctrinaire system of Godwin' (pp. 78-9). This is true ; but it was also Godwin's clear though cold presentment of the goal of human advance which, perhaps primarily, attracted Shelley and gave him a canvas, naked save for a few large outlines, for his Turner-painting. Prof. Dowden's view of Shelley errs, if at all, in making him too pathetic and pitiful a person ('children who stumble on the sharp stones and bruise their hands and feet, yet who can wing their way,' etc., p. 110). But Shelley was much tougher in brain, will, and temper than this would imply. See *post*, note to p. 196 ; and Paul Elsner, *Shelley's Abhängigkeit von William Godwin's Political Justice* (Berlin, 1906) for a methodical analysis.

p. 186, note **3. theoretical fatalism.** On this, and for a close and valuable exposition of Shelley's relation to the philosophy of his time, see the introduction by J. Shawcross to *Shelley's Literary and Philosophical Criticism* (1909). Mr. Shawcross traces Shelley's lines of thought in metaphysics, ethics, and politics, as well as in æsthetic matters, and points out that the doctrine of Necessity was attractive, because it seemed to guarantee the involuntariness, and therefore the innocence, of all opinions. For a hostile view of Shelley on the speculative side, see Leslie Stephen, *Hours in a Library*, vol. iii., 'Shelley and Godwin,' and note *post* to p. 423.

p. 188, note **1. Alastor.** Peacock says that he gave Shelley the title : 'The Greek word ἀλάστωρ is an evil genius, κακοδαίμων, though the sense of the two words is somewhat different. . . . The poem treated the spirit of Solitude as the spirit of evil.' ἀλάστωρ means (Liddell and Scott) 'avenging deity, destroying angel,' in its primary sense ; there is a further sense, 'he who suffers from such vengeance, a polluted or accursed wretch, parallel to ἄλαστος.' But the word *or* in Shelley's title is clearly a definition, and he calls his hero 'the Poet' throughout, and never 'Alastor,' so that Peacock's memory is confirmed. See the notes of A. Beljame in his edition and translation of *Alastor* (Paris, 1895) ; and R. Ackermann, *Quellen*, etc., *zu Shelley's poetischen Werken* (Erlangen, 1890), pp. 2-14, for probable traces of *Thalaba*, as well as of Wordsworth, in the piece ; and Clutton Brock, pp. 109-10, for analysis of the argument.

p. 188, note **2. the verse** of *Alastor*. See Saintsbury, *Hist. Eng. Prosody*, iii. 105, for a description ; 'plenty of trisyllabic feet ; very few, though some, redundant syllables ; a love for brilliant, opal-like spots of colour ; and a predilection for very strong full-stop pauses at or near the middle' ; and, it may be added, for hard abrupt stops at the end of the lines (ll. 11, 17, 624).

p. 190. **'The moon,'** etc. Clutton Brock, *Shelley*, p. 128, says this poem 'seems to refer directly to Harriet' ; and adds, as having perhaps the same reference, the lines 'That time is dead for ever, child,' and those beginning, 'Forget the dead, the past.' It may be so ; but the words in Shelley's letter of Dec. 16, 1816, which speak of Harriet after her death, as 'a human being once so nearly connected with me,' show apparently a curious remoteness of feeling, amidst the shock. It was more than two years since he wrote the astounding epistle (Aug. 1814), asking her to join himself and Mary, and to bring over certain documents, and describing the scenery and the miseries of the Swiss (Clutton Brock, p. 95).

p. 191, note 1. 'a very poetical circumstance.' *Prose Works*, iv. 143, in reference to Calderón's *Cabellos de Absalon* : see too *Prose Works*, iv. 181. For a full account of the change of title and consequential corrections, and for bibliography, see Forman, *The Shelley Library* (Shelley Soc.), part i., pp. 73-87. Peacock has till lately been the chief authority ; he states that 'Shelley was induced to submit to the required changes' by his publisher, Ollier, and by 'the advice of all his friends,' but that he 'contested the alterations step by step' (T. L. P. in *Fraser*, Jan. 1860). Ingpen, *Letters of Shelley*, ii. 574, No. 279, publishes for the first time a letter of Shelley to Moore which puts a slightly different colour on the tale. The seclusion in which he lived, says the poet, induced him 'to form for himself a very different measure of approbation or disapprobation for actions than that which is in use among mankind.' He found the subject would 'revolt' persons 'inclined to sympathise with my general view,' so he 'hastened to cancel,' and this 'not from any personal feeling of terror or repentance,' but from the 'sincere desire to do all the good,' etc.

p. 191, note 2. **Spenser's measure.** See Saintsbury, *Hist. Eng. Prosody*, iii. 106, 111. There are certainly some technical likenesses to the metre of *Childe Harold*, but the effect seems very different in the long run.

p. 193, note 1. **Rosalind and Helen.** The tie between the two women is partly suggested by that of Mary Shelley with Isabel Baxter, who had ceased friendly intercourse with her, but here the likeness ends. See Dowden, *Life*, and Forman's introduction to the poem, pp. xii.-xx., in *Shelley Soc. Publications*, 1888 ; Shelley's forfeiture of his children is also in his mind.

p. 193, note 2. **talk with Byron.** See Ingpen, *Letters of S.*, No. 304, ii. 619, Aug. 23, 1818, for the talk on the trip in question ; the subjects are not those in the poem, which draws no doubt on many memories. There is no juster view of Byron's character, and none more generous, than Shelley's, and it is only warped by his modesty about himself as compared with Byron. No one is a sharper witness at times ; there were grave differences, and there was the whole business of Claire and Allegra, to disenchant him ; but his perception and kindly tact in that matter speak for themselves. He saw Byron was 'as mad as the winds' at times ; but the character of Maddalo, in Shelley's prose ('it is his weakness to be proud . . . it is on his own affections only that he seems to trample') is apt, even if it reflect Byron's picture of himself overmuch. Of Byron's verse Shelley speaks discerningly. He disliked *Childe Harold*, except the address to the Ocean ; but Byron 'touched the chord to which a million hearts responded ; and the coarse music which he produced to please them *disciplined him to the perfection which he now approaches*' ; approaches, that is, in *Don Juan* and *Cain*, of which Shelley thought so much. To the latter poem he was biassed, no doubt, by the doctrine ; his appreciation of the former, so alien to his own usual mood, is a mark of his critical sense. Sometimes he is carried far : 'Space wondered less at the swift and fair creations of God when he grew weary of vacancy, than I at this spirit of an angel in the mortal paradise of a decaying body' (*Prose Works*, iv. 25).

p. 195. **Prometheus Unbound.** I adopt most of Mr. W. M. Rossetti's interpretations (*Shelley Soc. Papers*, part i., 1888). His discussion of the confusing dreams, temples, etc., should be consulted; but Shelley may simply have failed to revise some of these descriptive passages.

p. 196. **dethronement by the spirit of Christ.** See Sir Leslie Stephen, *Hours in a Library*, iii. 81-3. In his paper *Godwin and Shelley* he has written the most damaging of all criticisms of Shelley; the more so, as it is not from the orthodox side. Of *Prometheus* and its ideal he says: 'Man is to be made perfect by the complete dissolution of all the traditional ties by which the race is at present bound together'; and points to the perplexity caused when the poet tries to represent 'a fusion of the satirist's view, that all which is is bad, with the enthusiast's view, that all which will be will be perfect.' The answer is that if we like we can separate Shelley's picture of mankind filled with love and light, from his picture of the means by which this end is attained; though Shelley could not make this separation. In proportion, however, as we hold with him that the condition of progress is bound up with the abolition of dogma embodied in institutions, and that the result of moral progress is to make positive law superfluous *pari passu*, we shall sympathise with him. Stephen says that progress is won not by 'the annihilation of all the conditions of human life, but by the slow conquest of nature by the adaptation of the life to its conditions.' Shelley would have said this too, as his papers on practical reform, and his enthusiasm for political movements towards freedom, show. But *Prometheus* is an ideal and transcendental presentment of man as our dreams and hopes would have him when 'codes' are needless under the law of love.

p. 199. **delicacy in The Cenci.** Shelley hoped that the play might be acted by Miss O'Neill; but the subject was fatal, and *The Cenci* was first performed on May 7, 1888, under the auspices of the Shelley Society, at the Grand Theatre, Islington, Miss Alma Murray taking the part of Beatrice. See the Society's *Notebook* (1888), part i., pp. 50-80.

p. 205, note 1. **Epipsychidion.** See facsimile by Shelley Soc. (1887), preface by Stopford A. Brooke. Also Buxton Forman's remarks and introduction to *Mask of Anarchy* (in Society's publications, 1887), upon Mrs. Shelley's story, *The Last Man* (1826). Its heroine, he suggests, gives voice to Mary Shelley's own feeling on finding her husband's allegiance divided. On probable suggestions from Dante see Ackermann, *op. cit.*, pp. 20-4 (the parallels from the *Symposium* are weaker).

p. 205, note 2. **a soul that complements, etc.** This would seem the sense of Shelley's coined word *Epipsychidion*, an endearing diminutive form of the non-existent ἐπιψυχή: 'a soul upon my soul'; or over it, as Mr. Stopford Brooke explains. This second, or consummating soul, is Emilia Viviani. See *Lines to E—— V——*.

p. 207. **Adonais.** See ed. by W. M. Rossetti, 1891 and 1903.

p. 210. **Triumph of Life.** See careful expositions by Todhunter, *Shelley*; and by Stopford Brooke, *Selected Poems of Shelley*.

p. 217. **speculations.** For an account of these see Shawcross, *op. cit.*; and, on the side of Poetic, an article by A. C. Bradley, in *Oxford Lectures on Poetry*, pp. 151-74. See too Miss L. Winstanley's ed. of the *Defence of Poetry* and of Browning's *Essay on Shelley* (n.d.) in 'The Belles Lettres Series,' with introduction and notes.

p. 225. **James Henry Leigh Hunt.** See Alexander Ireland, *List of the Writings of Hazlitt and L. H.* (1868). There is no collected edition. The *Poet. Works* have been variously issued (*e.g.* by Moxon, 1883). *Autobiography*, ed. R. Ingpen (2 vols., 1903); *Letters*, ed. Thornton Hunt (2 vols., 1882). There are short memoirs by Cosmo Monkhouse ('Great Writers,' 1893), and R. B. Johnson (1896). See too T. H. Escott, *Masters of English Journalism* (1911), p. 139 foll., 'The Hunts, Perry, and Stuart.'

p. 230. **Keats.** Of many edd. of the *Poet. Works* may be named Buxton Forman's (first in 1888, 4 vols.); and E. de Sélincourt's (1905), with the fullest commentary, throwing much new light on the poet's reading, his language, and its sources; a work admirably initiated by W. T. Arnold in his ed. of 1888. For criticism see especially Swinburne's paper in his *Miscellanies*; M. Arnold, in *Essays in Criticism*, second series; and R. Bridges, introduction to G. Thorn Drury's ed. in the 'Muses' Library' (2 vols., 1896); also the comments in Sir S. Colvin's *Keats* ('Eng. Men of Letters,' 1887). A standard monograph is still that of Monckton Milnes (Lord Houghton), issued in 1848 (*Life, Letters, and Lit. Remains*). Sir S. Colvin edited most of the *Letters* in 1891; Forman those to Miss Brawne (1878). See too the ample monograph by Lucien Wolff, *John Keats, sa Vie et son Œuvre* (n.d., but after 1905).

p. 234. **Lemprière.** On this see De Sélincourt, pp. xliv., 499.

p. 237. **nineteen.** See De Sélincourt, p. 398.

p. 238, note 1. **actual dream of Keats.** See *Letters* (ed. Colvin), pp. 234-5.

p. 238, note 2. **ideal beauty.** See Bridges ('Muses' Library,' *Keats*), pp. xviii.-xxix.

p. 245, note 1. **Odes.** See the edition of the *Odes*, by A. C. Downer (1897), for useful analyses and illustrations.

p. 245, note 2. **On a Grecian Urn.** That the details in this poem are fused out of the memories of several distinct, and more or less traceable, works of art seems to be established by P. Wolters in an article on 'Keats's Grecian Urn,' *Archiv für das Studium der neueren Sprachen und Literaturen*, cxx. 53-61 (1907). (I owe this reference to Prof. R. C. Bosanquet.) Dr. Wolters reviews the evidence collected and set out by Forman, W. T. Arnold, Downer, De Sélincourt, and others, with the following conclusions: (1) the tracing of the 'vase of Sosibios' by Keats, made from a picture of Piranesi in the *Monuments antiques du Musée Napoleon*, contains an altar and a bacchanal and an 'attic shape'; and *may* have suggested to Keats's dream the three figures named in the *Ode to Indolence*; (2) the 'Holland House Urn' was probably seen by the poet in Piranesi's *Vasi e Candelabri* (1778), vol. xiii., which contains an engraving of it (see A. S. Murray's letter to W. T. Arnold, quoted in Arnold's ed., p. xxii.), and also of an urn in the Borghese Gallery, which shows 'men and gods' and a 'bold lover'; (3) Wolters suggests that the two urns in the Brit. Mus. numbered 2500 and 2501, which exhibit a mænad and two lovers who seem to kiss, might have been seen by Keats under the tutelage of Haydon; and that the 'lowing heifer' might have come from the Parthenon frieze of the Panathenaic procession. The heifer, however, is on the Holland House urn too. See the pictures in Downer's ed. Much of this must be guesswork, but it is plain that Keats was not transcribing from any *one* vase. See De Sélincourt, p. 476, and Colvin, *Keats*, p. 172.

p. 248. **traced by scholars.** On the Miltonic influence see De Sélincourt, pp. 488-93.

p. 249. **it breaks off.** For other explanations of the cessation of *Hyperion*, see the notes of De Sélincourt ; and Wolff, *op. cit.*, p. 407 note (seen since my text was printed) ; also A. C. Bradley, in Chambers's *Cyclop. of Eng. Lit.* (1903), iii. 100.

p. 250. **a living poet.** Bridges, *Keats*, vol. i. p. xlii.

p. 251. **disproves this supposition.** Lord Houghton, after some hesitations, treated the *Vision* as an early draft, and other editors followed suit. In 1887 Colvin (*Keats*, pp. 187, 232) stated the true nature of the work. For possible influence of Dante see Bridges' edition, introduction. See, generally, *Transliteration of the Fall of Hyperion* (from the Woodhouse transcript), ed. E. De Sélincourt (1905) ; and Wolff, *Keats*, p. 561 foll.

p. 253. **diction.** See W. T. Arnold's edition, pp. xxiv.-xxv., xxxii.-xxxvi., xl.-xlvi. ; and the exhaustive treatment by De Sélincourt (who corrects Arnold in some details) in his notes, and in App. C, pp. 570-600. The chief types of borrowing from older writers are : (1) actual or imaginary archaic words ; (2) extension of the normal formation of participial adjectives derived from substantives ('mountain'd' and 'penanced,' etc.) ; (3) rare or odd adjectives in *y* ('nervy,' 'rooty'), a Jacobean habit. The influence of Leigh Hunt as a cicerone in these paths is also worked out by the editors.

p. 257. **lesser practitioners.** For a number here excluded see the useful anthology of A. F. Miles, *Poets and Poetry of the* [nineteenth] *Century*, 10 vols., n.d.

p. 258, note 1. **Cary's Dante.** The last recension (1844) is reprinted, with notes, life of Dante, etc., in the 'Albion' ed. (1889). For previous English translators, and much information on Cary, see Paget Toynbee, *Dante in English Literature* (2 vols., 1909). There is a memoir of Cary by his son Henry (2 vols., 1847).

p. 258, note 2. **Ugo Foscolo.** See the work by F. Viglione (named *ante*, i. 456, in note on i. 418), pp. 212-4, as to this article in the *Ed. Rev.* Another story had it that Coleridge was the first to observe the merits of Cary's translation.

p. 258, note 3. **modern scholars.** See A. J. Butler, *The Hell of Dante* (1892), pp. ix.-x. : 'It remains, in text and commentary, unquestionably the best book to which the study of Dante in England has ever given birth.' Also Toynbee, *op. cit.*, vol. ii. pp. xxxvii.-xxxviii.

p. 262, note 1. **Sir Aubrey de Vere.** His *Mary Tudor, and Sonnets* (1875) were published by his son, Aubrey de Vere.

p. 262, note 2. **Heber.** Hymns by Heber, Montgomery, and Keble are to be found both in the *Church Hymns* and in *Psalms and Hymns of the Presbyterian Church of Scotland.*

p. 263. **James Montgomery.** The *Poet. Works* (1850) contain 'in a more concise form' matter previously published, with many notes and autobiographical comments.

p. 264. **hymns picked out of poems.** This explains the bad start, 'O timely-happy, timely-wise,' in the morning hymn, which is not the first verse of the poem. 'Sun of my soul' is a cento of stanzas chosen with wonderful felicity for the purpose.

p. 265, note 1. **Pollok.** Frere's inscription in his copy of the *Course of Time* has survived the work itself ('Robert Pollok, A.M., this work of yours Is meant, I do not doubt, extremely well,' etc.), and is quoted *e.g.* by Symons, *Romantic Movement*, p. 325.

p. 265, note 2. **Mrs. Hemans.** *Poet. Works* (1839, 7 vols., the first a *Memoir*).

p. 266, note 1. **Caroline Bowles Southey.** *Poet. Works* (1867). Her correspondence with her husband (ed. Dowden, 1881) is to be noted.

p. 266, note 2. **Burial of Sir John Moore.** For its fortunes see *Remains of the Rev. Charles Wolfe*, by J. A. Russell (2 vols., 1825, p. 25, etc.).

p. 266, note 3. **Blanco White's sonnet.** See the three versions printed by J. Dykes Campbell in *Academy*, Sept. 12, 1891. The poem seems to have appeared first in the *Bijou* for 1829. I am indebted for these references to Prof. J. Fitzmaurice-Kelly. Blanco White's *Life*, etc., ed. J. H. Thom (3 vols., 1845).

p. 267, note 1. **Kirke White.** His *Remains* were edited by Southey in 3 vols. (1808-22); there is an ed. of the poems in the 'Muses' Library,' by J. Drinkwater. See the stanzas 'imitated' from White by Sainte-Beuve in *Joseph Delorme* (ed. 1863, p. 140).

p. 268. **Clare.** See *Poems by Clare*, edited by A. Symons (1908), and the same writer's *Romantic Movement*, pp. 288-92. Mr. Symons was the first critic, I think, to value Clare in the right way and for the right things, and there is not much to say after him.

p. 269. **Elliott.** *Poet. Works*, ed. by his son Edwin (2 vols., 1876). Carlyle's article was in the *Edinburgh* for July 1832, and is in his *Misc. Essays*.

p. 271, note 1. **The Irish Muse.** See *A Treasury of Irish Poetry*, by Stopford A. Brooke and T. W. Rolleston (1900), books i. and ii. I have had to rely on this excellent anthology for Banim and Callanan.

p. 271, note 2. **Dermody.** *The Harp of Erin* (1807) and Dermody's *Life* (2 vols., 1806) were both edited by J. G. Raymond; and there are many references in Lady Morgan's *Memoirs*. In my text mention is wrongly omitted of Curran's gay sad ditty, 'If sadly thinking,' versified from an actual occurrence; see *Memoirs of J. P. Curran* (2 vols., 1819), i. 211 foll.

p. 272. **Thomas Moore.** He published his *Poet. Works* (10 vols., 1840-2); there are many modern editions, *e.g.* by A. D. Godley (1910). The *Memoirs, Journal, and Correspondence* were ill edited by Lord John Russell (8 vols., 1852-6); see Stephen Gwynn, *Moore* ('Eng. Men of Letters,' 1905).

p. 278. **to destroy Byron's memoirs.** The latest contribution to the long dispute on this matter may be seen in Lord Broughton (John Cam Hobhouse), *Recollections of a Long Life* (1910), ii. 326-52. This circumstantial 'narrative of events connected with the destruction of Lord Byron's memoirs' is hostile to Moore, reflecting on his candour and almost on his honour. It was written in 1825, but not published, so that no reply was then possible; and the story is a complicated one. But all Moore's other record shows him to be an honourable, if somewhat conventional, soul.

p. 280. **Rejected Addresses.** The sixteenth ed. was in 1819; the twenty-second in 1851. *James and Horace Smith*, by Arthur H. Beavan, 1899, contains much unpublished material, and gives a lively picture of the social and literary life of the brothers (also long extracts from Horace's work, *A Greybeard's Gossip about his Literary Acquaintances*). For 'samples of the poetic humour' of James, see *ib.*, pp. 191-3.

p. 281. **C. Fanshawe.** Her lines are to be found in Locker-Lampson, *Lyra Elegantiarum*.

p. 282. **Praed.** The first authorised edition of the *Poems*, with memoir by Derwent Coleridge, appeared in 1864. There are various reprints. The most important supplement is the *Political and Occasional Poems*, admirably edited by Sir George Young, Praed's nephew, in 1888. The editor gives a very full key to the endless allusions, and sifts the authentic pieces carefully from others that were long confused with Praed's, being written under the same initial by his friend and ally Edward Montgomery Fitzgerald. (Young, *Introd.*, pp. xxiv.-xxxi.). Praed's *Essays* are in Morley's 'Universal Library' (1887).

p. 286. **Hood.** The *Collected Works* were edited by Hood's son and daughter (11 vols., n.d.); for the *Poems*, see edition by A. Ainger (2 vols., 1897), with introduction. See the *Memorials*, edited by Hood's daughter (1860).

p. 292. **Reynolds.** *The Fancy* has been edited by J. Masefield with congenial pictures by Jack B. Yeats (1905). It is a pity that a selection from the other poems and prose pieces is not made. See art. by R. Garnett in *D. N. B.*, and Keats's letters to this poetic younger brother.

p. 294. **Wells.** The poem, with Swinburne's essay, has again been reprinted (1909). See E. Gosse, art. 'Wells,' in *Encycl. Brit.*, eleventh ed.

p. 295. **Procter.** Procter's work does not seem to have been reprinted save in anthologies; see Miles, *Poets and Poetry of the Nineteenth Century*, vol. ii.

p. 296, note 1. **Jeffrey on Procter.** See *ante*, i. 392.

p. 296, note 2. **Darley.** The complete *Poetical Works* were first collected in the 'Muses' Library' by Ramsay Colles, with an introduction (1906).

p. 299, note 1. **Beddoes.** The *Poetical Works*, edited with a memoir by E. Gosse (2 vols., 1890), supersedes the edition of 1851, and is complete, save for a few pieces included in *The Letters of T. L. B.*, ed. Gosse, 1894. Mr. Gosse was the first to tell the full story of Beddoes' life and the manner of his death, receiving the Beddoes papers from Robert Browning, to whom they were left by Kelsall. Most of the *Poems* are also edited in the 'Muses' Library' by Ramsay Colles, with an introduction and new collation and Kelsall's notes. Of the ten poems in Gosse's edition not at the disposal of Mr. Colles, two, namely *The Old Ghost* and *Lord Alcohol*, are given in Miles's *Poets and Poetry of the Century*, 'From Keats to Lytton.'

p. 299, note 2. **The Second Maiden's Tragedy.** *Letters*, p. 34 : 'Verily that is worth the whole heap of Horace Gwynn, L. E. L., Midsummer day dreams, and Bernard-bartonizings of this year's press' (1824).

p. 299, note 3. **'a haunted ruin.'** *Letters*, pp. 50-1 (1825).

p. 300. **none that is ultimate.** See *Poetical Works*, ed. Gosse, Pref., p. xi. The text of Kelsall, to which Mr. Gosse 'in the main adheres,' is compounded out of the three drafts, 'differing very considerably between themselves.' Mr. Gosse adds : 'It will always be possible to produce a variorum edition of *Death's Jestbook*, a demand for which, however, is hardly to be expected.' But the thing ought to be done.

p. 301. **engrossment with scientific ideas.** See *Letters*, p. 80, for a striking statement of the value to a dramatist of a study of 'phisolpsych.' (*i.e.* physiological psychology—this is written in 1825).

p. 302. '**Take of my youth.**' So Gosse and Colles; but should not 'of' read 'off'?

p. 304, note 1. '**his other characters.**' *Letters*, p. 194.

p. 304, note 2. '**a question of this nature.**' *Letters*, pp. 229-30.

p. 304, note 3. **the readable drama.** See the valuable chapters in Herford, *Age of Wordsworth*, pp. 135-45, and in Saintsbury, *Nineteenth Century Literature*, and in Walker, *Victorian Lit.*, pp. 263 foll. Mrs. Inchbald's collections, referred to in the text (especially *Brit. Theatre*, vols. xvii.-xx.), contain a number of the most popular stage pieces; others survive, more or less 'cut,' in Lacy's *Acting Plays*. See J. Genest, *Some Account of the Eng. Stage* (10 vols., 1832), vols. vi.-x. for this period. Genest gives a dated chronicle of plays acted at the chief theatres, with lists of the casts, and of the parts played by various actors throughout their careers; also many anecdotes and descriptions of the more noted performers.

p. 305. **Dibdin.** The *Songs*, 'chronologically arranged with notes' and the music, were edited by G. Hogarth in 1842. O'Keefe's ditties have not been reprinted save in fragments.

p. 307. **Kotzebue.** See Herford, *loc. cit.*; and Walter Sellier, *Kotzebue in England* (Leipzig, 1901) a useful monograph, full of matter drawn from the old magazines and theatrical notices, and giving lists of the representations of *The Stranger*, etc. See too J. E. Gillet, 'A Forgotten German Creditor of the English Stage,' in *Nineteenth Century*, April 1912, pp. 783-94. Dr. Gillet gives Kotzebue his full credit, or discredit, in moulding the popular drama. He proves, perhaps, too much in saddling Kotzebue with the subsequent divorce of the literary from the acting drama; the actual dearth of native dramatic talent was the prime cause. Inchbald's *Brit. Theatre* contains *The Stranger* (vol. xxiv.) and *Lovers' Vows* (vol. xxiii.).

p. 308. **Quadrupeds of Quedlingburgh.** I have not seen this production; the quotation is from Sellier, *op. cit.*, pp. 77-8. For other satires against the German drama see *id.*, pp. 39-40.

p. 310. **Joanna Baillie.** *Dram. and Poet. Works* (1851).

p. 311, note 1. **Milman.** *Poet. Works*, (3 vols. 1839).

p. 311, note 2. **Knowles.** *Dram. Works* (2 vols. 1841, and one vol. 1859); there is said to be a full list in the *Life* by his son R. B. Knowles (1872), but of this only a few copies were printed privately, and I have not seen one. See L. Hasberg, *J. S. K.'s Leben und dramat. Werke* (Lingen, 1883), for some bibliography.

p. 312, note 1. **De Quincey.** D. Masson's edition of the *Collected Writings* (14 vols., Edin., 1889-90) supersedes all earlier ones, including De Quincey's own uncompleted *Selections Grave and Gay* (14 vols., 1853-60), and the enlarged one (17 vols., 1863-78), as well as two American editions. Prof. Masson rearranged the whole material, and his prefaces explain the intricate bibliography. It is a pity he did not include (for his reasons see his edition, iii. 9-10) the first and much briefer edition of the *Confessions*; unless we can lay hands on one of its six re-issues (the last 1853), or on Dr. Garnett's reprint (now out of print, issued 1885), we are at a loss. A. H. Japp, under the name of H. A. Page, edited the *Posthumous Writings* (2 vols., 1891-3), wrote a full biography, second edition, 1879, and produced *De Quincey's Memorials* (2 vols., 1891). Masson's *De Quincey* (in ' Eng. Men of Letters' (1881) remains the best compact account. The article by J. R. Findlay in the *Encycl. Brit.* (ninth and eleventh editions) contains interesting personal memories.

p. 312, note 2. **Lake poets.** I do not forget the prose counterpart in 'Early Memorials of Grasmere' to Wordsworth's lines on George and Sarah Green.

p. 314. **had drafted.** De Quincey also drew up some *Prolegomena to all Future Systems of Political Economy.*

p. 316. **the Essenes.** On this see Masson's ed., vii. 2-3.

p. 317. **German romance.** For these details of sources, etc., see Masson, xii. 2-5.

p. 318. **The Somnambulist.** This appeared in *Knight's Quarterly* (Nov. 1824), and on internal evidence is attributed to De Quincey by Mr. W. E. A. Axon (in a note in the *Manchester Guardian*, March 15, 1912).

p. 320. **German work.** B. Bergmann, *Nomadische Streifereien unter den Kalmüken in den Jahren 1802 and 1803* (4 parts, Riga, 1804-5). I have not seen this book. For this and other sources see Masson, vii. 3-4.

p. 321. **The Spanish Military Nun.** This first appeared (1847) as *The Nautico-Military Nun of Spain.* De Quincey founded it on an article by Alexis Valon in the *Revue des Deux Mondes* for 1847. The whole business is fully unravelled by J. Fitzmaurice-Kelly, *The Nun-Ensign, translated from the Spanish with introduction and notes* (1908), in which De Quincey's doings are exposed with humorous clearness. Valon, it appears, had falsified the account of Ferrer, the producer of the autobiography of Catalina; De Quincey was deceived by Valon, not having read this original; but he suggests that he *had* read it and had looked into the question of its authenticity. But he did not even know that Ferrer had published the text for the first time; and he by no means makes a clean breast in his partial confession of ignorance, added in the 'postscript' of 1854. For all these data see Fitzmaurice-Kelly, especially pp. xxxii.-xxxvi., 296-7.

p. 331. **essay on death.** See Bacon's Works, ed. Ellis and Spedding, vi. 600-4.

p. 332. **Coleridge on English prose.** See *Lit. Remains* (4 vols., 1836), ii. 230-41 (Lect. xiv., 1818).

p. 334. **Charles Lamb.** The edition cited here of the *Works* of Charles and Mary Lamb is that of E. V. Lucas (7 vols., 1903-6, vols. vi. and vii. containing the letters; new and smaller ed. of the same, 6 vols., n.d.) Mr. Lucas has also written the *Life* of Lamb, sympathetically and exhaustively (2 vols. [1905]); and his *Charles Lamb and the Lloyds* (1898) is useful. There are valuable editions of the Works by A. Ainger and W. Macdonald; the original biographies and notices of Hazlitt, Talfourd, Barry Cornwall and others are absorbed in these later studies. See too J. C. Thomson, *Bibliography of the Writings of Charles and Mary Lamb* (1908).

p. 336 **Falstaff.** *Original Letters, etc., of Sir John Falstaff and his Friends now first made public by a Gentleman, a Descendant of Dame Quickly, etc.* (1796). In this year *Vortigern* had been played, and Ireland's *Confession* was published (apparently later than the *Letters*) in the same year. Southey wrote to Moxon in Feb. 1836 that Lamb and White were 'joint authors'; and Matthew Gutch, Lamb's schoolfellow and White's at Christ's Hospital, wrote in his copy that the work was by White, with 'incidental hints and corrections' by Lamb. See

Thomson, *Bibliography*, pp. 4-5 ; who, however, does not think the proof conclusive ; while Mr. Lucas (*Life of C. L.*, i. 85) has no such doubts, and states
his 'impression that the dedication is wholly Lamb's.' A reprint of the *Letters*
has been published. The title-page is facsimiled in *Works of Charles and Mary
Lamb* (ed. Lucas), i. 464.

p. 340. 'Mrs. Barbauld's stuff. . . .' See Lucas, *Life*, i. 232.

p. 350. an editor. Mr. E. V. Lucas.

p. 356. a letter of Coleridge's. See his *Letters* (ed. E. H. Coleridge), ii. 663
(May 13, 1816) : 'Add to this a voluntary lending of the will to this suspension
of one of its own operations (that is, that of comparison and consequent decision
concerning the reality of any sensuous impression), and you have the true
theory of stage illusion,' etc. See *ante*, p. 104.

p. 357. William Hazlitt. The standard edition in 13 vols. (1902-6) of A. R.
Waller and Arnold Glover with introduction by W. E. Henley (referred to
infra as *Works*) contains everything but the *Life of Napoleon*. The six vols.
in Bohn's Library contain most of the essays (except the political), criticisms,
and aphorisms. An excellent vol. of *Selections* from Hazlitt, with a memoir, by
Alexander Ireland, appeared in 1889 ; and the same veteran's *List* (1868) of
Hazlitt's writings is valuable. The catalogue (by J. H. Swann) of the Hazlitt
literature bequeathed to the Manchester Free Reference Library by Mr. Ireland,
is also of interest. The list of Waller and Glover is embodied with some
additions and modifications by J. Douady, *Liste chronologique des Œuvres de
W. H.* (1907), and the same writer's *Vie de W. H.* (1907) should be mentioned.
The chief biographical material is found in the *Memoirs* by W. C. Hazlitt
(2 vols., 1867), but there is much also in Crabb Robinson, in P. G. Patmore's
My Friends and Acquaintances (1854), and in the Lamb literature. Some of
Hazlitt's *Dramatic Essays* are reprinted in the 'Scott Library,' with preface
by W. Archer (1894).

p. 360, note 1. the French Revolution. See the papers *On the Feeling of
Immortality in Youth* (printed in *Winterslow*), *On Jealousy* (*Plain Speaker*,
No. xxxii.), and on *The Excursion* (*Round Table*, No. xxix), for lights on this
aspect of Hazlitt. In the last-named he says : 'We will never cease nor be
prevented from returning on the wings of imagination to that bright dream of
our youth, that glad dawn of the daystar of liberty,' etc.

p. 360, note 2. Owen. See *Works*, iii. 121 foll., and 'Bentham' in *Spirit of
the Age*, for amusing flings at Robert Owen.

p. 363. On the Clerical Character. *Works*, iii. 271 ; *A Reformer*, iii. 39.

p. 364, note 1. 'Chatham's eloquence.' *Works*, iii. 326. Hazlitt afterwards
said he had praised Burke in 'a fit of extravagant candour.' See his virulent
palinodes (1817) in *Works*, iii. 32, 170, 250.

p. 364, note 2. On the Pleasure of Hating. In *Plain Speaker*, No. xiii ; *Works*,
vii. 128.

p. 365, note 1. As we grow old. This text, quoted from *Winterslow*
(posthumously published), differs a good deal from the original one, *q.v.* in
Works, xii. 159.

p. 365, note 2. quotations. See *Works*, vol. i. p. xxviii. for the editor's
remarks. The inaccuracies of Hazlitt are not all unintentional.

p. 367. Notes of a Journey. In *Works*, ix. 83-303. The Grande Chartreuse is described in Ch. xiv., Rome in Ch. xix.

p. 368. **appreciations of art.** Many are in *Works*, vol. ix. (for the passage quoted in text, see pp. 7-8, also p. 27). See too the essay *On the Letter-Bell* (*Works*, xii. 235). In an essay prefixed to his ed. (1894) of the *Conversations of Northcote*, Mr. E. Gosse gives a judicious estimate of Hazlitt as an art critic.

p. 369, note 1. **Rousseau.** *On the Character of Rousseau*, in *Round Table*, No. xxiv. (*Works*, i. 88). See too the faithful dealing with Moore's strictures in *Plain Speaker*, No. xxxii. ; and a fervent judgment in *Conv. of Northcote*, No. xvi.

p. 369, note 2. **Liber Amoris.** Reprinted by R. Le Gallienne, 1893 ; and again in 1894, with enlargements which include eleven letters from Hazlitt to P. G. Patmore (one printed for the first time). Some of these letters vary from the text used, and authorised by Hazlitt, in the ed. of 1823 (reprinted in *Works*, vol. ii. ; see pp. 284, 436, for bibliography). See too W. Carew Hazlitt, *Lamb and Hazlitt* (1900), for passages from a MS. book in Hazlitt's hand ; chronicling, it appears, visits of Patmore's to the Walker *ménage*. One of the lady's admirers observes to her, 'Hang propriety !' 'Oh,' she replies, 'you would not hang propriety?' Hazlitt comments, 'She hangs it up and cuts it down again.' This is like a bit of Congreve, and is almost enough. See De Quincey's humane reference to the affair in 'Recollections of Charles Lamb' (*Works*, ed. Masson, iii. 80-1).

p. 371. '**I have undertaken . . .**' From *Dram. Lit. of the Age of Elizabeth*, Lecture vi. (*Works*, v. 301-2) ; the next passage quoted in text is from Lecture viii. (*Works*, v. 363-4).

p. 372. '**Genius is the power . . .**' From *Thoughts on Taste*, in *Works*, xi. 450 foll.

p. 375. '**In points where poetic diction . . .**' From *Plain Speaker*, No. xx. *On Reading Old Books* (*Works*, vii. 226).

p. 376, note 1. **Southey.** See various reviews and tirades in *Works*, iii. 192-232 ; the longest is on Southey's admirable *Letter to William Smith, Esq.*, in which he clears himself from the charge of apostasy and self-seeking, which Hazlitt unfairly reiterates. He praises, however, Southey's prose cordially (*Works*, vii. 16) ; *literature* usually brings Hazlitt to his senses.

p. 376, note 2. **Scott.** See *Plain Speaker*, No. xxvii. (*Old English Writers and Speakers*) ; and No. xxix. (*Sir W. Scott, Racine, and Shakespeare*), which contains a noble 'contrast' of Scott with Shakespeare ; also *Conv. of Northcote*, No. xvi.

p. 376, note 3. **Coleridge.** The many allusions are all vivid and curious. See the reviews (1816) of *Lay Sermons* and the *Statesman's Manual*, in *Works*, iii. 138-53 ; in the latter article is the first sketch of the famed portrait found in *My First Acquaintance with Poets* ; in the former, a wildly witty sally against Coleridge's mind and style ('his are all maiden ideas—immaculate conceptions,' etc.). In *Plain Speaker*, No. i., *On the Prose Style of Poets*, that of S.T.C. is only too shrewdly noted. But elsewhere he says, 'Till I began to paint, or till I became acquainted with the author of *The Ancient Mariner*, I could neither write nor speak.'

p. 376, note 4. **Byron.** For a contrast with Scott, see *Plain Speaker*, No. xxvii. Byron is one of the few writers upon whom Hazlitt is commonplace (see indeed *Commonplaces*, No. lii.). He makes one shrewd remark : 'Lord Byron *wills* to be sublime or pathetic,' in *Select Poems of Great Britain* (1824) (in the 'critical list of authors'). This curious collection, in its first form, infringed the copyright of living authors, and had to be curtailed in the next issue. One of the few original copies is in the Alexander Ireland collection in Manchester.

p. 377, note 1. **Hazlitt's excellence.** I may rescue (having found it in the Ireland collection) an opulent eulogy from the *Scots Observer* of September 28, 1889, which reads very like a piece of Henley : 'He was a better writer of English than all [his contemporaries]. No mere weaver of purple patches, when he is at his best his prose rolls out, solid and flexible, polished and luminous, as a chain of gold. It is dyed in the glow of poetic imagination, yet it never lapses into bastard rhythms. . . . It is concise but not involved ; full of vigour and fire ; direct, rich, and graceful ; epigrammatic on occasion ; each sentence firmly built, each period nobly cadenced. It touches one of the high-water marks of English.' A more critical and less lyrical account, fully just to Hazlitt as a writer, though, I think, over-hard on him as a man, can be read in G. Saintsbury's *Essays in English Literature.*

p. 377, note 2. **his death-mask.** A photograph of this is in the Ireland collection.

p. 378. **Parr.** See his *Works* (8 vols., 1828), ed. John Johnstone : this includes a memoir, and a *Life* by W. Field appeared in the same year.

p. 379. **Porson.** For the authorities, which are scattered, see the admirable articles by Sir R. Jebb in *D.N.B.* and by H. R. Luard and J. E. Sandys in *Ency. Brit.*, xxii. 106-9. J. S. Watson's *Life* (1861) is duller than befits the subject ; the notices in Beloe's *Sexagenarian* (1817) are not dull, but cannot be relied upon. The *Tracts and Criticisms* were edited by Kidd (1815).

p. 380. **Wakefield.** *Memoirs, by Himself* (2 vols., 1804). The *Observations on Pope* (1796) are eulogistic rather than critical, and represent a belated sort of enthusiasm : they are largely parallels and illustrations.

p. 381, note 1. **translations** (from the classics). The best list known to me is the old one of J. W. Moss, *Manual of Classical Bibliography* (2 vols., 1825). The following may be named as having been reprinted comparatively recently, or as keeping some kind of shadowy place : R. Potter's *Aeschylus* (1777), in blank verse, and his *Sophocles* (1788) ; Melmoth's *Cicero's Letters* (1773-1814) ; Charles A. Elton, *The Remains of Hesiod the Ascraean* (1812) ; J. and W. Langhorne, *Plutarch's Lives* (1770-1819). Before Frere came T. Mitchell as a translator of Aristophanes (1821). Cowper's *Homer* and Gifford's *Juvenal and Persius* are mentioned *ante*, i. 96-8 and i. 36-7.

p. 381, note 2. **Frere's Aristophanes.** In vol. ii. of his *Works* (1871).

p. 383. **Norse poetry.** See Georg Herzfeld, *William Taylor von Norwich* (Halle, 1891), Appendix, pp. 60-9, for a list of these efforts. I have failed to get sight of Cottle's *Edda* or of William Herbert's *Select Icelandic Poetry* (1804), described by Herzfeld (p. 67) as including translations of the *Song of Thrym*, the *Descent of Odin*, and many more well-known pieces, done from the Norse originals and not (as then usual) from Latin versions.

p. 384. **Lingard.** See the interesting memoir by Tierney prefixed to the tenth vol. of the *History* (1854-5). Lingard was attacked in the *Edinb. Rev.*, No. lxxxvii. (June 1826), and elsewhere. His *Vindication* is concerned with the passages in his *History* on the Bartholomew massacre and on Cranmer. The Edinburgh Reviewer, John Allen, signed a rejoinder briefly noticed by

Lingard in a later edition of the *Vindication*. Lingard leaves the impression of candour.

p. 386, note 1. **a grave ardour** (in Hallam). See his *Middle Ages* (ed. 1838), iii. 235 : ' God forbid that our rights to just and free government should be tried by a jury of antiquaries,' etc. The whole passage is in the spirit of Burke ; and a later one (*ib.*, p. 291 foll.) is a typical Whig defence of government settled by revolution ('however violent in its origin'), provided only it is 'uniformly obeyed and justly exercised—the position drawing after it the right.'

p. 386, note 2. **memoir of Arthur Hallam.** Prefixed to his father's ed. of his *Remains* (privately printed 1833, published 1863).

p. 389, note 1. **Hallam on Scott's Dryden.** In *Edinb. Rev.*, No. xxv., Oct. 1808.

p. 389, note 2. **mediæval chivalry.** See *Middle Ages* (ed. 1838), iii. 481 : ' the soul of chivalry was individual honour coveted in so entire and absolute a perfection,' etc.

p. 394. **library without a Hakluyt.** I do not at all profess to have covered this ground ; for one thing, many of the books have been out of my reach. Nor does there seem to be any ordered survey of English travel during the period. The nearest thing to Hakluyt's achievement is John Pinkerton's *General Collection of the most Interesting Voyages and Travels in all Parts of the World*, etc. (17 vols., 1814). Vol. xvii. contains a catalogue (pp. 1-255) of works in all languages, and a huge index. Many of the works Pinkerton includes are translations. Of this class the travels of the German pastor K. P. Moritz in England in 1782 are well known, and of high interest. The same vol. (ii.) contains H. Skrine's tours in Wales, J. Hassel's in the Isle of Wight, etc. (For list of books on the Lake country, etc., see E. de Sélincourt's ed. (1906) of Wordsworth's *Guide to the Lakes*.) Vol. xx. includes various interesting tours in India, and vol. xxiv. George Forster's important *Travels in India, Persia*, etc., in 1782-4. Coxe's *Switzerland* is in vol. xxiv. William George Browne's *Journey to Dar-Fûr* (travels published 1799, 1806) is in vol. xv., and is a heavily-penned but important work. (Thomas Pennant's *Tours* in Scotland, Wales, etc., appeared between 1770 and 1790.) The last five vols. of William Mavor's *Historical Account of the most celebrated Voyages, Travels, and Discoveries* (25 vols., 1796-1801) contains accounts (largely decoctions) of various works of our period. See too R. Kerr's *Collection*, etc. (18 vols., 1842). For list of county histories (1760-1800) see T. Seccombe, *Age of Johnson*, p. 104. The *Catal. of the Library of the Royal Geographical Soc.*, by H. R. Mill (1895), App. I., ' Collections,' shows the vastness of the material : see, for instance, *s.v.* ' Cavendish,' ' Sir R. Phillips,' ' R. Walpole.'

p. 395, note 1. **James Bruce.** See A. Murray, *Account of the Life and Writings of J. B.*, prefixed to the 1805 ed. of the *Travels*.

p. 395, note 2. **Mungo Park.** Parts of the *Travels* of 1799 are in Pinkerton, vol. xvi. The *Journal of a Mission to the Interior of Africa in the Year 1805* is prefaced by a judicious memoir by E. Wishaw, who explains Park's relations with his coadjutor, Bryan Edwards. The account in Mavor, vol. xxi., is in the third person and shows this other hand.

p. 397. **Alexander Wilson.** I have seen the ed. of 1831, re-arranged by Robert Jameson in four volumes, the fourth containing the continuation by Prince Lucien Bonaparte of Wilson's work. There is a memoir of Wilson in vol. i. (see art. in *D.N.B.*).

p. 399. **Crabb Robinson.** His *Diary, etc.*, was published in two vols. by Thomas Sadler in 1869 ; third ed., with 'corrections and additions,' 2 vols., 1872. Sadler only published a small fraction of the material—he says from one-twenty-fifth to one-thirtieth ; the entire MS., in many vols., is now in Dr. Williams's library in Gordon Square, London. Much still remains to be done by scholars with this priceless chronicle. For Bagehot's amusing account of Robinson see his *Lit. Studies* ; De Morgan's is printed by Sadler.

p. 404. **Georg Brandes.** See his *Main Currents in the Literature of the Nineteenth Century* (originally in Danish, 1872-5 ; Eng. trans., 1901-5).

p. 405, note 1. **coincidences.** See a striking sketch by A. C. Bradley, *English Poetry and German Philosophy in the Age of Wordsworth* (Manchester, 1909), being the Adamson lecture for that year given in the Manchester University.

p. 405, note 2. **influence of German.** Many of the facts are clearly set forth by Ernst Margraf, *Der Einfluss der deutschen Litt. auf die englische am Ende des achtzehnten und im ersten Drittel des neunzehnten Jahrhunderts* (Leipzig, 1901). Margraf traces the German studies, with their literary results, of Taylor, Lewis, Scott, Wordsworth, Southey, Coleridge (imperfectly), De Quincey, Crabb Robinson, Byron, Shelley, and Carlyle, and then summarises the effect of each of the chief German writers (excluding the philosophers) in England. For the philosophical influence, see the introduction and notes, already mentioned, to J. Shawcross's ed. of *Biog. Literaria*. The opening pages of Herford's *Age of Wordsworth* throw much light on the 'transcendental' movement. See too A. Brandl, *Die Aufnahme Goethes Jugendwerke in England*, in *Goethe-Jahrbuch*, vol. iii. (1882). Mme de Staël's *De L'Allemagne* (1810-13) was translated at once (1813), and a study of its reception in England is to be desired.

p. 405, note 3. **W. Taylor.** George Herzfeld, *William Taylor von Norwich*, named *supra*, gives a full description of this writer.

p. 406. **Carlyle.** The works mentioned, apart from the *Life of Schiller* and the version of *Wilhelm Meister*, are all in the seven vols. of his *Miscellanies*. The essay on 'Carlyle and his German Masters,' by C. E. Vaughan, in *Essays and Studies by Members of the English Association* (first series, 1910, edited by A. C. Bradley) is an admirable survey of this ground, which I have not pretended to go over in the text.

p. 407. **allusions to Dante.** Collected by Paget Toynbee, *Dante in English Literature*, c. 1380-1844 (2 vols. 1909).

p. 408. **Ugo Foscolo.** Besides Viglione's work (named *ante*, ii. 425), see the note of Eugenia Levi, 'Per Ugo Foscolo,' in *Rassegna bibliografica della lett. ital.* (1909).

p. 409. **Shakespeare.** See Ernest Walder, 'The Text of Shakespeare,' in *Cambridge Hist. of Eng. Lit.* (1910), xi. 275-7, and xi. 429, 445 foll. (bibliography) ; also Walder, *Shakespearean Criticism*, etc. (Bradford, 1895).

In the last two chapters the need of selection has been rigid. Amongst the names excluded with regret are those of Theobald Wolfe Tone, with his gallant *Autobiography* (1826), and of Isaac D'Israeli, whose *Curiosities of Literature* (1791-1817) was the first of many such miscellanies, motley and amusing, by this eager student of letters.

INDEX TO VOLS. I AND II

The letter **n** *following a page-figure shows that the reference is to be found in a note or notes occurring on that page.*